THE ATLANTIC WORLD

Artist, Henry Inman, 1828. From the *Colonization and Journal of Freedom* (1834), frontispiece.

THE Atlantic World

1450-2000

Edited by

Toyin Falola and Kevin D. Roberts

Indiana University Press

Bloomington & Indianapolis

This book is a publication of

Indiana University Press
601 North Morton Street
Bloomington, IN 47404-3797 USA

http://iupress.indiana.edu

Telephone orders 800-842-6796
Fax orders 812-855-7931
Orders by e-mail iuporder@indiana.edu

The paper used in this publication meets the minimum requirements of American National Standard for Information Sciences—Permanence of Paper for Printed Library Materials, ANSI Z39.48-1984.

Manufactured in the United States of America

Library of Congress Cataloging-in-Publication Data

The Atlantic world : 1450-2000 / edited by Toyin Falola and Kevin D. Roberts.
p. cm. — (Blacks in the diaspora)
Includes bibliographical references and index.
ISBN-13: 978-0-253-34970-5 (cloth : alk. paper)
ISBN-13: 978-0-253-21943-5 (pbk. : alk. paper)
1. History, Modern. 2. Civilization, Modern. 3. Atlantic Ocean—History.
I. Falola, Toyin. II. Roberts, Kevin D. (Kevin David), date
D210.A77 2008
909'.09821—dc22

2007043965

2 3 4 5 13 12 11 10

Dedication

For Paul E. Lovejoy

Contents

IV. Globalization and Its Discontents / 275

Introduction

Toyin Falola and Kevin D. Roberts

Created out of the desire for wealth and power, the Atlantic World possesses a history that is at once intriguing and difficult to grasp. Unlike national histories, which have definite dates for a nation's origins, the Atlantic World's history is less defined in terms of time, culture, and even space. But that is precisely what historians, other scholars, and students find so compelling about the Atlantic World. The imprecision in its history and the very absence of a nationalist entity and history—an idea which has fallen out of favor among historians—combine to make the Atlantic World one of the most popular subjects of study in the last twenty-five years. This volume is both the natural consequence of the field's maturing process and also an attempt to help define those nebulous aspects of the Atlantic World.

But what exactly *is* the Atlantic World? Its geography is easy enough to define, as it is bound by the four continents which lie on the Atlantic Ocean: North and South America, Europe, and Africa. Speaking in purely geographical terms, one would be most accurate in referring to this region as the "Atlantic world"—i.e., with a lowercase "w." But what makes the geographic "Atlantic world" something finite, something definable—indeed, the "Atlantic World"—are the processes of migration, colonialism, trade, and intellectual exchange that came to dominate the Atlantic region starting in the mid-fifteenth century. When they use the capitalized version, "Atlantic World," scholars are implicitly or explicitly connoting a sense of place, social identity, or political connection that extends beyond mere geography. Emigration movements from Europe, the settlements those migrants established in the New World, and the expansive involuntary migration of African slaves to the Americas all form the most popular Atlantic studies. Though political and economic considerations lay at the root of the Atlantic World, society, culture, and religion constitute equally important aspects of the field's history.

With millions of people from hundreds of cultures crossing the Atlantic since that time, the Atlantic World remains, in the twenty-first century, not only a scholarly entity but a social, political, economic, and intellectual system. Naturally, those people living in the Atlantic littoral today are descendants of people who migrated west from the Old World (Africa and Europe) or vice versa. To that end, this volume, which covers the entire span of the Atlantic World's history, says as much about modern societies and cultures as it does about the past.

The Atlantic World had its beginnings in Portugal's attempts to find an all-water route to India. During the fifteenth century, as Portuguese navigators made steady progress southward along the western African coast, they encountered societies which eventually became important trading partners. Some of the peoples whom the Portuguese encountered—such as the Guanches of the Cape Verde Islands—became "test cases" for the enslavement of non-whites by Europeans. By 1600, before the English established a single permanent settlement in North America, nearly 50,000 Africans had been sold from Africa to owners in New Spain. The subsequent 250 years shook West African societies to their core, draining at least 12 million humans from the continent and laying the foundation for European colonialism of the late nineteenth century. As an economic system with seemingly endless political, cultural, and social repercussions, slavery was the handmaiden of colonialism in the Atlantic basin. Together, they created the Atlantic World.

Between the Portuguese arrival in the Cape Verdes and the abolition of slavery four hundred years later, the Atlantic World evolved as a colonial and imperial system, with a handful of metropoles, or parent countries, establishing dozens of colonies in North and South America. The conquest of massive, intricate, and well-populated Amerindian cultures—by both warfare and disease—catapulted the economically, socially, and politically unstable European nations from backwaters to empires. Spain, Portugal, France, England, and Holland all used their Atlantic colonies to propel their own societies toward modernization. Without the raw goods and bullion from those colonies, the very appearance of the nation-state in modern Europe almost assuredly would have occurred later.

But this volume wholly rejects that traditional depiction of the Atlantic World being dominated by a handful of Europeans. In fact, the intellectual genesis of this book was the desire to move the field of Atlantic studies away from that misconception once and for all. As chapter after chapter shows, Africans, Amerindians, Creoles of the New World, poor Europeans, and women of all groups were active participants in the creation and shaping of the Atlantic World. Moving beyond mere "inclusion history" for the hollow sake of political correctness, the analyses that follow—and the crux of the book as a whole—demonstrate that one cannot accurately depict an "Atlantic world" without evaluating how all of the Atlantic basin's peoples interacted, counteracted, and reacted to aims, behaviors, and decisions by the others. Though what happened in the halls of Parliament and in the monarch's court in Spain are important, focusing only on those events skews not only the history of the Atlantic World but also the manner in which human beings behave.

That is not to say, however, that political authority was unimportant. Political and economic elites did, indeed, generate much of the structure within which the peoples of the Atlantic lived their lives. To be sure, Philip II of Spain—in a single whim—could alter the Atlantic World more profoundly than, say, a single African slave. But that truism misses the point about how diffuse power really is in human interactions, particularly in a chunk of the world as large as the Atlantic basin. As historians, we determine what our stage is: the king's court, the dock of a port city, the plantation house, the slave quarters, or the ship sailing across the Atlantic, just to name a few. In the Atlantic World, there were multitudinous, if not infinite, such "stages." Our useful example of Philip II's court might be a site of particularly concentrated power, and one that could affect smaller "stages" in most parts of the world. But to focus exclusively only on those historical "scenes" dominated by elites skews—and, dare we say, bastardizes—history. The decision of a young English woman to sail to America as an indentured servant, the decision of an indigenous American to go through the motions of conversion to Catholicism, and the decision of a West African leader to swap humans for European finished goods are but a handful of examples of how the Atlantic World was built by billions of individual decisions and actions. Examined individually, the indentured servant, the Amerindian, or the African created less documentation—which, of course, means less history—than, say, Philip II, but examined as a group, in an aggregate sense, those subaltern peoples become central figures in the Atlantic drama. Not only must we include them, but we must also demonstrate their interactions, counteractions, and reactions in Atlantic history.

In that sense, the popularity of Atlantic history may be understood by its reflection of trends in the field of history and other humanities disciplines, which in recent years have gravitated away from the study of elites toward the study of common people. New paradigms are necessary to the regeneration of the discipline of history. Since the early twentieth century, some of those paradigms have been based in social theory, political ideology, empirical methodology, and economic rubrics. Others, like the construct of the Atlantic World, have been based in geography while borrowing the social, political, economic, and cultural facets of others. The Atlantic World idea has helped scholars to see processes, events, and ideas with fresh perspectives unavailable with a more limited geographical and topical approach.

Yet, in spite of the popularity of Atlantic history and Atlantic studies, many questions—including the very definition of "Atlantic World" and "Atlantic history"—remain. This is undoubtedly the result of the plethora of scholars who claim to employ an Atlantic approach without ever defining what that entails, and how that is different from other approaches that historians use. The most spirited and lasting criticisms of the paradigm maintain that the so-called Atlantic World is merely a historians' creation; that is, the historical actors whom scholars study never possessed any sense of being an Atlantic "citizen." Rather, such criticisms allege, historians interested in the migrations, intellectual sharing, and political history of Atlantic peoples employ the language of this ephemeral Atlantic history to really mean something akin to comparative history. Now at loggerheads with some scholars promoting global history, Atlantic history is facing its fair share of critics.

The definitional challenges of the field are complicated by similar efforts to define two related fields of interest: the "African Diaspora" and the "Black Atlantic." As contributor Douglas B. Chambers argues in chapter 8, the coming-of-age of the Black Atlantic field suggests that the Atlantic World construction itself is a viable historical approach. Though the people whom we study in this volume may not have used the terms "Atlantic World" or "Black Atlantic," the ways in which they behaved indicate a strong connection among Atlantic peoples. Those individual decisions, when considered in the aggregate, allow us to draw composite sketches and make meaningful conclusions about the existence of an Atlantic World system of economic, cultural, religious, and social exchange. Failing to consider the importance of Africans in that story is an intellectually fatal enterprise.

With the vantage point of hindsight, the editors and authors of this volume have set out to answer those questions about the paradigm of Atlantic history. In so doing, we have also endeavored to fashion the first comprehensive synthesis of the history of the Atlantic World. On the surface, this is a seemingly improbable task, given the mastery of so many nationalist, regional, and local histories—not to mention the oft-cited problem of mastering multiple languages. Needless to say, we are guided by the spirit of *la longue durée*. Moreover, the burgeoning scholarship on Atlantic history—some of which has been produced by contributors to this volume—allows us to isolate the major themes, questions, and issues that have dominated Atlantic history since its reaching of a critical mass some time in the 1960s and 1970s. With a combination of established and junior scholars, the volume best represents both the roots of the Atlantic World paradigm and the seemingly limitless potential that the field has in the future.

The actual study of an "Atlantic World" began in the 1960s, when scholars of colonial British America began exploring the transatlantic context for the events that had been so well covered in their field. Bernard Bailyn, Edmund Morgan, Jack Greene, and John Eliot all contributed to this transition and unleashed—consciously or not—a field of history that now goes well beyond studying colonial British America. To be sure, some Atlantic scholars still see Atlantic World history as being synonymous with this original effort to expand the geographic scope of colonial U.S. history; for example, Nicholas Canny, a prominent Atlanticist, titled a recent excellent article "Writing Atlantic History; or, Reconfiguring the History of Colonial British America."[1] For the scores of

Atlantic scholars whose work does not deal with colonial British America, Canny's implicit definition of Atlantic World history with North America may come as a surprise.

But the very history of the phrase "Atlantic World" has its origins in North Atlantic relations, so altering this bias may take time. Bernard Bailyn observed that such terminology sprang into being in the aftermath of World War II, when the Marshall Plan and the creation of the North Atlantic Treaty Organization (NATO) prompted discussion of an "Atlantic community."[2] But for those Atlantic scholars who today are working on twentieth-century Atlantic topics, the subjects of diplomacy usually involve relations between African nations and the West, or efforts against Western economic and political hegemony in Africa and Latin America. As with most fields, then, Atlantic World history has evolved.

One reason that evolution has occurred with such speed is that several history departments have developed tracks, and even entire programs of study, dedicated to Atlantic history: Harvard University, Johns Hopkins University, Michigan State University, Florida International University, and the University of Texas at Arlington. At Harvard, Bernard Bailyn directs the annual Harvard Atlantic Seminar, which has provided a forum for dozens of Atlanticists in the early part of their careers. Though some scholars anticipated that the advent of global history studies spelled the demise of the Atlantic approach, the commitment of an increasing number of programs across the country to Atlantic history belies that notion.

Though Bernard Bailyn and Jack Greene ushered in waves of books and articles on the history of Atlantic World, the focus of subsequent scholarship has been tilted less toward the British Empire and more toward Africa and Amerindians. John Thornton's monumental work, *Africa and Africans in the Making of the Atlantic World* (1992), prompted scores of scholars to approach Atlantic history from the perspective of peoples whom previous historians had depicted as passive historical actors. As a result, Atlantic history, as this volume illustrates, has come to examine the interactions and influence that each of the three major continental groups had with the others. Moreover, historians have been much more careful in examining the sometimes wide differences within the term "African" and "Amerindian."

Constructing Atlantic history means more than simply adding the term "Atlantic" to the subtitle of one's book, article, or conference paper. Rather, it involves the conscious decision to examine one's specialized topic—however refined it is geographically, topically, or temporally—and connect it to the broader themes in Atlantic history. To that end, this volume represents an intellectual call to arms that we hope reverberates beyond the study of Atlantic history: rather than continuing down the slippery slope of hyper-specialization, in which the typical scholar is a master of the specific but an apprentice of the general, historians must do a better job of showing how their "micro-histories" fit with macro-level events and processes. There is perhaps no better field than Atlantic history to remind us that human behaviors do not occur in a vacuum.

What follows, then, is both our attempt to define the Atlantic World and also a concerted effort to re-connect elites and non-elites, Old World and New, early modern and modern, and economics and culture. For Atlantic history itself, there is perhaps no greater relevance than saving history from the cult of hyper-specificity.

Notes

1. Nicholas Canny, "Writing Atlantic History; or, Reconfiguring the History of Colonial British America," *Journal of American History* 86:3 (2002): 1093–1114.

2. Bernard Bailyn, "The Idea of Atlantic History," *Itinerario* 20 (1996): 19–44. Also see Peter A. Coclanis, "Drang Nach Osten: Bernard Bailyn, the World-Island, and the Idea of Atlantic History," *Journal of World History* 13:1 (2002): 169–82.

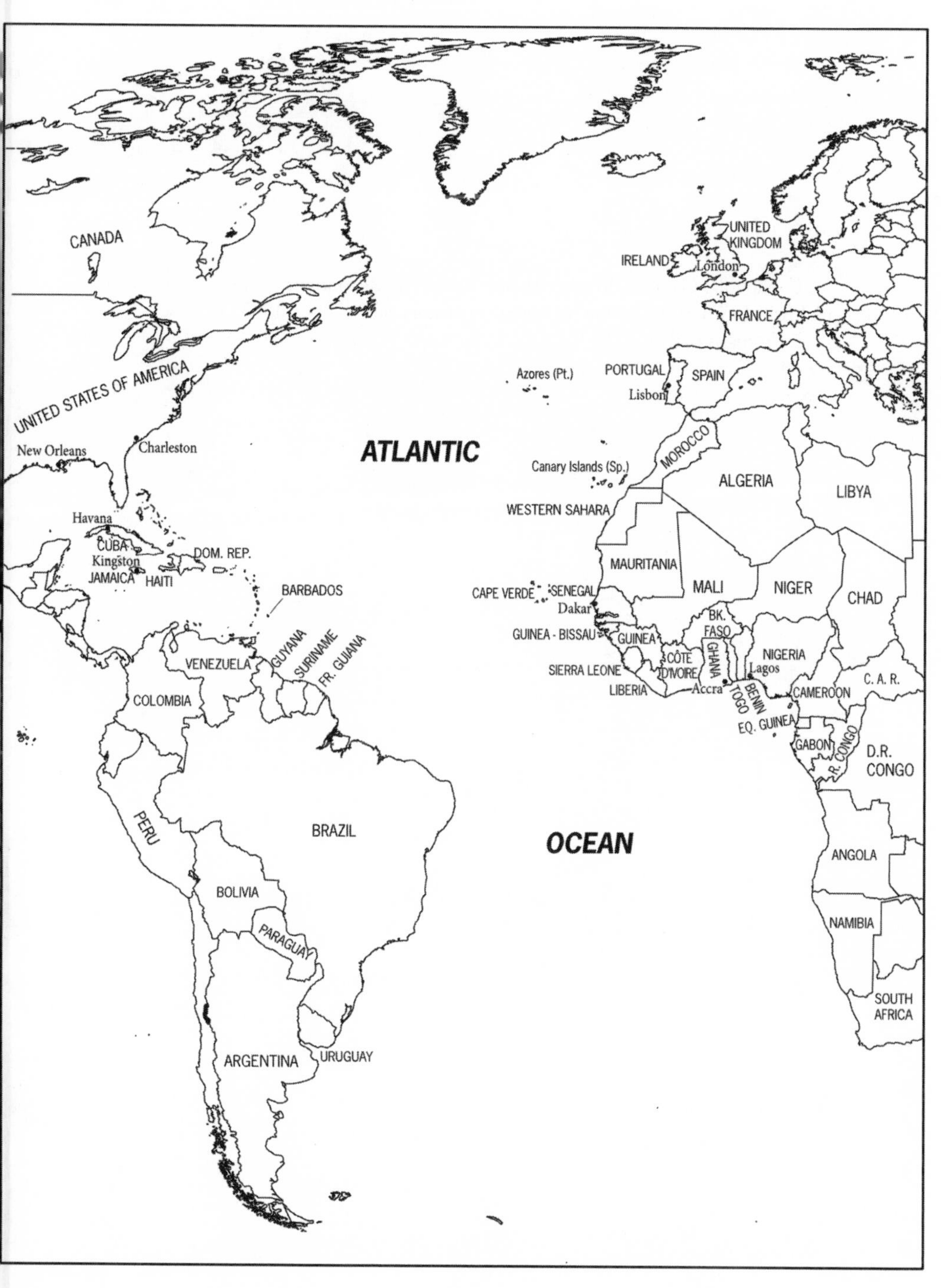

CANADA
UNITED STATES OF AMERICA
New Orleans
Charleston
ATLANTIC
OCEAN
Havana
CUBA
Kingston
JAMAICA
HAITI
DOM. REP.
BARBADOS
VENEZUELA
GUYANA
SURINAME
FR. GUIANA
COLOMBIA
PERU
BRAZIL
BOLIVIA
PARAGUAY
URUGUAY
ARGENTINA
Azores (Pt.)
PORTUGAL
Lisbon
SPAIN
IRELAND
UNITED KINGDOM
London
FRANCE
MOROCCO
Canary Islands (Sp.)
WESTERN SAHARA
ALGERIA
LIBYA
MAURITANIA
MALI
NIGER
CHAD
CAPE VERDE
SENEGAL
Dakar
GUINEA - BISSAU
GUINEA
BK. FASO
SIERRA LEONE
LIBERIA
CÔTE D'IVOIRE
GHANA
Accra
TOGO
BENIN
NIGERIA
Lagos
CAMEROON
C. A. R.
EQ. GUINEA
GABON
R. CONGO
D.R. CONGO
ANGOLA
NAMIBIA
SOUTH AFRICA

THE ATLANTIC WORLD

I

Nations and Migrations

Though scholars who focus on later periods often take for granted the existence of the Atlantic World, the processes from which that world was created are nonetheless crucial aspects of its history. In part 1, authors explore those events, ideas, and processes that laid the foundation for the creation of a transatlantic "world." Patricia Pearson gives readers a thorough understanding of societies in Europe, Africa, North America, and South America "on the eve of the formation of the Atlantic world." In so doing, Pearson establishes the groundwork from which the crux of the book—the interactions of Old and New World peoples—can be expanded. As she says, such interactions, given the experiences of cultures on all four Atlantic continents, would produce an Atlantic World that was "shaped by all parties involved."

Building upon that idea, Timothy P. Grady outlines the early history of the Atlantic World. Focusing on the initial contact among the societies of Africa, the Americas, and Europe, Grady provides a comprehensive view of the economic motives driving European exploration, as well as those influencing Africans to trade with Europeans. Linking the creation of the Atlantic World with earlier events in Europe, Grady concludes that European exploration was the logical "outgrowth of intellectual and technological progress" that occurred during the Renaissance. Unlike many previous histories of this earliest phase of the Atlantic World, however, Grady portrays both Africans and indigenous Americans as having considerably more agency. This theme, which has pervaded the scholarship of the youngest generation of Atlantic scholars, establishes one of the central purposes of this volume: exploding the centrism of Europe and Europeans in the story of the Atlantic.

The final chapter of part 1 illustrates the continued growth of the Atlantic

World, in terms of both population and conceptualization, by focusing on the two most significant processes in early Atlantic history: migration and slavery. Alison Games uses three Atlantic migrants—Barbara Wolfe, an English woman; Pierre Radisson, a Frenchman, and Abd al-Rahman, a West African man—as illustrative examples of the many threads of migration running through the Atlantic. In focusing on migration in the Atlantic Basin during this early period, Games reminds readers of the "profusion of languages" that enveloped the Atlantic World. She also provides that important yet often forgotten aspect of Atlantic history: that in spite of the term "Atlantic World" being a creation of historians, the people whose actions bound four continents together did share experiences and have some idea of a larger regional identity. Indeed, as Games argues, each person "who crossed the ocean had distinctive stories to tell, but common features shaped the larger trends in migration." A wholly necessary phenomenon to the creation and existence of the Atlantic World, migration remained a central feature of the identities that people living in that world possessed.

CHAPTER ONE

The World of the Atlantic before the "Atlantic World": Africa, Europe, and the Americas before 1450

Patricia Pearson

What historians call the Atlantic World began to form in the last half of the fifteenth century. In subsequent years the fortunes of four continents became intertwined and interdependent. The repercussions of these connections continue to be felt in the modern world. The complex history of the Atlantic World was not written on a blank slate. The peoples of Africa, Europe, and the Americas lived in diverse, complicated, and dynamic societies. While the advanced civilization of Europe is usually acknowledged by historians, the cultures of the Americas and Africa are often disregarded, neglected, or disparaged in scholarship. Inga Clendinnen, a historian of the Aztecs, criticizes this practice, saying, "Historians are the camp-followers of the imperialists."[1] Knowledge of the context in which the Atlantic World formed and functioned—that is, the past of *all* the regions involved—is required for complete and accurate understanding of the region and period.

Although this chapter addresses each region separately, their lands and peoples were not in isolation prior to the fifteenth century. Information, trade, and ideas moved throughout Africa and Eurasia, and between the Americas. People formed societies, adapted to their environments, fought in defense and aggression, worshipped devoutly, and seized opportunities for wealth and power. This chapter seeks to provide the reader with an impression of these regions as they were on the eve of the formation of the Atlantic World. Complete histories of each region would require far more than a single chapter to adequately tell, and the following is by no means intended to encompass the whole range of time, space, and human diversity of these continents. Although the text is heavily weighted toward the thirteenth, fourteenth, and fifteenth centuries, earlier events of significance and of lingering impact have been included wherever possible.

The Americas: Expansion, Interaction, and Enduring Cultures

Historians often represent the history of the Americas as being set in motion by the arrival of European explorers and colonizers, without recognizing the existence and influence of the history that had already happened—the background for the Atlantic World, the European colonies, and our own modern world. Historian Neal Salisbury has said, "As significant as is the divide separating pre- and post-Columbian North American history, it is not the stark gap suggested by the distinction between prehistory and history."[2] "Prehistory" implies that before the arrival of Europeans there was no "history" in the Americas. On the contrary, the inhabitants of North America, South America, and Mesoamerica developed sophisticated cultures, created and lost empires, produced stunning works of art, engaged in sophisticated agriculture, and had a rich history of their own before Columbus and colonization. History generally casts Native Americans in the role of inferior players in their encounter with Europeans.[3] Contact and subsequent interactions were shaped by Native Americans as well as Europeans. The inhabitants of the Americas met European explorers and colonizers as leaders and members of distinct and complex cultures. Their greatest disadvantage was medical, not cultural—they lacked immunity to European diseases and died by the thousands, some without ever seeing a European.

Pre-Columbian civilizations included the Olmec, Maya, Teotihuacán, Zapotec, Toltec, Aztec, Chavin, Moche, Chimor, Huari, and Inca in Mesoamerica and South America, as well as the Hopewell, Mississippian, Anasazi, Iroquois, Comanche, Sioux, and Athapascan in North America. Archaeologists are uncertain as to how long the Americas have been populated, although stone artifacts suggest Paleo-Indians occupied the land between 50,000 and 20,000 years ago. Settled agriculture was established by about 1000 BCE. Piecing together this history presents challenges, as most of the cultures in the Americas did not leave written records. The memories of the descendants of these peoples and the work of archaeologists and anthropologists provide invaluable tools in attempting to understand these civilizations.

The Maya, one of the most magnificent and long-lived societies in Mesoamerica, flourished from 200 BCE to around 900 CE. At its height in the eighth century, the central Mayan city of Teotihuacán anchored a military and commercial empire that dominated most of Mexico.[4] The empire was composed of a collection of states under a central authority. Controlling valuable Yucatan salt exports and sea commerce, the Maya practiced extensive trade throughout their empire and with neighboring powers. War constituted a fundamental part of Maya life, although they were skilled in diplomacy as well as conquest.

Mayan society emphasized hierarchical distinctions, war, and religious ritual. The Maya developed hieroglyphic writing, astronomy, mathematics, and two simultaneous calendars—a Long Calendar running from the distant past through to the end of the world, and a "vague year" of 365 days. Described as one of "the most sophisticated, exotic, and volatile cultures of ancient America," the Maya were fierce warriors and practiced ritual human sacrifice according to festivals prescribed by the Long Calendar.[5] Deeply religious, the Maya lived in a world defined by cyclical patterns of destruction and creation and controlled by rituals honoring a pantheon of gods. Their religious beliefs spread widely and remained influential for centuries. In addition to divisions based on status, labor was divided by gender. Successful warriors and elites practiced polygamy, and Maya women or female slaves could be given as gifts in diplomacy.

After a pinnacle in the eighth century, the Maya empire faded over the next hundred years. Ecological woes contributed to the social and demographic catastrophe. Rapid population expansion starting in the sixth century and the consequent overproduction of crops caused environmental degradation. The maintenance of Mayan imperial control depended upon the political charisma of the ruler and public rituals, resulting in an unstable system with natural volatility. Mayan society suffered continual stresses from intertribal conflict and war with outsiders. Increasingly tense alliances and internal revolts created additional instability in this period. The combination of declining crop production and political rumblings led to the disintegration of the empire and the collapse of many of its constituent states. The Maya did not disappear altogether, as their diplomatic and business skills preserved some states for centuries, even into the fifteenth century against the aggressive expansion of the Aztecs.[6] Mayan culture, particularly their religion, persisted into the colonial period. Canek of Tayasal, the last of the Maya kings, resisted incursions until 1697 when the Spanish conquered Tayasal by force. One historian writes, "it seems almost beyond belief . . . that while students at Harvard College had been scratching their heads over Cotton Mather's theology, Maya priests 2,000 miles away were still chanting rituals from hieroglyphic books."[7]

The Aztec empire also emerged in the fertile valley of central Mexico. The Mexica people, better known as the Aztecs, moved into the valley around the fourteenth century. They founded the city of Tenochtitlan in 1325. The Mexica overthrew their overlord in 1428 in a Triple Alliance with the Texcoco and Tacuba and established themselves as the dominant power in the region. During the fifteenth century, the Aztec empire grew in both size and prestige.[8] Temples, palaces, tribute warehouses, professional merchants, artisans, high-status elites, and vibrant markets stocked with luxury items filled Tenochtitlan, while miles of intensively cultivated, irrigated fields helped sustain the city's more than 200,000 residents—at a time when the largest city in Spain had only 70,000 residents.

Called *Huei Tlatoani*, or Great Speaker, the Aztec ruler held absolute control over the external side of Aztec life, including warfare, tribute, and diplomacy.[9] Military prowess drove expansion, but trade and tribute held together the empire; as Aztec armies conquered, collectors of tribute and taxes followed on their heels.[10] Their cultural commitment to warfare went beyond protection or expansion; an ethic of conflict dominated society. Professional warriors gained social and economic rewards for prowess in battle. Traders supported the warrior ethos, and priests provided spiritual power and sanction to the warriors. Conquest and empire comprised an essential part of the proper worship of their primary god, Huitzilopochtli. Human sacrifice was also fundamental to Aztec religious practices, and many victims were supplied by regular infusions of war captives. Despite their enthusiasm for warfare and their practice of human sacrifice, Aztec culture valued moderation, disapproving of intoxication and other losses of control. Reconciling the discrepancy between the "high decorum and fastidious social and aesthetic sensibility of the Mexica world, and the massive carnality of the killings and dismemberings: between social grace and monstrous ritual" presents a challenge ably taken up by Aztec scholar Inga Clendinnen.[11]

Aztec society drew sharp distinctions between lords and commoners, men and women, insiders and outsiders. Slaves, an integral part of Aztec life, were procured through warfare, traded in the markets, and sacrificed on the steps of the temples during rituals and celebrations. Female slaves were often given as gifts or as part of diplomatic negotiations. Called *tlacohtin*, slaves had certain rights under Aztec law, although little protection from the sacrificial knife. Aztec people lived in *calpullis* (big houses), often erroneously referred to as clans. The *calpulli* was a group of families related by kinship or proximity over time and resembled "localized, land holding corporations" run by elites for the benefit of all.[12] Within the *calpulli* children of both genders were educated, although separately. Upon birth, boys were celebrated as "captives" of the family and baptized as future warriors. Girls were equally celebrated, as supporters of warriors who labored at home. Skills were highly segregated by gender. Despite strict gender division and an emphasis on militarism, women's roles as well as men's were respected in Aztec culture, and women's contributions to society were valued highly. Marriage, a social bond arranged between families, occurred around the age of twenty and brought women more domestic duties and entrance into a wider world via the market. Many women represented their families as skilled traders.[13] Tenochtitlan remained a grand city until its destruction by the Spanish in 1521.

Farther south in the Andean highlands of South America, civilizations rose and fell in similar cycles. In the early fifteenth century, the Inca emerged from a morass of feuding societies.[14] The founder of the Incan empire, Pachakuti—"He who remakes the world"—reformed society and created a new ideology imparting both divine sanction and personal divinity to Inca rulers.[15] Over the next century, the empire expanded into Ecuador, Argentina, Bolivia, and Chile through military conquest and judicious exploitation of traditional Andean cultural practices. In an empire founded upon control and conformity, the Incas established relationships of reciprocity with conquered peoples, playing upon deeply ingrained notions about mutual aid and responsibility.[16] To ensure peace, the Incas scattered newly conquered populations through resettlement while shifting loyal subjects to the periphery to act as model citizens and staff imperial bureaucracies. Distant lands were often ruled indirectly, through hereditary local leaders called *curaca.* The Incas broke up potentially threatening local political structures and placed trusted elites in key positions.[17]

Specially trained officials moved into conquered territories after the armies, counting people, villages, animals, and household items. Although the Inca had no writing, they used systems of knotted strings to facilitate these records and possessed remarkable memories and oral histories. Sophisticated roads in combination with a communication system of way stations and runners facilitated governance over great distances and rugged terrain. A team of official runners could carry a message 125 to 150 miles a day. As part of a rigid social hierarchy, commoners were forbidden luxury goods, a practice that proved remarkably successful in controlling stealing as well as enforcing hierarchical status difference.

Although the Aztecs and the Inca are the most well-known cultures of Mesoamerica and South America, these civilizations were in some ways surpassed by others. Rivaling the Egyptians, the Maya surpassed the Aztecs in building and mathematics five hundred years earlier. The coastal cultures of Peru outdid the powerful Inca in their artistry in cloth and clay. The political structures of the Aztecs and Incas, however, did outshine other American cultures in size and complexity. Historian Peter Bakewell writes, "the Spaniards, encountering these states, were fearful, and rightly so. To master such peoples, however, would bring wealth and glory beyond anything that America had so far offered."[18]

The islands of the Caribbean, the first site of European contact, were probably settled around 5000 BCE, with subsequent waves of immigration from the mainland displacing and reforming populations. Peoples identifying themselves as Arawak, Ciboney, and Carib occupied different islands. Although contact with the mainland occurred, most Caribbean peoples seem to have been politically and socially independent from the continent. The Taino, a subset of the Arawak, lived in the Greater Antilles and on Puerto Rico, Hispaniola, and eastern Cuba. A pre-contact population of a million Taino lived on Hispaniola alone. By the fifteenth century alliances connected up to a hundred villages across the islands. Hierarchies were integral to society and politics. Chiefs called *caciques* ran groups of allied villages, assisted by a system of sub- and under-*caciques.* Politics and social interactions controlled by elites were structured by a complex set of principles. The importance of social bonding led to an ordering of relations designed to avoid conflict and preserve social control. Labor was certainly divided by gender, although sex segregation was not as severe as among other island peoples. The inhabitants of the Caribbean adopted agriculture as well as intensive fishing and gathering. West Indian subsistence practices demonstrated remarkable versatility, adapted to environmental conditions and cultural practices. Most economies were broadly based and included trade between islands. The Taino, like other Caribbean peoples, traveled widely and readily in their waters. By the fifteenth century the Taino constructed canoes that easily carried fifty to a hundred people.[19]

The other major island people, the Caribs, provided not only the name of the region but also the source of the word "cannibal," from *cannibales*, a name the Taino called them when speaking to Columbus. The Caribs probably practiced human sacrifice and cannibalism, in the form of ritual eating of flesh from their vanquished enemies. The extent and purpose of these practices remain hotly debated.[20] Using two languages, including a "men's language" for trade and ritual and a "women's language" for common use, the Caribs communicated with other islanders and mainland peoples.[21] The Caribs' extensive knowledge of wind, current, and oceanic geography proved of vital importance to Spanish explorers.[22] Island cultures flourished for over two thousand years in the Caribbean before Columbus's arrival, but in less than fifty years people scattered, languages diminished or died, and the survivors of disease and violence assimilated into the culture of the newcomers. Only a few islanders remained to resist the Europeans, raiding Spanish possessions throughout the sixteenth century and into the seventeenth.[23]

No civilizations of the sophistication and scale of those of Mesoamerica and the Andes existed in North America, due in part to less hospitable environments.[24] North of Mexico nearly three hundred different languages were spoken by almost 1.5 million people during the fifteenth century.[25] Ancient patterns of autonomous bands persisted in much of North America up to the time of contact, forming differentiated societies that engaged in constant interaction. The complexity of exchange relationships between societies contributed to cultural development and the concentration of political power. By the twelfth century, settled agriculture existed in the eastern woodlands and southwest, creating widespread exchange networks. Generally societies "progressed" from small, autonomous, and egalitarian communities to larger, more hierarchical, centralized political aggregations with vibrant economies—a pattern reminiscent of societies to the south.[26]

The Anasazi, one of the "Golden Age" peoples of North America, occupied the basin of the San Juan River in the Chaco Canyon in New Mexico. Peaking in the twelfth century, the Anasazi population centered around 15,000 people living in large planned towns surrounded by smaller villages. Renowned for their architecture, basket making, pottery, and agriculture, the Anasazi spread their influence throughout the Four Corners region of the United States. In the east, mound-building cultures such as the Adena, Hopewell, and Mississippian flourished in the first millennium of the common era. These cultures lasted for 1,700 years; the Mississippians declined around 1250. Their technology, mound building, and death cults were, from all accounts and archaeological evidence, advanced and intricate.

By the fifteenth century, most of the large settlements and centers of civilization were abandoned, their people dispersed and redistributed.[27] Intermittent and episodic coalescence as well as rapid growth and decline characterized the centuries following the peak of Anasazi and mound-building civilizations.[28] No satisfactory account or chronology of the period from 1250 to 1500 currently exists, due in part to the fluid nature of societies. Often people only briefly occupied settlements and communities established during this period. The Europeans reached a continent whose demography and politics were in profound flux. The collapse of centralized societies and established trading relationships left many cultures at levels below those previously attained.[29]

After the decline of the "Golden Age" cultures, the period from 1250 to 1500 was characterized by intense competition, insularity, defensiveness, and upheavals in exchange ties. Self-governing clans dominated the politics of most tribes. Some tribes confederated for mutual protection and general welfare, amassing considerable military strength and forming policy in common. Confederation was strongest among the eastern Algonquians—the Iroquois and Huron formed confederacies in the fourteenth century. The Iroquois League of Five Nations united the Seneca, Oneida, Mohawk, Cayuga, and Onondaga tribes. The Iroquois were unusual in that they were matriarchal. Each female-dominated nation was governed by a council of sachems, or chiefs, selected by the women of a family as the clan's representative. The senior women of each family had power of review and veto over council decisions. The League of Five Nations lasted from pre-Columbian times through contact and into the colonial period.[30]

Other North American Indian peoples known for their advanced cultural practices included the Cherokees for their sophisticated court system and the Wichitas and Caddoes for their advanced commercial skills. No North American peoples developed systems of writing, although many used substitutes such as pictographs, symbols, or wampum belts woven of strings and colorful shells as messages and records of important events. Many linguistically diverse neighboring tribes communicated with each other using sign language or the language of a dominant group in the region as a lingua franca for diplomacy and trade.[31]

Archaeological finds from the Americas evoke privileged social classes, long-distance trade, ritual, and art. Internal hierarchies, strict social stratification, and hereditary elites were common. Warriors, administrators of justice, and rulers came from elite families. Economies based on irrigated agriculture and hunting and gathering thrived. Many common foods were originally cultivated in the Americas, including potatoes, maize, and tomatoes. Resource exploitation among the peoples of South America reached highly developed levels, and they were among the most sophisticated plant breeders in the world. Indigenous peoples of the Americas possessed a vast knowledge of species and pharmacology which included the use of quinine, the anesthetic properties of coca, plants to prevent miscarriage, and other advanced medicinal uses. Most societies had a precise division of labor by gender. Warrior and hunter cultures predominated, while tribal conflict provided slaves to many societies. Religion and the supernatural were a part of everyday life. Spiritual ideas ranged from simple conceptions of deities to sophisticated theories and beliefs about holistic forces that ran through the entire world. Because the devastation wrought by European contact obscured the rich history of the peoples of the Americas, these complexities have not always been acknowledged. For many of these cultures, "the ultimate defeat of their societies was so overwhelming, and seemingly so final, that we forget their ultimate legacy to humanity."[32]

Africa: Trade, Islam, and Empires

Although often represented as static and unchanging, pre-colonial societies in Africa demonstrated evolution, adaptation, and change. European perspectives on pre-colonial Africa and its role in the Atlantic World often reflect a pervasive belief that the indigenous societies of Africa achieved low levels of development.[33] In actuality, Africa has long been home to sophisticated civilizations, from the magnificence of ancient Egypt to the power of Mali in the fourteenth and fifteenth centuries. No region of Africa has been without major states or empires at some time. The centuries directly preceding the formation of the Atlantic World were times of dramatic change in Africa. From 1100 to 1500, major territorial states rose and fell, expanding political control, cultural hegemony, religion, and trade over wide areas.[34] This time period was a crucial phase in the historical evolution of the continent as a whole. Africans assimilated outside influences and maintained their individuality, developing original cultures.

Islamic expansion in the centuries after the death of Muhammad fundamentally affected the course of African history. Early Islamic expansion was characterized by fast-moving nomadic warrior armies. By 1000 CE Islam had spread from Spain to northern India. Islam entered Africa by two routes: conquest in North Africa and via Muslim merchants and traders along trade routes running east and west. While Arabs swept down through Egypt and the Maghrib in North Africa, trade spread Islam in West Africa.[35] Moving steadily, Islam had spread into the western Sudan by the end of the tenth century, Chad by the eleventh century, and the Hausa lands (in the west) between the twelfth and thirteenth centuries. By 1200 many of the ruling elites of western and northern Africa had converted to Islam. Gold from western Africa financed Islamic expansion after the ninth century.[36] The mines of Africa allowed the widespread use of gold currency throughout the Muslim world. Possibly the most profitable branch of Muslim trade for centuries, trans-Saharan trade enriched Africans as well as Arabs.[37]

In conjunction with goods and economic prosperity, Muslim traders spread Islam, written record keeping, sophisticated accounting, and Arabic as a common commercial language. The name "the Sudan" is derived from Arabic—*Bilad al-Sudan*, the land of the black peoples. Islam profoundly affected Africa by connecting it to a vast commercial and cultural empire. Ties with the Islamic world caused previously established Christian connections to dwindle and in some cases dissolve entirely. In northeastern Africa the Christian states of Ethiopia and Nubia were weakened by incursions of Islamic culture. The Islamic way of life penetrated along trade routes far beyond any centralized political control. The importance of trade led Sudanese kings and other African rulers to guarantee security and freedom of worship for northern African and Arab Muslim traders within their kingdoms, regardless of whether or not the rulers converted to Islam. In 1067 CE the capital of the West African empire of Ghana was divided into two districts, one for Muslim traders and converts, the other for the king and his subjects, which still contained a mosque for Muslims visiting the king.[38] The centuries between 1200 and 1500 saw the greatest phase of Islamicization in Africa.

African relationships with the Muslim world were an integral part of an overall pattern of cultural and political connections. The cultural influence of Arabs and Islam brought about interconnected innovations in African society, some with profound consequences.[39] When elites and rulers converted to Islam, cultural practices adapted to the new faith. Gender relations changed to adhere to the precepts of the Qu'ran; some societies shifted from matrilineal to patrilineal reckonings of descent. Many ruling elites began to claim ancestral connections in the Arabic world, altering oral histories and professions of identity. Sometimes the Islamic network brought scholarship as well. Traders and teachers often set up their own settlements, acquiring slaves who worked farms and provided food and necessities for the settlement and passing caravans. These Muslim villages served as sites of Islamic scholarship, teaching, mysticism, and specialization.[40]

The Arab influence is easy to overemphasize due to the predominance of Arab written sources from this period and the comparative paucity of African sources. Many indigenous oral histories were disrupted by the events of subsequent centuries. For example, the contributions of local and regional trade to the development of the Sudanese states get neglected by historians focused on the impact of the trans-Saharan Islamic trade. Domestic trade provided the foundation for the development of societies and states in response to geographical, economic, and environmental factors. The civilizations of the Sudan and Sahel began as peasant societies but quickly evolved sophisticated trading systems. Before the spread of Islam, trade in the Sudan included brisk local trade, with regional networks stretching to the peoples in the north and south, as well as trans-Saharan trade with North Africa.[41] A network of established traders transported perishables throughout North Africa. Specialized traders functioned in specific areas, acting as brokers between societies living on the fringes of established states and empires, integrating them into the exchange networks. Rulers recognized the benefits of extensive trade, and traders occupied competitive positions, their movements both unrestricted and protected.

Trade networks linking North Africa, the Mediterranean world, Europe, the Sahara, regions of West Africa, and the Sudan existed before the coming of Islam, beginning in the third century CE. Islamic traders and imperial expansion greatly increased the scope and scale of these networks in the eighth century.[42] In this period, the Atlantic coast was marginal to major trade routes. The coast functioned much like a river system by connecting coastal cultures, but the nature of Atlantic currents discouraged long-range navigation.[43]

During the spread of the trans-Saharan trade, African traders profited enormously by acting as middlemen while rulers levied taxes and tariffs on goods passing through their lands and sold in their markets. Through centuries of indirect trade with North and West Africa through Muslim networks, Europeans became aware, though with much misinformation, of Africa and its riches and people, particularly its gold mines. A brisk continental slave trade supplemented other trades in luxury goods and exotic things from far lands. The slave trade supplied slaves to the Arabian peninsula and throughout Africa. In many parts of Africa, controlling labor rather than land led to wealth accumulation. Land was often held in common and distributed according to individual need and resources. Owning slaves increased one's ability to work the land, resulting in the allocation of more land and higher levels of production. A complex system with local, regional, and world ties, African trade fundamentally shaped the history of the continent before and after 1450.[44]

West Africa supported many notable empires. The empire of Ghana rose in the first millennium CE, controlling the coveted West African gold mines and fielding armies of over 100,000 troops in the eleventh century. The early history of Ghana, the first of the Sudanese kingdoms to rise to prominence, is obscure, but it traded gold with the outside world as early as the eighth century. Loosely organized, the empire began to decline at the end of the eleventh century, creating a power vacuum in the region.[45] In contests for power and battles for control, the empires and states that rose and fell throughout Africa's history relied on able and commanding leaders, military prowess, seizing the moment, and economic dominance. As Africans consciously attempted to maximize the advantages they gained from trade, their environment, and contact with Islam, large centralized kingdoms began to evolve. Some were brought down by internal and external problems, but others endured for centuries. After many years of states vying for power, Mali eventually took Ghana's place.

The Mali empire rose to prominence in West Africa and started spreading its influence over northwestern Africa and overland trade networks in the thirteenth century.[46] Conquering neighboring peoples with a formidable cavalry, Mali rulers gained control over river trade and the trans-Saharan routes, expanding their power and influence. The empire derived some of its wealth from a large agricultural base, but trade and mining played major roles in Mali's strength. Taxing trade was vital to the economic health of the empire. Rulers levied tolls on caravans and taxed commercial transactions in markets within their borders. Wise rulers understood that they could greatly increase their revenues by stimulating trade and gaining control of established trading routes.[47]

Mali's emperors, called *mansa*, combined Islamic and customary values. According to tradition, the ruler was the father of his people and wielded semi-sacred power. As a Muslim, the *mansa* was required to rule in accordance with the precepts of the Qu'ran. Leaders throughout Africa wove cultures together as they ruled over mixed populations. In Mali, justice was reserved as a royal prerogative and often split into two jurisdictions: Islamic law for Muslims and customary law for others. Populations in predominantly Muslim towns retained opportunities for customary justice through tribunals. The most famous leader of Mali, Mansa Musa, ruled from 1312 to 1337. In 1324 he made the pilgrimage to Mecca required of all devout Muslims. The size and splendor of his entourage made a dramatic impression on his contemporaries, while the amount of gold he lavishly spent and bestowed along his way spread word of the riches of Mali. His journey took him across 3,500 miles of Africa and Arabia, and after his passage the Egyptian markets were so flooded with gold that years passed before gold prices fully recovered.[48]

To run a vast empire, the *mansa* required assistance, men who enforced state policies and helped the empire run smoothly. This created a large court establishment composed of elites and bureaucrats serving specialized functions and needing to be supported by the state. Vast armies necessary for conquest and protection constantly demanded supplies, food, armor, and weapons. These and other state expenses were met through tribute, tax, and slave labor. Like most African societies, Malian society was centered on the family. Despite the faith of its rulers, most of the common people were deeply animistic, although Islam did spread beyond elites and merchants.

The inland heart of the empire revolved around Saharan "ports" servicing the caravan routes. During the fifteenth century, Mali faced threats from its neighbors. By the end of the 1400s the neighboring Songhay empire challenged Mali's dominance. Tuareg people from the north advanced upon the eminent city of Timbuktu, capturing it in 1433. Timbuktu was later absorbed by the Songhay empire. Threatened with economic suffocation, in the fifteenth century Mali's interest shifted toward the west. The focus of Mali trade turned in part from the Muslim world toward a developing coastal trade with Europe. The development of a profitable Atlantic trade alleviated some of the pressure on the state, and Mali maintained a measure of commercial importance through trade with the Portuguese, but expansion declined and the state became more inwardly focused. The Mali empire continued to decline in terms of its relative regional power and significance. Small regions on the periphery, such as Niumi on the Gambia River, remained connected to a larger world through trade.[49]

On the periphery of the great empires, small- and medium-sized kingdoms asserted their own sovereignty. Small kingdoms on the fringe of the real geopolitics of the fifteenth century controlled much of the West African coastline. A few relatively large states emerged with organized armies and bureaucracies.[50] On the coast of West Africa in the fourteenth and fifteenth centuries, kingdoms such as Oyo and Benin rose to prominence. Centered on independent cities with incorporated kingships, these states had less complex governments than the great empires. Still, they became powerful expansionist kingdoms. As in many societies, the process of state formation and expansion caused the diffusion of cultural institutions throughout their territory.[51] A large and powerful state at the end of the fifteenth century, Benin stood out in a region of small kingdoms. Benin's society was structured around a system of titles with sociopolitical implications.

On the eastern coast of Africa, Ethiopia endured as a Christian society despite the expansion of Islam. Europeans intrigued by the legend of Prestor John, a powerful Christian ruler standing alone against Islam, sought out Ethiopia as a potential aid in crusades against Muslim powers. The rulers of Ethiopia communicated with Europeans as equals, exchanging letters and emissaries with kings and popes. In 1306, King Wedem Ar-ad sent a delegation of thirty Africans to Europe in pursuit of a pan-Christian alliance. His envoy visited Spain, met the pope in France, and spent time in Rome.[52] Merchants from Venice visited Ethiopia in the fourteenth and fifteenth centuries. European maps from 1457 depict Ethiopia fairly accurately. In 1450, Ethiopia was ruled by Emperor Zara Yakob (1434–1468), a dynamic king zealous in his personal faith and forceful in his encouragement of Christianity throughout his lands. He exchanged warm letters with the Spanish king. Yakob encouraged writing, built churches, and supported public education. He also reorganized the government and suppressed provincial rebellions. His influence was felt widely: chiefs and kings of neighboring societies were forced to acknowledge him with tribute.[53]

South of Ethiopia, along the coast, a Swahili ethnic community emerged after the twelfth century. People descended from the wide migration of Bantu-speaking peoples south and east across the continent during the first millennium began to form a cohesive regional culture over several centuries. During the twelfth and thirteenth centuries the Swahili population grew steadily. Their economy was based on three occupations: farming, fishing, and trading. Swahili civilization bloomed through commercial development. Settlements grew into substantial towns as they became centers of trade. The city of Mogadishu, one of the most renowned cities in East Africa in the thirteenth century, had a cosmopolitan character and mixed population like many Swahili port cities. Contact with people from all over, including Arabs, Persians, Indians, and even merchants from China, in the early fifteenth century stimulated social and cultural development. Newly wealthy merchants competed with old elites for power and influence. Merchants often adopted Islam, followed by many elites and commoners despite Ethiopia's Christian heritage. Swahili became a language of commerce, displacing even Arabic in East Africa in the thirteenth century.[54] Trade was both a strength and a weakness, as the wealth of the region depended on trade rather than local production, creating some instability.[55]

Not all Africans lived within states or empires. The study of Africa tends to focus on large empires and kingdoms in contact with other areas of the world, resulting in the neglect of other peoples. By focusing on centralized rulers and institutions of government, researchers ignore societies organized in different ways. Doing credit to the diversity and extent of civilization in Africa presents a formidable challenge. Little written evidence of the peoples and states—even the large and formidable empires—exists of the parts of Africa unknown to Islam in this period. Archaeological evidence such as massive stone monuments provides evidence of skilled and complex cultures. In central Africa, chieftaincies organized politically on a large scale in the 1300s and 1400s, such as the Kongo people. Among the first to establish diplomatic relations with the Europeans in the 1480s, the Kongo disagreed intensely on the types of contacts they should establish with Europeans.[56]

Most African cultures emphasized the role of kinship in individual and collective identity, even considering the extensive diversity of the continent. Societies in organized kingdoms and empires were often highly hierarchical, most containing individuals or families with elite status. Slavery, practiced in many societies, varied widely from culture to culture. Often identified as those without kin, slaves inhabited a range of relationships of dependency. Warfare, another common experience, had its own cultural conventions. Captives from war provided a source of slaves for trade or labor. The Hausa people and others had regulations for war including a warning to their target followed by a three-day delay, allowing women, children, and elders to be sent to safety.[57] Most societies had distinct gender roles and a division of labor, which did not stop some elite women from wielding great power and prestige. Even in societies that enforced gender separation, such as the seclusion of married women in purdah, women of intelligence and influence rose to prominence.

External and internal dynamics affected the development of African states. Ideas about religion, government, art, commerce, agriculture, and manufacturing dispersed across state and ethnic boundaries. While facilitating this dispersal, trade networks provided access to goods and information from distant lands. Never truly isolated, Africa connected with the larger world through trans-Saharan trade and Islam. Black ambassadors resided in Cairo by the fifteenth century, and Timbuktu schools taught world geography. Africa hardly resembled the isolated backwater perceived by many historians of the past. Rulers and chiefs welcomed traders from Arabia, India, and eventually Europe, amassing wealth and resources to build their power and expand their states.[58] This commercial system, centered around Islamic expansion and stretching from Spain through Africa to South Asia and China, peaked around the year 1300. The centuries that followed were a crucial turning point in history, where the dominance of the world's trade and political power hung in the balance. The eventual control of this trade and power by Europe by the sixteenth century was by no means a necessary outcome.[59]

During the fifteenth century, when the Portuguese began exploring down the coast of Africa, their impact on the interior was negligible. Although they scattered and enslaved the inhabitants of islands in the Atlantic, the established trading systems and political powers of the interior remained fairly stable. As other

European traders ventured southward down the coast, Africans welcomed competition between Europeans. Rivalries provided opportunities to be turned to the advantage of skilled and experienced traders. Africans set the terms of exchange. Kings and chiefs levied high customs duties and created new fees and extractions, generating substantial profits for African middlemen and governments.[60]

Europe: Christianity, Identity, and Rebirth

Ancient civilizations clustered around the Mediterranean, including the Roman Empire. Interconnected by Roman rule, Africa and Europe had closer ties than many people now realize. Rome depended on the grain of Africa; Catholic theology was shaped by the African Augustine.[61] After the breakup of the Roman Empire, Africa and Europe developed separate spheres. Out of the collapse of the western half of the Roman Empire came the beginnings of Europe proper. The spread of Islam in Africa widened the breach, although Islam made incursions into Europe as well. In late antiquity Christianity transformed the Roman Empire, becoming the official religion by 400 CE. The spread of Christianity into the far reaches of the empire set the stage for the distinctive development of a European identity. In part a creation of the Middle Ages, Europe came to be distinguished by Latin Christianity from its Islamic, Byzantine, and Slavic neighbors.[62]

In the centuries after the fall of Rome, the core of Europe resisted invasions from Arabia, North Africa, Scandinavia, and Asia, all the while enduring internal division and chaos. Charlemagne's Frankish empire brought temporary stability and unity in the ninth century.[63] Charlemagne began to impose uniformity and harmony in the rites and chants of the church. The dominance of one liturgical language and one cultic form increased the homogeneity and unifying power of Christianity in Europe.[64] As the hierarchy around the papacy in Rome increased in scope and scale, a distinct Latin Christian/Roman Catholic culture began to emerge in Western Europe. By the end of the eleventh century, Western Europe began to assert itself on a larger stage—by going on Crusades to the Holy Land to reclaim Jerusalem. The Crusades, however impermanent their achievements, marked the beginning of Europe's aggressive engagement with the world outside its own continent.[65]

The rise of Christianity and Islam profoundly shaped ideas of the West and Europe as a distinct entity. People identified as part of a community of faith as well as subjects of a ruler and members of ethnic and linguistic groups. Called the "age of faith," Europe's medieval period was fundamentally shaped by Christian ideas, conflicts, and drives. Between 950 and 1350, Latin Christendom, characterized by rite and obedience, roughly doubled in size.[66] The late eleventh through thirteenth centuries were times of great vitality for Christianity in Europe. Christianity extended into distant parts of Europe through advances in territory and conversion. Scandinavia converted to Christianity in the eleventh century, despite the inhabitants' fierce independence. The establishment of local hierarchies directly subordinate to Rome accompanied conversion. Reforms, spiritual awakenings, and centralized governments strengthened and solidified its reach. As a common culture centered on the church spread, heretical groups were converted, exiled, or eliminated. The church flexed its power externally through the Crusades and inwardly by enforcing obedience to the hierarchy of the church. The church began to intervene in worldly affairs, leading to a degree of degradation in the fourteenth century.

Christianity was not the only faith on the move in the medieval period. From 750 to 1050, Latin, Greek, and Islamic empires spread political cohesion, religion, and language. Indeed, the Islamic empires extended into the European continent for centuries, mostly in the Iberian peninsula.[67] Until the twelfth century, the only gold coinage available in Europe originated in the Islamic world.[68] Even as Islamic power was driven back by the advance of Christianity, Arabic persisted as the language of record and official communication. For a hundred years after the Christian conquest of Toledo in 1085, Arabic, not Latin or a Romance language, dominated records and official documents. Early in the thirteenth century, Arabic documents became a minority for the first time, and by 1300 only two documents a year were written in Arabic.[69] The presence of Islamic culture in Iberia exposed Europeans to Arabic writing, modern science, forms of government, architecture, trade, navigation techniques, astronomy, and cartography. Many of these advances later aided the Atlantic exploration and expansion of the Spanish and Portuguese.[70]

After the ninth century, invasions into the heart of Europe ceased. Mongol and Ottoman expansion changed the boundaries of Europe, but unlike many other areas of the world, the center of Europe remained singularly free of invasion.[71] European trade received a boost from the Mongols in the thirteenth century. While not entering Western Europe, the Mongols invaded Russia and the lands of Eastern Europe. Sweeping westward from the central Asian steppes in 1223, the Mongol cavalry accomplished the only successful winter invasion of Russia in history. Their rule opened up stable trade routes from Europe all the way to China and fundamentally altered Asia and Eastern Europe. Marco Polo used the Mongol trans-Eurasian route, sparking the engagement of the Christian West with the East. Through trade under Mongol rule, gunpowder was introduced into European warfare from China. It was first used in artillery in the 1320s but would quickly become a staple of European warfare. The Byzantine Empire, the remnants of the eastern Roman Empire and the seat of orthodox Christianity, was hit hard by the Mongols. The expansion of the Islamic Ottoman Empire in the late fourteenth and fifteenth centuries hastened the decline of the Byzantines. The Ottomans expanded to forty times their original size by 1402. Sultan Mehmed II began to obliterate the last traces of the Byzantines in 1451, spreading into Eastern Europe.[72] Encounters with Mongols, Ottomans, and other cultures shifted the political and religious frontiers of Europe.

On the frontiers of Europe tensions between different groups were exacerbated by conquest, colonization, and conversion. European images of exclusion and inclusion in the twelfth century defined people as Christian or non-Christian, and barbarian or civilized. People could be Christian but still condemned for their barbarity. While the language of race is biological, its medieval manifestations were often cultural—matters of descent, custom, languages, and law.[73] Only descent is inherently biological. In medieval law, most individuals were subject to their own ethnic law regardless of where they resided. Images of natural and immemorial hostility came to dominate relations in the fourteenth century. Europeans perceived linguistic and cultural differences as representing essential opposition and antagonism. During the medieval period, discrimination against ethnic and religious groups increased as Catholic uniformity spread intolerance for heretics and non-Christians. Toleration of division within societies diminished considerably even on the periphery. In Spain, with its mixed Muslim, Jewish, and Christian population, high levels of tension existed. As Christian rulers solidified their power, Jews and Muslims faced expulsion or forced conversion. Other regions experienced similar problems, including the German borderlands in Eastern and Central Europe and the Celts in Ireland and Wales. The medieval world birthed the mental habits and institutions of European racism and colonialism.[74]

In the four centuries after 1050, three social institutions remained characteristic of medieval society through demographic and cultural changes: a system of personal loyalties associated with lordship and vassalage, an agricultural economy built on manors, and the demographic revival of cities with consequent economic growth. War also characterized the politics and culture of Europe. A strong secular martial culture, religious Crusades, and inter-ethnic conflict contributed to centuries of violence.[75] As people lived at times in a state of perpetual war, the community took priority over the individual in European societies. Invasions and internal strife contributed to the development of a reciprocal system of vassalage. Ties of dependence extended from the top to the bottom of the social scale, creating networks of loyalties and alliances ordering society in patterns of subordination and domination.[76] A small hereditary elite dominated the peasant majority engaged in manorial agriculture, supplemented by hunting and gathering. A period of dramatic urbanization occurred in the twelfth and thirteenth centuries. Older, established cities grew in population, while new cities and towns were founded. In the Mediterranean, mercantile mini-empires grew out of city-states on the Italian coast. Cities practiced localized imperialism starting in the thirteenth century, swallowing smaller neighbors and staking claims to the growing maritime trade. Aggression and alliances fed expansion, which created complex political-power relationships among the city-states. In response, the Italians invented aspects of modern diplomacy, including the practice of establishing permanent delegations to represent political and economic interests.

If Christianity united Europe, trade brought prosperity and cemented ties.

As Robert Bartlett has written, "The unity of the medieval West was, in part, a traders' unity."[77] Trade fueled expansion, development, and population increase. Europe emerged as an identifiable cultural entity by 1300. Relatively densely settled, Europe was productive and culturally innovative. Textile production, international banking, insurance, intellectual life, and political power advanced significantly. This dynamic society remained in flux at its periphery, where it engaged with other cultures and peoples far from its cultural centers. In contrast to its earlier flowering, the fourteenth and fifteenth centuries saw Europe drawing in upon itself in reaction to successive catastrophes.

Mongol power peaked in 1260 and subsequently declined.[78] Under the peace imposed by the Mongol invaders, European trade with the East flourished. The end of this trade caused economic displacement within Europe. The financial infrastructure of medieval Europe was tied to the international trade in luxury goods. Tensions from the economic pressures exploded in worker riots. A chilly beginning to the fourteenth century foreshadowed difficult years ahead for Europe. The Baltic Sea froze over in 1303 and 1306–1307, part of a wave of cold weather causing flooding and poor harvests. In the second decade of the century, two waves of crop failure struck much of Western Europe, possibly resulting in the death of 15 percent of the population from starvation and disease. The rise of food prices by as much as 800 percent triggered riots and unrest, adding to widespread suffering. The powerful reformer Pope Innocent III (pope from 1198 to 1216) was followed by Boniface VIII (pope from 1295 to 1303), whose personal vanity and excess helped weaken the papacy for nearly a century. Fleeing social chaos, the head of the church hierarchy relocated to France, becoming the puppet of the French kings. A weakened church offered little spiritual authority or comfort, adding to the social strain. The papacy eventually recovered from its weak position and left France to return to Rome. By the middle of the fifteenth century the papacy had returned to a position of power, although less absolute than in the thirteenth century.[79]

All of these blows paled in comparison to the greatest source of Europe's troubles in the fourteenth century. No event of the fourteenth century, perhaps of all European history, approached the devastation of the plague known as the Black Death.[80] In 1300 about 74 million people lived in Europe, a doubling of the population in 1000 and a sign of success. Mid-century, staggering losses from disease left a population of only 52 million.[81] Sailors returning from the East in the summer of 1346 told stories of terrible plagues and bodies stacked in the streets in India and China. At the time, people paid little attention to these accounts. But the disease, most likely the bubonic plague, first emerged in Italian ports in the spring of 1348. It quickly spread through the Italian peninsula and into the rest of Europe. Shipping and trade networks, a source of Europe's economic boom and development, only helped to spread the plague farther and faster. The plague reached Paris by summer, and England by the end of the year. The Netherlands, Norway, and Ireland were all struck in 1349, and by 1351 people in Russia were dying from it. From the late 1340s to the early

1350s the Black Death killed approximately one third of the population from Ireland to India, approximately 20 million people in Europe alone. Fatality rates varied widely—90 percent or more in some places, while only 20 percent in others. Entire towns were left empty. Spread by shipping, the plague reappeared sporadically about every fifteen to twenty years until 1721 in ports around Europe. Half the population of Florence died in 1400.[82]

In addition to these troubles, the Hundred Years' War contributed to the upheaval of the fourteenth century. The Hundred Years' War, a name coined by nineteenth-century historians, describes a prolonged period of trouble from 1337 to 1453. The conflict originated in disputes over territory between the kings of England and the French kings, precipitated by a succession crisis over the French crown. The "war" was less a sustained conflict than a series of pitched battles and truces interspersed with periods of exhaustion. The continuous conflict between France and England drained both powerful kingdoms and influenced their history and that of Europe. The identities of both countries became more solidified and distinct. The fighting spurred innovations in warfare and saw some of the first uses of gunpowder in European battles. Foot soldiers began to replace mounted knights as the main instruments of war. Large armies over long periods of time racked up high expenses, requiring rulers to find ways to pay for their endeavors. Moves toward government centralization were made on both sides. In England, Parliament became a more regularly meeting body due to the necessity of continually raising funds.[83]

Europeans responded to the upheaval and devastation of the fourteenth century by forming a profound cultural obsession with mortality. Art and literature reflected preoccupations with the universality and capriciousness of death. Dante's *The Divine Comedy* and Boccacio's *Decameron* stand as classics of literature and representations of this culture. Not all Europeans focused on death and destruction, however. Another cultural movement began in the midst of the chaos. Beginning in Florence, the Italian Renaissance (approx. 1350–1550) expressed a more hopeful view of life and the desire to improve the human condition. The Renaissance began as an attempt to imitate Latin styles but was pushed into a full-scale effort to refashion human society on the model of ancient cultures. This effort produced a critical approach to both the past and present. The identity of Europe became linked to ancient Hebrew, Greek, and Roman cultures as well as Latin Christianity.[84]

Independent Italian city-states, with their complex political and economic forces, nurtured the Renaissance.[85] Centers of trade such as Florence and Venice housed systems of patronage for artists and scholars. Such cities were quite cosmopolitan. Venice even had colonies abroad—a series of ports in the Mediterranean. This Renaissance, unlike earlier cultural flowerings, was not confined to monasteries and universities. It involved the educated laymen of the cities, intruding into and being affected by secular life, with manifold and extensive consequences. Artists, writers, philosophers, politicians, and scientists were inspired by the movement. The Renaissance and the fourteenth century also contributed to early feminism. Gender roles in Europe remained closely tied to Christianity, with notions that men were responsible for women, who were subservient. This ideology was challenged by a world where death came swiftly and often. Women found themselves without husbands or fathers, and the idea that men would and should always care for women was shaken. A young woman, Joan of Arc, claimed to hear voices of angels and saints directing her to put on men's clothing and lead a French army during the Hundred Years' War. She was convicted of witchcraft on the grounds that her refusal to wear women's clothing constituted a direct and serious challenge to women's place in the hierarchy of creation. Thus, the voices she heard must be demonic. In a sense, therefore, Joan was burned at the stake for challenging gender roles.[86] While the Italian city-states explored humanism and art, the Spanish kingdoms, France, and England maintained their agrarian, feudal, and clerical character for the most part. Despite common ties of Christianity, trade, and culture, Europe lacked internal cohesion.[87]

Following the travails of the fourteenth century, and on the shoulders of the Renaissance, the fifteenth century began more optimistically. The papacy emerged restored from its "Babylonian Captivity" in France. The plague, aside from sporadic and isolated outbreaks, receded into memory. The Renaissance inspired intellectual and scientific exploration, while tales of riches in the East and Africa spurred maritime exploration. Advances in sailing technology made ocean voyages feasible. Ship building developed greatly in the late fourteenth century; hybrid three-mast ships called *caravels* appeared around 1450 and would be in use for decades to come.[88] While the Portuguese were not the first to sail around Africa (that honor probably belongs to the Phoenicians), they led European advances southward in the fifteenth century.[89] Portuguese trips to Africa in the 1440s and 1450s followed over one hundred years of European seafaring around Morocco. On the Madeira and Canary islands sugar cane plantations were established and the inhabitants enslaved. Europeans were ready and able to fight for glory, God, and gold.[90]

Conclusion

While connected by the Mediterranean and Islamic world for centuries, direct contact between Europe and Africa (excluding North Africa) remained minimal until the mid-fifteenth century. Pursuing gold and slaves, the Portuguese began to venture down the coast of West Africa in the 1440s, conducting slave raids on the islands and archipelagos off the coasts of Mauritania and Morocco. The islanders not captured or killed usually scattered for survival. Emboldened by their successes, the Portuguese began to attack mainland settlements and sail inland up rivers. In 1444, a group of men led by Lancarote de Lagos sailed partway up the Senegal River, attacked a settlement, and seized captives. News of these and other raids spread among West African societies, and soon Portuguese vessels were met with heavy and effective resistance.[91] The naval forces of larger kingdoms maintained patrols, and many Africans looked upon all Europeans with mistrust and hostility. During the first contact between Europeans and the Niominka, both parties remained in their own ships, patrolling watchfully at a distance.[92]

Often Europeans found themselves at a fatal disadvantage in encounters with Africans. In the late summer of 1446, an armed Portuguese caravel led by Nuno Tristão sailed into the mouth of the Gambia River with a complement of twenty-eight men. Tristão launched two boats up the river, each containing twelve men. Riding the tide inland, the sailors sighted a settlement. Intending to attack the village and capture slaves, they failed to notice the approach of a dozen African vessels from the other bank. According to survivors' accounts, as many as seventy or eighty Africans sent the Portuguese sailors fleeing under a rain of arrows. Two days after the encounter, only seven of the original twenty-eight men were still alive—the Africans' arrows had been treated with a potent poison.[93] Limping slowly back to Portugal, the survivors brought with them a vivid tale of effective African resistance.

In some cases, contact between West Africans and the Portuguese involved peaceful trade rather than violence. Portuguese merchant seamen traded for gold with members of the Tuareg people in 1442. This trade, along with the sale of captives into slavery, fed the Europeans' intense interest in the West African coast, while the potential for profit and access to new goods interested Africans. For both sides, "survival and success depended not on force of arms, but on finding a mutuality of interests and then fostering those interests to the benefit of African states and foreign traders alike."[94] Over time, trading relationships were established, although they remained sites of conflict.

Trade interests often determined the shape of contact. Trading hierarchies prevailed between Europeans and Africans and within societies. Both sides possessed different advantages. Europeans had more access to capital than most African traders, they controlled shipping in the Atlantic with superior technology, and they offered access to new markets and goods. However, Europeans, outnumbered and unfamiliar with the continent, depended on Africans for basics such as water, food, and shelter. Powerful groups refused Europeans access to their lands. Europeans depended upon African traders, rulers, and intermediaries. They often lacked the upper hand in negotiations and could rarely survive long enough in the tropics to work independently. Africans provided cultural and commercial mediation, as well as access to ports and inland peoples in many cases. They also provided a steady and abundant supply of slaves, mostly captured from the interior of Africa.

Historian Donald R. Wright offers one perspective on the dynamics of power and exploitation that functioned in the mid-fifteenth century. As their contact with Africans expanded, Europeans came to understand "[w]hat should have been obvious from the beginning: that Africans were not going to wait passively until the next vessel of marauders arrived to fall upon their dwindling numbers; that Africans were not different from others in their interest in and willingness to exchange human beings for products they needed or wanted; and that Atlantic sailors could, therefore, more easily and safely acquire slaves by trade than by capture."[95] Slavery had been a part of African society for centuries, as had extensive trade networks and warfare—the Africans and Europeans in many ways were on the same page despite their cultural differences.

Contact between the people on the east side of the Atlantic and those in the Americas would not come until the end of the fifteenth century with Columbus. Still, these initial encounters were, as future ones continued to be, shaped by all parties involved. Understanding the depth and breadth of the continental backgrounds for the momentous events which followed the above early skirmishes between the Portuguese and West African coastal peoples helps to put the Atlantic World in perspective and in context.

Notes

1. Michael D. Coe and Rex Koontz, *Mexico: From the Olmecs to the Aztecs,* 5th ed., (London: Thames and Hudson, 1994), 225.

2. Neal Salisbury, "The Indians' Old World: Native Americans and the Coming of Europeans," in *Major Problems in American Indian History,* ed. Albert L. Hurtado and Peter Iverson (Boston: Houghton Mifflin, 2001), 43.

3. Brian M. Fagan, *Kingdoms of Gold, Kingdoms of Jade: The Americas before Columbus* (London: Thames and Hudson, 1991), 13.

4. Michael D. Coe, *The Maya,* 5th ed. (London: Thames and Hudson, 1993), 127.

5. Ibid., 5.

6. Ibid., 169; Fagan, *Kingdoms of Gold,* 137.

7. Coe, *Maya,* 158.

8. Coe and Koontz, *Mexico;* Inga Clendinnen, *Aztecs: An Interpretation* (London: Cambridge University Press, 1991); Peter Bakewell, *A History of Latin America: Empires and Sequels, 1450–1930* (Oxford: Blackwell, 1997), 20–25.

9. Coe and Koontz, *Mexico,* 201.

10. Clendinnen, *Aztecs,* 111.

11. Ibid., 2, 111–140.

12. Coe and Koontz, *Mexico,* 195.

13. Clendinnen, *Aztecs,* chapters 6, 7, and 8.

14. Friedrich Katz, *The Ancient American Civilizations,* trans. K. M. Lois Simpson (New York: Praeger, 1969), 263–309.

15 Bakewell, *A History of Latin America,* 44.

16. Ibid., 28.

17. Ibid., 31.

18. Ibid., 38.

19. Samuel M. Wilson, ed., *The Indigenous People of the Caribbean* (Gainesville: University Press of Florida, 1997).

20. Louis Allaire, "The Lesser Antilles before Columbus," in *The Indigenous People of the Caribbean,* ed. Samuel M. Wilson (Gainesville: University Press of Florida, 1997), 20–28.

21. Vincent O. Cooper, "Language and Gender among the Kalinago of Fifteenth-Century St. Croix," in *The Indigenous People of the Caribbean*, ed. Wilson, 186–196, 194.

22. John Thornton, *Africa and Africans in the Making of the Atlantic World, 1400–1800*, 2nd ed. (Cambridge: Cambridge University Press, 1998), 16.

23. Thornton, *Africa and Africans*, 40.

24. Fagan, *Kingdoms of Gold*, 202.

25. Salisbury, "Indians' Old World," 30.

26. Fagan, *Kingdoms of Gold*, chapter 18.

27. Salisbury, "Indians' Old World," 34–35.

28. Arrell Morgan Gibson, *The American Indian: Prehistory to the Present* (Toronto: D. C. Heath, 1980), 35.

29. Fagan, *Kingdoms of Gold*, 204–209.

30. Gibson, *American Indian*, chapters 3 and 4.

31. Ibid., 42–43.

32. Fagan, *Kingdoms of Gold*, 228.

33. Thornton, *Africa and Africans*, 3.

34. Funso Afolayan, "Civilizations of the Upper Nile and North Africa," in *Africa*, vol. 1, *African History before 1885*, ed. Toyin Falola (Durham, N.C.: Carolina Academic Press, 2000), 133.

35. I. Hrbek, "Africa in the Context of World History," in *General History of Africa*, vol. 3, *Africa from the Seventh to the Eleventh Century*, ed. I. Hrbek, abridged (Berkeley: University of California Press, 1992), 5.

36. David R. Ringrose, *Expansion and Global Interaction, 1200–1700* (New York: Longman, 2001), 25.

37. Hrbek, "Africa in the Context of World History," 4.

38. J. I. Dibua, "Sudanese Kingdoms of West Africa" in *Africa*, vol. 1, *African History before 1885*, ed. Falola, 145.

39. See I. Hrbek, ed., *General History of Africa*, vol. 3, *Africa from the Seventh to the Eleventh Century*, abridged (Berkeley: University of California Press, 1992), chapters 2, 3, and 4.

40. Ringrose, *Expansion and Global Interaction*, 35.

41. Dibua, "Sudanese Kingdoms," 141.

42. Ibid., 142.

43. Thornton, *Africa and Africans*, 21–22.

44. D. T. Niane, "Relationships and Exchanges among the Different Regions," in *General History of Africa*, vol. 4, *Africa from the Twelfth to the Sixteenth Century*, ed. D. T. Niane (Berkeley: University of California Press, 1984), 614–634.

45. Dibua, "Sudanese Kingdoms," 147.

46. See D. T. Niane, ed., *General History of Africa*, vol. 4, *Africa from the Twelfth to the Sixteenth Century* (Berkeley: University of California Press, 1984), chapters 6 and 7.

47. Donald R. Wright, *The World and a Very Small Place in Africa: A History of Globalization in Niumi, the Gambia* (New York: M. E. Sharpe, 2004), 37.

48. Dibua, "Sudanese Kingdoms," 148–149.

49. Wright, *World and a Very Small Place*, 139.

50. Ringrose, *Expansion and Global Interaction*, 55–66.

51. A. F. C. Ryder, "From the Volta to Cameroon," in Niane, *General History of Africa*, 4:370.

52. David Northrup, *Africa's Discovery of Europe, 1450–1850* (Oxford: Oxford University Press, 2002), 3–4.

53. Saheed A. Adejumobi, "Ethiopia," in Falola, *Africa,* 1:237–240.

54. Joel E. Tishken, "Central Africa: People and States," in Falola, *Africa,* 1:205.

55. See Niane, *General History of Africa,* vol. 4, chapter 18.

56. Joel E. Tishken, "Central Africa: People and States," in Falola, *Africa,* 1:215.

57. William C. Barnett, "The Geography of Africa," in *Africa,* ed. Falola, 1:31.

58. Funso Afolayan, "Kingdoms of West Africa: Benin, Oyo, and Asante," in Falola, *Africa,* 1:188.

59. Ringrose, *Expansion and Global Interaction,* 26.

60. George E. Brooks, *Landlords and Strangers: Ecology, Society, and Trade in Western Africa, 1000–1630* (San Francisco: Westview Press, 1993), 5.

61. Marc Bloch, *Feudal Society,* vol. 1, trans. L. A. Manyon (London: Routledge and Kegan Paul, 1962), xix.

62. Bloch, *Feudal Society,* xx.

63. Robert Bartlett, *The Making of Europe: Conquest, Colonization, and Cultural Change, 950–1350* (London: Penguin Press, 1993), 269.

64. Bartlett, *Making of Europe,* 19.

65. Brian Levack, Edward Muir, Michael Maas, and Meredith Veldman, *The West: Encounters and Transformations,* vol. 1, *To 1715* (New York: Pearson-Longman Press, 2004), 288–289; Rosemary Morris, "Northern Europe Invades the Mediterranean, 900–1200," in *The Oxford Illustrated History of Medieval Europe,* ed. George Holmes (Oxford: Oxford University Press, 1988), 216.

66. Bartlett, *Making of Europe,* 243, 292; H. G. Koenigsberger, *Medieval Europe, 400–1500,* (London: Longman House, 1987), 164–165, 234.

67. For an in-depth discussion, see Franco Cardini, *Europe and Islam,* trans. Caroline Beamish (Oxford: Blackwell, 2001).

68. Bloch, *Feudal Society,* 3.

69. Bartlett, *Making of Europe,* 204.

70. Michael L. Coniff and Thomas J. Davis, *Africans in the Americas: A History of the Black Diaspora* (Caldwell, N.J.: Blackburn Press, 2002), 17.

71. Bloch, *Feudal Europe,* 56.

72. Levack, *West,* 331–339; Robert Mantran, "A Turkish or Mongolian Islam," in *The Cambridge Illustrated History of the Middle Ages,* vol. 3, *1250–1520,* ed. Robert Fossier (Cambridge: Cambridge University Press, 1986), 278–283, 294.

73. Bartlett, *Making of Europe,* 23, 197.

74. Ibid., 240, 313.

75. Maurice Keen, "Introduction: Warfare and the Middle Ages," in *Medieval Warfare: A History,* ed. Maurice Keen (Oxford: Oxford University Press, 1999), 3.

76. Bloch, *Feudal Society,* 135, 281.

77. Bartlett, *Making of Europe,* 196.

78. Mantran, "Turkish or Mongolian Islam," 283–294.

79. Koenigsberger, *Medieval Europe,* 327.

80. Malcolm Vale, "The Civilization of Courts and Cities in the North, 1200–1500," in *The Oxford Illustrated History of Medieval Europe,* ed. George Holmes (Oxford: Oxford University Press, 1988), 325–329.

81. Levack, *West,* 326–330.

82. Ibid., 330.

83. Koenigsberger, *Medieval Europe*, 309.

84. Peter Denley, "The Mediterranean in the Age of the Renaissance, 1200–1500," in *Oxford Illustrated History of Medieval Europe*, ed. Holmes, 285–296.

85. Giorgio Chittolini, "Cities, 'City-States,' and Regional States in North-Central Italy," in *Cities and the Rise of States in Europe,* A.D. *1000 to 1800*, ed. Charles Tilly and Wim P. Blockmans (San Francisco: Westview Press, 1994), 28–43.

86. Levack, *West*, 346–7.

87. Koenigsberger, *Medieval Europe*, 385–386.

88. Koenigsberger, *Medieval Europe*, 294.

89. Coniff and Davis, *Africans in the Americas*, 31.

90. Ringrose, *Expansion and Global Interaction*, 30.

91. Thornton, *Africa and Africans*, 37.

92. Brooks, *Landlords and Strangers*, 126.

93. Wright, *World and a Very Small Place*, 11–12.

94. Ringrose, *Expansion and Global Interaction*, 62.

95. Donald R. Wright, *African Americans in the Colonial Era: From African Origins through the American Revolution*, (Arlington Heights, Ill.: Harlan Davidson, 1990), 23–24.

CHAPTER TWO

Contact and Conquest in Africa and the Americas

Timothy P. Grady

During the fifteenth and sixteenth centuries key developments in Western Europe led to an age of exploration and discovery that brought peoples of vastly different cultures into contact with one another for the first time. Explorers from Portugal, Spain, and other European nations slowly expanded their geographic knowledge southward along the coast of Africa and westward across the Atlantic to the shores of the Americas. The extension of European influence and power altered those societies which came into contact with the traders, missionaries, and soldiers who followed on the heels of those early explorers. In Africa the beginnings and growth of the slave trade changed the economies and political structure of peoples far inland from the small, isolated trading outposts that Europeans maintained along the coast, while in the Americas, disease, warfare, and abuse decimated the native population. Yet these events were not a foregone conclusion. Significant events in terms of political structures, economic impetus, and technological innovations allowed European nations, primarily Portugal and Spain, to successfully meet the challenges of exploration. As early European colonies grew, new institutions and ideas developed to aggressively exploit the new lands and inhabitants. This led to enormous changes all across the Atlantic World as native peoples sought to retain their lives and cultures in the face of overwhelming pressures applied in the name of king, country, and Christianity. Finally, with the spectacular success of the Spanish in the Americas, combined with Portuguese dominance along the coast of Africa, changes to European societies ensued as the wealth of the Americas and the new goods and foods of Africa and Asia flowed into Europe. In all, the events of the fourteenth through the sixteenth centuries set the stage for the Atlantic World as, for the first time, peoples from Europe, Africa, and the Americas became tied together into a larger whole.

In May of 1453, the Catholic cardinal Bessarion wrote to Francesco Foscari, the doge of Venice, relating the news that the capital of the Byzantine Empire, Constantinople, had been sacked by Ottoman Turks. "A thing terrible to relate, and to be deplored by all who have in them any spark of humanity, and especially by Christians," he wrote. "A city which was so flourishing, with such a great empire, such illustrious men, such very famous and ancient families, so prosperous, the head of all Greece, the splendor and glory of the East, the school of the best arts, the refuge of all good things, has been captured, despoiled, ravaged, and completely sacked by the most inhuman barbarians and the most savage enemies of the Christian faith."[1] The fall of the great city of Constantinople to the Muslim Turks shook the confidence of Christian Europe as the last vestige of the Roman Empire was lost. Additionally, the double setback of the loss of communication and trade ties to Asia as well as the presence of a large and powerful enemy in the Mediterranean was of great concern to all. The wealth of India, China, and other Far Eastern regions were well known to Europeans of the late Middle Ages. From Roman times, the flow of goods along the Silk Road, the trade route connecting the eastern Mediterranean to East Asia, had been a source of great wealth for all peoples along the trail. In addition to silk, the route carried many other precious commodities. Caravans heading toward China from the Mediterranean carried gold and other precious metals, ivory, precious stones, and glass. From India and Asia furs, ceramics, jade, bronze objects, lacquer, and iron were carried to the West. There was not a direct trade connection between the two ends, so many of these goods were bartered for others along the way, and most objects changed hands several times before reaching a final destination. Ideas and religion passed along the Silk Road as often as trade goods. Christianity, Buddhism, Hinduism, and Islam all spread to varying degrees along the route. From the European perspective, the connection to Asia also meant spreading Christianity. The Crusades brought Western Europeans into closer contact with the end points of these trade routes, and missionaries soon traveled eastward. By the mid-thirteenth century a fledgling Catholic population was established in China led by missionaries sent by the pope to the Mongol capital at Kharkoum, such as the Franciscan priest Giovanni Pian de Carpini, who traveled as an emissary from Pope Innocent IV to Asia from 1245 to 1247. The exotic tales of Asia in the European popular imagination reached their peak in the late thirteenth century with the widespread popularity of a book known at the time as *The Travels of Marco Polo* or as *The Description of the World*. These descriptions of the Mongol Empire, China (known as Cathay), and the cultures and peoples of various parts of India and Africa were related to a writer by the Venetian merchant Marco Polo, who, from 1271 traveled with his father and uncle to Asia, eventually entering the khan's service and living in China for some seventeen years before returning to Europe and relating his experiences. Polo's tales were met with much skepticism, but this did not prevent his book from attaining widespread fame and attention from most of European elites.[2]

The religious conflict between the Moslem and Christian worlds effectively severed the active connection between Asia and Europe. As the crusaders were slowly driven out of the eastern Mediterranean, it began to be more hazardous and more expensive to obtain the exotic goods from Asia that were in such demand. The rise of the Ottoman Empire culminated this trend. Beginning in the early fourteenth century the Ottoman Turks expanded their power throughout Anatolia, the Balkan provinces south of the Danube River, Syria, Palestine, and Mesopotamia over the next two hundred years. In addition, Egypt, Mecca, and the North African provinces were governed under special regulations imposed by the Turks, as were satellite domains in Arabia, in the Caucasus, and among the Crimean Tartars. This strategic position across the trade routes to the East slowly deprived the merchant houses of Venice, Genoa, and other European trading centers of this lucrative trade. Cut off from access to the East, merchants, sailors, missionaries, and rulers turned westward for new economic opportunities. Hence, the exploration of the Atlantic stemmed from a combination of motives. In the short term, merchants and nobles who sponsored most of the early voyages sought whatever immediate gain could be had from each voyage. In the process, these early traders became explorers as well, slowly expanding their knowledge of the Atlantic World and the possibilities therein. From these beginnings, the leaders of various nation-states that participated in this slow progression, particularly those of Portugal and Spain, sought to improve their economies through colonization of new-found territories and trade while at the same time looking for any opening or advantage in the ongoing crusade against their Moslem enemies.

Other developments in the late fourteenth through the fifteenth centuries had equally important effects on the beginnings of European exploration in the Atlantic World. Emerging from the social and political turmoil of the thirteenth and early fourteenth centuries, the beginnings of centralized nation-states provided the financial and political resources necessary for large-scale exploration. The expansion of trade and the rise of the merchant class would provide the impetus. An increase in trade throughout Europe and with the East before the Ottoman Empire interruption resulted in the growth of powerful trading centers in the Mediterranean such as Venice, Genoa, and Florence in Italy and others around Europe such as Bruges, Antwerp, and Lyon. The expansion of trade contributed to the growth of a large and influential merchant class and economic innovations such as the idea of corporations, stockholders, and joint-stock companies. The opportunity for economic gain encouraged many in the merchant and noble classes to sponsor voyages of exploration. The expansion of trade went hand in hand with the rise of centralized authority in many European states. Merchants preferred the uniform currencies, favorable trade laws, and fewer trade barriers that the growth of the early modern nation-state provided. During the late fourteenth century and throughout the fifteenth century European monarchs expanded their authority at the expense of the nobility, and by 1492 a map of Western Europe showed several united kingdoms, each of which would play a role in the exploration process, usually in rivalry with the others. In 1453 Louis XI emerged from the Hundred Years' War with England as the head of a unified France. In 1469 the marriage of Ferdinand of Aragon and Isabella of Castile united the two largest Iberian kingdoms to produce a unified Spain after centuries of warfare with the Moslems in which the various Christian kingdoms slowly re-conquered the Iberian Peninsula. In 1485 Henry VII of England was victorious in the War of the Roses, a thirty-year struggle over the succession to the throne, and became the first monarch of the Tudor dynasty. Earliest of all, in 1384, João I was victorious in a war with Castile and established a national identity for Portugal, which would quickly establish itself as a leader in Atlantic exploration.

A desire or motivation for exploration would be useless without the ability to overcome the significant challenges of navigation of the Atlantic. The exploration of the Atlantic can therefore, in many ways, be seen as an outgrowth of the intellectual and technological progress in Europe during the Renaissance. The Renaissance provided the stimulus for the expansion of Europe not only through technological advances allowing exploration but also through the spirit of learning and expansion of knowledge that is the crux of the Renaissance. Its roots are found in the contact between the Arab world and the Christian West beginning during the Crusades, from 1095 to 1270, and also in the Iberian Peninsula during the Reconquista, the century's long series of wars between Christians and Moslems that ended with the fall of Granada in 1492. After the fall of the Roman Empire, the knowledge of the classical Mediterranean world was preserved and expanded in Moslem centers of learning such as Cairo, Alexandria, and Seville. Despite the political and religious conflicts between the Christians and Moslems, over time the Christian world recovered previous knowledge of philosophy, medicine, geography, and astronomy and gained the technologies of Asia such as gunpowder and mechanical clocks. The rediscovery of the knowledge of the Greek and Roman worlds was enhanced by knowledge borrowed from the Arabs. Renaissance scholars revered these rediscovered ideas and used them to spur the expansion of all types of knowledge as some of the knowledge of the classical world was found to be incomplete or in error. Atlantic exploration was a part of this process as sailors, navigators, and shipbuilders took advantage of significant changes in key technological areas to improve their craft and ultimately allowed for the successful European exploration of the Atlantic.

The first of these were advances in the knowledge of geography. The Hellenistic world had produced a great body of knowledge relating to geography. Scholars such as Hipparchus (190–120 BC), Strabo (ca. 63 BC–ca. AD 24), and Erastothenes (ca. 276–196 BC) had produced remarkably accurate charts of the known world, and Erastothenes had calculated the circumference of the world with relative accuracy. However, the most significant influence on fifteenth-century scholars was Ptolemy's *Geography*, rediscovered in 1410. In that same year the treatise *Imago Mundi* by Cardinal Pierre D'Ailly melded the knowledge of Greek, Latin, and Arabic scholars on the size and nature of the world's geography. Despite the expansion of knowledge during this period, there were significant errors and variations in the various works produced. One such error was the general acceptance of Ptolemy's work, which claimed a much smaller circumference of the world than did Erastothenes. This miscalculation led many navigators, Columbus among them, to believe a westward passage to Asia possible. Nevertheless, this knowledge spurred explorers to push the boundary of the known world and led to the production of numerous charts and maps.

Other developments in the field of astronomy also assisted early explorers. The magnetic compass had been carried by European ships since at least the twelfth century, but its use for "dead reckoning" navigation was inadequate for long ocean voyages. While sailors in the Arab world had used the stars for navigation, the first recorded instance in Europe of figuring latitude by measuring the height of the Pole Star above the horizon was in 1462 by a Portuguese navigator. In 1484 a group of astronomers produced a set of declination tables at the behest of King João II of Portugal, allowing the use of the noonday sun to figure latitude more accurately. Combined with the concurrent production of increasingly accurate charts and maps, the ability to identify the latitude of one's position assisted mariners greatly in navigation.

Another area in which significant changes occurred during the fourteenth and fifteenth centuries was in the designs and capabilities of European ships. After 1300 in the European nations bordering the Atlantic there was widespread adoption of the use of a square rig on the main mast of larger ships. At the same time, ships began to more frequently adopt the use of a three-mast configuration rather than the earlier, smaller, single-masted ships. Finally, in Portugal, situated as it was at the crossroads of the Mediterranean and Atlantic worlds and therefore of different ideas regarding shipbuilding, designers borrowed the idea of a lateen sail used by most Arab ships and combined it with the square rig prevalent in the deep, round trading ships common in the north Atlantic, resulting in ship designs known as the caravel and the carrack. This new configuration provided these ships with unprecedented sailing power and stability required for sailing in all reasonable weathers. In addition to changes in ship designs, after 1300 European shipbuilders began to rely more and more on artillery as the main weapon of naval combat. This practice, in combination with the advances in design, resulted in the gradual replacement of the oar-powered galley as the main ship of European powers outside of the Mediterranean due to its inability to travel effectively in the rough Atlantic seas. The resulting vessel provided European merchants and explorers with a ship better able to protect itself and project armed might anywhere in the world. As the historian Carlo M. Cipolla has pointed out, "[b]y turning whole-heartedly to the gun-carrying sailing ship the Atlantic peoples broke down the bottle-neck inherent in the use of human energy and harnessed to their advantage, far larger quantities of power. It was then that European sails appeared aggressively on the most distant seas."[3]

Through the fourteenth and fifteenth centuries, using the slowly expanding capabilities of new maritime techniques and designs, European ships began to advance westward and southward from the Iberian Peninsula looking for trading opportunities along the African coast. The ability to penetrate far southward along the coast of Africa was assisted by the fortuitous accident of the Genoese trader Malocello, who had extensive commercial connections in the Moroccan town of Ceuta and in Cherbourg in northern France. On a trading voyage south of Gibraltar around 1312, Malocello was blown off course during a trading voyage and discovered, or perhaps rediscovered, the Canary Islands. He followed up on his accidental find by leading the colonization of these islands around 1335 with temporary trading and raiding camps. Malocello and those who followed his example found the islands to be filled with possibilities for economic gain. By the 1340s mariners and traders from various places in Europe regularly sailed to the Canaries looking for quick profits from slave raids among the native population known as Guanches or from dyes made from naturally occurring lichens and resins found on the islands. While numerous trading stations and small bases used for raiding among the islands were set up by groups from Aragon, France, and Portugal, it was the kingdom of Castile that sponsored the first permanent colony in the islands, though it was actually carried out by two Norman nobles, Gadifer de la Salle and Jean de Bethencourt from 1402 to 1405. By the end of the century, the Canary Islands profitably exported sugar, wines, sheep, and cattle. Castilian claims to the Canaries were contested by Portugal, which as early as 1341 laid claim to the islands as well as other groups of uninhabited islands in the Atlantic such as Madeira and the Azores.[4]

Portugal, in particular, looked at Atlantic trade as the method to increase its national wealth as well as a way to strike at the Moslems along the North African coast. Trading voyages to the Canaries and south along the African coast in the mid-1300s accelerated after Portugal's emergence as a unified nation in 1384. The double motivations of economic gain and a crusade against the Moslems are typified by the efforts of the Infante Henrique of Portugal, one of João I's younger sons. Not far up in the royal succession and thus with no realistic hope to ascend the throne, Henrique sought to expand his wealth and prestige through Atlantic exploration. His immediate goal was to improve his, and thereby Portugal's, share in the longstanding trade with North African merchants. Striking against the Moslems was merely an added benefit. Thus, the 1415 Portuguese attack and capture of the Moroccan port city of Ceuta served to advance both ends. During this campaign Henrique, named Henry the Navigator by later historians despite this being his sole overseas voyage, was active in capturing and defending the town from a Moslem counter-attack. It was at Ceuta that Henrique learned from Moslem merchants of caravan routes across the Sahara to Timbuktu, the Senegal and Niger rivers, and the Gold Coast, where a rich trade in slaves, gold, and spices would be found. Granted a license by his father, the Infante Henrique set about finding a route to these places sponsoring trading voyages that pushed ever farther south along the African coast. He pressed his father to launch an expedition against the Castilians and others in the Canaries as early as 1415, and in 1424 he organized a force of some two to three thousand soldiers to conquer the remaining un-colonized islands in the Canaries to serve as a base for trading voyages to the south. Henrique established an information service to collect charts and data on currents and winds brought back from expeditions along the coast of Africa. From here, events progressed steadily. In 1434 the Portuguese sailor Gil Eannes successfully passed the coast of Cape Bojador, and by 1444 the Portuguese were licensing traders of many nationalities. A rich trade in gold, slaves, malaguetta pepper, and other items developed in the Senegal region. By 1460 the Portuguese had reached the coast of modern Sierra Leone, and by the early 1470s the sharp southerly trend of the African coast had been recognized.

As efforts along the African coast expanded, the need for trading stations became apparent. The island of Madeira, known from the mid-1300s by the Europeans, was finally colonized around 1425. In 1448 the Portuguese established a small fort and warehouse on Arguim Island in order to facilitate trading expeditions along the coast in Guinea. The uninhabited Cape Verde Islands were claimed and colonized in the 1460s, serving as a crucial stopping point for journeys ranging further south. While established on uninhabited islands, these colonies soon became centers of agriculture, exporting wheat, wine, and sugar using first Canary Islanders as slave laborers and then slaves imported from the African continent as this trade became greater. These successful colonies provided both a model and an incentive for the continued exploration of the Atlantic in search of more unknown islands, and the combination of slave labor and plantation agriculture, primarily of sugar, would be carried westward into the Americas by both the Spanish and Portuguese. The motivation of finding new islands to colonize was at least as important, and probably more so, than the desire to find a route west to Asia, and most voyages sponsored by national leaders included the stipulation to search for new islands to claim.

As the profits from the African trade increased, the Portuguese government took a more active part in regulating and sponsoring voyages of exploration and trade along the African coast. In 1469, King Alfonso V granted a monopoly on the West Guinea trade to the wealthy Lisbon merchant Fernão Gomes. While gaining great wealth from this trade, a share of which he paid to the Crown, Gomes also organized voyages that pushed the known reaches of the African coast southward some five hundred leagues over five years.

In 1474, Alfonso granted the monopoly to his son, King João, who later succeeded his father as João II. João built Fort Elmina in 1482 in the heart of the Gold Coast to protect the small trading outpost that had grown there and gave financial support to expeditions into the interior. The early construction at Elmina provided a naval and commercial center that became the capital of an extensive trading network. This network provided gold, ivory, and pepper to Europe in exchange for iron, cloth, and other goods. More significantly, it also began a trade in African slaves that would accelerate and ultimately transport millions of African slaves across the Atlantic. Recognizing the importance of continuing to expand and claim a monopoly over the African trade, the Portuguese crown began funding its own voyages in the 1480s. The first explorer chosen by the crown was Diogo Cão, who, in two voyages in 1482 and 1484 attempted to find the route around Africa, succeeded in coasting as far south as modern Namibia, and found and penetrated a distance up the Congo River. These royal efforts broke the model followed for more than a century of private individuals funding and organizing expeditions only with royal sponsorship. As the exploration of the Atlantic World and the wealth of the trade along the African coast swelled the coffers of the Portuguese, the numbers of explorers searching for alternative routes to Asia increased, as did the desire of the Portuguese crown to be the ones who succeeded first. This hope swelled with the successes of the explorer Bartolomeu Dias, who sailed around the southern tip of Africa in 1488. He rounded the Cape of Good Hope and then Cape Agulhas, the southernmost point of Africa, landing at Mossel Bay on February 3, 1488. Finally, with the news of Columbus's discoveries spurring the effort, the Portuguese explorer Vasco de Gama achieved the long-sought quest of reaching India, where he landed at Calicut in May of 1498, and returned to Lisbon in September of 1499 after losing half his ships and a third of their crews. Yet he returned with a cargo of pepper, ginger, cinnamon, and cloves that paid for the voyage sixty times over. His achievement gained him a hero's welcome, and from this point the Portuguese Crown sought to monopolize trade between Asia and India, which they successfully dominated into the late seventeenth century. The trade with Africa, however, continued to be of equal if not greater value to the Portuguese and other European nations that sought to gain from it.[5]

The successful extension of European knowledge and trade, the advances in maritime technology, and the achievements in exploration of the African coast should not be interpreted to diminish the role of the African peoples who participated as equals most of the time in the commercial interaction with Europeans. Indeed, in many cases, the leaders of the African nations engaged in the trade controlled the access and terms under which Europeans were allowed to transact business, terms to which, in the majority of cases, the Europeans scrupulously attempted to adhere. The early voyages in the 1300s and early 1400s through the Canaries and along the African coast oftentimes relied on armed raids to obtain trade goods and slaves. Raids were effective against the Canary Islanders, but despite initial successes on the coast of Africa it soon became apparent that the Europeans, despite their inherent sense of superiority over the new cultures encountered, lacked the technological superiority to establish and maintain military dominance over the peoples of Senegal, the Gold Coast, and the others encountered further south.

The lack of European dominance and the ability of Africans to negotiate and often control the terms on which contact and trade occurred led Europeans to slowly adjust their tactics. Initial raids for slaves in the region of the Senegambian region gave way to negotiations and the presentation of gifts to local leaders as, over the space of a few decades, raiding expeditions were met more and more frequently with armed fleets of African boats carved from single logs and powered with oars. While the African boats were technologically inferior to European ships, there were large numbers of these African vessels, and some could carry fifty to one hundred men apiece, so the African boats were able to out-maneuver the larger ships in the shallow waters of the shore and in most cases could overwhelm European raiding parties attempting to seize slaves, spices, ivory, gold, and other trade items. It proved much easier to negotiate with the African inhabitants, leading the king of Portugal to dispatch Diogo Gomes to negotiate and establish diplomatic and trade relations with the African rulers along the coast in 1456. This policy of negotiation did not stop newcomers or rival nations from attempting to gain short-term economic benefit from raids along the coast, but those Europeans desiring to establish long-term relationships with African leaders respected the desires and rules of the African leaders who dictated the terms under which trade would be conducted. Failure to adhere to these rules often led to armed retaliation, as in the case of the French vessel seized by the king of Kongo in 1525 for trading illegally along his coast. The French traders had failed to pay the customs and duties required for such activities and violated the rule that all European ships should stand off the mouth of the Congo River and wait for a delegation of royal officials. The Portuguese reportedly made a regular practice of distributing trade goods along the coast by the 1490s to maintain their relationships with leaders of each region.[6]

Given the ability of African rulers to control the vast majority of trade with the Europeans, it is also important to note that the goods being traded by each side were not new or unique to either side. The trade goods that Europeans brought with them to exchange for African items consisted of cloth, processed metal both in raw and finished form (i.e., knives, swords, basins, etc.), alcoholic beverages, jewelry, and sundry items. None of these, however, were accepted in trade by Africans due to need. Africa during the first few centuries of trade with Europe produced all of these items, some of a better quality than that procured from traders. African rulers sought goods from Europe more from a desire for variety, the prestige attached to European goods, and perhaps a need for quantities of certain items, such as iron, greater than that available in certain regions. Nor did the arrival of European traders begin the commerce in many of these items. African states participated in a vibrant commerce between regions, oftentimes centered on large river systems such as that of the Senegal, the Niger, or the Congo. European traders on the Mediterranean coast had for centuries taken part in an active commerce in gold, ivory, and other items that were derived from caravan lines that penetrated deep into the African interior. Certainly, a desire to participate in this trade more directly, and bypass the Moslem traders who controlled the North African ports, was a prime motivation of much of the early exploration of the African Atlantic coast.

A prime example of Europeans tapping into already thriving markets is that of the slave trade. As the trade in African slaves across the Atlantic accelerated, European traders gained most of the slaves through markets already in existence. Slaves represented a prime source of wealth among many African cultures and the slave trade was widespread among African societies. Though it differed greatly in legal and societal structure from what it evolved into in the Americas, the pre-existence of slavery in Africa meant that Europeans infrequently gained slaves through raids, especially as the African trade grew in size and scope. The trade in slaves in Africa grew and changed as numerous African rulers responded to the increased demand for slaves, but Europeans did not instigate the traffic. Thus many myths of European-African trade can be dispelled. European goods were not vastly superior to those of African manufacture, at least in the first few centuries. African societies were not dominated or conquered by Europeans in search of trade but rather controlled much of this trade and relegated most Europeans to small, isolated outposts such as that at Elmina. Finally, European-African commerce did not begin with the exploration of the Atlantic coast nor did it begin trade in Africa. Long before European trade along the coast developed, numerous African nations existed connected through caravan lines across the Sahara to Mediterranean ports as well as a vibrant internal commerce along the Atlantic coast. It was this commerce into which European traders tapped to begin a new chapter which would grow in size and complexity as the Atlantic world expanded westward into the Americas.[7]

This westward expansion grew in large part out of the ongoing rivalries among European nations over the newly colonized Atlantic islands and the growing African trade, driven primarily by the competition between Spain and Portugal. In the fourteenth and most of the fifteenth centuries, before the unification of the thrones of Aragon and Castile, it was the kingdom of Castile that sought to follow the Portuguese example of exploration and trade in the Atlantic. It started with Castilian raids among the Canaries and along the African coast. The two Norman nobles, La Salle and Bethencourt, who led the colonization of the largest of the Canary Islands from 1402, exacerbated the tensions between Castile and Spain by giving homage to the king of Castile, a claim that was further supported by a papal grant given to Castile in 1344. From the early 1400s on, there were almost constant skirmishes and a few outright invasions as Portugal sought to expel the Castilian settlers from the Canaries. This hostility broke into open warfare in 1475 when King Alfonso V of Portugal contested the succession of Isabella, the daughter of Juan II, to the throne of Castile by supporting her sister Juana's rival claim. The civil war expanded beyond the shores of the Iberian Peninsula with the Portuguese assisting the Guanches in raiding Castilian settlements in the Canaries and Castile raiding the ships and trading outposts of the Portuguese in Guinea and along the Gold Coast.

The war ceased only with the entrance of the kingdom of Aragon into the conflict with the marriage of King Ferdinand of Aragon to Isabella. Diplomatic efforts began in 1479 to end the war and culminated with the Treaty of Alcacovas. This treaty, sanctioned by a papal bull issued by Pope Sixtus IV in 1481, significantly shaped the course of exploration in the Atlantic World. In it the unified kingdoms of Castile and Aragon, known collectively as Spain, agreed to recognize the Portuguese monopoly on trade and settlement along the African coast and in all islands in that part of the Atlantic except the Canary Islands, to which Portugal renounced all claims. In what seemed a steep price for peace at the time, the Spanish had effectively ended any hope to partake in the rich trade in Africa and had given up any claims to the Atlantic islands then known which promised opportunity for colonization and agricultural production. However, it did not give up claims for future discoveries of new islands further west, and in the 1480s the promise of these potential discoveries seemed great.

Rumors and sailors' stories of large islands, some perhaps the mythic Antille (Atlantis), gave the Spanish Crown hope for new lands westward. Even the success of Portuguese explorers beginning with Diogo Cão in hinting at a potential route to Asia and the East did not dissuade mariners such as Cristóbal Colón, more popularly known as Christopher Columbus. Columbus was a self-taught navigator from Genoa. Not a professional sailor, Columbus formed his ideas and theories based on his reading of most of the major treatises on geography of the time. From 1484 he began pitching his idea of sailing west to reach Asia to the various governments of Europe and was turned down by Portugal and England before he finally received the sponsorship of the throne of Spain. His proposal was nothing unique; others had theorized about the possibility of reaching Asia by sailing west, and certainly it was common knowledge that the world was round, despite the popular myth to the contrary. Columbus's great achievement was his salesmanship and the fact that he was the first to be recognized for reaching the coasts of those previously unknown (at least to the early modern Europeans) lands. His agreement with the Spanish Crown listed his goal of sailing west with the intention of searching out a route to Cathay and Cipangua, the names for China and Japan, as well as to discover and claim any islands encountered on the way.

He set out in his three ships, the *Niña*, the *Pinta*, and the *nao Santa Maria*, in August of 1492 and set course for the Canary Islands to set up stocks of water and provisions in what would become the standard practice for those sailing for the Americas. After leaving the Canaries, Columbus sailed westward, and after thirty-three days sighted an island of the Bahamas. From there he explored southwest, coasting along the island of Cuba, and finally reached the north coast of Hispaniola, modern-day Haiti. Here his hopes for wealth increased with his discovery of bits of gold worn by the native Taino Indians and their seemingly docile nature. His comments on their suitability for labor foretold their fate; but at the time Columbus was more intent on laying claim to these islands for Spain, and after losing one ship to grounding on the uncharted shoals, he determined to return with word of his discoveries. He left a small number of men behind with instructions to build houses and begin a search for gold, and he set course for Spain. He sailed northward until he found a westward wind, a practice once again followed by mariners for centuries to come in returning to

Europe from the Caribbean. On his return, poor weather forced Columbus to put in at Portuguese ports, first in the Azores and then in Tagus, where his reports of reaching Asia were met with skepticism and a touch of worry by Portuguese officials.

The Spanish received word of his finds with eagerness after Columbus's return to Palos on March 14, 1493. A new expedition was planned immediately, but Columbus's discoveries and their potential importance shared the stage with important Portuguese concerns: protecting their monopoly on trade with Africa and the anticipated route to Asia that Bartolomeu Dias's rounding of the Cape of Good Hope in 1488 had opened. What, if anything, Columbus had discovered was uncertain; but the Portuguese doubted his claims to have reached islands off the coast of Asia and sought a diplomatic solution to protect their interests. Ferdinand and Isabella may or may not have accepted Columbus's assertions; but, beyond doubt, a new archipelago of islands had been discovered that had produced at least a small amount of gold and was populated by a peaceful, if primitive, people. Spain's priority was to colonize these islands and to protect their claims, and they too sought to have their rights protected. What resulted was similar to the diplomatic resolution of the war between Portugal and Castile, first a papal declaration supporting Spain's claim to any lands discovered in the newly found regions. Pope Alexander VI, a Spaniard himself, issued the papal bull *Inter Caetera* in 1493 drawing an imaginary line from north to south a hundred leagues west of the Azores declaring that the sea and land west of that land would be Spain's to explore, settle, and Christianize the natives. The legal claim to this region provided by the pope's declaration set the basis for the diplomatic negotiations between Spain and Portugal that resulted in 1494 in the Treaty of Tordesillas. In this, Portugal successfully demanded the line of demarcation be pushed westward by 270 leagues to protect their trade in Africa. Overall, in the context of the knowledge possessed at the time, this treaty can be seen as a victory for Portugal, protecting as it did the African trade monopoly as well as the route to Asia. In retrospect, however, Spain's ability to explore and settle the Caribbean unimpeded, and from there to launch the conquest of the Americas, was relatively ensured, though Brazil would soon be found and claimed by Portugal from the early 1500s on and settled through the establishment of settlements such as those at Porto Seguro in 1535 and at Espiritu Santo in 1536.

While the question of the legitimacy of Spanish claims on the Americas rested in the hands of diplomats, Columbus and royal officials wasted no time waiting on the outcome of these deliberations. Columbus and Spanish officials outfitted a new expedition in a short five months, and the admiral left Cadiz in September of 1493 in command of seventeen ships, 1,200 people, and all the accoutrements of a small community. The Spanish had long since decided that it would be easier to establish a full colony to facilitate further exploration, to aid in prospecting for gold and other minerals, and to create an agricultural base to provide its own food and to supply future fleets. After the failure of a new but poorly positioned settlement named Isabela on the north shore of Hispaniola, Columbus and his brother Bartholomew, who was in charge of the settlement in Columbus' absences, moved the settlement about 1496 to the south coast of the island and there founded the city of Santo Domingo which served for some fifty years as the capital of the Spanish Indies.

Columbus's accomplishments as an explorer were overshadowed during his lifetime by his failures as an administrator of the new colony of Santo Domingo. He was unable to control the settlers on the island who exploited the native Taino Indians relentlessly in search of gold. Within a few years, Columbus was forced by rebellious colonists to buy off malcontents with land grants and a general division of Indian labor in a system assigning Indians to certain individual Spaniards who would then benefit from the goods, services, and property produced by those Indians. This system, known as *repartimiento*, was utilized in the Spanish colonies in the Canaries and became general practice throughout the Spanish Americas though modified over time. To quell the unrest and restore the colony to order, the Crown replaced Columbus and his brother with the royal official Francisco de Bobadilla in 1499 as governor of the colony, superceding Columbus's claims on the Americas. Columbus himself led two further expeditions to the Americas in 1498 and in 1502. In these voyages he succeeded in exploring further the islands of the Caribbean, the coasts of Venezuela to the Orinoco River, and the coast of Central America around Panama. Never succeeding in gaining the wealth he had hoped for, Columbus died in 1506 still believing that he had discovered the route to Asia.

Governor Bobadilla and to a greater extent his successor, Frey Nicolás de Ovando, were responsible for establishing a successful administration first of Santo Domingo, and from this base the rest of the Caribbean as the Spanish extended their explorations and settlements throughout the region. While the unification of the Spanish monarchy by Ferdinand and Isabella in 1474 had provided the economic backing for the first expeditions of exploration, the completion of the re-conquest of the Iberian Peninsula with the fall of the last Moslem kingdom of Granada in 1492 allowed the Spanish monarchs to turn their attention outward. In addition, Columbus's voyages spurred the imaginations of Europeans; numerous other explorers followed his example, and many books were produced by publishers eager to take advantage of the furor. One of the best known and most popular at the time was *Cosmographiae Introductio*, which among other accounts included several letters written by a Florentine merchant named Amerigo Vespucci describing four voyages he claimed to have made to the New World with expeditions ranging from the coast of Honduras to the middle of Brazil. While not contributing any major discoveries, Vespucci's voyages demonstrated that an entirely new continent existed between Europe and Asia. It was due to popularity of this book, and others like it that also included Vespucci's writings, that the new continent was named America in his honor.

Spain quickly exploited its new possessions, beginning on Hispaniola. By subduing the native populations of Arawak and Tainos, despite the fierce resistance and ongoing raids that lasted more than a century throughout the Caribbean, the Spanish settlers took advantage of small finds of placer gold in the rivers and quickly established sugar plantations and other agricultural endeavors such as cattle ranching borrowed from the successful example of the Canary Islands. Similar to the native Guanches, the Taino and other Indian populations of the island were decimated, and by the 1520s the Spanish were forced to seek labor through raids on Indian populations of other islands as well as from the North and Central American coasts. The growing population of settlers at Santo Domingo provided the impetus for the expansion of Spanish settlements as prime land on the island became increasingly scarce. Juan de Esquivel began the settlement of Jamaica in 1509, and two years later Diego Velázquez led an expedition brutally subduing native opposition on the island of Cuba and organizing the first settlement on that island. Within five years there were seven towns in Cuba producing quantities of gold and beginning the first sugar plantations and ranches.[8]

Spanish interests were not confined to the islands of the Caribbean, however. The first explorations of the coastline by Columbus and others demonstrated that lands found were not an isolated archipelago, but rather a continent that stood in the way of the long-sought westward passage to the Indies. Nevertheless, hopes for finding that passage were not abandoned entirely. In 1511, Vasco Núñez de Balboa seized control of an expedition exploring the northern coast of present-day Colombia, founded the town of Darién on the Atlantic coast of the Isthmus of Panamá, and two years later successfully crossed the narrow strip of land westward and found the Pacific Ocean on the other side. Balboa achieved victory over the fiercely resistant Indian population through a combination of terror, warfare, diplomacy, and outright bribery, and succeeded in making Darién a prime port for early trade in the Caribbean. Despite his successes, the king replaced Balboa as governor with Pedro Arias Dávila, who had Balboa arrested and beheaded for treason in 1519.

That same year, the most famous of all of the Spanish conquests in the Americas began as a small expedition organized and sent from Cuba by the founder and governor of that colony, Diego Velázquez, under the command of his former secretary, Hernán Cortés. Following up on previous expeditions that had explored along the coast of the Gulf of Mexico in 1517 and 1518, Cortés landed with his six hundred men, first on the coast at Tabasco and then at Veracruz, where he spent some four months setting up a base and beginning to establish relationships with the dense Indian populations in the region. Upon landing, Cortés took two significant steps. First he ordered his ships burned to prevent any calls for retreat; second, upon founding the settlement of Veracruz, he resigned his commission from the governor of Cuba and had his supporters installed as the town magistrates, who promptly gave Cortés a new commission. These two acts freed the sailors of the ships to march inland with him and cut his ties to Velázquez, allowing him to claim any finds for himself and his men. Cortés began his march inland to the capital of the dominant tribe in the Valley of Mexico, the Mexica, or as they are more popularly known, the Aztecs. The term *Aztec* is an imprecise term to describe the group that dominated the Valley of Mexico at the time of Cortés's arrival. All the Nahua-speaking peoples in the Valley of Mexico were Aztecs, while the group that dominated the area was a tribe of the Mexica (pronounced "Me-shee-ka") centered on the city of Tenochtitlan, or the place of the Tenochca, as this group named themselves. These "Aztec" rulers had migrated from the north as early as the twelfth century, and only in the century before the arrival of the Spanish had they been able to free themselves and achieve dominance over the entire region through open warfare and the threat of it. As the overlords of a huge area, the Aztecs held onto power only tenuously, and as Cortés discovered and took advantage of, many of the peoples subject to Tenochtitlan were in revolt against Aztec dominance. The arrival of the Spanish provided native leaders a method to overthrow their overlords, but Cortés managed to replace Aztec overlords with Spanish ones. He arrived in Tenochtitlan, or present-day Mexico City, in November 1519, promptly arrested the Aztec emperor Moctezuma, and ordered his execution. The city revolted, and Cortés had to retreat with disastrous results in 1520. He regrouped, and after persuading a large group of Spanish reinforcements sent from Cuba to join him, Cortés led his followers in defeating the Aztecs in 1521. In this he was greatly assisted by thousands of Indians eager to gain revenge on their former rulers and by the spread of a smallpox epidemic brought unwittingly by the Spaniards that decimated the Indians of Tenochtitlan and elsewhere.

Cortés was named governor and captain general of New Spain by Charles V, and Cortés distributed lands and Indian villages into tributary *encomiendas* for his followers. Cortés gained great wealth from his conquest of New Spain and organized expeditions to the north and south in search of new wealth. He lent support to Pedro de Alvarado, one of his officers, in the conquest of the Maya peoples in present-day Guatemala and Honduras from 1524, where Alvarado repeated the technique used with such efficacy by Cortés by playing the enmity of two of the larger Indian peoples, the Cakchiquel and the Quiché, against the other, allowing a quick and brutal campaign resulting in the establishment of Spanish rule in the region. Alvarado continued extending Spanish rule with the conquest of El Salvador and the founding of San Salvador as the capital in 1525.[9]

The conquest of South America was equally momentous in the spread of Spanish power through the Americas. From the base of the settlement of Darién, and later from the new capital on the Pacific side of the Isthmus at Panamá, the Spanish had been regaled with tales from the Indians in the region of rich native kingdoms to the south. The rumors of riches were enough to send groups exploring south almost immediately. In the late 1520s, Francisco Pizzaro set about organizing an expedition south along the Pacific coast. He finally set out from Panamá in January 1531 with some 180 men and 27 horses, sailing southward along the coast and landing in the Bay of San Mateo near the mouth of the Santiago River. The ships returned to Panamá for reinforcements while Pizarro headed inland in search of the rumored riches. This he found in abundance when he encountered the cities controlled by the Inca.

The Inca, like the Aztecs, had extended their control over numerous subject peoples over the course of the previous century. Their empire extended from northern Ecuador to central Chile and from the Andean mountain range to the coast. Unlike the Aztecs, who merely exacted tribute from their subject cities, the Inca placed their own officials in charge in each conquered community and exacted tribute mostly in the form of labor used to maintain an intricate system of roads, really footpaths, and storehouses that connected the entire empire with a remarkably effective system of communication in the form of runners stationed along the roads. This system also allowed the Inca to respond quickly to subdue unrest as the armies moved relatively easily along the roads using the pre-positioned stores for supplies. With all authority residing in the Sapa Inca, as the Incan ruler was known, and then disseminated through a bureaucracy consisting primarily of the family members of the ruler, the Inca ruled with efficiency unknown in other parts of the Americas.

For the Spanish, the timing of their arrival was fortuitous. After landing on the coast, Pizzaro explored the area around Puerto Viejo and went as far as the city of Túmbez, where they commandeered Indian rafts and passed over to the Island of Puna in the Gulf of Guayaquil. Here they were attacked by the islanders but survived thanks to the arrival of two vessels with an additional hundred men and some horses commanded by Hernando de Soto. Pizarro took time to replenish his forces and founded the settlement of San Miguel, establishing Spanish dominance over the Indians in the immediate region. Here, Pizarro received reports of the Inca and learned that the empire was currently seized by civil war between two half-brothers with rival claims to the throne. At the time of Pizarro's arrival, the Incan prince Atahualpa was in the final stages of defeating his brother, Huáscar, who had initially ruled as emperor. The confusion and rebellion that had paralyzed the empire was a perfect opportunity, and Pizarro left the Túmbez area in early in May 1532, heading into the heart of the Incan empire. In November he entered the city of Caxamalca (now Caxamarca) without opposition. Pizarro invited Atahualpa to a meeting at his camp where, with remarkable boldness and treachery, he had the emperor seized and his bodyguard slaughtered. In one swift stroke, Pizarro seized the sole power in the Incan empire in the person of the Sapa Inca; bereft of their leader, the Inca, though possessed of a large army outside the city, were unable to resist and retreated. Pizarro demanded a room be filled with gold in ransom for their emperor, and the Inca complied. Despite their capitulation, Pizarro had Atahualpa killed in June of 1534 after over a year of captivity. Reinforced from Panamá, Pizarro and his men marched on the Incan capital at Cuzco while his men set about subjugating the Indian population to Spanish authority. To quell dissent, Pizarro crowned Manco Capac as the Incan emperor and attempted with some success to rule through the same type of system that the Indians had traditionally used, recognizing the leaders of the individual communities and using them to organize and gain tribute for the Spanish overlords. Pizarro, furthermore, founded a capital city for the region at Lima, in January of 1535, which would become the seat of the Spanish royal government. Despite ongoing Indian resistance organized by Manco Capac and others, and almost constant fighting between rival Spanish leaders, Pizarro and his successors succeeded in adding a huge and rich area to the Spanish empire.[10]

The wealthy and densely populated areas of New Spain, Peru, and elsewhere had little similarity to the Spanish experience in North America, where—in spite of numerous expeditions through the mid-sixteenth century—the Spanish found no cities of gold or rich cities despite numerous rumors and hopes that continued well into the seventeenth century. The northernmost outpost of the Spanish during the sixteenth century was founded by Pedro Menéndez de Avilés in 1565 at San Augustine in Florida in response to a French Huguenot effort to establish a small fort and settlement in Florida. Despite the successes of Franciscan missionaries in establishing a chain of missions across northern Florida and along the coast as far north as Santa Elena through the seventeenth century, the outpost of La Florida remained a small, military oriented colony intended to protect the northern route for the Spanish treasure fleets. Other expeditions by the Spanish extended their knowledge and empire beyond the Atlantic, starting with a 1519 expedition commanded by the Portuguese Ferdinand Magellan, serving in the employ of the king of Spain. Although Magellan was killed fighting with natives in the Philippines, his expedition successfully rounded the southern tip of South America, and one of his ships managed to return to Spain with fewer than twenty starving crew members completing the first successful circumnavigation of the globe. Spanish influence would soon extend to the Philippines, making the Spanish Empire the first truly global domain, yet its heart would remain in the Atlantic World.

The startling success of the Spanish conquest should not be interpreted as a sign of the technological superiority of the Europeans. The ability of small groups of Spanish soldiers to usurp the authority of the Aztecs, Inca, and others typically came about with the active cooperation of many of the native peoples subjugated by unpopular overlords. Cortés benefited from allied Indian armies who made the eventual defeat of the Aztec armies possible. Pizarro used the same technique against the Inca as he played one side of the ongoing civil war against the other, allowing his seizure of power. Once having defeated the native rulers, in most cases the Spanish merely assumed the traditional role of overlord previously held by others, thereby easing their way into control. Second, by allowing many native leaders to remain in their customary positions of authority, the Spanish quickly brought about a cooperative relationship with many natives without whom the Spanish would not have been successful in establishing and maintaining their authority over time. A third, decisive factor was the staggering losses of the natives to disease, which weakened their ability to resist the Spanish effectively.

The imposition of Spanish control over a geographically vast and populated area also should not be seen as absolute. While political and military control in the centers of empire such as Mexico City and Lima tended to be strong, that control weakened as one approached the borderlands of the Spanish empire. In the borderlands, Europeans and natives negotiated an existence that drew from both peoples in terms of social, religious, economic, and military interaction. Even in the more populated areas, native villages and peoples retained a startling degree of independence and maintained cultural constructs and beliefs to a large extent, even as they were changing in response to the Spanish presence. Throughout, natives controlled and negotiated control over large parts of their lives and exercised a great deal of agency in their relationship with the new Spanish overlords.[11]

The effects of the expansion of Spanish power over the native populations of the Americas were severe and costly to natives. The cost to the Indian populations wrought by disease, carnage, and loss of life in this period was catastrophic. A population of almost one million on the island of Hispaniola was virtually wiped out. In Mesoamerica a population estimated by many historians at between 25 to 40 million in 1500 dropped to around 3 million by 1650, and in Peru a population of some 9 million dropped to around a half million during that same period.[12] Equally important was the spread of the disease into North American populations through trade and contact with European fishermen along the coast. Death by disease was not the only reason for the severe drop in the Indian population of Central and South America. Harsh treatment and labor demands placed upon native peoples by the *repartimiento* and *encomienda* systems used by the Spanish resulted in high mortality rates and high migration rates as many Indians fled their villages to avoid the quotas of laborers that these villagers were required to provide.

Spanish officials were not unaware of the severe decline in the numbers of subject Indians, nor did they ignore the abuses of laborers. Many complained of the brutal conditions imposed on the Indians by the Spanish conquistadores. One of the most notable was Bartólome de Las Casas, a former *Encomendero* on Hispaniola in 1502 who later became a Dominican priest and who became the most vocal advocate for the rights of Indians, claiming in numerous works and in many forums that the Indians held rights as subjects to the Spanish Crown. Despite a long evolution of legal protections provided the natives by Spanish law, first in the *Laws of Burgos* issued by the Spanish Crown in 1512 and later in the "New Laws" issued in 1542, Spanish officials in the colonies were unable to effectively end the abuse of the *encomienda* system, and abuse of Indian labor remained common.

Along with demographic collapse, natives in both North and South America saw drastic changes in mere decades to cultures which had evolved over thousands of years. Catholic missionaries from priestly orders such as the Jesuits, Franciscans, Augustinians, and others used various methods ranging from force to subtle persuasion to force native peoples into a semblance of Catholicism. While this altered traditional cosmography and religious beliefs in various ways, it never succeeded in eradicating vestiges of native convictions that survived in secret as well as in how many natives interpreted the Catholic teachings of the friars. The material culture of natives throughout the Americas also changed dramatically over time, even in areas not directly controlled by Europeans as traders voyaged along the coast and ranged far inland. Metal implements such as knives, pots, axes, and hoes took the place of stone implements. In North America, especially after nations such as England, France, and the Netherlands established outposts to the north of the areas controlled by the Spanish, a thriving trade in furs altered hunting patterns as Indians sought to meet the demand in order to gain greater access or control over the trade in these metal implements and other goods such as firearms, cloth, beads, and sundry items. Even the food they ate and the environment were changed for Native Americans by the coming of Europeans. In areas controlled by Spaniards and later by other Europeans nations, the new settlers imported domesticated animals such as sheep, cattle, horses, and pigs, which altered the dietary patterns of many groups as they sought to adapt to new food sources. Imported animals combined with a transformation of agricultural techniques as new methods were taught to the Indians and acted to alter the environment to a scale unknown in the pre-contact Americas. Land was divided and fenced-in, forests were cleared to make room for crops and pastures, and in some extreme instances herds of grazing animals turned formerly green, fertile lands into semi-deserts.[13]

The introduction of one new crop in particular, combined with the Americas' unwilling inclusion in the larger Atlantic World, wrought perhaps the greatest change to the Americas. The introduction of sugar and plantation agriculture to the Americas, brought by the Spanish to the Caribbean and later to Brazil by the Portuguese, led plantation owners to turn first to Indian laborers and then, as their numbers declined, to the newest and easiest source of labor, Africa. It was the sugar cultivation of the Americas and the plantation system of labor that came with it, copied by later Europeans in the Caribbean and then adapted to tobacco cultivation in the Chesapeake by the English, which provided the motivation for Portuguese traders to demand more slaves from their African trading partners. From its beginnings in the fifteenth century the African slave trade accelerated as demand grew. By 1700 it had reached around 36,000 slaves per year, and by 1780 it had grown to some 80,000 on average.

The areas that received the greatest numbers of slaves were the sugar-producing regions that demanded a constant flow of new slaves to replace those who fell victim to the high mortality rates suffered by laborers. Of the total number of slaves imported, roughly 38 percent of the total went to the Caribbean islands. Some 35 percent went to Brazil, and the rest of Spanish America accounted for 22 percent. Of the entire number, only about 4 percent went to North America.[14] The tens of millions of imported slaves became the foundations for the African American populations of numerous modern countries on both continents and in the islands of the Caribbean and changed demographics, language, religion, and ethnic composition in ways too numerous to describe in this short space.

As momentous as the effects of the conquest of the Americas were to the Indian populations of the Americas, the effects of the Atlantic World on Europe was equally great. Economically, the wealth of the Americas, especially in terms of precious metals, flowed into Europe and funded much of the growing African trade and subsequent trade with Asia. Between 1500 and 1660 Spain imported some 18.6 thousand tons of silver and 200 tons of gold, during which time the amount of gold and silver in Europe tripled. This increase in the amount of hard currency caused inflation on an unprecedented scale throughout Europe, affecting Spain worst of all. The economic activity spurred by this influx of wealth laid the beginnings of modern capitalism in the Netherlands, England, and elsewhere, including among other things the development of joint-stock companies, the rise of modern banking, and the introduction of maritime insurance. Another outcome of this economic expansion is the shift of the center of European economic activity from the Mediterranean to the Atlantic seaboard.

Politically, the major result of this early era of exploration was the dominance of Spain in European affairs from 1500 to the late seventeenth century and the subsequent rise of England, France, and the Netherlands as Spain's power eventually waned. Migration, the importation of new foods and goods, and new ideas had a tremendous influence on social developments in Europe. The outflow of settlers to the Americas involved hundreds of thousands of people and had a significant impact on the population of Spain and, to a lesser degree, on the population of England, France, and the Netherlands. From the trade with Asia, expensive spices, chinaware, and cheaper textiles, consisting mainly of cotton goods such as muslin, chintz, gingham, and calico, flowed into Europe and were eagerly bought by those who could afford them. New foods from the Americas accomplished a revolution in European diets through the use of foods such as corn, potatoes, tomatoes, pumpkins, and others that would become staples of the European population. Chocolate would become popular as a drink, and tobacco would become the vice of choice of many Europeans.

From the mid-fourteenth century, sailors and explorers in growing numbers increasingly looked outward from the traditional Mediterranean heart of European civilization. Impeded by implacable foes to the east, they turned westward to the Atlantic for new opportunities to expand both their knowledge and their wealth. Using new technologies and new methods, sailors discovered islands in the Atlantic that served as early colonies as well as bases to continue searching for previously unknown lands to the south and west. The Portuguese explored and traded south along the coast of Africa, opening up new avenues of commerce that ultimately specialized in human cargoes of slaves transported to the Americas. There, the Spanish took the early lead in exploring and conquering lands inhabited by highly cultured and wealthy natives. While exploiting these new lands for their wealth, the Spanish decimated the Indian population unknowingly through disease and intentionally through abuse, while at the same time transforming native cultures in numerous ways. It was in the Americas that sugar cultivation would spur the rise of the trans-Atlantic slave trade that resulted in the largest forced migration of humans in history with consequences on the evolution of American societies that echo to the present. In sum, the Atlantic World evolved from the fourteenth to the beginning of the seventeenth centuries to tie these three regions together economically, politically, and socially in such a way that their histories could no longer be considered individually but only as a single entity.

Notes

1. Cardinal Bessarion to Francesco Foscari, May 1453, cited in Carlo M. Cipolla, *Guns, Sails, and Empires* (Manhattan, Kans.: Sunflower University Press, 1965), 1.

2. See John Larner, *Marco Polo and the Discovery of the World* (New Haven, Conn.: Yale University Press, 1999).

3. Cipolla, *Guns, Sails, and Empires*, 81.

4. See Felipe Fernández-Armesto, *Before Columbus: Exploration and Colonization from the Mediterranean to the Atlantic, 1229–1492* (Philadelphia: University of Pennsylvania Press, 1988).

5. See M. D. D. Newitt, *A History of Portuguese Overseas Expansion, 1400–1668* (London: Routledge, 2005).

6. John Thornton, *Africa and Africans in the Making of the Atlantic World, 1400–1800* (Cambridge: Cambridge University Press, 1992), 36–42, 53–71.

7. See David Northrup, *Africa's Discovery of Europe, 1450–1850* (New York: Oxford University Press, 2002).

8. See Kathleen A. Deagan, *Columbus's Outpost among the Tainos: Spain and America at La Isabela, 1493–1498* (New Haven, Conn.: Yale University Press, 2002).

9. See Ross Hassig, *Mexico and the Spanish Conquest* (New York: Longman, 1994).

10. See Kenneth Andrien, *Transatlantic Encounters: Europeans and Andeans in the Sixteenth Century* (Berkeley: University of California Press, 1991).

11. See, for example, Inga Clendinnen, *Ambivalent Conquests: Maya and Spaniard in the Yucatan, 1517–1570* (Cambridge: Cambridge University Press, 1987).

12. For fuller discussion of demographic decline among Indians, see Noble David Cook, *Born to Die: Disease and New World Conquest, 1492–1650* (Cambridge: Cambridge University Press, 1998).

13. See A. W. Crosby, *The Columbian Exchange: Biological and Cultural Consequences of 1492* (Westport, Conn.: Greenwood, 1972).

14. For fuller estimates on numbers of slaves see David Richardson, "The Atlantic Slave Trade Scale, Structure and Supply Slave Exports from West and West—Central Africa, 1700–1810: New Estimates of Volume and Distribution," *Journal of African History* 30:1 (1989): 1–22; and Hugh Thomas, *The Slave Trade* (New York: Simon and Schuster, 1997).

CHAPTER THREE

Migrations and Frontiers

Alison Games

Three Atlantic Migrants

In a time when young men dominated European migration to America, Barbara Rolfe was something of an anomaly. She traveled to New England from England in 1635 at the age of twenty. The circumstances of her migration were also somewhat peculiar. Her father, George, had approached a ship captain, Thomas Babb, about his intractable daughter. He said he could not persuade her to pursue "a civil and orderly course of life." Instead, she disobeyed him repeatedly, and he feared the damage to his reputation that might ensue if she stayed in England. The new English colonies in North America offered a timely solution to his domestic problems. For the sum of five pounds sterling, Captain Babb agreed to transport Barbara to New England and to find a family to hire her as a servant once she arrived. But Barbara was disagreeable during the long journey to America and "so evil" that, by the time the ship reached Boston, no one there would take her in. Babb shipped her north to Maine with a merchant in hopes of finding a place for her there, and Barbara then vanished from history. If she was unusual in her gender, she was typical in her disappearance from historical records.[1]

Pierre Radisson was a teenager when his family made their transatlantic migration from France to Canada in the spring of 1651. They settled in Three Rivers and found themselves in a region at war. French incursions in Canada in the beginning of the seventeenth century had exacerbated pre-existing indigenous rivalries. When the French joined the Algonquins in an alliance, the tribes of the Iroquois Confederacy became their enemies. Pierre Radisson became ensnared in these conflicts. One day, a year after he had reached Canada, he set out to hunt ducks with two friends. They were attacked by a Mohawk party, one of the tribes of the Iroquois Confederacy. His two friends were killed, and Radisson was taken captive. And thus a new kind of migration began for Pierre, who had already survived one long trip across the ocean. A grueling and stressful journey brought him with his captors to his new life in an Iroquois village. As an Iroquois, Radisson took part in a long raiding party which necessitated a trip of hundreds of miles into the region of the Great Lakes. Although Radisson ultimately returned to his family near Montreal, the knowledge of the interior that he had gained from his Iroquois migrations eventually supported his and his brother-in-law's professions as fur traders, and he took several more long journeys into the North American interior and crossed the Atlantic again.[2]

Radisson and Rolfe traveled to an unfamiliar land but with the advantage of some familiar cultural practices: language, law, manners, religion, dress, and diet all journeyed with these two young people to their respective French and English homes in America. The African Abd al-Rahman's journey delivered him to an entirely alien world. He was a Muslim from the Futa Jallon region of West Africa. Seized during a battle, his enemies elected not to kill him (as was their right by custom), but instead to avail themselves of a profitable outlet for captured enemies and to sell him into slavery. Abd al-Rahman and fifty of his fellow soldiers were sold to some Malinke traders. They transported their human commodities down the Gambia River where they found an English trader who purchased the men and arranged their transportation across the Atlantic. In 1788, Abd al-Rahman's journey of six thousand miles ended in Louisiana, near Natchez, then under Spanish control. Although many slaves soon perished in the brutal conditions of frontier labor in the newly developing territory, Abd al-Rahman survived to cross the Atlantic one more time to return to Africa in 1829 as one of the ex-slaves who settled in the new colony of Liberia.[3]

These three figures all migrated across the Atlantic, but on the surface, too many other characteristics distinguished them to enable us to think of them as part of the same process: enslaved, captive, soldier, servant, male, female, French, English, African, white, black, Protestant, Catholic, Muslim. They spoke a profusion of languages: English, Iroquois, French, and Arabic. If Rolfe and Radisson came from families we might characterize today as broadly middle class, Abd al-Rahman was from a privileged, even aristocratic, background in Africa. Yet they were all a part of the same world, one shaped by imperial and local rivalries, by the demands of an emerging regional labor market, and by the cultural collisions and innovations created as strangers were forced to adjust to each other and to unfamiliar practices. However fractured the kingdoms and empires and villages of the Atlantic region remained from each other in a world characterized more by its continued diversity and heterogeneity than by its commonalities, migrants from and within each sub-region were affected by forces derived from patterns of interaction beyond their control.

Each one of the millions of people who crossed the ocean had a distinctive story to tell, but common features shaped larger trends in migration. Transatlantic migration was embedded in local economic and cultural developments, whether conflict between rival states or more intimate familial conflicts. The migrations of Rolfe, Radisson, and Abd al-Rahman were dictated by circumstances particular to their home cultures in Europe and Africa: a father's fear of public humiliation if he could not control his daughter, a family's hope for prosperity or warfare. Few people moved freely, either across the ocean or even within their home country, and as Radisson's and Abd al-Rahman's experiences as war captives reveal, their migrations introduced them in violent, unexpected, and often unwelcome ways to new populations. Although separated by 250 years, Rolfe and Abd al-Rahman also traveled as part of an expansive labor market, both bound to serve others who sought to extract profit from American soil and resources. They framed a larger transformation in the Atlantic labor market, from European to African workers. The migration of people and their intersecting paths, their forced meetings, shaped the Atlantic World.

The Atlantic World was created and defined by migration. Most people migrated as involuntary laborers, whether bound or enslaved, European, African, or Indian. Each of these migrant streams was linked to the other, and all were dictated by the demand for labor. The forced migrations of Europeans, Africans, and Indians within and around the Atlantic World provided the labor which shaped the Atlantic in every respect, from the environmental transformations which accompanied large-scale agricultural production to the new societies that emerged to support and sustain the extraction of wealth. Migration is thus inextricably linked to the commodities and minerals of the Atlantic and the consumer tastes which encouraged their production: rice, sugar, coffee, cotton, tobacco, indigo, gold, and silver.

Migration also redefined the cultures of the Atlantic. Populations that were once isolated became drawn into larger networks. In some places, languages, cultures, and the people who generated them disappeared altogether and were replaced by others from thousands of miles away or reorganized into new societies. Newcomers brought their own languages and cultures with them, and new forms evolved amid the cultural clashes and encounters of the period. The entire region became a series of frontiers, border regions where strangers confronted each other and were compelled to devise new strategies of co-existence.

The story of cultural encounters within the Atlantic world is also the story of cultural innovation. Historians continue to debate the ability of people to sustain and transmit home cultures from the eastern Atlantic across the ocean to the western Atlantic. In some instances, cultural attributes were muted; in others they disappeared altogether. At the same time that migrants endeavored to transport familiar cultural practices, residence in the western Atlantic forced and created cultural hybridity. The ability of migrants to sustain and transport old cultures was dictated largely by demographic features of migration—the age and gender characteristics of different migrating populations and the mortality regimes they encountered in new destinations. Almost all places that were affected by the exchange of people and commodities across and around the Atlantic acquired to different degrees the characteristics of frontier zones, places of exchange and interaction where different cultures met. Migration offers one vantage to examine this process.

The centrality of labor to the economic exploitation of the Atlantic's varied resources and the responses of people in the Americas to the invasions of Europeans were the basic motivations behind large-scale migration within and across the Atlantic in this period. They help us understand who migrated where, when, and why. But additional factors determined the *cultural* impact of migration, especially the demographic characteristics of migrant populations: How old were they? Were they predominantly male or female? How fully could young male populations replicate the cultures they had left? To what extent could migrants transmit familiar cultures from home, to what extent did they devise new ones? To what extent did migrants interact with other migrant populations? These were all features determined by the age and gender structures of migrant populations. The aggregate statistics for migration in the whole period anchor the discussion.

These numbers provide only a starting point, illustrating the extent of transatlantic migration and the people involved. Before 1800 an estimated 1.4 million Europeans migrated west across the Atlantic. They were joined by millions of enslaved Africans: an estimated 7.6 million departed Africa before 1800, out of a total, through 1867, estimated at 11 million. These numbers are only approximations, probably more reliable for Africans than for Europeans because of the record-keeping imperatives of the slave trade. The table not only indicates the stark differential between the numbers of European and African migrants but also points to the dominance of particular populations within this migration—Europeans from the British Isles dominated European migration, but they were dwarfed by Africans embarked from the Gold Coast, the Bight of Benin, the Bight of Biafra, and West Central Africa.

Three factors explain the total number of migrants and the dominance of Africans in this table: European patterns of exploration, population growth, and migration; the need for labor; and high mortality. Among European migrants, the British were the main population involved in transatlantic migration, followed by the Spanish. These population flows did not reflect the differential political dominance of these nations and of the empires which they controlled. Indeed, if we thought only in terms of the territory claimed by different European powers, we would certainly expect the Spanish, with their political claims to vast territory in Central and South America and the Caribbean, to have been the population most present in the Americas, or perhaps the Portuguese, whose territory in Brazil was similarly enormous. But colonial dominion was not so intimately linked with migration. The Portuguese did migrate from Portugal, for example, in huge numbers considering the kingdom's size. Between 1500 and 1640, some 580,000 people migrated from Portugal, a country with a population no higher than three million. But these migrants ventured to Portuguese

Table 3.1. Migrants to the Americas, 1500–1800

Country of Origin/ Region of Departure	Number	Date
EUROPEANS (Country of Origin)		
Spain	437,000	1500–1650
Portugal	100,000	1500–1700
Britain	400,000	1607–1700
Britain[1]	322,000	1700–1780
France	51,000	1608–1760
"Germany"[2]	100,000	1683–1783
Total Europeans	1,410,000	1500–1783
AFRICANS (Region of Departure)		
Senegambia	384,000	1519–1800
Sierra Leone	226,500	1519–1800
Windward Coast	144,000	1519–1800
Gold Coast	974,200	1519–1800
Bight of Benin	1,488,100	1519–1800
Bight of Biafra	1,058,800	1519–1800
West Central Africa	3,261,000	1519–1800
Southeast Africa	78,400	1519–1800
Total Africans	7,615,000	1519–1800

Notes:

1. Includes between 190,000 and 250,000 Scots and Irish.

2. Germany refers to emigrants from southwestern Germany and the German-speaking cantons of Switzerland and Alsace Lorraine.

Source: For Europeans, this table reproduces table 1.1 in Ida Altman and James Horn, eds., *To Make America* (Berkeley: University of California Press, 1991), p. 3; for Africans, David Eltis, "The Volume and Structure of the Transatlantic Slave Trade: A Reassessment," *William and Mary Quarterly*, 3rd ser., 58 (January 2001), table II, p. 44.

trade factories not only in Brazil but also in Africa and Asia.[4] Overseas holdings often vied with other lucrative destinations in the optimistic minds of migrants and investors.

This table masks the chronological changes in European migration over time. Between 1500 and 1650, Europeans, particularly the Spanish and English, dominated transatlantic migration. Most northern Europeans migrated across the Atlantic in a dependent status, answering a seemingly insatiable need for laborers to produce the agricultural commodities—tobacco, cotton, indigo, or sugar—which promised to provide profits to landowners and investors. They traveled as bound laborers (indentured servants or *engagés*) from France and Britain and as redemptioners from the Holy Roman Empire. Redemptioners were people, usually German-speaking migrants traveling as families, who were unable to fund their own voyage across the Atlantic, particularly after they endured the expensive journey from central Europe to major ports. When they reached American ports in New York, or especially in Philadelphia, they were free to find someone who might "redeem" them by repaying a ship's master or broker the cost of the voyage. If they were unsuccessful, they were bound out as servants and required to work until they had covered the cost of their journey.

Indentured servants and *engagés* (predominantly young and male) had agreed to serve for a certain number of years in America (anywhere from four to eight) in return for freedom dues that varied from colony to colony. Such dues might include the promise of land, agricultural equipment to start a new life as a farmer, a bushel of corn, or a new set of clothes. The ability of servants to extract their promised dues from masters always depended on the willingness of courts (themselves composed of masters) to support servants' claims. Many servants acquired this indentured status reluctantly: one study of late-seventeenth-century London found that people might wait in the metropolis a full year, first seeking employment in the city, before resigning themselves to failure at home and, out of desperation, boarding ships for the colonies as servants.[5] The colonies offered only one of many options for the poor, hungry, and desperate. Some migrants were lured onto ships with promises of opportunity in America. Others were tricked and kidnapped—the term "Barbadosed" was coined to describe these illegal methods of procuring servants. These servants were bought and sold in America at the will of their masters. One young man in Virginia, Thomas Best, who deplored his plight, wrote his brother and cousin in 1623 fuming that his master had "sold mee for 150 pounds [of tobacco] like a damned slave."[6] Real opportunity was rare except for those servants who ventured to healthier environments or who found good fortune and available land. For many, an early death ended the term of service.

Many migrants hoped to be able to return home. For example, some young English migrants hoped that a temporary term as a servant would give them enough money to afford to marry upon their return. Other migrants came with greater resources but still regarded colonial migration as the springboard to European prosperity and status. James Dering, for example, traveled to Barbados in the 1630s with credit sufficient to enable him to obtain land and servants. He hoped to make enough money through his tobacco crop to repay his debts and make a profit, and then he could take his earnings home with him to England; to his dismay, a poor crop kept him on the island. Europeans moved back and forth across the Atlantic in numbers that seem surprising when we consider the great discomfort and danger of transatlantic travel.

The Portuguese and the French constituted the smallest European migrant streams. They settled primarily in Brazil and in French settlements on the American mainland, in Canada, the Mississippi River valley, and Louisiana, in addition to the island colony of Saint Domingue. The Portuguese also traveled to trade factories in Africa, where they lived mostly at the pleasure of local rulers. The French and Portuguese in the Americas always lived as a minority among non-European populations, whether indigenous people in North America and Brazil or enslaved Africans in the West Indies and Brazil.

Spanish migration, strong in the first 140 years of conquest and settlement, started to decline in 1625. It was characterized initially by the young men who always dominate migration flows, although within decades of the initial conquest women and children joined men in migrating west. They came primarily from two regions in Spain, Extremadura and Andalusia, and particularly from the city of Seville. These Spanish migrants settled in the largest numbers in Mexico but also inhabited Peru, Bolivia, the islands of the Caribbean, and other regions. Unlike other European migrants, most of whom traveled as agricultural laborers, they settled especially in urban areas. By the seventeenth century the Spanish population was able to reproduce itself, and the pace of transatlantic migration from the kingdom dwindled.

Altogether as many as 700,000 British came from all over the British Isles, from England, Scotland, and Ireland. They poured into the eastern seaboard of North America and similarly ventured to the islands of the Caribbean, especially Jamaica and Barbados. Dominated by agricultural and artisan laborers, these migrants also contained family groups who settled especially in the northern British colonies. In some instances, entire communities migrated together, either en masse or one neighbor following another: the British, Spanish, and German-speaking migrants in particular demonstrated this pattern of "chain" migration. Some continued in this pattern once they reached American destinations. For example, in 1635 several families migrated to Massachusetts from adjacent towns in Buckinghamshire, England, a region known for religious dissent in these turbulent times (the minister himself followed his parishioners to New England), settling first in the town of Lynn, then moving again five years later to Long Island, re-creating a network of neighbors and families by then twice relocated and twice reconstituted.[7]

Governments regulated migration, then as now. If states perceived population loss to be a threat to national power, then overseas migration suffered. In the seventeenth century, for example, a growing English population led colonial promoters to propose colonies as solutions to overpopulation, underemployment, and poverty in England. But in the 1770s, British landlords who worried about losing their rent-paying tenants pressured the government to restrict migration. The French government was similarly hesitant to encourage the large-scale migration that would populate its American holdings with European settlers.

Some states relied on foreigners to settle their lands. The English recruited Protestants from the European continent (particularly the 100,000 German-speaking migrants noted in table 3.1), while the Dutch hired a range of European settlers and transients, and the Swedes in their experiment with colonization in New Sweden (modern Delaware) depended on the Dutch and others. The Spanish crown preferred to exclude other Europeans from its American holdings. Thus a range of factors shaped the actual flow of migrants overseas, including perceptions of population growth or decline and state attitudes toward population as a source of national power.

European invasions of America precipitated other migrations. Both the indigenous inhabitants of the Americas and Africans became enmeshed in the exploitation, extraction, and production of American resources and new agricultural crops. In the first 150 years of European invasion in the Americas, Europeans answered their need for labor primarily through European and Indian labor. But the demographic collapse of indigenous populations, the inadequate numbers of European laborers as European consumer preferences fueled demands for agricultural exports, and a range of cultural factors as well turned European interests to another labor source, enslaved Africans. The trade in African captives was embedded in existing migration and commercial patterns and generated new ones. The pre-existing slave trade in Africa followed established routes and markets. The rise in the Atlantic trade introduced new trade *entrepôts* where African traders might bring these human commodities for transshipment overseas. Captives were transported from their place of capture to the coasts, where they embarked on ships to cross the ocean. These initial land journeys could be hundreds of miles long and deadly. As many as 50 percent of captives might die during these treks. The gruesome and grueling middle passage was only one part of this dismal ordeal, and a slave's migration was not done yet when captives reached American ports. Some might find themselves sold to nearby planters or even to urban owners, but most slaves found themselves on the move again, chained and shackled and on the march to plantations in the hinterland. Labor and migration were inseparable in the Atlantic.

As table 3.1 makes evident, although Europeans initiated transatlantic migration in order to control American territories through conquest and colonization, Africans by far dwarfed Europeans among all transatlantic migrants. The vast majority of Africans journeyed to the islands of the Caribbean (especially Saint Domingue, Barbados, and Jamaica) and to Brazil. These places shared a single feature: they were colonial societies geared toward the production of agricultural commodities for export. In particular, these were the main locations for sugar production. Sugar and slavery were intertwined, and thus sugar, like other commodities, is part of the story of migration. Sugar production in the American tropics, a region which was transformed to facilitate sugar cultivation, was grueling and deadly.[8] High mortality of enslaved laborers, avaricious planters, and eager consumers fueled an almost insatiable need for more laborers. By the middle of the seventeenth century, the slave trade really took off, and showed no sign of abating during this period. The trade eclipsed European migration. Moreover, European populations in those regions of sugar and rice cultivation, the main destinations for captive Africans, were unable to reproduce themselves; nor, indeed, were the slaves. Only high migration replaced these agricultural workers. These tropical zones were characterized by African majorities.

Europeans traveled to particular destinations in clear patterns, and through the dynamics of the slave trade Africans did the same. Certain trade routes from Africa to different American ports became established over time, with the result that slaves from some African regions were predominant. Between 1658 and 1713, for example, Jamaica and Barbados were dominated by slaves from adjacent regions in Africa: the Gold Coast, the Slave Coast, and the Bight of Biafra. Eighteenth-century Saint Domingue contained large numbers of slaves who had been captured in the course of the long civil wars in the kingdom of Kongo. Luanda was a trading port dominated by the Portuguese, and thus slaves from Angola were particularly evident in Brazil, especially in Bahia. Some places, such as Cuba, had no single dominant population, while changes in the trade over time altered the numerical dominance and cultural impact of any one African region or population. Between 1701 and 1725, for example, 20.4 percent of slaves who survived to disembark from ships from West Central Africa went to the Dutch Caribbean, and 28 percent went to Brazil. In that same twenty-five-year period, of the slaves who survived their voyages from the Bight of Benin, 31 percent went to the English islands of Jamaica and Barbados, less than 1 percent went to Bahia in Brazil, and 8.71 percent went to the Dutch Caribbean. If European migration was heavily male, the forced migration of Africans was slightly more evenly balanced. Moreover, if European migration was dominated by people between the ages of fifteen and twenty-four, the forced migrants from Africa included more children. Thus African captives more closely approximated the societies they left than did the unfree Europeans who traveled across the Atlantic.

These core pieces of information—where European and African migrants came from and what age and gender they were—shaped the cultural impact migrants might have on new societies. Migration was defined by its demographic peculiarities, which joined with early death to hinder the growth of colonial societies: migrants tended to be young and male, as much as 90 percent male for indentured migrants from France and England in the seventeenth and eighteenth centuries. Given these demographic realities, it was obviously difficult for Europeans to transmit cultural practices intact: young male majorities were likely to bring recreations and cultures specific to their age and gender. Newcomers often tended to die at high rates. High mortality also determined that some places in the Atlantic remained migrant societies for the entirety of the early modern period, shaped by successive waves of newcomers who always outnumbered the native-born population. Elsewhere, locally born people—called Creoles if they were of European or African descent—predominated. Skewed gender ratios of European arrivals, high mortality, and the power dynamics of colonial societies generated complex social relations.

With the very first appearance of Europeans and Africans in the Americas new social and sexual relations and new mixed-race populations emerged. These relationships generally reflected the power dynamics of conquest and colonial societies, with European men claiming rights to women's sexuality as well as to the material riches of a conquered society. Indigenous and enslaved women occasionally derived benefits from these alliances as well, especially for their children. These unions, formal and informal, were direct consequences of migration patterns and, in some instances, the desire of Europeans to insinuate themselves in local political and commercial networks. The first waves of European migrants were almost entirely men, whether soldiers or servants. These men pursued romantic and sexual relations with local women. Male European traders in Africa sought alliances with prominent families through marriage or informal unions. The first Spanish conquistadors likewise secured their power and legitimacy in conquered territory in America through alliances with noblewomen. Isabel Moctezuma, the daughter of Moctezuma II, became a useful pawn for Cortés, who arranged for her to marry first her uncle and then a succession of Spaniards. Her marriage alliances established a pervasive pattern. The marriage of John Rolfe and Pocahontas in Virginia in 1614 suggested that the English might follow the same example; but, ultimately, English sexual alliances with indigenous women tended to be informal. Whether officially sanctioned or not, throughout the Americas and in coastal Africa European men found sexual partners among indigenous women, many of whom, along with their mixed-race children, came to play important roles as cultural mediators.

Demographic patterns within migration flows explain some of the varied unions and new populations that emerged in the Americas, but different nations and empires integrated these unions and their offspring into colonial polities in a variety of ways. In almost every part of the Americas, the children of enslaved women and European or Creole men could be legally and socially recognized by their fathers. Sometimes they were freed; sometimes they were educated. Thus, by the eighteenth century, the most violent slave societies, including Jamaica, Brazil, and Saint Domingue (all of which contained small white minorities), contained small but growing populations of free people of color, who participated in colonial society despite a range of legal and social encumbrances that hindered full participation. By the late eighteenth century, the free people of color of Saint Domingue constituted 5.2 percent of the colony's population, held one-quarter of the colony's slaves, and owned one-quarter of the real estate. The single notable exception to acceptance of these interracial unions was British North America and is best witnessed in the actions of Thomas Jefferson, the revolutionary and later third president of the United States who, DNA evidence, documentary sources, and oral tradition strongly indicate, had a long-term relationship with his deceased wife's half-sister, the slave Sally Hemings (1773–1835). A product of two generations of such unions, Hemings was, in the terminology of the time, a quadroon. Jefferson's public disavowal of this liaison, and his white descendants' bitter rejection of it, stand in contrast to the conduct of planters in other parts of the British Atlantic world and elsewhere in the Americas.

These sexual relations—coerced, voluntary, legal, or lacking in social recognition—point to the complexity of the societies that emerged in the Atlantic as a result of migration. The story of cultural encounters within the Atlantic is a story of the creation of ethnicity and of nationality: people developed heightened senses of who or what they were when they met those unlike themselves. At the same time that migrants endeavored to transport familiar cultural practices, residence in the western Atlantic forced and created cultural hybridity. New communities and ethnicities emerged out of amalgams of newcomers and old-timers in a process that was repeated throughout the Americas. Migration for all people—European, indigenous, and African—induced patterns of cultural adaptability, flexibility, and ultimately hybridity, in the same way that the circulation of commodities, information, and technology transformed all societies that surrounded the Atlantic Ocean.

A glimpse at the languages spoken in parts of the Americas reveals the enormous complexity of this question of the transmission of the Europe and Africa in America. Ethnic majorities did not necessarily impose their language, as in the case of Montserrat, where despite an Irish (and Irish-speaking) majority, English was the island's lingua franca. In Suriname, slaves spoke an English-based Creole, despite the fact that the country was English for no more than two decades and slaves always outnumbered planters, Dutch or English. Both examples indicate that language was intimately connected to migration patterns, but that configurations of settlement mattered as well.

In other places, migrants from one region could have a profound linguistic impact. In parts of eighteenth-century Saint Domingue, for example, the language of Kongo became the lingua franca because of the dominance of slaves from there. Elsewhere, in places with no ethnic (and linguistic) majority, pidgins emerged, such as Gullah and Geechee in the Sea Islands of North America (off the coasts of South Carolina, Georgia, and Florida). These two languages share African grammatical features and a mixture of vocabulary from numerous languages. Speakers used English words, but Gullah also contains words with origins in the parts of Africa from which most coastal slaves came, Sierra Leone, Senegambia, and West Central Africa (Angola and Kongo). To this day modern Americans have integrated words from these eighteenth-century pidgins into their own vocabularies: To "badmouth" (curse), for example, is a Gullah word which literally translates into English an African linguistic convention to use body parts to describe behavior. Such pidgins emerged in trading ports throughout the Atlantic and on plantations as well, where newcomers needed to find a common language out of variety of tongues.

Europeans from countries with political power in the Americas were obviously at an advantage in transplanting core features of their countries of origin. English, Spanish, French, and Portuguese migrants who settled in those regions claimed by their countries could continue to speak a familiar language. The law followed familiar practice. If the transmission of the features of local government was incomplete, it was for the most part functional. Everywhere the church provided a cultural glue that linked European migrants in the western Atlantic to the different ecclesiastical polities of the eastern Atlantic, whether Catholic or Protestant, even for dissenters. But at the same time no European power could transplant itself in its entirety in the Americas.

For Africans, cultural transmission was hindered by the circumstances of migration and the constraints of plantation production. Cultural autonomy varied greatly in different countries and colonies, from plantation to plantation, from one crop to another. Thanks to the compilation of the slave trade database, historians can talk with considerable certainty about the number of slaves who left from a particular port, but it is more difficult to link a particular slave to a specific place of origin.[9] The slave trade prompted its own patterns of internal migration within Africa in the same way that European invasions of America prompted different kinds of migration patterns by Native Americans. Historians who examine a single plantation often find that enslaved populations were characterized by their ethnic variety.[10] But at the same time, it is clear that slaves transported a great range of cultural attributes with them. The horrors of the slave trade did not destroy the vestiges of home cultures, seen through language, architecture, dress, worship, food preferences, music, art, animal husbandry, agriculture, and a host of other practices. Moreover, because of mortality most slave populations remained migrant populations, regularly replenished by newcomers from Africa for the entire period covered in this chapter.

Another impediment in the transmission of old world cultures was the peculiar age and gender structures of migrant populations. The colonial societies where most Europeans and Africans in the Americas lived were migrant societies. That is, they retained the peculiarities of migrant societies (young and male, with no natural increase, dependent on migration to sustain population) well beyond the first decades of settlement. The islands of the West Indies, Brazil, and the Carolinas remained migrant societies throughout this period. In other places such as New England and Mexico, European-born people and their descendants were able to reproduce themselves. Some of those places where migrants were able to reproduce themselves nonetheless remained migrant societies because of the continued influx of newcomers. The "middle colonies" of British North America—New York, New Jersey, and Pennsylvania—were healthy places to live. Families were able to sustain and reproduce themselves there. But these regions were attractive to newcomers throughout the colonial period. Pennsylvania continued to receive thousands of newcomers who brought European customs with them, thus ensuring the continued use of German, for example, over a century after the first German-speaking migrants appeared in the colony. Apart from these exceptions, the destinations for the overwhelming majority of migrants were places characterized by high mortality, low fertility, male majorities, and thwarted family formation. These features fundamentally shaped the ability of newcomers to transfer and to transmit their European or African cultures.

Indeed, for Europeans in the Americas an important theme is the creation, not the replication, of ethnic identity. German-speaking people from a host of distinct communities in the Rhinelands became "Germans," an ethnic identity they would have found alien in Europe in this period, and the polyglot people of New Netherland became "Dutch." Recent research reveals that the creation of ethnic identity was a complex process of interaction not only with other inhabitants of the colonies but also with the exigencies of a new environment. In New Netherland, Dutch West India Company officials consciously imposed a "Dutch" identity on the heterogeneous population of the colony.[11] For unfree migrants it was considerably more difficult to replicate home cultures. Those German-speaking redemptioners who bound themselves out to English-speaking families to repay the cost of their crossing found themselves learning English quickly.

Regional styles of vernacular architecture illustrate some of the complex processes at work. In the eighteenth century, wealthy English colonial merchants and planters sought to emulate the building styles of Britain, for example, but in places such as Boston's prosperous North Shore, they used wood in their colonial houses rather than brick, the common building material in England. Less prosperous rural New England colonists discarded the variety of regional building styles they transported from England for a single colonial style, constructing their homes out of wood (not the brick, stone, or thatch which were all commonly used in England), and similarly rejected the great variation in floor plans of England for a common one- or one-and-a-half-story house. For the most part, eighteenth-century immigrants from Europe to North America abandoned their old distinctive building styles, often characterized by cellars, large central chimneys, and steeply pitched roofs, for simple and functional cabins.[12]

If historians are able to approximate figures for transatlantic migration, particularly for those populations whose labor was a central economic undertaking, and to determine at least the general scope of migration and the cultural pressures migrants faced, the equally vast migration of indigenous people within the Americas in the wake of European conquests has been much more difficult to grasp. Yet those glimpses of Indian migration that have survived suggest that this migration was a major part of the settlement and reorganization of the Americas: Indians employed migration as a fundamental strategy to withstand conquest. The quest for labor primarily ensnared Native Americans before Europeans looked for other populations to exploit, and Indian migration within the Americas was in part a response to these labor demands. The Spanish, for example, took advantage of pre-existing labor and tribute requirements in the two main indigenous empires they conquered, the Aztec empire in Mexico and the Inca empire in Peru. But the Spanish modified some of these practices. The Spanish required Indians in the former Inca empire to work one out of every seven years in the silver mines at Potosí (a practice called the *mita*). Families often moved with the men who were burdened by this obligation, and thus what started as temporary labor migrations became permanent family migrations. Other people fled the labor requirements altogether, leaving home communities and joining new ones.

Forced migration took other forms as well. Communities that were fragmented and dispersed after conquest were reassembled into towns under Spanish rule. Other populations were resettled in mission communities under the protection of Catholic missionaries. Efforts to convert Indians to Catholicism often necessitated the wholesale rejection of indigenous customs and culture. The social and religious reorganization of Indian communities and economies was dependent on migration.

It is hard to appreciate now the cultural significance of migration for populations whose sacred beliefs were inextricably linked to specific locales. People in the Americas, Europe, and Africa alike often had local beliefs, gods, and practices that supplemented or replaced beliefs in universal deities. Europeans, Protestant and Catholic alike, believed in fairies and demons who lived nearby and were associated with local natural features, whether streams, caves, or forests. In those places where much religious practice was local, the associations were even more important. The Andean people affected by the *mita* lived in interdependent and cooperative residential units that enabled people to take advantage of the different growing seasons at different altitudes. Each unit was sustained by its own local gods and sacred objects, all of which were essential for the protection and well-being of a community and its resources. When people moved away from their homes, they had to abandon their families' gods and all of the religious practices associated with sustaining the cosmos. For such people, migration had enormous cultural, social, and religious consequences.

The story of Indian migration in the Atlantic world has often been obscured by an emphasis on transatlantic migration and by another demographic story historians focus on for native people, that of high mortality in the wake of conquest. These two narratives are actually intertwined. Europeans reached the Americas eager to extract whatever riches they could identify, and they set Indian laborers to work for them, panning for gold, mining silver, cutting trees, tending crops. They acquired labor through barter and through force. The Spanish and Portuguese were particularly dependent on Indian labor in the islands of the Caribbean and the American mainland. The Portuguese and the English joined with Indian allies in Brazil and North America, respectively, to create a slave trade to meet their labor needs. These slaves took part in a migration that was as forced as that pursued by Indians whose preferred strategy was to avoid Europeans altogether through migration farther from the coasts.

New epidemic diseases joined the social, political, and cultural dislocations of conquest and colonization to reduce Indian populations by as much as 90 percent in some areas. These deaths had two important consequences in terms of migration. First, Indians whose bands had been ravaged by illness and death often could not sustain themselves as a corporate entity. Squanto, one of the most famous North American Indians of the seventeenth century, experienced such a fate: of his entire tribe, he was one of a handful of survivors. Unable to reconstitute his society or his political power, Squanto found a temporary haven among the English at Plymouth. Other Indians assembled in new bands composed of the remnants of a variety of groups. The Catawba, who live in the southeastern part of North America, were a people composed of refugees from other tribes. Some tribes undertook long migrations to evade Europeans. The Saponis of Virginia, for example, moved a number of times. They first joined the Catawba before returning to Virginia and then finally made a longer migration to join the Iroquois of northern New York, Canada, and the Great Lakes.[13] The Iroquois themselves were a population composed increasingly of outsiders over time. Through the mechanism of captivity, the Iroquois incorporated newcomers (European and Indians alike) into tribes depleted by disease and warfare. By the 1660s, one Jesuit observer remarked that there were more foreigners than Iroquois in Iroquois country. Two-thirds of the Iroquois by then were adopted.[14]

Indians constitute the great overlooked migrant population of the period largely because their numbers are so hard to calculate and their activities so dimly revealed in the sources on which historians depend. Migration was a crucial strategy as Indian populations considered how best to respond to the new circumstances of conquest and colonization. While some tribes migrated toward Europeans, eager to engage in trade and to procure commodities that were desirable not only for their practical use but also for their social prestige, others migrated away from Europeans. In the middle of the sixteenth century, some Tupinamba in Brazil were engaged in just such a migration north away from areas of Portuguese settlement when they found themselves moving toward the French, who proved to be useful allies. Four thousand Indian refugees migrated away from areas lost by the Dutch to the Portuguese after the Dutch surrender in 1654. The picture that emerges of the Americas during the age of conquest and European settlement is of Indian populations in steady motion, as forced laborers and as refugees. Although the numbers are often difficult to calculate with certainty, any wave of European migration across the Atlantic set off a similar movement on the American continent.

If migration within America offered one strategy for Indians who wished to avoid or engage European incursions, migration across the Atlantic offered another strategy for a small but politically powerful Indian population. In the mid-seventeenth century, the Tupis of Brazil greeted the Dutch as a potential ally against the Portuguese and their policies of forced labor and forced migration. Some of these Tupi-speaking allies, the Potiguars, asked the Dutch to take them to Holland so that they could escape from the Portuguese, and so they commenced a long journey across the Atlantic, reversing the trip that had brought so many Europeans to Brazil. This small group of Potiguars lived for several years in the Low Countries, where they learned Dutch and mastered as well the political and diplomatic language of the period. One of these Indian leaders, a man named Anthonio Paraupaba, later deployed his linguistic and cultural skills to secure political power in Brazil, and in the wake of the Portuguese revolt that signaled the end of Dutch rule in Brazil, Paraupaba returned to Holland to secure continued Dutch support in their struggles with the Portuguese. Many of the Dutch-allied Tupi had converted to Protestantism, and they migrated into the mountains to form a refugee community.[15] Migration in all its forms was a central response to conquest.

Violence underpinned the majority of migration flows, seen vividly in the physical restraint necessary for the transportation of enslaved laborers. Violence of another kind, warfare, dictated migration as well. It generated captives to be sold into slavery, as was the case for Abd al-Rahman. European conflagrations similarly caused economic dislocation and religious conflict which prompted refugees to seek new homes in the Americas. The Atlantic World was a region beset by warfare. All European conflicts had their own manifestations in the western Atlantic. Three places where European conflicts regularly provoked local upheavals were the Caribbean, the southeastern part of North America, and northeastern North America. Wars prompted people to move from areas engulfed in violence, while the peace that followed each war and the redistribution of territory that was part of treaties produced new waves of migration. Some of these refugee populations are well known in modern United States culture. The Cajuns of Louisiana, for example, derived from a population of French inhabitants of newly acquired British territories in Canada. The British first dispersed and then expelled these Acadians, who journeyed to France and attempted colonial settlements in Saint Domingue and Guyane, before some survivors found their way to Louisiana. Any war and any peace treaty in which territory was swapped generated similar waves of migration. When the British claimed Florida in 1763 at the end of the Seven Years' War, the colony's Spanish inhabitants, free and enslaved, evacuated to Cuba. The proximity of rival powers could also prompt migration apart from overt conflict. The Spanish government in eighteenth-century Florida offered incentives to enslaved blacks in the nearby Carolina colonies, under British control, to migrate to Florida. With promises of freedom and legal privileges to Carolina slaves, the Spanish hoped to weaken Britain's power in the region. These incentives inspired small numbers of migrants, all slaves, including those who slipped away one by one to a new life in Florida and those who in 1739 took part in an uprising in South Carolina called the Stono Rebellion.[16]

These wartime migrations were typical of the violence and coercion that governed migration in the Atlantic World between 1500 and 1800. Migrants were predominantly laborers and were thus always vulnerable to the coercive powers of masters and governments. "Free" migrants were the minority. European conquests compelled the social and political reorganization of indigenous economies. Labor demands on Indian populations joined high mortality to prompt waves of migration and the reconstitution of Indian communities. Waning Indian populations and inadequate European migration alike led to the rise in the Atlantic slave trade. Migration within the Atlantic was defined by its African majority, those men, women, and children whose journeys were entirely involuntary. For all the merciless violence that drove migration, the forced relocation of people across and around the Atlantic World generated innovation and heterogeneity that defined the cultures of the Atlantic.

Notes

1. Alison Games, *Migration and the Origins of the English Atlantic World* (Cambridge, Mass.: Harvard University Press, 1999), 80–81.

2. Arthur T. Adams, ed., *The Explorations of Pierre Esprit Radisson* (Minneapolis: Ross and Haines, 1961).

3. Michael Gomez, *Exchanging Our Country Marks: The Transformation of African Identities in the Colonial and Antebellum South* (Chapel Hill: University of North Carolina Press, 1998), 71–72, 86; Terry Alford, *Prince among Slaves* (New York: Harcourt Brace Jovanovich, 1977).

4. Stuart B. Schwartz, "Formation of Identity in Brazil," in *Colonial Identity in the Atlantic World, 1500–1800*, ed. Nicholas Canny and Anthony Pagden (Princeton, N.J.: Princeton University Press, 1987), p. 20.

5. John Wareing, "Migration to London and Transatlantic Emigration of Indentured Servants, 1683–1775," *Journal of Historical Geography* 7 (1981): 356–378.

6. Thomas Best to his brother and cousin, April 12 (1623), Virginia Colonial Records Project, reel 50 (original in the Manchester Papers, Public Record Office, London).

7. Games, *Migration*, pp. 179–181.

8. J. R. McNeill, "Yellow Jack and Geopolitics: Environment, Epidemics, and the Struggles for Empire in the American Tropics, 1650–1825," *OAH Magazine of History* 18:3 (April 2004).

9. David Eltis, Stephen D. Behrendt, David Richardson, and Herbert S. Klein. *The Trans-Atlantic Slave Trade: A Database on CD-ROM* (Cambridge: Cambridge University Press, 1999).

10. Lorena S. Walsh, *From Calabar to Carter's Grove: The history of a Virginia Slave Community* (Charlottesville: University Press of Virginia, 1997). See for Jamaica Trevor Burnard and Kenneth Morgan, "The Dynamics of the Slave Market and Slave Purchasing Patterns in Jamaica, 1655–1788," *William and Mary Quarterly*, 3rd ser., 58 (2001): 205–228.

11. James H. Williams, "How Dutch Were the Dutch: The Cultural Struggle for New Netherland," unpublished paper presented to the American Studies Association, Kansas City, 1996. Joyce Goodfriend has demonstrated the extraordinary tenacity of this created Dutch identity in New York City in *Before the Melting Pot: Society and Culture in Colonial New York City, 1664–1730* (Princeton, N.J.: Princeton University Press, 1992), chapter 5. For the Germans, see Aaron Spencer Fogleman, *Hopeful Journeys: German Immigration, Settlement, and Political Culture in Colonial America, 1717–1775*

(Philadelphia: University of Pennsylvania Press, 1996), and Philip Otterness, *Becoming German: The 1709 Palatine Migration to New York* (Ithaca, N.Y.: Cornell University Press, 2004).

12. Stephen Hornsby, *British Atlantic, American Frontier: Spaces of Power in Early Modern British America* (Lebanon, N.H.: University Press of New England, 2005), pp. 86, 143, 173.

13. James Merrell, "The Indians' New World: The Catawba Experience," *William and Mary Quarterly*, 3rd ser., 41 (1984): 537–565.

14. Daniel K. Richter, "War and Culture: The Iroquois Experience," *William and Mary Quarterly*, 3rd ser., 40 (1983): 528–559.

15. Mark Meuwese, "Native American Reponses to the Portuguese (Re)Conquest of Dutch Brazil, 1654–1656," paper presented in Philadelphia, March 26, 2004, at a conference on Lost Colonies.

16. Jane Landers, *Black Society in Spanish Florida* (Urbana: University of Illinois Press, 1999).

II

Empires and Slavery

Part 2 focuses on the institutions, economic and otherwise, that led to the construction of European empires across the Atlantic Basin. But rather than center on European elites—an idea that has dominated Atlantic history for far too long—the chapters of this section highlight the numerically more important subaltern groups whose labor, repression, and actions helped shape the eighteenth- and nineteenth-century Atlantic World.

Also central to the accelerated creation of the Atlantic World was slavery. In that institution scholars and students of Atlantic history may have the best single example of the distinctiveness of the Atlantic World. As Michael Guasco shows poignantly, the transition to slavery from slavery-like precursors—such as indentured servitude and *encomienda*—resulted in a slavery system that, while based on the European model, necessarily took on a more racialized tone in the New World. Guasco homes in on the point near the end of his chapter: "With the articulation of an Atlantic World in which wealth and power were premised on agricultural production and the extraction of precious metals, race and slavery were intertwined and racism and human bondage evermore exploitative and arbitrary." Equally important is that Guasco's portrayal of the important transition from servitude to slavery focuses not on the over-covered region of the Chesapeake but on regions in New Spain, New France, and other parts of the British Atlantic.

Timothy R. Buckner reveals the binding force of the transatlantic slave trade, which reached its peak in the eighteenth century. While providing a brief statistical overview for readers, Buckner focuses on those issues that were more important in the daily lives of people living that trade, living slavery, and living mastery: social relations, culture, and economic behavior. As an economic and cultural force, the slave trade became the mechanism by which Atlantic societies were more closely intertwined.

Building upon Buckner's examination of the slave trade, Aribidesi A. Usman provides an overview of Black Atlantic culture in the nineteenth and early twentieth centuries through the slave trade and other movements to the Caribbean, to the Americas, and in Africa. Usman focuses on the rise and transformation of African culture whose outlook spanned the Atlantic during the era of the slave trade. The scale and intensity of these bonds were such that some African groups, or at least their commercial and ruling elites, may be considered as participating in what can reasonably be termed an "Atlantic community." By emphasizing the slave trade in the nineteenth century and the Atlantic societies it helped to create, Usman illustrates the African influence in the cultural syncretism of the Atlantic.

The theme of cultural syncretism is also evident in Ken Aslakson's chapter on gender in the early modern Atlantic. Focusing on the interplay of race and gender in the construction of Atlantic slave societies, Aslakson offers a different dimension to the early Atlantic World from most typical histories. Aslakson argues, "cultural constructions of gender and race did much to determine the demographic and social make-up of the Atlantic Worlds. Perceptions of what it meant to be a woman in these societies were not necessarily rooted in biology, but they shaped the experiences of women nonetheless." Indeed, the Atlantic World emerged in large part because of these differences.

Since the early 1990s scholars have been re-thinking the African Diaspora, often re-conceptualizing the subject as the "Black Atlantic." Douglas B. Chambers traces these developments, with a special emphasis on several "turns" in the historiography: a critique of creolization as an organizing concept; a generalized focus on the circum-Atlantic world; and a particular focus on cultural history. His chapter suggests a theory, a method, and a practice for studying the Black Atlantic in the era of the slave trade, slavery and post-emancipation.

CHAPTER FOUR

From Servitude to Slavery

Michael Guasco

There may be no more definitive image of the colonial Atlantic World than that of half-dressed, bedraggled, and emaciated Africans toiling away on a plantation. Countless images survive from nineteenth-century magazines, eighteenth-century tobacco labels, seventeenth-century maps, and sixteenth-century books that attest to the ubiquity of slavery. Africans cut cane in Pernambuco and Barbados, cultivated tobacco in the Chesapeake and Bermuda, waded through rice paddies in the Carolina low country, distilled rum in Antigua, and otherwise carted goods, cleared land, and built the world anew as the slaves of Europeans. In the simplest terms, historians have noted that "slaves worked."[1] We might add to this truism, from the perspective of our collective historical imagination, the reality that Africans were enslaved. The sweat on the brow of the African slave and the blood on the hands of European slave traders and planters fueled the Atlantic World. European wealth and nascent empires were constructed on the remains of the broken bodies of human beings ripped from their native soil and compelled through violence to labor against their will.[2]

In the beginning, however, this brutal reality was hardly a foregone conclusion. When European navigators first set sail across the Atlantic in the late fifteenth century, the development of expansive plantation colonies was unimaginable. Few European nations, before the English beginning in the late sixteenth century, anticipated the large-scale migration of their fellow countrymen to the New World. Moreover, when Europeans thought about the ways they might profit from America, they assumed that the resources of the two continents could be had through trade or conquest or by compelling Indians to provide for the newcomers. In some cases, particularly among the French and English, European colonizers imagined that their own people would be sufficient to meet the labor demands in their new overseas possessions. Africa and Africans were certainly integral to the early modern Atlantic World, but most often as trade partners in the developing trade in gold, ivory, and pepper. Nonetheless, although Indians and many poor Europeans would be compelled to labor throughout the Americas, enslaved Africans would bear the brunt of mercantile colonialism in the long run. A combination of demographic, economic, political, and cultural factors would combine to transform how, and by whom, labor was performed in the Atlantic World by the dawn of the eighteenth century.

Indian Slavery

Typically, historians portray the indigenous inhabitants of America as a people who, once encountered by Europeans, were conquered or displaced over the course of nearly two centuries by military conflicts, disease, and cultural genocide. To the conquering Europeans, however, Indians represented an invaluable source of labor. Thus, during the decades that followed the planting of Spanish, Portuguese, French, and English colonies, Indians were systematically preyed upon and regularly reduced to slavery. Famously, Christopher Columbus initiated this pattern when he returned several hundred Indians to Spain in 1496 to be sold into slavery. In some ways, this episode did not represent a dramatic historical departure. Several forms of slavery could be found in the Americas in the pre-contact era. Slavery was also quite common in the fifteenth-century Iberian world, and Moors, sub-Saharan Africans, and Canary Islanders (among others) were held in bondage in significant numbers, particularly in the coastal cities. Thus, in the absence of immediately identifiable quantities of gold and silver, Columbus transported a familiar commodity across the ocean sea: human beings.

More commonly, Indians were enslaved in post-conquest America rather than Europe, though this issue was complicated within the Spanish Empire. Ferdinand and Isabella, for example, evidenced their concern with the legality of Indian slavery when they drafted a letter to Pedro de Torres in Seville in 1500 ordering the release of the Indians in his custody and their return to the Americas. Even so, Indians continued to be enslaved during the first half century of the Spanish conquest, especially in peripheral zones where the practice was justified as a natural outgrowth of an ongoing just war. Between 1515 and 1542, historians estimate that as many as 200,000 Indians were captured in Nicaragua and sold into slavery in the West Indies. In 1542, however, the Council of the Indies issued the famous New Laws, which effectively abolished legal Indian slavery.[3] While they represented an important ideological statement in a European context, the New Laws were not popular with Europeans living in the Americas. When the Spanish viceroy Blasco Núñez Vela attempted to enforce the laws in Peru, he provoked an insurrection and was eventually killed.

The delicacy of the issue was appreciated by leaders in New Spain, who chose to phase out the practice of Indian slavery more gradually in the region around Mexico City. Nonetheless, in the absence of close controls over latter-day *conquistadores* and, perhaps, with a desire to mollify the local populace, less-than-scrupulous slave raiders continued to be tolerated in frontier regions well into the nineteenth century. The ban on Indian slavery was reasserted by decree in 1681. Still, in the 1850s, at least 2,000 predominantly Navajo Indians were enslaved in the New Mexico territory acquired by the United States from Mexico.[4]

The New Laws were designed to end indigenous slavery and offer a whole spate of imperial protections to Indians, but they did not signify a departure from the idea that Indians were, and should be, bound laborers. In Peru, Indian labor was extracted through the *mita*, or a compulsory rotational labor draft that was used throughout the Andes but most famously in the silver mines of Potosí. In other parts of Spanish America, authorities continued to countenance the *encomienda* system, which had been formalized in the Laws of Burgos in 1513. An *encomienda* was a grant to an individual (*encomendero*) of the right to the labor of a group of Indians in exchange for the promise to protect Indians and see to their conversion to Christianity. Abuses in the system had been evident from the beginning, and famous defenders of native rights such as Bartolomé de las Casas attacked the system vigorously. The New Laws attempted to reign in the prerogative power of *encomenderos* as part of their effort to address the catastrophic demographic losses being suffered by Indians. Labor demands, however, continued to be placed on Indians through the *repartimiento*, a tribute system like the *mita* that funneled labor to private individuals through government mechanisms. This system, too, was abolished in 1635.[5]

Indian slavery was not confined to the Spanish-American world—every European nation either participated in, or abetted, the practice. Almost as quickly as the Portuguese began to establish coastal outposts in Brazil, for example, they began to deal in Indian slaves. As early as April 1503, a fleet returned to Portugal with a cargo of brazilwood and Indian slaves. As Stuart Schwartz has revealed, the description of Indians as *negro da terra* is indicative of the servile role sixteenth-century colonists, secular and religious alike, envisioned for Indians. Since the Portuguese waited several decades to establish permanent settlements, however, it was not until the middle of the sixteenth century that they began to enslave Indians in larger numbers to knock down brazilwood trees or, increasingly, to toil away on the developing sugar plantations.[6]

Though Indian slavery persisted longer in Brazil than it did in the core areas of the Spanish empire, the practice was not without its critics or consequences. Already in the second decade of the sixteenth century, the Portuguese crown placed Indians under its protection, asserting that Indians must be treated well in order to facilitate their conversion. To this end, the Jesuits were brought in at mid-century, and for the next century they proved to be the most vocal opponents of the use of indigenous peoples as slaves. Rebellious Indians, however, were considered fair game, and so, even as the Jesuits sought to gather together Indians into settlements (*aldeias*) to promote religious instruction, Portuguese settlers conducted "just wars" to augment their supply of slaves. Such a precarious policy that encouraged conversion yet condoned enslavement was important in Brazil since both religious and economic justifications were at the heart of sixteenth-century colonialism. Thus, the Portuguese imagined that they were in Brazil to gather souls, but they also needed bodies to work in the sugar fields and factories (*engenhos*), and so Indian slavery was tolerated so long as it did not prove to be socially disruptive.[7]

Even as they imposed restraints on their slave raiding and slave trading, the Portuguese presence in Brazil had tragic consequences. Arguably, proselytization and enslavement equally challenged the ability of Indians to live out their lives in any kind of traditional fashion. Matters were further complicated in 1562 when epidemic disease first struck the local population. By some estimates, perhaps half of the coastal Indian population was killed, which effectively intensified the labor demands Portuguese colonists placed on Indian peoples during subsequent decades. Therefore, in 1570 King Sebastião, in order to alleviate the pressure, decreed that Indians could only be enslaved in a just war declared by the king or his governor or if Indians were found guilty of cannibalism. In effect, the law represented an effort to diminish Indian slavery by ending the corrupt practice of *resgate*, whereby the Portuguese "ransomed" Indians who were captured in inter-tribal warfare and subsequently held them as slaves. But just as Spanish settlers had reacted negatively to the New Laws in 1542, Portuguese settlers protested angrily. The Crown heard these complaints and modified the law in 1574, once again allowing *resgates*, so long as Indians were registered officially. Though their numbers diminished steadily, and they were soon subsumed by the enslavement of Africans, Indians continued to suffer enslavement in Brazil and reeled from organized slave-raiding expeditions (*bandeiras*) on the frontier throughout the colonial era.[8]

Indian slavery also factored into French and English colonialism in North America, though in different ways and in much smaller numbers. In the English colonies, colonial promoters and early settlers sought to promote better, less destructive relationships with the natives than had their predecessors to the south. Even so, Indian resistance to English incursions sparked violence in the Chesapeake (1622, 1644, and 1676) and New England (1636 and 1675) that resulted in the enslavement of hundreds of conquered Indians based on the prevailing wisdom of the early modern era that captives in a just war could be held in bondage. During the seventeenth century, perhaps 1,000 Algonquian Indians from the eastern woodlands were transported to the West Indies as slaves. Not all Indian slaves, however, were reduced to such a condition through traditional mechanisms. In the Carolinas, during the late seventeenth and early eighteenth centuries, thousands of Indians were sold into slavery by rival Indian peoples interested in profiting from their new trading relationship with English settlers. Although historians tend to overlook this episode in colonial history, Indian slavery was crucial to Anglo-Indian relations in the southeast.

By one estimate, between 30,000 and 50,000 Indians were either enslaved or purchased as slaves by the British in this region before 1715.[9]

French colonialism also encouraged Indian slavery, even as the practice was outlawed in the Caribbean and Louisiana. In the St. Lawrence River Valley, French settlers acquired slaves like their English counterparts to the south—through warfare, kidnapping, and trade. Thus, in spite of the colony's small size and substantially less invasive presence (when compared to the interventions of other European nations), several thousand Indian men, women, and children were turned into merchantable commodities in New France. In Montreal in 1725, half of the property owners residing in the commercial district possessed at least one slave. Throughout Canada, however, slavery was much more closely linked to Franco-Indian diplomacy and gift giving than a product of labor demands or market necessities. Indeed, as Brett Rushforth has argued, by so thoroughly embracing slavery in this manner, the French in North America may have been responding to, and adopting, indigenous customs in which human bondage served as a mechanism to foster relationships and preserve peace. In other parts of North America where the European presence was either distant from colonial population and administrative centers or weakly held, like the southwest borderlands, the cultural imperatives of Indian slavery seem to have held the economic principles of Euro-Atlantic slavery at bay for several generations.[10]

Indentured Servitude

While Indians were enslaved by Europeans throughout the Americas, northern Europeans tended to rely more heavily on another labor system during the seventeenth century—indentured servitude. The use of fellow Europeans as bound laborers was not entirely new. Countless Europeans served out terms of bound service as apprentices during this era, but in the early decades of the seventeenth century Europeans, particularly the English and French, began entering into contractual arrangements that promised not to transmit specific marketable skills, but to transport human beings across the ocean. Beginning in the 1620s in the English colony of Virginia, in order to solve the labor problem generated by the development of tobacco as a cash crop (as well as the incredibly high mortality rates among English settlers), migrants began to sell their labor for a period of four to seven years, literally condemning themselves to bondage, in exchange for passage to the Americas.

Though indentured servitude was primarily an English phenomenon, other European colonizers relied on the bound labor of their own countrymen. Most male emigrants to the French colonies, for example, were servants known as *engagés*, who typically served for a period of three years. Most French servants went to the West Indies in the early seventeenth century, where they labored in agricultural endeavors that made their lives little different from English servants and subsequent generations of enslaved Africans. Indeed, one observer concluded that they were "worse treated than the slaves—they have to be forced to work, since they are so miserable and hungry—with blows from the stave."[11] Other, perhaps more fortunate, servants were shipped to New France, where they performed a wider variety of tasks related to fur-trading enterprises. Ultimately, however, the number of migrants to the French colonies was much smaller than those who journeyed to the English colonies. Moreover, a majority of servants returned to France after their term expired. By 1700, the French West Indies had made the turn to African slavery, and only 15,000 settlers could be found in Canada.

Most indentured servants in the colonies, however, were either English or destined for service in British America. On the whole, the vast majority of servants were young, unskilled men. During the entire period of the indentured servant trade, men may have accounted for 80 percent of the total. In a list of 2,010 names from London in 1635, women account for only 14 percent of the whole. Surviving lists from eighteenth-century London, with 6,896 names, record the presence of only 524 women, or less than 7 percent of the total, among servants bound for America. Most indentured servants were also young; perhaps two-thirds of all immigrants were between the ages of fifteen and twenty-five. Very few children under ten or adults over forty ever emigrated as servants to America. Skill levels are more difficult to summarize. In the early seventeenth century, unskilled laborers, many of whom were already domestic migrants at home, clearly predominated in the trade. Even so, there were significant numbers of journeyman artisans who found their way across the Atlantic. By the eighteenth century, evermore indentured servants came from nonagricultural backgrounds and instead were more likely to have occupational skills. By the eve of the American Revolution, more than 80 percent of registered male emigrants to the colonies were listed as skilled workers.[12] Significant numbers of people found their way to the English colonies in the Americas as indentured servants. Roughly 200,000 people emigrated to North America during the seventeenth century, and about 60 percent went to the Chesapeake colonies of Virginia and Maryland. Strikingly, 90,000 of the 120,000 emigrants to the Chesapeake were indentured servants. Another, somewhat more elusive body of servants set out for the West Indian colonies, particularly Barbados and, later, Jamaica during this era. While no firm number is available, surviving registers from the seventeenth century suggest that perhaps 50,000 to 75,000 white indentured servants went to the islands. During the first three-quarters of the eighteenth century, during which time Scots-Irish and German immigrants were increasingly in the majority of new arrivals, more than 150,000 Europeans (about 50 percent of the total) came in bondage. In all, some 350,000 emigrants to the English colonies were bondmen.[13]

Few generalizations can, or should, be made about this massive pool of European immigrants. Several points, however, deserve mention. First, there was a significant difference between the seventeenth- and eighteenth-century servant populations. During the seventeenth century, most indentured servants were of English origin. By the eighteenth century, the sources of bound labor were much more diverse, with Irish, Germans, and Scots accounting for roughly three-quarters of the total. Second, slightly more than 50,000 convicts were transported to the American colonies. As a group, felons actually represented more than half of all English immigrants to the American colonies between 1718 and 1775. Convicts typically had no choice in their destination, though four out of five went either to Virginia or Maryland, and could be bound for up to fourteen years of service. If there were "white slaves" in colonial America, these young, unmarried, and unskilled convicted criminals came closest to fitting the mold.[14]

Third, while most indentured servants were transported to either the Chesapeake or West Indies during the seventeenth century, the potential destinations for laborers were more numerous in the eighteenth century. Moreover, destination was shaped by national origins. English and Welsh indentured servants, though they numbered only about 30,000, continued to migrate to the Chesapeake. Irish emigration concentrated on the Delaware River Valley, though large numbers also entered the colonies through New York and Baltimore. Perhaps three in four German immigrants funneled through Philadelphia into the American interior. Finally, tens of thousands of emigrants were servants of a different sort. Among Germans, specifically, many people came as redemptioners. Like indentured servants, redemptioners were contractually obliged to serve a number of years, but unlike previous servant groups they often traveled as families and were usually granted a two-week grace period to find a relative or benefactor to purchase their labor contract before it went on the open market. Therefore, whereas the experience of convicts could be characterized in dramatically unfortunate terms, redemptioners clearly fared much better than the average indentured servant.[15]

As these examples suggest, the experience of indentured servitude could be quite varied depending upon location, but time mattered even more. During the first half of the seventeenth century the conditions under which indentured servants labored were more "slavish," and their chances of even surviving their term of service more unlikely than would be the case in the eighteenth century. This situation was partly circumstantial—colonial mortality rates as a whole were dramatically worse in the Chesapeake colonies and West Indies during the early seventeenth century, and indentured servitude was initially localized in these two regions. Additionally, however, the contractual agreements that bound masters and servants declared that both parties had rights and obligations, but servants were fundamentally regarded as chattel property, and seventeenth-century legislation and court verdicts seem to have favored masters' rights in this earlier period. Servants could be sold away without cause, their contracts passed down through the generations, and they could be treated quite brutally by harsh masters. By the eighteenth century the labor climate had changed, and colonial governments increasingly interceded on behalf of servants. In

Pennsylvania, for example, a 1700 statute limited the ability of masters to sell their servants across colony lines without judicial approval. Servants in other colonies were also granted greater protections under the law and could find relief, perhaps even freedom, in the courts when their masters were found guilty of criminal offenses.[16]

The earliest generation of servants complained with some legitimacy that theirs was an exceptionally precarious existence. Throughout the early seventeenth century, critics bemoaned conditions in the colonies with graphic depictions of harsh climates, poor Indian relations, poverty, disease, and tenuous food supplies. Perhaps most troubling for colonial sponsors of the labor-starved American plantations, however, was the popular recognition that life as a servant in the colonies was not simply unpleasant, it could be inhumane, life threatening, and slavish. As the former indentured servant and colonial promoter George Alsop revealed in 1666, the "clappermouth jaws of the vulgar in England" seemed to believe that "those which are transported over thither, are sold in open Market for Slaves, and draw Carts like Horses." Conditions in the West Indies, where masters did not hesitate to label their servants as "white slaves" were probably worse. At mid-century in Barbados, Richard Ligon expressed shock at the "cruelty there done to Servants," which he could not believe "one Christian could have done to another."[17]

The rhetorical value of slavery served the needs of people interested in drawing public attention when they commented on life in the colonies in such dramatic terms. And though defenders of the propriety of indentured servitude resisted the notion, the suggestion that Anglo-Americans practiced slavery *among themselves* could not be easily dismissed. For one, slavery was in fact a part of early Anglo-American penal law. Governor Samuel Argall determined in 1617 that individuals found guilty of price gouging could be punished with "3 years Slavery to the Colony." In 1618, an Englishmen could "be a slave" for failing to attend church, not planting corn, or wasting ammunition without due cause. Virginia was not exceptional in this regard. A Bermudian court sentenced Nicholas Gabriel to be "a slave unto the colony" for slandering the governor. In Massachusetts at least eight men and one woman were condemned to slavery for assault, rape, and theft between 1638 and 1642. During the 1650s, Parliament even debated two petitions submitted by more than seventy Englishmen claiming that they were "freeborn people of this nation now in slavery" in Barbados. While the claims of these servants were contested by members who argued that nobody was "sent without their consent," and those who went "were civilly used, and had horses to ride on," other English officials expressed outrage at the prospect of "buying and selling [English] men."[18]

Not only did the notion that Englishmen should not be slaves assume special importance in the Americas, but *why* they should not be termed as such also underwent a fundamental transformation because of the expansion of racial plantation slavery. After slavery became inextricably intertwined with race in the mentality of most Englishmen and their American cousins, the concept lost much of its flexible and inclusive character. Thus, when Morgan Godwyn noted in 1680 that "[t]hese two words, *Negro* and *Slave* [have] by Custom grown Homogenous and Convertible," he shed considerable insight not just on the changing status of Africans in the Anglo-Atlantic World but also on the disaggregation of Anglo-American ideas about slavery.[19] In that sense, by the late seventeenth century, slavery was much less of a problem than it had been earlier in the century. Once Anglo-Americans settled on one peculiar variant of slavery, closely allied with social and cultural conclusions about race and labor, the ideological complications visited upon early settlers vanished.[20]

Whether or not their lives were slavish, most indentured servants seem to have believed their lives were "very hard." William Moraley, who was indentured in the mid-Atlantic during the early 1730s, believed that "the Master is generally heard before the Servant, and it is ten to one if he does not get his Licks for his Pains." Moraley, and other servants like him, correctly pointed out that his prospects were not particularly bright in the eighteenth century, since, it seems, that while servants' lives may have been more precarious in the prior century, once free they had stood a reasonable chance of achieving some measure of respectability in colonial society. Indeed, during the initial decades of the seventeenth century, some former indentured servants even went on to become prosperous landowners. But by the eighteenth century, economic opportunities for former servants were much narrower, and the general absence of skills of the servant class meant that a large percentage of freedmen lived out their subsequent lives as renters and laborers. William Moraley, like a few others, "embrace[d] the first Opportunity that offer'd" and "struck a Bargain" that allowed him to return to England. It may be the case, as some historians have claimed, that as indentured servants were increasingly drawn from non-English populations and the institution was defined and constrained by impersonal market considerations in the mid-eighteenth century, servitude became more brutal and exploitative—especially in those colonies where the lives of European indentured servants were not offset by the exploitation of enslaved Africans.[21]

Africans in the Early Atlantic World

It is an interesting historical irony that, in contrast to the experiences of European servants and Indians whose early ordeals in the Americas were slavish, African peoples often had greater personal and legal freedoms in the early Atlantic World than they would later on. Thus, as European colonialism developed during the seventeenth and eighteenth centuries, European laborers and the surviving indigenous peoples were increasingly able to exact concessions from European governments and rely on imperial policies that generally sought to reign in the excesses of colonial elites. Africans, however, were gradually subjected to greater abuse, intensifying labor regimes, and evermore constricting social policies as American slave owners and European slave traders were given the latitude to treat sub-Saharan African peoples with impunity. By the eighteenth century, while there continued to be significant numbers of European servants and bound Indians, the definitive institution of the Atlantic World was the plantation complex fueled by enslaved Africans.

Still, there was another model in the early Atlantic World. As Ira Berlin has argued, many of the earliest African peoples in the Atlantic World, what he terms "Atlantic Creoles," were much more than brute laborers. Among the many conquistadores and early colonizers in the Atlantic World were large numbers of free blacks. By all accounts, black mariners sailed with Christopher Columbus in the 1490s, and black soldiers aided Hernán Cortés in the conquest of the Aztec empire during the subsequent generation. Where enslaved, evidence from the sixteenth and seventeenth centuries suggests that large numbers of Africans were freed unconditionally—more than 33 percent in Lima and in excess of 40 percent in Mexico City between 1524 and 1650. Even in North America, free blacks could be found in significant numbers, at least as a percentage of the total black population. New Netherland, for example, a Dutch colony situated at the mouth of the Hudson River for forty years during the seventeenth century, became home to large numbers of Africans who were able to bridge the divide between slavery and freedom by their "genius for intercultural negotiation." By 1664, at the time of the English conquest, roughly 20 percent of the black population in New Amsterdam was free.[22]

Because the legacy of slavery has left such a deep imprint in our collective historical imagination, we do not routinely emphasize the degree to which Africans in the early modern Atlantic World were often both powerful and free. It is useful, therefore, to remind ourselves that the history of African peoples begins on the African continent, not in the fetid hold of a slave ship or under the whip of an overseer on a New World plantation. As a new generation of historians has emphasized, Europeans depended on African rulers and merchants to conduct diplomacy and trade; Africans, not Europeans, were the power brokers on the coast of West Africa. Many Africans in Africa, from diverse nations, sought out Europeans for material, cultural, and even spiritual gain. Similarly, the European presence in Africa often created opportunities for common men and women—the very first generation of Atlantic Creoles—to facilitate relations on the continent. Richard Jobson noted that he was accompanied during his time in West Africa in the early 1620s by "a pretty youth called *Samgulley*, who . . . had always lived with the English, and followed their affaires, so as hee was come to speake our tongue, very handsomely, and him I used many times as an Interpreter." Another young Khoikhoi woman named Krotoa, also known as Eva, served the Dutch in modern-day South Africa as an interpreter in the mid-seventeenth century. Eventually, she began dressing in western clothing and even adopted Christianity, yet she also continued to practice traditional Khoikhoi rites. Other Africans similarly exploited opportunities for personal advancement that otherwise would not have been available.[23]

Africans were also much more than slaves in other parts of the Atlantic World.

A number of Africans, free and enslaved, were armed for militia service in the colonies, particularly in Latin America. Indeed, sixteenth-century English privateers reported that they were confronted by free black militias during their raids on the Spanish Main. Free blacks were particularly visible to English eyes as military personnel, a capacity in which many of them had served since the conquest. During Drake's 1585–1586 large-scale assault on the West Indies, his ground forces were opposed by a company of free blacks and mulatto musketeers in Santo Domingo. The company operated under the command of an illiterate free black named Augustin. Unlike their experiences with runaways and *cimarrones*, the English found in this resistance African peoples engaged in defending Spain's grip on America. This circumstance was not remarkable; the English who sailed to the coast of West Africa commonly encountered indigenous peoples who also fought them off, often to defend the Portuguese or Dutch with whom they had closer relations.[24]

The fluid nature of the conquest and settlement era created extraordinary opportunities for Africans to exert themselves throughout the entire Atlantic World. Some historians have suggested that the peculiarities of the Iberian world, shaped as it was by Roman law, Catholicism, and its unique multi-racial heritage, created opportunities for Africans to prosper as free individuals in the subsequent Iberian–Atlantic World. In contrast, the argument goes, the early modern English world, with its common law tradition, Protestant exclusivity, and comparably insular homogeneity, did not create an environment that allowed for much more than an abject and dehumanized existence for Africans.[25] Although it is true that the English experience with Africans was limited before the late sixteenth century, England effectively inserted itself into an Atlantic World defined by more than a century of Iberian precedents by the time Jamestown was settled in 1607. Moreover, African peoples were not the powerless subjects some Europeans would have liked to imagine they were. Thus, although most Englishmen encountered Africans in the Americas as a people whose lives were defined by slavery, and although anti-black prejudice was already in evidence, there were exceptional opportunities for the people listed, almost casually, in English sources as "negros" to carve a space for themselves, beyond the confines of slavery, in Anglo-America through the late seventeenth century.

One way of conceptualizing the influence of the customs of the Atlantic World on the lives of blacks in early Anglo-America is the existence of a notable free black population. One of the distinguishing characteristics of early modern slavery, particularly as it existed in both the Iberian Peninsula and North Africa, was the opportunity for, and ready access to, freedom through manumission. Even more, blacks who attained their freedom seem to have done so by creatively exploiting patron-client relationships. The structure of this relationship might even be traced directly to Hispanic precedents in the way it paralleled ritual godparentage. The most vivid example of this occurred in Bermuda where James Sarnando, "Commonly Called olde James the Nigro" and his wife engaged Hugh Wentworth in a ceremony designed to cement a fictive familial bond. At the time, Saranando and his wife were the parents of a seven-year old daughter, Hanna. The Sarnandos appeared at the Wentworth home sometime in 1639, whereupon "the sayd James did take the Childe by the hand & delivered it into the hande of Mr. Wentworth saying heere Master mee give you this Childe take her & bring her up & mee give her to you freely." At the end of the ceremony, the Sarnandos clearly imagined that they had formed a bond that would enable them and their daughter to live fuller lives and, perhaps, might open the door to manumission at a later date.[26]

The tacit acceptance of free blacks in early Anglo-America (especially on the mainland) was the source of at least three additional structural concessions that typified the practice of slavery throughout the early modern Atlantic World. First, English settlers in New England, the Chesapeake, and the West Indies all broached the idea of arming slaves for colonial defense during the 1640s and 1650s. Providence Islanders, in particular, celebrated "with due gratitude and wonder" the "loyalty in adversity of the negroes who had often rebelled in times of prosperity" when they helped fend off a Spanish invasion in 1640. In 1652, the Massachusetts General Court ordered "that all Scotsmen, Negeres and Indians . . . shal be listed, and are hereby enjoyned to attend traynings as well as the English." Even in Virginia, free blacks possessed arms and were, apparently, eligible for the militia during much of the seventeenth century. When, in 1640, the general assembly passed an act requiring "all masters of families" to furnish "themselves and all those of their families which shall be capable of arms (excepting negroes) with arms both offensive and defensive," it clearly chose not to arm slaves but it did not disarm the small free black population.[27]

Second, the existence of a free black population forced Englishmen to deal with the question of whether or not it was either appropriate or desirable to introduce African peoples to the tenets of Protestant Christianity for the purpose of religious conversion. The Hispanic world, with the complicity of the Roman church, and Islam had long since moved beyond this particular problem, but incipient Protestant traditions, combined with the peculiarities of English law, militated against holding co-religionists as slaves. Some Englishmen, however, did not see this as a particular problem. Richard Ligon apparently believed that African slaves could be introduced to Christianity yet continue to toil as slaves in Barbados. He was particularly taken with an African slave named Sambo who demonstrated (in Ligon's opinion) a remarkable intellect compared with other slaves on the island. When Sambo declared his intention to become a Christian, Ligon took the slave's case to his owner. The slave owner, however, informed Ligon that "the people of that Island were governed by the Lawes of *England*, and by those Lawes, we could not make a Christian a Slave." Ligon responded that it was not his intention to enslave Christians, rather he "desired . . . to make a Slave a Christian." The Barbadian sugar planter agreed that there was a difference, but continued to object on the grounds that "being once a Christian, he could no more account him a Slave, and so lose the hold they had of them as Slaves, by making them Christians; and by that means should open such a gap, as all the Planters in the Island would curse him."[28]

Third, the existence of a free black population forced early English colonists to consider the issue of race and racial intermixture as the result of the gradual, but steady, emergence of a mulatto population. Intimate relations between people of different racial, ethnic, and religious backgrounds were common in the early Anglo-Atlantic World, as they had been throughout the Mediterranean beforehand. Mulattos provide dramatic evidence of the willingness of many English and Africans to form personal bonds across racial lines. Since most of these children were the product of illicit relationships (though certainly not all), there were a number of efforts to curb fornication that were enacted in a fashion consistent with the common law. Yet, in most places, racial intermixture was problematic not because it was perceived as immoral or illegitimate, but because it complicated property considerations. In 1660 the Bermuda Court addressed this problem when it ruled that John Davis was "permitted to marry Penelope Strange one of the Companys molatto women upon condition that every other child born of the marriage shall be the property of the Company—reserving to the said Davis the right to put in a negro child in lieu of any one of those so falling to the company." Davis was also allowed to pay for Penelope's freedom, "but in the interim he is to pay 40s per annum for her wages." This solution was not very satisfactory, and in the long run it was determined that in order to prevent "the great mischiefe & anger which otherwise is like to happen by the multyplication of malattoes," it was ordered in early 1664 that "from henceforth if any mallato shall be made free, such p[er]son doe within twelve months after depart the Islands."[29]

During a long and dynamic two-hundred-year period, roughly the mid-fifteenth through the mid-seventeenth centuries, human bondage—slavery, even—was something that shaped the lives of Europeans, Indians, and Africans. After 1650, when 95 percent of the enslaved Africans involved in the history of the transatlantic slave trade would make their treacherous crossing in the holds of European slave ships, it is impossible to comprehend the history of sub-Saharan Africans without acknowledging the pervasiveness of slavery. Before 1650, however, the story of African peoples in the Atlantic World is one that can only be understood by imagining them as powerful, knowledgeable, influential, and quite often free.

From Servitude to Slavery: The Rise of African Slavery

Although *racial* slavery may not have been pervasive in the early modern Atlantic World, the institution of slavery was ubiquitous. During the sixteenth century, various forms of slavery flourished in Africa, the Mediterranean, and southern Europe. Even more, the idea of slavery or the notion that human beings could be held against their will, compelled to serve, and bought and sold like livestock was taken for granted even in those parts of Europe (such as England, the Netherlands, and France) where the institution had long since faded into insignificance. Among the English, for example, there was a self-congratulatory tone to the notion, in 1567, that "England was too pure an air for slaves to breathe in." Yet, during that same decade, four English expeditions (three under the command of Sir John Hawkins) sailed to Africa, where they acquired more than 1,200 human beings and sold them into slavery in the Spanish West Indies.[30]

In the main, there were two powerful streams of thought that buttressed European notions of slavery—religion and the law. The Bible was filled with references to slaves and slavery and established human bondage as an apt metaphor, particularly in sermons, for the complete submission of mankind and particular individuals to God. Throughout the book of Exodus, one could read of the children of Israel who "sighed for the[ir] bondage and cryed" in an Egypt so miserable and cruel that when Moses told them that Yahweh would free them of their burdens and lead them to a better place they could not listen, "for anguish of spirit & for cruel bondage." The entire Old Testament, in fact, granted tacit justification for the legality of human bondage, provided it conformed to certain religious precepts. The book of Leviticus made it clear that slaves should come from foreign nations and that "ye shal take them as inheritance for your children after you, to possesse them by inheritance, ye shal use their labours for ever: but over your brethren the children of Israel ye shal not rule one over another with crueltie." Similarly, the New Testament, particularly the letters of Paul, reveals a certain recognition of slavery as a legitimate human institution and contains sentiments that upheld the status quo, such as that slaves must "counte their masters worthie of all honour, that the Name of God, and *his* doctrine be not evil spoken of."[31]

Roman law also buttressed the legitimacy of slavery among Europeans, particularly as evidenced by Justinian's *Digest*—a work that informed not only early modern conceptions of slavery but also of freedom. Indeed, as some historians have argued, the idea of freedom was born out of slavery. Thus, according to Roman law, "Manumission means sending out of one's hand, that is, granting freedom. For whereas one who is in slavery is subjected to the hand (*manus*) and power of another, on being sent out of hand he is freed of that power. All of which originated from the *jus gentium*, since, of course, everyone would be born free by the natural law, and manumission would not be known when slavery was unknown." But as St. Augustine argued in his *City of God*, the state of nature had not existed since Adam's fall, and slavery had been normalized by God's punishment of Cham. Therefore, although slavery was not part of God's original intent, Augustine maintained that slavery "as a punishment" was "ordained by that law which enjoins the preservation of the order of nature, and forbids its disturbance." In an important sense, slavery had become a natural part of the Fallen World, and masters and slaves alike were obligated to respect their condition in order to ensure peace and harmony.[32]

European law and Christian religion therefore normalized the notion that there were three classes of men: "free men, and set against those slaves and the third class, freedmen, that is, those who had stopped being slaves." Even where the institution of slavery was not formally in evidence, as in northern Europe, other customary forms of servitude granted masters the authority to circumscribe their servants' lives. Among the northern European nations could also be found the relics of the system of serfdom that had risen up in the ashes of the slave system that had survived into the medieval era. Northern Europeans also employed penal slavery, particularly in the galleys, as a form of punishment for criminals and political prisoners. Finally, some Europeans even imagined that there might be a progressive, even educational, use for slavery. Thomas More's *Utopia* described a carefully crafted, idyllic society where slavery offered a way for convicted criminals to be reformed through "mild and practicable" punishment in order "to destroy vices and save men." This conception of slavery was expressed most famously in Tudor society in 1547 when parliament passed legislation to attack "idle beggars and sturdy vagabonds." With this short-lived act, slavery could be imposed on recalcitrant individuals who refused to work. The master would have absolute control over the diet of his bondmen and could "cawse the saide Slave to work by beating, cheyninge or otherwise in such worke and Labor how vyle so ever it be." The slave could also be leased, sold, or bequeathed, as "any other of the master's movable goodes or Catelles."[33]

Regardless of medieval legacies and flexible notions of human bondage, the enslavement and transportation of African peoples was already commonplace during the sixteenth century among northern and southern Europeans alike. Yet, while every European colony in America was familiar with racial slavery from early in its history, each initially relied on either Native Americans or other Europeans as their primary labor force. Every European nation in America, however, would eventually turn to enslaved Africans. By the eighteenth century, although indentured servitude and Indian labor systems continued to operate, work—especially in the cultivation and production of cash crops and the mining of precious metals—and racial slavery became virtually inseparable notions. How, when, and to what degree this transformation occurred, however, depended upon a number of factors, including the increasing willingness to exploit Africans as slaves, European politics, mortality rates among indigenous peoples, the evolution of the transatlantic slave trade, European labor concerns, and even choice.

Racial slavery, or the subjugation of one particular group of people because of their perceived phenotypical and biological characteristics, was not common in the early modern Atlantic World. The most common justification for slavery in places such as the Mediterranean, where the institution flourished, was religious. Nonetheless, Europeans increasingly embraced the idea that sub-Saharan Africans were suitable, perhaps even desirable, slaves. This idea may have been buttressed by the reality that slavery was already part of the social structure of many African societies. Slavery, however, could mean many things in Africa. Some slaves in Africa clearly were laborers, while others might be soldiers, concubines, criminals, or even tributary peoples. In West Africa, slavery was most commonly a minor local institution, in which slaves were often integrated into kinship networks, and slave status was ameliorated over time. Slavery was a more intensive, large-scale enterprise in west-central Sudanic states, such as Mali and Songhai. As John Thornton has argued, slavery was intrinsic to most African societies because of the absence of private property in land. Ownership of people's labor, therefore, served the same claims to wealth and power that the ownership of land produced in Europe. Thus, while historians continue to argue about slavery's relative significance within Africa, there is evidence to suggest that the institution was widespread and functioned, at least initially, independent of the Atlantic slave trade.[34]

The transition to a labor force made up, predominantly, of enslaved Africans occurred first in the Iberian American colonies. Before 1580, African slaves were somewhat rare in the Americas, though they were quite common in the Atlantic islands—where many were already laboring on sugar plantations—and in Iberian port cities such as Lisbon and Seville. During the last third of the sixteenth century, however, there were two important developments that increased the potential supply of African slaves for American markets. First, although more than 2,000 slaves per year were being exported from Africa after 1500, and more than 264,000 Africans would be transported on Portuguese ships during the sixteenth century, European access to African markets was insecure until Portugal established a permanent presence in the Kongo during the 1570s. European exploitation of enslaved Africans by direct access at the source began during the 1440s, but the first century of the transatlantic trade featured intermittent activity concentrated in the northern region of Senegambia and the more southern Gold Coast, Bight of Benin, and Bight of Biafra. Once the Portuguese were entrenched in West Central Africa, their access to slaves and their ability to transport larger numbers of Africans across the ocean expanded exponentially. Thus, most slave exports during the sixteenth century occurred during the last twenty-five-year period and emanated, specifically, from West Central Africa (more than 83 percent).[35]

The second factor that increased the availability of enslaved Africans for Latin American markets occurred in 1580 when the crowns of Spain and Portugal were united under Philip II. Previously, since the Treaty of Tordesillas in 1494, Spain and Portugal were content to rule their separate spheres of interest. Therefore, while Portugal exercised a virtual monopoly in Africa, Spain—with the significant exception of the Portuguese colony in Brazil—was the sole player in the Americas. Thus, in order to acquire enslaved Africans, Spanish colonists had to go through Portugal, which the Spanish crown was reluctant to do. After 1580, however, the organization, experience, and resources of the greatest supplier of slaves in the African world were placed in the hands of the nation with the greatest potential demands on bound labor. Between 1595 and 1640 (when Portugal regained its independence) Spain granted six monopolies on the slave trade to Portuguese merchants. In excess of 268,000 Africans were imported into Spanish colonies during this time, and between 1600 and 1650 another 150,000 slaves arrived in Brazil. If we account for mortality rates that averaged around 20 percent during this era and the minor involvement of early English and Dutch traders, more than 500,000 Africans were exported from Africa during the first half of the seventeenth century, about 92 percent of these from West Central Africa.

While supply-side considerations increased the availability of enslaved Africans by the mid-seventeenth century, two issues concerning labor demands were equally significant. First, the Spanish and Portuguese transition to racial slavery was concentrated in regions where Indians initially served Iberian labor needs. During the sixteenth century, however, indigenous populations experienced a "virgin soil epidemic" in which they were subjected to waves of new European and African diseases, such as smallpox, the plague, measles, influenza, yellow fever, and malaria. Historians disagree on the precise number of people living in the Americas in 1491, so the intensity of the demographic decline that occurred in the wake of Christopher Columbus is unclear. While 10–12 million indigenous inhabitants could be found in Mexico before Europeans arrived, merely 750,000 remained in 1630. In Peru, the pre-contact population may have been 6 million, or it may have been 10 million, but there were only about 670,000 indigenous inhabitants alive in 1620. Very conservative estimates place the pre-contact population in the West Indies at 500,000. Still, no more than 22,000 Indians were alive in this region in 1570. An Indian population of perhaps 2.5 million living in Brazil would decline to 800,000 by 1570 and continue to decline in subsequent decades as a result of disease, war, dislocation, and slavery. Thus, whatever disagreements exist about specific numbers, native populations seem to have declined by about 90 percent during the sixteenth and early seventeenth centuries. In Latin America, where conquerors and settlers relied upon the local inhabitants as workers, the result was, in part, the search for an alternate labor supply.[36]

Second, just as the indigenous labor pool wilted away over time, the production of cash crops and the extraction of mineral wealth grew rapidly in different parts of the Americas. In Peru, the growth of silver mines like Potosí increased overall labor demands so that Africans were funneled into a variety of tasks. Thus, the slave population of Lima expanded from 4,000 to 20,000 between 1586 and 1640. Africans were also drawn into Mexico during the late sixteenth century by the discovery of new silver mines, though their numbers were never large—merely 35,000 or 2 percent of the population in 1646—because of the relative vitality of the indigenous population. At its peak, roughly 100,000 enslaved Africans could be found in Peru, which represented perhaps 15 percent of the local population. By 1650, neither region would continue to be an important importer of African slaves, though roughly 340,000 Africans would be imported to the mainland colonies of Spanish America by 1650.[37]

While the majority of slaves transported out of Africa before 1650 were destined for mainland Spanish America (about 57 percent), the West Indies and Brazil, primarily as a result of sugar cultivation, emerged as the two centers of plantation slavery. With some exceptions, the West Indies would not come into their own until the eighteenth century, but an increase in the demand for enslaved Africans as a result of new economies did occur in Brazil very early. Sugar was a familiar crop in the Atlantic World and had been associated with slave labor for centuries in the Mediterranean and Atlantic islands. Sugar plantations began to appear at mid-century in Brazil and gradually came to replace the brazilwood trade as the prime economic activity. By the 1570s, scores of mills were in operation, and labor demands grew rapidly. Several factors, however, complicated the labor supply at this juncture, including the imperial restrictions and onsets of epidemic diseases discussed above. Portuguese planters also suspected that Indians were not particularly efficient laborers, which encouraged the *senhores de engenho* to look across the Atlantic for slaves at precisely the same time as their cousins in Spanish America. Although the full transition to a reliance on enslaved Africans would not occur until the third decade of the seventeenth century, already by 1600 some 40,000 Africans had been sold into slavery in Bahia and northeastern Brazil. During the subsequent fifty years another 176,000 would be added to their numbers.[38]

The transition to slavery in Latin America, then, represented a transition from exploiting the labor of Indians to exploiting the labor of Africans. Still, two qualifications deserve mention. First, while enslaved Africans clearly came to dominate in Brazil and, in later years, the West Indies, Spanish colonists continued to expropriate the labor of Indians in both Mexico and Peru. Mexico's Indian population was particularly large and even began to recover from the devastation wrought during the first century and a half of conquest and colonization. Second, the transition to enslaved Africans represented more than a demographic shift at the beginning of the seventeenth century; it was a cultural transformation as well. During the early part of the sixteenth century, most of the Africans who were transported to Spain's American colonies were actually *ladinos*, or Africans who were already assimilated into European society and culture by pre-residence on the Iberian Peninsula. By the middle of the sixteenth century, however, *bozales*, or Africans who had been exposed to neither European culture or Christianity, were increasingly being shipped to America directly from Africa. In that regard, the nature of the slave population was significantly transformed once the transatlantic slave trade intensified.

By the middle third of the seventeenth century, then, Brazil and several parts of Spanish America were fully committed to slave labor. The colonial possessions of other European nations, however, continued to rely on their own distinctive labor systems, primarily indentured servitude. Neither Spain nor Portugal relied on their fellow countrymen as laborers during the colonial period. Spain's population was large enough—in excess of 7 million people in the mid-sixteenth century—but much of the population was fully engaged and adequately employed in continental enterprises, both civil and military. Portugal was a different story. With a population of less than a million, demand for labor at home was intense, and there was little incentive to export the members of the already strained labor force. The English, on the other hand, had a profound population problem. From the late sixteenth century, English colonialism was imagined as an enterprise that would not only enrich the nation and advance the cause of Protestant Christianity, but would also help rid the land of the idle, underfed, and unemployed masses. England, as well as France and the Netherlands (the former, like Spain, having a large population but plenty of domestic opportunities, and the latter, like Portugal, with few people to spare), also had few other choices since the West Indies and North America did not possess the high concentrations of native peoples encountered by the Iberians.

The transition to racial slavery for northern Europeans, particularly the English, therefore amounted to the gradual replacement of European indentured servants with enslaved Africans, especially in plantation agricultural zones, during the second half of the seventeenth century. Once again, there were at least four factors related to supply and demand that coincided to make this possible. For example, North American Indians experienced a similarly dramatic population decline as a consequence of their encounter with Europeans. Of course, northern Europeans never relied on Indian labor like the Spanish and Portuguese, but Indian slaves were nonetheless exploited in small numbers, particularly in the southwestern frontier region. Indian slavery, however, proved to be an unattractive option in the long run because Indians were relatively scarce in North America even before the English and French arrived. There were probably fewer than 2 million native inhabitants east of the Mississippi River in 1492, and that number declined to roughly 250,000 in subsequent centuries. Additionally, the people most likely to profit from Indian slavery quickly developed the idea that Indians were poor workers. Thus, Englishmen engaged in Indian slavery, but only as a secondary or tertiary enterprise and usually in a role as slave traders (i.e., to the West Indies) rather than slave drivers.[39]

The need for labor, enslaved or otherwise, intensified in English North America and the West Indies throughout the seventeenth century. In the West Indies, economic prosperity hinged on sugar agriculture beginning by the 1640s when Barbados experienced an agricultural boom that would subsequently occur in virtually every English, French, and Dutch West Indian colony. Initially, the northern European colonies in the West Indies were hardscrabble settlements where small planters and their indentured servants cleared the land, cultivated tobacco, and raised livestock for export. In the 1640s, however, with the technological and financial assistance of Dutch traders who had been chased out of Brazil, English planters began to develop sugar plantations. Almost immediately, the sugar economy transformed the island, and within two decades Barbados would be more profitable than all other English colonies combined. Visions of potential riches also attracted immigrants. Between 1640 and 1660 the English West Indies were the most popular destination of English emigrants, free and indentured.[40]

As the European population expanded in the West Indies during the middle decades of the seventeenth century, so too did the enslaved African population. Part of this growth was a product of the commercial relationship between primarily English planters and Dutch traders who, in addition to transporting English sugar to European markets, imported African slaves to American plantations. Indeed, during the first half of the seventeenth century, no single nation was more responsible for coordinating slave trading, sugar cultivation, and colonialism than the Dutch, particularly the energetic Dutch West India Company after it was chartered in 1621. As Robin Blackburn has argued, the Dutch invasion and occupation of Brazil seems to have contributed to a decline in the Brazilian sugar industry and created an opportunity for French and English colonists to assume a leading role in the production of sugar in the West Indies. In order to do so, however, they needed more laborers than they could generate from their domestic populations. Sugar cultivation was dangerous and degrading work that required many more laborers than the tobacco crop. Relying on Dutch resources, then, the number of enslaved Africans in Barbados would climb to about 25,000 by 1660. At the same time, there were probably no more than 5,000 additional Africans in all of the other English colonies combined, with Virginians possessing only 1,000 slaves.[41]

Tobacco was another boom crop in the English Atlantic World, particularly in Virginia. Beginning in the 1610s, soon after John Rolfe began cultivating a transplanted West Indian seed variety in Virginia soil, Chesapeake planters discovered that they had a valuable commodity on their hands. In subsequent decades, as the price of tobacco soared, plantations appeared in dizzying numbers, and settlers began clearing the countryside almost as quickly as they could push back the native populations. The desperate English land grab prompted an equally desperate Powhatan Confederacy, desirous of preserving its traditional hunting grounds, to launch a surprise attack in 1622, killing nearly 350 English settlers. Indians would rise up again in 1644 under the leadership of the aged Opechancanough, killing even more colonists, but their efforts were ultimately futile. From a little more than 1,000 in 1622 the English population expanded to 13,000 by 1650 (even as staggering mortality rates decimated the ranks of new arrivals) as promises of tobacco riches fueled a "gold rush" mentality. More than 40,000 English men and women could be found in the Chesapeake in 1670. The growth of tobacco was equally impressive. In 1624, Virginia produced 200,000 pounds of tobacco for the English market. By 1638, Virginia had surged ahead of West Indian planters with 3 million pounds of tobacco. Even as prices dropped from overproduction, much of it in the Chesapeake as Bermuda and the West Indies ceased cultivating much tobacco, the growth was astounding. By the end of the century some 28 million pounds of tobacco would be produced.[42]

Barbadian sugar planters and Virginia tobacco growers may have needed an increasing number of laborers, but their ability to acquire workers was constrained at mid-century by the limits of the English domestic labor force. After

1650, however, a labor supply problem of crisis proportions pervaded the Anglo-Atlantic World. Where once thousands of Englishmen looked to America as a place to alleviate their economic difficulties as a result of rapid population growth and high unemployment levels at home, by the mid-seventeenth century economic growth in the wake of the English Revolution discouraged many potential emigrants from risking an oceanic crossing and disinclined people from considering the radical step of temporary bondage in the Americas as an avenue toward prosperity. Moreover, there were an expanding number of more attractive options than those available in the much derided Barbados and Virginia settlements. New York, Pennsylvania, Carolina, and Jamaica all became viable alternatives for potential migrants in the course of two decades after the 1650s, and laborers looked to these upstart colonies with greater favor. Predictably, then, servants became an increasingly rare and expensive commodity in late-seventeenth-century Virginia and, especially, Barbados. Where once a planter could own the services of another Englishman for four to seven years by paying the £6 fee for crossing the Atlantic, servants were going for £12 in the West Indies at mid-century and £15 on the mainland at the end of the seventeenth century.[43]

Other problems may have also made indentured servants increasingly less attractive to planters during the seventeenth century. For example, wherever English colonists employed rigorous labor regimes, they invariably stirred up animosity, resistance, and even rebellion among the lower orders of society. Access to land had always been the central motivation for indentured servants who willingly subjected themselves to harsh labors in the West Indies and the Chesapeake. By the mid-seventeenth century, however, the dream of becoming a landowner in Barbados disappeared for former servants. In a 1675 petition, Barbadians protested that "[i]n former tymes wee were plentifully furnished with Christian servants from England and Scotland, but now wee gett few English, having noe lands to give them at the end of theire tyme, which formerly was their main allurement."[44] With no land to grant servants as their freedom dues, servitude became an unattractive option in Barbados, and running away, resistance, and even small-scale rebellion increasingly characterized master-servant relations on the island. Not coincidently, the settlement of additional English colonies in the Leeward Islands, Jamaica, and Carolina was energized by the shortage of land and the difficulty of accommodating poor whites and recently freed servants.

The prospects of servile insurrection in combination with the limited availability of land were also experienced on the mainland, most famously in Virginia during the 1670s when a full-scale insurrection threatened to tear apart the colony. In the summer of 1675, western settlers, many of whom were recently freed servants, began agitating against what they perceived to be Governor William Berkeley's lenient Indian policies. When frontiersmen began looking for a leader more willing to condone their virulent anti-Indian measures, recently arrived Nathaniel Bacon embraced the opportunity to elevate his local standing and agreed to lead volunteer militia units. Bacon secured by threat of force a commission from Governor Berkeley in June 1676 to lead his volunteers in military action against the Indians, but the governor would soon insist that he had granted the commission under duress, leading Bacon to chase the governor and his small band of allies across the Chesapeake to the Eastern Shore. By July, the Old Dominion was firmly in Bacon's hands. His forces crushed a group of friendly Occaneeches in May and scattered a bedraggled band of Pamunkeys hiding out in a swamp in the fall, but they were never able to do anything about the Susquehannocks beyond their frontier. Soon after torching the colonial capitol at Jamestown and allowing his men to plunder the property of Berkeley's loyalists, the rebellion dissipated when Bacon—like so many other new arrivals to the Chesapeake in the seventeenth century—died.

Bacon's Rebellion was more of an insurrectionary movement for control of the colony than it was an external conflict with Indians. As such, it highlighted the inherent instability in a colonial society, as in the West Indies where the subjugation of fellow countrymen who believed they possessed inherent rights as Englishmen clashed with the desire of the incipient planter class to maximize profits by controlling labor relations and land policies on their own terms. Some historians have argued therefore that the prospects of even more widespread class warfare necessitated the replacement of white indentured servants with African slaves in subsequent years. While overly simple, the transition to racial slavery clearly coincided in both the West Indies and the plantation colonies on the mainland with mounting problems related to the control of indentured servants, access to land, Indian relations, and the rise of large-scale plantation agriculture that benefited an increasingly narrow stratum of English society.[45]

None of these factors would have generated a full-scale transition to a reliance on enslaved Africans, however, were it not for an important development in the supply of slaves for the transatlantic trade. One of the main reasons why enslaved Africans appeared in such small numbers in the early northern European American colonies is that those colonies were largely denied regular access to the African market by Portugal's monopolistic pretensions. Slaves who initially appeared in English colonies were therefore either pilfered on the high seas or brought in through illicit channels, often by the Dutch, who had dislodged the Portuguese from many of their West African trading forts during the 1630s. After the English Restoration in 1660, however, the English government took a much greater interest in the African trade. In 1663 the English Company of Royal Adventurers Trading to Africa was authorized to transport 3,000 Africans per year across the ocean. In 1672 the Royal African Company was chartered as a joint-stock company and granted a monopoly on the English slave trade. Similarly, France organized two slave-trading monopolies: the Senegal Company and the Guinea Company. Northern European slave traders became so successful that Spain granted the cherished *asiento*, or license, to organize trade into the Spanish colonies to the Dutch in 1662, the French in 1701, and the British in 1713. With the additional step, particularly among the

English in 1698, of allowing private traders to participate in the slave trade, the supply of bound laborers escalated dramatically.[46]

The numbers tell the story in particularly revealing terms. Before 1650, England, France, and the Netherlands combined to transport 64,000 Africans across the Atlantic, while the Portuguese were responsible for nearly 440,000. Between 1651 and 1700, however, northern Europeans were responsible for roughly 540,000 enslaved Africans, while the Portuguese shipped only about 215,000 to the Americas. During the eighteenth century this disparity, and particularly the prominent role of British slave traders, would be in even greater evidence. Between 1701 and 1800, British traders shipped nearly 2.5 million Africans to the Americas. French slave traders transported 1.1 million, and the Dutch an additional 363,500. During the same era the Portuguese would add nearly 1.9 million African souls to the miserable trade. The effect was catastrophic for Africans, who were increasingly extracted from Senegambia, Sierra Leone, the Windward Coast, Gold Coast, Bight of Benin, and the Bight of Biafra (roughly 3.7 million), as opposed to West Central Africa (perhaps 2.3 million). The effect was viewed in profoundly different terms by American planters, who saw the increasingly availability of laborers and the decline in price of enslaved Africans as economic boons.

Conclusion

Although the transition from competing labor systems to racial slavery in the Americas largely represented a demographic and economic shift, the transition that occurred in Anglo-America was also marked by significant legal and cultural transformations. Pre-plantation Anglo-Americans may have relied primarily on indentured servants, but they also willingly adapted slavery to their specific circumstances before it was written into positive law. When they did so, however, it involved social and cultural practices generally at odds with their own English heritage (at least the one they espoused). Yet the practice of slavery in the early English colonies was perfectly consistent with the prevailing customs of the Atlantic World as laid down primarily by the Spanish and Portuguese in Africa and the Americas, but also by Christian Europeans and North African Moors in the Mediterranean. Regardless, when English colonists in Virginia, Barbados, and other colonies began to inscribe slave laws, they enacted legislation that contrasted with how slavery tended to function under Roman law in Spain and Portugal, in Latin America, and—initially—even in Anglo-America. High manumission rates, significant numbers of free blacks, the tacit acceptance of racial intermixture, and the acceptance of African peoples in the Christian community were consistent with patterns of slaveholding throughout the broader Atlantic World. Therefore, when English colonial legislatures passed laws that clamped down on manumissions, limited African access to the Christian community, and attacked racial intermixture, they were not merely authorizing a transition that was already occurring as a result of autonomous demographic and economic factors; they were also inventing slavery anew.

The decimation of the indigenous peoples of the Americas and the limited capacity of Europeans to fill labor needs, combined with the expanding demand for a secure labor force that could be compelled to work in harsh circumstances in the wake of the development of sugar, tobacco, and silver mining, prompted Europeans to turn to enslaved Africans. Neither plantation agriculture nor slavery were invented in the Americas, however. Slavery was an ancient institution, practiced in Greece and Rome and authorized in the Christian Bible. The use of slaves in plantation agriculture, particularly for sugar, also dates back to at least the medieval era. When Europeans began to exploit the people and resources of the Americas, they were accustomed to thinking about slavery as an institution that was buttressed in both natural and positive law, even if northern Europeans had turned away from the practice. Predictably, then, Indians were regularly enslaved until such time as the ideological and spiritual qualms of Christian Europeans—combined with the diminishing number of Indians—made them less attractive subjects. The use of fellow Europeans, too, was consistent with the prevailing laws and customs of the Europeans nations, even if the specific parameters of indentured servitude were invented to address American labor problems.

The role of Africans, however, represented a radical departure from European norms. As the third party in a drama enacted on American soil by European invaders, Africans could be found, at least initially, in any number of possible roles. Quite often, Africans appeared in the Americas as the slaves of the European newcomers, but other Africans were free. Africans could be quite valuable to Europeans as military allies, guides, and translators. As long as Indians and Europeans satisfied the labor demands of colonizing powers, Africans who found themselves in the Atlantic World could exercise some measure of power and independent authority. With the transition that occurred during the seventeenth century, however, Africans were reconceptualized as consummate slaves and, increasingly, a race apart. Arguably, in early modern Europe, slavery was incidental, and race hardly mattered. With the articulation of an Atlantic World in which wealth and power were premised on agricultural production and the extraction of precious metals, race and slavery were intertwined, and racism and human bondage were evermore exploitative and arbitrary.

Notes

1. Ira Berlin and Philip D. Morgan, eds., *Cultivation and Culture: Labor and the Shaping of Slave Life in the Americas* (Charlottesville: University Press of Virginia, 1993), 1.

2. This characterization of slavery is broadly based on Orlando Patterson's classic definition of slavery as "the permanent, violent domination of natally alienated and generally dishonored persons." See *Slavery and Social Death: A Comparative Study* (Cambridge, Mass.: Harvard University Press, 1982), 13.

3. John H. Parry and Robert G. Keith, eds., *New Iberian World: A Documentary History of the Discovery and Settlement of Latin America to the Early Seventeenth Century*, 5 vols. (New York: Times Books, 1984), 1:348–359.

4. James F. Brooks, *Captives and Cousins: Slavery, Kinship, and Community in the Southwest Borderlands* (Chapel Hill: University of North Carolina Press, 2002).

5. Peter Bakewell, "Mining in Colonial Spanish America," and Murdo J. MacLeod, "Aspects of the Internal Economy of Colonial Spanish America: Labour; Taxation; Distribution and Exchange," in *The Cambridge History of Latin America*, vol. 2, *Colonial Latin America*, ed. Leslie Bethell (Cambridge: Cambridge University Press, 1984), 105–151, 219–264 [hereafter *CHLA*]; M. C. Mirow, *Latin American Law: A History of Private Law and Institutions in Spanish America* (Austin: University of Texas Press, 2004), 82–90.

6. Stuart B. Schwartz, *Sugar Plantations in the Formation of Brazilian Society: Bahia, 1550–1835* (Cambridge: Cambridge University Press, 1985), 52.

7. José Eisenberg, "Antonio Vieira and the Justification of Indian Slavery," *Luso-Brazilian Review* 40:1 (2003): 89–95. More generally, see John Hemming, *Red Gold: The Conquest of the Brazilian Indians, 1500–1760* (Cambridge, Mass.: Harvard University Press, 1978).

8. Schwartz, *Sugar Plantations*, 51–72.

9. Alan Gallay, *The Indian Slave Trade: The Rise of the English Empire in the American South, 1670–1717* (New Haven, Conn.: Yale University Press, 2002), 294–299.

10. Brett Rushforth, "'A Little Flesh We Offer You': The Origins of Indian Slavery in New France," *William and Mary Quarterly*, 3rd ser., 60:4 (October 2003): 777–808.

11. Cited in Robin Blackburn, *The Making of New World Slavery: From the Baroque to the Modern, 1492–1800* (London: Verso, 1997), 286.

12. David W. Galenson, *White Servitude in Colonial America: An Economic Analysis* (Cambridge: Cambridge University Press, 1981), 23–64.

13. Abbot Emerson Smith, *Colonists in Bondage: White Servitude and Convict Labor in America, 1607–1776* (Chapel Hill: University of North Carolina Press, 1947).

14. A. Roger Ekirch, *Bound for America: The Transportation of British Convicts to the Colonies, 1718–1775* (Oxford: Clarendon, 1987).

15. Aaron Spencer Fogelman, *Hopeful Journeys: German Immigration, Settlement, and Political Culture in Colonial America, 1717–1775* (Philadelphia: University of Pennsylvania Press, 1996).

16. Kenneth Morgan, *Slavery and Servitude in Colonial North America: A Short History* (New York: New York University Press, 2000), 56–64.

17. George Alsop, *A Character of the Province of Maryland* (London, 1666), reprinted in *Narratives of Early Maryland, 1633–1684*, ed. Clayton Colman Hall (New York: Charles Scribner's Sons, 1910), 378, 357; Richard Ligon cited in Hilary McD. Beckles, *White Servitude and Black Slavery in Barbados, 1627–1715* (Knoxville: University of Tennessee Press, 1989), 90.

18. Susan Myra Kingsbury, ed., *Records of the Virginia Company of London*, 4 vols. (Washington, D.C., 1906–1933), 3:69, 93 (2); J. H. Lefroy, ed., *Memorials of the Discovery and Early Settlement of the Bermudas or Somers Islands, 1515–1685*, 2 vols. (Toronto: University of Toronto Press, 1981), 1:127; Nathaniel B. Shurtleff, ed., *Records of the Governor and Company of the Massachusetts Bay in New England*, 5 vols. (Boston, 1853–1854), 1:246, 269, 284, 297, 300, and 2:21; and John Noble and John F. Cronin, eds., *Records of the Court of Assistants of the Colony of Massachusetts Bay, 1630–1692*,

3 vols. (Boston, 1901–1928), 2:78–79 (3), 86, 87, 90, 94, 97, 118 (2); Thomas Burton, *Parliamentary Diary, 1656–1659*, 4 vols. (London, 1828), 4:255, 260–262, 268.

19. Morgan Godwyn, *The Negro's & Indians Advocate, Suing for Their Admission into the Church* (London, 1680), 36.

20. Michael Guasco, "Settling with Slavery: Human Bondage in the Early Anglo-Atlantic World," in *Envisioning and English Empire: Jamestown and the Making of the North Atlantic World*, ed. Robert Appelbaum and John Wood Sweet (Philadelphia: University of Pennsylvania Press, 2005), 236–253.

21. Susan E. Klepp and Billy G. Smith, eds., *The Infortunate: The Voyage and Adventures of William Moraley, an Indentured Servant* (University Park: Pennsylvania State University Press, 1992), 96, 124; Sharon V. Salinger, *"To serve well and faithfully": Labor and Indentured Servants in Pennsylvania, 1682–1800* (Cambridge: Cambridge University Press, 1987).

22. Ira Berlin, " From Creole to African: Atlantic Creoles and the Origins of African-American Society in Mainland North America," *William and Mary Quarterly*, 3rd ser., 53:2 (April 1996): 251–288; Frederick P. Bowser, "Africans in Spanish American Colonial Society," in *CHLA* 2:357–379.

23. Richard Jobson, *The Golden Trade* (London: Dawsons of Pall Mall, 1968; orig. 1623), 105; David Northrup, *Africa's Discovery of Europe, 1450–1850* (New York: Oxford University Press, 2002), 61. See also John Thornton, *Africa and Africans in the Making of the Atlantic World, 1400–1800*, 2nd ed. (Cambridge: Cambridge University Press, 1998).

24. Matthew Restall, "Black Conquistadors: Armed Africans in Early Spanish America," *The Americas* 57:2 (October 2000): 171–205. See also Ben Vinson III, *Bearing Arms for His Majesty: The Free-Colored Militia in Colonial Mexico* (Palo Alto, Calif.: Stanford University Press, 2001).

25. Frank Tannenbaum, *Slave and Citizens: The Negro in the Americas* (New York: Random House, 1946).

26. Virginia Bernhard, *Slaves and Slaveholders in Bermuda, 1616–1782* (Columbia: University of Missouri Press, 1999), 76–80.

27. Alison Games, "'The Sanctuarye of our rebell negroes': The Atlantic Context of Local Resistance on Providence Island, 1630–1641," *Slavery and Abolition* 19:3 (December 1998): 16; George H. Moore, *Notes on the History of Slavery in Massachusetts* (New York, 1866), 243; Warren Billings, *The Old Dominion in the Seventeenth Century: A Documentary History of Virginia, 1606–1689* (Chapel Hill: University of North Carolina Press, 1975), 172.; T. H. Breen and Stephen Innes, *"Myne Owne Ground": Race and Freedom on Virginia's Eastern Shore, 1640–1676* (New York: Oxford University Press, 1980), 26.

28. Richard Ligon, A *True & Exact History of the Island of Barbadoes* (London, 1673), 50.

29. Lefroy, *Memorials*, 2:141, 178–179.

30. Helen Tunnicliff Catterall, ed., *Judicial Cases Concerning American Slavery and the Negro* (Washington, D.C.: Carnegie Institution, 1926), 1:9; Kenneth R. Andrews, *Trade, Plunder, and Settlement: Maritime Enterprise and the Genesis of the British Empire, 1480–1630* (Cambridge: Cambridge University Press, 1984), 121–125.

31. Exodus 2:23, 6:1–9; Leviticus 25:44–46; 1 Timothy 6:1; see also Titus 2:9–10. All biblical citations taken from *The Geneva Bible: A facsimile of the 1560 edition* (Madison: University of Wisconsin Press, 1969).

32. *The Digest of Justinian*, 4 vols. Latin text edited by Theodor Mommsen, En-

glish translation edited by Alan Watson (Philadelphia: University of Pennsylvania Press, 1985), 1:2 (bk. 1, pt. 1, no. 4); Orlando Patterson, *Freedom in the Making of Western Culture* (New York: Basic Books, 1991); St. Augustine, *Concerning the City of God against the Pagans*, trans. Henry Betterson (Middlesex: Penguin Books, 1972), 874–875 [bk. 19, ch. 15].

33. *Digest of Justinian*, 1:2 (bk. 1, pt. 1, no. 4); Thomas More, *Utopia*, 2nd ed., trans. and ed. Robert M. Adams (New York: W. W. Norton, 1992), 16, 7; C. S. L. Davies, "Slavery and Protector Somerset; the Vagrancy Act of 1547," *Economic History Review*, 2nd ser., 9 (1966): 533–549.

34. Thornton, *Africa and Africans*, 72–97.

35. David Eltis, "The Volume and Structure of the Transatlantic Slave Trade: A Reassessment," *William and Mary Quarterly*, 3rd ser., 58:1 (January 2001): 17–46. Statistics for the slave trade in subsequent paragraphs, unless otherwise noted, are drawn from this article.

36. Nathan Wachtel, "The Indian and the Spanish Conquest," in *CHLA* 1:204–248; Nicolás Sánchez-Albornoz, "The Population of Colonial Spanish America," and Maria Luiza Marcílio, "The Population of Colonial Brazil," in *CHLA* 2:3–63.

37. Herbert S. Klein, *African Slavery in the Latin America and the Caribbean* (New York: Oxford University Press, 1986), 28–37.

38. Schwartz, *Sugar Plantations*. See also, Philip D. Curtin, *The Rise and Fall of the Plantation Complex: Essays in Atlantic History* (Cambridge: Cambridge University Press, 1990).

39. Daniel K. Richter, *Facing East from Indian Country: A Native History of Early America* (Cambridge, Mass.: Harvard University Press, 2001); Gallay, *Indian Slave Trade*.

40. Richard S. Dunn, *Sugar and Slaves: The Rise of the Planter Class in the English West Indies, 1624–1713* (Chapel Hill: University of North Carolina Press, 1973).

41. Blackburn, *Making of New World Slavery*, 187–215, 252–55.

42. Edmund S. Morgan, *American Slavery, American Freedom: The Ordeal of Colonial Virginia* (New York: W.W. Norton, 1975).

43. Richard S. Dunn, "Servants and Slaves: The Recruitment and Employment of Labor," in *Colonial British America: Essays in the New History of the Early Modern Era*, ed. Jack P. Greene and J. R. Pole (Baltimore, Md.: Johns Hopkins University Press, 1984): 157–194.

44. "Grievances of the Inhabitants of Barbados" (November 25 , 1675), cited in Hilary McD. Beckles, *White Servitude and Black Slavery in Barbados, 1627–1715* (Knoxville: University of Tennessee Press, 1989), 10.

45. Anthony Parent, *Foul Means: The Formation of a Slave Society in Virginia, 1660–1740* (Chapel Hill: University of North Carolina Press, 2003).

46. K. G. Davies, *The Royal African Company* (London: Longmans, 1957).

CHAPTER FIVE

The Slave Trade's Apex in the Eighteenth Century

Timothy R. Buckner

The idea that the slave trade profoundly altered the economic, cultural, and social composition of four continents from around 1450 through the nineteenth century is not new to historians. What is new, and perhaps surprising to some, is the degree to which Africans controlled both the source of slaves for the Atlantic market and the amount of agency that these slaves, both men and women, asserted within their new communities. Despite the distaste that we have for slavery in the modern world and the tacit acceptance by many that enslavement represented an aberration, it was bondage—not freedom—that typified the way labor was performed throughout human history until the later years of the eighteenth century. Through feudal relations, indentured servitude, concubinage, serfdom, and apprenticeship, bound labor, not free, was the norm. This is not to suggest that chattel slavery as performed in the Americas was not distinct. Although bonded laborers in other systems could be traded or even pass their status on to their progeny, chattel slavery in the Americas differed significantly. In the Americas, slavery was a racialized system condemning those captured from Africa or born into the institution to a permanently debased status that largely excluded them as people in favor of categorizing them as property. As such, the enslaved lacked control over their circumstances, no choice of occupation or location, no right to own property or marry, and no ability to create a different life for their children. Essentially, the image of the chattel slave is the opposite of freedom.

Historians have rightly noted that the Atlantic slave trade in the eighteenth century presented one of the more confounding paradoxes in world history; that is, just as the slave trade reached its highest volume, the process that would bring it to an end began. The explanation for this seeming contradiction rests in both the cultural and legal heritage of the Old World, both European and African, and the New World realities of producing commodities while consuming people. By 1700, the sugar trade of the Caribbean had generated enough wealth to justify large-scale importation of enslaved laborers and had transferred this labor system throughout the Americas just as other forms of bound labor had become unfeasible. The profitability of sugar made enslaved labor available to other regions producing other commodities that could not have justified the expense. Nevertheless, while the usage of enslaved Africans spread across the Americas and became firmly entrenched by the last quarter of the century, the rationalizations for the institution of slavery came under increasing attack from various groups, including the enslaved.

This chapter focuses on the growth of slavery in the Americas during the eighteenth century, the influence of Africans in every part of the trade, and the beginnings of the abolitionist movement.

Africa and the Slave Trade

Europeans tapped into the internal African trade in humans, and though some apologists have mentioned that these men and women already were enslaved, the gulf separating slavery in Africa and the Americas was very wide. As Suzanne Miers and Igor Kopytoff have argued, African societies were open to bringing in outsiders as dependents or retainers, but this was very different from chattel slavery that developed in the Americas. Treatment of the enslaved in Africa varied based on the circumstances surrounding enslavement (capture in war, kidnapping, birth, etc.) and divergent societal mores. Moreover, slaves within these societies could achieve levels of influence and power never available in the Americas. This is not to suggest that slavery in Africa was compassionate, but rather that in many ways it more closely corresponds to slavery in the larger scope of world history rather than to the peculiarities of the American chattel system. Most slaves in West Africa had been captured as a result of expansion of territory through warfare; however, the marginality of slaves within particular societies was not fixed. Enslaved men and women in West African societies could be incorporated into families and eventually could wield a high degree of authority within their communities. Thus slavery in these communities could be considered an historical accident rather than a permanently debased condition.

People taken into slavery in West Africa through warfare, kidnapping, or other means were used in a variety of ways. Slaves were used for labor in agriculture, as domestic servants, and as soldiers. In some cases women or children were integrated into families to enlarge existing families or to replace those lost by death or capture by another nation. Slaves in these societies were "outsiders" in the sense that they were strangers to the particular society or kin group that enslaved them, but the outsider status did not have to be permanent. Detachment from one group could lead to a sense of belonging to another, at first as a dependent or a servant, but that role might morph into one with a more significant role, "bonding" the slave to the society while also being "in bondage" to it. As Miers and Kopytoff argue, creating new bonds within the enslaving society reduced the marginality of the slave, but while the slave might want to become a complete "insider," that role could not be completely achieved. Within most West African cultures, insiders were not individuals but rather members born into a kin group. Individual slaves could achieve certain levels of "social mobility," attaining legal rights and obligations, a sense of emotional attachment and high regard from the family that owned him or her, and even an improvement in lifestyle, through material wealth or political influence. Individual slaves would usually remain outsiders unless they were incorporated into a kinship group.

This contrasted sharply with slavery in the Americas, where identities and freedom were connected to a sense of individuality, not kinship relations. In the Americas, Europeans created a system in which enslaved Africans represented a racialized underclass in which slave status was perpetual and inheritable. While slave societies in Ancient Rome or across Africa might have allowed for the buying and selling of human property, the status of "outsider" did not remain constant. One could achieve freedom and be completely incorporated within these societies. In transferring a labor system to the New World, Europeans had determined that while exploitation of their own people was acceptable, actual slavery was not. Bound labor, in the form of apprenticeship or indentured servitude, was a temporary condition and entered into, for the most part, by choice. Those who entered into these relationships did not lose their status as cultural and social "insiders." For example, men and women who became indentured servants or were apprenticed in England remained English, remained Christian, and remained "free" in the sense that they had sold their labor by choice and thus were not outside the social order. When their period of indenture expired, these people could be incorporated back into free society.

The peculiarities of the American system forbade this for Africans. Voluntary European immigrants could not satisfy the need for labor in the Americas. Conditions, discussed below, made it difficult, if not impossible, to convince Europeans to sell their labor. If coerced labor was necessary, then it would seem that the easiest economic solution would be to enslave other Europeans and force them to the Americas to labor. While men and women of other nations might have been long-time enemies, ideas about freedom and who was eligible for enslavement had been firmly established in legal systems and cultural practice. Those of other nations might have been different, but they were not different enough. Early justification for enslaving Africans rested on the notion that these people were pagans and hence more available for enslavement. As Christianity began spreading among Africans especially in the New World, the rationalization for enslavement moved away from religion and toward a notion of racial difference. Across the Americas, skin color came to be the dividing factor between insider and outsider. Although freedom could be achieved, ideas about racial difference and white supremacy led to a separation between those who were formerly enslaved and those who formerly enslaved them.

Assumptions by Western scholars of earlier generations about the cultural and racial inferiority of Africans incorrectly led to the conclusion that Europeans dominated the trade in Africa either by military superiority or through creating African dependency on European goods. Actual control of the trade rested upon differing notions of "control." Some historians argue that African slavery was changed by external, rather than internal, stimuli. In other words, the export of around 11 million people from Africa could not have occurred without a transformation of the political economy of Africa. External demand for slaves in the New World fueled internal rivalries within the continent of Africa, which, in turn, led to a dependency on the Atlantic slave trade. European alliances and patronage, then, encouraged and furthered conflicts between cultures, and the resulting prisoners taken from those conflicts could end up on board a slave vessel bound for the Americas. "Control" of the trade in this sense could be linked to European sponsors of warfare between African cultures. Though the operation of the trade had shifted among European powers multiple times by the eighteenth century, the experience had led Africans to internalize the notion of the trade as a viable means of gaining wealth and power.

Historians of Africa have countered some of the arguments made by this earlier generation by pointing out that while Africans were drawn to European goods, it was more out of a sense of novelty or variety than any kind of real dependency. Firearms, alcohol, and clothing did provide a medium of exchange but hardly represented reliance. Further, if Europeans possessed such overwhelming power, it begs the question: why not simply enslave all Africans and set up plantations in West Africa rather than transport them to the Americas? David Eltis has turned these assumptions about African weakness on their head by proposing that it was actually African strength that created the Atlantic slave trade. Certainly it would have made more economic sense to develop plantation agriculture in West Africa as it was both much closer to Europe than the Americas and would not require the additional dangers and expenses involved in transatlantic shipping. European powers, however, found it impossible to penetrate beyond the coastline of Africa as the various nations in the interior proved far too strong for conquest. The best situation slaving companies could hope for was maintaining a close and mutually beneficial relationship with a powerful coastal nation. This along with European naval power could protect the local "factories"—the bases of operation for slave traders. Since controlling Africa proved cost prohibitive in monetary and military terms, men and women were captured and shipped across the Atlantic to replace dwindling Amerindian and bound European labor.

Africans along the coast resisted the voyage across the Atlantic. Some coastal Africans allied themselves with European slave traders, but others opposed the trade. In a study of slaving voyages undertaken between 1689 and 1807, Joseph Inikori has found that seventy-nine ships were lost as the result of a shipboard insurrection or conflict with Africans on the coast. The study suggests that insurrections occurred much more frequently along the coast of Africa than while crossing the Atlantic. There is little doubt that proximity to the African coast convinced captives that a revolt could be successful and that they would be able to return to their homes, but it seems that free Africans, those not involved with the trade as either partners of the slavers or slaves themselves, may have offered assistance to those onboard slave ships. Inikori notes that incidents in which free Africans offered support to those taken aboard slaving ships may not reflect the dominant attitude of these people toward the trade and European traders, but the treatment given slave traders who were shipwrecked on the coast could indicate that the hostility level was fairly high.[1]

But if the Atlantic slave trade had been in place since the time of Columbus, why did the apex of the trade occur in the eighteenth century? Portugal became the first European nation involved in the African slave trade but had allowed the trade to remain controlled by individual trading companies rather than a state-sponsored monopoly. Only in 1692 did Portugal create the Portuguese Company of Cacheo, but by that point, other European nations had marginalized the Portuguese influence in Africa. The Dutch West India Company had effectively challenged the Portuguese by the 1620s in Africa and brought the first Africans to Spanish, French, and English colonial ventures in the New World. Conflicts with France and England in the late seventeenth century damaged the hold that the Dutch had in Africa and their ability to maintain control over the Atlantic trade.

Though it would not be correct that declining Dutch authority had created a power vacuum, it did leave an opening for the English to assert their authority in the slave trade. In 1672, the Royal African Company was chartered to secure English investment in the slave trade and to satisfy the growing market for slave labor in the English colonies. England's domination of the slave trade spanned the next fifty years during which time it provided enslaved Africans to English as well as Spanish colonies. Even after the Royal African Company had shifted its interest away from slavery, the English continued to rule the slave trade, especially with non-English markets. As late as 1788, two-thirds of slaves brought to the New World by the English were sold to other nations. England's mercantile ventures had come to dominate world commerce by the eighteenth century by securing the source of enslaved Africans, the New World markets, and by having the world's most powerful navy to protect both.

This is not to suggest that the English dominated Africa any more than earlier European powers had. Despite their strength, even the English could not simply sail to a coastal port, fill their ships with enslaved people, and then leave for the New World. In order to obtain human property, the English first had to cultivate relationships with local cultures in West Africa to secure permission to trade and to establish a source for enslaved people. Often slaving ships had to visit several ports before enough men and women had been captured to fill the hold. Negotiations with local authorities could also delay the process. If goods brought for trade did not match local demands for quality and quantity, English slavers could be turned away just as prior European traders had.

Africans vigorously resisted enslavement both from other tribes and from European slavers. Perhaps one of the best primary sources detailing the trade in the eighteenth century is the narrative of Olaudah Equiano. Equiano, born an Ebo, relates in his autobiography the precautions his people took to avoid being enslaved by others. As he described, "generally, when the grown people in the neighborhood were gone far in the fields to labour, the children assembled together . . . and commonly some of us used to get up a tree to look out for any assailant, or kidnapper, that might come upon us; for they sometimes took those opportunities of our parents' absence to attack and carry off as many as they could."[2] In spite of the caution, Equiano and his sister were captured by two African slavers, carried first to another African slaving tribe, and then brought to the coast for sale into the Atlantic market.

Equiano's experience on the coast with English slavers demonstrates both the shock of the Atlantic trade and the differences between European and African notions of slavery. Upon arrival, Equiano was understandably shaken by the vastly different appearance of English sailors and himself. Once taken on board the ship, he admitted to himself that he would much prefer living as a slave within an African community than what he currently experienced. While on board, men and women, bound to one another by chains, were forced to endure living below deck in oppressive heat with little ventilation. The brutality whites exercised upon the Africans on board the ship caused him to believe that he would be put to death; but as the journey continued, Equiano became convinced that death would be preferable to life on board the ship. Several others on the ship agreed and actually chose to jump overboard and drown rather than submit to life in this type of slavery.

Enslaved Africans such as Equiano endured these gruesomely harsh conditions because it had proved to be the only way for European slavers to prevent onboard mutinies. Of all the ships crossing the Atlantic in the eighteenth century, none were more heavily armed than slave ships. Resistance to slavery by those on board thus drove up the cost of operating the slave trade. Captains and crew onboard slave ships received higher wages than those on other transatlantic voyages in the eighteenth century. Consequently, notwithstanding the success of shipboard slave revolts, the resistance altered the operations of the trade. Since this increased the costs of shipping human commodities from Africa, it necessarily drove up the costs of slaves in the Americas and thus lowered the total numbers of Africans who might have been forcibly taken across the Atlantic had it been otherwise. According to the most recent and detailed study of the slave trade, approximately 5.5 million Africans were taken between 1700 and 1800. The same study estimates that resistance lowered the total numbers during this period by 9 percent. In other words, just during the eighteenth

Table 5.1. Volume of the Transatlantic Slave Trade by Century

Century	Enslaved Africans brought to the Americas
1519–1600	266,100
1600–1700	1,253,300
1701–1800	6,096,200
1801–1867	3,446,900
Total (All years)	11,062,500

century, resistance prevented around 500,000 Africans from enduring the Middle Passage and American chattel slavery.

Despite the difficulties the traders had in securing and transporting slaves across the Atlantic, the trade had become hugely profitable by the eighteenth century, but only through cooperation between Europeans and some Africans willing to enslave others. Europeans, especially the English, had developed ideas about economics and individual property rights, which prevented them from enslaving each other, but not Africans. By the eighteenth century no nation had a more advanced economic system nor a more closely defined sense of individual rights than England. Interestingly, it was these two factors that enabled England to become the most dominant power in the slave trade's history. The expansion of the English colonies, the demand for New World products, and the accompanying need for labor drove the numbers of Africans taken from their homes and forcibly transferred across the Atlantic ever higher, but one crop in particular fuelled the engine of the British economy. That crop was sugar.

The Sugar Revolution and Its Consequences

It could be argued that sugar is the most important crop in world history. Sugar consumption in Europe began as a novelty reserved for the elite, but as with most things novel, the demand for it created a supply which could reach a much larger demographic. Unlike other crops consumed in the Old World, the demand for sugar rarely, if ever, lapsed. Moreover, when combined with other "exotic" products such as tea, coffee, or cocoa, its value only increased. Like tobacco, sugar is addictive and thus, by its nature, drove its own expansion; but unlike that weed (at least during this period) the refinement of sugar only enhanced both its rate of consumption and its addictiveness. Raw sugarcane was far less appealing than either molasses or granulated sugar that could more easily be incorporated into one's diet. Distilling molasses into rum not only enormously increased its value but also added to its addictive properties and created an entirely new industry.

The inelastic demand for sugar and the profits that could be realized from the product justified to its producers the expenditures of large sums of money on both land and labor. Those who sought to enter this industry, however, found that it became simply impossible to convince free people to work in Caribbean climates performing the monotonous and dangerous labor needed on a sugar plantation. Though other crops grown in the Americas were labor intensive, nothing matched the demanding nature of work on sugar plantations. Along with the ubiquitous threat of disease and backbreaking labor, numerous other pitfalls could cripple or kill workers; a slip of the cane knife, being trampled by a cart, and getting caught in the grinding mechanism were all risks heightened during harvest season as the work environment intensified. In other words, just as these "factories in the fields" produced sugar, they consumed human lives. Replacing the workforce lost through such conditions required constant importations as mortality rates and demanding work schedules checked the formation of families and the raising of children. As a result, the cultural compositions of these islands retained heavy influences from Africa, not only through a memory of tradition but also through a continued reinforcement of those traditions by the continued importation of enslaved Africans.

Demand for sugar, and the profits created by that demand, massively increased the volume of the Atlantic slave trade. As Europeans' desire for New World products grew, so too did the labor needs of the Americas. Warfare between West African nations became the means through which most Africans were brought into the trade. By the eighteenth century, the powerful Ashante Empire on the Gold Coast and the Dahomey Empire on the "Slave Coast" (Bight of Benin) came to dominate the trade in enslaved Africans. Through the traditional practice of enslaving enemies captured in war, these empires sold their captives into the Atlantic market in exchange for firearms, allowing for more prisoners to be taken and a consolidation of power by these empires.

Though sugar did not reach all New World colonies at the same time, everywhere it did arrive it created profound changes within each respective colonial economy and society. Whereas sugar production began early in places such as Barbados (1640) and relatively late in such places as Cuba (the 1760s), everywhere it was introduced it changed societies in similar ways. The production of sugar in these places led to the displacement of other New World cash crops such as tobacco or indigo. In most cases, as with the British West Indies, food crops also would be ousted in favor of using all available land for sugar production, the rationale being that it was more profitable to import food from elsewhere than to waste land by growing it. Further, as sugar production grew, so did the slave population through continuous importation, and so too did the ratio of enslaved over free. In the decade of 1752–1762, sugar-producing Jamaica imported approximately 71,000 enslaved Africans. Guadeloupe imported 40,000 slaves between 1759 and 1762. Large plantations came to dominate and push out the smaller ones that could not compete. Thus, everywhere that sugar took hold, slave labor pushed out free, and wealth became concentrated in the hands of a few individuals or families. As an example, near the end of the eighteenth century the *average* sugar plantation in Jamaica contained around two hundred slaves. For comparative purposes, the largest U.S. factories would not reach a similar size until well into the nineteenth century.

Of course, the elite individuals who gained this wealth from the operation of sugar plantations in the eighteenth century did not remain on their plantations; rather, they chose to extract their wealth as absentee landowners. Many of these families employed overseers to run their plantations while they enjoyed the enormous wealth produced by them in their own home countries. Not surprisingly then, these owners cared less about the societies from which their wealth came than they did about the societies in which they spent their wealth. As a result, the small white populations of the sugar-producing regions dominated the men and women they enslaved with brutally repressive punishments and legal codes so as to protect both their investments and their own lives.

The system of enslavement developed in sugar production would guide the ways in which slaveholders of later generations would understand the nature of the institution. Perhaps nowhere was the transfer of sugar plantation slavery more complete than in the Low Country of South Carolina and later Georgia. South Carolina had been settled largely by whites who had been pushed out of Barbados because of the expansion of sugar and slavery. This "colony of a colony" would come to resemble Barbados not just because of the first settlers' origins, but also because of their growing reliance upon the Atlantic slave trade to fill their labor needs. Though South Carolina had been founded in 1670, it did not become a true producer of wealth until the eighteenth century, when rice became a viable commodity to be grown there and sold into the Atlantic market. Rice was not a crop familiar to the English, but it was to the peoples of West Africa. The knowledge of how to cultivate this highly profitable crop, then, came along with those who were forced into bondage in Africa.

As was the case in sugar-producing countries such as Brazil, specific ethnicities among enslaved Africans were recognized and sought after by people purchasing slaves in coastal areas of South Carolina and Georgia. As was true in Latin American countries, slave buyers associated work habits, temperament, and physical characteristics with geographical regions. While South Carolinian buyers and slave traders in Africa may have confused specific ethnicities or cultures, it is clear that the buyers in this colony preferred men and women from the Niger Delta because of agreed-upon characteristics assigned by white purchasers in South Carolina. Specifically, it seems that South Carolinian rice planters preferred "Gambians" to other Africans. The attention paid to regional differences of Africans in South Carolina differed substantially from other British mainland colonies, specifically Virginia, where buyers seemed indifferent to the origins of those they enslaved. Demand for specific enslaved groups certainly influenced traders in Africa who supplied these men and women through violence.

Just as slavery and concerns with African ethnicities were transferred to South Carolina, so too were demographic conditions. Once rice production took hold, as with sugar in Barbados and other locales, white masters began acquiring large tracts of land and acquiring massive amounts of enslaved Africans to work the plantations. While other forms of labor had been available to these planters, such as white indentured servants or even bound Native Americans, the familiarity of Africans with the crop led to the continued importation of Africans via the Atlantic slave trade. Unlike tobacco, but again much like sugar, rice cultivation required not only intensive but inherently dangerous labor. In order to grow rice, fields required flooding, and thus enslaved workers could expect to toil most of the day nearly knee-deep in standing water in coastal Carolina heat. The standing water attracted mosquitoes, spreading illnesses such as yellow fever and malaria to both the white and black populations. Free white masters could and did choose to relocate away from their plantations to healthier regions, usually to the city of Charles Town, leaving an overseer in charge of the workforce. Of course, the enslaved did not have this option, and they suffered and often died as a result. As with sugar culture, high mortality rates and work schedules slowed the formation of families and reproduction. Still, the slave population grew quickly in South Carolina as these descendants of Barbados searched for profits while working their labor force to death. Continued and increased importation—rather than improving conditions—led to this rapid growth in the African population of the colony until, as was the case with the sugar islands, it had come to outnumber the white population by the first decade of the eighteenth century.

Along with demographic similarities, the legal code followed these Barbadian colonists to the mainland. Whereas the slave code of Barbados took time to develop on that island, it transferred almost completely to North American societies just as slave populations grew. These laws stressed the ability of Europeans to compel their enslaved labor force by any means necessary. Consequently, slave-owners were given the power of life or death over enslaved Africans. The slave code removed plantation owners from charges if a slave were killed while being punished or compelled to work. These laws removed the humanity of the enslaved in order to secure the ability of whites to command the labor of Africans.

Some historians have argued that even in the sugar-producing regions of Latin America enslaved men and women found better treatment than those held by the English and their descendants. This contention was based on the idea that the Catholic Church provided a buffer between the slave and the master, thus preventing the cruel treatment found in other parts of the Atlantic World. As a result, this generation of scholars argued that in Latin America those of African heritage were not permanently saddled with an inferior status, and once slavery was abolished, these men and women were incorporated into society in a way that did not happen in the United States. Others have suggested that a three-caste system of racial distinction existed in Latin American changing racial meanings in both social and legal contexts. By focusing on institutions these historians miss the larger demographic and social consequences of African slavery in Latin America. Later generations of scholars would demonstrate that, if one can compare levels of cruelty, Latin American nations such as Brazil were far harsher in their treatment of the enslaved than in the U.S. South in terms of punishment and work.

Perhaps a more compelling reason for the misconception over treatment between these regions has to do with the development of sugar culture in Latin America and a tendency to see New World slave societies as completely distinct entities. Just as with British colonies, sugar culture in the Spanish Caribbean did not transfer immediately throughout the Spanish and Portuguese empires. While Brazil represents an exception to this, political conditions and competing industries throughout Latin America prevented the transmission of sugar culture circumstances to other locals. Most slaves in the Spanish colonies worked in small-scale operations compared to the production of sugar and rice. In Mexico and Peru, slaves produced agricultural products for domestic consumption rather than for sale in the Atlantic market. Others were employed as skilled artisans or miners. As was the case in places in the British Empire such as New England, conditions did not call for the same type of work or controls as existed in sugar-producing societies. Maybe even more importantly, slave treatment in the Spanish Empire in the eighteenth century was not determined locally, but largely by the Crown. The Spanish government restricted the number of slaves that could be imported and prosecuted masters who punished excessively or killed the men and women they enslaved. This governmental control collapsed in Cuba by the 1760s with the shift from tobacco to sugar production. Between 1763 and 1790 about 41,000 Africans were imported into Cuba, but even this would be dwarfed in the next three decades as sugar production grew. As was the case elsewhere, planters took over control of slave regulation and the slave trade, resulting in both higher importations and harsher conditions.

Cultural Implications of the Sugar Revolution and the Slave Trade

The largest change sparked by the slave trade and sugar revolution was cultural. Relying upon the Atlantic trade to maintain slave labor in sugar- and rice-producing areas created a stronger connection with Africa than in regions that produced tobacco. In Virginia, the model for a tobacco society, work conditions and climate made it possible for the enslaved to survive and create relatively stable families. Thus, Virginia became the earliest place in the New World to have a "creolized," African American culture. Subsequent generations of enslaved people born in Virginia would identify Virginia, not African regions, as their home. By the mid-eighteenth century, this Afro-Virginian identity was reinforced by natural population increase, leading slave-owners to rely less on the Atlantic trade. As a result, the connection to older African heritages was diminished, which necessarily increased adaptation to life in the New World.

In sugar and rice cultures, connections to an African past remained strong.

Continued importation allowed for a greater chance of Old World cultural traits being passed down through generations. The children of involuntary immigrants to the New World not only would have their parents' teachings to connect them to their heritage, but they also would be exposed to others who shared their languages, religious beliefs, food ways, and other traditions that crossed the Atlantic with the constant new arrivals. A creolized culture, then, developed more slowly in these regions and looked very different from those in tobacco cultures. For example, whereas large numbers of African slaves had been brought to Jamaica beginning in the mid-seventeenth century, a hundred years later, those customs that had been African—religion, music, and dress, for example—remained African, though altered somewhat by new circumstances. The explanation of this is at least two-fold. First, these customs did not die crossing the Atlantic. Men and women accustomed to living in these ways did not abandon them in the New World. Second, even in the first half of the eighteenth century, the majority of enslaved people living in Jamaica had been born in Africa. While certainly these people had to adjust to a new environment, they did so in particularly African ways. Description of enslaved life in Jamaica during the seventeenth and eighteenth centuries appear very similar.

Still, in some areas, creolization proved a necessity. This came about particularly in the case of language. Olaudah Equiano recalled that upon arriving at Barbados, he and his shipmates were greeted by "Africans of all languages" and were relieved. On sugar islands and rice-producing regions such as the South Carolina Low Country, enslaved men and women like Equiano might be lucky enough to live with others with whom they could communicate. However, on individual plantations, this luxury often was not present, and the language of the slavers remained foreign. Across the Atlantic World distinct Creole forms of European language appeared, usually carried by enslaved men and women born in the New World to those born in Africa rather than directly from Europeans. These creolized, or "pidgin," languages enabled Africans from different language groups to converse with one another more easily. Of course, all of these languages had substantial African components to them. Just as these creolized languages made their way "down" to the African-born slaves, so too did they move "up" the social ladder to whites. John Atkins wrote of Jamaican whites in 1736 that "they are half-Negrish in the Manners, proceeding from the promiscuous and confined Conversation with their Relations, the Servants and Plantations, and have a language especially pleasant, a kind of Gypsy Gibberish, that runs smoothest in swearing."[3] From those first-enslaved people who had begun speaking creolized versions of European languages the numbers would spread such that the children of both whites and blacks in the Americas would use these languages, or versions of them, on a daily basis.

Nowhere was this type of language more apparent than in the Low Country region of South Carolina. Some have convincingly argued that Gullah, as this dialect has come to be known, along with other creolized languages, first appeared on the coast of Africa as those who worked for slave traders used them to communicate with both Europeans and Africans. Those captured into enslavement also continued this process onboard slaving vessels. Evidence suggests that the Wolof speakers of Senegambia having closer contact with Europeans often served as interpreters in the slave trade and transferred specific words such as *banana* and *yam* into non-African vernaculars. For slave-owners in South Carolina, the idea of having the men and women they enslaved speaking English held both advantages and perils. Some felt that Africans were unable to master the language while others feared that they could and would do so, thus taking away some of the master's power. Knowing the masters' language could allow the enslaved to eavesdrop on conversations not meant for them, but not being able to communicate with slaves also could lead to gross inefficiency on plantations. Slaves also had misgivings about learning the dialect of the slave-owners. While speaking the language could lead to other, perhaps less abusive positions on the plantation, there also could be benefits in ignorance. As enslaved men and women came to realize, seeming to not understand instructions could justify their not carrying out instructions. Moreover, acceptance of the slave-owners' language could also imply another level of subservience which some might have resisted. Gullah, then, served multiple purposes: it blended several African languages with English, allowing enslaved Africans to more easily communicate with one another; it retained aspects of African dialects, making it more appealing to enslaved speakers; and it provided a way of understanding the language of slave-owners without totally capitulating to their lifestyle.

As with Creole languages elsewhere, Gullah gained in both the number of speakers and in complexity as generations of enslaved people were born in the Low Country. In the same way as in sugar-producing regions, the continued importation of slaves into the Low Country reinforced the African components of this tongue. Further, aspects of African languages made their way into the white community through their usage by the enslaved. Naming practices in the Low Country retained elements of this type of compromise. In the case of children born to enslaved couples, often owners and parents found ways of satisfying both cultural impulses. A practice common among several nations of Africa was to name their children after the day of the week when they were born. If parents chose to name their son *Cudjo* (Monday) the slave-owner might be willing to compromise by calling him "Joe." An even easier case for compromise might be made for girls born on Friday and thus named *Phibbi*, which English speakers would simply translate into the more Britannic "Phoebe." Geographic terms used in African languages also made their way into Gullah and then to common usage for whites and blacks in the Low Country. *Tai bi* of the Hausa dialect, which means "fertile, low-lying farmland," was translated as *Tybee* by the English and remains the name of an island off the Georgia coast. Similarly the Mende word *sasi* ("proud one") and the Yoruba term *wahu* ("to trill the voice") found easy correlations in English.

The slave trade, then, did not bring just forced labor to the New World; it also brought rich and varied cultures and practical knowledge, which would lead to new and different societies in the Americas. These transfers would be of at least equal importance as European influences to the development of New World societies. Just as European ways have survived and adapted in the Americas, so have the African. Despite the importance of the slave trade to the continued success of New World colonies and the highest levels of importation of enslaved Africans during the eighteenth century resulting from the spread of sugar culture and the growth of rice production, this century would also mark the beginning of the end of the trade.

The Rise of Abolition

That the "apex" of the slave trade occurred in the eighteenth century represents a paradox in world history: just as the slave trade had become one of the most profitable ventures in human history, the movement to end it also began. Why and how the abolition movement began and ultimately ended the trade is directly related to the conditions that allowed European nations, particularly England, to succeed in the business of slavery in the first place.[4]

The largest problem for an antislavery movement in the eighteenth century or prior was the very history of slavery. The foundation of every Western society in social, political, and even religious mores rested on the accepted notion that humans could own other humans. Slavery had not been considered "wrong" throughout recorded history; rather, going back to the thought of Aristotle, some were destined for ruling, while others were for service. This had been one of the cornerstones of Western society from before the Roman Empire through the eighteenth century. Early Christianity condoned slavery not only by arguing it was a corporal rather than a spiritual condition but also through example: the Catholic Church itself owned slaves. Even eighteenth-century secular thinkers supported the notion of slavery. Though John Locke's idea of "inalienable rights" would inspire later abolitionist thinkers, he defended slavery.

Beyond this were the material and cultural benefits that supporters of slavery could cite in relation to slave-owning societies. Ancient Greece, it could be argued, became the cradle of Western civilization because of the wealth generated by slavery. The same could be said of Rome. European nations of the eighteenth century could point to the wealth garnered from the trade itself as well as from the Americas as evidence that slavery had resulted in power for each of these nations. In the Americas, the European setters could point to slavery as the reason why they enjoyed better material conditions than they had in the Old World.

Why and how England, the nation most closely associated with the slave trade in the eighteenth century, could become the most powerful force for ending the trade within the first decade of the nineteenth century has been a subject of much debate. Essentially, there are two main arguments. The first suggests that England began its drive for ending the slave trade and later for full-fledged abolition of slavery because of economic imperatives. Increased competition in the late eighteenth century, especially from the French, caused a drop in the price of sugar, lowering the profits of British sugar planters. At the same time, West African slave traders began increasing the price of slaves. Accordingly, despite the constant demand for sugar, the lower returns on investment and the increasing cost of enslaved labor made sugar less lucrative for the British. The lack of return on sugar plantations and the rising cost of enslaved Africans also eroded the profitability of the slave trade for the English. Without sugar to invest in, English banks chose to put their money into new English manufacturing interests that had begun as a result of the Industrial Revolution. The idea was that it would be more efficient to pay workers low wages to work in English factories rather than continue to operate overseas plantations. Manufacturing required raw materials that were unavailable in England but plentiful in other parts of the world, especially Africa. By ending the slave trade to the Americas, the British did not intend to abandon trade with Africa, but rather to switch from human commodities to others that could be used in manufacturing. Switching from slave to wage labor would allow for higher profits and a new market provided by free workers with purchasing power.

The second explanation for England's turn against the slave trade rests in what could be called the humanitarian impulse stemming from the Enlightenment. Prior to the end of the eighteenth century, those who opposed slavery were viewed as religious radicals. Samuel Sewall, a judge in Puritan Massachusetts, wrote one of the earliest anti-slavery tracts in 1700 with *The Selling of Joseph*. Sewall's position as a Puritan marginalized the work's import, as most Europeans found this group to be extremely radical and easy to ignore. The Society of Friends, who would become powerful antagonists of the trade by the end of the eighteenth century, did not condemn the trade as a group until 1775. In fact, Quakers in Pennsylvania participated in chattel slavery and the slave trade itself prior to the order's ruling that one could either be involved with slavery or be a Quaker, but not both. Neither of these movements publicly called for an end to the trade itself, but rather contended that it was one sin among many that right thinking people should avoid.

Still, how would these thinkers on the fringe of British social and religious thought affect the slave trade? The answer has its roots in several movements across the Atlantic World, and as with all other aspects of the Atlantic slave trade, Africans were crucial. The Enlightenment and the egalitarian revolutions in the Americas that it spurred influenced the creation of a vocal and public anti-slavery slavery movement. These movements closely fit into the notions prescribed by religious thinkers contending that the slave trade, and later the practice of slavery, were morally wrong. Moreover, the transatlantic nature of both the Quakers and their new allies, the Methodists, created an influential voice against the trading of humans.

The Quakers, along with other dissenting groups, enlarged the campaign by establishing the non-sectarian Society for Effecting the Abolition of the Slave Trade. Though Ignatius Sancho's *Letters* had been published in England in 1782, it was this society's expansion that led other Afro-Britons to contribute to the movement against the slave trade. Although Sancho had exposed the terrible conditions under which enslaved Africans had to live, *Thoughts and Sentiments on the Evil and Wicked Traffic of the Commerce of the Human Species, Humbly Submitted to the Inhabitants of Great Britain* by Ottobah Cugoano, published in 1787, became the first explicitly abolitionist work by an Afro-Briton. Cugoano's account provided the populace of England a firsthand account of the evils associated with the slave trade. Two years after the release of Cugoano's work, Olaudah Equiano's *Interesting Narrative* was published and became a bestseller. Both men had been kidnapped from West Africa as children and endured the middle passage and slavery in the Americas, but perhaps of equal importance to their readers, both clearly identified themselves as British.

Though they could never be ethnically English, the assumption of British identities of these two authors clearly offered a different perspective of the trade for English readers in the eighteenth century. Equiano's work became especially powerful in that he could offer testimony about the trade both as an outsider while an African slave and now as an insider—culturally British. While still enslaved, Equiano served in the Royal Navy during the Seven Years' War and, though denied the freedom he was promised in return for his service, managed to use the skills he had learned as a sailor to purchase his freedom while working as a ship captain for an American merchant. Once earning his freedom, he moved to London, where he continued to work as a sailor and converted to Methodism. In London, Equiano married an English woman named Susanna Cullen. Aside from his skin color and the fame he gained from his public support of abolishing the slave trade, he lived a relatively common life for a British subject. The notion that a person so incorporated into British culture had been enslaved no doubt resonated with the English reading public.

The religious aspect of his narrative also offers a powerful indictment on the trade. Because his autobiography is retrospective, that is, he is telling his story several years and even decades after the fact, he can present events he experienced as a young man both in a factual way and through a retrospective religious lens. That is to say, though he did not know it while living through his time as a slave, by retelling his story from a Christian perspective and knowing its ending, Equiano could impart specific religious meaning that was particularly poignant with his Christian abolitionist audience. Though his narrative is written in a highly descriptive form in which it is easy to sympathize with his struggle, he makes it clear that temporal freedom only had been half his battle; he did not become truly free until he embraced Christ and converted. The book, then, turns both racial and religious justifications for the slave trade on their heads. An African clearly had the ability to compose this book and, when given the opportunity, embraced Christianity fully and certainly more completely than any of the whites within his narrative.

Judging how influential the works by Afro-Britons were in comparison to those by other eighteenth-century abolitionists might be an impossible prospect; however, it is possible to note who personally read and were influenced by *The Interesting Narrative*. Through ads and published arguments with pro-slave trade thinkers, Equiano promoted the book before its release and, as such, could sell the book by subscription. This required that buyers put down at least a portion of the price of the book prior to its publication. As reviews of the book came out, subscriptions lists grew, and more men and women wanted to be associated with the author, who by the late 1780s and early 1790s had established himself as the leading black abolitionist in England. The subscriber lists included not only other famous abolitionists such as Thomas Clarkson and Granville Sharp but also famous social and political figures, aristocrats, and even members of the royal family.

Even though the British would not officially end their part in the slave trade until 1807, the foundations for the abolitionist movement had been created by the end of the eighteenth century. Any full explanation for why this happened must rely on both the economic and the humanitarian arguments. Certainly changing economic realities led to a decline in support for the slave trade, but slavery remained a widely used economic system well beyond the Industrial Revolution in England. Likewise, while the humanitarian impulse of the abolition movement exposed the grim realities of the trade to the English reading public, it alone could not create the political power necessary to end the trade. Had the trade and the sugar industry not begun to suffer from competition and overproduction by the end of the eighteenth century and had the profits remained high, it is less likely that the movement against the trade would have been as successful. Still, as with all other aspects of the trade, Africans shaped the beginning of the trade's end. West Africans who controlled the prices of enslaved Africans raised prices as profits from British sugar plantations declined. Had the British actually dominated the trade, they could have maintained stable labor costs and better managed the economic downturn. Moreover, Africans, perhaps more than any other group, popularized the abolitionist movement. Cugoano and Equiano offered firsthand accounts of the trade and presented them in ways that English readers not only would understand but also could relate to in important ways. Though Africans, these men had adopted a British identity just as their readers had. The idea that British subjects and, especially in Equiano's case, devout Christians had been enslaved inspired a more direct condemnation of the trade than the work of other abolitionists.

Conclusion

When African agency is taken into account, perhaps the slave trade reaching its highest point and the beginning of the abolitionist movement occurring in the same century are not quite as paradoxical as some have thought. The huge profits realized from the sugar revolution allowed for the expansion of slavery in sugar-producing regions and also brought enslaved men and women to other plantation ventures. Sugar became the economic engine by which Europeans were able to drive their colonial ventures. More than just providing labor, Africans captured and taken into slavery brought knowledge and customs with them that led to the development of unique Creole cultures throughout the Americas. These cultures did not remain confined to the slave quarter; rather, they directly influenced the growth of their colonies as much, if not more, than the Europeans who founded them.

Though notions of individual freedom held by Europeans, especially the English, both forbade the enslaving of other Europeans and allowed for enslaving Africans, it could be argued that it was the Africans who were most influential in convincing others that the slave trade should end. Shipboard revolts as well as actions by those that placed them on the ships in the first place created a situation that prevented Europeans from exporting as many enslaved men and women as they would have liked at prices that made sense economically. This, along with economic problems toward the end of the eighteenth century, led to smaller profit margins for British investors. These declining profits, along with an increasingly vocal abolitionist movement, spearheaded by Afro-Britons such as Equiano, eroded popular and political support for the trade. With the British openly opposing the slave trade by the first decades of the nineteenth century, other less powerful nations often found themselves at loggerheads with the British for continued importations of Africans to the New World. Still, without African actions against the trade, it is doubtful that Europeans would have been willing to part with an enterprise that had remained so integral to the creation of wealth and power both at home and in their colonies.

Notes

1. Joseph E. Inikori, "The Unmeasured Hazards of the Atlantic Slave Trade: Sources, Causes, and Historiographical Implications," in *From Chains to Bonds: The Slave Trade Revisited*, ed. Doudou Diène (Paris: UNESCO, 2001), 86–102.

2. This quote is taken from Olaudah Equiano, *The Interesting Narrative and Other Writings* (New York: Penguin Books, 1995), 45.

3. Quote from John Atkins, *A Voyage to Guinea, Brasil, and the West Indies*, reprinted in Richard D. E. Burton, *Afro-Creole: Power, Opposition, and Play in the Caribbean* (Ithaca, N.Y.: Cornell University Press, 1997), 24.

4. It should be noted that "abolition" in the eighteenth-century British context meant the ending of the slave trade, not the ending of slavery itself.

CHAPTER SIX

The Nineteenth-Century Black Atlantic

Aribidesi A. Usman

It is generally agreed that commercial links were established by the slave trade between Africa, the Americas, and Europe, but the trade also generated transatlantic social and cultural connections. "Black Atlantic" in this chapter refers not to a definite region or specific period, but to a "multidimensional" and "trans-cultural space" continually crisscrossed by movement and networking of black people. A cultural pattern can be deemed "Atlantic" if a substantial portion of it is shared by two or more groups or societies living at considerable distance and in different geographical regions. The hyphenated "Afro-Atlantic culture" as used by John Thornton is in recognition that this culture forms on both sides of the Atlantic.[1] Through retention and adaptation, African cultures were able to survive in areas outside their birth place. Also, the degree of involvement in this interaction sphere or the intensity of the Black Atlantic bond varied from society to society and from period to period. So, the issue here is not the identification of a uniform culture at all times and in all places throughout Africa and the Diaspora, but that Africans and their descendants tapped from the same cultural values and modes of expression in their struggle to retain some authentic sense of themselves as people. The Black Atlantic itself was also subject to transformation, with the importance of links specifically between certain areas in Africa and the New World increasing over time.

There has been a growing body of literature concerned with the study of the "Black Atlantic."[2] In his studies of the Anglophone world and from the perspective of the North Atlantic Diaspora, Paul Gilroy has proposed the "black Atlantic" identity as a single, complex unit of analysis, where blacks are agents equally with whites.[3] He conceived the Atlantic as "continually crisscrossed by the movements of black people—not only as commodities but engaged in various struggles towards emancipation, autonomy, and citizenship."[4] Robin Law and Kristin Mann, focusing on the nineteenth-century slave trade from Africa, see the Atlantic community as "transracial," rather than specifically "black."[5] With the Slave Coast and Brazil as their case study, their main concern was the development and maintenance of continuous commercial, social, and cultural links across the Atlantic.

This chapter provides an overview of Black Atlantic culture in the nineteenth and early twentieth centuries through the slave trade and other movements to the Caribbean and Americas and in Africa. The nineteenth century is unique not only because it marked the end of the Atlantic slave trade, but because it was a period that saw the largest export of Africans across the Atlantic and the solidification of African cultures in the New World. The focus here is to document the rise and transformation of African culture whose outlook spanned the Atlantic during the era of the slave trade. The scale and intensity of these bonds were such that some African groups, or at least their commercial and ruling elites, may be considered as participating in what can reasonably be termed an "Atlantic community." This chapter examines 1) the slave trade in the nineteenth century and the Atlantic societies it created; and 2) the syncretism cultures that emerge with significant African influence.

Slave Trade in the Nineteenth Century

Several societies in Africa became part of a wider Atlantic World through their participation in the slave trade. We now know enough about the parts of Africa involved in the slave trade, about the organization of the trade, and about the history of the societies in the Americas to which slaves were taken before the nineteenth century. A chapter in this volume is devoted to the slave trade before the nineteenth century. My concern in this essay is to examine the events in the nineteenth century. Although some of these events started prior to that period, the nineteenth century witnessed an upsurge in the slave trade from Africa. That period saw the largest human migration to date and has been regarded as the first of the world's modern migrations.[6] It has been estimated that slave exports from all parts of Africa amounted to 5.6 million, about 1.6 million fewer than total exports for all sectors (i.e., Atlantic, Saharan, Red Sea, and Indian Ocean) in the eighteenth century.[7] There were almost 3.5 million slaves sold across the Atlantic, representing about 62 percent of all slave exports.

The nineteenth century is also associated with the period of the abolition of the slave trade. For a combination of humanitarian, political, and economic motives, the last decades of the eighteenth century witnessed increasing attempts to abolish the slave trade. The United States passed its laws in 1791 and 1794, Denmark in 1802; in 1807 Great Britain, the largest carrier of slaves to the Americas before 1800, made it illegal for its citizens to trade in slaves. Britain pressured other Europeans to outlaw the slave trade and instituted naval action against violators. The naval blockade, which was ineffective early in the nineteenth century due to violations, increasingly became a major obstacle for European ships attempting to purchase slaves easily in many places. But the slave trade continued and increased in proportion until about 1850, although it had become a secret operation after 1830. Traders devised various means of hiding their trade, such as building barracoons or stockades to hold slaves in isolated and remote locations such as on the Gabonese coast and in the creeks of the lower Zaire.[8] Several areas of Africa in the nineteenth century witnessed an increased proportion in the slave trade. Areas chosen for consideration in this essay are West Africa (e.g., the Bight of Benin, Biafra), Central Africa, and Eastern Africa.

For most of the slave trade, Ouidah was the principal slave port on the West African coast; it was replaced by Lagos as the dominant port in the 1830s and 1840s. The majority of slaves were initially supplied by the inland kingdom of Allada with proximity to the coast until the eighteenth century, when Dahomey conquered the kingdom and became the dominating force on the coast. The Slave Coast also supplied slaves from the Yoruba kingdom of Oyo.[9] The collapse of the Oyo kingdom in the early nineteenth century, the Dahomey, Nupe, and Fulani invasions of the Oyo area, and the various Yoruba wars launched in an effort to re-establish a centralized state in the region supplied many more slaves to the market between 1818 and 1823.[10]

The Aro commercial system in the Igbo-Ibibio area reached its fullest development and contributed to the rise in slave exports in the nineteenth century. Probably more than three-quarters of the exported slaves came from the Igbo-Ibibio area including those brought by the Aro from further inland.[11] In central and northern Igbo areas most slaves were taken in village raids and wars carried out by warriors from Abiriba, Ohafia, Abam, and Edda who served as mercenaries for the Aro.[12] In the southern and central Igbo districts, people were enslaved through pawns, kidnapping, or capture for oracles. Parents sold their children because of debts, laziness, and insubordination. In places such as Nguru, slaves and pawns were no longer differentiated, and both are called *ohu*, the local name for "slave."[13] Traditional laws prohibiting sale of domestic slaves or those born into slavery at such places as Enugwu-Ukwu were violated or completely ignored. Kidnapping was a common occurrence, and parents became wary of their children playing too far from their homes. Stories of kidnapping in the nineteenth century are reported in various oral traditions collected by Elizabeth Isichei.[14] The oracles, despite their roles in stabilizing the segmentary political system, contributed to enslavement by requiring slaves as payments for certain offences committed and services received by the people.[15] Slave exports from the Niger delta declined in the late 1830s as a result of British embargoes and the increases in the sale of palm oil to European traders. The British navy liberated 17,622 slaves from the Bight of Biafra in the 1830s, which helped end the trade. Also, palm oil exports rose from 3,000 tons in 1819 to almost 8,000 tons in 1829 and to 12,800 tons in 1839; exports topped 24,000 tons per year by the mid-1850s and 41,000 tons annually in the 1860s.[16]

The unwillingness on the part of the Portuguese to enforce anti–slave trade laws helped extend the trade in Central Africa late into the nineteenth century, although on a reduced scale. It has been suggested that from 1800 to 1850 as many slaves as in the last half of the eighteenth century were exported from Central Africa, often quietly supported by Britain.[17] Major changes occurred in the Central African interior as a result of increasing slave exports. For example, the Lunda and Luba warlords captured slaves from the interior, while the inland Lunda state of Kazembe experienced growth and acquired wealth on a large scale.[18] During the nineteenth century, U.S., Portuguese, and Spanish traders serving Cuba after about 1810 concentrated their trading along the mouth of the Zaire River. The increasing volume of the trade produced additional slaves from the central and northern equatorial forests to the already large multitudes of Central Africans. Before the nineteenth century, slaves came mostly from the savanna to the south of Zaire. With high demand for slaves in the nineteenth century, Bobangi fishermen and traders to the northeast of the Malebo Pool began to bring slaves down the river.[19] The spread of cassava cultivation was related to this commercial growth, as cassava could be carried easily on riverboats as food for the traders and slaves being transported.

The greater demand for slaves in the nineteenth century also led to the emergence of the Cokwe as an important force in trade and politics.[20] The Cokwe were hunters and possessed good knowledge of the forest country between Kasanje and Lunda. This placed them in an advantageous position to trade and profit from the increasing demand for ivory and beeswax, an important export from Angola in the 1830s. The Cokwe used the proceeds from ivory and wax sales to buy guns which they used to raid for slaves and served as warriors and raiders to rival factions in the succession disputes of the Imbangala, Ovimbundu, and Lunda polities.[21]

East Africa did not experience a British naval blockade of the slave trade until the eradication of the West African trade. Even when Britain secured treaties with the Portuguese, the French, Uman, and the Hova rulers of Madagascar, the country was still faced with other problems that made the eradication of the slave trade in the region difficult until the second half of the nineteenth century. For example, there were limitations on the authority of the naval squadron to seize and search suspected ships. Other problems include the shortage of anti-slave patrols in the Indian Ocean, the lack of desire among traders in East Africa to abandon the trade, and the independence of Brazil in 1822.[22] By the nineteenth century slaves had overtaken ivory as the most lucrative trade commodity in Mozambique Island. For example, ivory exports in 1809 fell to about 7,300 arrobas and in 1817 to less than 4,000 arrobas, while the revenue from slave exports was five times more than the ivory export and other commodities.[23] The British inability to eradicate slave trading in Portuguese territories in Africa until the second half of the nineteenth century, and the restriction in 1815 and 1817 of the Portuguese trade to Portuguese possessions in Eastern Africa, diverted much of the trade from West Africa to Portuguese

East Africa. Also important in this period was the Arab and Swahili slave trade to Madagascar, much of which came from the coast close to Mozambique. The slaves transported to several ports on the northwest shore of Madagascar were mostly Makua who were absorbed by the Sakalawa and sometimes sold to the Hova in the interior of the Island.[24]

Slaves' Destinations

The question of where the nineteenth-century slaves were taken is of some significance, especially in the identification of heterogeneous cultures and societies that emerge with significant African influence. On the Slave Coast in the nineteenth century, traders from a number of nations traded slaves and shipped exports primarily to their own countries' settlements in the Americas, but Portuguese from Brazil and native-born Brazilians dominated the trade. In the final three decades of the trade, Spanish Cuba became a major market. Yoruba men and women captured by the Dahomeans turned up in Haiti and Brazil, while other captives of the Fulani were brought to Cuba, Brazil, and the Caribbean, notably Trinidad.[25] The Yoruba of Cuba were called Lucumi. Ulkami may be a word of Gun (a Ewe group language) origin and be cognate with Lucumi, which has been found to be the Cuban name for the Yoruba.[26] Lucumi is said to be derived from an Ijesha salutation (*oluku-mi*, "my friend") and dates from the mid-nineteenth century when it was given by their fellow slaves to Ijesha slaves captured by raiders from the newly founded Oyo town of Ibadan and shipped at the very end of the slave-trading period to Cuba, one of the last importers of slaves.[27]

The Rio traders' dominance at Luanda and Benguela and the large number of captives taken to south-central Brazil made Central Africans the dominant group among the slaves in and around the city of Rio de Janeiro. By the end of the transatlantic slaving in the 1850s in the Spanish Caribbean, Central Africans formed the most recent and very large cohort of immigrants among the plantation workers alongside an urban slave population of much older and more diverse origins.[28] Most of the slaves from Mozambique were taken to Brazil. However, Brazil was not the only source of demand for slaves from Mozambique. Mozambique slaves were also carried on Arab and Swahili vessels to Comoros, where French traders purchased and then transported them to the Seychelles, Bourbon, and Mauritius.[29] Also in 1819 Spanish vessels from Havana entered Mozambique harbor to take on slaves before continuing on to Zanzibar to complete their cargoes. Cuban slavers, and even a few American slavers, continued to put in occasional appearances at Mozambique right through the 1840s.[30]

It is difficult to come up with exact figures for the nineteenth-century slave exports or even the previous periods, largely because of lack of the adequate records, and partly because the slave trade lasted much longer than people often thought. For example, slaves continued to be exported from the Zaire estuary until well into the 1870s, and from the delta of the Ogooué until 1900.[31] Also in the Yoruba hinterland, slavery was an expansive institution from the 1850s through the early 1890s. Both of these areas contributed a large proportion of slaves exported from 1801 to 1867, and West-Central Africa accounted for two-thirds of the slaves shipped after 1847. It is estimated that about 3.2 million slaves crossed the Atlantic in the first half of the nineteenth century; exports declined to just under 180,000 slaves in the 1850s and 50,000 in the 1860s before the trade ceased altogether.[32]

African Cultural Transformation

The survival of African culture in the Atlantic World has long interested anthropologists and historians alike. Melville Herskovits, an anthropologist, coined the term "Africanism" to describe African cultural traits in African Americans.[33] "Culture" in anthropological terms means a total life way, including elements such as kinship, political structure, language and literature, religion, art, music and dance, technology, and art. Culture also changes at different rates and by various factors. As explained by John Thornton, culture change can be of two types: through its own internal dynamics (e.g., political shift, environmental changes, population growth) and through contact or interactions with other cultures (e.g., trade, politics, alliance).[34] In the period of the slave trade several major changes occurred in the pottery traditions of some of the West African societies.[35] Also, archaeological excavations at Elmina in Ghana, where Europeans interacted intensely with Africans, have recovered a large number of European imports as well as new items of local manufacture (e.g., smoking pipes) that had not been produced before. These items in turn diffused in all directions in West Africa, affecting societies that had no contact with Europeans.[36]

The recognition of change explains why scholars have explained African culture in the Atlantic in terms of "traits." In this case, there is a tendency to examine specific "Africanisms" in American life rather than the cultural totality.[37] "Black Atlantic" culture resulted from struggle and adaptation over time that extend into the present through the slave trade and voluntary migration. Most important, by embracing the phenomena of change and hybridity and rejecting the notion of African culture as a "fixed essence," the "Black Atlantic" construct not only reflects the reality of the past but also allows for the possibility of continuing cultural "evolution" through ongoing cultural interaction, exchange, and development.[38]

The enslaved Africans from the continent included artisans, priests, soldiers, chiefs, princes, and princesses. The process of cultural transformation in the New World may have been difficult and complex since white slave owners opposed the transfer and perpetuation of African traditions on the plantations. The white opposition "extinguished" some African practices, forced the re-working of others, and forced still others "underground."[39] However, these experiences challenged and encouraged the enslaved Africans to develop new techniques and strategies of self-expression. For instance, the traditional African cultures that could not be openly displayed were made into craft objects both for white consumption as well as for enslaved African household consumption or personal use. Most of these objects were associated with African religious practices.

There remains another important question: Which African culture constitutes the Black Atlantic? There was a policy of mixing slaves on plantations so that slaves of the same ethnic group would not find themselves together. Equally noted is that West Africa is an area of great cultural diversity with an underlying unity which has led a number of scholars to consider it a culture area established on the basis of a number of shared cultural features.[40] However, one cannot rule out the possibility of a specific culture or ethnic group being the foundation of Atlantic culture. The dominant group in the formative period would have set the pattern to which other groups then and later would have had to conform. Also, the African cultural practices created in the Diaspora did not survive intact over time. In fact, how well an African cultural element fared in the New World depended on a number of factors, such as the degree of contact between African and Euro-American groups, the length of separation from the African homeland, the degree of acceptance among Euro-Americans of African customs, and the demographic composition of the African community.

The coming of African icons to the black New World accompanied an affirmation of philosophical continuities. The African cultural practices recognized in the New World are particularly in the areas of language, burials, naming, music, dance, rituals, festivals, folklore, religion, and spirituality. Due to the limitations on this essay, only a brief discussion of some of these cultural elements is possible. More detailed examinations of African cultures in the Atlantic have been attempted by various scholars.[41] The African cultural practices discussed in this chapter include religion and rituals, burial, architecture, and technology (e.g., ironworking and pottery).

Religion and Rituals

Selected aspects of the African practices remained alive in icons of the goddesses and gods on New World shrines or altars. The Yoruba deities or *orisha* such as Ifa, Ogun, and Sango were introduced to the New World by the enslaved Africans who probably came from the Oyo region. The survival of Yoruba tradition through its turbulent history depended in large measure on a cadre of wise and disciplined diviners steeped in the secrets of the ancestors and gods.[42] Ifa is one example of Yoruba religion brought to the New World. Ifa divination permeated every aspect of life in Yoruba society as it is performed on occasions such as naming and marriage ceremonies, funeral rites, and the installation of kings. Thus, Yoruba rely on Ifa divination to place their problems in perspective. In Yoruba society in the past, the authority of Ifa was respected because the people regard Ifa as the voice of the divinities and the wisdom of the ancestors.[43]

Among the Yoruba of Nigeria the Ifa diviner *babalawo* uses different methods of divination. Two of these methods reported in the New World are the Ikin, the "sixteen sacred palm-nuts," regarded as the most ancient and important instruments of divination; and the divining through the use of a divining chain, *ọpẹlẹ,* made of string or metal with four half-nuts of the *ọpẹlẹ* fruit attached to each of the chains. In Cuba the continuity of Yoruba *odu, or* sacred Ifa verses, has been suggested in which the *babalao* (the Creole equivalent to the Yoruba diviners) had reinstated the *odu* with names and explanatory tales virtually intact.[44] The Cuban divination trays are round (as in northern Yorubaland in Nigeria) or rectangular, and some are called *atẹfa* as in Ketu-Yoruba and Bahia in Brazil.[45]

Ogun is one of the deities carried to the Americas by Africans during the Atlantic slave trade. Ogun is regarded as the god of war and iron in West African pantheon. Ogun lives in the flames of the blacksmith's forge, on the battlefield, and, more particularly, on the cutting edge of iron.[46] As an arbiter of human actions, Ogun also relentlessly pursues truth, equity, and justice. It is a popular saying among the Yoruba people in Nigeria that "If someone stole something and that person is in a lorry, that motor will simply kill the person . . . Ogun will kill him there. Anytime you see something that belongs to another, you must not take it, otherwise you will be killed by Ogun."[47] Besides punishing offenders, Ogun facilitates interactions between humans and supernatural forces. Worshippers of various cults frequently assert that Ogun is essential for the creation of any altar to an otherworldly being (*ara orun*). "Anywhere you are going to put any shrine on earth, Ogun will first of all work there." The Yoruba have the proverb *Ogun lo sale f'orisa do,* meaning "Ogun is the one who clears the place where a shrine for the gods is established."[48] Ogun is also involved in procreation. He gives life as dramatically as he takes it away. Ogun presides over the beginning of life and the cutting of the umbilical cord, and he is there at the end, for "Ogun is the hoe that opens the earth (to bury you)"; *Ogun okoko yeri ogu.*[49]

Ogun survives today in a number of West African countries and New World societies in the Caribbean, South America, and North America. Ogun ritual paraphernalia in Cuba today includes the bucket-shaped iron cauldron (*caldero de ogun*) which contained various expressions of ironwork, such as nails, iron bows and arrows, horseshoes, and fetters.[50] The Cuban migration to North America resulted in the establishment of the *caldero de ogun* in Miami and New York, with other additions, such as a shrine in the New York area in 1979 that contained a pistol. In Brazil, as in Nigeria and the Benin Republic, Ogun is honored by placing on his shrine pieces of iron as well as miniature implements called in Bahia *ferramentas de ogun* (Ogun irons).[51]

Sango is known in Yoruba traditions as one of the early kings (Alaafin) of

Oyo. He is considered violent, temperamental, and vindictive, yet handsome, loving, caring, and generous.[52] He was a great warrior and magician who had the power to attract lightning, with which he vanquished his enemies on the battlefield. The circumstances surrounding Sango's death and deification are not clear. One story claimed that Sango voluntarily abdicated the throne after a long reign in the fifteenth or sixteenth century and disappeared through a hole in the ground as a sign of his transformation into an *orisa* (deity). Others allege that his subjects forced him to abdicate after becoming tired of his political intrigues and military escapades. In the end, Sango committed suicide. But shortly after, according to one legend, Oyo-Ile, capital of Oyo Empire, experienced a series of unprecedented and devastating thunderstorms that the king's former subjects interpreted as a manifestation of Sango's retributive justice and wrath. As a result, the people dedicated shrines not only to pacify him but also to harness his power for communal benefit. Since his military successes reportedly laid the foundation for the political ascendancy and economic prosperity of Oyo, Sango worship was a state religion from the seventeenth century to the early nineteenth century, when the kingdom was at the apex of its power.

The devotee of Sango places carvings (*ere*) on altars dedicated to him. As the controller of rainfall, Sango represents the dynamic, fecund principle in nature. This explains the emphasis on the female in Sango art and rituals.[53] The double-axe motif associated with Ogun devotee is a metaphor for the thunderbolt (in the form of a polished stone axe) that, according to popular belief, Sango hurls down from the sky during thunderstorms. The double-axe motif also signifies the male-female interaction in Sango symbolism, recalling the stage during initiation ceremonies when a novitiate has a polished stone axe tied to his or her head to symbolize the union of the human and super-human. In Cuba and Brazil the enslaved Africans were introduced to the cult of Roman Catholic saints. The power of Christian saints was then considered analogous to the forces and power of the African deities. For example, Shango, the Yoruba god of thunder and lightning, in Cuba was often equated with Saint Barbara, whose killers were struck dead by God with lightning.[54] Metaphoric fire balanced on the head of the worshipper is an aspect of Sango sacred features that traveled to Bahia in Brazil. The balancing of twin bolts of meteoric fire on the head of the devotee is meant to convey a promise of moral vengeance. In Bahia in the late nineteenth century, the butterfly-like shape of the thunderstones balanced on the devotee's head revealed influence from Ketu-Yoruba, where Sango axes are designed in this form.[55]

Nail and mirror fetishes are unique and important religious items of the Kongo. This consists of figures with magical substances embedded in various parts of the body. In the Kongo, a fetish is called *nkisi* (plural: *minkisi*).[56] *Minkisi* are made in various forms such as leaves, shells, ceramic vessels, wooden images, and cloth bundles, among others. The carved *nkisi* statuettes can be divided into four functional specialties: *Nkondi* or "hunter" are fetishes of ill omen, usually brandishing a spear or a knife; *Npezo* are just as evil, but less menacing in attitude; *Na moganga* are benevolent figures which protect against sickness and dangerous spirits. Finally, there is *Mbula*, which protect against witchcraft. The *nkisi*, properly endowed with magic substances by the *Nganga* or doctor, had the power to identify and hunt down individuals or villages guilty of perpetrating some evil or wrong through secret means. A punishable offense could range from bringing illness to bringing death on an individual.

Kongo-inspired *nkisi* vessels and bundles have been reported in Cuba and among the Afro-Cubans of the United States, especially in Miami and New York in the nineteenth century. Many *minkisi* produced in Cuba and in United States today contain large three-legged iron cooking pots.[57] The *nkisi* vessels among Afro-Cubans are called *prendas* (pawns), reflecting the ritual obligations shared by the owner of the charm and the spirit within. In the nineteenth century in Cuba the *minkisi* figurines were produced to attack slaveholders and other enemies and for spiritual reconnaissance.[58] They have been described as "magic doll-like figurines with magic substance inserted in a small cavity similar to the *Nkisi nkondi* (hunter) image of Kongo. Also present in Cuba is the *matiabo* image with horn (*mpoka*) that is said to represent runaway slaves who sometimes allied with rebel forces in Cuba's nineteenth-century war of independence against Spain. In Haiti, Western Hispaniola, *nkisi* objects are known as *pacquets-congo*, and the Kongo spirits of the dead, *bisimbi*, were said to direct its production in Haiti.[59]

The Kongo-Angola presence in Brazil produced another form of *nkisi* tradition in the form of charms for love and war. The *ponto de segurar* ("securing point") was a small charm in a cloth container designed to "arrest a spirit or attract a person to its owner." In form and function *pontos de segurar* resemble the miniature Haitian charms called *pwe* ("points"), both of which are similar to the Kongo-Cuban *nkangue* charms made to "tie" a lover for a client. *Nkangue* in Ki-Kongo literally means "one who arrests" and in religious connotation referred to the moment when the shaman *nganga* says, "I close the door," and the spirit is thereby contained.[60]

Voodoo (*vodun*) first elaborated in Haiti is a synthesis of the African traditional beliefs with Roman Catholicism. The Africans who populated Haiti came primarily from Kongo and Angola, but also from the Republic of Benin (formerly Dahomey), Yorubaland, Igboland, Bamana, and Mande territories in West Africa. The religion emerged in Saint Domingue (now Haiti) as early as the mid-eighteenth century and became more popular with large arrivals of slaves from the Bight of Benin between 1760 and 1790.[61] The Vodun religion has two parts: Rada, named after slaves taken from Arada (i.e., Allada), on the coast of Dahomey; and Petro-Lemba (or Petro) after a messianic figure, Don Pedro, from the south peninsula of what is now Haiti and the northern Kongo society, Lemba.[62] *Vodun* religion represents the pantheon of deities under one supreme creator. Their manifestation was through spirit possession (mounting) of the bodies of their worshippers. This aspect of *vodun* worship—possession—was reinforced by contact with Roman Catholic saints who were associated with miracles.

The Haitian term for spirit, *loa*, encapsulates the hidden nature of the syncretism that took place in this religion. In Abomey in the Republic of Benin, deities are called *vodun* (mysteries); in Yoruba, diviner-herbalists are called *babalawo*, a term creolized by Haitians into *papaloi*, the name for a *vodun* priest. The Haitian words for deity, *loa* or *mystère*, therefore may derive from the Yoruba *l'awo* for "mystery."[63] On the Kongo influence of *vodun* in Haiti, he became the Petro spirit Ogun-Bonfire. Dahomeans know Gu as the personification of iron's cutting edge. United with Ogun, the Yoruba god of iron and war, from whom Gu himself originally derived, Gu became Papa Ogun. Papa Ogun was, in turn, associated with the warrior saints of the Roman Catholic Church.[64]

Burial

Kongo-Angola influence in the New World was very pronounced in black burial practices, especially in the decoration of graves with different objects. This is a confirmation of the Kongo notion of the tomb as a charm for the persistence of the spirit.[65] Several items have been used as grave decorations (e.g., pottery, glass containers, cups, saucers, bowls, sea shells, clocks, salt and pepper shakers, medicine bottles, spoons, pitchers, white pebbles, statues, razors, soap dishes). Seashells, believed to enclose the soul's immortal presence, have been reported on graves in the Carolinas; St. Louis, Missouri; Mississippi; New Orleans; Jacksonville, Florida; Haiti; and Guadeloupe. This practice of decorating graves is derived from the African belief that the dead continued to be involved in the lives of the surviving relatives. It is important that proper or adequate burial is made for their departure. Graveyard goods are therefore a statement of homage and affection. Rosa Sallins of Harris Neck, Georgia, explained the rationale for the treatment of grave goods: "You broke the dishes so that the chain will be broke. You see, the person is dead and if you don't break the things, then the others in the family will die too."[66] In other words, the surface "decorations" frequently function as "medicines" of admonishment and love. Such materials are broken and must not be disturbed because they are the property of the deceased person.

The similarity to Central African practices has been mentioned in different accounts. E. J. Glave, who traveled through Zaire in 1884, wrote in 1891, "natives mark the final resting places of their friends by ornamenting their graves with crockery, empty bottles, old cooking pots, etc., all of which articles are rendered useless by being cracked or penetrated with holes."[67] Recent anthropological studies in the same region also suggest several graves with diverse objects for the dead to assist them in the next world. One example is a chief's grave with ten baskets, an iron pot, a large cloth, broken pottery, and terracotta figurines of an elephant, tiger, and crocodile.[68] Similar practices have also been reported in some parts of West Africa. Among the Ekoi of southeastern Nigeria, devotees of the goddess Nimm were buried under a stick framework from which were suspended the belongings of the deceased. The Akan people of Ghana and Cote d'Ivoire also honored their dead with terracotta portraits of the deceased person. As Roy Sieber notes, "After dark on the last day of the ceremonies [funeral], the hearth, the pottery and wooden cooking vessels and utensils, the shelter, and the terracottas were all taken to the royal cemetery and placed on the grave."[69] From the above, it appears that the pattern and practice of burial customs across West and Central Africa is roughly equivalent, and such ideas have accompanied the enslaved Africans to different destinations in the New World.

Architecture

A house as a spatial phenomenon is an important expression of the individual and group, and the values upon which culture depends are in many ways derived from house form.[70] Africans arrived in the New World equipped with ideas and skills for building their own houses. Some planters allowed the enslaved Africans to design and build their own houses, though others were hostile to any such expression of African culture. One finds in these houses evidence of African continuities in the construction and types of materials and in the definition of space. In the houses built in the seventeenth and eighteenth centuries, there is a strong resemblance with West and Central Africa. In the Bight of Benin region in Nigeria, the nine-by-nine-foot units used are very similar to the ten-by-ten-foot and eight-by-eight-foot units found in Angola.[71] While the traditional African architecture forms brought to the New World varied, the most important and most widespread African house form in the New World is the "shotgun house." The term "shotgun" was probably derived from the Yoruba *to-gun*, meaning "place of assembly."[72] The Yoruba house forms varied from a small two-room module of ten by twenty feet to a series of small houses arranged end to end or built around an open courtyard that is generally called a "compound" or *agboile* (flock of houses). But no matter the sizes and forms of these houses in Yorubaland, they are still considered as single dwelling units.

Shotgun houses were common in the southern part of United States because of their efficient use of land, modest cost, and suitability to the climate. The size of each house was ten or twelve feet (three to four meters) square, and a general preference for small square rooms was seen as an important means of African cultural preservation. They contain floors plastered of beaten dirt called *pise*, thatched reed or palmetto leaf roofs, and wattle-and-daub or clay wall construction.[73] Unlike the major convention of American folk housing, the shotgun's gable side, rather than its long side, faces the road. Each shotgun house has three or more small rooms all connected directly to each other. This arrangement forces inhabitants into prolonged, immediate interaction with one another in the porch or street, thus eliminating privacy and emphasizing strong communal focus. In the United States, by the middle of the nineteenth century, the shotgun proved very popular for economic reasons, and by the 1870s it was commonly built as a cheap, rental house. A number of modified versions of the basic house form had also developed, most notably a double shotgun built side by side under one roof and a "camelback" house, which is a shotgun with a two-story rear section.[74]

The Afro-Haitian architecture, an amalgamation of Yoruba and Arawak Indian plans and elevation provides another example of African building concepts in the New World.[75] The common slave house in Haiti was a rectangular gable-roofed house made with wattle-and-daub walls and roofed with thatch. More importantly, it was built to the same dimensions as in Yorubaland, while the repetition of the ten-by-twenty-foot farm represents the impact of a West and Central African architectural concept. Between 1760 and 1790, 28 to 42 percent of slaves in Haiti came from areas dominated by the Yoruba, followed by slaves from Angola-Zaire origins, which constituted between 32 and 37 percent of the total imports. Since the Yoruba arrived first and in the greatest numbers, it has been suggested that the culture that produced Haiti's architecture is primarily Yoruba, with supportive influences provided by Central Africans.[76]

Ironworking and Pottery

The earliest evidence of ironworking in Africa suggests both external and possible indigenous sources involving a variety of techniques such as smelting and smithing. In West Africa blacksmiths made ritual objects of iron. In local village communities in Mali, the Senegambian region, and northern regions of Burkina Faso, Cote d'Ivoire, and Ghana, blacksmiths held some of the highest political and spiritual authority. The spread of iron occurred as part of larger cultural complexes, including kingship and ritualized production of iron.[77] Just as iron can be used as a tool for creation or for destruction, the ironworker was regarded by his community with feelings of love and hate. It has been claimed that the greater complexity and perceived dangers of smelting as more fundamentally transformative contributed to the greater incorporation of ritual in smelting as compared to ordinary smithing activities.[78] In Nigeria, particularly in Yorubaland and among the Nupe, anyone could smelt iron, but the smiths were "a people apart" because of their specialized knowledge.[79] Much of the symbolism revolved around the concepts and imagery of fertility, sexuality, and reproduction. Knowledge associated with African traditional iron technology was in the hands of men, while women and children provided supportive, less transformative activities such as mining and charcoal production. Ironworking was carried out in small pit furnaces, sometimes in low shaft furnaces, and sometimes in tall, natural-draft furnaces.

By the time of the Atlantic era (c. 1508 to 1850), most African technologies were affected by the European presence. Increased coastal trade with Europeans brought in large quantities of cheap European metal goods produced by the Industrial Revolution. These competed with indigenous iron manufactures that were facing high labor costs in the wake of the slave trade and the scarcity of charcoal fuel after centuries of exploitation. Europeans on the coast also employed African ironworkers and introduced new production methods such as coal fuel, European-style raised forges, and iron anvils. Some local iron industries in Africa, such as in Togo, resisted European pressures and survived into the twentieth century, but they were eventually banned by the Europeans, who feared competition might end their monopoly over manufactured goods.[80]

Various metalworking techniques, whether in iron, copper-based alloys, or gold, have been identified with African metallurgists in the New World. Besides woodworking, there was no occupation in which the enslaved African's talent in the Americas was expressed more often than in blacksmithing. Slave records (e.g., ship cargo lists, auctions, runaway notices) show that approximately 20 percent of the Africans brought to America between 1650 and 1740 were Mande and Wolof peoples (Senegal-Gambia), with some of them probably blacksmiths.[81] Also, auctions and runaway notices were full of references to blacksmithing as the occupation of the slaves.

The charcoal-fueled bloomery process survived into the nineteenth century in some parts of the Caribbean and North America. Documentary evidence also suggests high status was accorded slaves with metalworking expertise. These slave artisans were rarely used for agricultural tasks. Some of them even became church leaders in post-abolition Jamaica and in the antebellum South of North America.[82] As transformers of metal to weapons, the slave artisans' status was significant in resistance and rebellions. In Jamaica, the 1774 law that forbade slaves from trading in metal goods was probably because of the fear of metal goods in the hands of slaves.[83] The successful slave revolts against slave masters at Winkle Village, Guyana, or in Maroon communities from Jamaica to Suriname, suggests the potential for empowerment of slave ironworkers. In North America the famous rebellion led by Gabriel Prosser of Richmond, Virginia, in 1800 included the support of a slave blacksmith whose duty was to make swords.[84] And in Charleston in 1822, Denmark Vesey's insurrection had abundant weapons produced by two slave blacksmiths, Mingo Hearth and Tom Russell.[85]

Archaeology provides the most promising source for investigating African cultural transformation and continuities in the New World. Archaeologists in the Caribbean have identified objects which were either manufactured in Africa or in African style as well as behaviors that reflect African traditions.[86] Two examples of African technological transformation in the Caribbean are the site of Reeder's Foundry in Morant Bay, Jamaica, and the Fort King George blacksmith shop site in Tobago, both identified with African metalworking activities. The Reeder's Foundry site is an iron and brass foundry that made cannon balls and repaired other metal objects during the late eighteenth century (1774–1782). As described by Goucher, the excavated iron slag, pieces of metals, and pottery corresponds with the documentary evidence of the presence of Africans at the Reeder's Foundry site, which had more than 267 African ironworkers. The local pottery, an African-associated "Yabba ware" in Level Two represented about half of the pottery excavated from levels date to the period between 1775 and 1825. Blacksmithing at the Reeder's Foundry site had ceased since the site was abandoned in the beginning of the nineteenth century. However, the Morant Bay area where Reeder's Foundry was located is well known for a powerful African religion, the Kumina, whose worshippers may have been iron and ritual experts. The ethno-archaeological study of the religion has revealed other information on the Reeder's Foundry, such as the role of fire in political, social, and spiritual transformation, the dancing of the iron cutlass, and even the African vocabularies for specialized metal objects (*afana*, an Akan word for a ceremonial cutlass).[87]

The other archaeological site relating to ironworking in the Caribbean is the eighteenth- to early nineteenth-century Fort King George blacksmith shop site in Tobago.[88] The excavations of the site revealed furnace fragments, iron slag, a smithing workshop, pottery, smoking pipes, and other artifacts. Also, a carved ornament, probably a hip mask, recovered from a surface collection is said to be similar to masks worn by the Edo warrior chiefs in the eighteenth-century Benin kingdom. The identification of a blacksmith shop at the find site of the Edo-style mask is suggestive of the African presence.

Archaeologists studying pottery from New World African sites must constantly attempt to determine whether the pottery production represents the choices and economics of the planter or that of the enslaved Africans. Sometimes the design motifs on slave pottery assemblages may be suggestive of African aesthetic or cultural traditions. Decoration types such as geometric lines, chevrons, bands, and lines of dots are common elements of West African pottery traditions. In the 1930s, archaeologists recovered undecorated pieces of low-fired pottery at slave sites at colonial Williamsburg and nearby plantations in Virginia. The excavations at Kingsmill plantation, near Williamsburg, in 1978 confirm that the pottery was made at plantations by blacks from the 1670s to mid-1700s. Leland Ferguson proposed the term "colonoware," which recognized the mergence of two cultural traditions, North American Indian and African American.[89]

On some plantations in South Carolina, the excavated pottery exhibited design styles found in Africa. For example, X's and X's cross-cutting circles were carved on the exterior and interior bases of some bowls. The Bakongo cosmogram is a circle, quartered by an X, with smaller circles on the branch ends of each X, representing the circle of life and death and the progression of the seasons.[90] It explained that these X's may represent New World versions of the Bakongo cosmogram. Prior to the arrival of Europeans, cross forms had been perceived by the Kongo people as a visual analogy of their own relationship to their world: a crossroads, that is, between "this world" and "the land of the dead." Also, when this is placed on the interior or exterior base of a bowl it indicates a bowl used to create *nkisi*, or sacred medicine.[91]

The Bakongo symbol of "crossroads" (i.e., the Kongo sign of cosmos and the continuity of human life), "remains an indelible concept in the Kongo-Atlantic World, as the point of intersection between the ancestors and the living."[92] One of the hand-painted ceramic shards recovered from the slave quarters at Clifton Plantation, Bahamas, bears a design remarkably similar to the Bakongo cosmogram.[93] Also, these symbols have been identified in Haiti and Cuba. The isolated rural Yaughan and Curriboo plantations in South Carolina with sizeable black communities have yielded the most colonoware in the state.[94] Here blacks had minimal contact with whites during the slave era. So blacks held onto African pottery techniques and forms, which were also very similar to those of the North American Indian. These marks found on the bases of colonoware bowls from slave sites and other contexts indicates that 150 years ago African American priests used similar symbols of the cosmos.[95]

Conclusion

The nineteenth century appears to have achieved two things in regard to the Atlantic slave trade and the migration of African peoples to the Americas. First, the period recorded the largest export of Africans to the New World of any single period in the history of the Atlantic slave trade. The increased slave exportation during this period was not only due to the increasing demand by the Europeans but also to socio-political changes in Africa such as warfare triggered by political collapse of some African polities. The increasing trade in slaves led to the growth of heterogeneous populations in the New World that helped shape Atlantic culture. Second, the nineteenth century is the period of legal abolition of slave trading and slavery. This enabled some former slaves to return to their homes in Africa or to travel back and forth between societies in the New World and Africa. Hence, the Black Atlantic community was transformed as links to Africa increased over time, with greater social and cultural consequence. For example, the return of freed slaves created a large population on the coast of West Africa that identified with Bahia (Brazil) and its language, religions, and cultures. Continuing commercial, cultural, and intellectual communication among the members of this group and family, friends, co-religionists, and business associates in Bahia kept the transatlantic community alive when it might otherwise have perished following the abolition of the slave trade.[96]

The slaves exported to the New World in the nineteenth century provided a fresh face to the Black Atlantic culture. Being mostly born in Africa, they made more direct contributions to the transformation of African cultures in the New World than the slaves who preceded them and who faced much greater obstacles in self-expression and cultural preservation. Already by the late eighteenth century the concentration of slaves from the Slave Coast in Brazil had created a market for products from West Africa, such as Yoruba cloth, which was "held . . . in much esteem by the black population" not only for its quality but also "because it is manufactured in a country which gave many of them, or their parents, birth."[97] In the nineteenth century the trade from West Africa to Brazil also included palm oil, kola nuts, black soap, calabashes, and various spices. The growth of Yoruba cults among slaves and ex-slaves in Brazil further created a demand for religious and ritual objects made in West Africa.[98] The two largest and most important groups that created the black Atlantic were the slaves forcibly shipped across the Atlantic to places like Haiti, Brazil, Cuba, and other places in the Caribbean, as well as the freed slaves who in the nineteenth century returned, such as from Brazil, Sierra Leone, and Liberia. Both groups continued to look across the Atlantic to define their identity and way of life. The decline in African-born slaves in North America after the American Revolution appears to have made African culture less strong (or more diluted) in North America than in the Caribbean, and especially Brazil and Cuba.[99]

The "Black Atlantic" was a demographic shift driven largely by commercial motives of the slave trade. The cultural consequences were profound for both white and black people. Europeans, Africans, and Native Americans were faced with multiple tasks of surviving and forging structures of meaning and value in the societies of the New World. Africans enslaved in the New World were brought from different societies with varied cultural, linguistic, political, and religious traditions. These differences tended to blend together, creating a body of cultural perspectives, values, and practices that came to define the black Atlantic cultures. In stressing the Black Atlantic as an interactive term, it should be seen as involving reciprocal rather than "unidirectional" (Africa to America) links. The regular communication back and forth between Africa and the New World societies created networks that facilitated the exchange of culture as well as trade. Just as enslaved Africans carried African religions (traditional and foreign), languages, material culture, and architectural practices in their varied forms into the New World, so European slave traders and freed African returnees also brought literacy, numerics, Christianity, European languages, new consumer goods, artisan knowledge, and building styles to Africa.

Notes

1. John Thornton, *Africa and Africans in the Making of the Atlantic World, 1400–1800* (Cambridge: Cambridge University Press, 1998).

2. Ibid.; Bernard Bailyn, "The Idea of Atlantic History," *Itinerario* 20:1 (1996): 38–44; Ira Berlin, "From Creole to African: Atlantic Creoles and the Origins of African American Society in Mainland North America," *William and Mary Quarterly*, 3rd ser., 53 (1996): 251–288; Paul Gilroy, *The Black Atlantic: Modernity and Double Consciousness* (Cambridge, Mass.: Harvard University Press, 1993); Robin Law and Kristin Mann, "West Africa in the Atlantic Community: The Case of the Slave Coast," *William and Mary Quarterly*, 3rd ser., 56:2 (1999): 307–334; Robert F. Thompson, *Flash of the Spirit* (New York: Vintage Books, 1983); Pierre Verger, "Nigeria, Brazil, and Cuba," *Nigeria Magazine*, October (1960), 113–123.

3. Gilroy, *Black Atlantic*, 7.

4. Ibid., 16.

5. Law and Mann, "West Africa," 308, 310.

6. Paul Lovejoy, *Transformations in Slavery: A History of Slavery in Africa* (Cambridge: Cambridge University Press, 2000).

7. Ibid., 142.

8. Jan Vansina, *Paths in the Rainforests: Toward a History of Political Tradition in Equatorial Africa* (Madison: University of Wisconsin Press, 1990), 209.

9. As suggested by Law and Mann, the "Slave Coast" extended from the River Volta to Lagos (or sometimes further east), corresponding roughly to the Bight of Benin (or, in terms of modern political geography, the coast of Togo, Benin, and western Nigeria), 307.

10. A. G. Hopkins, "Economic Imperialism in West Africa, Lagos, 1880–92," *Economic History Review* 21:3 (1968): 580–606; Patrick Manning, *Slavery, Colonialism, and Economic Growth in Dahomey, 1640–1960* (Cambridge: Cambridge University Press, 1982).

11. David Northrup, *Trade without Rulers: Precolonial Economic Development in South-Eastern Nigeria* (Oxford: Clarendon Press, 1978), 133–134; Elizabeth Isichei, *Igbo Worlds: An Anthology of Oral Histories and Historical Descriptions* (Philadelphia: Institute for the Study of Human Issues, 1978), 132–135.

12. Elizabeth Isichei, *The Ibo People and the Europeans: The Genesis of a Relationship to 1906* (New York: St Martin's, 1973), 49; see also Lovejoy, *Transformations in Slavery*, 148.

13. Lovejoy, *Transformations in Slavery*, 148.

14. Isichei, *Igbo Worlds*, 45, 51, 152.

15. Lovejoy, *Transformations in Slavery*, 148; Northrup, *Trade without Rulers*, 133–134.

16. Lovejoy, *Transformations in Slavery*, 149; David Northrup, "The Compatibility of the Slave and Palm Oil Trades in the Bight of Biafra," *Journal of African History*, 17:3 (1976): 353–364.

17. Joseph Miller, "Central Africa during the Era of the Slave Trade, c. 1490s–1850s," in *Central Africans and Cultural Transformations in the America Diaspora*, ed. Linda Heywood, 21–69 (Cambridge: Cambridge University Press, 2002), 35.

18. Jan Vansina, *Kingdoms of the Savanna* (Madison: University of Wisconsin Press, 1966), 155–248; see also Joseph Miller, "The Slave Trade of Congo and Angola," in *The African Diaspora: Interpretive Essays*, ed. Martin Kilson and Robert Rotberg, 75–113 (Cambridge, Mass.: Harvard University Press, 1976), 108–111.

19. Miller, "Central Africa," 58.

20. Lovejoy, *Transformations in Slavery*, 150.

21. Ibid.

22. Edward Alpers, "The Impact of the Slave Trade on East Central Africa in the Nineteenth Century," in *Forced Migration*, ed. J. E. Inikori, 242–273 (New York: Africana, 1982), 243; Leslie Bethell, *The Abolition of the Brazilian Slave Trade: Britain, Brazil, and the Slave Trade Question, 1807–1869* (Cambridge: Cambridge University Press, 1970); for comprehensive information on the British anti-slavery campaign in the Western Indian Ocean, see G. S. Graham, *Great Britain in the Indian Ocean, 1810–1850* (Oxford: Oxford University Press, 1967), especially chapters 2, 3, and 5.

23. Alpers, "Impact of the Slave Trade, 242–273.

24. Ibid., 248.

25. Thompson, *Flash of the Spirit,* 17.

26. William Bascom, *Shango in the New World* (Austin, Tex.: African and Afro-American Research Institute, 1972), 13.

27. Peter Morton-Williams, "The Oyo Yoruba and the Atlantic Trade, 1670 to 1830," in *Forced Migration,* ed. J. E. Inikori, 167–186 (New York: Africana, 1982), 169; see also William Bascom, "Two Forms of Afro-Cuban Divination," in *Acculturation in the Americas,* ed. Sol Tax, 169–179 (Chicago: University of Chicago Press, 1952), 13.

28. Miller, "Central Africa," 35.

29. Alpers, "Impact of the Slave Trade," 244.

30. Ibid., 248.

31. Lovejoy, *Transformations in Slavery,* 149.

32. Ibid., 145.

33. Melville Herskovits, *The Myth of the Negro Past* (Boston: Beacon, 1941), 9–32; see also John Vlach, *The Afro-American Tradition in Decorative Arts* (Cleveland: Cleveland Museum of Art, 1978), 2.

34. Thornton, *Africa and Africans,* 206–207.

35. Merrick Posnansky and L. B. Crossland, "Pottery, People and Trade at Begho, Ghana," in *The Spatial Organization of Culture,* ed. Ian Hodder (Pittsburgh: University of Pittsburgh Press, 1978), 10.

36. Christopher DeCorse, "Historical Archaeological Research in Ghana, 1986–1987," *Nyame Akuma* 29 (1987): 27–31.

37. Herskovits, *Myth of the Negro Past,* 9–32.

38. Blaine Hudson, "The African Diaspora and the 'Black Atlantic': An African American Perspective—Cover Story," *Negro Bulletin,* October–December (1997).

39. Ibid.

40. Alan Cobley and Alvin Thompson, eds., *The African-Caribbean Connection: Historical and Cultural Perspectives* (Barbados: University of West Indies, 1990), 113.

41. Some relevant works are Dale Bisnauth, *A History of Religions in the Caribbean* (Jamaica: Kingston Publishers, 1989); Cobley and Thompson, *African-Caribbean Connection;* Albert Raboteau, *Slave Religion: The "Invisible Institution" in the Ante-bellum South* (New York: Oxford University Press, 1978); Thompson, *Flash of the Spirit;* Margaret Drewal, "Dancing for Ogun in Yorubaland and in Brazil," in *African's Ogun: Old World and New,* ed. Sandra T. Barnes, 199–234 (Bloomington: Indiana University Press, 1997); Sidney Mintz and Richard Price, *An Anthropological Approach to the Afro-American Past: A Caribbean Perspective* (Philadelphia: Institute for the Study of Human Issues, 1976); and Vlach, *Afro-American Tradition.*

42. Wande Abimbola, *Ifa Divination Poetry* (New York: Nok, 1977), 5.

43. Ibid.; Thompson, *Flash of the Spirit,* 32.

44. Bascom, "Two Forms of Afro-Cuban," 169–179.

45. Thompson, *Flash of the Spirit,* 37.

46. Robert Smith, "Yoruba Armament," *Journal of African History* 8:1 (1967): 87–106.

47. John Drewal, "Art or Accident: Yoruba Body Artists and Their Deity Ogun," in *Africa's Ogun: Old World and New,* ed. Sandra T. Barnes, 235–260 (Bloomington: Indiana University Press, 1997), 236.

48. Margaret Drewal, "Dancing for Ogun," 210.

49. Verger, "Nigeria, Brazil, and Cuba," 193.

50. Thompson, *Flash of the Spirit,* 54.

51. Ibid., 56.

52. Babatunde Lawal, "Yoruba Sango Sculpture in Historical Retrospect," Ph.D. diss., Indiana University (1970); see also Ulli Beier, "Festival of the Images," *Nigeria* 45 (1954): 14–20.

53. Beier, "Festival of the Images," 14–20.

54. Bascom, *Shango in the New World,* 16–17.

55. Thompson, *Flash of the Spirit,* 87.

56. Wyatt MacGaffey, *Art and Healing of the BaKongo: Commented by Themselves* (Stockholm: Folkens Museum, 1991; Bloomington: Indiana University Press, 1991).

57. Thompson, *Flash of the Spirit,* 121.

58. Ibid., 125.

59. Ibid., 127.

60. Ibid., 128.

61. Kevin Roberts, "The Influential Yoruba Past in Haiti," in *The Yoruba Diaspora in the Atlantic World,* ed. Toyin Falola and Matt Childs, 177–184 (Bloomington: Indiana University Press, 2004), 180.

62. Thompson, *Flash of the Spirit,* 164.

63. Ibid., 167.

64. Ibid.

65. Ibid., 132.

66. Vlach, *Afro-American Tradition,* 141.

67. Ibid., 142.

68. Ibid.

69. Roy Sieber, "Kwahu Terracottas, Oral Traditions and Ghanaian History," in *African Art and Leadership,* ed. Douglas Fraser and Herbert Cole, 173–183 (Madison: University of Wisconsin Press, 1972), 178–179.

70. Vlach, *Afro-American Tradition,* 123.

71. Ibid., 124.

72. Ibid., 131.

73. Sharon Patton, *African-American Art* (Oxford: Oxford University Press, 1998), 28.

74. Vlach, *Afro-American Tradition,* 131.

75. Patton, *African-American Art,* 59.

76. Vlach, *Afro-American Tradition,* 125.

77. Candice Goucher, "African-Caribbean Metal Technology: Forging Cultural Survivals in the Atlantic World," in *African Sites Archaeology in the Caribbean,* ed. Jay B. Haviser, 143–156 (Princeton, N.J.: Markus Wiener, 1999), 145.

78. Eugenia Herbert, *Iron, Gender and Power: Rituals of Transformation in African Societies* (Bloomington: Indiana University Press, 1993), 146.

79. Siegfried Nadel, *A Black Byzantium: The Kingdom of Nupe in Nigeria* (London: Oxford University Press, 1942); see also L. M. Pole, "Decline or Survival? Iron Production in West Africa from the Seventeenth to the Twentieth Centuries," *Journal of African History* 23:4 (1982): 503–513.

80. Goucher, "African-Caribbean Metal Technology," 147.

81. Patton, *African-American Art,* 38.

82. Monica Schuler, *Alas, Alas, Kongo: A Social History of Indentured African Immigrants into Jamaica, 1841–1845* (Baltimore: Johns Hopkins University Press, 1980), 383; Dennis Dickerson, *Out of the Crucible: Black Steelworkers in Western Pennsylvania, 1875–1980* (Albany: SUNY Press, 1986), 66–72.

83. Sidney Mintz and D. Hall, *The Origins of the Jamaican Internal Marketing Sys-*

tem, Publications in Anthropology no. 57 (New Haven, Conn.: Yale University, (1991), 327; Goucher, "African-Caribbean Metal Technology," 149.

84. Joseph C. Caroll, *Slave Insurrections in the United States, 1800–1865* (Boston: Chapman and Grimes, 1938), 49.

85. Vlach, *Afro-American Tradition*, 110.

86. Jay B. Haviser, "Identifying a Post-Emancipation (1863–1940) African-Curacaoan Material Culture Assemblage," in *African Sites Archaeology in the Caribbean*, ed. Jay Haviser, 221–263 (Princeton, N.J.: Markus Wiener, 1999); see also Laurie A. Wilkie, "Evidence of African Continuities in the Material Culture of Clifton Plantation, Bahamas," in *African Sites Archaeology*, ed. Haviser, 264–275; Kofi Agorsah, "Ethnoarchaeological Consideration of Social Relationship and Settlement Patterning among Africans in the Caribbean Diaspora," in *African Sites Archaeology*, ed. Haviser, 38–64; Jerome Handler, "An African-Type Healer/Diviner and His Grave Goods: A Burial from a Plantation Slave Cemetery in Barbados, West Indies," *International Journal of Historical Archaeology* 1:2 (1997): 91–130.

87. Goucher, "African-Caribbean Metal Technology," 150–152.

88. Ibid., 153.

89. Leland Ferguson, *Uncommon Ground: Archaeology and Early African America, 1650–1800* (Washington, D.C.: Smithsonian Institution Press, 1992), 18–22.

90. Wilkie, "Evidence of African Continuities," 274; Ferguson, *Uncommon Ground*, 110.

91. Wilkie, "Evidence of African Continuities," 274.

92. Thompson, *Flash of the Spirit*, 109.

93. Wilkie, "Evidence of African Continuities," 274.

94. Patton, *African-American Art*, 39.

95. Ferguson, *Uncommon Ground*, 110.

96. Law and Mann, "West Africa," 315.

97. Ibid., 314; see also John Adams, *Remarks on the Country Extending from Cape Palmas to the River Congo* (London: G. and W. B. Whittaker, 1823), 97.

98. Law and Mann, 314; also, Freyre Gilberto, *The Masters and the Slaves: A Study in the Development of Brazilian Civilization*, trans. from the Portuguese by Samuel Putnam (New York: Alfred A. Knopf, 1964), 274; Verger, "Nigeria, Brazil, and Cuba," 113–123.

99. Sterling Stuckey, *Going through the Storm: The Influence of African American Art in History* (New York: Oxford University Press, 1994).

CHAPTER SEVEN

Women in the Atlantic World

Ken Aslakson

In the spring of 1791, a few months before thousands of enslaved Africans rose up in rebellion on the northern plains of St. Domingue, Melanie Chalon was born free in the small town of Miraguane, on the southern coast of the French colony.[1] Chalon was of mixed African and European ancestry: her black mother was the mistress and former slave of her white father, Victoire Chalon.[2] After Melanie's mother died in 1793, Victoire entrusted his infant daughter to a wealthy merchant named Jean Baptiste Carvin. But the person truly responsible for Melanie's care was Carvin's housekeeper, a white woman named Claire Lafitte Drouin. Sometime in the mid-1790s Carvin fled the rebellion in St. Domingue for Charleston, South Carolina, taking Drouin and young Chalon with him. Because Carvin's business took him away from his Charleston home for long stretches of time, Melanie was almost entirely dependent on Drouin.

Within a few years after arriving in Charleston, Drouin ran away to New Orleans, Louisiana, taking Chalon, not yet a teenager, with her. Once in New Orleans, Chalon's already tumultuous life took a turn for the worse. In her early teens she became pregnant and had a child whom she named Celestin. The identity of Celestin's father remains unclear, and the circumstances surrounding Chalon's pregnancy lead to the inference that Drouin may have been exploiting the girl as sexual labor. When Chalone became pregnant, Drouin began to claim that the girl was her slave, and after Celestin was born Drouin had the child baptized as a slave.

Melanie Chalon's childhood experience epitomizes the cultural mélange, political chaos, and social conflict of the Atlantic World in the Age of Revolution. She was of mixed African and European descent and had lived through the initial stages of what would become the Haitian Revolution, the only successful slave rebellion in the history of the Americas. Before her eighteenth birthday, Melanie had experienced freedom, slavery, and then freedom again. Her early childhood also illustrates the difficulties of being a woman in the eighteenth-century Atlantic World. Women of color were much more likely than men of color to be illegally enslaved during these chaotic times, and men were not subject to sexual exploitation. Finally, Chalon's story shows the interconnectedness of the various Atlantic World slave societies despite their cultural and political differences. The Atlantic Ocean was well traveled in the eighteenth century. In less than a decade, Chalon had lived in three different regions of Atlantic World, the Caribbean, the South Carolina Low Country, and the Lower Mississippi Valley.

Slavery was the common socio-economic bond of all Atlantic World societies; and patriarchal and racist ideologies helped to explain and support their social hierarchies. Yet the interplay of gender and race played out differently in different contexts. This chapter examines how constructions of gender and race shaped both the demographics of migration to the New World and the organization of Atlantic World societies. It also explores the diverse experiences of women in the Atlantic World during the Age of Revolution. White women, enslaved women, and free women of color occupied different stations within the social hierarchies, but their relative positions varied from region to region. In these hierarchies, most black women were enslaved, all black women were subordinated to whites, and all women were subservient to white men. Nevertheless, women in each of these groups found some maneuverability within the socio-economic and cultural structures that bound their lives.

Gender, Race, and the Politics of History

The focus on women in history (or "her-story" as some scholars have called it) is intimately linked with feminism. As the play on the word "history" implies, the point of "her-story" is to tell the story of people who have been traditionally ignored in the writing of history (women) and hence to give value to their historical experiences. The writing of "her-story" has several uses. It demonstrates that women, too, participated in history. For example, women played a large role in most moral reform movements in Western societies. It also serves as a departure from the traditional narrative of history. A focus on women, for instance, re-directs historians away from political, military, and diplomatic history toward social and cultural history. Finally, "her-story" challenges traditional notions of progress in history by demonstrating that women were often the victims of "progress" rather than its beneficiaries. Many studies have demonstrated, for example, how technological innovations have contributed to the further subjugation of women. Ultimately, "her-story" emphasizes the agency of women by demonstrating that, despite their subjugation and oppression throughout history, women have been able to exercise a remarkable amount of control over their lives and influence the world around them.

Nevertheless, "her-story," as well as most feminist scholarship in the liberal arts fields, becomes problematic when it grapples with issues of race and deals with relations between the sexes outside the West. In pursuit of the goal of exposing the oppression of women in its many different forms, Western feminist scholars studying non-Western parts of the world have tended to focus on the various forms of female subjugation there that, for the most part, do not exist in the West, such as polygamy, foot binding, and the wearing of the veil. Much of the feminist scholarship in the West, therefore, carries with it assumptions about the normalcy of Western culture.

Beginning in the late 1980s, however, some African scholars began to criticize the assumptions of Western feminism, arguing that the criteria upon which African societies are measured with regard to their treatment of women are racist and ethnocentric. According to these scholars, patriarchy is a Western-imposed construct that does not accurately reflect the relations between the sexes in Africa. Western scholars, these Africanists argue, focus on the unfamiliar forms of subjugation but fail to recognize the opportunities for women in African societies. In the Igbo culture of Nigeria, for example, women traditionally have had more social mobility than women in the West. African women historically have played a greater role in politics and the economy, and African societies tend to have more flexible gender systems than in the West. In the end, the African rebuttal claims, race must be given priority over class and feminist issues to counter the effect of racism in gender studies.

Rather than giving priority to race over gender (or vice versa), however, scholars should attempt to see how these two cultural constructs work together to create and perpetuate or re-organize social hierarchies. Feminist historians must move beyond "her-story" and make gender a category of analysis. In the words of one well-known historian of gender, "feminist history then becomes not the recounting of great deeds performed by women but the exposure of the often silent and hidden operations of gender that are nonetheless present and defining forces in the organization of most societies."[3] Gender is especially useful in the study of race and slavery. Both race and gender were "present and defining forces" in the making of Atlantic World slave societies. Operating together in different contexts, they helped to shape the experiences of women.

Gender, Race, and the Demographics of Early Migration to the Americas

Different European and African constructions of gender and race combined to profoundly shape the different demographics of European immigration and the transatlantic slave trade. If patriarchy is defined as a social organization in which males hold the power, then, to be sure, societies in both Europe and Africa tended to be patriarchal. Gender constructions on both continents facilitated males' control (to a limited degree) over females. However, they affected different aspects of women's lives. In Africa, the man controlled the woman's reproductive function, and hence her sexuality, while in Europe he controlled her productive function, or her labor.[4] These different gender ideologies had a profound impact on the demographics of early migration to the Americas. Women composed a much higher percentage of forced migrants from Africa than of immigrants from Europe.

In early modern Europe, women had limited occupational opportunities. They worked in light agricultural labor, produced goods for consumption in the household, and occasionally worked outside the household for pay. However, the heaviest labor and the skilled trades were reserved for men. While many scholars link the exclusion of women from the trades with the Industrial Revolution, apprenticeship records show that there were very few female coopers, weavers, blacksmiths, or other artisans in any period in Europe. When women did work in traditionally male occupations, their pay was typically three-fifths that of men. Although European women were just as physically capable as men to perform all but a few of the same tasks, they were precluded from performing these tasks by gender constructions about what was and was not "women's work." To be sure, women had ambivalent attitudes about these cultural limitations since hazardous and even life-threatening occupations, such as mining and soldiering, were among the jobs precluded to women.

Opportunities for European women appear to have been much greater in the reproductive than in the economic zone of gender relations. Early modern Western European marriage patterns were exceptional in relation to the rest of the world. Compared to women in Asia and Africa, Western European women married late, they had considerable choice over when they would marry, and a large proportion of them never married at all. Their reproductive practices were also exceptional. Western European women waited longer in life to give birth to their first child and had fewer children overall. Furthermore, while a double standard for sexual morality did exist in Europe, the discrepancy was not nearly as great as it was in the rest of the world. According to the letter of the law, husband and wife in Europe each owned the sexual property of the other.

While data with regard to Africa are rare and difficult to come by, the evidence that exists leads to the conclusion that women in eighteenth-century Africa performed a much wider variety of economic tasks than women in early modern Europe.[5] Female labor was (and still is) general in Africa. There were few communities where women were exempt from heavy physical tasks. African women were sailors, soldiers, and even slave traders, occupations that were virtually unthinkable for European women. African women utilized a wider range of skills and played a much greater role in economic decision making than anywhere in early modern Europe.

In the reproductive sphere, however, African gender constructions placed severe limitations on women. The most obvious example of the African man's control over the reproductive capacity of the African woman is the common practice of polygyny. Most African societies placed (and still place) great emphasis on the acquisition of new members to a kinship network, and polygyny was a fast way to accomplish this. However, just as there were positives for European women in the occupational limitations created by European gender constructions, the practice of polygyny had an upside for African women. Polygyny meant that work could be shared among many wives, lessening the workload for each individual wife.

Different gender constructions on the two continents help explain the different demographics of European and African migration to the New World. Since most European immigrants initially came across the Atlantic as indentured servants, convicts, or soldiers, early European migration to the New World was overwhelmingly male. There were no women at all on Columbus's first three voyages, and throughout the sixteenth century women made up less than 10 percent of Spanish emigrants. In the seventeenth and eighteenth centuries, moreover, more than eight of every ten immigrants from England, Ireland, and France to the Caribbean were men. In almost every New World colony the sex ratios of early European immigration were close to the same. The sex ratio of European immigrants to the Americas approached the natural ratio only in those colonies that were settled for religious rather than economic reasons, such as New England. Despite high demand for labor in the Americas, and corresponding high wages, women did not (or could not) take advantage of this opportunity. There were no more female artisans in the Americas than there were in Europe.

While early European immigrants to the New World were overwhelmingly male, the forced migrants from Africa were much more demographically representative of the societies they left behind. Just over six out of ten African slaves arriving in the Americas were men, despite evidence that European planters and slave traders would have preferred a much higher male to female ratio. Thinking that men made better workers, the Royal African Company of Great Britain ordered its traders to obtain at least two males for every one female. But they were rarely able to achieve these ratios because slave traders in Africa, where women had a central productive role, offered a similar ratio of males to females. Though Europeans did not view labor on sugar plantations as the work of women (even African women), they were willing to bend their attitudes in the face of the supply offered by the African traders. In the arena of the slave trade, European racism proved stronger than male chauvinism.

Gender, Race, and Women in the Atlantic World

Just as gender and race shaped the demographics of migration to the New World, they also played a large role in the organization of the developing slave societies of the Atlantic World. Women of European, African, and mixed ancestry occupied different positions within the social hierarchies of these societies, but they were all subordinate to white men. Despite this cultural and social subordination, however, women could, and did, make choices affecting their lives. Claire Lafitte Drouin, for example, had been subject to the control of Jean Baptiste Carvin in St. Domingue and Charleston, but she took charge of her life by running away to New Orleans. Unfortunately for Melanie Chalon, Drouin also took charge of her. But fortunately for Chalon, the New Orleans court system provided her with the opportunity to escape Drouin's control. The rest of this chapter examines the lives of white women, enslaved women of African descent, and free women of color, respectively, in the Atlantic World. Dealing with both the myths of race and gender as well as actual social relations between the different sexes and races, it discusses the cultural constructions bounding the lives of women as well as the opportunities for maneuverability within these boundaries.

White Women

Of all three groups, women of European ancestry were the most advantaged legally, culturally, and socially. They couldn't be enslaved (because of their skin color they could not suffer the same fate as Melanie Chalon), and they were the only group of women who could marry white men, which provided opportunities for upward social mobility. Nevertheless, European gender ideologies held that women were physically and mentally weaker then men. Thus, even white European women in the New World were legally, politically, and socially subordinated to men. They could not enter the professions or the skilled trades; nor could they hold public office, take part in government, or vote.

Moreover, European cultural myths held that women tended to be more emotional and nurturing than men. Thus European men valued women for their mothering instincts and contributions to the family rather than their labor and contributions to the polity. As a result, European and Euro-American laws and customs deprived women of economic opportunities, legal standing, and political power. Married white women were under the authority of their husbands, while unmarried white women remained under the authority of their fathers. Furthermore, the property of a woman became that of her husband upon marriage (although there were legal mechanisms for regaining property upon legal separation).

Some white women were in better circumstances than others, however, as class differences went a long way in determining quality of life. As an unmarried housekeeper in the Caribbean, Claire Lafitte Drouin was at the bottom rung of the white social ladder. More than likely, Drouin came to the New World as one of the relatively few female indentured servants, as in this instance economic necessity modified cultural norms. Prior to the rise of African slavery, most female indentured servants, like most male indentured servants, worked in the fields. The willingness of white women to work in the fields, and of men to allow them to do so, varied depending of the type of crop and the climate. Tobacco was less labor intensive than most New World staple crops. Therefore, planters in the Chesapeake, where tobacco was grown, were less reluctant to contract with white women to work in the fields. The sugar islands of the Caribbean, however, where working conditions were generally the harshest, had a lower percentage of female indentured servants, and those white women who did work in agricultural labor in the Caribbean were spared the most difficult tasks. By the late eighteenth century, after slavery had become entrenched in most of the sugar islands, female indentured servants most often worked as domestic servants. No doubt Drouin was stigmatized for being single, yet her role as Melanie Chalon's caregiver fit within European and Euro-American understandings of the "natural" role of a woman.

The personal lives of indentured servants in all periods were restricted in many ways. Planters discouraged the formation of family and emotional ties among indentured servants because they thought this would prevent them from being good laborers. Some colonies passed laws preventing indentured servants from getting married. In Barbados, men who married indentured women had to buy the women out of servitude at twice the market value, and men who got indentured women pregnant had to supply the owner with a replacement.

After completing their period of service, most female servants continued to do the same sort of work they did as indentured servants. Those few who worked in the fields, however, tried to move into the towns to work for wages in taverns and inns or in other areas of the urban service sector. Some, like Drouin, became housekeepers for wealthy men. Drouin was probably not an indentured servant by the time she ran away from Carvin's Charles Town home, but her everyday life had changed very little. Working-class white women also worked as teachers, traders, midwives, and governesses. Some white women ran boarding houses, though, in the Caribbean at least, this business venture became increasingly dominated by free women of color. Some boarding house operators had female slaves that they hired out as prostitutes. These female brothel owners made a practice of selling the children of their enslaved prostitutes once they were weaned. Certainly Drouin was aware of the Caribbean practices. Perhaps she ran way from her job as Carvin's housekeeper to pursue a more lucrative career as a "madam." Melanie Chalon's mysterious pregnancy and Drouin's attempts to sell Celestin lend credence to this speculation.

As Atlantic World societies matured, the reality of white working-class women existed in increasing tension with the ideal of a white woman in a slave society. White women were supposed to be wives and mistresses of the household. In *Good Wives, Nasty Wenches, and Anxious Patriarchs*, Kathleen Brown sheds light on this tension by showing how gender and race interacted in conjunction with the rise of racial slavery in colonial Virginia. Gender helped to determine the construction of racial categories while, at the same time, ideas about race were transforming gender relations. Prior to the rise of African slavery the distinction between "good wives" and "nasty wenches" was a class distinction. The latter label was reserved for female indentured servants in Virginia who, for the most part, worked in the tobacco fields. Female indentured servants could not be "good wives" because law forbade them to marry so that their time could be devoted to useful labor. They were "nasty wenches," a term that carried the implication of sexual promiscuity, because there was no way of ensuring that they would not bear children out of wedlock. "'Good wives' and 'nasty wenches' reflected elite English judgments about differences between moral and respectable women—married and domestically employed— and depraved, degenerate women who were barely fit for the manual labor of men."[6] With the rise of African slavery, however, as fewer and fewer white women and more and more enslaved black women worked in the fields, the distinction between "good wives" and "nasty wenches" become a racial distinction. Black women were portrayed as promiscuous, while white women were thought to be naturally monogamous, dependent, weak, and in need of the protection of men.

Marriage was the key avenue to upward mobility for white women in the Atlantic World. Many elite white women achieved their status through marriage to wealthy planters, merchants, or professionals. In general, elite white women lived lives of leisure. Domestic servants or slaves did the housework and other domestic chores and even raised the children, while the mistresses of the household lived off the income produced by slave labor. Elite white women more closely resembled the ideal of the "good wife."

Though most elite European women in the Atlantic World gained their wealth through marriage, some were independently wealthy. Often these women were widows who had inherited their deceased husband's assets. Some of the wealthiest women had been married several different times and accumulated the assets of several different estates. Many white women were slave owners themselves. White female slaveholders tended to own more female slaves than male slaves. Contrary to images of the gentleness and passivity of women, however, white women slaveholders were not significantly kinder to their slaves than white men. Drouin, though by no means elite, certainly did not treat Chalon kindly either before or after she claimed Chalon to be her slave. Slave narratives and traveler's accounts contain numerous stories of cruel slave mistresses. This may have been the only way that some white women knew how to exercise power and control in a society dominated by white men.

Enslaved Women

Though Melanie Chalon was never legally a slave, she certainly lived as one for much of her early childhood. If Drouin did indeed force her to have sex for money, and then appropriate this money on the pretense that she was Melanie's mistress, it is hard to imagine a greater economic exploitation or deprivation of freedom. If not for the courage of Melanie, the benevolence of her attorney, and the sensibility of the New Orleans Parish Court, Melanie and her son could have been slaves the rest of their lives. And this very real possibility could only have happened because some of Melanie's ancestors were from Africa.

In Africa, female slaves were more numerous and more expensive than male slaves. Some historians have argued that women were preferred as slaves in Africa because of their potential for reproduction. Yet Claude Meillassaux and Martin Klein have demonstrated that female slaves in Africa had very few children, and, in fact, did not even ensure simple reproduction of the slave population. According to these historians of Africa, it was the productive, not the reproductive, capacity of the female slave that determined her price. In Africa, enslaved women were valued more highly than male slaves because in African societies women's participation in labor was greater than that of men.

Westerners trading in African slaves, shaped by the Christian image of female fragility, considered the grueling physical labor required of slaves incompatible with the "nature" of women. Since African slave traders, for the most part, determined the supply side of the transatlantic slave trade, however, female slaves constituted a significant percentage of the labor force on New World plantations. Most enslaved women were field workers and were just as likely as enslaved men to be assigned to the most grueling tasks in the plantation system. Most plantations operated under a "gang system" in which there were usually three gangs: the first gang did the heaviest work, and the third gang did the lightest. A higher percentage of enslaved women than enslaved men worked in the first gang.

As European-Americans became accustomed to female Africans working long hours at heavy labor in the fields and being punished with the whip, they came to believe that black women were not subject to the same physical and emotional limitations as white women. The collision of European gender constructions about the impropriety of heavy labor for women with the socioeconomic and demographic reality of the enslavement of black women produced what Michelle Wallace calls the myth of the superwoman. In describing the myth, Wallace writes:

> From the intricate web of mythology which surrounds the black woman, a fundamental image emerges. It is of a woman of inordinate strength, with an ability for tolerating an unusual amount of misery and heavy, distasteful work. This woman does not have the same fears, weaknesses, and insecurities as other women, but believes herself to be and is, in fact, stronger emotionally than most men. Less of a woman in that she is less "feminine" and helpless, she is really more of a woman in that she is the embodiment of Mother Earth, the quintessential mother with infinite sexual, life-giving, and nurturing reserves. In other words, she is a superwoman.[7]

By all accounts, female slaves were just as productive as enslaved men, and their productivity did much to create and perpetuate the superwoman myth.

Some historians have argued that female slaves were particularly suited to be workers in a plantation system because they came from societies in Africa where women, traditionally, were the mainstay of agricultural production. While African women were more accustomed to agricultural labor than European women, no person is, or ever was, particularly well suited for the type of work slaves were forced to do on sugar, cotton, and tobacco plantations. The fact that white slaveholders could subject their slaves to such brutal working conditions shows the extreme power of the profit motive. But the fact that an ideology could support or justify a system in which such brutality took place underscores the prominence of gender and race in the ideological structure of the eighteenth-century Atlantic World. Planters (and indeed almost all of white society) had come to accept the myth of the superwoman.

While the myth of the superwoman served to justify the use of women in grueling field labor, the "mammy" stereotype soothed the planter's conscience by creating an image of the kind, gentle, happy, and content domestic slave. The mammy myth held that the female domestic slave was the caregiver with infinite nurturing reserves and expertise in all household matters. All of the other house servants were her subordinates. Mammy was portrayed as a close and loyal friend of the family, a confidant of the mistress, and a second mother of the children.[8]

Like the myth of the superwoman, the mammy stereotype was only partially based on reality. To be sure, with the exception of the French colonies, the majority of domestic slaves in the Atlantic World were female. In Barbados in the last half of the eighteenth century, 70 percent of all domestics in plantation households were women. These female domestic slaves performed the functions within the plantation household traditionally associated with "women's work." They laundered clothes, sewed, cooked, cleaned, and took care of the children. Relative to field hands, they enjoyed more comforts and had closer relationships with their masters and mistresses. Yet the suggestion that female domestic slaves were "content" and "loyal friends of the family" ignores the special difficulties they faced. Although there were clear material benefits to being a domestic slave, there was also a downside to being so closely supervised by the master and mistress, having their every move scrutinized and subject to criticism. For female domestics (especially young and attractive ones), their proximity to their masters created a risk of sexual abuse.

As much as any other aspect of its culture, attitudes about miscegenation (or sexual relations between blacks and whites) demonstrate the operations of gender and race in the Atlantic World. In the racialized power relationships imbedded in slave societies, white men were in a unique position to sexually exploit their black slaves. There were enough sexual relationships between white men and black women to have produced a significant population of people of mixed ancestry (or mulattoes) early on in the development of the Atlantic World. But miscegenation was never legally or culturally sanctioned. Therefore, a third stereotype developed to explain its existence, that of "Jezebel," the black female seductress with infinite sexual reserves.

The attitudes and behavior of Thomas Jefferson are representative of the central dilemma of miscegenation in slave societies as well as the psycho-sexual transference that helped to produce the Jezebel myth. Jefferson often wrote about the evils of the mixing of the races. Yet, to the dismay of some curators working at Monticello, new DNA evidence proves that Jefferson himself had sexual relations with one of his black slaves, Sally Hemmings. Jefferson was not alone in this hypocrisy. Many slaveholders had sexual desires for their female slaves, and since these slaves were legally their property, the slaveholders were in a unique position to act on these desires whether or not the slave woman was complicit. Though the sexual attraction itself was natural, it could not be condoned in a racially based slave society. Therefore, white men projected their desires onto the objects of their affection and, indeed, onto all black women.

Of course, not all relationships between white men and black female slaves were the result of rape. The laws of the Spanish territories protected female slaves against sexual exploitation by their masters. The Siete Partidas, the laws governing the Spanish colonies, stated that enslaved women could be compulsorily freed if they were sexually abused or used for prostitution by their owners. In the early years of colonization, moreover, the high ratio of European men to European women dictated that some men, at least, would seek lasting relationships with African or African American women. Recently historians have begun to document and study voluntary partnerships between white men and black women in slave societies, and they are numerous. Just as a white woman might have used marriage as a path to upward mobility, some enslaved women may have seen a relationship with a white man as an opportunity to escape the cruelty of slavery.

In the slave societies of the Atlantic World, field slaves worked almost incessantly Monday through Saturday, but in most places they were given Sundays off. With their free time, most slaves celebrated, worshiped, or simply relaxed. However, some slaves used their time off from the fields to work their own plots of land or to produce goods for sale at market. Enslaved women dominated marketing in New World slave societies, a survival of the West African custom that women manage the household economy. Slave women had a great deal of liberty to buy and sell commodities in the market. But the market also had another social aspect, as gossip, as well as goods and money, was exchanged there.

While the participation of enslaved women in the markets was most pronounced in the Caribbean, most Atlantic World societies had their own "black markets." Slaves participated to a great extent in the public markets of Charles Town, South Carolina, in the late eighteenth and early nineteenth centuries, and most of the participants were women. The slaves' participation in the marketplace, however, produced a great deal of anxiety among whites, who saw the market activity as a challenge to white authority. One elite Charles Town resident complained that black women with "large sums of money, purchase quantities of flour, butter, apples, etc . . . , all [of] which they retail out to the inhabitants of Charles Town, by which means leading lazy lives, and free from the government of their masters."[9] Another complained in his local newspaper that

> Women have such a connection with and influence on, the country Negroes who come to market, that they generally find means to obtain whatever they may chuse,

> in preference to any white person; . . . I have seen the country Negroes take great pains, after having been first spoke to by those women to reserve whatever they chose to sell to them only, either by keeping the particular articles in their canuws, or by sending them away and pretending they were not for sale; and when they could not be easily retained by themselves, then I have seen the wenches so briskly hustle them about from one to another that in two minutes they could no longer be traced.[10]

Whites, therefore, felt that slave participation in the market undermined their authority because it produced slaves with money and facilitated potentially dangerous contacts with plantation slaves. Nevertheless, the fact that the market traders were female slaves (as opposed to male slaves) mitigated against the perceived threat to white authority. According to historian Robert Olwell, "as long as the actions of slave marketers could be read as a female challenge to male authority, rather than as a challenge by blacks or slaves to the authority of whites or masters, they could be fit into [the] tradition of 'unruly women' and contained within the parameters of what constituted acceptable manifestations of social conflict. To some degree, therefore, the female market slaves may have been 'hiding behind their sex' in their defiance of laws and statutes."[11]

Although whites may have been less fearful of female than male slaves, historians have shown that enslaved women were just as rebellious as enslaved men; they just resorted to different tactics. Certainly, female slaves, who were generally subject to the same grueling working conditions and cruel punishment as male slaves, had plenty of incentive to resist slavery. Resistance to slavery can be categorized into three different types: running away, violent resistance, and day-to-day resistance. Women resisted slavery as much as men and participated in all three types. But statistics show that women were less likely to run away or to resort to violence. Perhaps women did not run away as much as enslaved men because they had closer ties to their own children. Historians have recently argued, however, that enslaved women facilitated conspiracies and escapes by providing the meeting places for the planning stages of these events because masters and authorities were less suspicious of women than men. In the end, slavery itself provided enough incentive for resistance to it.

Free Women of Color

When Melanie Chalon was born in 1791 she became one of over 28,000 free people of African descent in St. Domingue, a colony with a total population of just over 400,000. Every slave society in the Atlantic World had some free blacks. In terms of percentages, St. Domingue was average in this category. The Spanish colonies tended to have the highest percentages of free blacks. In 1827, for example, free blacks made up 20 percent of Cuba's population. The English colony of Barbados, on the other hand, never had a large number of free blacks, with only 2,000, or less than 1 percent of the total population, at the end of the eighteenth century. In most Atlantic World societies free women of color outnumbered free men of color. Barbados, again, seems to be the exception. By 1830, Barbados, unlike any other British-colonized territory, had more free black men than free black women. As the slave societies matured, the number of free people of color rose, primarily due to natural increase, and free blacks began to develop a collective identity distinct from enslaved blacks.

When contemporaries described someone as a "person of color" they meant that the person was of mixed European and African ancestry, or a "mulatto." Indeed, by the end of the eighteenth century, most free blacks in Atlantic World slave societies were, like Melanie, of mixed ancestry. The distinction between free Negroes and free mulattoes was more significant in some areas of the Atlantic World than in others. While British North America was a bi-racial society, the Caribbean slave societies tended to be tri-racial.[12] The Spanish colonies had an elaborate system of racial categorization based on the perceived degree of European and African blood: octoroons were said to be one-eighth African; quadroons, one-fourth; mulattoes, one-half; and griffes, three-fourths. But such attempts to identify the exact degree of African blood were never completely successful. It was sometimes difficult to trace a person's ancestry, and skin color can reveal only so much in this regard. Moreover, perceptions of a person's ancestry were shaped by factors other than their complexion, such as behavior, dress, education, and, most importantly, status as enslaved or free. Since planters justified slavery with the claim that it was the natural condition of blacks, freedom tended to whiten.

Free people of African descent or their ancestors obtained their freedom in a variety of ways. Sometimes slaves, their friends, or their relatives purchased their freedom. Under the Spanish practice of *coartacion*, masters in Spanish colonial possessions were required to sell their slaves their freedom at an agreed upon or administratively determined market value. Some masters granted freedom to their slaves without any monetary compensation. Masters "gratuitously" freed their slaves for any number of reasons: as a reward for good service, as repayment for a heroic deed, as a way of soothing the master's conscience, or as part of a religious conversion, to give just a few examples. Masters also commonly granted freedom to slaves who were their own children by a slave mother, which helps to explain why so many free blacks were of mixed ancestry.

Although free people of color were not slaves, they were not entirely free, at least not as free as white people. In all Atlantic World societies, free people of color faced many restrictions. These restrictions were designed to keep them from achieving the same status as whites in the highly racialized societies of the Atlantic World. Restrictions on free blacks existed in all slave societies but varied in severity a great deal across culture and region. Ira Berlin refers to free blacks in the antebellum United States as "slaves without masters" in a book by the same title, because their lives were so severely limited. In these societies, free blacks were not allowed to vote or hold public office; they could not testify in court except against other blacks and could never serve on juries; they could not join the professions or the skilled trades; and they were subject to curfews and limitations on their mobility.

In other societies, however, free blacks enjoyed many more privileges. In St. Domingue, where Melanie Chalon was born, the distinction between free and enslaved blacks was vigorously enforced. Free blacks were called *gens de couleur*, and as in many West Indian societies, they served as a middle caste that whites saw as a buffer between themselves and enslaved blacks. In New Orleans, too, free blacks retained many of the privileges of whites. They could work in the skilled trades, own real property, serve in the militia, and even testify in court against whites. Suffice to say that Melanie might not have won her lawsuit had she brought it in Charles Town rather than New Orleans.

Most free women of color had the same types of occupations that working-class white women had. They were domestic laborers or worked in the urban service sector. Others, especially in the Caribbean, used their knowledge of medicinal herbs and made their living as herbal practitioners, nurses, or doctresses. In the Caribbean and New Orleans, free women of color held a virtual monopoly on the boarding house business. A few free black women made enough money in their occupations or married well enough to become slaveholders and even plantation owners themselves.

Throughout the Atlantic World significant numbers of free women of color had intimate relationships with white men, and a great deal has been written about these relationships, though most of it tends to simplify their meaning. Since laws prohibited whites and blacks from getting married, every interracial relationship was illicit, but in some parts of the Atlantic World they were promoted and institutionalized nonetheless. New Orleans and parts of the Caribbean, for example, were home to the "quadroon balls," to which free women of color and white men were invited while black men and white women were excluded. Historians interpreting these events have taken opposing views as to their significance and character. Some claim that the gatherings were disreputable and violent assemblies that deserved nothing more than the proper title of interracial orgies. Others argue that they were respectable affairs at which refined women of color exhibited social graces and charms that won the favor of white gentlemen. To be sure, some free black women lived in lasting relationships with white men. One Captain Cornishe, from Jamaica, was said to have kept a "genteel mulatto girl." A Matthew Gregory Lewis wrote that the Coloured "wife" of his attorney was faithful and an example of the decent manner in which these women conducted their relationships. Finally, Thomas Thistlewood believed that the majority of white men were faithful even to death to their Coloured mistresses. The evidence suggests that the social dynamic of relationships between white men and free women of color was something more complex than either of these interpretations. Of course, the concubinage of free women of color was grossly exploitative, but it also provided women of color a means of social and economic advancement that was otherwise unavailable.

Conclusion

The story of Claire Lafitte Drouin and Melanie Chalon presented at the beginning of this chapter illustrates how gender and race created boundaries that shaped the experiences of women. Yet the lives of these women also demonstrate that despite these cultural limitations, women retained some ability to take charge of their lives. Further, the extent to which and the way a woman could exercise her choices depended on her race and socio-economic position as well as her geographic location within the Atlantic World.

As an unmarried white woman in the Caribbean, Drouin had very few opportunities for economic advancement. According to European gender constructions, white women were supposed to be "good wives," and those that never married most often worked, like Drouin, as domestic servants. Yet Drouin recognized opportunities, as well as limitations, within the gendered and racial boundaries of the Atlantic World. Hence she ran away to New Orleans, a slave society in which she was an unknown newcomer, claimed that Melanie Chalon, a woman of African ancestry, was her slave, and attempted to create a new identity for herself as a madam.

Unfortunately for Chalon, she was the victim of Drouin's attempts at economic advancement. Free people of color, especially free women of color, like Chalon, lived precarious lives in that they always faced the possibility of being illegally enslaved, a possibility that did not exist for whites. But Chalon did not accept this fate that was apparently thrust upon her. She took advantage of a legal system in New Orleans that was much more receptive than Charles Town of freedom suits by people of African descent who claimed to be illegally held as slaves. Chalon pursued her claim in the New Orleans city court and won back her freedom.

Cultural constructions of gender and race, therefore, played an important role in the demographic and social makeup of the Atlantic World, but they did not determine the lives of individuals. Women such as Drouin, Chalon, and the enslaved women in the fields, households, and markets were severely confined within the socio-economic and ideological structures bounding their lives. But they were not powerless. They acted even as they were acted upon, and they impacted the shaping of the Atlantic World.

Notes

1. This rebellion became the Haitian Revolution.

2. For the purposes of this discussion, a "black person" and a "person of color" both refer to a person who is of at least partial, though not necessarily total, African ancestry.

3. Joan Wallach Scott, *Gender and the Politics of History* (New York: Columbia University Press, 1988), 27.

4. Of course, these are broad generalizations. Production and reproduction are re-

lated functions. And men controlled the reproductive function of women in Europe, just to a lesser degree.

5. On both continents, most labor was performed within the household.

6. Kathleen M. Brown, *Good Wives, Nasty Wenches, and Anxious Patriarchs: Gender, Race, and Power in Colonial Virginia* (Chapel Hill: University of North Carolina Press, 1996), 104.

7. Michelle Wallace, *Black Macho and the Myth of the Superwoman* (New York: Dial, 1979), 107.

8. The mammy image survived well into the twentieth century. In addition to being a key figure in the classic movie *Gone with the Wind*, she showed up on everyday consumer goods such as pancake boxes and syrup bottles.

9. "Petition of Sundry Inhabitants of Charles Town," JCHA, February 5, 1747, 154–155, as quoted in Robert Olwell, *Masters, Slaves and Subjects: The Culture of Power in the South Carolina Low Country, 1740–1790* (Ithaca: Cornell University Press, 1998), 171.

10. *South Carolina Gazette*, September 24, 1772, quoted in Olwell, *Masters, Slaves and Subjects*, 172.

11. Olwell, *Masters, Slaves and Subjects*, 176.

12. This chapter assumes that race is a cultural, rather than a biological, category. Most of the antebellum United States South followed a "one-drop" rule, by which all persons deemed to have any "African blood" in them were considered to be "black." Other slave societies, especially in the Caribbean and Brazil, however, held mulattoes, or people of mixed African and European ancestry, to be in a different racial category from Negroes, or people perceived to be entirely of African descent.

CHAPTER EIGHT

The Black Atlantic: Theory, Method, and Practice

Douglas B. Chambers

In 1816, a runaway enslaved Jamaican woman named Bessy turned herself into the St. George Workhouse, claiming that she had no owner. When interrogated by the workhouse supervisor, Bessy also claimed that she was "an Eboe." Later it was determined that Bessy had not been born in Africa but was in fact born on the slave ship during the Middle Passage. When she was listed in the local newspaper, nearly a decade after the British abolition of the transatlantic slave trade, the supervisor noted that Bessy "formerly said she was an Eboe, but [was] now found out to be a salt-water creole." Though her age was not given, Bessy likely was an adult as she had at some point in the past been branded (*WB*) on her left shoulder, presumably in Jamaica. She also claimed that she did not know her master's name.[1]

That this desperate woman had reached back beyond the Atlantic to an imagined part of Africa to "identify" herself, even though she had been born on the Crossing (or shortly afterward), is remarkable. It is especially so as she could not (or would not) name her master, and, that she claimed to be Eboe perhaps two decades after she had been born in the African Diaspora, and indeed nearly a decade after the slave trade to Jamaica had ended.

Perhaps despite (or perhaps because of) being "masterless" she seemingly sought to identify with a particular kind of African in Jamaica, and certainly she did not seek to identify with those born on the island. But if she sought solidarity with other slaves on the basis of being "Eboe," which seems plausible given the "prismatic" nature of slave society in Jamaica,[2] and perhaps as a liminal person (not Igbo/Eboan and not exactly Creole), indirect evidence on fugitive slaves suggests that she would have found enough other "Eboe" in such workhouses, including St. George, to do so.[3] In any case, her diasporic claim to a particular

African-derived consociation (or fellowship, or nationality) in her particular historical circumstance is a "clue" to a new history of the African Diaspora, one that embraces both sides of the Black Atlantic in newfound specificity (in this case of Igboland in Nigeria and Jamaica in the West Indies). As such, and as with so much else in recent research on the African Diaspora, this micro-event can be taken as a sign of "a larger, but hidden or unknown, structure."[4] Increasingly, that structure is being conceptualized as the Black Atlantic.

A Theoretics of the Black Atlantic

It is now possible to think through the current "conceptual impasse"[5] in the historiography of the African Diaspora by outlining a working theory of the Black Atlantic as an historical phenomenon, and to do so from an Africanist perspective. Since the 1990s historians have been rediscovering the agency of particular groups of Africans in the Atlantic World as part of a larger critique of anthropological creolization. To distinguish this new body of work, scholars increasingly talk about the "Black Atlantic."[6] We have now reached a point where one can recount the historiographical construction of the Black Atlantic and to synthesize these disparate approaches into a conceptual statement of theory, method, and practice in writing the subject.

This chapter introduces a theoretics designed to distinguish the Black Atlantic from the African Diaspora. I do so by exploring a series of contrasts in basic assumptions about the forced migrations of Africans in the era of the slave trade and historical consequences for the cultural and social development of slave societies in the Americas. These contrasts include heterogeneity (Black Atlantic) versus homogenization (African Diaspora); transnational (or circum-Atlantic) versus North American-centric (or simply comparative); agency as bounded rationality versus agency as resistance; Africa as generative versus Africa as background (that is, creolization as Africanization rather than as Americanization); and punctuated equilibria (contingency) versus a tendency toward presentism. The chapter argues for the utility of distinguishing between the vast majority of Atlantic Africans (and initial neo-African diasporic ethnogenesis) and the relatively obscure Atlantic Creoles (early cosmopolitan intercultural brokering),[7] and for understanding creolization itself as a historical, multi-generational process.

Making the African Diaspora

The modern concept of the African Diaspora developed in the 1950s–1970s in large part by a new generation of African American scholars in concert with a romanticized and politicized pan-Africanism and Black Nationalism, themselves reflections of the civil rights era in the United States. The original and clearly generative concept was explicitly comparativist, emphasizing change over space and time. In perhaps the most succinct definition of the subject, Joseph Harris wrote:

> The African diaspora embodies the following: the voluntary and forced dispersion of Africans at different periods in history and in several directions; the emergence of a cultural identity abroad without losing the African base, either spiritually or physically; the psychological or physical return to the homeland, Africa. Thus viewed, the African diaspora assumes the character of a dynamic, ongoing and complex phenomenon stretching across time and geography.[8]

The foundational thinkers of the modern African Diaspora concept were also explicitly contributionist (in seeking to recover an anti-racist useable past). Scholars such as Elliott Skinner, George Shepperson, St. Clair Drake, and, of course, Joseph Harris argued specifically against the older racist metaphor of black inferiority and historical invisibility, and they tied their understandings to not only anti-racist but also anti-colonial struggle movements, especially Pan-Africanism and Black Nationalism. And they self-consciously built on earlier generations of "Negro" activist-scholars such as Edward Blyden, W. E. B. Du Bois, and C. L. R. James, and, of course, others (who were equally anti-racist, anti-colonial, and pro-contributionist), most notably Melville Herskovits.[9]

In the 1970s a third component of mature African Diaspora theory—creolization—refocused efforts on social or cultural history squarely in the Americas. As scholars incorporated the arguments of Kamau Brathwaite and of Sidney Mintz and Richard Price on the essential "newness" of New World black societies, African Diaspora studies became increasingly creolist. The prime concern became explaining how discontinuity from Africa, and the imperative of cultural creativity among diasporic populations in their resistance against white hegemony in the crucible of slavery, created basically sui generis societies throughout the Americas. Though Brathwaite's creolism had more room for African influences, in both particular and generic senses, and indeed Mintz and Price recognized the historical importance of deep or structural (or vague) African principles in diasporic cultural systems, the creolist position was based fundamentally on discontinuity. The three key creolist assumptions were (1) that the slave trade was largely random, (2) that populations of enslaved African arrivants constituted crowds of cultural strangers, and (3) that out of their extremity the mutual strangers forged, rather quickly, basically ad hoc social and cultural arrangements, which then sustained them.[10] An added assumption is that once in place, these Creole societies persisted as folk or peasant or traditional societies into the present and thus can be studied ethnographically as well as historically.[11] An intellectual logjam broke, and a flood of remarkable and brilliant studies resulted.

The success of (anthropological) creolization in redirecting African Diaspora studies by the 1980s also rendered rather old-fashioned work which had flowed from the original comparativist and contributionist wellsprings. For creolists, Africanisms became largely anathema.[12]

One sign of the creakiness of the classic diaspora concept was the appearance in the late 1980s and early 1990s of critical "intellectual archaeologies" of the concepts of Africa, of Pan-Africanism, and of racial ideology in Black Nationalism, particularly by African-born scholars.[13] For V. Y. Mudimbe, Europeans (and the West) constructed Africa as an index of difference, as the Other, in a continuing discourse of prejudice made opaque by the apparent triumph of cultural relativism. Even (or especially) Melville Herskovits's anthropology of cultural relativism was re-cast as rooted in an epistemology of totalizing or essentializing Africa and Africans, dependent on definitions of collective "types" rather than understandings of individual consciousnesses.[14] Kwame Anthony Appiah interrogated the degree to which the idea of Africa and especially Pan-Africanism and Black Nationalism all were grounded in a racialist discourse and, in rejecting such racialized thought, how one might re-think what it meant and means to be "African" in the first place.

The anthropological bases of African Diaspora studies, and clearly anthropology had provided the foundational vocabulary for the basic meta-narrative of culture change, and its fusion of contributionist and creolist discourses had, by ca. 1990, made it possible to equate *both* the Herskovits and Mintz/Price works and to criticize them for the same supposed error (as in David Scott);[15] that is, the contestation of a "lack" of history by trying to write "what really happened" in the diaspora. In effect, Scott argued for the rejection of the anthropological, contributionist, and creolist pillars of diaspora theory, all at the same time, arguing further against the construction of useable pasts for a discourse of memory and tradition rather than of history. At roughly the same time, there was a growing recognition that the pan-Africanist project itself had broken down, that cultural and political distance between black Americans and Africans had increased since the 1960s, the appellation of "African American" notwithstanding. Following Appiah's lead, Tunde Adeleke saw an essential racism in the whole project to "redeem" Africa.[16] Adeleke's evocation of the many-sided divide in the contemporary diaspora, that is, the deep sense of separation between Africans and African Americans in the U.S., including in academia, underscored not just the need to "revive" Pan-Africanism as a cultural-nationalist project but the failure of [small-p] pan-Africanism in classic African Diaspora discourse.[17]

By the early 1990s the comparativist, contributionist, and pan-Africanist pillars of African Diaspora theory were clearly showing signs of age; in the 1990s the creolist pillar would come under sustained reevaluation, and indeed devastating refutation.

Constructing the Black Atlantic

The re-publication in 1992 of Mintz and Price's *The Birth of African-American Culture* (originally published in 1976) ironically marked the beginning of the demise of the anthropological (or classical) creolization theory of the African

Diaspora. The publication in the same year of John Thornton's *Africa and Africans in the Making of the Atlantic World* and Gwendolyn Midlo Hall's monograph on Africans in colonial Louisiana, all on the heels of David Scott's critique of the general effort to recover *what really happened*, opened what turned out over the following decade to be a systematic interrogation of the key concepts of creolization theory, itself a hegemonic discourse in the study of the African Diaspora for the previous generation of scholars.[18]

This intervention came in the middle of a general series of "Atlantic turns" in early modern historiography and in concert with a more proximate "cultural turn" in the 1990s. By the end of the decade, new research tools such as Eltis et al.'s CD-ROM database on the entirety of the transatlantic slave trade and Gwendolyn Midlo Hall's on slaves in Louisiana, among others, further pushed this new tendency to integrate particular African and American histories in systemic (transnational) Atlantic contexts.[19]

The Black Atlantic has been brought into focus in the past decade or so through the convergence of two major trends in the historiography of the early modern Western world. One, rooted in the 1980s, was a generalized "Atlantic turn," in which historians of the colonial Americas (and of the relevant metropolitan European merchant-empires and later of Atlantic Africa and African America) have been responding to an increasingly globalized world by rescaling their research efforts to encompass large segments of, or indeed the entirety of, the Atlantic basin in ambitious transnational studies. This generalized "Atlantic turn" has produced a large and impressive body of scholarship. In the initial stage, however, much of it was also essentially "white."[20] Even major exploratory works from the latter 1980s which had centered Africa and Africans in an Atlantic context were, by the mid-1990s, subject to criticism as being essentially Eurocentric.[21]

A corresponding (or perhaps compensatory) "Atlantic turn" among pre-colonial Africanists also gained coherence in the 1990s. A renewed interest in the transatlantic slave trade, both on the continent and in the diaspora, reopened the "numbers game" (which had seemed to be settled a generation after publication of Philip D. Curtin's *Census* in 1969), and which was pushed in part by a systematic effort to document the Atlantic slave trade through extant shipping records.[22] This secondary "Atlantic turn" extended to a new appreciation of the manifold effects of the slave trade on continental African societies, but perhaps even more so turned the attention of Africanists to the diaspora.[23] A number of key scholars in the current development of the Black Atlantic as an emerging field of study are Africanist-trained historians.[24]

Likewise there has been a concerted "Atlantic turn" among African Americanists (broadly considered). In the past fifteen years scholars increasingly have turned their attention to the several centuries before ca. 1800–1820, or the era of the transatlantic slave trade, a return to the colonial period, when diasporic Africans inhabited the social and cultural landscape, and to transnational studies of slavery and slave societies.[25] By ca. 2000 the several Atlantic turns, of colonial Americanists and early modern Europeanists, of Africanists (increasingly scholars of Atlantic Africa), and of black people in the Americas, were so complete that one could write, as David Armitage did (albeit in the context of the British Atlantic but *à propos* a wide range of disciplines), that "we are all Atlanticists now."[26]

Furthermore, Atlantic studies since the mid-1990s have often put slavery at the fore of systemic analysis. As Rebecca Scott wrote, regarding David Brion Davis's call in 2000 for studying slavery in broader perspective, "Atlantic Studies has indeed emerged as an organizing principle under which multiple phenomena within and outside metropoles and colonies can be linked, often with slavery at the core."[27]

These several Atlantic turns coincided with a second prevalent trend: a generalized "cultural turn" in the 1990s. As one prominent intellectual historian wrote recently, "in the 1990s, everyone appeared to become a cultural historian."[28] By 1999, even the economic historian par excellence David Eltis was moved to write, "To make sense of Atlantic history we still have to break out of the materialist paradigm and focus on the cultural, not the economic, or, to put it another way, to make sense of the economic, scholars should re-examine cultural patterns."[29] As such, questions of identity, agency, and what Bernard Bailyn long ago termed "the description of internal states of mind and their relation to external circumstances and events" are newly burning ones.[30] And for the Black Atlantic world, increasingly this "cultural turn" means centering Africans in the development of slavery, slave culture, and plantation societies. As John Thornton long ago argued, African slaves may have been marginal to the formation of political and print-based intellectual life in the Atlantic world, but they were central to economic, cultural, and social development, especially before ca.1800.[31]

A first basic fact is that between ca.1580 and 1820, some 8.7 million Africans versus 3 million Europeans crossed the Atlantic to the New World, and like those from Europe, African arrivants came in waves from particular continental regions. Though the Americas would in fact "whiten" over the course of the nineteenth century, with some 13.3 million Europeans flooding the New World between 1820 and 1880 (compared to a further 2.1 million Africans), before ca. 1820 much of the western Atlantic World was black.[32]

A second basic fact is that the great majority of these Africans came from a relatively small set of sub-regional peoples in West and West Central Africa. Everywhere in the diaspora, the vast majority of enslaved arrivant peoples resolved into no more than ten to twelve main named groups. Historians have been rediscovering the agency of these particular groups of Africans in the Atlantic world, of particular named groups, and are doing so as part of a larger critique of anthropological creolization.[33]

To distinguish this new body of work, scholars are increasingly moving beyond a terminology of the African Diaspora to write about the "Black Atlantic." Though Robert Ferris Thompson introduced the term to capture cross-Atlantic connections, Paul Gilroy appropriated it; but Gilroy's conception of the subject as a sociology of late modernism, as a sort of postmodernist hyper-hybridity, is at odds with much of the *historical* work since, other than his central point of "the instability and mutability of identities which are always unfinished, always being remade."[34] Deborah Gray White, in an article written simply to "affirm the *idea* of the Black Atlantic" (emphasis in original), also reminds that for historians of earlier periods Gilroy's central ideas of the importance of *movement* (cross-oceanic and sub-regional), of the *formation* of essentially new compound political and cultural identities among descendants of displaced Africans in the New World, and of the necessity of paying attention to *regional* and national histories and cultures so as to not essentialize all black people as simply "black" (i.e., the importance of historicizing race) are quite useful as we reconceive the diaspora in fully Atlantic terms.[35] In the baker's dozen years since Gilroy's book, however, we can see the construction of a Black Atlantic world not in a swirling sociology of (post)modernism but rather in an ever-escalating set of historiographical critiques of the early modern African Diaspora between ca.1991 and 2001.

In 1991, David Scott bemoaned the historiographical rut that a focus on recovering a "lost past" in African Diaspora studies had wrought, for which he would have substituted postmodernist concerns with discourses of memory and tradition instead of trying to recover "what really happened." But in his account he maintained a generic Africa and a static slavery; in the same year Allan Karras lamented that even ca.1990 transnational and comparative works on slavery in the Atlantic world (and beyond) were still essentially Eurocentric and focused on whites.[36] By 1993, Patrick Manning (extending his 1990 transnational study of the several slave trades out of Africa) underscored the larger point that the settlement of the Americas can be studied as a single unit of analysis, in terms of migration, and that the transatlantic (Occidental) slave trade was part of a larger set of forced migrations, in which these millions of people crossed the Atlantic in a "number of distinct stages."[37] In looking at Cuba in particular, Stephan Palmié argued directly that the orthodox "rapid creolization" theory (from Mintz and Price) increasingly could not account for historical realities such as the continuing relevance of selected neo-African ethnicities and African-derived consociations in Afro-Cuba (and Brazil, and Trinidad, and perhaps even Suriname), but concluded only that these apparently (and perhaps fleetingly) socially meaningful "aggregates" were worthy of study as such.[38] But at this early moment perhaps Palmié was closest to a real breakthrough on the key issue of ethnicity, seeing a perhaps short-lived historical process of regrouping in the Afro-Cuban *cabildos de nacion* and the religious consociations of *abakuá*, *palo mayombe*, and *regla de orisha* (Santería), in which first displaced Africans and then their Creole descendants created and sustained connections along specific ethnic-African lines but later through initiated fictive kinship. By the mid-nineteenth century it was possible for even white Cubans to become *Carabalí* [Calabars], that is, by being initiated into *abakuá*.

This theme of specific ethnic-African agency (among and between Africans) was picked up by Colin Palmer, who found that marriage choices among African-born slaves in sixteenth-century Mexico, especially among "Angolans," argued against the old creolist assumption that "African slaves arrived in the Americas culturally *tabula rasa*"; and that in fact for the first generation(s) such ethnic affiliations remained significant and meaningful. At first, he noted, "African ethnic loyalties and attachments were nothing if not tenacious."[39] But Palmer's insight was still transitional, suggesting that African influences and especially the meaningfulness of African ethnicity (still seen as a carry-over, a transfer, a continuity, a survival) was perhaps fleeting. And because his argument was for a very early (charter) generation, his evidence begged a *historical* explanation.

For Jamaica over the *longue durée* from the eighteenth through the twentieth centuries, Jean Besson and Barry Chevannes rejected the basic dichotomy of "African continuity" and "Caribbean creation" as relational categories for an argument of revivalism throughout Jamaican history. But they did so in only vague ways; they still wrote of a generic Africa. In trying to split the difference between "continuity" and "Creole" for a vague revivalism even by the mid-1990s, they did not yet have the terminological tools to do it effectively.[40]

The complete breakdown of the classic African Diaspora concept by the mid-1990s is represented by Carlton Wilson's 1997 article, "Conceptualizing the African Diaspora." He explicitly questioned the basic assumptions of the classic theory by asking, some forty years after they were first formulated, "where do we go from here?":

> Have we continued to move forward in our approach or conceptualization of the African diaspora? In the face of so many diaspora studies, departments, and programs, we would be remiss if we do not continue to reexamine the parameters of the African diaspora. . . . Do people of the diaspora share an emotional bond? Are they aware of the alienation that may accompany the voluntary or involuntary leaving of one's homeland? How prevalent is the sense of return to the homeland? Once again why do some return and others not? And there is always the important issue of identity.[41]

In the end, Wilson's principal conclusion was that diaspora studies must be African-oriented: "Africa must be maintained as the center or focus. Diaspora studies or programs that do not conceptualize Africa as the center are fundamentally flawed."[42] And yet he curiously closed by commending a recent popular account of the transatlantic African Diaspora by Ronald Segal, which was written specifically against academic concerns with "tracing African tracks" (and clearly written *for* introductory college courses) as "of particular interest to students of diaspora."[43] But in Segal's *Black Diaspora*, Africa, and Africans, have barely a presence and in only the most cursory of background ways. Segal's larger narrative (organized along the lines of African background, resistance/revolution, national colonies, pan-Africanism and racism, and then contributions) was nothing if not the African Diaspora ca.1970, a quarter-century later. Clearly by the mid-1990s the larger concept had hit an interpretive wall.

Even though throughout the 1990s (and beyond) John Thornton has been uncovering the manifold influences of Africans throughout the Americas,[44] between 1997 and 2001 the key development in the writing of the newly emergent Black Atlantic was the intervention of Paul Lovejoy (initially with Robin Law and Elisée Soumonni) and the wide array of scholars from throughout the modern Atlantic world associated in one way or another with the scholarly network of the York/UNESCO Nigerian Hinterland Project (York University, Canada).[45] With its global scale (trans-Sahara as well as trans-Atlantic connections), its centering of Africa, its plethora of conferences and workshops (at least a dozen in the first five years), and its focus on theoretical and methodological innovations to move beyond the classic African Diaspora concept but from Africanist perspectives, the Nigerian Hinterland Project moved the debate in substantive ways.

In an early statement in 1997, Lovejoy laid out a tentative revisionist model identifying the need for scholars to (1) unravel basic patterns of movement (origins, distributions) to understand the many historically contingent reasons that people were caught up in enslavement, (2) apply a comprehensive knowledge of African history and the usual rigorous method of historical analysis (instead of the sloppy generalizing of most diaspora scholars when introducing "the African background"), (3) be careful about using twentieth-century ethnography and focus on change over time, and (4) understand collective diasporic identities as "ethnicities" (neo-African) and not as tribes (survivals), that is, to decipher the collective names used in the diaspora historically rather than ethnographically.[46] In numerous succeeding publications, mostly from the Nigerian Hinterland Project conferences, Lovejoy has continued to explore these central themes, though most recently he has tended to fall back on a basically ahistorical concept of "charter generations."[47] And though the Nigerian Hinterlands Project to date has not produced its major promised products (a biographical database of enslaved Africans and a historical atlas of slavery, both to be accessible on-line, as well as an archival inventory of primary source materials), it has been a qualified success in highlighting the importance of historicizing ethnic identity and individual experience throughout the Black Atlantic.[48]

In the same five years there were, of course, other important scholarly networks and conferences, often similarly regionally focused. One of the best conceptual statements for an African-centered, circum-Atlantic and historical approach (and which entirely avoids the term "African Diaspora") is Joseph Miller's Black Atlantic vision for reconnecting West Central Africa and the Americas, originally from a 1999 conference at Howard University. He introduced four basic issues, organically related, as a sort of précis of an African-oriented Black Atlantic project (and connected them in his essay on Central Africa in the era of the slave trade):

> Understanding the Central Africans who reached the New World as slaves requires consideration of at least four phases in their disrupted lives: (1) how the Bantu-language-speaking people living in Africa south of the Equator thought about themselves and the many local worlds they lived in, from the sixteenth through the mid-nineteenth centuries, (2) how those captured coped with removal from their home communities, the hardships of being marched into unknown coastlands and eventually loaded onto ships, and the trauma of the oceanic Middle Passage, and (3) how they might have remembered and drawn on these experiences once forcibly resettled in Spanish mainland colonies, in Brazil, in the West Indies, and in North America, depending (4) on what from their former lives in Africa they recognized as relevant to forging new senses of community in the Americas, with others of different backgrounds enslaved alongside them, under specific challenges of surviving that varied enormously throughout the continents and over the centuries.[49]

By 1999–2000, then, one could say that the concept of the Black Atlantic was accepted by a wide range of scholars and was being pushed forward at a remarkable pace in a series of scholarly networks. From the publication of Eltis et al.'s comprehensive database on the slave trade and Debra Gray White's affirmation that "yes, there is a Black Atlantic" to Gwendolyn Midlo Hall's publication of her rich database of enslaved individuals in pre-1820 Louisiana and David Eltis's panoramic study of the 'English Atlantic slave system' (2000), as well as a new "The Black Atlantic" book series by Cassell/Continuum publishing house of London, the turn of the millennium marked a turning point.[50] The Black Atlantic had arrived as a coherent unit of study, with a basic narrative approach focused on the importance of Africans in the development of Atlantic societies in the several centuries before ca.1800–1820.[51]

Writing the Black Atlantic

By 2001, then, there had been sufficient theoretical movement, Kristin Mann's "Africanist-creolist impasse" notwithstanding, to make new research along distinctly Black Atlantic lines more than simply "plausible." By writing Africa and Africans directly into the emerging Black Atlantic world, in the past half-decade a wide range of scholars have been consolidating a new vision of the early modern Atlantic based on four central concepts: (1) that there was something we can term the Black Atlantic, and that one may approach the general subject in *systemic* (transnational) as well as *comparative* ways; (2) that the African Diaspora was in fact a series of many over-lapping sub-diasporas, in which the sum of the parts in many ways was greater than the whole; (3) that the central analytical points of the Mintz/Price "creolist" theory (the randomness of the slave trade, arrivant Africans as "crowds" of cultural strangers, and that they rapidly formed largely ad hoc cultures) are contestable on fact as well as on interpretation,[52] in that many displaced Africans re-connected themselves in many ways and indeed often seemed determined to create connections of solidarity, even intentional communities in times and places, and often on the basis of shared experiences as people from particular regions on the African continent, regions which together comprised something we may term "Atlantic Africa"; and (4) that therefore ethnicity in the diaspora mattered, including (or especially) African or more precisely neo-African ethnies, which in fact may be the key to understanding historically the social-cultural formation of regional African/American societies.

By re-scaling the basic subject, disaggregating the diaspora (and Africa, and the Americas) and re-casting agency along Africanist lines, it has become possible to map out the contours of the Black Atlantic by writing it on global, transnational, inter-regional, and even local levels. It is now possible to move beyond the generalized Africanist-creolist debate to see the outlines of a theory, a method, and a practice of writing the Black Atlantic.

Theory

A theory of the *Black* Atlantic must begin with Africa. Though embedded in multiple trans-oceanic historical matrices of movement, event, and memory that made up the Atlantic world as ecumene (*oikoumen*), it is possible to see the Black Atlantic in terms (at least partly) of African history. Therefore it should be possible to see the key process of change, that is, creolization, as *Africanization* (again at least in part and necessarily selectively). By following dynamic waves of people, rather than defining static "charter generations," we can begin to identify and understand something beyond schematic "stages of creolization" (of which I have been guilty).[53] Patterns of change need not have been continuous, a slow upward curve from homogenized African backgrounds to, in effect, "the Negro," but were just as likely to be discontinuous, with perhaps relatively long periods of cultural stability (or at least slow change or perhaps cultural conservatism) juxtaposed with dramatic moments of systemic change.

Perhaps the best example is in the de-centering of Christianity in the grand narrative of North American black history. The basic fact is that before ca. 1800–1820 (and indeed perhaps mid-century), Christianity was of only minimal importance in the lives of the vast majority of African Americans (or before ca. 1750, of *American Africans*). The sacred worlds of those several generations of the "long eighteenth century" (ca.1680s–1820s) is still a black box; but from a tiny vanguard in the late eighteenth century through the emergence of free blacks in the nineteenth century, and then momentously with the coming of the Civil War and general emancipation, Christianity became one of the pillars of African American political and social culture. As the children of the Exodus, this seventh generation saw all the prophecies come true. But it may have happened largely in one generation.

For the several arrivant generations, moreover, the central challenge of displacement and enslavement was to assert one's humanity among fellows; the central challenge of displaced Africans was to re-create individual connections. In seeking solidarity and thereby resisting isolation, the first fact of agency was that survivors sought to achieve what they wanted, what they hoped they could achieve in their circumstances. They rarely sought to "maximize" (to re-create the totality of their lost worlds or, alternatively, to violently overthrow slavery in its totality), but rather chose to "satisfice," doing what they hoped will succeed. The basic argument (from rational-choice theory) is that to understand agency we need to assume that enslaved Africans and their immediate descendants made choices (even under their extreme duress) because they hoped to achieve something, in the immediate case of re-connecting, based on situational logics in which what they hoped to achieve made sense to them at that time. Different situations would have called for different historical logics.[54]

A basic rational-choice approach helps to explain the central anomaly of the Black Atlantic's diasporic African-derived "named groups." The names of these groups are generally meaningless or of only limited meaning in continental terms, but meaningful in the Black Atlantic. In terms of "bounded rationality," they were assertions of belonging to counter the dehumanization of cultural and social isolation; they expressed hopes for solidarity, but sometimes with the unintended consequence of creating divisions. African agency for individual and communal solidarity among slaves was neither racial ("Negro") nor status ("Slave"), but of multivalent and historically contingent ethnicity (and African-derived at that). These "named groups" could be seen as rational choices of collective re-grouping within a situational logic of countering isolation. Names, therefore, became instruments of belonging and indexes of agency.

An alternative way to consider these named groups is in terms of what has recently been called the "new history."[55] As a set, they could be understood as a discourse of ethnicity (us/them), rooted in locally or regionally shared historical experience, but in a new land and a new violent world of slavery. The diasporic claims to identity were regional, and thus they embodied meta-narratives that were regional. But as meta-ethnies they expressed an ideology of belonging; they were a system of signs, of relational categories, of contingent meanings.

Either way, whether as practices (historical creolization) or as representations (discourse theory), they point in large part to Africa. They reflected waves of Africans from particular regions at particular times and subsequent reinventions of ancestral traditions into living common traditions. Or else they were simply "brand names," devoid of any enduring practical meaning.[56]

Gender must also be central to a theory of the Black Atlantic. Jennifer L. Morgan's recent sweeping book on the significance of enslaved women in the emerging plantation societies of pre-1750 Anglophone America (in particular, Barbados and South Carolina) provides useful ways of thinking about gender and slavery in the Black Atlantic.[57]

White male assumptions about black women and their sexuality in the construction of racism, the reality of commercial consequences of childbirth for the slave master and the slaves, and the centrality of slave women (in Africa as well as the diaspora) in actual work and their laboring as cultural actors in the creolization of slave populations over time, all suggest that the study of slavery (and by extension the Black Atlantic in general) must *account* for women, not simply *include* them. This is especially true for Africans, particularly when their numbers were proportional to those of men, such as before ca.1750. In the slave-trade era and beyond, the depth of white stereotypes about African sexuality and the sexuality of African American women in particular underscores the importance of gender, of a *gyneo-logos* of racial slavery. What most directly distinguished enslaved women from men was the female body and its potential for reproduction; how it was represented, appropriated, exploited (and resisted), defended, and deployed. But in the end, except for physical reproduction, much the same applied to men but with perhaps an *andro-logos*.

Method

Black Atlantic historical artifacts such as diasporic named groups (on a transnational level of analysis), or of a runaway in early nineteenth-century Jamaica such as our "Eboe" Bessy (on the individual level of analysis), can be seen as "clues" to heretofore obscured past realities. Such a "method of clues" uses words, things, and events as a starting point. Microhistorical (micrological) methods take small, indeed formally anomalous, things as signs of "a larger, but hidden or unknown, structure. A strange detail is made to represent a wider totality."[58] And if the historiography of the African Diaspora/Black Atlantic in the past fifteen years suggests anything it is that the anomalies are piling up at such a rate that they can no longer be simply explained away but demand explanation. In effect, by way of microhistory one can see a universe in a grain of sand, if you know how to look. The challenge is always to connect the micro with the macro, and to do so by focusing on the marginal, the borderline, and the exceptional. Microhistorians seek to explain the *typical exception* (or, one could say, the *exceptional typical*).[59] To be done well, the study must use the exceptionality to explain its typicality; of course, some things are simply exceptional, no doubt. If done poorly, microhistories can approximate antiquarianism. It would be useful to apply the general assumption from archaeology, for example, that seemingly anomalous bits and pieces are in fact "small things forgotten," that finding one cowrie shell probably means that there were many more in social use; this exceptional find therefore reflected a larger historical structure (and the ideas behind its usage). There can indeed be a whole "world" embedded in one pierced cowrie shell or in an incised spoon handle.[60] The particular can signify the universal.

The first-order methodology is to follow groups of Africans into the Atlantic World. We now have so much better control over the basic numbers of the slave trade (in annual, quinquennial, quarter-century, and centennial series at least for the cross-oceanic trade) from the *Trans-Atlantic Slave Trade* database that it is now possible to dissect the New World slave trade in remarkably fine slices and document waves of exports and imports with new assurances of plausibility.[61] As importantly, transnational (rather than strictly comparative) analyses are called for; in effect, to stand in Africa and look outward rather than from the Americas and look backward. But it is not enough to simply connect the particular with the general; by disaggregating the Black Atlantic it is possible to mediate the micro and the macro with the regional.

Practice

One practice of writing the Black Atlantic, therefore, is to initially define circum-Atlantic connections by identifying flows of peoples in time and space and historical impacts on various societies including in Atlantic Africa. Such clusters or waves of imports/exports enable event-level analyses of how people created connections "on the move" and on both the African and American landfalls of the Atlantic. Students of the Black Atlantic, or parts thereof, now have the tools to identify with greater assurance particular regions of Atlantic Africa in which to ground their research on specific parts of the Americas and Africa, and beyond. At a minimum Black Atlantic studies should incorporate two basic historiographies, one African and the other American (broadly speaking), should be interdisciplinary (engaging oral-historical, literary, folkloric, archaeological, archival, and ethnological and other sources), and should move from the general to the particular to the regional.

If we extend our perspective to seeing the Atlantic as a bridge as well as a barrier to cross-oceanic connections, especially in the era of the slave trade and slavery, and thus center Africa and Africans, we can envision the early modern Black Atlantic (appropriating Shakespeare's metaphor for the early settling of the maritime Americas)[62] as a grand tempest or hurricane originating off the coasts of Atlantic Africa. Revolving counterclockwise as it spins west, the original tropical depression was propelled by trailing feeder bands extending from the coastal entrepôts of stone forts and associated villages in Senegambia and the Gold Coast to the barracoons of Whydah and Bonny and Calabar and southward on to Loango, Benguela, and Luanda, past the various "doors of no return," expanding to storm strength while violently pulling in peoples and polities from the localized successor kingdoms of old Mali and Songhay in Upper Guinea, later radicalized by new jihadist Islamic movements, to the newly rising empires of Asante and Dahomey and lesser predatory states, or by the collapse into civil war of other empires such as Kongo in the seventeenth century and Oyo in the nineteenth, or to the regional clash of local civilizations such as between the pacifistic Nri and the mercenary Aro in Igboland (the principal hinterland of the Calabar Coast), the latter tied to the storm surge of slaving and the former lost in swimming against the rising tide of violence that became a tsunami in which millions would suffer.

And all carried involuntarily along the Equatorial Current across the Atlantic, gathering force until crashing into the coasts of Brazil and the islands of the Caribbean, wave after wave, from Barbados onward back to Jamaica, St. Domingue, the Lesser Antilles, and finally Cuba, not to mention Suriname, wreaking havoc and depositing these swells of enslaved people in chains across a landscape flattened by the gale force winds of slavery and then periodically rebuilt, plantations financed by quotidian stimulants such as sugar and coffee and tobacco; and finally pushing on up the coasts of North America to the flatlands of Louisiana, the rice swamps of Carolina, the rolling tobacco farms of the Chesapeake, and stony New England, the tail ends of a much larger creative destruction.

This great tensile southern arc was carried on further by its own immense momentum, its fury largely spent, recrossing the Atlantic on the westerly trade winds to warm the great port cities of maritime Europe, from London and Bristol and Liverpool to Lisbon and Amsterdam and Nantes. The violent circulation of peoples and things and ideas was not simply a commercial system, nor the carving out of spheres of imperial influence—not just the competition among mercantile empires for territory and trade; nor a single central culture linked with a series of colonial societies or subcultures—not just a collage of centers and peripheries; nor an endless collection of roughhewn outlands where "the rules" were suspended and people reinvented themselves in their extremity—not just marginal marchlands; the Black Atlantic was all of these and more. Peoples, places, and products became interlinked in an ever-shifting mosaic that conjoined the three basic western worlds, the European and African and American littorals of the Atlantic, into a single dynamic "world," pushing the pace of change in each and increasingly so along the transnational fault lines of slavery and freedom, those twinned midwives of modernity.

Within this ongoing storm, displaced Africans like others forged new identities wherever they found themselves, asserting their humanity by establishing connections among each other, hoping to achieve what they could in the crucible of slavery, with the arrivants piecing together a collective discourse of belonging by renaming themselves according to regional historical logics, their very names *lieux de mémoire*.[63] Throughout the Black Atlantic, as Shakespeare himself intuitively understood even at his early moment, Euro/American "Prosperos" may have owned the magic books and commanded center stage, ultimately controlling the weather, but they closed out by declaiming "set me free" (the last three words of *The Tempest*). In the eye of the storm, however, it was the enslaved African/American "Calibans" who would most directly embody the contradictions of freedom and slavery, and in the most concrete ways, they made the New World. As Shakespeare had Caliban say, "you taught me language and my profit on't is, I know how to curse." Of course, African "Calibans" brought with them their own languages and linguistic curses, as well as secret knowledges of *cursing* (for example, *ôbia*/obeah) throughout the Americas. Their Creole descendants drew on these ancestral ideas, words, and things and adapted them to the realities on the ground to survive their harrowing ordeal with their essential humanity intact.

Conclusion

Though it may sound overly optimistic, as the study of the Black Atlantic is still in its infancy, I am convinced that we are on the collective threshold of a remarkably productive (even generative) opening in the history of the early modern world. A spate of new books structured along transnational (that is, cross- or even circum-Atlantic), African-centered, and what can at this point only be called post-creolist lines, and the continuing work of a wide range of scholars on at least four continents and in many languages are revealing new vistas. From James Sweet's study of the manifold significance and influences of West Central Africans in the ongoing formation of Afro-Brazilian culture and society in the context of the South Atlantic world to my own attempt at linking particular American microhistories with general African macrohistories for the region of the Chesapeake to Gwendolyn Midlo Hall's new work to render visible the dozen or so major African groups in their clusterings throughout the Black Atlantic world, and to do so systematically from all regions of Atlantic Africa to all regions in the Americas, historians of many different stripes are writing the Black Atlantic anew.[64] In doing so they are also developing theories and methods and practices that will enrich the entire discipline.

Nearly a quarter-century ago, Bernard Bailyn closed his meditation on what he termed the challenge of modern historiography with a call that still reverberates today:

> Historians must be, not analysts of isolated technical problems abstracted from the past, but narrators of worlds in motion—worlds as complex, unpredictable, and transient as our own. The historian must re-tell, with a new richness, the story of what some one of the worlds of the past was, how it ceased to be what it was, how it faded and blended into new configurations, how at every stage what was, was the product of what had been, and developed into what no one could have anticipated—all of this to help us understand how we came to be the way we are, and to extend the poor reach of our own immediate experience.[65]

Some twenty years earlier in *Shadow and Act* (1964), the American writer Ralph Ellison demanded, in a *cris de coeur,* that those who would write on "the Negro" tell the whole story. "Everybody wants to tell us what a Negro is," wrote Ellison, "yet few wish, even in a joke, to be one. But if you would tell me who I am, at least take the trouble to discover *what I have been.*"[66] This is the project of the Black Atlantic.

Notes

1. *Cornwall Chronicle* (February 5, 1816, et seq.); abstracted in Douglas B. Chambers, ed., "Jamaican Runaways, 1718–1817: A Compilation of Fugitive Slaves" (typed manuscript, 2003), 467. She had said that her master had lived at Black River but had died.

2. Edward Kamau Brathwaite, *The Development of Creole Society in Jamaica, 1770–1820* (Oxford, UK: Clarendon Press, 1971); Brathwaite, *The Folk Culture of the Slaves in Jamaica*, rev. ed. (London: New Beacon Books, 1981).

3. Over the course of the year in St. George Parish workhouse Bessy would have encountered over a dozen other captured runaways who were born in the hinterlands of the Bight of Biafra; Eboe specifically constituted fully one-quarter of the 36 Africans advertised in the parish in 1816. Indeed, between 1810 and 1817, Eboe were the most numerous African-born group among the 1,767 Africans advertised in workhouse lists in Jamaica, accounting for one in five of all such Africans. See Chambers, "Jamaican Runaways."

4. Quotation from Matti Peltonen, in describing the "new history" approach of a "method of clues," developed by Carlo Ginzburg, Giovanni Levi, and other European "micro historians"; Matti Peltonen, "Clues, Margins, and Monads: The Micro-Macro Link in Historical Research," *History and Theory* 40:3 (2001): 349. See also Carlo Ginzburg, *Clues, Myths, and the Historical Method*, trans. John and Anne C. Tedeschi (Baltimore: Johns Hopkins University Press, 1989).

5. Kristin Mann, "Shifting Paradigms in the Study of the African Diaspora and of Atlantic History and Culture," *Slavery and Abolition* 22:1 (2001): 3.

6. Though Paul Gilroy reintroduced the term, he conceived the subject as a sociology of (post) modernism at odds with much of the historical work since; *The Black Atlantic: Modernity and Double Consciousness* (Cambridge, Mass.: Harvard University Press, 1993), xi. Other works still think in "diaspora" terms though on an Atlantic scale; see James Walvin, *Making the Black Atlantic: Britain and the African Diaspora* (London: Cassell, 2000). Cf. an example of an explicitly "Atlantic" perspective, in this case of Central Africans in the diaspora; see Joseph C. Miller, "Central Africa during the Era of the Slave Trade, c. 1490s–1850s," in *Central Africans and Cultural Transformations in the American Diaspora*, ed. Linda M. Heywood (Cambridge: Cambridge University Press, 2002), 21–69; and for a recent regional study of the South Atlantic that centers on Central Africans, see James H. Sweet, *Recreating Africa: Culture, Kinship, and Religion in the African-Portuguese World, 1441–1770* (Chapel Hill: University of North Carolina Press, 2003).

7. Cf. Ira Berlin, "From Creole to African: Atlantic Creoles and the Origins of African-American Society in Mainland North America," *William and Mary Quarterly*, 3rd ser., 53:2 (1996), 251–288.

8. Joseph E. Harris, introduction to *Global Dimensions of the African Diaspora*, ed. Joseph E. Harris (Washington, D.C.: Howard University Press, 1982), 5.

9. See programmatic statements by Skinner, Shepperson, Harris, and Drake in Harris, *African Diaspora*: Elliott P. Skinner, "The Dialectic between Diasporas and Homelands," 17–45; George Shepperson, "African Diaspora: Concept and Context," 46–53; Joseph E. Harris, "A Comparative Approach to the Study of the African Diaspora," 112–124; St. Clair Drake, "Diaspora Studies and Pan-Africanism," 341–402. Herskovits, *The Myth of the Negro Past* (New York: Harper, 1941).

10. Brathwaite, *Creole Society in Jamaica;* Sidney W. Mintz and Richard Price, *The Birth of African-American Culture: An Anthropological Perspective* (Boston: Beacon Press, 1992; originally published under a different title, 1976).

11. For concise restatements of the basic creolist position and its application to slave social and cultural history, to North America in particular, see Charles Joyner, *Down by the Riverside: A South Carolina Slave Community* (Urbana: University of Illinois Press, 1984), xx–xxii; Allan Kulikoff, *Tobacco and Slaves: The Development of Southern Cultures in the Chesapeake, 1680–1800* (Chapel Hill: University of North Carolina Press, 1986), 317–319; and, more recently, in Philip D. Morgan, *Slave Counterpoint: Black Culture in the Eighteenth-Century Chesapeake and Lowcountry* (Chapel Hill: University of North Carolina Press, 1998), 442–443, to wit, "*After all* [my emphasis], slaves did not arrive in the New World as communities of people; they had to *create* [original emphasis] communities. The slave trade irrevocably severed numerous social bonds that had tied Africans together. Unable to transport their institutions, slaves were forced to rebuild a society in the New World. They brought a few building blocks with them, but they had to fashion the foundation and framework of their new lives *from scratch* [my emphasis]" (442). In his synoptic account of slavery in North America before 1800, Ira Berlin tended to see Africans as social and cultural agents, but only within relatively limited time frames, or an "African moment"; Berlin, *Many Thousands Gone: The First Two Centuries of Slavery in North America* (Cambridge, Mass.: Harvard University Press, 1998).

12. For example, Philip Morgan concluded an important article from the mid-1990s with: "The homogenizing tendency of stressing cultural unity in Africa, of emphasizing the non-random character of the slave trade, and of seeing the dominance of particular African coastal regions or ethnicities in most American settings, is at variance with the central forces shaping the early modern Atlantic world. This tendency should be resisted." Morgan, "The Cultural Implications of the Atlantic Slave Trade: African Regional Origins, American Destinations and New World Developments," *Slavery and Abolition* 18:1 (1997): 142.

13. V. Y. Mudimbe, *The Invention of Africa: Gnosis, Philosophy, and the Order of Knowledge* (Bloomington: Indiana University Press, 1988); Mudimbe, *The Idea of Africa* (Bloomington: Indiana University Press, 1994); Kwame Anthony Appiah, *In My Father's House: Africa in the Philosophy of Culture* (New York: Oxford University Press, 1992). For a recent lament on the apparent failure of the political-cultural aspect of this research program, that is, to unite black Americans and Africans, see Tunde Adeleke, "Black Americans and Africa: A Critique of the Pan-African and Identity Paradigms," *International Journal of African Historical Studies* 31:3 (1998): 505–536.

14. Mudimbe, *Idea of Africa,* 40–55.

15. David Scott, "That Event, This Memory: Notes on the Anthropology of African Diasporas in the New World," *Diaspora* 1:3 (1991): 261–284.

16. Adeleke's "Black Americans and Africa" was written in response to a 1992 student conference on the need to revive Pan-Africanism.

17. In "Black Americans and Africa," Adeleke takes pains to deny the "Africanness" of black Americans and stresses their Americanism in basic cultural assumptions and practices; they share only "racial" rather than any "ethnic" connections with Africans (525–529).

18. John Thornton, *Africa and Africans in the Making of the Atlantic World, 1400–1680* (Cambridge: Cambridge University Press, 1992; 2nd ed., 1998); Gwendolyn

Midlo Hall, *Africans in Colonial Louisiana: The Development of Afro-Creole Culture in the Eighteenth Century* (Baton Rouge: Louisiana State University Press, 1992); David Scott, "That Event, This Memory."

19. David Eltis, Stephen D. Behrendt, David Richardson, and Herbert S. Klein, eds., *The Trans-Atlantic Slave Trade: A Database on CD-ROM* (Cambridge: Cambridge University Press, 1999); Gwendolyn Midlo Hall, ed., *Databases for the Study of Afro-Louisiana History and Genealogy, 1699–1860* [CD-ROM] (Baton Rouge: Louisiana State University Press, 2000).

20. See, for example, Bernard Bailyn, *Voyagers to the West: A Passage in the Peopling of America on the Eve of the Revolution* (New York: Knopf, 1986); D. W. Meinig, *The Shaping of America: A Geographical Perspective on 500 Years of History*, vol. 1: *Atlantic America, 1492–1800* (New Haven, Conn.: Yale University Press, 1986); David Watts, *The West Indies: Patterns of Development, Culture, and Environmental Change since 1492* (Cambridge: Cambridge University Press, 1987); Jack P. Greene, *Pursuits of Happiness: The Social Development of Early Modern British Colonies and the Formation of American Culture* (Chapel Hill: University of North Carolina Press, 1988); David Hackett Fischer, *Albion's Seed: Four British Folkways in America* (New York: Oxford University Press, 1989); and the recognition of this early Eurocentric emphasis in Alan L. Karras, "Of Human Bondage: Creating an Atlantic History of Slavery," *Journal of Interdisciplinary History* 22:2 (1991): 285–293; and Karras, "The Atlantic World as a Unit of Study," in *Atlantic American Societies: From Columbus through Abolition 1492–1888*, ed. Alan L. Karras and J. R. McNeill (London: Routledge, 1992), 4–5.

21. Paul E. Lovejoy, "Identifying Enslaved Africans: Methodological and Conceptual Considerations in Studying the African Diaspora" (TMs., 1997), 11, advanced such criticism of Joseph C. Miller because Miller defined his subject in terms of "a marginal institution on the margin of the Atlantic system"; quotation from Miller, "A Marginal Institution on the Margin of the Atlantic System: The Portuguese Southern Atlantic Slave Trade in the Eighteenth Century," in *Slavery and the Rise of the Atlantic System*, ed. Barbara L. Solow (Cambridge; Cambridge University Press, 1991); and compare Miller, *Way of Death: Merchant Capitalism and the Angola Slave Trade, 1730–1830* (Madison: University of Wisconsin Press,1988), xix, 452–59. Lovejoy, however, failed to understand what Miller meant by "marginality," both in the strict economic sense and in terms of the larger dynamics of change in the South Atlantic system; see also Lovejoy, "Identifying Enslaved Africans in the African Diaspora," in *Identifying Enslaved Africans: The "Nigerian" Hinterland and the African Diaspora*, ed. Paul E. Lovejoy, proceedings of UNESCO/SSHRCC Summer Institute, 1997 (London, 2000), 25n11.

22. Philip D. Curtin, *The Atlantic Slave Trade: A Census* (Madison: University of Wisconsin Press, 1969). Cf. Paul E. Lovejoy, "The Volume of the Atlantic Slave Trade: A Synthesis," *Journal of African History* 23:4 (1982): 473–501, a confirmatory article regarding Curtin's basic numbers, with the following: David Richardson, "Slave Exports from West and West-Central Africa, 1700–1810: New Estimates of Volume and Distribution," *Journal of African History* 30:1 (1989): 1–22; Joseph Inikori, "The Volume of the British Slave Trade, 1655–1807," *Cahiers d'Etudes africaines* 32:4 (1992): 643–688; David Eltis and David Richardson, "West Africa and the Transatlantic Slave Trade: New Evidence of Long-Run Trends," *Slavery and Abolition* 18:1 (1997): 16–35; David Eltis, "The Volume and Structure of the Transatlantic Slave Trade: A Reassessment," *William and Mary Quarterly*, 3rd ser., 58:1 (2001): 17–46.

23. A recent example of the former is Walter Hawthorne, *Planting Rice and Harvesting Slaves: Transformations along the Guinea-Bissau Coast, 1400–1900* (Portsmouth, N.H.: Heinemann, 2003).

24. Senior scholars (writing in English) include John Thornton (seventeenth-century Kongo); Joseph C. Miller (precolonial Angola); Paul Lovejoy (nineteenth-century Sokoto/Hausa); Michael Gomez (precolonial Senegambia); Robin Law (eighteenth-century Dahomey); Patrick Manning (precolonial Dahomey). Others such as Gwendolyn Midlo Hall, Colin A. Palmer, and Rebecca Scott trained as Latin Americanists.

25. For a sample of the literature see Hall, *Africans in Colonial Louisiana;* Michael Mullin, *Africa in America: Slave Acculturation and Resistance in the American South and the British Caribbean, 1736–1831* (Urbana: University of Illinois Press, 1992); David Eltis and David Richardson, eds., *Routes to Slavery: Direction, Ethnicity and Mortality in the Atlantic Slave Trade* (London: Frank Cass, 1997); Robin Blackburn, *The Making of New World Slavery: From the Baroque to the Modern, 1492–1800* (London: Verso, 1997); Lorena S. Walsh, *From Calabar to Carter's Grove: The History of a Virginia Slave Community* (Charlottesville: University Press of Virginia, 1997); Michael A. Gomez, *Exchanging Our Country Marks: The Transformation of African Identities in the Colonial and Antebellum South* (Chapel Hill: University of North Carolina Press, 1998); Morgan, *Slave Counterpoint;* Berlin, *Many Thousands Gone;* J. Lorand Matory, "The English Professors of Brazil: On the Diasporic Roots of the Yoruba Nation," *Comparative Studies in Society and History* 41:1 (1999): 72–103; Walvin, *Making the Black Atlantic;* Judith A. Carney, *Black Rice: The African Origins of Rice Cultivation in the Americas* (Cambridge, Mass.: Harvard University Press, 2001); Sheila S. Walker, ed., *African Roots / American Cultures: Africa in the Creation of the Americas* (Lanham, Md.: Rowman and Littlefield, 2001); Heywood, *Central Africans and Cultural Transformations;* Sweet, *Recreating Africa;* Douglas B. Chambers, *Murder at Montpelier: Igbo Africans in Virginia* (Jackson: University Press of Mississippi, 2005); Gwendolyn Midlo Hall, *Slavery and African Ethnicities in the Americas: Restoring the Links* (Chapel Hill: University of North Carolina Press, 2005).

26. David Armitage, "Three Concepts of Atlantic History," in *The British Atlantic World, 1500–1800,* ed. David Armitage and Michael J. Braddick (New York: Palgrave Macmillan, 2002), 11. For recent synoptic statements on Atlantic history, see Bernard Bailyn, "The Idea of Atlantic History," *Itinerario* 20:1 (1996): 19–44; David Eltis, "Atlantic History in Global Perspective," *Itinerario* 23:2 (1999): 141–161; Wim Klooster, "Introduction: The Rise and Transformation of the Atlantic World," in *The Atlantic World: Essays on Slavery, Migration, and Imagination,* ed. Wim Klooster and Alfred Padula (Upper Saddle River, N.J.: Pearson/Prentice Hall, 2005), 1–42; Bernard Bailyn, *Atlantic History: Concept and Contours* (Cambridge, Mass.: Harvard University Press, 2005).

27. Rebecca Scott, "Small-Scale Dynamics of Large-Scale Processes," *American Historical Review* 105:2 (2000): 472; David Brion Davis, "Looking at Slavery from Broader Perspectives," *American Historical Review* 105:2 (2000): 251–280. Philip Morgan was more succinct: "Slavery was a central feature of the emergent Atlantic system"; "Cultural Implications of the Slave Trade," 122.

28. Ronald P. Formisano, "The Concept of Political Culture," *Journal of Interdisciplinary History* 31:3 (2001): 395.

29. Eltis, "Atlantic History in Global Perspective," 143–144. In part this was from the recognition that before ca.1820 nearly three times more Africans than Europeans

went to the Americas; but also that the European shift from legally coerced (penal, indentured, and so forth) to slave labor, or, rather, the refusal to enslave "other" whites, reflected cultural choices rather than strictly economic ones.

30. Bernard Bailyn, "The Challenge of Modern Historiography," *American Historical Review* 87:1 (1982): 22.

31. Thornton, *Africa and Africans in the Making of the Atlantic World*. Cf. Gomez, *Exchanging Our Country Marks*; and largely contra Philip Morgan, *Slave Counterpoint*.

32. David Eltis first highlighted this contrast in "Free and Coerced Transatlantic Migrations: Some Comparisons," *American Historical Review* 88:2 (1983): 251–280. Ten years later Patrick Manning extended the analysis from an Africanist perspective in "Migrations of Africans to the Americas: The Impact on Africans, Africa, and the New World," *History Teacher* 26:3 (1993): 279–296. The final revised numbers are from Eltis, "Atlantic History in Global Perspective," Table 1, 151.

33. For relevant general arguments and citations see Douglas B. Chambers, "'My Own Nation': Igbo Exiles in the Diaspora," *Slavery and Abolition* 18:1 (1997): 72–97; Chambers, "Ethnicity in the Diaspora: The Slave Trade and the Creation of African 'Nations' in the Americas," *Slavery and Abolition* 22:3 (2001): 25–39; Paul E. Lovejoy, "The African Diaspora: Revisionist Interpretations of Ethnicity, Culture and Religion under Slavery," *Studies in the World History of Slavery, Abolition and Emancipation* 2:1 (1997), 1–21, online at http://www2.h-net.edu/~slavery/essays, and now available at http://www.yorku.ca/nhp/publications/ under "Articles and Chapters" (accessed August 15, 2007); Lovejoy, "The Conditions of Slaves in the Americas," in *From Chains to Bonds: The Slave Trade Revisited*, ed. Doudou Diène (Paris: UNESCO, 2001), 125–138; Lovejoy and David Trotman, "Enslaved Africans and Their Expectations of Slave Life in the Americas: Towards a Reconsideration of Models of 'Creolisation,'" in *Questioning Creole: Creolisation Discourses in Caribbean Culture*, ed. Verene A. Shepherd and Glen L. Richards (Kingston, Jamaica: Ian Randle, 2002), 67–91; Lovejoy, "Methodology through the Ethnic Lens: The Study of Atlantic Africa," in *Sources and Methods in African History: Spoken, Written, Unearthed*, ed. Toyin Falola and Christian Jennings (Rochester, N.Y.: University of Rochester Press, 2003), 105–117; Lovejoy, "Trans-Atlantic Transformations: The Origins and Identity of Africans in the Americas," in Klooster and Padula, *Atlantic World*, 126–146. And in reference to Brazil see Joseph C. Miller, "Retention, Reinvention, and Remembering: Restoring Identities through Enslavement in Africa and under Slavery in Brazil," in *Enslaving Connections: Changing Cultures of Africa and Brazil during the Era of Slavery*, ed. José C. Curto and Paul E. Lovejoy (Amherst, N.Y.: Humanity Books, 2004), 81–121.

34. Robert Ferris Thompson, *Flash of the Spirit* (New York: Vintage, 1983); Gilroy, *Black Atlantic*, xi.

35. Deborah Gray White, "'Yes,' There Is a Black Atlantic," *Itinerario* 23:2 (1999): 128–140.

36. David Scott, "That Event, This Memory"; Karras, "Of Human Bondage."

37. Patrick Manning, *Slavery and African Life: Occidental, Oriental, and African Slave Trades* (Cambridge: Cambridge University Press, 1990); Manning, "Migrations of Africans," 281.

38. Stephan Palmié, "Ethnogenetic Processes and Cultural Transfer in Afro-American Slave Populations," in *Slavery in the Americas*, ed. Wolfgang Binder (Würzburg, Germany: Königshausen and Neumann, 1993), 337–363.

39. Colin Palmer, "From Africa to the Americas: Ethnicity in the Early Black Com-

munities of the Americas," *Journal of World History* 6:2 (1995): 223–236, quotations 224, 236.

40. Jean Besson and Barry Chevannes, "The Continuity-Creativity Debate: The Case of Revival," *New West Indian Guide* 70:3/4 (1996): 209–228.

41. Carlton Wilson, "Conceptualizing the African Diaspora," *Comparative Studies of South Asia, Africa and the Middle East* 17:2 (1997): 120.

42. Ibid.

43. Quotations, Ronald Segal, *The Black Diaspora* (New York: Black Diaspora Communications, 1995), xiii; Wilson, "Conceptualizing the African Diaspora," 121.

44. A select bibliography for John Thornton: "On The Trail of Voodoo: African Christianity in Africa and the Americas," *Americas* 44:3 (1988): 261–278; "African Dimensions of the Stono Rebellion," *American Historical Review* 96:4 (1991): 1101–1113; *Africa and Africans in the Making of the Atlantic World*; "Central African Names and African-American Naming Patterns," *William and Mary Quarterly*, 3rd ser., 50:4 (1993): 727–742; "'I Am the Subject of the King of Congo': African Political Ideology and the Haitian Revolution," *Journal of World History* 4:2 (1993): 181–214; "The African Experience of the '20. and Odd Negroes' Arriving in Virginia in 1619," *William and Mary Quarterly*, 3rd ser., 55:3 (1998): 421–434; *Warfare in Atlantic Africa, 1500–1800* (London: UCL Press, 1999); "Religious and Ceremonial Life in the Kongo and Mbundu Areas, 1500–1700," in Heywood, *Central Africans and Cultural Transformations*, 71–90; "Cannibals, Witches, and Slave Traders in the Atlantic World," *William and Mary Quarterly*, 3rd ser., 60:2 (2003): 273–294.

45. The initial International Advisory Board (1997–2001) included representatives from Bénin, Nigeria, Togo, and Tunisia in Africa; Barbados, Costa Rica, Cuba, and Jamaica in the Caribbean; Brazil; the United Kingdom; and the United States and Canada. The Project was formally affiliated with the UNESCO Slave Route Project (founded 1994), and funded by a five-year grant from the Social Sciences and Humanities Research Council of Canada. See "York/UNESCO Nigerian Hinterland Project" (brochure, n.d. [ca.1999]); York/UNESCO Nigerian Hinterland Project *Newsletter*, no.1 (May 2000).

46. Lovejoy, "African Diaspora: Revisionist Interpretations," 7–10.

47. Lovejoy, "Trans-Atlantic Transformations," 127–129.

48. See various edited volumes resulting from sponsored conferences: Robin Law, ed., *Source Material for Studying the Slave Trade* (Centre of Commonwealth Studies, University of Stirling, Scotland, UK, 1997); Lovejoy, *Identifying Enslaved Africans*; Paul E. Lovejoy and David V. Trotman eds., *Trans-Atlantic Dimensions of Ethnicity in the African Diaspora* (London: Continuum, 2003); Curto and Lovejoy eds., *Enslaving Connections: Changing Cultures of Africa and Brazil during the Era of Slavery* (Amherst, N.Y.: Humanity Books, 2004).

49. Miller, "Central Africa during the Era of the Slave Trade," 21. Miller further elaborated these themes in "Retention, Reinvention, and Remembering," 81–121.

50. Eltis et al., *Trans-Atlantic Slave Trade*; White, "'Yes,' There Is a Black Atlantic"; Hall, *Databases for the Study of Afro-Louisiana History*; David Eltis, *The Rise of African Slavery in the Americas* (Cambridge: Cambridge University Press, 2000).

51. Perhaps the best sign of this conceptual triumph was the 2000 article by Tiffany Patterson and Robin Kelley in which they sought to re-orient African diaspora studies away from the earlier period and the cultural ("Afro-Atlantic") to later periods and to the expressly political ("black internationalism"); "Unfinished Migrations: Reflections

on the African Diaspora and the Making of the Modern World," *African Studies Review* 43:1 (2000): 11–45. Meanwhile, younger scholars such as James H. Sweet were by then teaching the "Modern African Diaspora" directly in terms of the transatlantic slave trade; "Teaching the Modern African Diaspora: A Case Study of the Atlantic Slave Trade," *Radical History Review* 77 (2000): 106–122.

52. Eltis, *Rise of African Slavery*, 252.

53. Chambers, *Murder at Montpelier*, 17–18.

54. Rod Aya, "The Third Man: Or, Agency in History; Or, Rationality in Revolution," *History and Theory* 40:4 (2001): 143–152; Herbert A. Simon, *Economics, Bounded Rationality and the Cognitive Revolution* (Aldershot, UK: E. Elgar, 1992).

55. For example, see Miguel A. Cabrera, "On Language, Culture, and Social Action," trans. Anna Fagan and Marie McMahon, *History and Theory* 40:4 (2001): 82–100.

56. Cf. David Northrup, "Igbo and Myth Igbo: Culture and Ethnicity in the Atlantic World, 1600–1850," *Slavery and Abolition* 21:3 (2000): 1–20.

57. Jennifer L. Morgan, *Laboring Women: Reproduction and Gender in New World Slavery* (Philadelphia: University of Pennsylvania Press, 2004).

58. Peltonen, "Clues, Margins, and Monads," 349.

59. Ibid., 351–358.

60. On the latter see Patricia Merk Samford, "Power Runs in Many Channels: Subfloor Pits and West African-Based Spiritual Traditions in Colonial Virginia" (Ph.D. diss., University of North Carolina at Chapel Hill, 2000).

61. Though there are other putative slave-trade "databases" that serve as object lessons on the subject of manipulation of statistics; for example, James A. McMillen, *The Final Victims: Foreign Slave Trade to North America, 1783–1810* (Columbia: University of South Carolina Press, 2004).

62. William Shakespeare, *The Tempest* (1612).

63. "Sites of Memory"; Chambers, *Murder at Montpelier*, passim.

64. Sweet, *Recreating Africa*; Chambers, *Murder at Montpelier*; Hall, *Slavery and African Ethnicities.*

65. Bailyn, "Challenge of Modern Historiography," 23–24.

66. Ralph Ellison, *Shadow and Act* (New York: Random House, 1964), 115 (my emphasis).

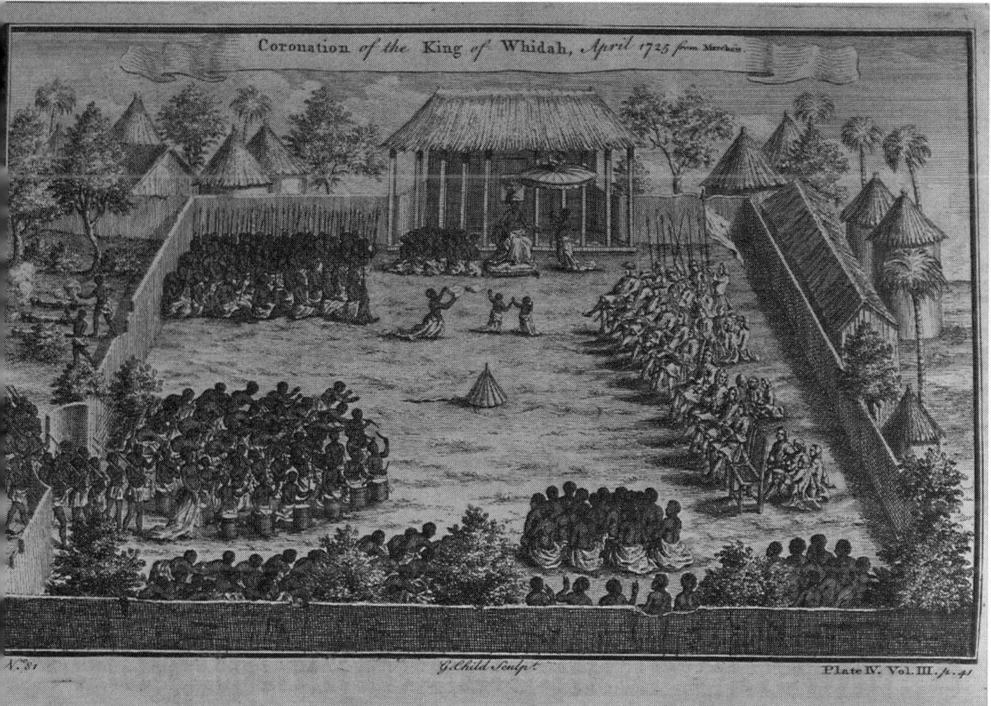

Jean Baptiste Labat, Voyage du Chevalier des Marchais en Guinee . . . fait en 1725, 1726, & 1727 (Amsterdam, 1731), vol. 2, after p. 57. In A *New General Collection of Voyages and Travels*, ed. Thomas Astley (London, 1745–47), vol. 3, plate 4, facing p. 41.

Copies in Special Collections Department, University of Virginia Library, Charlottesville, and Library Company of Philadelphia.

James Edward Alexander, *Narrative of a voyage of observation among the colonies of Western Africa . . . in 1835* (London, 1837), vol. 1, facing p. 76.
Courtesy of The Mariners' Museum, Newport News, Virginia.

Henry Chamberlain, *Views and costumes of the city and neighborhood of Rio de Janeiro, Brazil, from drawings taken by Lieutenant Chamberlain, Royal Artillery, during the years 1819 and 1820, with descriptive explanations* (London, 1822). The illustration shown here is taken from the Brazilian (Portuguese) edition, *Vistas e costumes de cidade e arredores do Rio de Janeiro em 1819–1820* (Livaria Kosmos, Rio de Janeiro, 1943), p. 95 (plate 34 in the 1822 London edition).
Copy in University of Florida Library, Gainesville.

Two soldiers with weapons, Nigeria, 1820s.
Special Collections, University of Virginia Library.

Carrying a sedan chair (palanquin), Brazil, 1853.
Special Collections, University of Virginia Library.

Free woman of color, Martinique, 1826.
Special Collections, University of Virginia Library.

III

Independence and Abolition

Part 3 explores the nineteenth-century period in Latin America and the twentieth-century period in Africa during which colonies challenged their subservience to parent states. The section also explores the twinned outcome of abolition, which in some Latin American colonies was part of their independence efforts from the beginning. In his chapter on independence in Latin America, David Cahill explores how Atlantic processes, events, and ideas played upon the revolutionaries in Latin America; fittingly for a book on the Atlantic World, Cahill adopts a perspective that places Latin America on an equal footing with Europe during the tumultuous period of Atlantic Revolutions.

Building upon Cahill's chapter on Latin American independence, Maurice Jackson explores the era of Atlantic Revolutions, particularly in the manner that the period saw tremendous efforts to end slavery. Writing that the effort to abolish slavery "was truly an Atlantic one," Jackson demonstrates the various ways in which slavery was attacked. Not only was the institution under attack from those forces that immediately come to mind—state legislatures, individual activists, the British Parliament—but, as Jackson emphasizes, slavery was also under attack from slaves themselves. Centering the efforts of slaves adopts a perspective that furthers a rather typical assessment by recent Atlantic histories.

Though African independence movements occurred in the next century, as Joel E. Tishken illustrates, most of the same factors—Atlantic, regional, and local—that impacted American independence efforts played key roles across the Atlantic. Claiming that "Africa's independence movements represent the most significant constellation of events in the continent's modern history,"

Tishken connects those events with the major themes of Atlantic history. With every region of Africa involved in self-determination efforts, an important sense of pan-Africanism emerged. A force in both independence movements that Tishken discusses, and in modern critiques of the Atlantic and global systems, pan-Africanism is one of the most important themes to emerge in the modern Atlantic World.

CHAPTER NINE

Independence Movements in the New World

David Cahill

Between 1808 and 1830 the modern nations of Latin America came into being, carved out of a crumbling Spanish imperium thrown into crisis in 1808–1814 by the Napoleonic invasion of the Iberian Peninsula. The subsequent Peninsular War wrought radical changes in both Spain and Portugal, and their repercussions in Hispanic America proved fatal, for all that the issue of Latin American emancipation from European rule was left in abeyance by more than a decade of protracted, ruinous wars in Spain's American possessions. The divisions that had demarcated the viceroyalties, *audiencia* jurisdictions, and captaincies-general of Spanish America were often blurred and dictated by administrative convenience such that the definitive resolution of national boundaries was not resolved until after independence; indeed, even today there are boundary disputes dating from that time; for example, the 1995 war between Ecuador and Peru. In any event, when Napoleon had been driven from Iberia and the artillery smoke had cleared, there were nineteen new republics plus two Spanish possessions (Cuba and Puerto Rico) while the Philippines, hitherto part (with Mexico) of the Viceroyalty of New Spain, also remained in Spanish hands, until in 1898 all three fell to the expansionist ambitions of the United States. The Republic of Panama was created in 1903, hived off from Colombia at the urging of the United States. Meanwhile, Brazil almost unobtrusively slipped into independence from Portugal, occasioned by instability on the peninsula after 1808, as Portugal underwent a *via crucis* similar to that of its Spanish neighbor. This massive political transformation in Iberian America was the product of nearly two decades of war, often civil war, but the roots of these Wars of Independence may be traced further back, to at least the mid-eighteenth century.

There is dispute as to how deep those roots went; modern revisionists allege they were shallow. Latin American independence is now understood as part of the Atlantic Revolutions, but some historians go beyond this by insisting that the Latin American upheavals of the era were merely reactive to European developments.[1] In particular, the repercussions of the French Revolution and especially its Napoleonic aftermath in Spain and Portugal are regarded as causative and not merely contextual for events in Iberian America; curiously, the North American Revolution does not appear to have been a major inspiration to the separatists elsewhere in the Americas, although it exercised some influence in Mexico and Brazil. Even more limited in its influence was the spectacularly successful Haitian Revolution of 1791, though it did instill fear into Cuban and Brazilian elites.[2] If this was in many respects a reflex of the French Revolution, it had its own agenda, its foremost issue being freedom from slavery, and its sui generis character sets it apart as a special case. Revolutionary events in the Spanish and Portuguese possessions lagged well behind European and North American insurrections; it was not until the crisis of 1808–1814 in the Iberian Peninsula before its avatars found the courage to act decisively.

Certainly, it is only from 1808 that events move forward, but to conclude from this that Latin American independence had shallow roots is to infer a high degree of spontaneity to the post-1808 elections, insurrections, and wars—an abrupt break with the past that appears to deny Latin Americans a primary role in their own emancipation.[3] The entire independence era is presented as a complex civil war, a working out of a new relationship in which adult Americans assert their grown-up identities against the wishes of their mother country—a family squabble between *españoles europeos* and *españoles americanos*. Certainly, the crisis of 1808–14 provided an unparalleled opportunity for Americans to assert their sovereignty, or at least to claim a measure of control over their own destiny. This "top down" or "trickle down" interpretation, currently favored by many historians, has rightly restored the peninsular storyline to the history of the independence era; earlier historiography had often downgraded (although not overlooked) the role of events in Spain and Portugal. However, one can err too far in the opposite direction. Its importance can be exaggerated to the point where Americans' agency in making their own history is devalued. Recent revisionist interpretations of the independence era tend to privilege "white" American participants over their indigenous, African, and mixed-race counterparts. Indeed, some of the most vigorous proponents of this interpretation base their case on Spanish archives alone; Latin American documentation often tells another story in which subalterns forge their own history.[4]

To assign Latin Americans the role of belated followers but not vanguard leaders is thus a top-down, Eurocentric model, one which in many respects reflects the old dependency model of the continent's economic development and state-building. Like the dependency paradigm, it diminishes the motive power of social conflict as a creative rather than reactive force and unnecessarily privileges outside forces. It views Latin Americans on the eve of nationhood as the playthings of a transformative, international political logic, where dependency theorists once saw them as helpless victims of the international economy that guaranteed the development of the Northern Hemisphere at the cost of Latin American underdevelopment.[5] In any case, while generalizations are unavoidable, a "one size fits all" explanation of Latin American independence hardly embraces the variety of radical political movements and military campaigns between 1808 and 1830 and discounts the many episodes of rebellion, radical protest, conspiracy, and subversion prior to 1808. This interpretive model largely elides cultural difference as well as any notion of the cultural basis of politics. Yet Spanish American political culture had its own flavor that was distinct from its Iberian counterpart. Above all, its rich ethnic mixture comprised populations that had their own good reasons to seek freedom from Creole as well as peninsular domination, and that bore a disproportionate share of the financial cost of running an empire and, not least, of providing the resources to feed Spain's chronic appetite for foreign wars. They were perhaps less enamored of *Hispanidad*, and they felt less of an affinity with peninsular Spaniards than did Creole elites who admired and imitated aristocratic values and modes of behavior: not many indigenous, slave, "free black," or other subaltern groups aspired to be *caballeros* and *damas*. Yet elite and subaltern groups in the Americas shared a common set of grievances as well as having their own, divisive sectional interests. In the long term, these divergent group interests often proved irreconcilable but in the short term might be set aside to fight a common foe. For Creole elites, the foe comprised immigrant Spanish bureaucrats, miners, and merchants, patronizing toward American-born Spaniards and disdainful of the society and cultures that surrounded them. Anti-peninsular feelings were widespread among all classes. Indeed, the despised *chapetones* or *gachupines* were convenient scapegoats for Iberian American elites. In the colonial era, exploitation of subaltern groups and all manner of ills could be ascribed to their influence. After independence, however, it rapidly became obvious that the worst exploiters of indigenous and African underclasses were the Latin American elites themselves—exploitation began at home.

An alternative, broad-brush explanation of the independence era would see the 1808–1814 imperial crisis as a golden opportunity of which Americans availed themselves in order to assert their long-simmering desire for sovereign self-government free from imperial shackles; this aspiration had been ruthlessly constrained by an oppressive colonial régime. The incipient nations had grasped this opportunity to forge their respective nations; it was no gift, then, from a generous metropolis. This was nationalism in action.[6] Whatever the glaring weaknesses of the later independent republics, these were fully nations, however disparate the social and ethnic identities of their citizens, and notwithstanding their limited suffrage. After all, the European nations of that era contained many small nationalisms within them, a primordial ethnic mosaic in which few enjoyed even limited suffrage. Moreover, much American blood had been spilled long before Napoleon's regiments marched onto Iberian soil. Of the many rebellions, revolts, and violent protests of Bourbon Spanish America, the great Andean rebellion of 1780–1781 in the southern Andes was the most sanguinary.[7] Contemporary estimates put its death toll above 100,000 combatants and civilian bystanders. This estimate is probably exaggerated, but it is certain that tens of thousands died. Many of these gave their lives for freedom—from local Creole exploitation, from taxes, from forced labor, from imperial rule. Manifestly, some rebels died in the king's name, but others died to rid themselves of the king entirely. The majority of combatants were indigenous, and many of these *indios* fought to free themselves from non-Indians forever. In 1780, genocidal discourse stemmed from the rebel camp.[8] This was a sharply delineated case of the Empire Fights Back. This indigenous "empire" sought no accommodation within a revamped imperial system. Rather, it wanted to kill all imperialists, the homegrown as well as the imported species. These rustic rebels wanted no place in the Hispanic family of nations. They just wanted to be left alone.

This essentially nationalistic view of Latin American independence is heavily tinged with a fascination for its Great Men—women scarcely appear in this vision—and their supposedly galvanizing courage. Unlike its polar opposite, that interpretation which privileges peninsular events, the nationalist "school" allows for peoples being present at the making of their own history rather than having it handed down from on high. As usual, the truth probably lies somewhere in between—a golden mean between the "home made" and the "trickle down" interpretations. It would be misleading, however, to give the impression that the revolution wrought in Iberian America by the catastrophic upheavals in Europe was primarily military in character. Well before Iberian Americans had recourse to arms, they had made plain their collective resentment against the unremitting tide of reforms that washed over the Iberian world, once the Bourbon dynasty had consolidated its rule in Spain. Parallel reform measures were implemented in the Luso-Brazilian world and provoked dissension, which, however, was more muted than in Spanish America, appropriately so given that these "Pombaline" reforms were on the whole more pallid and less thoroughgoing than their Bourbon counterparts. While some reforms benefited the colonies or, at least, some colonial sectional interest groups, many others were deleterious to local interests, as imperial reformers sought to wrest control of administration and resources from its colonial subjects. The resentments generated thereby provided a fertile seedbed—the cliché here seems justified—that increasingly nurtured separatist ideas and alternative political projects in the colonies.

Wellsprings of Independence

Origins lie deep; causes are often just catalysts, perhaps chains of events that run out of control and, in their turn, overflow into events of "great pith and moment." It is most useful to distinguish between such "triggers" and concatenations of events that generate their own momentum, on the one hand, and the longer-term or contextual roots of independence-era rebellions and wars, on the other. It might be argued that the change from Habsburg to Bourbon dynasties in 1700 set in train events and produced policies guaranteed to alienate the monarchical affections of Americans. Certainly, the relative lassitude and non-confrontationist approach of the Habsburg administrations allowed the colonies, on the whole, a great deal of latitude to arrange governmental, legal, and fiscal matters to suit their own convenience. A leitmotiv of the Habsburg era was the formula *obedezco pero no cumplo*—"I obey but do not comply"—that was used by colonial officials to avoid compliance with royal decrees from the metropolis that inadvertently might damage royal interests or those of selfish colonial elites allied to colonial officialdom. While this slackness continued under Bourbon administrations, the leeway available for what was, effectively, dereliction of duty or insubordination was progressively constrained. Americans were on the whole comfortable under the Habsburg dispensation; however, they increasingly bridled as the Bourbons tightened the reins.

The intellectual climate of the late eighteenth century and the turn of the nineteenth was propitious for Americans who chafed under their activist Bourbon rulers. The Enlightenment was the "usual suspect" for Crown policymakers suspicious of Creole dissent and propensity to subvert royal interests and laws "so kindly meant." Some feared it: the "current of the century" (as one American bishop called it) was seen to drive some of the more contentious Bourbon policies. The central question hovering over the topic of the influence of the Enlightenment on Iberian American constitutional projects, rebellions, and independence is whether the (usually French) canonical texts circulated in the Americas and, if so, were they read and digested by colonial subjects spoiling for a fight with a distant monarch and his ministers? For colonial subjects, there was much to welcome in *ilustrado* thought. Voltaire's *Mores* dispensed with a hierarchy of cultures, opening a new perspective in which Americans might consider themselves equal to Europeans, rather than, as hitherto, cringing before the mother culture. This perhaps prosaic perspective took on a special edge in the context of the perennial colonial rivalry between peninsular Spaniards and Creoles over public appointments. The writings of D'Alembert and the Abbé Raynal posed the question of popular sovereignty in a way designed to provoke colonial American readers.[9]

Other Encyclopedists, especially Rousseau and Diderot, reinforced this re-evaluation of American cultures, above all Amerindian cultures. If this was hardly enough to fuel a pro-indigenist movement within the wider stream of alternative political projects, especially those associated with "Creole Nationalism," the drift of Enlightenment ideas to the Americas was a fillip to native elites and their public profile. This too had political implications for an incipient American nationalism. In the Enlightenment world of "noble savages," indigenous noble descendants of Aztecs and Incas were overdue for a re-evaluation of their nobility. This overhaul of the conventional view of indigenous peoples could only enhance the sense of identity or *conciencia de sí* of the native nobility. That nobility was strongest in the erstwhile capital of the Inca empire, Cuzco, with its hundreds of descendants of former Inca emperors who displayed their livery, "pagan" symbols and all, on civic and religious festive occasions.[10] In France, two contemporaneous popular novels appeared on the Incas, depicting a utopian Inca world and their unjust colonial condition, respectively: Marmontal's *Les Incas* and Mme. de Graffigny's *Lettres d'une Péruvienne*. While there is no record of the colonial Inca nobles having read these, there is record of the influence of a new edition of Garcilaso ("El Inca") de la Vega's *Royal Commentaries of the Incas*, now with a new, inflammatory prophetic introduction. We know that the leader of the Great Rebellion of 1780, an Inca noble called José Gabriel Túpac Amaru, carried Garcilaso on his travels; similarly, Mme. de Graffigny's novel was inspired by her reading of Garcilaso's *Commentaries*. Indeed, these colonial Incas drew on European histories and genealogical treatises in order to compare themselves with the aristocracies of older empires—quite like, in fact, Voltaire had done. These nobles, thus emboldened, were to play a central role in the American response to the constitutional crisis of 1808–1814.

As for Creole elites, the private libraries of the era did include proscribed French texts, though to what effect is not immediately clear. There is good evidence from some colonies (such as Mexico and Brazil) that the leading French authors were read and had a direct impact on the political *engagement* of some colonial dissidents.[11] It is also evident that a popular literature existed (and was read) that ordained an imminent chiliastic era in which Americans would rule themselves. This literature probably comprised, at least in part, some of the canonical *ilustrado* texts reframed for a non-elite audience, akin to what has been called the "literary underground of the Old Regime."[12] The existence of such potentially subversive elite and popular literatures, if not catalysts to insurrection, nevertheless contributed to the impression of an Atlantic World in flux, beset by endemic war at the very time when the civil, ecclesiastical, and religious bases of the ancien régime compact were being shaken to their foundations. These Enlightenment literatures were both symptom and cause of a world turned upside down.

The American subjects of the Castilian and Portuguese monarchies in any case did not need the nourishment of Enlightenment imaginaries for their intellectual armory. Subversive literature had long been at hand which prescribed a formula for popular sovereignty in the event that the monarch should be absent or else prove himself unworthy of his divine oath. These medieval and early modern treatises were familiar to American clergy and jurists.[13] Perhaps most influential was the "constitutionalist" or "Probabilist" social contract theories of Francisco Suárez (1548–1617), the early seventeenth-century Jesuit theologian who, however, built on firm scholastic foundations, notably those of the Dominican St. Thomas Aquinas (1225–1274). The key Spanish Renaissance texts were overwhelmingly religious in character. All these classic texts, instruments of political persuasion, were canonical texts in American universities and seminaries. There was thus a subversive potential innate to traditional scholasticism, with its Aristotelian theories of natural rights and Thomist ideas of devolution of sovereignty to the people, such as reversion to tyranny by a divinely ordained monarch, who thereby forfeited his divine right to rule. Every clergyman had imbibed these ideas in the seminary, and the clergy, for good or ill, wielded great authority in Iberia and Iberian America. There is much truth in the contention that the social contract that influenced separatist Americans was that of Suárez, rather than Rousseau's more modern version. Nonetheless, a late colonial Spanish envoy to New Spain alleged that Mexico City was awash with the most controversial French Enlightenment texts and warned Madrid that their dissemination could have the direst political consequences, especially in light of the recently successful northern War of Independence.[14]

Not that Spain lacked its own homegrown Enlightenment authors of "new ideas," some of whom were indeed Crown ministers.[15] From the American perspective, this was cause not for compliment but rather for complaint, given that the fertile practicality of reformist intellectual ministers such as Aranda and Campomanes was the *fons et origo* of the Bourbon Reforms. Such men were open to fashionable ideas flowing from abroad, especially from Spain's Bourbon sister state to the north. Not all Spain's ideas were derivative, however. The prodigious output of the Spanish Benedictine Fr. Benito Jerónimo Feijoo (1676–1764) was compiled as the *Teatro Crítico Universal*, in effect a one-man encyclopedia to rival that of the northern *philosophes;* the *Teatro Crítico* was widely available and influential throughout Iberian America. The most potent revolutionary force of the era was the incipient Liberalism, something new that throughout the nineteenth century would destabilize many a European throne. Conservatives in Spain, Portugal, and their respective American possessions hardly knew how to handle it. Its utility as a source of practical modernizing ideas and projects was offset by its politically destabilizing tenets, above all concerning representative government or constitutionalism. The principal conduit in Spain for the flow of such unsettling ideas was the *Sociedades Económicas de Amigos del País.*[16] This peculiar institution was akin to a Masonic lodge—yet another movement born of this era and which influenced many patriots in Spanish America and Brazil—but its *salon* included clergy as well as lay members. There was a network of these societies throughout Spain, the most important being in Sevilla, Valencia, and Zaragoza. Indeed, Francisco Carrascón, a Jansenist clergyman member of the Zaragoza Society, later became the principal ideologue of Cuzco's (failed) "patriotic revolution" of 1814–1815. These societies spread rapidly throughout Spanish America after 1780, under a variety of names. In any case, if scholastic and Enlightenment texts failed to enthuse the politically disaffected, there were always the Bible passages invoking justice and especially its more radical books such as Revelations, its dire prophecies of the "last things" being especially potent when applied to this-worldly matters. When the crisis years of 1808–1814 arrived, neither Iberian nor American agitators would overlook its apocalyptic message. Indeed, whatever their ideological disposition, they had an entire palette of colorful ideas from which to construct a separatist rationale: the Bible, Scholasticism, Enlightenment, and Liberal texts. The reason why they delved into such texts for political guidance was the felt impact of the Bourbon and Pombaline reform agendas.

The Imperial Reform Agenda

The Bourbon Reforms have been called the second conquest of the Americas. In the Luso-Brazilian world, the reforms under the aegis of the Marquis de Pombal had less of an impact, because they were fewer in number and their time span shorter, but nevertheless they substantially reconfigured colonial government and economy, always to the mother country's advantage. These represented the collective attempt of the Iberian kingdoms to modernize themselves, to restructure and reform their sclerotic foundations: the military, governmental, administrative, ecclesiastic and religious, and economic and commercial bases of their dynastic power and commonweal. They also stood for metropolitan determination to reform radically their American possessions so as to increase, exponentially if possible, the resources they could extract from their colonial subjects while simultaneously reinforcing the defenses of the colonies against the designs of other European powers as well as putative internal enemies. These reforms are usually presented as a coherent block of major reforms trailing in their wake innumerable petty regulations designed to implement the overall agenda. How monolithic they were is open to doubt. Some reforms seemed timid and piecemeal (the taxation reforms of the 1770s); at other times bold (the 1776 creation of the Viceroyalty of Río de la Plata). In many areas of reform, there was an appearance of two steps forward, one step backward. Do what historians call "the Bourbon Reforms" include all of the reforms introduced after 1700, or just the major structural reforms after 1740? Or does it make sense to restrict the term to the most radical reform conjuncture under Charles III (1759–1788), above all the major imperial restructuring following Spain's humiliating defeat in the Seven Years' War (1756–1763)? The difference translates into choosing between a steady trickle of colonial sympathy for long-distance rule over several generations and a relatively sudden alienation arising from a conjunctural reform program, like that which occurred in the southern Andes in the wake of radical reforms that inter alia transferred Upper Peru with its rich mines of Potosí and Oruro to the new viceroyalty centered on Buenos Aires. It makes better sense to see them as a series of structural reforms, for the most part coherent, which transformed the fundamental bases of metropolitan and imperial rule. For their American victims, however, they might rather have appeared as an inchoate, unremitting rain of rules and regulations that harassed them throughout their lives. As reform piled upon reform, the sense of grievance provoked by one reform was compounded by each successive measure.

Some reforms were shocking and counter-productive. Perhaps the best example of this was the expulsion of the Jesuits from Portuguese (1759) and Spanish (1767) domains, as also from Bourbon France (1764). The Jesuit order was the doyen among educators in the Iberian world. Even Creoles of anti-clerical disposition regarded this measure as damaging to their *patria* and, not least, the future education of their sons (their daughters were instructed privately or by nuns). Manifestly, many Americans benefited by individual reforms, while being disadvantaged by others. Thus the merchants and textile producers who were the immediate beneficiaries of greatly expanded trade opportunities—the *comercio libre* measure of 1778 resulted in a ten-fold increase in exports to Spain and only a four-fold increase in imports—simultaneously found themselves victims of more rigorous tax collection, their market share reduced by a flood of imports, and their market position challenged by a host of new, small-scale traders and producers.[17] The net result was that even major beneficiaries of the reform were usually also its victims, such that each and every American, to greater or lesser extent, had ample cause to be disillusioned with, or alienated from, metropolitan rule. Nor were the costs and benefits shared equally among social classes and interest groups: the clergy took a disproportionate buffeting, while those perennial colonial losers, the Indians, were even worse put upon by the reforms. Eventually there was no one left who did not have several grievances against the metropolis, generally, and the Council of the Indies and its ministers, specifically. For the most part, though, Americans seemed willing to regard the king as another victim of an imperial administration, to all appearances either incompetent or malevolent, or both.

In reconfiguring the fundamental structures of colonial rule, the reforms in some measure presaged the independence era. In particular, they redrew the map of Latin America by creating two new viceroyalties—New Granada (1717, 1739), Río de la Plata (1776)—consolidated the *corregimientos* and *alcaldías mayores*, seen as inefficient and venal, into an intendant system, raised Venezuela (1777) and Chile (1778) to the status of captaincies-general, and revitalized local government. Such measures contained within them the seeds of national identity, raising as they did questions concerning regionalism and representative government. The creation of new political entities also raised the question of incipient national boundaries. There was much food for thought as Iberian Americans were left to ponder whether they would be best served by smaller or larger political entities—whether, for example, one chose to identify with Colombia or New Granada. One might, of course, choose both identities equally, but to ask the question was to raise the specter of a nation state. From there, it was a small step to consider whether one wanted to be a citizen rather than a subject of Colombia, to dispense with the viceroyalty altogether.

Such meditations were easily provoked by, for example, thrusting guns into the hands of a reformed and burgeoning colonial militia.[18] The Indies had never been a military domain. Even the conquest was little more than a private venture sanctioned by the Crowns of Castile and Aragon. It was not military occupation that guaranteed continuing Iberian hegemony, but rather a colonial compact under which the colonies were merged within the metropolis and in which the defense of the empire was underwritten by small garrisons at strategic points, by a chain of fortresses, and reinforced by the conflicting interests of the myriad caste, class, and ethnic subdivisions within the colonies. Put simply, those Iberian Americans who yearned for emancipation from European hegemony had to balance such utopian ideas against the threat posed to them by the overwhelming numbers of indigenous peoples who, once the metropolitan yoke was lifted, might well turn on their Creole and mestizo "siblings." Racial violence turned against themselves was the nightmare of Iberian American elites who, after all, had no clear conscience as regards their treatment of indigenous Americans—exploitation existed prior to the Iberian conquests, was introduced by Spaniards and Portuguese, but was maintained, refined, and exponentially increased by Iberian American "white" elites. The fear of bloody retribution from below was as good a guarantee of continued European hegemony in the Indies as a dozen crack Spanish *tercios*.

The military reforms of the eighteenth century should have made those Hispanic elites think anew their second-class status vis-à-vis their peninsular counterparts, as well as ameliorating their lurking fear of the surly resentment of the subaltern masses of Amerindian and African descent, not to mention the many poorer *españoles* and castes who had never shared in the spoils of colonial rule. Modern research has cast considerable doubt on the thesis that the praetorian tradition of modern Latin American history had its origins in these swingeing military reforms, suggesting instead that it should be sought in the independence wars themselves. Contemporaries were less certain than modern historians, however, and complained bitterly of "imaginary" and "fantastic" military corps that acted and were, in fact, above the law. These were the newly created militias that burgeoned from the 1760s. They comprised all classes, estates, and castes, but their armaments, of whatever caliber, were controlled by the overwhelmingly "white" elites. At a distance the innumerable militiamen looked like tin soldiers, ridiculous Don Nadies strutting small-town streets in impromptu uniforms of many hues. Some were absurdly young: for example, the future Liberator Simón Bolívar was an officer at the age of fourteen. Yet, however comical they appeared to foreign travelers, they had won the right to bear arms, formerly the preserve of nobles or caballeros, and with those arms went menace. The militias were to make their presence felt in civil disturbances and, later, in the great wars from 1808 to 1825—now in favor of the monarchy, now against it. Overnight creations, they went forth and multiplied.

Spain was at war during every decade of the eighteenth century, but the incidence of war involving Portuguese forces was much less. By the same token, it cost much less. The obverse of military glory was its expense. Vast sums were required to maintain a standing army and navy, to mobilize fresh cannon fodder when war threatened, and to mount a campaign, especially expeditions to far-flung trouble spots. This was true even when a war was successfully prosecuted, but this knack eluded Spanish forces more often than not. On grounds of cost alone, it made good sense to create colonial militias, largely self-supporting, to complement the scanty battalions of Spain's colonial standing army. These militias were created to augment imperial defenses against possible incursions or even invasion by Spain's European rivals, notably Great Britain and France. In practice, creation of the militias meant that Spain had mobilized a large civilian standing army that might be turned against its creator. At the outset of the great Túpac Amaru rebellion of 1780–1781, the provincial militia comprised the core of the rebel army. In 1806 and 1808, British forces invaded the River Plate only to suffer humiliating defeats, at the hands of not regular regiments but Creole militia detachments. Two years later, these militias provided the nucleus of an independent Argentine revolutionary army. Spain had provided a rod for its own back.

Policymakers in Europe perhaps anticipated that the overhaul of imperial defense would be kept in check by coeval reform of the governmental apparatus in the colonies. Yet this, too, brought collateral damage in its wake. Much resentment was created from the 1760s by wide-ranging reform of the colonial bureaucratic machinery and a correspondingly vast increase in the numbers of bureaucrats. Whether such reforms were entirely beneficial is open to doubt, but manifestly they generated an increase in colonial disaffection. First, improved bureaucratic efficiency meant improved fiscal efficiency, and taxation increased markedly in the area of the royal mining "fifth," in sales tax (*alcabala*), in the Crown monopolies (*estancos*), tithes, and other charges; Indian tribute in Peru increased exponentially after 1770. Part of this improved fiscal harvest was due to the fact that tax avoidance, for long a sport among elites, was heavily curtailed. Separately, the manner of collection was often heavy-handed. The increased fiscal burden aside, colonial elites bitterly complained about the prevalence of peninsular Spaniards in the bureaucracy. New posts were often filled by peninsulars and other outsiders, such as big-city Creoles transplanted to the provinces, who were perceived to be arrogant in their behavior toward local residents. These appointments exacerbated a long-festering Creole complaint, that of the preferential treatment of peninsulars. This grievance was general throughout the Americas and produced real hatred among the Creoles, a sore point that did nothing for American affections toward the "mother country."

For every winner in the Bourbon reform lottery there were many losers. Native Americans were colonialism's perennial losers, but their condition worsened only slightly during the reform era; it had long been abysmal. Their fiscal burden increased, but on the whole their oppression and exploitation levels fluctuated little. The big losers from the reforms were the clergy, whose considerable wealth and extraordinary privileges were particular targets of reforming ministers.[19] The first to go under the knife were the regular orders, and they never recovered. The secularization decrees of 1747 and 1753 transferred most of the rural parishes (*doctrinas de indios*) controlled by the regular clergy to the secular parish clergy. Because the rural indigenous peoples were the principal source of ecclesiastical income, this measure impoverished the orders while simultaneously enriching many secular priests. Whereas in Europe Church wealth derived principally from ecclesiastical landholding, in the Americas the bulk of clerical incomes came from sacramental fees (*obvenciones*) and a Crown subvention (*sínodo*) to beneficed parish priests (*curas*). There were other sources of income such as tithes and testamentary dispositions, especially chantries, but the richest earnings by far came from parochial fees and the subsidy. However, it was only from around 1790, with the succession of Charles IV, that the Crown dared tax ecclesiastical earnings directly. This it did in three steps, with two further measures added after 1808, courtesy of the Junta Central and the Cortés of Cádiz, respectively. First, two subsidies (*subsidios eclesiásticos*) of 1790 and 1800 directly taxed (about 12 percent) the incomes of all diocesan, parochial clergy and the regular orders. Second, while this was being collected from clergy, the episode of the consolidation of the *vales reales* was introduced in 1798 in the peninsula and from 1802 in Spanish America. Third, several ad hoc imposts—forced "donations"—on clergy between 1796 and 1808 raised funds to feed the insatiable Bourbon appetite for war finance. After the fall of the monarchy, the Supreme Junta Central in 1809 introduced another compulsory "voluntary donation" that stripped away most of the chantries and property liens left after the swingeing consolidation measures had devastated clerical and local church incomes; this appalling new tax was collected from 1810 to 1813. Finally, the hard-pressed Cortés decreed an impost impounding most gold and silver church plate, including that used in the celebration of the holy mass—this was frankly tantamount to sacrilege. Now an older, anti-Moorish *reconquista* discourse attacking the new "saracens" in their midst was resurrected and was to be increasingly heard in Iberia and Iberian America.

Some clergy regarded even such prosaic reforms as taxing tithes and first fruits as sacrilegious, as interfering in God's divine plan. The post-1808 imposts were therefore especially horrendous, enraging many clergy and directly fueling the desire to be freed from either the imperial monarchy or the liberal regime, or both. All of these fiscal measures merged into a wider radical reform process that targeted Church and clergy. Most notably, they were imbricated in what has been called the "crisis of ecclesiastical privilege," the gradual but damaging erosion of ecclesiastical jurisdiction—over civil, criminal, ecclesiastical, and even strictly religious matters—by a succession of royal decrees ranging over several decades. These reforms severely reduced the Church's authority over family matters, control of delinquency, local disputes, and (most damaging of all) litigation concerning real property, property loans, and liens. Harshest of all ecclesiastical reforms, the clergy's right (*fuero eclesiástico*) to have their legal affairs heard before Church tribunals was seriously eroded by numerous decrees, to the point that, in the independence era, they found themselves subject to military tribunals, which sometimes summarily executed insurgent clergy. The clergy's power over indigenous Americans—not least to extract taxes and free labor service, and to mete out corporal punishment—was similarly constrained by successive decrees. Even in the religious sphere, there was a series of decrees that reformed liturgical practice, especially as regards public rituals and processions, for the good reason that these might be exploited by political activists; religious confraternities (*cofradíasain*) and the religious orders were also targets of several reforms. These meshed with a curtailing of sacramental charges, especially the exorbitant funeral fees. The overall effect of the myriad ecclesiastical reforms was vastly to enhance the power and authority of Crown officials, royal tribunals, and local government authorities, with a consequently severe weakening in the secular and regular clergy, the low clergy as well as the prelacy. The affronts to Church and clergy were unending, each outrage compounding the previous, until political alienation eventually was attained. In this all-out assault on the bases of the Church's temporal authority, the Crown ministers, ingenious in most respects, appeared to have overlooked two eternal verities: that religion harnessed as ideology is especially potent; and that the clergy constituted the colonial information network, above all to the rural masses. Before and after 1808 the Crown would pay the price for such obtuseness, as some clerics opted for insurgency and many others evinced sullen indifference to the fate of the distant metropolis.

Bourbon imperial restructuring had better luck in its economic and commercial reforms. Here again, though, the obverse of success was that many colonial elites acquired a certain self-confidence and *conciencia de sí* from sharing in the commercial, mining, and textile manufacturing growth spurts of the late colonial era. Creoles were more than capable of flexing their commercial muscle: the Bourbon *comercio libre* reform of 1778—"free trade" so restricted as to be anything but free—witnessed a ten-fold increase in American exports to Spain, while imports increased four-fold. While a success, it was hardly the result anticipated by reformers. In any case, Creole profits tended to obscure the fact that imports still comprised mainly specie and primary produce; there was growth, but precious little economic development. Economic success stories often had an opportunity cost. In 1776 the Crown created the new Viceroyalty of Río de la Plata with Buenos Aires as its capital. Simultaneously, it ordered the silver from the rich mines of Upper Peru (later Bolivia), the lifeblood of Spanish South America's internal market, to be transported to Buenos Aires rather than, as previously, to Lima. This severely damaged grain and textile production in the Viceroyalty of Peru, though the impact was assuredly much less than alleged by its ostensible victims. Within less than a decade, these reforms produced a boom in Buenos Aires that lasted to independence, but at the cost of alienating the influential elites in Peru. Ironically, it was in Buenos Aires that the first independent Spanish American republic was declared. Nor, for that matter, did booming mining production in Mexico and the individual fortunes it generated do much to douse Creole enthusiasm for, at least, a vastly enhanced control of its own destiny. It was precisely in Mexico that "Creole Nationalism" is first detectable, for all that the Argentines moved quicker to act on their own separatist convictions.

Straws in the Wind: Rebellion, Revolt, and Protest

Security at home and abroad provided the essential rationale for the Bourbon Reforms. Yet the era witnessed frequent outbreaks of danger—many brushfires, a few great conflagrations. Local protest increased markedly after mid-century, usually village revolts directed against high-handed local officials or avaricious village notables. Official venality went hand in hand with coercive tax collection operations, transgressing a notional "moral economy" that defined the limits beyond which a community would tolerate no further exploitation. These were similar to those European peasant jacqueries of the seventeenth century rebelling against royalty tightening its grip on regional affairs, typically involving abusive tax farmers, forcible military recruiting, steepling taxes, and local administrations that were more inflexible and less ad hoc than previously. In a sense, the wave of village and town riots in eighteenth-century Iberian America were the counterpart of those in seventeenth-century Western Europe: collective protest against the beginnings of modernization and the growth of the absolutist state. These riots and revolts perhaps represented something more, colonial subjects beginning to test the limits of imperial or vice-regal power. A number of violent protests, at times verging on political alienation, were clearly designed to challenge royal officials' attempts to implement some or other tax innovation, manifestly markers of discontent with specific Crown policies. Others simply responded to traditional local grievances, a world away from policy protests. Some spectacular outbursts with revitalization overtones, such as sudden Maya uprisings, merged with unease produced by the reform conjuncture. Still other localized violent protests were more ominous, portents or earnests of more serious storms long in the making. The numerous Mexican village protests of the era fizzled out quickly, even those with a messianic flavor. It was in the Andes that the river of protest finally burst its banks.

It is not entirely clear why the popular onslaught against the perceived excesses of colonial rule should have struck there rather than in Mesoamerica, but several reasons suggest themselves. First, the Andes were at a far greater remove, and it was difficult access for the manpower and resources necessary to suppress a large-scale rebellion, especially in the highlands. Second, there was a much larger ratio of indigenous to non-indigenous subjects in the Andes, and the region's "Indians" suffered incomparably greater exploitation than other social sectors, at home or abroad. Third, some research suggests that the royal and ecclesiastical tax burden was significantly heavier there. Fourth, the use of forced corvée labor (*mita*) was much more widespread in the Andes. Fifth, there was no exploitative mechanism in Mesoamerica to match the devastating Andean forced sale of merchandise (*repartimiento de mercancías*) that struck at poorer rural Creoles and castes as well as native Andeans. Finally, there were "deep rivers" of messianism and millenarianism in the Andes. Although Mesoamerica did not lack revitalization movements, large and small, cognate Andean instances centered on the shimmering figure of an Inca redivivus who would restore either the old Inca empire (Tahuantinsuyu) or a cross-class and cross-racial alliance, headed by an Inca or Incan confederation. There was simply no comparable Aztec or Maya or Chibcha personage to match this Incan specter.

The Age of Andean Rebellion is usually viewed as running from 1730 to the great insurrection or rebellion (*levantamiento general*) of 1780–1781, although similar insurgent patterns of behavior suggest that this "Age" should also embrace the long wars of independence in the southern sierra.[20] This firestorm was long in the making, smoldering conspiracies and occasional brushfires littering the half century, above all the never-defeated, quasi-messianic Santos Atahuallpa rebellion on the eastern edge of Peru's central sierra. To greater or lesser extent, these revolts and conspiracies featured Incan ideology, discourse, and symbolism: they kept the idea of an Inca messiah alive. In 1780 the remarkable happened: a massive rebellion led by one who claimed not just to be an Inca noble—there were hundreds of descendants of the erstwhile Inca emperors—but to be primus inter pares among Incas and thus first in line to inherit a Peruvian throne, whether entirely independent of Spain or as ruler of a dominion answering only to the Castilian monarch. In fact, the "Great Rebellion" consisted of two discrete uprisings that gradually merged in mid-1781. The more compelling within the wider Atlantic context was the eponymous rebellion of José Gabriel Túpac Amaru, which at its inception appealed for alliance between all American social groups, though, after military reverses and splits within its shaky interracial coalition, it eventually curdled into an increasingly nativist rebellion. Even more ferocious was its southern counterpart, the Túpac Catari movement. Both movements were anti-peninsular—indeed, they decreed the death of all European Spaniards—and were marked by atrocities committed by both rebel and royalist forces, especially once Creoles and mixed-race combatants and civilian bystanders, caught in the vortex, also became generalized targets of violence. One contemporary estimate set the rebellions' mortality at 100,000; another claimed that 120,000 died in the *catarista* insurgency alone. Both figures are probably exaggerated, but it is beyond doubt that tens of thousands of deaths resulted from pitched battles, skirmishes, and unbridled massacres of civilians. The Great Rebellion and its precursors made clear that the foundations of Spanish rule in the Americas were shaky. It also underlined just what American elites themselves had to fear from the collapse of those foundations: the specter of a vengeful indigenous flood willing to spill Creole blood to avenge the exploitation and humiliation of three centuries of colonial subjection. Even without this moral, should the revolutionary example of North America exert an appeal on incipient Creole nationalism, they would be given pause by the sanguinary Haitian Revolution. The terrible end of the French colonists there would remind them of what they might expect from an indigenous peasantry freed of its shackles, aided by free black and slave populations.

Not that Andean insurgency always, or only, involved indigenous protestors and rebels. The Great Rebellion was preceded by several urban riots crewed mainly by Creole and mixed-race groups; where they were joined by "Indians," these mostly belonged to the deracinated urban *indiada*. Yet it was the northern Andes, in the Viceroyalty of New Granada, that revealed most clearly the extent of Creole disaffection with Bourbon innovations. The so-called Rebellion of the Barrios in the city of Quito in 1765 was a well-organized and largely successful revolt that presaged the extraordinary Comunero Rebellion of 1781, to a degree influenced by the Túpac Amaru rebellion but primarily a non-indigenous protest movement.[21] It was the culmination of numerous village riots throughout New Granada over two decades. Unlike the Túpac Amaru rebellion, it evinced no real desire for an alternative to continued Spanish hegemony. All of these rebellions and revolts brought at least temporary relief from exploitation, fiscal impositions, and official high-handedness. Even as the Túpac Amaru rebellion got underway, the hated *reparto* was abolished followed by the abolition of the *corregimientos*. Such alleviation, though, was short-lived, as indigenous communities fell victims to local elites—notably the clergy of the rural parishes—as avaricious as the *corregidors* they replaced. Nevertheless, improved military and bureaucratic efficiency bolstered by Creole fears of a hostile and vengeful *indiada* combined to ensure a period of relative peace. Until, that is, the watershed years of 1808–1814 transformed the Hispanic world.

The Window of Opportunity

The first phase of the Latin American independence struggle had Napoleon Bonaparte as its ringmaster. This simile seems especially apt, given that the disintegrating Spain of 1807–1808 resembled a circus.[22] Its régime was an embarrassment at home and abroad, especially given the widespread belief that King Charles IV had for long been cuckolded by the royal favorite, Manuel de Godoy. Napoleon's interest in the peninsula sprang directly from his war with Britain. The only remaining gap in the continental blockade was Portugal, Britain's long-time ally. Ineluctably, Portugal had to yield or be defeated militarily. By the Treaty of Fontainebleau in 1807, France and a craven Spain conspired to conquer Portugal; the treaty allowed Napoleonic forces to be stationed in Spain preparatory to invading Portugal. Spain's economy had recently been wracked by a devastating famine, the popular classes had suffered badly, resentment was rising, and such was the magnitude of the disaffection that an alternative was sought, actively so by the so-called *partido fernandista* whose members rallied round Charles's son, Ferdinand, Prince of Asturias, in a bid to undermine the king, Queen María Luisa, and her favorite Godoy. Fortuitously, popular hopes coincided with military plans in the belief that Ferdinand (*el deseado*) on the throne would be the saving of Spain. Both parties wooed Napoleon for his support. In the case of Ferdinand, conspiring with a foreign power to overthrow the king was tantamount to treason. Drawing Napoleon even closer to court machinations was foolish in the extreme: both factions merely won his contempt. By this stage of his career, the emperor was the French Revolution incarnate: if 1789 had destroyed the Bourbon dynasty in France, why should its Spanish branch be permitted to survive?

The Spanish Bourbons destroyed themselves; Napoleon merely delivered the coup de grâce. Even at this remove it seems remarkable that Spaniards could have seen Ferdinand as *el deseado*. Of him it was written that he learned nothing and forgot nothing. His will to power was subverted by his obtuseness, notwithstanding that he grabbed the throne by force (1808) and was twice restored (1814, 1823) after having been overthrown by first the French (1808) and then his own Spanish subjects (1820). Charles IV abdicated in the wake of the Aranjuez riots, orchestrated by Ferdinand, his *partido*, and the military. It is this event that marks the beginning of the long and sorry history of military involvement in the making and breaking of Spanish governments. Ferdinand entered Madrid triumphantly, anticipating popular acclaim and a French benison. Instead, he was seized and, with his parents, was transported to Bayonne, whence both son and father (for the second time) abdicated in favor of Napoleon, who offered the throne to his brother Joseph Bonaparte, king of Naples, now become king of Spain. Spanish humiliation was complete.

European Spaniards and American Spaniards resolved to act politically and militarily. Here began two great movements: the Spanish War of Independence to expel the invader from Spanish domains, and the Latin American Wars of Independence, more ambiguous in their aspirations even when prosecuted in the name of Ferdinand VII. In 1808, however, the Hispanic world was united in the great enterprise of ridding itself of French invaders. Events in Spain now moved rapidly. The political vacuum was filled by the juntas that sprang up across the length and breadth of the peninsula to direct and coordinate local and regional defense. These rapidly gave way to a Junta Central based in Seville, which in 1810 dissolved into a Council of Regency, which in turn convoked a parliament or Cortés. The Cortés met in the near-impregnable city of Cádiz, and here began a constitutional experiment that would transform the Atlantic World. Its deliberations and the Constitution of 1812 that it promulgated spelled out, for the very first time, the rights of Americans. Indeed, it decreed the full equality of their rights with those of Spaniards. Elections were held under the provisions of the Constitution and Creole deputies began arriving in Cádiz to take full part in the forging of a liberal Spain, but one still loyal to the missing king. This was all to the good, but the abdication of two kings without demur, the Peninsular War itself, and the devolution of sovereignty inhering in the popular institutions of the Juntas, the Regency, and the Cortés, posed for Americans some tricky questions. If Americans enjoyed full constitutional equality, why should they not form or elect their own Juntas to encode their sovereignty during the captivity of their sovereign? Why, indeed, bother with a monarch at all, given the pusillanimity of Charles IV and Ferdinand VII—and his blatant treachery—who had not deigned to consult any of their subjects before meekly abdicating in favor of a godless foreigner? Spanish Americans had reached a crossroads.

The Making of Latin America: The First Phase

The extraordinary peninsular events and their constitutional implications came as a bolt from the heavens. The news galvanized Americans; some moved promptly, others warily, still others were paralyzed by indecision. Loyalties were split; factions formed; occasionally, naturally antipathetic liberals and conservatives joined forces in a show of reformist loyalty. It did not take long, however, for blood to flow. There were ambiguities in the first phase of the independence process, which lasted until 1817.[23] In the decisive second phase, such doubts evaporated. The issue was now starkly posed: full independence or nothing. The sharpening of focus was for two reasons. First, the restoration of Ferdinand VII no longer permitted the indecision or obfuscation of using the king's name to cloak separatist aims; now it was a case of whether one was for or against the monarch. Second, bloody reprisals awaited those who were found in the wrong camp as battle lines shifted. Even Simón Bolívar, the greatest of the "liberators" and a liberal hero, had 800 prisoners cold-bloodedly executed en masse; the previous year, Bolívar had perpetrated another atrocity by executing 60 Creole and peninsular captives.[24] As retaliation followed massacre, the death toll continued to rise. No one has calculated the entire human cost of the independence wars between 1808 and 1825, but it was enormous. These were not only wars against Spain but were to a very great degree also civil wars.

It took some time for Spanish Americans to digest the news of the European disaster. Then, in 1809, the Upper Peruvians (Bolivians in prospect) broke ranks. The cities of La Paz and Chuquisaca (also called La Plata, after 1825 renamed Sucre) formed independent juntas.[25] Although these were ostensibly to rule in Ferdinand's name and were pacific, they were brutally crushed by Goyeneche and the leaders executed. Shortly after, Quito declared its own junta; then Bogotá followed suit; in Mexico, leading Creoles conspired in Valladolid (modern Morelia) to seize power, again to rule in Ferdinand's name. All these minor and largely pacific projects were suppressed in a heavy-handed manner. Americans were left to ponder what their alleged equality with Spaniards was worth, if their blood was to be shed when they tried to form comparable juntas which aimed to rule in the name of the deposed king. There was manifestly a contradiction between peninsular liberal proclamations and American aspirations. This reflected tensions between the Spanish juntas and American viceregal administrations even before the Cortés of Cádiz came into being. Its inauguration hardly improved liberals' relations with the viceroys.

Then, in 1810, the Junta Central collapsed. Americans promptly responded by creating juntas in Río de la Plata (Argentina, Uruguay, Paraguay), Chile,

New Granada (Colombia, Ecuador) and Venezuela. The emerging *conciencia de sí* of Buenos Aires and its inhabitants had been on the rise since the reforms of 1776, when it became, overnight, the seat of a new viceroyalty, which then witnessed a period of unbroken prosperity and growth into the new century. The self-confidence of *bonaerenses* or *porteños* increased exponentially when its militias defeated successive British invasions in 1806 and 1808. When news of the collapse of the Junta Central arrived, the viceroy was deposed and a junta was formed—popular sovereignty acting in the deposed king's stead. A rampant Buenos Aires then joined war with both Paraguay and Montevideo, in the Banda Oriental. Paraguay emerged victorious, proclaimed independence in 1811, and then settled down to an unbroken, relatively prosperous twenty-six years of dictatorship (1814–1840) under José Gaspar Rodríguez de Francia. Meanwhile, the movement in Buenos Aires bogged down, mired in differences between constitutional monarchists and the partisans of a more radical political solution to the imperial crisis, and between centralists and provincial interests. These strains were eased by a change of personnel on the junta, and by a somewhat fragile accord between the *bonaerenses* and *provincianos*. Adoption of the name United Provinces of the Río de la Plata helped to quell the latter's fears. Full independence from Spain—from its king, liberals, and conservatives—was declared at the Congress of Tucumán in 1816. Uruguay's birth was more protracted and crucially assisted by Great Britain in the unlikely role of midwife. However, the independence movement was driven by the landowner José Gervasio Artigas, in the face of stiff opposition from both Buenos Aires and Brazil. It was incorporated into Brazil from 1817 to 1828, whence the Banda Oriental became Uruguay.[26]

In Chile, a national junta was elected (by limited suffrage) following the resignation of the captain-general.[27] It claimed limited sovereignty in the name of the king and eschewed any separatist pretensions. Nevertheless, the election of a new national congress seems to have radicalized the political sphere, and clear evidence of separatist tendencies began to emerge. Accordingly, the viceroy of Peru, José de Abascal, sent an expeditionary force, which routed patriot forces at Rancagua in 1814, marking the end of Chile's Patria Vieja and three years of repressive royalist government. However, Bernardo O'Higgins, the Creole patriot leader and illegitimate son of the erstwhile viceroy of Peru, Irishman Ambrosio O'Higgins, was still at large with his rump army, ensconced beyond the cordillera and now under the command of José de San Martín, who was mounting an invasion of Chile preparatory to liberating Lima, the main bastion of royalist rule in Spanish South America.

Mexico's response to the fall of the Junta Central was violent. The viceroyalty's death knell was tolled on September 16, 1810, by the priest Miguel Hidalgo.[28] His call to arms or *grito de Dolores* sparked a popular, mass insurrection in central Mexico. Largely confined to the Bajío region—densely populated, wealthy, prostrated by famine, its victims at the mercy of rising prices and falling wages—it nevertheless quickly engulfed towns and villages. Its fury, however, soon alienated Creole sympathizers, as soon as it became clear that Mexican elites would face a social revolution, clearly underlined by the massacre of Guanajuato's Creole as well as peninsular defenders. Hidalgo was run to ground by royalist forces in 1811 and executed. His successor, José María Morelos, a *cura* from the poor *tierra caliente,* had greater rapport with his insurgent troops and better military nous and martial prowess than Hidalgo. He met the same fate, however, being captured and executed in 1815. Mexico's separatist aspirations appeared to have run out of steam. The numerous village riots and provincial revolts that speckled the half century to 1810 established a tradition of collective violence in the region, but their limited goals and short duration suggested that they could prove no real threat to continuing Spanish hegemony. The events of 1810–1815 had disabused elite Mexicans of that comforting assumption, not least when Hidalgo stood at the gates of the capital with 80,000 non-elite Mexicans, only to turn away. This was to draw the moral with a vengeance; its *quod erat demonstrandum* came a century later, in the Mexican Revolution, one of the great civil wars.

The spectacle of priests as insurgent leaders was the most salient feature of the 1810–1815 uprising. In the Atlantic World of the era, this was not quite so extraordinary as it might appear. The French Revolution witnessed insurgent priests in both the royalist and revolutionary forces, the "constitutional priests"—also known as *curés patriots, curés rouges, curés democrats*—as well as the defenders of the traditional faith, above all the martyr priests of the Vendée. In Ireland, the Wexford Rebellion of 1798 was partly directed by rebel priests. During the Peninsular War, Spanish priests bore arms in the guerrilla corps against the Napoleonic invaders. Further south, there were numerous combatant priests for and against independence in the Viceroyalty of New Granada and Venezuela; in the latter, royalist *curas* were instrumental in turning the rebel tide during the ferocious campaigns of General Morillo. However, the most exemplary case of ecclesiastical insurgency was in the Viceroyalty of Peru, during the failed Cuzco Revolution of 1814–1815.[29] The revolution encompassed southern Peru in its entirety, revolutionary forces occupying the cities of Arequipa and Guamanga (modern Ayacucho); indeed, a revolutionary expedition conquered, and for a time held, the city of La Paz. Many clergy joined the revolution—although these were a minority of clergy, as in Mexico—and served not only as military chaplains but also as insurgent leaders. Ildefonso de las Muñecas, a beneficed cathedral priest, continued to operate as a warlord (like Morelos) even after the royalist suppression of the movement. He led the nominally independent provinces or *republiquetas* until his capture and death in 1817. One of the revolution's leading cadres was a peninsular prebend of the cathedral of Cuzco, Francisco Carrascón y la Sota, but perhaps even more remarkable was the enthusiastic support for the revolution by the bishop and most of the cathedral chapter of Cuzco, a movement which aimed at full independence from Spain and its monarchy.

Far north, innumerable battles, unparalleled atrocities, and fluctuating fortunes characterized the struggle for ascendancy in Venezuela and New Granada after 1810. Paradoxically, Venezuela produced several of the most remarkable figures of the unfolding Latin American independence movement—Miranda, Bolívar, Bello, Sucre, and Santander—and yet was unrivaled as a killing field. Both armies in the Venezuelan campaigns willingly engaged in a declared war of extermination, high battlefield mortality crowned by summary mass executions of prisoners. Bolívar, "El Libertador," was unsurpassed in the massacre of prisoners. Yet it began peaceably enough, with both Miranda and Bolívar in the ascendant. Caracas embraced the news of the Junta Central's fall by establishing its own junta to rule in Ferdinand's name, but its momentum was such that full independence was declared on July 5, 1811. However, this First Venezuelan Republic rapidly crumbled in 1812 when confronted with a Spanish expedition sent by the Council of Regency; in extremis, Spain was fighting a war on the home front against the French and a war abroad against its American subjects. Meanwhile, in New Granada, several cities formed juntas, two governments were formed centered on Bogotá and Tunja, respectively, the latter called the Confederation of New Granada. Then Bolívar arrived, an army was raised, and the Second Republic was inaugurated. It lasted until 1815, prostrated by several crushing defeats at the hands of the fearsome *llanero* cavalry led by José Tomás Boves. In prospect, too, was a major expeditionary force led by General Pablo Morillo, the greatest of the royalist military commanders of the era, ordered from Spain by Ferdinand VII, now restored to his throne. By the end of 1815, Venezuela and New Granada were once again securely under royalist control.

The Consummation

Simón Bolívar was the greatest of all independence heroes.[30] After 1815 he improved as a military leader, learning the hard way from numerous reverses. An inspirational and ruthless commander, he could lead men where few others dared: his route march to Bogotá in appalling conditions, whence countless followers died from privation, is one of the great victories in the entire history of warfare. In the independence campaigns, only San Martín's odyssey in crossing the Andes into Chile bears even the slightest comparison. His political vision encompassed the entire continent, but it was a dictatorial imaginary that fell before centrifugal, regionalist forces. Bolívar's goals owed much to Francisco Miranda, one of the extraordinary figures of the era.[31] Miranda's peregrinations through Europe and the Americas were epic in scale. He was a French revolutionary general, commanding a division in battle. He fought in the southern theater of the North American Revolution. He inculcated Enlightenment ideas of liberty in a generation of Spanish Americans, even founding a Masonic chapter in London, where he talked independence with Bolívar, San Martín, Bello, and O'Higgins. He was the intimate of many luminaries of the period: Robespierre, Pitt, Bentham, James Mill, Alexander Hamilton, and many others. He devised a bicameral constitution for an independent South American republic, notable for its inclusion of indigenous nobles or *caciques*, a mixture of British, French, and Spanish constitutional precepts that would be ceremonially headed by an Inca. It was only on home soil that he was found wanting. Greeted as a hero in Caracas, he met successive military defeats, only to flee with patriot monies to the Caribbean; intercepted en route, he died in a Spanish prison in 1816. He had personified the Atlantic Revolution. However, Miranda's sometime protégé, Simón Bolívar, was far from finished. Lessons learned, the second phase of his career was to be decisive.

The Liberator launched a fresh attempt from emancipated Haiti in 1816. It failed ignominiously, but he tried again, once more supported by the Haitian Republic. This time his luck held; it was reinforced through his skill as a coordinator of disparate commands, including the feared *llaneros* who had switched to the patriot cause, and who were now under the command of José Antonio Páez, the implacable Boves having been killed in battle. He was fortunate, too, that his forces were swelled by a foreign legion of some 4,000 adventurers, most veterans of the Napoleonic Wars, about 500 of them British. These combatants played a leading role in Latin American independence well out of proportion to their number, the most prominent being Thomas, Lord Cochrane, in Chile, Peru, and Brazil; Bernardo O'Higgins, second-generation Irish, in Chile; and General William Miller and Daniel O'Leary in Bolívar's army. Their influx was most opportune, because their leading royalist adversary was the formidable General Morillo. To a degree, Bolívar and his indispensable general, Antonio José de Sucre, fought him to a standstill, but it was clear by now that the patriot star was in the ascendant. Bogotá and other New Granadan provinces had already fallen to the patriots at the Battle of Boyacá in 1819. However, it was only when Morillo set sail for Europe, undefeated, that the patriot army proved irresistible, crushing royalist forces at the battle of Carabobo in 1821. Venezuela was now triumphantly independent. Less than a year later, it was joined by New Granada, with the Quito region liberated by Sucre at the battle of Pichincha. The Viceroyalty of New Granada was now the Republic of Colombia. The key to South American independence was the Viceroyalty of Peru, Spain's continental nerve center. The road to Lima now stood open.

Two other dominoes needed to fall: both Chile and Charcas (Upper Peru) harbored considerable separatist sentiment. The defeat of O'Higgins at Rancagua in 1814 had quelled Chilean hopes in the interim, but the invasion of Spanish troops dispatched from Lima did nothing to strengthen ties to the metropolis. Chile was ripe for the taking. While the separatist political aspirations of Charcas liberals remained undimmed, there was markedly less enthusiasm for independence in Upper Peru given the brutal reprisals meted out to the vanguard liberals of Chuquisaca and La Paz by the royalist Goyeneche in 1809, and especially following the region's "liberation" by the *porteño* army in 1811. The patriot army of Buenos Aires under Castelli arrived in Charcas to eradicate the remaining royalist presence, a potential threat to the River Plate, but proved as bad or worse than Goyeneche's troops, destroying property, looting houses, and attacking, raping, and killing their ostensible allies. The royalist Goyeneche ordered executions; the patriot Castelli authorized rapine. The hapless Upper Peruvians were caught between two armies, their friends as savage as their enemies.

As in Venezuela, indeed like in any civil war, military advantage ebbed and flowed as armies advanced and then retreated. After 1814, however, the fortunes of war favored the royalist occupiers. This followed another invasion by the ostensibly liberating *porteño* army, who retreated south; royalist forces that tracked them were in turn defeated by the *porteños* under General Belgrano. Stalemate had been reached, and Upper Peru remained in royalist hands until 1825 when Sucre successfully engaged a depleted royalist army led by General Pedro Antonio de Olañeta. Upper Peru became Bolivia in honor of El Libertador, who entered his now eponymous republic from southern Peru. In 1814, however, the royalists in Upper and Lower Peru had faced a greater threat than that posed by the patriot army of Buenos Aires, far from its principal supply lines and living off the land. The initially triumphant Cuzqueño *revolución de la patria* seemed to sweep all before it, with victorious expeditions winning all of southern Peru. Its 1814 expedition to La Paz was also successful, but the revolutionary army was pursued north by forces under General Ramírez, a seasoned Peninsular War veteran, who in 1815 crushed the Cuzqueños at the battle of Umachiri. The Cuzco revolution rejected government from the peninsula, whether liberal or monarchical, and aimed at a complete break with Spain—full independence, in fact.

Royalists and patriots both were surprised by the outbreak in 1820 of the radically liberal Riego Revolt in Spain. If this emboldened patriots, it dismayed the royalists and left them in some disarray. By this time Chile had been liberated by the extraordinary expeditionary march over the Andean cordillera led by San Martín, with O'Higgins and his remnant Chilean army under his command. Chilean independence was declared in 1818 and O'Higgins installed as supreme director. San Martín then mounted the great liberating expedition to Peru, borne to Lima by a navy under Lord Cochrane. The patriots made landfalls, met no opposition, entered into prolonged negotiations with the royalists, and took Lima when the royalists abandoned the city. San Martín was proclaimed protector, but without much popular acclaim, indeed, with a great deal of indifference. Lima was beset by political torpor. The royalists, meanwhile, controlled the central sierra and the south, where the vice-regal government re-established itself in the ancient Inca capital, Cuzco. By this time, the southern military commander, José de la Serna, had, in a bloodless coup with ex post facto blessing from Spain, replaced the vacillating Joaquín de la Pezuela as viceroy of Peru. The independence movement in Peru was at a standstill, the water-borne invasion becalmed.

This should have been a galvanizing moment for Peruvian patriots, but there were precious few of these in Lima. It had been the *serranos*, especially in the southern sierra, who had fought hard in the "great uprising" of 1780–1782 and the "patriotic revolution" of 1814–1815. Yet Lima was and remained the seat of power, and it was to be the *limeños* and not the *serranos* who were the heirs and beneficiaries of independence, which was delivered to them in 1824 by Bolívar and Sucre. With Bolívar organizing in the north, San Martín's landfall near Lima should have been the defining moment of Peruvian Independence, a pincer movement in which the southern and northern movements came together—a trap shutting on the vice-regal army. This lost opportunity worked, though, to Bolívar's advantage. At a celebrated meeting between Bolívar and San Martín in Guayaquil in 1822, San Martín, ill and out of ideas, ceded command of the Peruvian expeditionary force to Bolívar. The Liberator arrived in Lima to be acclaimed as dictator—perhaps *limeños* prudently recalled his mass executions of prisoners in Venezuela—and fresh preparations were made to give battle, at last, to La Serna's vice-regal forces. It was Sucre, however, who delivered Spanish South America to Bolívar. His great victories at Junin and Ayacucho in 1824 were followed by the viceroy's unconditional surrender. General Rodil held out at the Fortress of Callao until 1826, but this siege was but a footnote to Peruvian independence, albeit one in which over two thousand died from starvation and disease. With Peru seized, Upper Peru was the only remaining royalist redoubt, but after two small military engagements, General Olañeta surrendered to Sucre. Sucre had again delivered victory to Bolívar, the absentee commander. This victory was the capstone of independence in Spanish South America.

In Mesoamerica, meanwhile, independence was reached raggedly, a distinct anti-climax after the heroics of the Hidalgo-Morelos insurrection, for all that there remained insurgent activity in several Mexican provinces, notably that led by Vicente Guerrero in the south. The five soon-to-be Central American states—Guatemala, Honduras, Nicaragua, Costa Rica, El Salvador—were hitched to Mexico's destiny, unwillingly dragged along like refractory children. By 1820 repression was the principal characteristic of government in Mexico, a contrast with the relatively benevolent policy of a decade earlier. This darkening of attitude was a direct consequence of the fright to Creole and peninsular life and limb posed by the insurgency of 1810–1816, although Creoles had also been culpable in several massacres of *gachupines*. With Guerrero and other rebel leaders posing a continuing threat to the central power, repression was stepped up, especially with the appointment of Agustín de Iturbide as commander of the army of the south. At this point the Riego Revolt occurred, and Ferdinand VII was obliged to reintroduce the Constitution of 1812 and convoke a Cortés. The new Cortés, radically liberal, issued a stream of decrees attacking the vested interests of clergy, landowners, military, and others. Many conservative Creoles now took a new separatist line, supported by the Church, which was the prime target of the new liberal reforms. On February 24, 1821, the Plan de Iguala was proclaimed declaring independence and guaranteeing the Catholic faith and national unity but still, at this point, loyal to Ferdinand VII. Madrid rejected these developments, a five-man regency was instituted, led by Iturbide as *alteza* or "highness," and a thirty-eight man junta was formed. In 1822 Iturbide and soldiers loyal to him engineered a popular demonstration demanding his proclamation as Emperor Agustín I. This was uncannily similar to the way Ferdinand had arranged his own elevation to the throne by instigating the Aranjuez riots; it was fitting, then, that Iturbide's coronation marked the end of Ferdinand's rule in Mexico. Mexico was now its own empire. In 1824 Iturbide, dictatorial and lacking judgment, was ousted, and a federal republic was proclaimed in the Constitution of 1824. Mexico was now independent, but after the élan and vigor of the insurgency of 1810–1816, it had merely crept over the line, wracked with division and disharmony.

The Central American provinces were even less united within and among themselves.[32] The independence process there was fissiparous, centrifugal. The 1812 Constitution had been popular among the region's elites, especially in Guatemala, pre-eminent among the nascent states. Liberal tendencies were given renewed emphasis from the Cortés of 1820–1823. Aspirations to independence rapidly became evident, as region after region declared itself emancipated, a process brought to a sudden halt when Emperor Agustín invaded from the north to secure his imperial possessions. When Iturbide fell in 1823, Mexican interest in the region lapsed, and the five provinces declared themselves absolutely independent but yoked together under the Constitution of 1824 as the United Provinces of Central America. Yet the underlying separatist tendencies soon made themselves felt, and by 1830 each province had declared its independence from the others. The confederation was at an end, and the independent republics of Guatemala, Honduras, Nicaragua, El Salvador, and Costa Rica emerged. The circle was complete: Spanish Middle America and Spanish South America reached full-fledged nationhood almost simultaneously, but only after a decade and a half of ruinous, bloody war. The portents for a prosperous and peaceful independent existence for the newly hatched republics looked poor. Coeval with this, and in contrast to warring Spanish America, Brazil had devised an ingenious and graceful solution to the Atlantic crisis—it domesticated the imperial court. The Braganzas became Brazilian.

Brazil: A Special Case?

Brazil's independence was triggered by the same set of events that provoked its insurrectionary Spanish American neighbors to action: a radical imperial reform program that restructured metropolitan-colonial relations, the forces unleashed by Bonapartism, notably the Peninsular War with its concomitant regime of disarray and disruption to imperial administration, and the spread of a transforming liberalism spawned by the Enlightenment and tempered in revolution.[33] Like Spanish America, Brazil proved especially fertile ground in which radical new ideas and revolutionary thoughts would quickly strike deep roots. Although the political harvest was similar, change in Brazil had its own rhythms and flavor. Prior to the 1770s, regional fragmentation and dispersion of political authority rendered the country relatively impervious to change. Indeed, the country had consisted of two states, Brazil and Maranhão, until these were merged in 1772.

This was the first of several crucial structural reforms by the Marquês de Pombal (Sebastião José de Carvalho e Melo), who for nearly thirty years directed Portuguese policy at home and abroad.[34] Pombal then moved to reorganize the regional governments, abolishing the hereditary captaincies and introducing a hierarchy of ten principal and six subordinate captaincies. However, the base of local power was the municipal council (*senado da câmara*), which often exercised authority over a large region. Pombal sought to restrict councils' authority, but without much success. The *câmaras* served as the power base of the Brazilian-born "whites" or *mazombos*, the counterparts of the Spanish American Creoles; there was often great hostility between the *mazombos* and the Portuguese-born *renóis*, just as in Spanish America the Creoles and *peninsulares* were often at loggerheads. This latent tension between European-born and American-born was of fundamental importance in both Spanish and Portuguese America, in determining the eventual political allegiance of Americans when they came to decide between metropolitan rule and full independence. This tension was especially aggravated by the continuing exclusion of native-born Brazilians from senior government and ecclesiastical posts; such exclusion was a perennial gripe in the Spanish colonies also, but the extent of exclusion seems to have been extreme in Brazil. So, too, Portuguese mercantilism seems to have been more thoroughgoing than its Spanish counterpart in the degree to which it discouraged secondary production, barred foreign imports, and enforced metropolitan commercial control to the detriment of *mazombo* interests. Just how deleterious were the effects of Portuguese mercantilism was brought home to Brazilians by the spectacular effects of Spain's quite modest *comercio libre* reform of 1778. Buenos Aires commenced an era of unprecedented prosperity and growth while Brazilian port traffic remained steady. Free trade remained for decades at the top of the reform agenda of *mazombo* activists. Fortuitously, it came overnight; when in 1808 the royal family decamped to Rio de Janeiro with British support, Brazil's ports were at a stroke opened to British trade. This was a new commercial master, perhaps, but a modernizing one; mercantilism as such was dead.

The Pombaline reforms had integrated government and administration, a process that would be accelerated by the relocation of the royal court to Brazil. Political independence in Brazil, however, had a longer lineage. While there was no university in the country—a deliberate decision by Portuguese policymakers, fearful of creating over-mighty subjects—and *ilustrado* political treatises were proscribed, Brazilian intellectual life appears to have been unusually vigorous, especially in comparison with Spanish America. Brazil had its university graduates, but educated at the University of Coimbra in Portugal, and not a few of these elites took a leading role in Brazil's earliest phase of independence; indeed, some had been involved in conspiracies against the Crown. There were also graduates of other European universities, especially from Paris and Montpellier, but after 1789 these were barred, at least officially, from returning to Brazil. The banned French texts, though, appear to have circulated widely and were discussed freely. Alert to the intellectual and political currents of the era and resentful of their perennial exclusion from office, Brazilians were developing a heightened self-esteem to match their disillusionment with metropolitan policies. Consequently, the translocation of the royal court to Brazil was a marvelous fillip to their political self-confidence.

This burgeoning sense of national identity was already evident before 1800. Several conspiracies or *inconfidência*—notably in Minas Gerais (1789) and Bahia (1798)—suggested that the patience of many Brazilians with their subordination to Portuguese interests was exhausted. The conspiracy in Minas Gerais was entirely an elite affair and chiefly remarkable for the conspirators' thorough acquaintance with the European intellectual fashions. These were "white" Brazilians, for slaves and mixed-race and indigenous Brazilians never formed part of their political equation; as the Haitian Revolution attested, these social groups were to be feared. In Bahia in 1798, however, it became clear that fashionable European political ideas had also penetrated to the underclasses: all forty-nine members of this conspiracy were "mulattos," many of them soldiers or artisans. One of its leaders was a young soldier, Lucas Dantas do Amorim Tôrres, who was thoroughly imbued with French revolutionary ideas—he freely invoked "liberty, equality, fraternity"—while another young officer read Enlightenment political tracts aloud to his men in barracks. Although royal authorities had little difficulty in crushing these conspiracies, they were symptomatic of undercurrents of resentment and, perhaps, also of a feeling that the time for a renegotiation of the colonial compact had arrived. Brazilians increasingly felt themselves entitled to full partnership in the enterprise of empire. Some wanted more, and their numbers rapidly swelled when in 1807 Portugal was plunged into crisis. With Napoleon advancing on Lisbon, the Portuguese royal family, encouraged and abetted by Great Britain, fled to Brazil, establishing their court in Rio de Janeiro.

This year marked a watershed moment. Brazil's independence is sometimes portrayed as a gift from the visiting Braganzas. While simplistic, this view does capture something of the fortuitousness of Brazil's accelerated progress to nationhood, because once the royal court had set up in Rio de Janeiro, it was clear that the metropolitan-colony relationship had been fundamentally transformed. Indeed, in a very real sense Brazil had become the metropolis and Portugal its dependency. It was historically unique that an imperial dynasty set up headquarters in a colony, and the only time in Latin American history that a member of the royal dynasty set foot in a colony at all. In 1815 Brazil went from a colony to a kingdom with status fully equal to Portugal itself. The defeat of

Napoleonic forces in Portugal in 1811 should have seen the repatriation of the royal family to Lisbon, but they lingered. Prince João, regent for his mentally incompetent mother until his 1816 coronation as King João VI, seemed entirely comfortable with his tropical Versailles in Rio and in no mood to heed the importunities of his increasingly angry Iberian subjects, above all the emerging liberal breed, who now made common cause with the military.

The Portuguese military, imbued with radical liberal ideas and riding a tide of post-bellum popular discontent, seized power in August 1820 from the king's regents, all the while pledging allegiance to the absent monarch. They now began to reprise the Spanish liberal experiment. This was something of a "copy cat" revolution, sparked by Spain's military Riego Revolt of January 1820, such that the liberal officers now promulgated Spain's liberal Constitution of 1812 in Portugal and its empire. Accordingly, in 1821 a Cortes was elected, and as in Spanish America in 1812, Brazilian deputies were invited to participate. Portuguese liberalism now showed its false colors: while claiming enhanced rights for its fellow nationals, it treated Brazilians contemptuously and not only abolished privileges accorded them during the Braganza sojourn but installed military governors in all regions. It was a curiously reactionary liberalism. Those Brazilian deputies who arrived in Portugal in 1821 were roundly abused by their peninsular counterparts, who perhaps were overly sensitive to the 1815 constitutional downgrading of Portugal vis-à-vis Brazil. They intensified demands that *their* king return home. King João succumbed to demands that were now more threats than entreaties. In his stead he left his son Pedro on the Brazilian throne. Pedro spurned similar demands that he return to Lisbon and in 1822 declared Brazilian independence in his famous "Cry of Iparinga"—"Independence or Death!" Brazil now declared itself an empire, and Pedro was crowned as Emperor Pedro I. In 1825, following financial concessions, Portugal formally accepted Brazil's independence, and Pedro granted his father, the king of Portugal, the right to use the honorific title "emperor of Brazil." Such stipulations appalled Brazilians; Pedro's political honeymoon was over. He abdicated in favor of his five-year-old son Pedro de Alcântara in 1831, who was now supervised by a three-man regency; Pedro assumed the throne at the age of fourteen, ruling for forty-nine years until his exile in 1889 (he died in Paris in 1891), a year after the abolition of slavery. The old regime had been entirely swept away.

The Meaning of Independence

The Atlantic Revolution has often been reified and used to explain events that are, in a circular argument, used as evidence for its very existence. There is a danger that the Atlantic Revolution can serve as a Hegelian "idea" or Zeitgeist that infuses and explains everything that happened in the Atlantic World for the half century from 1776. A synoptic view of the era does indicate that the Latin American independence process accorded well with the historical currents of the Age. European rivalries were increasingly fought out in the Western Hemisphere, not least because of the domino effects of the French Revolution in the Hispanic world. To take just one example, even such a new phenomenon as the military mobilization of clergy in France, Spain, and Ireland was writ large in the Americas, especially in Mexico, Venezuela, and Peru. Perhaps the most remarkable feature of the epoch was the transformation of political authority and sovereignty through the rise of liberalism. Its radical nature was of a magnitude perhaps difficult for us to grasp, because to modern eyes Liberalism in its several incarnations has long seemed a relatively tame ideology. It was, however, electrifying for Americans hitherto bereft of rights and consistently led to believe that they were second-class subjects both in law and because of their colonial status, a pejorative view most evident in the pervasive anti-Creole discourse of the Habsburg and Bourbon centuries. However, the view that independence in the Americas was the inevitable outcome of the Atlantic Revolutions seems excessively essentialist, denying Latin Americans of that era the ability to have forged their own historical destiny. To a degree, such a condescending view describes the political and military activities only of a "white" elite, largely excluding indigenous, African, and mixed-race groups as ideologically conscious protagonists. Several leading revisionist studies give the impression that these subaltern groups had little to do with the independence process, except perhaps as cannon fodder. However, it is clear from such events as the great Andean insurrections of 1780 and 1814, the Bahian conspiracy of 1798, and the political and military engagement of the *llaneros* in Venezuela, that there existed a fierce desire for independence, cogently argued, among subaltern groups. It is surely simplistic to say that great anti-colonial insurrections aimed at liberating a colony not just from *afrancesado* liberals and Napoleonic usurpers but also from the Bourbon dynasty are symptomatic of little more than a political realignment or redefinition of the metropolitan-colonial relationship within the wider Hispanic world. Creole nationalism there certainly was, but it was only part of the picture; lower-class groups were perhaps just as likely to press for full independence. Indeed, a post-independence insurgency in the Peruvian highlands aimed at a return to a monarchical form of government, suggesting that poor, indigenous, and mixed-race populations were perfectly willing and able to conceptualize the political and ideological choices offered them by a new political conjuncture. The activities of such subaltern groups strongly suggest that independence was more than a long overdue re-alignment within the Hispanic family of nations, and that independence did not merely represent the moment when Spain's adopted children finally reached their legal majority. Americans of all social stripes knew how to choose, and they did so.

To be sure, deriving generalizations as to the nature of Latin American independence is extraordinarily difficult because one finds exceptions to the rule at every turn. The universal validity of any single characterization of this era can be no more than provisional, given the morass of erratic military campaigns and mixed ideological signals emanating from the patriot and even royalist military camps. Similarly, within the political endeavors and military campaigns are to be found bitter internecine disputes within regional and national movements. Moreover, the many patriotic movements rarely marched in lockstep, and this differential timing undermined the overall patriotic political process. So, too, the diverse military responses from beleaguered viceroys make it difficult to discern a consistent royalist policy toward American demands for enhanced Creole rights, especially during the crucial 1808–1814 crisis, a pattern that came to be repeated in the 1820–1823 liberal-military experiment in Spain. It is also tempting to overemphasize the elections of American representatives to the Cortés of Cádiz. To a degree, these elections were a red herring, something of a sideshow to the main patriotic drive for independence. This is suggested by the fact that the elected deputies were rarely drawn from the cream of Latin American political or intellectual elites. While the imperial electoral process looked impressive to foreign observers (and to some modern historians), especially in its invocation of democracy in bloom, it was in certain measure a tale "full of sound and fury" signifying very little at all. The Constitution of 1812, which provided for the election of American deputies, was nevertheless of transcendent importance in radically redefining American, especially Creole, identity and in fuelling wider aspirations to independence. This process eventually occurred even in Brazil, when Spain's liberal-military Riego Revolt and its fresh adoption of the Constitution was exactly mimicked by Portuguese military and liberals who then implemented the 1812 Constitution in Portugal, a key moment in Brazilian independence as it was in Spanish America. Brazil's trajectory from colonial to monarchy to empire within the space of a few years, if at first sight a peculiar outcome, was also consonant with another significant constitutional trend of these years. The desire for an independent monarchy was the preferred option for many Spanish American elites, Miranda and San Martín being the best-known proponents of a monarchical model for an independent Latin America.

Latin American independence produced revolutionary outcomes, both in the short and long term, even though there was little in the way of a true social revolution. For the most part, Creole and (in Brazil) *mazombo* elites now ruled the roost without fear of contradiction from Madrid or Lisbon. For underclasses, this often meant more of the same exploitation, with the difference that a patriotic discourse replaced the earlier imperialist discourse, but to much the same effect—the "same horse, different rider" thesis seems especially apposite in this context. Notwithstanding, slavery was progressively abolished, albeit in a sometimes piecemeal fashion. If much was made of liberalism and constitutionalism in the creation of the new republics, this was also accompanied by frequent (and legendary) political instability, because the removal of the traditional allegiance to the monarch created a vacuum of consensual sovereignty. Still, at least it was rule by nationals for nationals, a great advance on the unrepresentative authoritarianism that had prevailed during three centuries of imperial rule. There were other drawbacks. This instability was accompanied by the rise of militarism, the canker in Latin American history to the present day, and its early republican manifestation as *caudillismo*, in which regional and even national societies at times appeared to be ruled by warlords, whose power was based on patron-client relationships rather than springing from any representative consensus. The economies of the nascent republics were on the whole prostrated by the Wars of Independence and in this condition had to confront the radical structural transition from a restrictive (even after 1778) Hispanic mercantilism to the need to compete in international markets. Latin America began modernization and especially industrialization well behind northern Atlantic powers. Yet, even here, the transformation wrought by independence introduced positive outcomes: economies became more export-oriented and manufacturing was slowly but measurably transformed.

For all the political instability and violence injected into the new republics by the Wars of Independence, the post-colonial era ushered in manifold positive innovations in political representation, law, and economic and commercial life, and opened the way to cultural enrichment as Latin Americans moved from a certain cultural hermeticism of the imperial centuries to a closer engagement with the non-Hispanic world. In the event, a cost-benefit analysis of the outcomes of independence indicates a clearly positive balance in favor of Latin America. Once comfortably ensconced as full members of the Atlantic community of nations, Latin Americans were free to enrich culturally the wider world; whatever benefits they took from three centuries of colonial rule, they also gave in equal measure. Nationalism came first, but the new republics now could begin to build nations, a right and a duty they had been denied under colonial rule.

Notes

1. There are four excellent introductions to Spanish American independence: John Lynch, *The Spanish American Revolutions, 1808–1826*, 2nd ed. (New York: W. W. Norton, 1986); Jay Kinsbruner, *Independence in Spanish America: Civil Wars, Revolutions, and Underdevelopment* (Albuquerque: University of New Mexico Press, 1994); the splendidly written, more "popular," but generally reliable synthesis by Robert Harvey, *Liberators: South America's Savage Wars of Freedom 1810–30* (London: John Murray, 2000); and the wide-ranging revisionist essay by Brian R. Hamnett, "Process and Pattern: A Re-examination of the Ibero-American Independence Movements, 1808–1826," *Journal of Latin American Studies* 29:2: 279–328. An excellent collection of primary texts and excerpts from secondary sources is John Lynch, ed., *Latin American Revolutions, 1808–1826: Old and New World Origins* (Norman: University of Oklahoma Press, 1994). For the "continuity" interpretation, Jaime E. Rodríguez O., *The Independence of Spanish America* (Cambridge: Cambridge University Press, 1998). A fine introduction to Brazilian Independence is Leslie Bethell, ed., "The Independence of Brazil," in *The Independence of Latin America*, ed. Bethell (Cambridge: Cambridge University Press, 1987), 155–194.

2. For recent reassessments, see David P. Geggus, ed., *The Impact of the Haitian Revolution in the Atlantic World* (Columbia: University of South Carolina Press, 2001).

3. For an extreme example of this approach, see O. Carlos Stoetzer, *The Scholastic Roots of the Spanish American Revolution* (New York: Fordham University Press, 1979), 150: "The reforms of the Bourbon regime during the reign of Charles III prepared the way for the Revolution; the Napoleonic invasion of the peninsula was its immediate cause. But the so-called Spanish American Revolution was no revolution at all, merely the echo of events which began in Spain on May 2, 1808. As in Spain itself, so in the territories overseas, citizens acted in defense of the fatherland, in the name of the deposed King Ferdinand VII and against the Napoleonic usurpation, with deepest loyalty and in keeping with old and accepted traditions."

4. For an example, see David Cahill and Scarlett O'Phelan Godoy, "Forging Their Own History: Indian Insurgency in the Southern Peruvian Sierra, 1815," *Bulletin of Latin American Research* 11:2: 125–167.

5. The controversy over "dependency" is cogently summarized in Rory Miller, *Britain and Latin America in the Nineteenth and Twentieth Centuries* (London: Longman, 1993), 13–23.

6. An important re-evaluation of nationalism and nationality in the Americas is Benedict Anderson, *Imagined Communities: Reflections on the Origins and Spread of Nationalism*, 2nd ed. (London: Verso, 1991).

7. The Andean rebellion comprised the northern Túpac Amaru rebellion and the southern Túpac Catari rebellion, which gradually merged; for the former, see Charles Walker, *Smoldering Ashes: Cuzco and the Creation of Republican Peru, 1780–1840* (Durham, N.C.: Duke University Press, 1999) 55–83; for the latter, Sinclair Thomson, *We Alone Will Rule: Native Andean Politics in the Age of Insurgency* (Madison: University of Wisconsin Press, 2002).

8. Nicholas A. Robins, *Genocide and Millennialism in Upper Peru: The Great Rebellion of 1780–1782* (Westport, Conn.: Praeger, 2002), argues that the rebellion was an instance of genocide from below.

9. Arthur P. Whitaker, ed., *Latin America and the Enlightenment*, 2nd ed. (Ithaca, N.Y.: Cornell University Press, 1961), remains a valuable introduction to, inter alia, the effects of *ilustrado* ideas on independence. On this and related themes, see also the engaging D. A. Brading, *The First America: The Spanish Monarchy, Creole Patriots, and the Liberal State, 1492–1867* (Cambridge: Cambridge University Press, 1991).

10. Peter T. Bradley and David Cahill, *Habsburg Peru: Images, Imagination and Memory* (Liverpool: Liverpool University Press, 2000).

11. For concrete examples, see Peggy Liss, "Atlantic Network," in Lynch, *Latin American Revolutions*, 264–265; E. Bradford Burns, *A History of Brazil*, 2nd ed. (New York: Columbia University Press, 1980), 140–142.

12. Robert Darnton, *The Literary Underground of the Old Regime* (Cambridge Mass.: Harvard University Press, 1982). For a concrete example, Alberto Flores Galindo, "In Search of an Inca," in *Resistance, Rebellion, and Consciousness in the Andean Peasant World, 18th to 20th Centuries*, ed. Steve Stern, 193–210 (Madison: University of Wisconsin Press, 1987).

13. Stoetzer, *Scholastic Roots*, is an outstanding study of the influence of this literature in the Americas.

14. Liss, "Atlantic Network," 264–265.

15. Brading, *First America*, passim. The classic study of the Spanish Enlightenment

is Jean Sarrailh, *La España Ilustrada de la segunda mitad del siglo XVIII,* trans. Antonio Alatorre (1954; reprint, Mexico: Fondo de Cultura Económica, 1957), long overdue for an English translation. Bourbon ministers Gaspar Melchor de Jovellanes and the Conde de Campomanes made notable contributions to Enlightenment thought.

16. Robert J. Shafer, *The Economic Societies in the Spanish World, 1763–1821* (Syracuse, N.Y.: University of Syracuse Press, 1958).

17. For economic change in the era, see especially John R. Fisher, *The Economic Aspects of Spanish Imperialism in America, 1492–1810* (Liverpool: Liverpool University Press, 1997); and Dauril Alden, "Late Colonial Brazil, 1750–1808," in *Colonial Brazil,* ed. Leslie Bethell, 284–343 (Cambridge: Cambridge University Press, 1987).

18. Christon I. Archer, *The Army in Bourbon Mexico, 1760–1810* (Albuquerque: University of New Mexico Press, 1977), analyses the military reforms of the era.

19. For ecclesiastical reforms, see especially Adriaan C. Van Oss, *Catholic Colonialism: A Parish History of Guatemala, 1524–1821* (Cambridge: Cambridge University Press, 1986); D. A. Brading, *Church and State in Bourbon Mexico: The Diocese of Michoacán, 1749–1810* (Cambridge: Cambridge University Press, 1994); William B. Taylor, *Magistrates of the Sacred: Priests and Parishioners in Eighteenth-Century Mexico* (Stanford, Calif.: Stanford University Press, 1996).

20. This long conjuncture is best approached through the essays collected in Stern, *Resistance, Rebellion, and Consciousness,* complemented by John Fisher, "Royalism, Regionalism, and Rebellion in Colonial Peru, 1808–1815," *Hispanic American Historical Review* 59:2 (1979): 232–257.

21. On insurrection in New Granada, see especially Anthony McFarlane, "Civil Disorders and Popular Protests in Late Colonial New Granada," *Hispanic American Historical Review* 64:1 (1984): 17–54; John Leddy Phelan, *The People and the King: The Comunero Rebellion in Colombia* (Madison: University of Wisconsin Press, 1978).

22. The disintegration of Spain is elegantly conveyed by John Lynch, *Bourbon Spain, 1700–1808* (Oxford: Blackwell, 1989); see also the cogent account by Simon Barton, *A History of Spain* (New York: Palgrave Macmillan, 2004), 149–171.

23. I here follow the dual-phase approach of Kinsbruner, *Independence in Spanish America,* rather than John Lynch's strictly regional approach. It should be noted, however, that there was a great lack of synchronicity between the several independence movements, and that they were sometimes interlocked, as, for example, the Bolivarian campaigns in New Granada and Venezuela or the way that the Platine (Argentinian) and Charcas (Bolivian) movements merged and split.

24. Kinsbruner, *Independence in Spanish America,* 54–55; his account (46–57, 77–95) of the extraordinarily complex Bolívarian campaigns in the north is excellent. See also Rebecca A. Earle, *Spain and the Independence of Colombia, 1810–1825* (Exeter, UK: University of Exeter Press, 2000).

25. The Bolivian independence process is dealt with by Charles Arnade, *The Emergence of the Republic of Bolivia* (Gainesville: University of Florida Press, 1957).

26. On the intricately related developments in the soon-to-be Argentina, Bolivia, Uruguay, and Paraguay, see especially Lynch, *Spanish American Revolutions,* chapters 3 and 4.

27. Simon Collier, *Ideas and Politics of Chilean Independence, 1808–1833* (Cambridge: Cambridge University Press, 1967), remains the best account of Chilean independence.

28. The historiography of Mexican Independence is extremely large, with many stud-

ies of high quality. The best place to start is the outstanding compilation by Christon Archer, ed., *The Birth of Modern Mexico, 1780–1824* (Wilmington, Del.: Scholarly Resources, 2003). Eric Van Young, *The Other Rebellion: Popular Violence, Ideology, and the Mexican Struggle for Independence, 1810–1821* (Stanford, Calif.: Stanford University Press, 2001), is a masterwork that has reset the agenda for studies of the independence era. Events in Mexico City are perhaps best approached via Timothy E. Anna, *The Fall of the Royal Government in Mexico City* (Lincoln: University of Nebraska Press, 1978).

29. This important, though failed, revolution is overlooked by the key syntheses of Latin American independence history and several studies of Peruvian independence that focus on events in Lima. Fisher, "Royalism, Regionalism, and Rebellion" is a valuable corrective.

30. Bolívar has not found the biographer he deserves. The best introduction is a special issue of the *Hispanic American Historical Review* 63:1 (1983), with articles by John Lynch, David Bushnell, Simon Collier, and Germán Carrera Damas. The "Liberator" is perhaps most accessible through his own writings: David Bushnell, ed., *El Libertador: Writings of Simón Bolívar,* trans. Frederick H. Fornoff (Oxford: Oxford University Press, 2003).

31. See especially Karen Racine, *Francisco de Miranda: A Transatlantic Life in the Age of Revolution* (Wilmington, Del.: Scholarly Resources, 2003).

32. There is a paucity of studies on Central American independence; the best place to start is Lynch, *Spanish American Revolutions,* 333–340. See also Mario Rodríguez, *The Cádiz Experiment in Central America, 1808 to 1826* (Berkeley: University of California Press, 1978).

33. For the Brazilian case, see especially Bethell, "Independence of Brazil"; A. J. R. Russell-Wood, *From Colony to Nation: Essays on the Independence of Brazil* (Baltimore: Johns Hopkins University Press, 1975); E. Bradford Burns, *A History of Brazil* (New York: Columbia University Press, 1980), pp. 115–186, who privileges the influence of European ideas.

34. Kenneth Maxwell, *Pombal: Paradox of the Enlightenment* (Cambridge: Cambridge University Press, 1995).

CHAPTER TEN

The Rise of Abolition

Maurice Jackson

W. E. B. Du Bois, the magisterial voice of those formerly enslaved, wrote, "the rough and brutal character of the time and place was partly responsible for this [harsh punishment for rebellious slaves], but a more decisive reason lay in the fierce and turbulent character of the imported Negroes." He added, "the docility to which long years of bondage and strict discipline gave rise was absent, and insurrections and acts of violence were of frequent occurrence."[1] Quoting from the Slave Codes of South Carolina and the Quaker abolitionist Anthony Benezet's *Some Historical Account of Africa*, Du Bois documented the "rapid importation" of Africans, harsh slave conditions, and the danger whites faced. This fear of discontented blacks caused their captors to impose even harsher conditions and penalties on their captives. It was this fear, not concern for enslaved Africans, that in part caused whites to seek biblical reasoning and undying support for their deeds. Some historians have labeled their actions "paternalistic." Yet, the masters treated the slaves more like beasts than children. Others tried to find a "benevolent" strain among the whites. There was nothing kind, charitable, or sacrificial about their actions. They did not bring Africans to the New World to "save" and "civilize" them but to exploit and oppress them in order to turn a profit. With a Bible in one hand and a book of Justinian codes and philosophical tracts in the other, whites kidnapped tens of millions of Africans, without guilt. And untold millions died during the horrible "Middle Passage." Slavery, with the blood of the Africans dripping across the Atlantic Ocean, sapped the life out of the blacks and robbed the whites of their souls and their humanity.

The slaves first showed resistance to their imposed slavery aboard the slave ships, as they were kidnapped and forcibly taken to the New World. Many Africans starved themselves by refusing to eat even though the crewmen tried to force-feed them. At other times, the whites muzzled them like dogs, chaining them, one atop the other. Some slaves jumped overboard, choosing to die rather than to be beaten, raped, and possibly dismembered. They believed that in death the "transmigration of the soul" in African tradition would allow them a final freedom, one they could not find in life. While these first acts of resistance were most often individual in nature, the minute a second slave took such action, the acts represented an early collective consciousness against forced enslavement. And so, from the first day of captivity until the final slave was manumitted in Brazil in 1888, the enslaved Africans fought against their captivity and their oppression any way they could. Whether they resisted as individuals or as members of a collective, there was at all times a most common thread among the enslaved Africans: the yearning for freedom.

In the Beginning

Portugal brutally ushered in the modern slave trade era in 1441, as the explorer Antao Gonçalvez captured a dozen Africans from a market near the Guinean coast and gave them to Prince Henry "the Navigator." In 1444 another 240 African men, women, and children were captured and shipped, from the port of Lagos, to Portugal. In the next thirty years, 2,500 more slaves would be forcibly taken to Portugal and another 12,500 to other places in Europe. A little over a hundred years later Sir John Hawkins, the Elizabethan-era ship captain, brought Britain into the buying and selling of human beings. By 1619 the Dutch got involved in the "business," sending the first captured "twenty and odd" Africans to the Virginia colony. Although Britain did not become a major destination for the trade, by the end of the seventeenth century, with the development of the Royal African Company (1672–1750), it became the world's leading supplier of human flesh. The Crown became the leading beneficiary. If it is true that the process of death begins at birth, then is also true that the seeds of the demise of slavery were spread at its beginning. The four-hundred-year-old struggle to end slavery can be seen as one of the highest and the lowest points of human existence. From the beginning contradictions abounded. Anthony Benezet (1713–1784), the French-born exiled Huguenot and Quaker-convert wrote *A Caution and a Warning to Great Britain and Her Colonies in A Short Representation of the Calamitous State of the Enslaved Negroes in the British Dominions:*

> How the *British* nation first came to be concerned in a practice, by which the rights and liberties of mankind are so violently infringed, and which is so opposite to the apprehensions *Englishmen* have always had of what natural justice requires, is indeed surprising. It was about the year 1563, in the reign of Queen *Elizabeth* that the *English* first engaged in the *Guiney* Trade; when it appears, from an account in *Hill's* Naval History, page 293, That when Captain *Hawkins* returned from his first voyage to *Africa*, that generous spirited *Princess*, attentive

> to the interest of her subjects, sent for the Commander, to whom she expressed her concern lest any of the *African* Negroes should be carried off without their free consent, *declaring it would be detestable, and call down the vengeance of heaven upon the undertakers.* Captain *Hawkins* promised to comply with the Queen's injunction: nevertheless, we find in the account, given in the same History, of *Hawkins'* second voyage, the author using these remarkable words, *here began the horrid practice of forcing the Africans into slavery.*[2]

As the queen, who was not as innocent as Benezet might have imagined, saw her empire enslave millions "without their consent," Pope Leo X, in 1514, issued a papal bull condemning both slavery and the slave trade. Later slave-holding men such as Thomas Jefferson would proclaim "equality for all." For the oppressed these statements were "just words," yet for others, if these words could be used to attain freedom, then they had meaning.

The struggle to end slavery took many forms, from open resistance by the enslaved Africans to high philosophical ideas from European Enlightenment-era thinkers. Oddly enough, as with any quest for freedom and dignity, those forms would often pass each slave on the journey; sometimes speaking but most of the time not. Many whites who wanted to end the slave trade and even the practice of slavery had no desire to win equality for the blacks. William C. Nell, one of the first great African American historians, wrote in 1855 about a "well known antidote" dating to the American Revolutionary War. When General John Sullivan of New Hampshire told his slave that the whites were forming an army "to fight for liberty," the black "shrewdly suggested that it would be a great satisfaction to know they he was indeed going to fight for *his* liberty." So, "struck with the reasonableness and justice of this suggestion, Gen. S. at once gave him his freedom."[3] In another mainland colony a black man, upon seeing his master grab his firearm to fight the British, mustered his own gun. The "master" admonished the "slave," asking indignantly, "boy where are you going with that gun?" The enslaved African forcibly answered, "master, I wants my freedom just like you wants yours." This statement, by an illiterate slave, was as profound as anything the nation's founders ever uttered.

Crispus Attucks, a 6'2" man whose father was said to be African and mother Natick Indian, heard the call of the American patriots and joined with a force of fifty to confront British forces at Boston Harbor and help start the American Revolution. Attucks, who calmly told his fellow revolutionaries, "don't be afraid," was one of five men killed in the confrontation now known as the Boston Massacre. The future second president, John Adams, referred to the men as "as a motley rabble of saucy boys, negroes and molattoes, Irish teagues and outlandish jack tars." He also understood the role of Attucks: "this Attucks . . . appears to have undertaken to be the hero of the night; and to lead this Army, with banners." Adams clearly knew the significance of Attucks's color as he proclaimed that Attucks stood at the "head of such a rabble of Negroes, & c. as they can collect together."

The famed British writer Samuel Johnson, noting the contradiction between the American revolutionaries' desires for their liberty and the continued enslavement of the Africans, sarcastically proclaimed, "how is it that we hear the loudest yelps for liberty among the drivers of Negroes."

Beginning in 1858, blacks and whites in Boston began celebrating Crispus Attucks Day. At the first celebration the white abolitionist Wendell Phillips proclaimed, "I place, therefore, this Crispus Attucks in the foremost ranks of the men that dared. When we talk of courage, he rises, with his dark face, in the clothes of a laborer, his head uncovered, his arms above him defying bayonets." Philips concluded his March 5, 1858, speech declaring, "when all the proper symbols are placed around the base of the statue of Washington, one corner will be filled by the colored man defying the British muskets." Indeed, thirty years later, in 1888, a monument to Crispus Attucks was dedicated on Boston Common.

At the time of the American Revolution there was a total population of 2,600,000 people in the British region of mainland North America, of which 500,000 were black. According to Gail Buckley, "only a fraction of that population went to war. Some five thousand blacks served under George Washington, and about a thousand, mostly Southern runaways, fought for George III." She adds, "although the percentage of the black population who served was small, by 1779 as many as one in seven members of Washington's never be very large army were black."[4]

However, many blacks fought with their feet. John Hope Franklin tells us that "Thomas Jefferson estimated that in 1778 alone more than 30,000 Virginia slaves ran away. David Ramsay, South Carolina historian, asserted that between 1775 and 1783 his state lost at least 25,000 blacks. It has been estimated that Georgia lost about 75 percent of its 15,000 slaves."[5] Jefferson would later estimate that up to one-sixth of Virginia's slaves fled during the war years.

In the struggle for freedom "the contagion of liberty" knew no bounds. The enslaved developed their own rhetorical freedom themes with music, words, rituals, and sermons. In 1928 U. B. Phillips, author of the 1918 work *American Negro Slavery*, gave a speech to the American Historical Association titled "The Central Theme of Southern History." Phillips declared that the main goal of white people and their historians was "a common resolve indomitably maintained—that it [the South] shall be and remain a white man's country." Many years later Herbert Aptheker, one of the first historians to document the resistance struggles of enslaved Africans, challenged Phillip's thesis. Aptheker declared that the central theme of African American history "is the struggle for freedom against an oppressing class."[6] This struggle would include members of the African Diaspora throughout the Americas.

The many justifications used to enslave black people—among them, skin color, race, and religion—have been well documented, and all made the blacks heathen and less than human. Even well-meaning men such as Bartholomew de las Casas, the bishop of Chiapa, who came to find the oppression and forced servitude of the indigenous Native American peoples offensive, could nevertheless justify the enslavement of the African, arguing that "their temperament

[was] best suited for hard labor." His words were used by proslavery proponents to justify their actions.

Religious leaders such as Morgan Godwyn, an Anglican bishop and missionary, and George Fox, founder of Quakerism, both while residing in Barbados, began in the late 1680s to challenge, on religious grounds, the proslavery justifications. Yet, there simply was no need to justify slavery until an opposition to the institution appeared. Since most of the first organized opposition came from the church, proslavery arguments had to counter using biblical arguments, the most common being that the Bible did not condemn the keeping of slaves. The most frequently used were biblical references to the enslavement and oppression of the Israelites by the Egyptian pharaoh, Ramses. If God's chosen people could be enslaved, then certainly the scriptures did not condemn the practice. Those opposing slavery found a quick retort in Exodus 9:1 and God's order to "Let my people go." The legend of the "curse of Ham" was a main source of proslavery rhetoric. But as Robin Blackburn has asserted, "reference to the 'son of Ham' sometimes served to acknowledge the humanity of the Africans, to affirm the need for humane enslavement, and to deny the ultra racist notion that black slaves were simply beasts of the field—a notion that was to gain ground . . . in the plantation colonies."[7]

One of the first attacks against slavery in the Atlantic World came from the Quaker founder George Fox, who wrote in 1676, "do not slight them, to wit the Ethyopians; he died for the Tawnies [the indigenous Native Americans] the Blacks now, neither any Man of Woman upon the face of the earth, in that Christ died for all, both Turks, Barbarians, Tartarians, and thyopians; he died for the Tawnies and for the Blacks, as well as for you that are called whites."[8]

Morgan Godwyn had seen the Fox tract, in Barbados, and became angry because it accused Anglicans of neglecting the religious training of blacks. He later penned the *Negro and Indians Advocate* in 1680, arguing that "the Negros (both slaves and others) have naturally an equal right with other men to exercise and Privileges or Religion." Godwyn helped open the debate about slavery by arguing that "these two words *negro* and *slave* are by custom grown Homogeneous and Convertible; even as *Negro* and *Christian*, and Englishman and Heathen then, are by the like corrupt Custom and Partiality made opposites." He did not challenge the legality of slavery but stressed the humanity of the blacks. He did acknowledge that "some may perchance object against my spending Time in this discourse to prove the *Negro's Humanity*, and to show that neither Complexion not Bondage, Descente nor County, can be any impediment thereto."[9] Religion could make them Christians but would not make them free. If religion could no longer serve as the only justification for slavery, then what? The answer was skin color.

According to historian Winthrop Jordan:

> What had occurred was not a change in the justification from religion to race. No such justifications were made. There seems to have been within the unar-

> ticulated concern for the Negro as a different sort of person, a highly significant shift in emphasis. Consciousness of the Negro's heathenism remained through the eighteenth century and into the nineteenth and twentieth century, and awareness, at the very least of his different appearance was present form the beginning.[10]

As British historians Paul Edwards and James Walvin noted, "it needs to be stressed moreover that arguments where blacks were things or humans were no mere abstractions, debated in the rarefied atmosphere of the courts. Blacks were after all *treated* as objects in everyday social practice. They were bought, sold and bartered."[11]

In 1688, the Quakers of Germantown (Philadelphia), Pennsylvania, began the first organized activity by whites against slavery. In the *Germantown Protest* they laid bare their arguments against slavery, declaring, "these are the reasons why we are against the traffic of men-body as followeth. Is there any that would be handled at this manner? Viz, to be sold or made a slave for all the time of his life." But it was not until the Quaker *Epistle of 1754*, over sixty years after the *Germantown Protest*, with a "proposal of making that Rule of our Discipline respecting the Importation of Negroe's or the Purchasing of them after imported, more public, together with some reasons to discourage that practice," that Quakers took any official actions against their members' slaveholding. Finally, in 1776, at the Philadelphia Annual Meeting, it was declared that ownership of slaves was incompatible with membership in the Society of Friends (Quakers) and that final action was taken against their own slaveholders. This condemnation was the culmination of almost a hundred years of Quaker action and inaction. Thus if the battle against slavery was so difficult, even for the Quakers who were the leading organization against the institution, one could imagine the difficulty within society as a whole throughout the Atlantic World. It took men such as Anthony Benezet and his continental cohorts, Thomas Clarkson, John Wesley, and Granville Sharp in England. They were joined by Jacques Pierre Brissot de Warville, Etienne Clavière, the Marquis de Condorcet, founding members of the Société des Amis de Noirs in France, and newly freed Africans such as Olaudah Equiano and Ottobah Cugoano in proving the fallacy of the bishop's logic. Indeed, these men showed proof that "before the Europeans came the Africans lived in peace" and harmony and worked to produce what they needed before the advent of slavery and commodity production.

Sources of Antislavery Thought

Just as slave revolts occurred in response to the inhuman institution, so intellectual ideas developed to combat slavery. The years from the mid-1750s until the 1780s, just after the American Revolutionary War, were an era of such intellectual activity. It was Charles-Louis de Montesquieu (1689–1755) who gave the antislavery forces one of their initial enlightened voices against slavery. Montesquieu observed in *Espirit des Lois* (1748):

> That the state of slavery is in its own nature bad. It is neither useful to the master nor to the slave; not to the slave because he can do nothing through a motive of virtue; nor to the master because by having an unlimited authority over his slaves he insensibly accustoms himself to the want of all moral values, and then becomes fierce, hasty, severe, choleric, voluptuous, and cruel.[12]

Among the most cited Western thinkers was the noted University of Glasgow professor Francis Hutcheson. His *A System of Moral Philosophy* (1755) insisted that blacks as human beings had never forfeited their freedom and were therefore entitled to the same liberty, happiness, and benevolence as were the Europeans. Proclaiming that "no endowments, natural or acquired, can give a perfect right to assume power over others, without their consent. . . . the subject must have a right of resistance, as the trust is broken, beside the manifest plea of necessity."[13] Many antislavery leaders such as Benezet and Benjamin Rush in the mainland colonies and Sharp, Clarkson, and Wesley in Britain agreed with Hutcheson in his condemnation of slavery. However, these men differed on the "right to resistance" by the slaves, fearing violent revolts.

The Scottish jurist George Wallace, the son of a legendary Scottish barrister, also gave an intellectual compass to freedom's cause. Wallace's major work was *A System of the Principle of the Law of Scotland* (1760), in which he argued, "all that inequality, which is to be found among the human race, is derived from political and arbitrary institutions alone. . . . all inequality, all dependence, all servility, all superiority, all subjugation, all pre-eminence, which is not necessary to the welfare of Society, is unnatural; and that if it could, it ought to be destroyed." Like Hutcheson, he went further and challenged the right of one person to hold another human being as chattel, arguing that any slave or transaction of human flesh was *ipso jure void*. His most potent claim in *System*, and one used by antislavery leaders in America, Britain, and France, was the following:

> Men and their liberty are not in commerce; they are not either saleable or purchasable . . . for everyone of those unfortunate men are pretended to be slaves, has a right to be declared free, for he never lost his liberty; he could not lose it; his Prince had no power to dispose of him.[14]

The third of these Scottish moral philosophers was James Foster, who, in *Discourse on all the Principle Branches of Natural Religion and Social Virtue* (1749), proclaimed that chattel slavery "is much more criminal, and a more outrageous violation of *natural rights* than preceding forms of slavery." In essence he served to rebut those who made exception for the enslavement of Africans. Foster was also one of the first philosophers to argue against slavery, countering the religious arguments of Christian thinkers in writing that "we sacrifice reason, our humanity, our Christianity, to an *unnatural sordid gain*." Of course, the gain he referred to was the drive for maximum profits. Seeing that slavery debased the morals of his fellowmen, he argued that "we teach other nations to despise, and trample under foot, all the obligations of *social virtue* . . . and prevent the propagation of the *Gospel* by representing it as a scheme of *power* and *barbarous* oppression, and an enemy of the *natural* privileges and rights of men."[15]

Adam Smith, the Scottish philosopher, first weighed in on the issue of slavery in 1759 with *The Theory of Moral Sentiments.* However, it was in *The Wealth of Nations* (1776) that he made his real imprint in the antislavery dialogue. He believed that from an economic standpoint slavery was simply not profitable within the free market system. It reduced the incentive of the master because it did not force him to seek new productive methods. It made poor use of fertile land. It made whites lazy because it did not encourage them to work. After all, their labor was their own, and they were "free" to sell it, yet they could not sell it because the forced slave labor of the blacks negated the value of the white man's labor. Thomas Clarkson in *An Essay on the Impolicy of the African Slave Trade, in Two Parts* (1788), had shown that the slave trader had lost money and, more importantly, innumerable white lives aboard slave-trading vessels. Men such as Clarkson and Benezet strived to show that slavery distorted the white soul just as it mangled the black body. Above all, Smith believed slavery cost more than using wage labor. He showed how it stalled even the white's drive for maximum profits.

In 1758 a Portuguese priest, Manoel Ribeiro Rocha, published *Etiope Resgatado empenhado, sustenado corrigido, instruido e libertado* (The Ethiopian Redeemed, pledged, nurtured, corrected, educated and emancipated). Celia M. Azevedo has shown that there existed a "context of Receptions" between the priest and the Philadelphia Quakers in action and in their use of religious and philosophical ideas. Rocha used as his guide the writings of two famed Jesuits, the Spanish Luis Molina (1535–1600) and the Portuguese Fernando Rebelo (1546–1608). Azevedo has shown that "both accused Portuguese merchants of purchasing slaves who had been unjustly enslaved by African rulers, and therefore of disrespecting liberty as a natural right of all people." The two men believed that "human beings could be legitimately enslaved only by right of conquest in a publicly declared just war."[16] Ideas concerning freedom knew no national or geographical boundaries, and men like Rocha were also influenced by ideas of the Enlightenment.

Many proslavery forces in the Americas and on the Continent during the Age of Revolutions (1776–1848), found their intellectual justification in the works of John Locke. Although Locke died in 1704, his ideas were ingrained in proslavery propaganda. A strong proponent of slavery, Locke believed that in most cases the institution arose as the natural condition of the inferiors. He argued in *Second Treatises of Governments* (1689) that "slavery is so vile and miserable an Estate of Man, and so directly opposite the generous Temper and Courage, of our nation; that tis hardly to be conceived that an *Englishman*, much less a *Gentleman*, should plead for it."[17] Yet he and his fellow English gentlemen did plead for slavery. Locke, who owned stock in the Royal African Company, justified slavery when he wrote a clause in the Fundamental Constitution of the South Carolina Colony (1669) stating that "every freeman of Carolina shall have absolute power and authority over Negro slaves, of what opinion or Religion soever."[18] For Locke, property defined the man. If men had the right to buy and sell Africans as chattel slaves, then that right was by law supreme and inalienable.

Other philosophers of the time, such as the Scotsman David Hume, wrote in his essay "Of Natural Characters" (1748, 1754) that "there never was a civilized nation of any complexion other than white, nor an individual eminent in action or speculation."[19] On the other hand, conservative thinkers such as Edmund Burke implicitly challenged the notion of absolute authority in relation to slavery. Burke wrote, "if we undertake to govern the inhabitants of such a country, we must govern them upon their own principles and maxims, and not upon ours."[20] Burke was voicing a notion that could be applied to any subject people. Showing the contradiction of antislavery leaders who relied solely on their philosophical training or political bent, he pronounced his opposition to the French Revolution, French abolitionist actions, and British radicalism. Burke declared in 1792, just as the first British parliamentary debates on the slave trade commenced, "the cause of humanity would be far more benefited by the continuance of the trade and servitude, regulated and reformed, than by the total destruction of both or either."

In short, many leaders in the colonies and Britain and France could challenge some aspects of slavery. But when antislavery ideas joined forces with those who wanted more radical social reforms, conservative men, even those with antislavery ideals, put those ideas in the background. Yet, at times, the philosophical debate over slavery found the French absolutist thinker Jean Bodin and the English conservative scholar Edmund Burke in basic agreement with Montesquieu and more radical Scottish thinkers, such as Hutcheson and Wallace. Their ideas placed great social responsibilities on humankind. Their ideas traveled from Bodin to the men who fought in the English Civil War to the Quakers to the American and the French revolutionaries to the leader in Saint Domingue.

Revolutionary ideals were at the center of the French *Encyclopédie,* which, according to Diderot, was "to collect the knowledge collected on the surface of the earth, and to unfold its general system." In volume 16 published in 1765, Chevalier Louis de Jaucourt wrote "Traites de Negres." Jacourt took the words almost verbatim from Wallace, just as Wesley took most of his *Thoughts on Slavery* (1774) from Benezet's *Some Historical Account of Guinea.* What did it matter to them that their words were so liberally borrowed, for as Frederick Engels once wrote, "an idea is nothing until it reaches the masses." And when Jacourt so liberally borrowed from Wallace, ideas of reason, science, and "human rights" spread throughout the learned Atlantic community.[21]

These ideas were rational, secular, and religious. They were about the freedom of the whites as well as the blacks. Many of these ideas were transmitted through men on both sides of the Atlantic who, like Benezet (who was both French and American), best summed up their thoughts in *Notes on the Slave Trade* (1783): "liberty is the right of very human being, as soon as he breathes the vital air. And no human law can deprive him of the right which he derives from the law of nature."[22]

The antislavery ideas developed during the later half of the eighteenth century were the products of the Scottish moral philosophers, the French materialist thinkers, English political economists, and men such as Father Rocha. They had a tremendous intellectual impact on those who would lead the fight culminating with the ban on the international slave trade in 1807–1808.

Revolts and Revolutionaries: They "Came in Waves"

Herbert Aptheker wrote in *American Negro Slave Revolts* (1943) that slave revolts often "came in waves." Such were the examples of the event in the mainland colonies and the Caribbean in the middle of the eighteenth century and the early to middle nineteenth century. When he wrote this he was roundly criticized for exaggeration and for finding a slave revolt "under every rock" or every time three blacks gathered. He was also criticized because he had an openly Marxist bent, using both a class (materialist) analysis and one that showed the self-agency of the oppressed. Aptheker also listed what he termed "precipitants and . . . other causes of rebellion" linking the harnessing of plantation labor and slave punishment and the political and economic climate to existing social conditions. As Eugene Genovese wrote in *Roll, Jordan, Roll* some thirty years later, "Aptheker demolished the legend of the contented slave . . . and unearthed much evidence of insurrection, maroon activity, and other forms of physical resistance and compelled a new departure in the historiography."[23] Indeed, a brief look at several interrelated slave revolts shows that the links in the fight against oppression were as conjoined as those which held that oppression together.

In 1737 a revolt in Antigua shook both the Caribbean and the mainland colonies. This was documented by one proslavery writer who wrote of the "catching of the King, that is, he who was to have been King of the Blacks, had the plot succeeded and his two generals." This planned revolt became well known throughout the British Empire. The authorities meted out extreme punishment to discourage future revolts. "King" and "general" were titles given to the plot's leaders, who gave orders to kill all the whites. The Antiguan blacks, living closely together on the small island, had retained their "Africanisms" longer than many of the slaves in the mainland colonies and used their links with their African past to plot for their freedom. They represent the model established by Eugene Genovese of "restorationist" rebels as those who sought to restore the African state of being and African state of mind. What shook the authorities even more was that Will, one of the Antiguan leaders, ended up in New York in 1741 and played a major role in its revolt. According to the 1741 trial record, the *Journal of the Proceedings*, kept by one of the judges, Daniel Horsmanden, a slave named "Ward's Negro" testified "that this criminal has within a few years past, been concerned in two conspiracies in the West Indies, the first at St. John's, the last at Antigua, in the year 1736 where (as it was said) he became an evidence, and from thence he was shipped to this city."[24] Will had been accused of being involved in the plot but also of informing on eighty-eight of his fellow Antiguan conspirators, and he was transported to New York. Slave masters, fearing the loss of profits, often resisted the death penalty for their slaves, choosing instead to sell and transport them to other slave-holding regions.

The Stono Rebellion of 1739 in South Carolina was the largest slave revolt in colonial North America. South Carolina had a total population of 56,000. The 32,000 blacks outnumbered whites by a few thousand short of two to one. Just as British leader Lord Dunmore offered freedom to slaves in 1774 during the American Revolutionary War, so the Spanish in Florida offered liberty to slaves in the British possessions. Enslaved Africans, hearing of this offer, conspired to runaway to Spanish lands. On Sunday, September 9, 1739, twenty slaves seized a store, executed its owners, and burned several plantations. Led by an African slave, Jemmy, and proclaiming "liberty," the slaves gathered at St. Paul's Parish and moved south, picking up recruits and burning plantations as they marched, killing more than twenty-five whites. Outnumbered by the heavily armed militia, the slaves were captured a few days later. In the end, forty-four of the insurgents were killed or hanged. Many of their heads were placed on pikes at the entrance to the city's port, as was later done in New York.[25]

Many of South Carolina's slaves came from Angola. They spoke the same languages or dialects and were able to communicate secretly with each other. Some of the slaves were said to have been trained in the use of firearms and military regimen by the Portuguese. Some had been taught the tenets of Catholicism by their Portuguese captors. They were also proficient in rice production, South Carolina's staple, just as they had been in Angola.[26]

Some four years after the events in Antigua, and two years after the uprisings in South Carolina, the "rumor of revolt" swept New York City in the first few months of 1741. The paranoia that overwhelmed the city lasted from May 11 until August 29. Historians are divided over whether the events that so engrossed the city constituted a real slave revolt, white hysteria, or a criminal conspiracy. The city had a population of 11,000 of which 20 percent were black. Because of the "long winter" of 1740–1741, the War of Jenkins' Ear (Britain against Spain), and the inability to conduct normal trade because of the freezing of the Hudson River, tensions were high. In 1741, a "combination of villains" made up of groups of enslaved and free Africans, indentured Dutch, British and Irish servants, and Irish, Cuban, and West Indian sailors, along with Haitian "voodoo priests," African Obeah, and several Dutchmen, "conspired" to revolt against the New York authorities. As in other slave rebellions, the slaves, knowing where the center of authority and the munitions armories were, attacked Ft. George. The conspirators set a number of fires over a ten-day period.

White merchants claimed to have heard blacks scream the words "Fire, Fire, Scorch, Scorch, A LITTLE, damn it, BY-AND-BY." The New York conspirators had planned to name a king and a general, just as they had in Antigua. In New York, in a reverse of positions for blacks and whites, the general was an Akan (from southern Ghana) named Caesar, and the general a Dutchman named John Hughson. In the end, thirty slaves were executed, thirteen blacks were quartered and burned at the stake, and seventeen others were hanged. Four whites were hanged, and their bodies, along with those of the blacks, were left to rot in public at the entry ports of the city, so as to strike fear in other would-be conspirators. By the end of the events (with similarities to the Salem, Massachusetts, witch trials of 1692), more than seventy people had been expelled from the city and two hundred others were questioned and arrested. Seventy other blacks were sent out of the colony. Whereas in Stono the authorities did all they could to keep the matter silent, in New York the trials and hysteria made the events known throughout the western Atlantic World. Yet like Stono, the events were in part blamed on the high concentration of blacks in the city.

The demographics of the 1,429 slaves in the city shifted drastically after the revolt. Prior to the events of 1741, 70 percent of the slaves had come from the West Indies, and the other 30 percent from Africa. At the end of the trials only 30 percent of the slaves arrived in New York from the West Indies, with the other 70 percent coming directly from Africa. This was the opposite of what happened in South Carolina, where slaves arriving directly from Africa had led the protests. This shift was caused by the authorities' fear that other rebellious blacks transported from Jamaica and Antigua would again end up in the city. Indeed, if goods could travel across Atlantic waters, so could ideas, including revolutionary ideas about freedom.

Gabriel's revolt, occurring at the beginning of the nineteenth century, was influenced both by the ideals of the American and Haitian revolutions. Gabriel Prosser (ca. 1776–1800) lived in Henrico County, Virginia, near Richmond, the capital city. A blacksmith by training and a man who taught himself to read the Bible, he was well versed in the revolutionary rhetoric of the period. He began to recruit, arm, and train slaves in Richmond. Seizing the treasury and the armory in late August, he freed prisoners and prepared for open revolt. But a severe thunderstorm and fearful slaves who revealed his plot to the whites betrayed him. The whites quickly armed and mobilized themselves, and in the next day or so they arrested hundreds of slaves. Gabriel was able to escape with the help of a white antislavery Methodist ship captain by hiding aboard a schooner in Norfolk, many miles by foot to the south. However, he was soon betrayed by two of the ship's crew, who collected a $300 reward. Gabriel, along with twenty-six other slaves, was quickly convicted of insurrection and executed on October 7, 1800. Many others were jailed for long periods. As they would whenever revolt or fear of revolt occurred, the authorities tightened existing laws and prevented blacks from gathering, praying, or reading together.

The next large revolt came in 1822 in and around Charleston, South Carolina, a major southern seaport. The revolt was led by Denmark Vessey (ca. 1767–1822), who was said by some to have been born in Africa and by others in St. Thomas. Vessey had also spent considerable time on ships as the slave of the Bermuda slave trader Joseph Vessey, and when his master settled in Charleston, Denmark Vessey remained with him. As a trusted slave in an urban setting, Vessey experienced "relative freedom." He won the Bay Street Lottery in 1800 and with the $600 prize purchased his "real freedom." There were already about 1,000 free blacks in the city. The number would rise to 3,600 by 1822. Most worked on the docks, as apprentices to tradesmen, or as house servants. The majority of the 260,000 slaves still worked, as they had in 1739, in the rice fields. By 1822, Denmark Vessey had accumulated around $8,000, along with seven wives and countless children. Like Prosser, he was also a literate man, longed for information about the events of his time, and was well versed in the rhetoric about rights, freedom, and liberty from the American and French revolutions and about the heroic actions of the men and women in Haiti. He also knew about the discord among white Americans over the Missouri Compromise, which allowed Missouri to enter the Union as a slave state and Maine as a free state (free of slavery). Deciding that his freedom meant nothing as long as his brethren remained enslaved, he organized a revolt, quickly mobilizing fellow tradesmen while secretly meeting in black churches. It was said that as many as 9,000 blacks were involved in the plot. But just as with the earlier Prosser plot, he was betrayed by fearful slaves. On July 2, 1822, Vessey was captured and executed along with thirty-four co-conspirators. Thirty-seven others were sent out of the state. The authorities, fearful of another revolt, clamped down on the blacks, especially free blacks. The legislature quickly passed a series of Seamen Acts, requiring all seamen to be jailed as long as their ships were docked or in port. Similar acts were passed throughout the South. Perhaps the greatest fear which was held by whites was that blacks had invited people in Haiti to join the rebellion and that Vessey's own escape plan involved going to the island.

The last of the three major mainland revolts occurred in Southampton, Virginia, starting in February 1831 and led by Nat Turner (1800–1831). Turner's mother had come from Africa only seven years before his birth and told him often of her native land. Known as an eccentric and a God-fearing zealot, he had tried to escape in 1821, only to be recaptured and severely punished. But this experience led him to believe that his calling was to lead his people to freedom. Turner organized his plot through the black churches and camp meetings throughout the area. He became ill on the day the revolt was to begin, August 13, so it was postponed until August 22. Beginning with five slaves, with another seventy-five or so joining along the way, they moved from plantation to plantation, and house to house, killing more than sixty whites. However, the whites quickly organized a well-armed militia which soon defeated the rebels. In the end, more than a hundred blacks were killed. Turner escaped to the swamps of Dismal Creek near Norfolk, Virginia, a site of a previous maroon community. Captured a month later, Turner was hanged on November 11, 1831.

All three of the rebellions involved careful planning by charismatic and learned leaders. All involved spreading revolutionary ideas. All involved men who had worked near the sea or in some trade. All fell victim to both the unpredictable weather and betrayal by blacks. Perhaps those blacks who betrayed them felt that their conditions were far better that those of the plantation blacks and did not want to risk their positions. All were in some way inspired by the events in Haiti, both the slave rebellion and the revolution.

Coming amid these three rebellions, and influenced by the same events and conditions, was a fiery pamphlet, *One Continual Cry: David Walker's Appeal to the Colored Citizens of the World 1829–1830.*[27] Walker (1785–?) was a free black, born to a black mother and a white father, and had immigrated to Massachusetts from North Carolina. He was a contemporary of Frederick Douglass and Martin Delaney. The *Appeal,* according to Vincent Harding, a noted scholar and close associate of the martyred Dr. Martin Luther King Jr., must be considered the first black nationalist statement in the United States. Walker's appeal addressed ten major themes and demands which have been documented by Harding.[28] Among them were that blacks must end complicity with slaveowners and resist oppression, violently if need be. He called for solidarity with and unity among all Africans, "free" and captive throughout the African Diaspora. He demanded that blacks resist the African Colonization Society's bid to rid America of its free people among them. He saw the education of blacks as a weapon for freedom and equality. He called for action by whites to help acquire peace and justice and to end racism. Near the end of the *Appeal* he told his readers that he and others who fought against slavery and oppression would be persecuted and killed.

Walker, a used-clothes salesman, personally raised funds to distribute the tract. Southern whites so feared its distribution that the state of Georgia placed a $10,000 bounty on his head if captured alive and $3,000 if dead. Those caught distributing the pamphlets were threatened with death. A northern paper called it "one of the most wicked and inflammatory productions ever issued from the press." Southern governors demanded that the Massachusetts authorities arrest Walker and seize all copies of the publications, but Massachusetts alerted its counterparts that they were powerless to do so. Using the solidarity of seamen, black and white, who came to his shop seeking cheap clothing and news, Walker sealed copies of the pamphlet in their wide bottomed pants and found other means of smuggling the work to southern blacks. Walker, as he had predicted, did not live long after the publication, dying mysteriously. But the *Appeal* alerted whites to the intelligence of blacks and warned them that slavery would be challenged in the North and in the South, violently if need be. This is where the real fear lay.

Additionally, in New York in 1741, in Boston in 1828, and in incidents at intervals between and thereafter, whites were given something else to fear: the cooperation of other whites, among them seamen who had traveled the Atlantic World with blacks, had themselves been oppressed, had worked and socialized with black sailors, and knew that the basis of their oppression was the emerging commodity production system and the system of slavery. More importantly, the nation and the world now knew that blacks would act, and many whites would join them, to end the institution of slavery.

In Barbados fear of revolts arose as officials enacted a series of stringent "Black Codes" from 1661 to 1688. Seeing the blacks use music to communicate and as a weapon for freedom, the officials later banned the beating of drums or the playing of instruments. As in many places, they sought to bar slaves from speaking in their native language if they had retained it. Yet the slaves fought back, most notably in 1675. Here they were led by Fortuna, a black woman who had plotted the insurrection over three years. When the plot was uncovered, 100 slaves were arrested; 50 were found guilty of conspiracy and executed. Six of them were burned at the stake, 5 committed suicide, and, as was often the case, 11 others were beheaded, and their heads displayed in the city of Speightstown. Another plot was discovered in 1693 before the slaves could act. More than 300 slaves were arrested, and 93 were executed. There were scattered revolts in the following years, but it was not until 1816 that blacks in Barbados staged one of the largest revolts in the British West Indies. It became known as Bussa's revolt, after the African-born slave who led it, or as the Easter Rebellion of 1816. Twenty thousand slaves mobilized to take over dozens of estates. The revolt lasted three days. In the end nearly 1,000 slaves had been killed, 300 were tried, 140 were executed, and more than 130 were transported to other colonies. British fears forced the Barbadian planters, known as the most brutal in the region, to enact after years of debate the Consolidated Slave Law of 1825, which gave the slaves the "three rights law." They were allowed to own some property, to testify in court cases, and to seek cheaper manumission prices.

Jamaica also had a long history of slave rebellion during this period. The first revolt began in 1522, and from the 1670s the revolts were continuous. The first Maroon War with its origins in 1663 lasted through seventy years of irregular skirmishes, with the main battles from 1730 to 1740. Many of these battles were led by the legendary Nanny, who it was said could catch bullets with her bare hands. In 1739 the British offered peace to the Cockpit County Maroons if they would agree to help recapture runaway slaves. The British also conceded to maroon communities where "free towns" were established. The Second Maroon War of 1795 saw 300 maroons battle with 1,500 British soldiers. Although the Maroons eventually surrendered, they still maintained control of their territory, existing as a "nation within a nation."

It is true that not all Maroons saw the abolition of slavery as their main goal. Most Maroons sought to restore their identity and cultures in separate and independent communities. At the same time other slaves in Jamaica wanted the revolutionary overthrow of slavery.[29] But make no mistake, they wanted freedom from the whites and from slavery one way or another. In 1760, Tacky's revolt, one of the largest in Jamaican history, was led by Akans, or Coramantees (as in New York). Starting on Easter Sunday, 150 blacks led by the slave Tacky first attacked the main fort at Port Maria, just as slaves had done in New York a few years earlier. Choosing to attack at the height of the French and Indian Wars (1757–1763), the slaves no doubt felt that the British could not wage full battle on both fronts, on the mainland and in the Caribbean. The center of the revolt was in the parish of St. Mary's, which had a high concentration of Akan slaves. The rebellion was not suppressed until October of 1761. In the end almost 400 slaves, 60 whites, and 60 free blacks were killed. As was the colonial pattern, those participating slaves who were not hung or shot were "transported" out of the colony. On December 25, 1831, more than 20,000 slaves revolted, which led to the British Emancipation Act providing for the gradual manumission of 500,000 slaves in the British West Indian colonies.

Waves of slave unrest continued throughout the West Indies between 1816 and 1834. In Demerara, British Guyana, slaves revolted between August and September 1823. Tensions were high. The planters were edgy because of the abolitionist debates in Britain. Indeed, in Britain in 1823 the Society for Mitigating and Gradually Abolishing Slavery Throughout the British Dominions, or the Anti-Slavery Society, was formed. The London Missionary Society, which disapproved of slavery, had been active in Demerara since 1803. This caused tension among the white elite and the missionaries. Tension had been high, in fact, ever since an earlier revolt in 1795. Economic conditions were unsettling, with the planters heavily in debt and the price of sugar low.

And the slaves became more restless and fiery as word spread of recent revolts in Jamaica. They also became more discontented as work conditions grew harsher. The blacks also had a united sense of identity. Emilia Viotti da Costa has documented the many tensions in Demerarain society. The missionaries wanted to teach the slaves to read, while the colonists prohibited it. The missionaries wanted the Sabbath to be obeyed, while the whites wanted to work the slaves. And as the missionaries "organized night meetings and attracted to their chapels large numbers of slaves from different plantations, then most colonists treated missionaries as enemies and did everything in their power to stop them."[30] Da Costa also noted that "among the slave practices that whites feared the most was what they called 'obeah'" and other African rituals and retentions.[31] Thus Demerara was ripe for revolt: unity of being and thought among the blacks, increased social hardship, rumors of revolts and political tensions, and economic strife among the whites.

Historian Michael Craton has estimated that "nearly all the 30,000 slaves on the sixty estates over a thirty-mile stretch east of Georgetown were involved." in the revolt.[32] The slaves, who held one white captive, attempted to negotiate their demand of "land and three days work in the week for themselves . . . and others their freedom" with the unbending white leaders who quickly mobilized their militias. The blacks refused to surrender to the well-armed white militia, and between 100 and 150 rebels were killed, and 2 white militiamen were injured.

Restorationists and Rebels: Maroons and Revolutionaries

There were many different forms of slave resistance within the Atlantic World. Among these were maroonage, open revolts, sabotage of the "masters'" property, suicide, fires, poisoning the master and his family, and work slowdowns. Genovese in *From Rebellion to Revolution* places the forms of resistance in categories: restorationist and revolutionary. The restorationists sought to restore the system of their African pasts. The revolutionaries, on the other hand, had the goal to overthrow slavery, and if need be the entire existing social order. Their goal was no less lofty than the American revolutionaries or others who wanted freedom. Often these forms overlapped, and "the authorities understood that unchecked Maroons presented a constant temptation to the slaves to rise in revolt or to desert en masse. Maroon resistance, in which the Maroons sought to restore their African identity, took place in many forms. Some took "to the hills," others to the "swamps." Those who had not been "seasoned" or broken in by the slave masters often ran away in groups. These Maroons, hoping to retain their family or tribal structure or restore their African ancestries, often took their whole families with them. Slaves who had been in the area for a while, or who had been "acclimated" to the terrain, may have run off individually or in small groups. The goal always was to come back and get their wives, children, and elders. They wanted to establish their own "nation within a nation": to establish their own independent communities. Recent scholars have shown that some, in fact, collaborated with and made treaties with the whites in turning away rebel slaves. They did so in order to preserve their maroon homelands. They existed as *palenques*, and as *quilombos*, *cumbes*, and *cimarrones*. They were most common in parts of the Caribbean, Latin America, and Brazil, where there were both higher proportions of blacks to whites and land conditions that included mountains, swamps, and forests. Maroons escaped to places where they could more easily defend themselves and where their former masters would have difficulty navigating the terrain. Maroons, as in the case of the Jamaican communities in the eighteenth century, paid special attention to the colonial conflicts and often ran away at the peak of the conflict. This was also the case in South Carolina and Georgia where, during the French and Indian Wars, slaves used the conflict to escape, knowing that the colonialists would have problems fighting on two fronts, just as the leaders of Tacky's revolt had predicted.

Brazil, the largest country in South America, also witnessed hundreds of attempts by enslaved Africans to win their freedom. From the Portuguese arrival in 1500, tensions developed between the colonizer and the several million indigenous people of the country. As in North America, the Native American indigenous people were seized and decimated, their lands depopulated and taken over. Much of this was done in the name of Christianity. The first blacks were taken there in 1538, although the Portuguese had first taken slaves from Africa in 1433. In Brazil, as elsewhere, the Europeans fought among themselves for control—in this case the Portuguese, Dutch, and Spanish. It is estimated that, 3.5 million slaves, or more than 35 percent of all slaves captured from Africa, ended up in Brazil, with 100,000 in the sixteenth century, 600,000 in the seventeenth century, and 1.3 million enslaved Africans in the eighteenth century. Yet it was during the debates over the transnational slave trade in Britain, France, and America in the early 1800s that Brazil dramatically increased its drive for slaves. In 1820 Brazil had 1.5 million slaves (40 percent of the population). From the turn of the century until the 1850s Brazil imported more than 1.6 million slaves, or 40 percent of the total imports. However, here politics and economics clashed. Britain had banned the slave trade in 1803 and put pressure on Brazil to do likewise, yet Brazil still overtook Britain in sugar exports.

Quilombos (runaway slaves), or *mocambos* were the earliest forms of revolts and were led by Bantu-speaking enslaved Africans, the first lasting from 1603 until 1694. The runaways existed as a federation of thousands of residents and challenged Portugal's authority. Another of these restorationist slaves established an African-like state, the Republic of Palmares, in Alagoas in northeastern Brazil. The Male uprisings led by Muslim insurgents occurred between 1807 and 1835 in Salvador and Bahia. Brazil also had revolts in its Balem, Maranhão, and Rio Grande regions.

The most famous and last of these revolts occurred on January 25–26, 1835, and became known as the Husua Uprising (named after slaves from Nigeria) or the Great Male (African Muslims) Revolt, as the slaves attempted to gain control of Bahia. Between 400 and 6000 slaves attempted to gain control of Bahia. The enslaved Africans came from various ethnic groups and tribes from West Africa. Some were Hausa, while some were Yoruba, Muslim, or of different African religions. Most held on to their religion, their culture, their music and song; in short, their Africanism. The day of the planned revolt was Our Lady of Guidance (a feast day for the whites), and as with Turner's rebellion in Virginia, several slaves informed the whites of the plot. The militia quickly mobilized and encountered a large number of African fighters. Soon other rebels took to the streets of the capital city, Salvador, and the slaves and the whites engaged in fierce battle in which 70 of the rebels were killed. When the Africans were captured they were wearing their tribal clothing and had with them bracelets and other ornaments containing passages from the Qur'an, written in Arabic. In the end more than 230 enslaved Africans were arrested, tried, and punished. But after this uprising Brazil passed a law that freed all slaves entering the country and decreed that participation in the international slave trade was illegal and equivalent to piracy; but as with many laws allowing for gradual manumission, it was ignored. National independence leaders such as Simon Bolivar of Venezuela and José Artigas of Uruguay fought valiantly against slavery. Bolivar wanted to attract slaves to his army, and in 1816 he promised the president of Haiti he would abolish slavery in the entire hemisphere. In Chile, Jose de San Martin, like Bolivar and Artigas, promised freedom to any slave who joined his army for independence.

In 1815 Portugal accepted £750,000 from Britain to restrict the slave trade in Brazil, and in 1817 Spain accepted £400,000 to abandon the trade in Cuba, Puerto Rico, and Santo Domingo. But that did nothing to diminish the Brazilian planters' drive to acquire slaves. José Bonifacio de Andrada e Silva, the father of Brazilian independence, wrote an appeal in 1830 condemning slavery and calling for free labor. Shortly after, in 1833, the antislavery newspaper *O Homem de Cor* (the Colored Man) appeared. It was similar in force to David Walker's *Appeal to the Colored Citizens of the World* (1829). Yet it differed in that it demanded that, "every citizen may be admitted to civil, political, and military public offices, with no qualifications except those of his talents and virtues." Walker had no hope that authorities in the United States would listen to such a plea. But then again, neither did the rulers of Brazil listen to the pleas of the slaves; and it was not until September 4, 1850, that a law was passed requiring penalties for slave traders. In 1852 Brazil joined other nations in the suppression of the transatlantic slave trade. Finally, in 1864, Brazilian Emperor Pedro II emancipated slaves, which were a part of his daughter's dowry, and acceded to the French abolitionist request that the government commit itself to end slavery. In 1871, the Brazilian Congress approved the Rio Branco Law of Free Birth, which conditionally freed the children of slaves. Yet slavery persisted. In 1883, Joaquim de Araujo, the Brazilian abolitionist, issued his *O absolicionism*, which helped launch a final campaign against slavery and establish the Brazilian Abolitionist Confederation, which issued its manifesto, *Confederação abolicionista.* But it was not until 1888, when the senate passed a law establishing unqualified emancipation, that slavery was at last abolished.

The events of Haiti and in Latin America have been discussed elsewhere in this volume. Yet it needs to be constantly stated that perhaps more than any other revolution before or since, the occurrences in Haiti (1791–1804) brought together two important strands: the desire for colonial independence and the desire to overthrow colonial slavery. Never before had blacks who fought for independence and against slavery been one and the same people. And never before had the French and the American leaders united so much to suppress a movement which used both of their ideas as models. The Haitian leaders sought to link American oppression by the British with their own. Yet never before had the ideas of men such as Thomas Jefferson, who had inspired both Toussaint L'Ouverture and Henri Christophe, been so clear: Ideals about liberty, equality, and independence were "FOR WHITES ONLY." Never before had one movement done so much to inspire a people.

Africa and Freedom

Whites who justified slavery proffered an image of Africa as a dark and foreboding place. This image of Africa, as a place of savagery and heathenism in need of both Christian conversion and European-style civilization, provided a necessary foundation for arguments legitimizing African slavery. By presenting the "Negro nations" as barbaric, degraded, and deeply uncivilized, writers such as John Locke could argue that Western Christians served the interests of Africans themselves by introducing them to the benefits of Christianity. On this point, Locke and the Society for the Propagation of the Gospel could agree. The first person to publicly counter this image of Africa was Anthony Benezet, first in 1762, with *A Short Account of Africa*, and then in 1771 with a longer edition, *Some Historical Account of Guinea*. This is generally recognized as the first history of West Africa in the English language. This book was first used to teach African history to blacks in Reconstruction schools in the aftermath of the Civil War and to students at Quaker colleges. Using the journals of men who had traveled to Africa, many of whom went to study the flora and fauna of the various regions, Benezet developed positive images of Africa "before the arrival of the Europeans." He also used the works of Leo Africanus, who wrote in 1526, "they lived in common, having no property in land, no tyrant or superior, but supported themselves in an equal state; upon natural produce of the country, which afforded plenty of roots, game and honey. That ambitions and avarice never drove them into foreign countries to subdue or cheat their neighbors. Thus they believed without toil or superfluities."[33]

Former slave Ottobah Cugoano (1757–?), whose *Thoughts and Sentiments on the Evil and Wicked Traffic of the Slavery and Commerce of the Human Species* (1787) referred his readers to "the worthy and judicious" Benezet as giving "some very striking estimations of the exceeding evil occasioned by that wicked diabolical traffic of the African slave trade."[34] Cugoano arrived in England shortly after the Somerset decision had been made and witnessed the debates surrounding the decision. However it was his own voice, that of an African commenting on the evils of slavery and on the beauty of his native land, that gave his work an impact. As an African he wrote, "and we that are particularly concerned would humbly join with all the rest of our brethren and countrymen in complexion [in] imploring and earnestly entreating the most respectful and generous people of Great Britain." As an Englishman or an Afro-Brit he denounced the Christian theory of the Great Chain of Being and challenged those who argued "that an African is not entitled to any competent degree of knowledge, or capable of imbibing any sentiments of probity; and that nature designed him for some inferior link in the chain."

Olaudah Equiano (1745–1797), who had been kidnapped into slavery as a child, also relied upon Benezet when describing his native Nigeria. His *Interesting Narrative of the Life of Olaudah Equiano or Gustavas Vasa, the African* (1789), became necessary reading in the antislavery community. Equiano was truly a man of the Atlantic, visiting numerous countries in Africa, Asia, Europe, and North and South America. By adding *the African* to the book title, just after his "slave name" he asserted his heritage. He was a musician, linguist, navigator, hairdresser, accountant, astronomer, sailor, and author. He studied Islam, Methodism, Quakerism, Catholicism, the ideas of George

Whitefield, and several eastern religions. Few people of his time had such a rich life. The African wrote:

> When I came to Kingston, I was surprised to see the number of Africans who were assembled together on Sundays, particularly at a large commodious place, called Spring Path. Here each different nation of Africa meet and dance after the manner of their own country. They still retain most of their native customs; they bury their dead, and put victuals, pipes, and tobacco, and other things, in the grave with the corpse, in the same manner as in Africa.[35]

Both Equiano and Cugoano gave their visions of Africa, of their "country" and of their "countrymen," and traveled widely denouncing the slave trade and proclaiming their humanity and that of their fellow Africans. John Wesley also learned of Africa from Benezet's work. William Wilberforce quoted Benezet of Africa in Parliament. Thomas Clarkson wrote of Benezet's description of Africa: "in this precious book . . . I found almost all I wanted. I obtained by means of it a knowledge of, and gained great access to the great authorities of Adanson, Moore, Barbot, Bosman, and others."[36] People, who read Equiano, Cugoano, Clarkson, Benezet, and a few others thus came away with a vision of Africa that countered that of the proslavery writers.

In colonial North America, Samuel Hopkins, a Congregationist pastor, wrote *Dialogue Concerning the Slavery of the Africans* (1776), a fiery attack on the Second Continental Congress, supporting freedom for the enslaved Africans. However, it was in his lesser-known work "To the Public" (1773), issued with Ezra Stiles, that he first called for a moderate colonization plan to send freed slaves out of the mainland colonies. Their goal was to "send to light . . . to these nations in Africa, who have been injured so much by the slave trade . . . to promote the most important interest, the Kingdom of Christ." They promised to send two blacks with distinct African names, Bristol Yamma, an enslaved African, and John Quamine [Quamino], a free man, to Guinea. Both men still spoke African languages. The original intent was to train a total of forty blacks for this and other missions, but the plan was aborted because of revolutionary war hostilities. Thomas Jefferson first wrote about his support for colonization for blacks in 1776; and in 1781 he feared that "the slave, when made free, might mix with, with staining the blood of his master . . . when freed, he is to be removed beyond the reach of mixture." The difference between Hopkins and Stiles, on the one hand, and Jefferson and many later supporters of colonization, on the other, is that the former proponents were genuinely bitter enemies of slavery and did what they thought was in the best interests of blacks according to their Christian beliefs. As Lamin Sanneh, historian of blacks who went back to West Africa, has shown, Hopkins "supported a scheme in which Christian blacks would be repatriated to Africa where they could live as free men and enjoy the fruit of their labor."[37]

At its height, there were never more than 14,000 blacks, referred to as "body servants" in Britain. For Britain the slave trade was not about meeting its own labor needs. It was about meeting its crass needs for profits and New World goods, which kept it at the center of the slave trade. Yet British humanitarians such as Sharp and Clarkson knew that the slave trade corrupted British society. In 1787 British reformers and abolitionists founded Sierra Leone and began the process of repatriating former slaves in London to Africa, sending 377 settlers. Its first town was named Granville Town, after Granville Sharpe, who had supported the effort. Later, 1,200 blacks who had immigrated to Nova Scotia were resettled in 1792 in Sierra Leone. Whereas most of the early antislavery leaders such as Benezet and Wolman opposed colonization, Sharp supported the concept. His *Short Sketch of Temporary Regulation* was seen as setting the founding ideas for the colony.

In 1815 Paul Cuffe, a free black and wealthy merchant from Massachusetts, lent his support by spending $4,000 of his own money to finance an expedition of thirty-eight black colonists to Sierra Leone. He later boasted that thousands more had sent him pleas, begging for passage to Africa. It must be said that Cuffe had different reasons for supporting the "Back to Africa" movement: he genuinely believed that blacks would never find equality in racist America.

Black leaders in Philadelphia were vehemently opposed to Cuffe's plan. Richard Allen, the founder of the African Methodist Episcopal Church, and Absalom Jones, leader of the Protestant Episcopal Church, formed the Free African Society on April 12, 1787. Along with James Forten, another black leader in Philadelphia, they led the opposition to colonization. All had been former students at the African Free School headed by Anthony Benezet. Some Quakers had also argued against colonization, and in *Short Account of Africa* Benezet rhetorically asked, "What shall be done with those Negroe's already imported and born in our Families? Must they be sent to *Africa?* That would be to expose them to a strange land, to greater Difficulties than many of them labor under at present."[38]

In December of 1816 the Virginia Assembly adopted a resolution authorizing the governor to request from the president a place outside the United States to send free blacks. Shortly thereafter, on December 21, 1816, an "unholy alliance" of emancipationists and slaveholders who wanted to rid the hemisphere of free blacks founded the American Colonization Society. Its full name was the American Society for Colonizing the Free People of Colour of the United States. The ACS was led by Robert Finley, a white minister from Princeton, New Jersey, who believed that resettlement to Africa would bring about an end to slavery. Supporters of the ACS included former American presidents James Monroe and James Madison and Supreme Court Justice John Marshall. However, the most ardent supporter was Henry Clay, the Kentucky senator and slaveholder. The humanitarian Finley wrote that the society's mission had three basic goals: "we would be cleared of them; we would send to Africa a population partially civilized and Christianized. . . . [and] blacks would be put in a better condition."[39] Finley left his home in New Jersey and traveled to Washington to meet with Clay, who was to give the keynote address at the founding meeting of the ACS. However, on his way Finley met with James Forten and other Philadelphia black leaders. To his dismay they opposed his plan.

In January 1817, Forten, Richard Allen, and Absalom Jones organized a convention in Philadelphia, attended by 3,000 blacks, to express their opposition to colonization. Forten wrote Cuffe, "I must mention to you that the whole continent seems to be agitated concerning Colonising the People of Colour." He further told Cuffe that just as the ACS was meeting a month before, "the People of Colour here was very much fritened at first," adding, "they were afraid that all the free people would be Compelled to go, particularly in the southern States."[40] The Philadelphia blacks knew that the chief aim of the ASC was to deport all blacks who had won their freedom or could read and write. These blacks, most of them former slaves, would most likely come to aid their enslaved brethren, and the whites knew this.

In 1821 the ACS sent the first expedition of blacks to Liberia. The land, about a thousand miles square, was purchased in 1822 for six gallons of rum, a hogshead of tobacco, and other assorted goods worth about $300. Around 20,000 blacks were relocated. Its capital, Monrovia, was named after former president James Monroe. Later that year Benjamin Lundy, the noted white abolitionist, first published *The Genius of Universal Emancipation*, in which he advocated colonization.

It was obvious from the start that there were broad divisions among those who wanted colonization. In 1827, just as Lundy used his paper to support the efforts of black leaders, John Russwurm and Samuel Cornish began publication of *Freedom's Journal* to oppose the ACS. George M. Frederickson has observed that white abolitionists had as "their purpose to bring about emancipation in a way that was congenial to conservatives." Black leaders, such as Cuffe, on the one hand, and Forten, Allen, Jones, and later Russwurm and Cornish, on the other, desperately wanted black freedom yet found different ways to fight for it.

Although the high point for colonization was during the 1820s and 1830s in the United States and Britain, the Fugitive Slave Act of 1850 re-ignited the quest for emigration to Africa. Around that time more than 30,000 blacks sought refuge in Canada. Others went to Haiti, where President Abraham Lincoln supported their migration. Martin Delaney (1812–1885), with his fiery brand of Black Nationalism, issued his *The Condition, Elevation, Emigration and Destiny of the Colored People of the United States* (1852). Delaney took his family to Canada in 1856 and began to organize the emigration of blacks to Africa. As a writer, orator, and medical practitioner, he was a skillful leader but had often been criticized for his lack of organizational follow-through. In 1858 and 1859 he visited Nigeria to investigate emigration to West Africa, but the pending Civil War led him back to America, where he became an officer and later a Freedman's Bureau official during the Reconstruction years.

Another emigration proponent during that period was Edward Blyden (1832–1912), who was born in St. Thomas, U.S. Virgin Islands, and immigrated to New York where he was recruited to the New York Colonization Society. He was the first to call for "Africa for the Africans." Like Benezet, he saw an Africa rich in resources and people. Immigrating to Monrovia, Liberia, in 1850, he became a school headmaster and minister. A self-educated man who read voraciously to develop his concepts of emigration and "African" freedom, he later became a professor of classics at Liberia College. In most cases colonization was based on the hope and optimism of the blacks and the fears and pessimism of the whites. Yet blacks in the main had long since rejected the concept of colonization. Most agreed with the statement signed by Richard Allen and Absalom Jones at the anti-colonization meeting of April 12, 1787, in Philadelphia: "we will never separate ourselves voluntarily from the slave population of the country; they are our brethren by the ties of consanguinity, of suffering, and of wrong."

Conclusion

Lawrence Tise, a historian of the proslavery movements, has written that "not until the decade before the American Revolution did anything like an extended intercolonial and international debate on slavery get underway." He further observed that "impelled by the new and widely circulating writings of a small coterie of Quaker emancipationists led by Anthony Benezet of Philadelphia various colonial thinkers used proslavery ideas to counter the first major attack in the new world."[41]

In England during the conflict between the colonies and Britain, the Somerset case arose. James Somerset, the slave of Boston customs official Charles Stewart, escaped from his master upon their arrival in London. Granville Sharp had been looking for a case to test English law on whether a person could be held a slave on English soil. He came to the aid of Somerset, proclaiming that slavery "was so odious that nothing can be suffered to support it." He legally challenged Stewart and the captain of the ship, James Knowles, over Somerset's freedom. The issue, however, went beyond this. Could one human being be the property of another? Lord Chief Justice Mansfield soon issued his famous Somerset decision of 1772 which stated that a slave could not be forced to leave England for a life of slavery anywhere else. Mansfield ruled that "whenever the inconveniences, therefore, may follow from a decision, I cannot say this is allowed or approved by the law of England; and therefore the black must be discharged."[42]

The larger issues of property rights were carefully avoided. He did not declare, as was thought by some antislavery activists, that all slaves brought into a non-slaveholding territory be declared free. Mansfield, no doubt, knew of Wallace's *A System of the Principles of the Laws of Scotland,* written twelve years earlier. Wallace had asserted that "as soon as therefore he comes into a country in which the judges are not forgetful of their own humanity, it is their duty to remember that he is a man and to declare him to be free."[43] Nonetheless, slaves in North America gave the Somerset decision their own positive interpretation by attempting to file countless "freedom suits" in the northern courts. Most times they were denied the right to file their petitions. So inspiring was Mansfield's decision that slaves who fled to non-slaveholding areas should be free that North American blacks fled northward. In 1773 an advertisement in the *Virginia Gazette* for runaway slaves asserted that a couple fled to Britain, "where they imagine they will be free (a Notion now to prevalent among the Negroe's, greatly to the vexation and Prejudice of their Masters)."

In the words of legal scholar James Oldham, "popular history often credits Lord Mansfield with freeing the slaves in England by his decision in the Somerset case. That he did not do so is by now agreed and is a point featured in modern scholarship on slavery."[44] Nonetheless the case did provide a legal precedent and hope for enslaved Africans.[45] For example, as late as 1836 the state of Massachusetts adopted the decision as law. Some southern states even adopted the basic ruling of Somerset but abandoned it by 1850.

Enslaved Africans had many times before had their hopes dashed. Thomas Jefferson in a first draft of the Declaration of Independence had called for the freedom of slaves, only to withdraw his plan in the face of southern opposition. In *Notes on the State of Virginia* he also expressed misgivings about slavery and his belief that blacks were inferior. Even Granville Sharp had asserted that "I am far from having any particular esteem for the Negro; but as I think myself obliged to consider them as men, I am certainly obliged to use my best endeavors to prevent their being treated as beasts by our unchristian countrymen." The 1770s and 1780s saw the development of antislavery societies throughout America and Britain. Manumission and abolition societies were formed in Pennsylvania, where Benjamin Franklin later became a leader (1784). Societies were also formed in Rhode Island (1785) and New Jersey (1793). By 1827, there were 130 Abolition Societies, and by 1838 the American Antislavery Society claimed more than 1,350 members. The British Society for Effecting the Abolition of the Slave Trade was formed in 1787 with Thomas Clarkson, Granville Sharp, William Wilberforce, and others, with both Quakers and non-Quakers playing leading roles. In 1792 they led a massive campaign in which antislavery activists collected more than 400,000 signatures and presented them to the House of Commons. That same year, the parliamentary leader William Wilberforce, citing passages from Benezet and Clarkson, proclaimed before the Commons that "since the trade had been used, all punishments are changed into slavery. . . . Never before was another system so big with wickedness." Prime Minister William Pitt the Younger closed the proceeding, as Wilberforce offered a motion, "that it is the opinion of this committee, that the trade carried on by British Subjects, for the purpose of obtaining Slaves on the coast of Africa, ought to be abolished."[46] Although the motion did not pass the whole house, it was the first of its kind in the world. This action in 1792 led to the eventual abolition of the slave trade in 1807–1808. In 1833, some 5,000 petitions were handed to Parliament containing 1.5 million signatures. This campaign was led by the Society for the Mitigation and Gradual Abolition of Slavery, which was formed in 1823 with Wilberforce, Clarkson, and others at the head. Their efforts and petitions led to the passage of the British Emancipation Act, which provided that, as of August 1, 1834, slavery would cease to exist in the British colonies.

In 1770 the Abbè Guillaume-Thomas Raynal published *Historie deux Indies*. Taking evidence from Montesquieu, he believed that there "was nothing inherently inferior about Blacks and it was slavery that made them seem so." Raynal also predicted a "Black Spartacus" would arise in the colonial world leading his people in the fight for freedom. Some years later, in 1788, the French formed the Société des Amis des Noir. The leaders were Jacques Pierre Brissot de Warville, Abbè Henri Grégoire, Antoine de Condorcet, Marquis de Lafayette, Count Honore de Mirabeau, and Abbè Emmanuel Sieyes. Lafayette had fought with the patriots at Yorktown with the future leaders of the Haitian Revolution under his command. Condorcet had written *Réflexions sur l'esclavage des negres* in 1781. He attacked the slave trade and slavery on humanitarian grounds, and like Adam Smith he asserted the free labor was more productive and beneficial to the whites. The Société advocated the immediate end of the slave trade and an end to slavery in all French possessions. At the March 13, 1788, meeting of the Société, Brissot, in urging international unity of action against slavery, gave a presentation about the work of Anthony Benezet, whom the society "venerated." Several of his works had been translated into French. Having read Benezet's *Some Historical Account of Guinea* (1781), Brissot said it is the "foreign corruption introduced in their country [Africa] by the avarice and cupidity of Europeans" with their "thirst for gold."[47] France abolished slavery in the colonies in 1791, the same year that Abbè Grogorie issued his famous words to the Haitians, "you were men, you are now citizens." By 1794 France emancipated it slaves in the colonies, which totaled over 650,000, although, as in most places, illegal trade continued until the *Société Française pour l'aboliton de l'esclavage* helped to secure its end in 1831. Slavery officially ended in the French colonies in 1848.

In the United States the debates over means and methods to end slavery lasted from the 1820s until the end of the Civil War. Was it to be gradual or immediate? Some white abolitionists even debated whether or not to allow blacks to speak up for their own freedom or even to fight in the Union Army. At the beginning of the Civil War Abraham Lincoln issued a call for 75,000 men to join the Union Army. Many blacks responded, only to be denied the "right to fight" for their own freedom. They then began a campaign, a "fight to fight." By the time he issued the Emancipation Proclamation, Lincoln realized that to win the war black troops would have to be mustered. In Massachusetts a call was issued: "To Colored Men—Wanted. Good men for the 54th Regiment of Massachusetts Volunteers of African Descent." Another group, the Second South Carolina, was also formed. To his credit Lincoln enlisted black leaders such as Frederick Douglass and Martin Delaney to help recruit black soldiers. Lincoln once wrote to Andrew Johnson: "the bare sight of fifty thousand armed and drilled Black men in uniform on the banks of the Mississippi would end the rebellion at once. And who doubts we can present that sight, if we but take hold in earnest."[48] By the war's end more than 180,000 blacks had served in the Union Army. They had fought in more than 450 battles including 40 major battles.

Many white abolitionists found it difficult to accept black women abolitionists such as Harriet Tubman and Sojourner Truth and black men such as Frederick Douglass. The great abolitionist William Lloyd Garrison, publisher of the leading antislavery paper the *Liberator*, called for immediate end to slavery and racial discrimination in 1831. Yet he roundly criticized Douglass when the ex-slave spoke at Seneca Falls, New York, in July 1848, on behalf of the rights of women, including their right to vote. Garrison had opposed women's rights and some of Douglass' more radical abolitionist ideas. Others could not accept Douglass's demand that blacks be enlisted in the Union Army or his call "for men of color to arms." Still others found it difficult to accept Douglass's work to internationalize the struggle and link it with oppression wherever he witnessed it. Thus his immortal words, "a blow for freedom anywhere is a blow for freedom everywhere," and "he who wants freedom must strike the first blow." Once in England, Douglass encountered a poor Irishman who used drink for food and who had fallen in a ditch. Half of the man's face had been bitten off by rats that were as hungry as he was. When Douglass linked the British oppression of the Irish with the British and American complicity in slavery, he was criticized by white abolitionists, just as he was when he spoke up for women's rights. Although Douglas refused to go with John Brown to Harper's Ferry, Virginia (now West Virginia) in 1859, believing himself more valuable alive than dead, he understood his friend Brown's belief that he (Brown) would be worth more to the cause dead than alive. Brown, along with several of his sons and other men, died as they attempted to take the military arsenal on October 16, 1859. But the blacks knew, as Douglass said in a memorial service to his friend, that it was old Osawatomie "who began the war that ended American slavery and made this a free Republic." And just as blacks mourned the martyred Brown, Douglass refused the demands of white abolitionists that he denounce Brown. Instead Douglass later said of his friend, "his zeal for the cause was far greater than mine—it was the burning sun to my taper light."[49] Douglass had remembered the words of President Abraham Lincoln that "there must be a position of superior and inferior and I as much as any other man am in favor of having the superior position assigned to the white race." Douglas remembered Lincoln's *Address on Colonization to a Delegation of Black Americans*, where on August 14, 1862, he told them "it is better for us both, therefore to be separated" Encouraging free blacks to immigrate to Central America. Lincoln said, "the political affairs in Central America are not quite as satisfactory condition as I wish" but as "to your colored race they have no objections." Lincoln also told them that Central America "is nearer than Liberia . . . and within seven days run by steamers" and "because of the similarity of the climate with your native land—thus being suited to your physical presence."[50] Douglass and his allies, black and white, in America and abroad, compared Lincoln's words with the deeds of old Osawatomie John Brown.

With the 1860s came the American Civil War and the Emancipation Proclamation of 1863. Slavery had ended in the United States, and gradual manumission laws were enacted by degrees in many countries in Latin America. But slavery still remained on North American soil when Dr. Carlos Manuel des Céspedes freed his slaves at La Demajagua in Oriente Province, Cuba, on October 10, 1868. With thirty-seven planters at his side, he proclaimed Cuban independence from his own plantation. The *Grito de Yara* started the Revolutionary War for independence just as the insurrectionist proclaimed freedom for all slaves. The war lasted ten years. In 1870 the Spanish introduced the Moret Law freeing the newborn offspring of slaves, all those sixty years old, and those who had fought for Spain in the Ten Years' War with Cuba, but widespread slavery still existed. Although Spain abolished slavery in Puerto Rico in 1883, it was not until 1886 that the Spanish government abolished slavery in all of its colonial possessions, including Cuba. Brazil soon followed with its "Golden Law" and freed its last 70,000 slaves in 1888. Frederick Douglass had watched events in Cuba, just as he had in Britain, and noted the actions of de Céspedes and his comrades. He wrote, "the first gleam of the sword of freedom and independence in Cuba secured my sympathy with the revolutionary cause."[51] That revolutionary cause included the ending of slavery in the Americas, and that revolutionary cause was truly an Atlantic one.

Chronology of the Fight against Slavery

1514	Pope Leo X issues a papal bull condemning the slave trade and slavery.
1521–1572	In 1521, forty slaves on the Hispaniola estate of Christopher Columbus's son revolt. There are more uprisings in Hispaniola in 1533, 1537, and 1548. Revolts follow in México (1523, 1527, 1537), Puerto Rico (1527), Cuba (1533, 1538), Colombia (1545), Honduras (1548), Panamá (1555, 1572), Ecuador (1570).
1562–1567	Englishman Hawkins trades and plunders in Spanish America and carries 300 slaves from West Africa to Hispaniola.
1595	In Brazil, Amador leads slaves to devastate sugar plantations and capture the city of São Paulo.
1598	In Colombia, following a series of small slave uprisings, thousands of slaves revolt in the gold mines near Zaragoza.
1619	The first Africans arrive in Virginia. The first representative assembly meets. Dutch ship delivers "twenty and odd" Africans to the English settlement of Jamestown, Virginia, where they are sold by bid as indentured servants.
1639	Revolt in St. Kitts, 500 whites mobilize and kill 60 rebellious slaves.

1656	Angolan and Senegambian slaves rebel in Guadeloupe.
1663	In the North American colonies, black slaves and white servants plan a rebellion in Gloucester County, Virginia, but they are betrayed by one other servant. This marks the first major slavery in English North America.
1673	In Jamaica, the British Colony has its first major slave uprising.
1690	In Jamaica, 300 slaves seize their master's house and weapons and kill onlookers from the neighboring estate. The militia kills 200 slaves and hangs the survivors, while a few manage to escape into the mountains.
1692	(October) In Barbados, Ben, Sambo, and others lead an Afro-Creole plot
1702	Slaves attempt to commandeer the slave ship *Tiger* off of the coast of Gambia. Forty slaves and two whites are killed.
1712	Slaves in New York rebel, killing 9 whites.
1730	Slaves revolt in Norfolk and Princess Anne counties of Virginia.
1732	In Venezuela slaves periodically rebel over the next seventy years.
1730–1740	In Jamaica, the first Maroon War involving Cudjoe the younger, Nanny, and many other leaders
1735	In Great Britain, the British North American colony of Georgia bans slavery, but later restores it.
1735–1736	(October) In Antigua, Tackey and Tomboy lead an island-wide Afro-Creole plot. Over 90 slaves are executed.
1737	In a mass suicide attempt, 30 slaves die when 100 of them jump from the *Prince of Orange* on the British Caribbean island of St. Kitts.
1739	At the Stono Uprising, 80 slaves seize weapons and revolt in South Carolina with hopes of escaping to Florida and gaining freedom. Twenty-five whites are killed and 30 slaves executed.
1741	"The Great Negro Plot" of New York. "Rumors of revolt" bring New York City to standstill. Thirty slaves are executed (13 are quartered and burned at the stake, 17 are hanged), and 4 whites are hanged.
1744	In the United States, a law is passed to allow blacks to serve as witnesses in criminal or civil suits.
1748	Charles Louis de Secondât, baron de la Brede et de Montesquieu, publishes *The Spirit of the Laws*. He declares "that the state of slavery is in its own nature bad. It is neither useful to the master nor to the slave."
1749	Scottish philosopher James Foster publishes *Discourse on all the Principle Braces of Natural Religion and Social Virtue*. He proclaims that chattel slavery "is much more criminal, and more outrageous violation of natural rights than preceding forms of slavery."
1750	In Curacao, 30 plantation slaves, including 13 women, are killed following an uprising. In Philadelphia, Anthony Benezet, along with his Quaker brethren, establishes a school for free blacks.

1751	Rebellion begins in St. Domingue that lasts until 1757. Up to 6,000 people die.
1753	Slaves seize, take ashore, and destroy the *Adventure*, a British slave-trading vessel, off the coast of West Africa.
1755	University of Glasgow professor Frances Hutcheson publishes his *System of Moral Philosophy*, proclaiming "no endowments, natural or acquitted, can give a perfect right to assume power over others, without their consent . . . the subject must have a right of resistance, as the truest is broken, beside the manifest plea of necessity."
1760	In Jamaica, Tacky's revolt is dominated by Coromantee slaves, originating in St. Mary's parish at Easter, but spreading widely through the island around Whitsun. Sixty whites are killed, 400 blacks are executed, and 600 others are sent to Honduras. Scottish jurist George Wallace publishes A *System of the Principles of the Law of Scotland.* He writes that "men and their liberty are not in commerce; they are not either salable or purchasable . . . for everyone of those unfortunate men are pretended to be slaves, has a right to be declared free, for he never lost his liberty; he could not lose it; his Prince had no power to dispose of him."
1762	Anthony Benezet publishes his first antislavery pamphlet, A *Short Account of that Part of Africa.* Benezet's pamphlets have great impact on men and women in Britain, the mainland colonies, and France. He offers a new look on Africa and Africans and declares that they lived in peace and abundance "before the arrival of the white man."
1763	Over 3,000 participate in Cuffee's rebellion in Dutch Berbice, Guyana. Preceding revolts took place in 1733, 1749, 1752, and 1762. Many of the slaves are executed.
1765	Slave rebellions take place in Jamaica and Grenada. Antislavery article "Traites des Negres" by Louis de Jaucourt is published in Denis Diderot's *Encyclopédie.* Rebellions in Grenada and Jamaica.
1766	In Jamaica, a Coromantee uprising occurs in Westmorland Parish. In July, an Afro-Creole plot in Hanover parish is led by Sam, Charles, Caesar, and others.
1768	Slaves revolt in Montserrat.
1769–1773	St. Vincent, First Carib War, with black Caribs led by Chatoyer.
1769	Granville Sharp publishes A *Representation of the Injustice and Dangerous Tendencies of Tolerating Slavery in England.*
1770	France—Abbè Raynal publishes *Histoire philosophique et politique des ètablissemens et du commerce des Européens dans les deux Indes.*
1771	Anthony Benezet publishes *Some Historical Account of Guinea,* a longer and more detailed version of his A *Short Account of that Part of Africa.*
1772	In the Somerset case, Lord Chief Justice Mansfield decides English law does not allow for slave James Somerset to be returned

to his "master slavery" once he enters Britain. In Britain, the Somerset decision is popularly interpreted as outlawing slavery in England. Slaves in North America begin to petition the court in "freedom suits." Correspondence between Granville Sharp and Anthony Benezet begins, opening the way for continuing communication between Anglo-American abolitionists.

1774 John Wesley, the founder of Methodism, publishes *Thoughts upon Slavery.*

1775 In Madeira, slavery is abolished. In the British North American colonies, Lord Dunmore, the royal governor of Virginia, promises freedom to any slave who deserts and serves in the king's forces, whereupon 800 blacks join the British Ethiopian Regiment. Blacks serve in colonial militia in the battles around Boston. Philadelphia Quakers help organize a Society for the Relief of Free Negroes Unlawfully Held in Boston.

1775–1804 Gradual abolition: American Revolution begins when shots are fired at Lexington and Concord, Massachusetts. Free blacks are among those who take part in the battles. On April 14, Quakers in Philadelphia organize the Society for the Relief of Free Negroes Unlawfully Held, the first secular antislavery society in the American colonies. Gradual abolition laws are passed in the northern states: Vermont, Massachusetts, New Hampshire, Pennsylvania, Rhode Island, Connecticut, New York, New Jersey.

1776 British troops evacuate Boston; Battle of Long Island, Battle of Trenton. In Williamsburg, Virginia, a group of free blacks organize the African Baptist Church. In Philadelphia, the Society of Friends approve a measure urging other Quakers to shun fellow Quakers who refuse to manumit their slaves. In Jamaica in July, Afro-Creole plot, Hanover parish, is led by Sam, Charles, Caesar, and others. Adam Smith publishes *The Wealth of Nations,* declaring chattel slavery unprofitable and harmful to whites. Dutch slave ship is captured by enslaved Africans off the Gold Coast. Ship explodes, and 400 are killed.

1777 In North Carolina, the assembly re-adopted an older colonial statute that had prohibited the manumission of slaves by private citizens except for cases of meritorious service that were documented and verified by a local magistrate. In Vermont, the constitution abolishes slavery. In France, a royal decree prohibits the immigration of Negroes or mulattoes, whether slave or free.

1780 In Pennsylvania, the state decides to gradually end slavery with the adoption of a gradual emancipation law. In Massachusetts, the constitution outlaws slavery.

1782 Virginia enacts a law allowing private manumissions.

1783 In Great Britain, British Quakers form committees to work against the slave trade. Quaker petition to end the slave trade is presented to Parliament. Quakers print more than 10,000 copies of *The Case of Our Fellow Creatures, the Oppressed Africans,* and distribute them to pubic figures. Granville Sharp helps publicize the facts

	of the *Zong*, in which 133 blacks were thrown overboard at sea. The ship's captain, claiming insufficient provisions to feed the white crewmen, let alone the blacks, throws the blacks overboard and then seeks insurance compensation for the slaves. Judge Mansfield rules in favor the ship-owners who, claiming the lost blacks as private property, are compensated for their loss.
1784	Gradual abolition laws are passed in Rhode Island and Connecticut.
1785–1790	In Dominica, the first Maroon War begins under the leadership of Balla, Pharcell, and others.
1786	In Great Britain, Thomas Clarkson, British abolitionist, publishes *An Essay on the Slavery and Commerce of the Human Species*, a pamphlet influenced by the work of Anthony Benezet.
1787	Quobna Ottobah Cugoano publishes his *Thoughts and Sentiments on the Evil of Slavery.*
1788	Thomas Clarkson, British abolitionist, publishes *An Essay on the Impolicy of the African Slave Trade* to show the negative effects of the slave trade on whites. In France, the Société des Amis des Noirs is established and initiates contact with abolition societies in London, Philadelphia, and New York. Connecticut, New York, Massachusetts, and Pennsylvania forbid their citizens from participating in the slave trade.
1789	Pennsylvania Abolition Society is organized by Benjamin Franklin. Delaware bans its citizens from engaging in the slave trade. The Providence (Rhode Island) Society for Abolishing the Slave Trade is formed. In France, the Amis des Noirs, upon the convening of the Estates General, call for freedom for all slaves in the colonies and for the universal abolition of the slave trade. Thomas Clarkson visits France and works with the Société. At the Assembly white colonists and merchants prevent debate on the slave trade. Olaudah Equiano publishes *The Interesting Narrative of Olaudah Equiano, or Gustavus Vassa, the African: Written by Himself.*
1791	In France, suffrage rights are granted to all colonists, regardless of color, who are born of free parents and own sufficient property. Haitians begin popular revolts. Events lead to the establishment of the first independent black state in the Americas.
1792	Dutch ban slave imports in its colonies by 1803. British House of Commons votes to terminate the slave trade by 1796. House of Lords votes the measure down. Sierra Leone Company sends black refugees from the American Revolution to Africa. Many had first been sent to Nova Scotia.
1793	Upper Canada enacts a gradual emancipation law.
1794	French Convention outlaws slavery in all the French colonies and extends the rights of citizenship to all men. The U.S. Congress prohibits American citizens from engaging in the slave trade with foreign countries.
1795	In Guyana, a slave revolt begins in Dutch Demerara, in conjunc-

tion with Maroons. In St. Vincent, the Second Carib War under the leadership of Chatoyer and Duvalle occurs. In Grenada, Julien Fèdon's rebellion begins, involving the majority of the island's slaves. Slaves revolt in Dutch colony of Curacao.

1796 St. Lucia, the Briogands' War, begins, involving many slaves. Delaware forbids its citizens from engaging in the slave trade. The Providence (Rhode Island) Society for Abolishing the Slave Trade is formed. William Wilberforce's bill for abolition of the slave trade is defeated.

1798 In Salvador, Brazil, the Tailors' Revolt is discovered. British forces begin withdrawal from St. Dominique after treaty with L'Ouverture; the struggle begins between mulattoes and blacks (led by L'Ouverture).

1799 New York passes gradual manumission law.

1800 L'Ouverture forces take control of French St. Domingue. Gabriel Prosser's rebellion occurs in Virginia.

1801 L'Ouverture captures Spanish Santo Domingo, unifies the island, and publishes a constitution prohibiting slavery.

1802 L'Ouverture is betrayed and sent to France. Blacks resist the re-establishment of slavery in Guadeloupe, which had been abolished in 1794. Thousands are killed.

1804 Haiti is declared independent and abolishes slavery. A bill for abolition proposed by Wilberforce is passed by the House of Commons but is tabled by William Pitt's cabinet.

1805 House of Commons defeats a bill proposed by Wilberforce for abolishing the slave trade.

1806 British Parliament passes a law to ban the British slave trade to foreign countries. Haitian leader Dessalines is assassinated and succeeded by Henri Christophe.

1807 The United States and Great Britain pass laws prohibiting slave importation after January 1.

1808 In Great Britain, Thomas Clarkson publishes his two-volume *History of the Rise, Progress and Accomplishment of the Abolition of the African Slave Trade by the British Parliament.*

1809–1814 In Dominica, the Second Maroon War is led by Quashie, Apollo, Jacko, and others.

1810 In Latin America, the Supreme Junta of Caracas proclaims the abolition of the slave trade. In Mexico, Hidalgo issues an emancipation decree before his rebellious movement is crushed.

1811 Cuba protests proposals debated in the Spanish Côrtes to prohibit the slave trade and to provide for gradual emancipation in the colonies. Great Britain passes a law making participation in the slave trade a felony. The largest slave revolt in the United States is suppressed in New Orleans. It begins in St. John the Baptist Parish in Orleans Territory and involves about 300 slaves. The intention seems to have been to march down along the river to New Orleans, but the slaves are intercepted and suppressed by local militia and U.S. military forces before they get there.

1814 Public pressure mounts in Great Britain to force France to abolish the slave trade after the first Treaty of Paris sanctions a five-year postponement of French abolition.

1815 Napoleon decrees the abolition of the slave trade.

1816 Bussa's Easter Rebellion is centered in St. Philip Parish. In France, Simòn Bolìvar secures arms and supplies from Haiti after promising Pètoin that he will promote the cause of emancipation in South America. The American Colonization Society is formed in the United States to promote the colonization of free blacks in Africa.

1817 Great Britain signs a treaty with Portugal prohibiting the slave trade north of the equator but sanctioning the Portuguese-Brazilian trade south of the line. In the United States, blacks led by the Philadelphia abolitionist James Forten protest the policies of the American Colonization Society.

1819 The Congress of Angostura rejects Simon Bolivar's pleas to ratify his military emancipation policies.

1820 Missouri Compromise is adopted admitting Missouri to the Union as a slave state but prohibiting slavery in all other states "north of latitude line 36 degrees, 30 minutes." Britain uses its navy to prevent international slave trading.

1821 Colombian Congress of Cúcuta adopts a gradual emancipation act for Gran Colombia. San Martìn proclaims an end to the slave trade and provides for gradual emancipation in Peru.

1822 Denmark Vesey's rebellion in South Carolina is uncovered. Slavery is abolished in the Dominican Republic.

1823 Chile enacts a general emancipation plan. Jamaica is the scene of widespread plots and unrest, especially in Hanover parish, where it was popularly called the Argyle War. In Guyana in August, a rebellion takes place on the east coast in Demerara led by Quamina, Jack Gladstone, and many others.

1825 African and Creole slaves rise in Cuba, killing whites and destroying plantations.

1829 David Walker's *Appeal* is published.

1831 New England Anti-Slavery Society is founded in Boston. Nat Turner leads a slave insurrection in Southampton County, Virginia. Turner and 31 blacks are executed. In Jamaica during Christmas, Samuel Sharpe and others lead Baptist War in western Jamaica, where up to 60,000 blacks are involved. In Antigua, there is widespread unrest and arson after banning of the Sunday markets.

1833 The American Anti-Slavery Society is founded in Philadelphia.

1834 The British Empire ends slavery throughout but allows for a short-term apprenticeship system.

1835 In St. Kitts, there is widespread unrest over the apprenticeship system. Five hundred slaves revolt in Salvador da Bahia, Brazil.

1839 Blacks led by Cinque seize the ship *Amistad.* Pope Gregory XVI issues a papal bull condemning slavery.

1840 American Anti-Slavery Society begins publication of the *National Anti-Slavery Standard.*

1841 The *Amistad* Case, involving the status of certain slaves who had mutinied and were brought to Connecticut, was tried in federal court. En route to New Orleans from Hampton Roads, Virginia, slaves revolt and seize the vessel *Creole.* They sail to the Bahamas, and all except those accused of murder are freed.

1842 Paraguay's passage of the Law of the Free Womb begins the end of slavery. However, it is not until 1862 that all slaves in the region are freed.

1843 In India, British courts are denied claims for slaves. A series of slave uprisings take place in Venezuela and Colombia in the gold-mining region of the Cuaca River valley.

1845 French and Danish colonies abolish slavery.

1850 Peru begins importing a large number of Chinese coolies to serve as indentured servants.

1852 In Ecuador, slavery is abolished. In Brazil, slave trading ends.

1854 Peru and Venezuela end slavery. Argentina's program for the gradual ending of slavery, which began in 1825, is finally completed. The Portuguese government frees all of the slaves in its empire who are on royal grounds.

1861 Argentina abolishes slavery. In India, holding a slave is made illegal.

1862 Cuba ends slave trade. Paraguay's program for ending slavery, which began in 1825, is completed.

1863 Slavery ends in all Dutch colonies. January 1, 1863, the Emancipation Proclamation is issued by President Abraham Lincoln, freeing all slaves living in territories or states not in rebellion.

1865 Thirteenth Amendment to U.S. Constitution formally abolishes slavery. A system of Black Codes is established in former Confederate states to regulate and control newly freed backs.

1867 The last shipload of Africans arrives in Cuba, marking the end of the Middle Passage, which began in 1502. The Reconstruction Era begins in the United States with congressional passage of Reconstruction Acts, which place the South under military rule and enfranchise African Americans.

1868 Cuban landowner Carlos Manuel de Cespedes releases his slaves with the "Declaration of Yara." Blacks in Cuba join with independence forces.

1870 Spain frees slaves over the age of 60 in Cuba with the "Moret Law" leading to the gradual abolition of slavery.

1871 Brazil announces gradual end to slavery.

1873 Puerto Rico abolishes slavery.

1877 The Reconstruction Era ends in the United States. Southern whites retain control of state governments, and federal troops pull out of the South. An era of white on black terror begins.

1880 The Brazilian Anti-Slavery Society is established in Rio de Janeiro.

1882	Reliable statistics are first collected about lynching in the United States. Between 1882 and 1968, 3,446 black persons are lynched.
1886	Cuba finally abolishes slavery.
1888	Brazil abolishes slavery on May 13 with enactment of the Golden Law.

Notes

1. W. E. B. Du Bois, *The Suppression of the African Slave Trade to the United States of America, 1638–1870* (New York: Russell and Russell, 1898), 6.

2. Anthony Benezet, A *Caution and Warning to Great Britain and Her Colonies in A Short Representation of the Calamitous State of the Enslaved Negroes in the British Dominions* (Philadelphia: Henry Miller, 1766; reprint, London, 1767), 36.

3. William C. Nell, *The Colored Patriots of the American Revolution* (New York: Arno Press, 1968), 119–120.

4. Gail Buckley, *American Patriots: The Story of Blacks in the Military from the Revolutionary War to Desert Storm* (New York: Random House, 2001), 5–6.

5. John Hope Franklin and Alfred A Moss, *From Slavery to Freedom History of African Americans,* 8th ed. (New York: McGraw Hill, 2000), 87.

6. Herbert Aptheker, "The Central Theme of Southern History: A Re-Examination," *Afro-American History: The Modern Era* (Secaucus, N.J.: Citadel Press, 1971), 19–27.

7. Robin Blackburn, *The Making of New World Slavery: From the Baroque to the Modern Era, 1492–1800* (London: Verso, 1997), 75.

8. George Fox, *Gospel, Family-Order, Being a Short Discourse Concerning, the Ordering of Families, Both of Whites, Blacks and Indians* (London, 1676) 13–14.

9. Morgan Godwyn, *The Negro's and Indian's Advocate* (London, 1680), 20.

10. Winthrop D. Jordan, *White over Black: American Attitudes towards the Negro, 1550–1812* (New York: W. W. Norton, 1968), 97.

11. Paul Edwards and James Walvin, *Black Personalities in the Era of the Slave Trade* (Baton Rouge: Louisiana State University Press, 1983), 40.

12. Baron de Montesquieu, *The Spirit of the Laws* (Paris, 1748; reprint, Cambridge: Cambridge University Press, 1989), book 15, chap. 1, 246.

13. Francis Hutcheson, *A System of Moral Philosophy* (1755; reprint, New York: Augustus M. Kelley, 1968), book 2, chap. 5, sec. ii, 301.

14. George Wallace, *A System of the Principles of the Laws of Scotland* (Edinburgh: W. Millar, 1760), 95–96.

15. James Foster, D.D., *Discourses on All The Principle Branches of the Natural Religion and Social Virtue* (London, 1749), 1:158–159.

16. Cecelia M. Azevedo, "Rocha's 'The Ethiopian Redeemed' and the Circulation of Anti-Slavery Ideas," *Slavery and Abolition* 24:1 (April 2003): 109.

17. John Locke, *Two Treatises of Government,* ed. Peter Lasslett (Cambridge: Cambridge University Press, 1960), 159.

18. Statues at Large of South Carolina, 1:55.

19. David Hume, "Of National Characters," from *Enquiry Concerning Human Understanding,* in *Race and the Enlightenment: A Reader,* ed. Emanuel Chukwudi Eze (Cambridge, Mass.: Blackwell, 1997), 37.

20. Edmund Burke to Henry Dundas (Viscount Melville), Easter Monday, 1772, in Edmund Burke, *Collected Works* (London, 1852), 5:587.

21. Louis Jacourt, Chevalier de, "Traites des Negres," in *Encyclopédie, ou, Dictionnaire raisonne des sciences, des arts des métiers* (Neufchatel, 1765), 16:532, quoted in David Brion Davis, *The Problem of Slavery in Western Culture* (Ithaca, N.Y.: Cornell University Press, 1966), 416.

22. Anthony Benezet, *Notes on the Slave Trade* (Philadelphia, 1783), 8.

23. Eugene Genovese, *Roll, Jordan, Roll: The World the Slaves Made* (New York: Vintage Books, 1972), 597.

24. Daniel Horsmanden, *The New York Slave Conspiracy* (1744; reprint, New York: Beacon, 1771), 265–266. See also Thomas J. Davis, *A Rumor of Revolt: "The Great Negro Plot" in Colonial New York* (Amherst: University of Massachusetts Press, 1985), and Serena R. Zabin, ed., *The New York Conspiracy Trials of 1741: Daniel Horsmanden's Journal of the Proceedings and Related Documents* (Boston: Bedford/St. Martin's, 2004).

25. Peter Wood, *Black Majority: Negroes in Colonial South Carolina from 1670 through the Stono Rebellion* (New York: W.W. Norton, 1972).

26. John Thornton, "African Dimensions of the Stono Rebellion," *America Historical Review* 96:4 (October 1991): 1101–1113.

27. *One Continual Cry: David Walker's Appeal To the Colour Citizens of the World, but in particular, and very expressly, to those of The United States of America*, ed. Sean Wilentz (New York: Hill and Wang, 1995); see also Peter Hinks, *To Awaken My Brethren: David Walker and the Problem of Antebellum Resistance* (University Park: Pennsylvania State University Press, 1997).

28. Vincent Harding, *There Is a River: The Black Struggle for Freedom in America* (New York: Harcourt Brace Jovanovich, 1981), chap. 4.

29. For a brief yet insightful analysis see Eugene D. Genovese, *From Rebellion to Revolution: Afro-American Slave Revolts in the Making of the New World* (New York: Vintage Books, 1981).

30. Emilla Viotti Costa, *Crowns of Glory: The Demerara Slave Revolt of 1823* (New York: Oxford University Press, 1994), 113.

31. Viotti Costa, *Crowns of Glory*, 107.

32. Michael Craton, "Emancipation from below? The Role of the British West Indian Slaves in the Emancipation Movement, 1816–34," in *Out of Slavery: Abolition and After*, ed. Jack Hayward (London: Frank Cass, 1985), 116–117.

33. Anthony Benezet, *Some Historical Account of Guinea: Its Situation, Produce, and the General Disposition of Its Inhabitants with An Inquiry into the Rise and Progress of the Slave Trade* (Philadelphia, 1772), 43.

34. Quobna Ottobah Cugoano, *Thoughts and Sentiments on the Evil and Wicked Traffic of the Slavery and Commerce of the Human Species*, ed. Vincent Carretta (1787; reprint, New York: Penguin, 1999), 75.

35. Olaudah Equiano, *The Interesting Narrative of the Life of Olaudah Equiano: Written by Himself*, ed. Robert J. Allison (Bedford: Boston, 1995), 145. Originally published in 1789 as *Interesting Narrative of the Life of Olaudah Equiano or Gustavas Vasa, the African*.

36. Thomas Clarkson, *The History of the Rise, Progress and Accomplishment of the Abolition of the Slave Trade by the British Parliament*, 2 vols. (London 1808), 208–209.

37. Lamin Sanneh, *Abolitionists Abroad: American Blacks and the Making of Modern West Africa* (Cambridge, Mass.: Harvard University Press, 1999), 46.

38. Anthony Benezet, *A Short Account of that part of Africa Inhabited by the Negro's, and the Manner by which the Slave Trade Is Carried On* (Philadelphia, 1762), 69.

39. Philip Foner, *History of Black Americans* (Westport, Conn.: Greenwood, 1975), 585–586. See also Sanneh, *Abolitionists Abroad,* 190.

40. Julie Winch, *A Gentleman of Color: The Life and Times of James Forten* (New York: Oxford University Press, 2002), 190.

41. Lawrence E. Tise, *Proslavery: A History of the Defense of Slavery in America* (Athens: University of Georgia Press, 1987), 16.

42. Carl Stephenson, *English Constitutional History* (New York: Harper and Row, 1937); T. B. Howell, ed., *A Complete Collection of State Trials to 1783,* 2nd ed. (London, 1816–1826); State Trials, Somerset Case # XX, 82, Somerset v. Stewart, in W. Cobbett, T. B. Howell, et al., eds., *State Trials,* 34 vols. (London 1809–1828), vol. 20, 1–82.

43. George Wallace, *A System of the Principles of the Laws of Scotland* (Edinburgh: W. Millar, 1760), 95–96.

44. James Oldham, "New Light on Mansfield and Slavery," *Journal of British Studies* 27:1 (January 1988): 45.

45. Steven M. Wise, *Though the Heavens May Fall: The Landmark Trial That Led to the End of Human Slavery* (New York: Da Capo, 2005).

46. The Debate on a Motion for the Abolition of the Slave Trade, 2nd April, 1792 in the House of Commons, Wilberforce and Pitt Present, Parliamentary Debates, British Library, London, England, 40.

47. Marcel Dorigny and Bernard Gainot, *La Société des Amis des Noirs* (Paris: UNESCO, 1998), 91.

48. Roy P. Basler, ed., *The Collected Works of Abraham Lincoln,* 9 vols. (New Brunswick, N.J.: Rutgers University Press, 1955), 4:517–518.

49. Merrill D. Peterson, *John Brown: The Legend Revisited* (Charlottesville: University of Virginia Press, 2002), 49.

50. "Abraham Lincoln: Address on Colonization to a Delegation of Black Americans, August 14, 1862," in *Abraham Lincoln, Slavery and the Civil War: Selected Writings and Speeches,* ed. Michael P. Johnson (Boston: Bedford, 2001), 201–202.

51. Frederick Douglass to S. R. Scottern, Esq., March 29, 1873, in *The Life and Writings of Frederick Douglass,* ed. Philip S. Foner (New York: International, 1975), 4: 303.

CHAPTER ELEVEN

African Independence Movements

Joel E. Tishken

Without question, Africa's independence movements represent the most significant constellation of events in the continent's modern history. The form and magnitude of these events still shape political developments in many African nations to the present day. Independence occurred in four general, and overlapping, stages:

Phase 1: Before 1960: North Africa, Ethiopia, Ghana, and Guinea
Phase 2: 1960–1977: French Africa, Belgian Africa, Spanish Africa, non-settler British Africa, and Indian Ocean territories
Phase 3: 1962–1975: Lusophone Africa and settler colonies
Phase 4: 1980–1994: Settler colonies and Eritrea

In general, the first two phases transpired peacefully. The later two phases turned violent, principally due to the presence of white settlers. This chapter explores various case studies from each of these phases.

No path to independence, whether peaceful or violent, proved easy. Millions of Africans protested in various ways throughout the colonial era. Each colony tended to have a single leader who became a focal point of the independence movement, and who often became the new nation's first president as well. These leaders became symbols of national resistance to both the populace of the colonies/nations and to the colonial powers who directed their negotiations to these individuals. It is important to remember that African independence was not achieved in isolation. Decolonization was part of a global trend that dissolved empires across Asia, Oceania, and the Caribbean. Independence for any imperial possession took some willingness, however small, from the colonial power to let go. Some colonial powers refused to consider independence for their colonies, and these independence movements turned violent until imperial consent was forced. At the most fundamental level, African independence movements reflected a growing desire for African self-determination. As Africans redefined their identities in the twentieth century, many chose to pursue political sovereignty within new nation-states. This chapter presents the story of these independence movements and how they achieved their goals of political autonomy.

The Roots of Independence Movements: Early Nationalism

The previous chapters on empires discussed how all parts of Africa were colonized by Western European powers (Britain, France, Germany, Belgium, Portugal, Italy, and Spain) in the late nineteenth and early twentieth centuries, except Liberia, which enjoyed protection from the United States. As a result, independence movements developed in all parts of Africa (except Liberia) under colonial rule. Ethiopia experienced Italian imperial rule for only a short time and provides a special case that is discussed in greater detail in the next section.

The roots of independence movements took the form of nationalism. Nationalism in Africa coalesced around agitation against colonial states. Nationalism assumed three forms:

1 Agitation within a colony (or colonies) directed at a specific colonial power.
2 Agitation aimed at colonialism in general on behalf of many, or all, subject Africans—this form of nationalism is also called Pan-Africanism.
3 A combination of the previous two forms where agitation was organized within a colony but with local as well as Pan-African goals (the most common variant of nationalism).

This section explores early nationalism in all three of the manifestations mentioned above by looking at the Industrial and Commercial Workers' Union (ICU), Négritude, and the National Congress of British West Africa (NCBWA), respectively. Early nationalists employed a variety of tactics, including constitutional reform, political parties, ethnic unions, newspapers, independent churches, trade unions, work hold-ups, migration, and symbolic resistance. For the most part, early nationalist agitation, though often illegal according to colonial law, still took place within peaceful parameters and was generally aimed at reform, not revolution.

The ICU was a nationalist labor organization aimed at bettering economic conditions in South Africa. It was formed in South Africa in 1919 by a dockworker from Nyasaland named Charles Kadalie. Its early membership was largely drawn from Coloured dock workers in Cape Town. However, the ICU grew all across South Africa, particularly in Natal due to the recruiting efforts of ICU secretary George Champion. Almost from its inception, the organization suffered from an ideological division between Communists and more moderate members. Kadalie expelled the Communists in 1926. To compensate for the loss in numbers, the ICU began a successful recruiting campaign in rural areas. With the addition of the rural members, the ICU began to become less of a labor organization and more of a nationalist one dedicated to a vague platform of land repossession and Black liberation. By 1927–1928, the ICU claimed 100,000 African members, 15,000 Coloured, and several hundred whites.

Despite its initial popularity, the ICU never succeeded in bringing its membership together, physically or philosophically. The geographic distribution of the membership in a country as large as South Africa made it difficult to bring sizeable numbers to a single rally or mobilization. Philosophically the organization found it difficult to address the interests of different racial and ethnic groups split by class differences and an urban-rural divide. The ICU's sporadic work stoppages, work desertions, cattle raiding, and sabotage had little impact except to feed white fears, which it did greatly. The membership began to accuse the leadership of losing touch with their interests and drawing large salaries from the ICU. The organization died out in the early 1930s largely due to the resignation of Kadalie in January 1929 and the banishment of Champion from Natal in 1930. The ICU's dreams of redressing the needs of South Africa's blacks went unfulfilled. However, the organization must be remembered for its efforts in organizing black South Africans at a time when it was not easy to do so. It helped pave the way for the emergence of other organizations later in South African history.

Négritude was a Pan-African movement that emerged in the French-speaking world in the 1930s. At the most fundamental level, Négritude represented a reaction against the assimilation policy of French colonialism that tried to turn its African and Caribbean subjects into proper French citizens who adored French culture while abandoning their own. This reaction glorified Africa's past and celebrated the essence of the African "race." Its three founding theorists were Aime Cesaire of Martinique, Léon-Gontran Damas of French Guiana, and Leopold Senghor of Senegal. The term Négritude derived from a poem written by Cesaire in 1939, "*Cahier d'un Retour au Pays Natal*" (Diary of my return to my homeland), which became the most authoritative source of Négritude philosophy.

Cesaire, Damas, and Senghor were themselves products of the French colonial system: they were Christian, received Western educations, mastered impeccable French, and served in the French Constituent Assembly. But it was also their closeness to the French system that provided them with their intense dissatisfaction. Négritude argued that colonialism was based on alienation and forced its subjects to live in exile within their own countries. The founders of Négritude argued that there was such a thing as a "black soul" composed of humor, rhythm, emotion, and linkages to the social world. This made it different from the strict rationalism of Hellenistic Europe and the soul of white people. In other words, the thinkers of the Négritude movement asserted that there was such a thing as an African "race" which was based in the biological reality of "blackness." This fundamental difference meant that European civilization had no resonance with African peoples whose entire make-up was utterly different.

In later years critics would argue against such a biological essentialism that assumed all black peoples were alike and incapable of strict rationalism. This biological essentialism was largely abandoned after World War II, and from that date Négritude became defined in increasingly cultural terms. For the most part Négritude has disappeared as a cultural movement in recent decades. But Négritude was a vitally important movement that attempted to regain pride for African peoples through a glorification of their cultural heritage and vitality.

The National Congress of British West Africa (NCBWA) was an organization that encompassed four British West African colonies (Gambia, Sierra Leone, Gold Coast, and Nigeria) and expressed both national and Pan-African ideals. It was founded in 1920 by forty-five delegates from the above four colonies. These delegates shared an elite status and a common background of Western education and Christianity. Their chief goal was to pressure Britain to permit Africans to join the colonial parliaments of each of their respective colonies. Though these parliaments were not particularly powerful, the delegates hoped that the parliaments could be used as a platform for creating four democratically based parliaments and then, later, a single national parliament. In this sense, the efforts of the NCBWA were like the ICU in largely being aimed at the level of the colony. However, the NCBWA also had goals that were Pan-African. For instance, the organization pushed for the political unification of Gambia, Sierra Leone, Ghana, and Nigeria. Their first president, Ghanaian lawyer J. A. Casely-Hayford, also endorsed the notion of Pan-Africanism, saying there was a need to create an international feeling among all black people. In this way, the NCBWA believed they could create change by working with other educated Africans across colonial frontiers.

The NCBWA held meetings until 1933, but the organization suffered from two shortcomings. The first was that critics accused them of being out of touch with average Africans because of their elite educated status. While this was true, in the end most of the first leaders of independent African nations also shared this status. Secondly, their platform of gradual reform did not resonate with more radical nationalists who wanted greater change at a faster rate. Though the NCBWA lasted just thirteen years, many of its members would later reemerge in other nationalist organizations.

These three nationalist organizations, and thousands of others like them, were the precursors of Africa's independence movements. Many of the ideas and people involved in nationalist agitation in the 1920s and 1930s would reemerge in the 1940s and 1950s with greater popular support and stronger ideological platforms. In fact, many of the ethnic unions, labor unions, women's groups, and so forth of the 1920s and 1930s would become transformed into political parties around World War II. For instance, the Yoruba cultural organization

Egbe Omo Oduduwa, founded by Obafemi Awolowo, was transformed into the political party Action Group in 1951. Thus, demands for change and self-determination by Africans were not born in the 1950s but have earlier roots. Let us now examine how various nations gained their independence before 1960.

Phase One: Independence Gained Prior to 1960: North Africa, Ethiopia, Ghana, and Guinea

Just like the early nationalist movements before them, agitation for independence contained a variety of goals that differed for various groups of people. Some groups, such as the Association des Bakongo (ABAKO) in the D. R. Congo, the Action Group of Nigeria, or the Inkatha Freedom Party in South Africa, were grounded in ethnicity and worked for independence for better conditions of their ethnic group or region. Other groups were national in character, such as the African National Congress of South Africa or the Frente de Libertação de Moçambique (FRELIMO) in Mozambique, whose goals concerned all peoples within the boundaries of a particular colony or nation. And still other organizations, such as the Conference of African Independent States, had Pan-African objectives. But, as with most early nationalist organizations, most organizations agitating for independence combined ethnic, regional, national, and supra-national goals, to some degree. For example, the National Liberation Movement (NLM) in the Gold Coast, an Asante ethnic union, alternated its demands for Asante autonomy within an independent federated Gold Coast with Asante's complete secession.[1] The "Land and Freedom Army" of Kenya, or the Mau Mau army as it is more commonly known, was a constellation of rebel groups whose concerns included land dispossession, African poverty, white dominance, and national liberation. Many national leaders such as Kwame Nkrumah of Ghana, Julius Nyerere of Tanzania, and Patrice Lumumba of D. R. Congo fought for the independence of their particular colony at the same time that they held Pan-African goals of continental unity.

Thus, while most Africans were united in a desire to free Africa of colonial rule, the strategies and goals they had in doing so varied widely, with differences based on colonial history, ethnicity, race, education, income, religion, generation, and gender. These differences manifested themselves at local, national, and international levels and are evident in the case studies that follow throughout this chapter.

The independence of a handful of nations prior to 1960 occurred because of a variety of factors, but World War II played a large role for many. In fact, liberation by Allied and indigenous armies and the withdrawal of German and Italian armies led to the independence of Ethiopia in 1942 (see the special case of Ethiopia in the next section), Libya in 1951, and Tunisia, Sudan, and Morocco in 1956. Thus the independence of most of North Africa was a direct result of World War II.

But even before World War II, Liberia had managed to maintain its autonomy since the creation of its constitution in 1847. Moreover, Egypt gained a nominal independence in 1922 with the dissolution of the British protectorate over Egypt that had been declared in 1914. This independence was only nominal, however, because the Reserved Points in the February 1922 Declaration of Independence left Britain to maintain the status quo in the security of imperial communications, the defense of Egypt, the protection of minorities and foreign interests, and protection of Sudan. Consequently, control of much of Egypt's external affairs remained in British hands. Thus some scholars and Egyptians are inclined to see the 1956 nationalization of the Suez Canal as the true liberation of Egypt from Britain.

The most surprising independence celebrations transpired not in North Africa but in the colony of the Gold Coast (which became Ghana). The Gold Coast had a long history of nationalist agitation. The NCBWA's first president, J. A. Casely-Hayford, was from the Gold Coast. Cocoa farmers had withheld their crops on numerous occasions (1914, 1916, 1921, and 1937) to protest prices set by companies such as the United Fruit Company. Many farmers' cooperatives were established to break economic dependency on the companies and European banks. During the last protest in 1937, which enjoyed 100 percent participation by cocoa farmers, the British broke the companies' ability to set prices. In 1947 a group of WWII veterans held a rally to protest their disappearing veteran's benefits. The rally, though peaceful, was dispersed by gunfire, and several veterans were killed. The rally of the veterans coincided with the formation of the United Gold Coast Convention (UGCC), whose goal was self-government in the shortest possible time. A young man named Kwame Nkrumah was invited home from the United States (where he was at Lincoln University) to become its general secretary.

Outrage at the death of the veterans led to widespread rioting and looting in the Gold Coast. British authorities blamed the leaders of the UGCC and jailed them in 1948, though Nkrumah was spared that fate for the moment. With the UGCC leadership gutted, Nkrumah, K. A. Gbedemah, and Koto Botsio formed the Convention People's Party (CPP), with the slogan "self-government now." Inspired by the non-violent strategy of Mahatma Gandhi, the CPP's plan of action for self-government now, termed "positive action," involved non-violent protest through general strikes, boycotts, and demonstrations.

The CPP enjoyed an instant popularity. When the party called a colony-wide strike and boycott in January 1950, it was met with strong popular support. The CPP's leadership, including Nkrumah, was arrested and charged with sedition. Elections were held in 1951 for a newly created Legislative Assembly. Despite being in jail, Nkrumah won 98.5 percent of the vote for the Accra delegate position. He was released in order to help form the new governmental body. The CPP assisted the Legislative Assembly in creating a plan for a new constitution. This constitution was adopted in 1954 and provided for an unofficial all-African cabinet. While Britain remained the ultimate authority, peoples of the Gold Coast were slowly gaining more internal authority. In the elections following adoption of the 1954 constitution, the CPP won 79 of 104 seats. In 1956 the CPP proposed a motion in the new legislature for complete independence, which passed.

Every colony had similar agitations taking place. What made the Gold Coast different? The independence efforts taking place in the Gold Coast in 1954–1956 enjoyed the endorsement of the colonial governor, Sir Charles Noble Arden-Clarke. Arden-Clarke could not have single-handedly held back independence for Gold Coast, but he certainly could have delayed it. So while the majority of credit for independence must be given to decades of agitation by peoples of the Gold Coast, we must not forget also that the early timing of Gold Coast independence was largely due to Arden-Clarke. Without his support, the Gold Coast probably would have gained its independence in 1960, when most of Africa's British colonies did. The Gold Coast became independent on March 6, 1957, taking the name Ghana. It was the first country in sub-Saharan (or Black) Africa to gain its independence from a colonial power (aside from the special situation with Ethiopia). At independence, British Togoland (the Trans-Volta Togo which had become British territory after World War I) was joined with Ghana. Nkrumah said Ghana's independence meant nothing until the rest of the continent was free. And by the late 1950s, the independence of large portions of Africa seemed not far away.

In French Africa, nationalist protest before World War II was not as deep and rich as that found in British Africa. France viewed its African territory as extensions of France and the colonial citizens as French subjects. French colonial law was intolerant of African traditions and indigenous leadership and promoted French culture and institutions above all. Many of those who questioned French colonial policy found themselves arrested, imprisoned, and often exiled. But as the discussion of Négritude demonstrated, this did not prevent others from protesting against French colonialism. As in North Africa, World War II proved to be a turning point for Africa's French colonies. The post-war government of France promised to eliminate *indigénat* (arbitrary arrest and detention), cease forced labor, and reorganize the colonial system to provide greater African representation. The first two were carried through, but the last was not. Political parties such as the Rassemblement Démocratique Africaine, Indépendents d'Outre Mer, and Mouvement d'evolution sociale de l'Afrique noire began to form when France's post-war promises evaporated.

Three strategies for self-rule and independence emerged in French Africa. The first position, led by Leopold Senghor of Senegal, favored a strong federation of self-governing African states with continued links (in defense, foreign affairs, and development) to France. Barthélémy Boganda of Ubangui-Chari favored a similar federation of French Central African states with the eventual dream of integrating other Central African states as well. The second was led by Felix Houphouët-Boigny of Cote d'Ivorie, who favored a loose federation of African states with continued ties to France. This position was favored by many leaders from Senegal, Cote d'Ivorie, and Gabon. For the wealthier of the French colonies a decentralized system meant that these richer colonies would not have to finance the poorer ones such as Mauritania and Ubangui-Chari. The third position was advanced by Sékou Touré of Guinea, who favored federation with total independence (i.e., no ties to France).

As Francophone African leaders were debating their relationship with France, Charles de Gaulle had assumed the French presidency. In 1958 he called a referendum of French Africans to determine the outcome of the federation debate. The voting options provided to the voters revealed de Gaulle's agenda. The voters were not given the three options above. Instead, voters received only the latter two. They could vote *oui* (yes) for a loose federation of separate territories with links to France through the French Community (the idea of Houphouët-Boigny), or they could vote *non* (no) for total independence with no links to France (Touré's strategy). By eliminating Senghor's plan of a strong federation from the voting, it forced his supporters to vote for the Houphouët-Boigny plan. This plan worked to the advantage of France because it maintained ties to the colonial power while simultaneously keeping French African territories from uniting. In the end only Guinea voted *non*. Guinea became independent in 1958, but de Gaulle showed Guinea and the rest of French Africa that independence would come at a cost. France severed its ties with Guinea immediately and completely. France made an object lesson of the new country by sabotaging its administration. For example, departing French administrators destroyed civil records and infrastructure and even went so far as to pull government phone lines from the wall, deeming them property of France, not Guinea. The story of the rest of French Africa is discussed in the next phase of independence.

Ethiopia: Symbol of Black Pride and Resistance

Ethiopia (also called Abyssinia) is a special case in the history of modern Africa. It was the only African nation to successfully defend its autonomy against a European power. This event made Ethiopia a source of racial pride throughout the black world, empowering nationalist movements inside and outside of Africa.

Designs against Ethiopia can be traced to 1869, when an Italian missionary, Giuseppe Sapeto, purchased the port of Assab, which was in turn purchased by the Italian shipping company Societa Rubattino. In 1885 an Italian army seized the Red Sea coast province of Massawa. They did so with the blessing of the British, who felt Italian expansion might help counter their chief rivals, the French. By 1889 the Italians had expanded their territory to include the territory of what is now Eritrea. They were able to capitalize on a number of factors: the threat of the Sudanese Mahdist state to the north, threats from Britain on the side of Italy, chaos due to the unexpected death of the Ethiopian

Emperor Yohannes in 1889 in battle against the Mahdists, and epidemics of rinderpest, smallpox, and cholera.

The new emperor, Menelik, signed a treaty with the Italians on May 2, 1889, at the town of Wuchale. Under the Wuchale Treaty (Uccialli in Italian), the Italians believed they were creating a protectorate over Ethiopia. This is not what Menelik understood from his Amharic version of the treaty. He thought he was delineating boundaries between sovereign powers. In January 1890 the Italians marched into the province of Tigre and said they would not leave until Menelik agreed to their interpretation of the treaty. Menelik entered into several years of diplomacy with the Italians. In time he discovered that the two versions of the treaty were not the same. He finally renounced the treaty in February 1893. The emperor made the renunciation from a position of strength because he had used the past few years to import the best firearms and artillery available. Fighting broke out between Italy and Ethiopia in December 1894. The Italians were beaten back to the town of Adowa, where the final battle took place in 1896. Menelik enjoyed superiority of numbers (100,000 to the Italian 17,000) and had the support of the local population, who aided his army with geographic knowledge and intelligence on Italian movements. The battle was a decisive victory for the Ethiopians. The Italians lost 40 percent of their army, all their artillery was captured, and 11,000 of their rifles were taken. On October 26, 1896, the Treaty of Addis Ababa was signed which recognized the sovereignty of Ethiopia and annulled the Treaty of Wuchale. Italy remained in control of Eritrea.

The victory had huge ramifications beyond the preservation of Ethiopian independence. Many nations created embassies and signed treaties with Ethiopia including Britain, France, Russia, the Ottoman Empire, and even the Mahdist state, a sign of Ethiopia's surging international prestige. But its greatest consequence was the impact it had upon African racial pride, inside Africa and beyond. Travelers to Ethiopia noted the pride Ethiopians felt about defeating and ousting a European power. And they were the only nation of Africa to do so. (Liberia maintained its sovereignty by close association with the United States, not by military power.) Peoples of African descent in the Americas, particularly intellectuals, also expressed pride in Ethiopia. Some of them, including the Afro-Cuban William Ellis and Haitian Benito Sylvian, even made several visits to Ethiopia with plans for development and the resettlement of black peoples from the Americas.[2]

A new Ethiopian emperor was installed in 1930. Ras Tafari took the throne name of Haile Selassie I. Pictures of the coronation were printed throughout the world. Many peoples of African descent saw in Selassie the epitome of power and dignity. Peoples of the African Diaspora, especially in the United States and Jamaica, began to announce that they were citizens of Abyssinia and subjects of Selassie. In Jamaica, Leonard Percival Howell began to preach that Selassie was the king of all black peoples and a divine messiah sent to initiate their liberation. The religion of Rastafarianism would form around his teachings.

Italy reinvaded Ethiopia in 1935. The invasion was fueled by fascist plans of colonial expansion and the desire to recover lost national pride. Outrage was voiced throughout the African world. An arbitration commission from the League of Nations was unsuccessful in preventing war. The capital, Addis Ababa, fell in 1936, and the emperor of Ethiopia, Haile Selassie, took refuge in England. Ethiopia was integrated into Africa Orientale Italiana with Eritrea and Somaliland. Italy's East African empire was a reality for a few years, 1935–1941. The nations were liberated by Allied forces and indigenous rebels. Ethiopian independence was declared in 1942. In 1950 a UN resolution created a confederation between Ethiopia and Eritrea (that would later collapse in 1993). Ethiopia remained a source of racial pride, and for many peoples of African descent the term *Ethiopian* became synonymous with *African*.

Thus, by 1960 Africa possessed nine independent nations. The majority of them were in North Africa, and their independence was due to WWII. Each of the others (Liberia, Ethiopia, Ghana, and Guinea) had a unique story of independence. The first assembly of independent African nations took place in Accra, Ghana, in April 1958 and was entitled the First Conference of African Independent States. At the meeting, Egypt, Ethiopia, Ghana, Liberia, Libya, Morocco, Sudan, and Tunisia promised their assistance to Africa's independence and liberation movements and promoted the dream of a colony-free continent. The assistance they provided varied, but it was sometimes generous indeed. For instance, Ghana gave ten million pounds to Guinea in 1958 to help Guinea create an effective administration and bureaucracy. The map of Africa changed dramatically over the next few years, and these nine nations were soon joined by many more.

Phase 2: 1960–1977: French Africa, Belgian Africa, Spanish Africa, non-settler British Africa, and Indian Ocean Territories

In just a decade and a half, many African colonies became independent nations, transforming the map of Africa. The year 1960 is often called the "heyday" of African independence because so many nations achieved independence at that time. These new nations arose from five kinds of colonies: French Africa, Belgian Africa, British Africa, Spanish Africa, and Indian Ocean territories. For the most part, the independence of these nations came about peacefully, because none had a sizeable population of white settlers. As described in the next section, settler colonies were not relinquished peaceably. Of course, many people risked their lives to achieve even these "peaceful" transitions. Still, independence in this phase was achieved without bloody and prolonged liberation struggles like those covered in the next sections.

As discussed in the prior description of Guinea, France had held a referendum among French Africans in 1958 to vote *oui* for continued association with

France or *non* for total independence and a severing of ties with France. Only Guinea, led by Sekou Touré, voted for total independence, with an 80 percent *non* vote. The rest of French Africa voted *oui* for continued association. But the independence of Guinea broke up the territorial integrity of French West Africa (Afrique Occidentale Français), making plans for a strong federation more difficult. To prevent the break-up of French West Africa, Senghor pushed forward with his plan of federation. Senegal, French Soudan (now Mali), Upper Volta (now Burkina Faso), and Dahomey (now Benin) created the Federation of Mali. Upper Volta and Dahomey quickly withdrew under pressure from Cote d'Ivorie. But the two remaining colonies within the Mali Federation petitioned France for independence in September 1959. Preoccupied by the Algerian War and interested in ridding himself of troubles in West Africa, de Gaulle encouraged the French Parliament to approve the independence petition. Mali and Senegal were granted independence in June 1960, and the rest of French West Africa as well as French Central Africa (Afrique Centrale Français) followed from August through November 1960. Thus by 1960 French-speaking Africans had succeeded in gaining independence in virtually all French colonies, but the dream of a strong federation of French West African states was dead. Houphouët-Boigny's plan of a loose federation, endorsed by de Gaulle's 1958 referendum, caused French West Africa to gain independence individually and at slightly different times. As de Gaulle had intended, this worked to the advantage of France because it left the colonies fractured into multiple states, ensuring their continued dependence upon France.

Britain did not have an overall policy of decolonization. The independence of British colonies worldwide was conducted in a rather piecemeal fashion, with Britain responding to individual cases as they arose. By the late 1950s Britain had granted independence to several nations in North Africa and to Ghana. Throughout the 1960s, independence was granted to others: Nigeria and Somaliland in 1960, Sierra Leone in 1961, Tanganyika and Zanzibar in 1961 (which unified into Tanzania), Malawi and Zambia in 1964, Gambia in 1965, Botswana and Lesotho in 1966, Swaziland and Mauritius in 1968, and Seychelles in 1975. The timing of each was influenced by the nature of the independence campaign of each colony and its proximity to sizeable numbers of white settlers. For instance, the later independence of Botswana, Lesotho, and Swaziland was due to these colonies' geographic proximity to South Africa. South Africa was holding on to hope that these territories might be relinquished by Britain to its control, as Namibia had been after World War I.

Belgium's three African colonies (Congo, Rwanda, and Burundi) had haphazard independence. In the Congo, Belgium had banned all political parties. Thus, nationalist agitation developed in alumni associations (such as ASSANEF, the Association des anciens élèves des Frères des écoles chrétiennes) and ethnic unions (such as ABAKO, the Association des Bakongo). The Belgians felt such organizations were innocuous, but in fact they provided a forum for nationalist leaders to meet. However, these types of organizations would complicate the future of Congolese politics because their leaders were elitist and regional or ethnic in orientation.

Interestingly, the boiling point for Congolese independence came in December 1955 with the publication of "Plan de trente ans pour l'émancipation politique de l'Afrique belge" (Thirty-year plan for the emancipation of Belgian Africa) by Professor A. A. J. Van Bilsen. The "Plan" was endorsed by many colonial administrators and more conservative nationalist leaders, such as those in Conscience africaine, who were comfortable with a gradual emancipation. However, other nationalist leaders, such as Joseph Kasavubu of ABAKO and Patrice Lumumba, rejected the slow timetable. They demanded immediate independence. The Belgian administration compromised by calling for local elections in December 1957. However, they placed restrictions on voting in rural areas, thus creating an urban-rural tension. That tension kept the Congolese fighting among themselves along ethnic lines instead of devoting all their energy to attacking the colonizer. Nonetheless, by 1958 political parties had begun to emerge. These political parties were grounded in ethnicity with one exception, the Mouvement national congolais (MNC), founded by Patrice Lumumba, which was the only truly national party.

The Belgian colonial strategy of paternalism (treating colonial subjects like children in need of proper guidance) meant that little thought had ever been given to independence. Many colonial administrators assumed that the Congolese would need Belgian supervision for decades, if not centuries, to come. Likely due to developments elsewhere in Africa, a meeting was called in Brussels in January 1960, which set a date of June 30, 1960, for Congo independence. While most independence leaders were delighted with the announcement of independence, six months left little time for planning. The short amount of time did not permit nationalist leaders to bridge a serious ideological gulf between more moderate leaders who favored a federal system with strong regional governments (like Kasavubu) and more radical leaders who favored a strong national system with Pan-African goals (like Lumumba). Because this ideological gulf was never bridged, it resulted in tension that broke out immediately after independence, leading to political assassinations and a long civil war. Independence did come in June 1960 with Kasavubu as president and Lumumba as prime minister. However, fears for the new country's stability soon proved well founded.

Rwanda and Burundi (united until independence in a single territory, Ruanda-Urundi) had been League of Nations, and later United Nations, Trust territories under Belgian oversight since World War I. Political parties began to emerge there from 1957 onward. Both Rwanda and Burundi suffered from ethnic tensions between the Tutsi and Hutu. This tension had escalated during the years of colonial rule because the Belgians had placed the Tutsi into positions of political and ecclesiastical power. Influenced by developments in the Congo, the Belgian government announced a timetable for independence on November 10, 1959. Political violence followed for the next several years, complicated by the fact that the Belgians now began backing the Hutu. Prompted by the political violence and the UN General Assembly, the Belgian government cancelled local elections planned for January 28, 1961. Rwandans gathered at the city of Gitarama to dethrone the Tutsi king Mwami Kigeri V, create a republic, and adopt a new constitution. When general elections were held under UN supervision in September 1961, the results legitimized the January 28 coup. The Belgians gave up control of Ruanda-Urundi in December 1961 to the United Nations, which granted the colony full independence in early 1962. Upon independence Rwanda and Burundi separated despite pressure from the UN to stay together. Unfortunately, independence did nothing to solve Hutu-Tutsi ethnic tensions, with disastrous consequences on more than one occasion since.

Spain possessed just one colony in sub-Saharan Africa: Equatorial, or Spanish, Guinea. A campaign for independence began there in 1950 with the formation of the Cruzada Nacional de Liberación composed largely of teachers and colonial elites. Spain maintained a repressive posture and crushed any discussion of independence. This repression culminated in the late 1950s with the assassination of the two most prominent independence leaders, Acacio Mañe and Enrique Nvó. Spain's hard-line stance forced many independence supporters into exile in Cameroun and Gabon where they formed the political parties MONALIGE (Movimiento Nacional de Liberación de Guinea Ecuatorial) and IPGE (Idea Popular de Guinea Ecuatorial). After 1960 these two parties enjoyed critical support from many newly independent African nations. This support, coupled with growing social unrest, forced Spain to legalize political parties in 1963 and to grant self-rule in 1964. A constitutional convention was convened in 1967–1968 and full independence was proclaimed on October 12, 1968.

Independence came later to some of the Indian Ocean territories. The French had greater interest in Madagascar than the Comoros and so granted greater autonomy to the four-island colony composed of Grande Comore, Anjouan, Mayotte, and Moheli. In 1946 France made the Comoros a Department Outre-Mer (French Overseas Department), thereby conferring greater internal autonomy. This higher level of autonomy dampened nationalism for a time. But nationalist sentiment did emerge in the 1970s. In 1975 Grande Comore, Anjouan, and Moheli voted for independence. Mayotte, with a highly Christian population, feared inclusion in a Muslim-dominated state and voted against independence. Independence was granted, without Mayotte, on June 5, 1975. The Comoros have since been plagued by numerous coups and inter-island disputes. British strategic concerns delayed the independence of Mauritius until 1968 and the Seychelles until 1976. In 1965 the British government regrouped a number of islands previously associated with Mauritius and Seychelles into the British Indian Ocean Territory. Independence for both nations became dependent on their recognition of the new British Indian Ocean Territory. The Indian Ocean territories of Reunion and Mayotte remain under French control, and the British retain control of the British Indian Ocean Territory.

These nations had to struggle to achieve their independence. Millions of Africans—some whose names we easily recognize, such as Touré and Lumumba, and others whom history has forgotten—risked their livelihoods and safety for their dream of a liberated Africa. Although their independence came about without prolonged liberation wars, individuals still died to establish these new nations. From the veterans shot in the Gold Coast to the assassinations of Mañe and Nvó, it took many brave people to stand up to the various colonial powers. But despite some deaths, for the most part the above two phases of African independence took place peacefully.

In all cases, independence was eventually achieved due to some willingness on the part of the colonial powers to abandon control. And the independence of these nations had a cumulative affect. As nations around the world gained independence, including many in South Asia, Southeast Asia, Oceania, and the Caribbean, as well as Africa, decolonization proved a force too strong for most colonial powers to resist. This became particularly true as the United States and Soviet Union began to promote decolonization and exerted pressure upon the colonial powers. However, there were two types of colonies that did fight this global trend: colonies possessed by Portugal and colonies with large white-settler populations. The next sections discuss the bloodiest two phases of African independence, those that involved violence within these two types of colonies.

Phase 3: Lusophone Africa and Settler Colonies, 1962–1975

By the 1960s, the map of Africa had changed dramatically. Newly independent nations could be found in every region of the continent. The new African states had increased the membership of the United Nations by about one-quarter, giving the UN General Assembly a whole new atmosphere. In alliance with Asian member states, the Afro-Asian group, as they became called, had adopted an ardent anti-colonial stance. Most of southern Africa and parts of Central Africa remained under colonial or white minority control. Throughout the 1970s and 1980s the UN General Assembly passed countless resolutions on Angola, Namibia, Apartheid South Africa, and other territories under colonial control. Additionally, anti-colonial struggles of the 1970s received support from the Organization of African Unity (OAU). Founded by thirty-two member nations in May 1963, and headquartered in Addis Ababa, Ethiopia, the OAU deserves great acclaim for the role it played in assisting the liberation of Portuguese colonies and territories under white minority rule.

The first two prolonged liberation conflicts took place in Kenya and Algeria because of their large white settler populations. In Kenya the position of the white settler population had been strengthened by World War II, when they supplied materials to the war effort in Southwest Asia. This economic dominance was reflected politically as well as with white settlers dominating colonial committees. In 1952 a revolt broke out known as the Mau Mau revolt, a peasant uprising with a strong ethnic flavor. Most of the members were drawn from the Kikuyu ethnic group, one of Kenya's largest and a group that had suffered the brunt of land dispossession from white settlement. Thus some of the motivations behind the insurgency included land dispossession, African poverty, white dominance, and anti-colonialism. But because the Mau Mau was actually a constellation of various rebel groups, the goals varied slightly from group to group. This "Land and Freedom Army" (perhaps it would be more accurate to say armies) used the mountainous areas of the Central Highlands as their base of operations. They systematically attacked white settler farms and killed Europeans. However, they also targeted Africans they viewed as collaborators. The colonial authorities grossly underestimated the depth of African disgruntlement and saw the Mau Mau rebels as a small group of malcontents being fueled by the Kenya African Union (KAU) led by Jomo Kenyatta.

The colonial government declared a state of emergency in October 1952. Kenyatta was convicted as the mastermind of the rebellion and sentenced to jail in 1953 (where he served seven years). But it does not appear that the KAU and Kenyatta had much to do with the Mau Mau. Although both the KAU and Mau Mau voiced anti-colonialism, there was a cultural gap between the educated Christian elites of the KAU and the impoverished peasants of the Mau Mau. The colonial authorities gathered a force of 100,000 to put down the rebellion. Despite the massive size of the counterforce, the rebels enjoyed military success until the end of 1953. The colonial army gained the upper hand by 1954. Large numbers of rebels were captured and placed in detention camps, and food supplies were cut off. Popular support for the rebellion began to dwindle when the authorities employed mass arrests against those suspected of harboring sympathy for the Mau Mau. The movement collapsed on October 21, 1956, with the capture of Dedan Kimathi, one of the most respected Mau Mau leaders. The Mau Mau might have enjoyed greater success if it had cached a better supply of weapons, appealed to more ethnic groups, and put forth a stronger ideological platform. Colonial propaganda had also successfully painted the rebellion as barbaric and primitive, thus alienating it from the educated Christianized elite.[3]

Despite the eventual military failure of the Mau Mau, it did arouse intensified nationalist feelings throughout Kenya. The cost of the war, monetarily and in human lives, also made the British question their degree of dedication in maintaining the control of the white settler population of Kenya. A constitutional convention was convened in 1959. The Kenya African National Union (KANU—the newly named KAU) won a landslide victory in 1963, and Kenyatta became the nation's first prime minister. While Kenya did experience great violence in its independence struggle, it paled next to what happened in Algeria at roughly the same time.

The Algerian path to independence was among the bloodiest the world has seen. It began on November 1, 1954 (All Saint's Day), when *mujahids* (in Arabic; *maquisards* in French; *guerrillas* in English) launched attacks in various parts of Algeria against military installations, police posts, warehouses, communications facilities, and public utilities (all non-human targets). The attacks followed shortly after French withdrawal from Indochina, and Algerian rebels were demanding they also withdraw from Algeria. Many Algerians had been in negotiation with France throughout the early 1950s, principally through the Mouvement pour le triomphe des libertés democratiques (MTLD). When frustration built among Algerians over the lack of progress, the MTLD dissolved into several factions. More violent tactics were adopted by some of the former MTLD members, leading to creation of the Front de libération nationale (FLN). Nine leaders in particular, referred to as the *chef historiques* (historic leaders), formed the core of the movement, including future Algerian president Ahmed Ben Bella. The guerrilla forces were later restructured into the Armée de liberation nationale (ALN) in August 1956.

French minister of interior François Mitterrand responded sharply to the November 1 attacks, saying that the only possible negotiation was war. On November 12, Premier Pierre Mendés-France insisted that the Algerian departments were part of the French republic, and calls for independence threatened the integrity of France itself. Thus the French government had made it clear from the beginning that Algeria was simply part of France, and independence in any form was not an option. This policy that Algeria was France was boosted by the presence of one million French settlers (*colons*) in Algeria as well as the discovery of oil and natural gas deposits in the Sahara in the 1950s. The French military strategy was three-fold. It involved the "regrouping" (or forced removal) of villages as a way to destroy the FLN's popular support, the psychological use of terror to alienate the average Algerian from the FLN, and the erection of wire barriers (later electrified) on the Moroccan and Tunisian borders to prevent support from arriving across those frontiers.

French intransigence was more than matched by Algerian dedication to independence. In fact, the French radicalized the average Muslim Algerian by making no distinction between the *maquisards* and Algerian civilians—all were subject to French reprisals. The FLN grew from an initial 2,000–3,000 armed insurgents to about 130,000 at the height of the fighting from 1956 to 1958. Even more critical than the number of fighters was the mass support the FLN enjoyed throughout Algeria. Other Algerian political parties slowly dissolved and were absorbed by the FLN. The first congress of the FLN was held at Kabylie in August 1956. The delegates adopted a radical line. They decided that independence was not enough. Algeria must become a socialist republic based on sweeping agrarian reform with a fundamental Arab and Muslim character. Support, including weapons, from Arab, Asian, and socialist nations began to be given to the FLN and ALN.

But the lines of battle were far more complicated than France versus the FLN. The FLN was also engaged in civil war with the Mouvement National Algérien (MNA) founded by Messali Hadj. The MNA had a similar policy of violent revolution and total independence, but the FLN largely wiped out the MNA in Algeria. The MNA's remaining support was among Algerians within France (one in seven Algerian males lived in France because of a lack of employment opportunities in Algeria). Tension between the FLN and MNA culminated in what was later called the "café wars," where FLN and MNA supporters assassinated one another on French streets. Nearly 5,000 people were killed through the "café wars" throughout the Algerian war of independence. The French *colons* added another dimension as well. Many *colons* felt the French army was not doing enough to protect them and formed their own vigilante groups. The vigilante *colons* carried out *ratonnades* (literally, rat hunts; synonymous with Arab killings) against suspected FLN members. These vigilante groups enjoyed passive support from the French authorities, who did little to stop them. Thus in the Algerian independence war little distinction was made between combatant and civilian, and the citizens of Algeria, both French settler and Algerian Muslim, suffered the consequences.

In January 1955, Jacques Soustelle arrived in Algeria as the new governor general. Determined to restore peace, he began an ambitious reform program (the Soustelle Plan) aimed at improving economic conditions for the Muslim population. An important watershed in the war took place in August 1955 when the FLN massacred 123 French civilians near the town of Philippeville, which was in stark contrast to their earlier policy of attacking military and government installations. The French responded with a counter-massacre that killed 12,000, and all-out war erupted. Soustelle was replaced by Robert Lacoste, who abolished the Algerian Assembly, ruling by decree and adopting force as the rule of law. In the first two years FLN guerrillas killed about 6,000 Algerian Muslims (viewed as collaborators) and about 1,000 French.

Under constant attack by the French, the FLN shifted its tactics again by taking its fight to urban areas, principally to the capital, Algiers. On September 30, 1956, the FLN planted bombs in downtown Algiers, killing several *colons*. The French responded brutally with arrests, interrogations by torture, assassinations of suspected FLN members, and aerial bombardments of cities suspected of harboring FLN rebels. Events in late 1956 brought the Algerian War to the attention of the entire world. France would eventually commit 400,000 troops to Algeria, including 170,000 Muslim Algerians, while the FLN fielded about 15,000 rebels. By summer 1957 the destructive measures of the French had succeeded in rounding up many of the insurgents. But despite France's military edge, the FLN rebels never ceased their actions, and the French never gained a political victory.

Events in France, more than Algeria itself, brought an end to the Algerian War. In spring 1958 dissident army officers, disaffected *colons*, and sympathetic Gaullists staged a coup d'état. Charles de Gaulle became premier of the Fifth Republic in February 1959 despite FLN attempts to sabotage the election through acts of terrorism in France and Algeria. With the stability of France threatened, de Gaulle began to move Algeria toward independence. Some *colons* organized the Organisation Armeé Secrete (OAS) and led coups against de Gaulle in January 1960 and February 1961 in an attempt to dislodge him and derail the negotiations. Troops loyal to de Gaulle easily crushed both coup attempts. A peace agreement was signed at Evian (Evian Accords) on March 18, 1962, recognizing the Algerian right to self-determination, calling for a referendum on the question of independence, and giving *colons* three years to leave or accept Algerian citizenship. In June 1962, some 350,000 *colons* left Algeria, leaving fewer than 30,000 in Algeria. Algeria was declared an independent nation on July 3, 1962.

It is not likely we will ever know the precise number of casualties from the Algerian War. Most estimates calculate that over one million people were killed. The physical devastation was enormous as well: farms were burned, villages were leveled, and a great deal of infrastructure was lost from aerial bombardment. What can be said without question is that the war was a very brutal and bloody affair and the deadliest moment of decolonization in French imperial history.

Like the French in Algeria, Portugal viewed its African territory as simply Portugal overseas. The Portuguese claimed that their five African colonies formed part of Portugal itself, not colonial territories. Additionally, the Portuguese had been in Africa since the sixteenth century and had come to depend on these colonies as places to build entrepreneurial and bureaucratic careers. Brought to power by a military coup in 1926, Antonio Salazar served as the Portuguese prime minister from 1932 to 1968. He was followed by Marcelo Caetano, who was prime minister from 1968 to 1974. Both men governed through a form of authoritarian fascism and refused any discussion of independence for Portuguese African possessions. In time nationalists within Angola, Mozambique, Guinea Bissau (Portuguese Guinea), and Cabo Verde felt violent overthrow of the Portuguese was their only option. Fighting broke out in Guinea-Bissau and Cabo Verde in 1963 led by the PAIGC (Partido Africano da Independencia da Guiné e Cabo Verde) under Amilcar Cabral. War broke out in Mozambique in 1964 led by FRELIMO (Frente de Libertação de Moçambique) under the leadership of Eduardo Mondlane. He was assassinated by a letter bomb in 1969, and Samora Michel assumed FRELIMO's leadership. Both PAIGC and FRELIMO waged successful wars against the Portuguese, and their humiliation of the Portuguese army was a critical factor in the independence of all the Portuguese territories. The MLSTP (Movimento de Libertação de São Tomé e Principe) formed in 1972 and operated from exile in Gabon. São Tomé and Principe achieved its independence without violence, though its fate was intrinsically linked to the violent struggles taking place in the other Portuguese territories.

In Angola, fighting broke out in February 1961 led by the MPLA (Movimento Popular de Libertação de Angola) under the leadership of Antonio Agostinho Neto. Other organizations later joined in the liberation struggle, including FNLA (Frente Nacional de Libertação de Angola) in 1962 under Holden Roberto and UNITA (União Nacional para a Independência Total de

Angola) in 1966 led by Jonas Savimbi. The Portuguese responded with a brutal military campaign to crush the guerrilla armies. Within the space of a few months, 30,000–50,000 people were killed, and 150,000–200,000 people (mostly BaKongo in the northwest) were forced into exile in Zaire. A stalemate resulted: the Portuguese could not crush the Angolan liberation armies, but neither could the liberation armies expel the Portuguese.

The MPLA, FNLA, and UNITA might have had greater military success had they united their efforts. But the three armies were plagued by ethnic, regional, and ideological divisions. The MPLA drew its greatest support from among the Mbundu and the country's center, the FNLA from the BaKongo and the country's north, and UNITA from the Ovimbundu and the country's south. Ideologically the MPLA was Marxist and received support from the Soviet Union and Cuba, the FNLA espoused a liberal laissez-faire ideology and drew its chief support from Zaire, and UNITA was initially backed by China but soon turned to the United States and South Africa. Thus, though the three groups shared a common goal of defeating the Portuguese, they did not work together to form a common front of resistance. The ideological gulf and lack of interaction between the groups would continue to plague Angola's future.

Angola's war of liberation lasted for fourteen years, 1961–1975. It was a particularly bloody and complicated war. Ultimately, like the Algerian situation, it would take events in the metropolis to determine the final course of the independence struggle. In 1973 disaffected military forces, weary from the multiple liberation wars they were being forced to fight, created the Armed Forces Movement (AFM). The AFM was on the political left and was willing to let the colonies go. It staged a bloodless coup on April 25, 1974, now referred to as the Revolution of the Carnations. With AFM in power, the Portuguese government was now willing to negotiate independence. The PAIGC declared the independence of Guinea-Bissau on September 24, 1973, just nine months after the assassination of Cabral. The new AFM regime recognized Guinea-Bissau's independence in September of 1974 as well as that of Cabo Verde. São Tomé and Principe gained independence on July 12, 1975, and Mozambique did as well on June 25, 1975. Because there were more liberation parties involved in the negotiations, Angola was the last to gain independence from Portugal on November 11, 1975.

Unfortunately, Angola's transition to independence proved far from simple. From the time the peace accords were signed in January 1975 until independence was attained in November, the ideological gulf between UNITA, FNLA, and MPLA escalated into full-fledged fighting. The MPLA drove the FNLA and UNITA out of the capital Luanda. Thus when independence was finally declared in November the declaration was made from two capitals; from Luanda by the MPLA and from Huambo by the FNLA and UNITA. A civil war ensued where the war of liberation left off. The Organization of African Unity (OAU) was spilt 22–22 with two abstentions about which Angolan government to recognize. With a series of MPLA victories in early 1976 (due in part to Soviet and Cuban military aid), the MPLA government, led by Agostinho Neto (José Eduardo dos Santos followed him from 1979 until the present), became the internationally recognized government at the OAU (as of February 1976) and the UN (as of November 1976). But several regions remained under control of UNITA, and international recognition of the MPLA did not make them stop fighting. UNITA received support from the United States and South Africa. Even the ending of the Cold War and the withdrawal of Cuban and South African troops in 1991 could not resolve Angola's long-standing internal divisions. The Angolan civil war continued until February 2002, when the head of UNITA, Jonas Savimbi, was killed in a gunfight. A ceasefire was signed in April 2002 which remains in effect. UNITA forces have been integrated into the Angolan army. Angola entered the twenty-first century dealing with the legacy of forty years of combat from 1961 to 2002. It is estimated that about 1.8 million people were killed and about 2.5 million people were displaced during that time.

Phase IV: 1980–1994, Settler Colonies and Eritrea

Even after the independence of Kenya, Algeria, and the former Portuguese colonies, several significant nations remained under colonial or white minority control: Zimbabwe (Southern Rhodesia), Namibia (Southwest Africa), and South Africa. And Eritrea was engaged in a liberation struggle against Ethiopia.

Zimbabwe (Southern Rhodesia during white minority rule) had been a self-governing British Crown Colony since 1924. It was briefly federated with Northern Rhodesia and Nyasaland in 1954. Feeling this was a tactic to perpetuate white minority control, Africans in the three territories opted for separate independence, which was granted by the British to Northern Rhodesia (which became Zambia) and Nyasaland (which became Malawi) in 1963. In 1965, the Rhodesia Front party, led by Ian Smith, announced its Unilateral Declaration of Independence, severing all ties to the British and renaming the country Rhodesia. Britain did not recognize the regime, but neither did they attempt to counter it. The UN passed sanctions against Rhodesia. However, the sanctions had little bite because South Africa and the United States traded with Rhodesia, as did Angola and Mozambique while under Portuguese control. In 1966 two Black Nationalist organizations declared an all-out war against Rhodesia: Zimbabwe African People's Union (ZAPU), led by Joseph Nkomo, and Zimbabwe African National Union (ZANU), led by Robert Mugabe. The independence of Angola and Mozambique in 1974 helped the cause of independence in Zimbabwe as both were used as bases for guerrilla fighters. In 1976 the two organizations joined forces as the Patriotic Front (PF). Constitutional settlement talks took place throughout the 1970s without success. It was not until 1979 that the PF and Rhodesian government agreed on a new constitution, transitional arrangements, and a ceasefire. Zimbabwe became fully independent in 1980. Bob Marley performed at the independence celebration, giving an immense boost to the popularity of reggae music in Africa. Robert Mugabe and his ZANU-PF party have dominated Zimbabwe's government to this day. Since 1999, Mugabe has encouraged veterans from the independence struggle to occupy white-owned farms as part of a land redistribution scheme. Zimbabwe was once a food exporter, but millions of Zimbabweans are at risk of famine as Zimbabwe's agri-business has become subsistence farming at best. Mugabe has been criticized for choosing short-term political goals over long-term economic planning. Opposition candidates and international observers accused the 2002 presidential election (that maintained Mugabe's power) of being fraudulent.

Originally a German colony, Southwest Africa (what would later be called Namibia) was taken by South Africa during World War I and administered by them as a League of Nations mandate. With the end of the League of Nations and creation of the United Nations in 1945, mandate territories came under the control of the UN. South Africa refused to recognize UN authority over Namibia and insisted instead that it be integrated as a fifth province of South Africa. In 1966 the UN General Assembly removed South Africa's right to administer the territory. Rightly believing that none of the major world powers would go to war with South Africa over Namibia, South Africa continued to rule Namibia as it wished. This rule included the implementation of Apartheid and the establishment of separate black homeland governments. Liberation organizations emerged in the years 1957–1960. The two largest, the South West Africa National Union (SWANU) and the South West African People's Organization (SWAPO), joined forces in 1960 against the Apartheid South African government. After nearly thirty years of guerrilla war, a peace plan was drafted in 1988–1989. The collapse of the Cold War assisted the peace plan as South Africa no longer enjoyed unilateral support from the United States. Elections took place in November 1989. Independence was achieved March 21, 1990, under President Sam Shafishuna Nujoma, the leader of SWAPO. Namibia has been among the most stable of African nations since 1990 and remains under the leadership of Nujoma.

The presence of white colonists in South Africa made their history similar to that of Namibia and Zimbabwe. However, the white population of South Africa was much larger, with greater political and economic power. The roots of white supremacy go all the way back to the first white settlers who arrived at the Cape in 1652. But as an official governmental philosophy, white supremacy was not instituted until after the Union of South Africa was created in 1908. Non-white South Africans (Africans, Coloureds, and Indians) suffered from segregation, discrimination, and land dispossession. Non-white South Africans campaigned against white supremacy by every means at their disposal. However, this protest resonated more with educated elites than with the average non-white and rarely transcended ethnic lines.

Apartheid was created in 1948 by the Nationalist Party. While it had a new name, Apartheid did not differ much from the governmental philosophy evident in South Africa during 1908–1948. Agitation against Apartheid increased through the 1950s and 1960s. There were several important moments in the anti-Apartheid movement. One was the creation of the Freedom Charter in 1954. The Charter envisioned a multi-racial South Africa with equitable treatment and voting for all created by peaceful means. The Charter was drafted by a multi-racial delegation and supported by a host of anti-Apartheid organizations such as the African National Congress (ANC), South African Indian Congress (SAIC), South African Coloured People's Organization, Congress of Democrats, and South African Congress of Trade Unions. In 1959 Robert Sobukwe formed the Pan Africanist Congress of Azania (PAC) under the slogan "Africa for the Africans." Sobukwe and the PAC believed cooperation with Indians and Coloureds weakened the African position. But Sobukwe did feel that non-Africans could become Africans in their goals and mentality.

In 1960 large numbers of Africans arrived at police stations, inviting arrest for traveling without their passes. At Sharpeville, outside Johannesburg, police fired into the crowd, killing 67 and wounding 186. In response, strikes and protests rippled across South Africa. The Apartheid government declared a state of emergency and outlawed anti-Apartheid organizations, forcing them underground. Frustrated by the futility of their previous peaceful efforts, several anti-Apartheid organizations decided a change of tactics was necessary. From 1960 onward the anti-Apartheid struggle became partly a guerrilla war. Formed in 1960 were the Armed Resistance Movement, composed largely of white Communists, Poqo, the violent wing of the PAC, and Umkhonto we Sizwe, the violent wing of the ANC. South African intelligence forces infiltrated all three organizations, gutting their leadership with imprisonments. But they did not succeed in destroying the organizations. Membership in violent anti-Apartheid organizations climbed after 1976. To campaign against enforced education in the Afrikaans language, thousands of non-whites formed protests. Several children were killed at Soweto when police opened fire on the crowd. By February 1977 a total of 575 people were killed in ongoing protests. The Black Consciousness Movement, and its founder, Steve Biko, were blamed for the continuing disturbances in the country.

In an effort to weaken the anti-Apartheid movement, the Apartheid government began granting "independence" to separate black homelands. The independence was limited, as the Apartheid government still meddled in the affairs of the homelands, which had little legitimacy and no territorial integrity. By the 1980s the anti-Apartheid movement had taken on strong international dimensions with sanctions passed by the United Nations. The collapse of the Cold War at the end of the 1980s meant the Apartheid government's loss of support from the United States and United Kingdom. The white population of South Africa was shrinking, and the economy was weakening. And while the anti-Apartheid movement had never succeeded in toppling the Apartheid government, neither had the Apartheid government succeeded in destroying the anti-Apartheid movement.

In February 1990 the ban on the ANC, PAC, and others was lifted. Nelson Mandela and other political prisoners were freed. In September 1991 the Convention for a Democratic South Africa (CODESA) was held. Though CODESA suffered from numerous setbacks, a final agreement was reached in September 1992. Elections were set for April 1994. Nelson Mandela, with an ANC landslide victory, was elected as the first president of a multi-racial South Africa. Mandela remained president from 1994 to 1999, when he was followed by Thabo Mbeki from 1999 to the present.

With no white minority population, Eritrea had a significantly different history than Zimbabwe, Namibia, and South Africa. Eritrea was federated with Ethiopia in 1952, but the Ethiopian emperor Haile Selassie annexed it in 1962, triggering a civil war. Because of their differing colonial histories, Eritrea and Ethiopia were never suited for perfect combination into a single nation. The civil war continued until 1993 when a referendum in Eritrea (supported by Ethiopia) produced an almost unanimous vote for independence. With Eritrean independence in 1993, Ethiopia became a land-locked nation. Border disputes broke out in 1998 near the town of Badme, largely over which version of the Treaty of Wuchale delineated the boundaries of Eritrea. A brutal war followed in which tens of thousands died before a peace settlement was reached in June 2000.

African Independence: Past, Present, and Future

There was nothing easy about Africa's independence. As these cases have illustrated, independence came about through a combination of nationalist agitation combined with global decolonization. No colony achieved its independence solely by agitation; the colonial power had to have some willingness, though small, begrudging, and often late, to release the colony from imperial control. Even in violent situations such as in Algeria, Angola, and Mozambique, it was internal coups in France and Portugal that led to the final achievement of independence. This is not to understate the decades of agitation and resistance by countless millions of Africans. Independence would not have happened without them. Only by forcing decolonization onto the forefront of the colonial powers' agenda was any independence possible; surely empires do not normally dissolve unless they are forced to. As part of a global trend of decolonization, these new African nations joined a wave of independence struggles that swept across South Asia, Southeast Asia, Oceania, and the Caribbean.

Most territories in North, West, East, and Central Africa were transformed into newly independent nations with minimal violence. Portuguese territories and colonies with a sizeable number of white settlers (primarily in Central and Southern Africa) followed a different trajectory. These territories became independent only after prolonged violent liberation struggles. Many of these places still struggle with the legacy of the violent nature of their nation's birth.

The entry of so many new nations into the United Nations forever changed the geopolitics of the globe. But these fledgling nations were also born during the Cold War, and the ensuing ideological struggle between West and East both helped and hampered their development.

Not every independence movement and liberation organization has been successful. Given the artificiality of the borders of African nations, constructing strong national identities has proven to be a challenge for most African nation-states. Some former colonies have had independence movements erupt from within their own borders. Biafra represents perhaps the best-known case of this. Biafra seceded from Nigeria in March 1967. Fearing domination by the north and continued mismanagement within a federal system, this eastern province of Nigeria, largely dominated by the Igbo, declared itself the independent nation of Biafra. The federal army commanded far greater strength and was able to impose a blockade upon Biafra. Biafra won a great deal of sympathy from foreign nations with a successful propaganda campaign. The war lasted for thirty months, during which an estimated one million people died, largely from starvation. When independence failed, Biafra was reintegrated into a newly redefined Nigerian federal system in 1970.

Other portions of Africa remain under colonial control. Reunion and Mayotte in the Indian Ocean are still French, the British Indian Ocean Territory is still British, and the cities of Ceuta and Melilla in northern Morocco are still Spanish. In addition, Morocco conquered the Western Sahara in 1976, and the area remains in dispute. A UN referendum to determine control of the Western Sahara continues to be postponed. For the moment, independence campaigns do not seem likely to emerge in the other territories mentioned above.

Of course, other independent nations may be in the making. The Democratic Republic of the Congo spent most of the past decade in civil war. A peace agreement signed at the end of 2003 led to a transitional government, but the agreement is a fragile one in a nation that is no stranger to internal and regional conflicts. In similar fashion, few can predict what the eventual outcome may be in Sudan's on-going civil war. Territorial integrity may be maintained, or perhaps two or more nations may emerge. Though it enjoys little international recognition, the northern part of Somalia (the former British Somaliland) has declared itself independent as Somaliland. It may survive, or it may even pave the way for the creation of additional nations from the former Somalia.

The breakup of the Soviet Union and Yugoslavia, along with the violent struggles in Kashmir, Palestine, and Northern Ireland, show that the impulse for self-determination is not peculiar to Africa. The imposition of political rule, and agitation against that political rule, are as old as human history. As Africans continue to define and redefine their identities in the twenty-first century, we can expect continued political change. Such change may be intra-national, resulting in the creation of additional nation-states from existing nations. Or that change may be supra-national, involving new roles and power for regional bodies such as the Southern African Development and Co-ordinating Conference (SADCC) and the evolution of the African Union into a "United States of Africa." If the political map of Africa continues to change, as seems likely, new developments will be profoundly influenced by colonial and independence-era experiences.

Timetable of African Independence[4]

B=British F=French I=Italian P=Portuguese Bl=Belgian S=Spanish

Phase I: before 1960: North Africa, Ethiopia, Ghana, and Guinea

1847 Liberia [incorporated from a number of Afro-American settlements]
1922 Egypt
1942 Ethiopia (I) [Italian occupation, 1935–1942]
1951 Libya (I)
1956 Sudan (B&Egypt), Tunisia (F), Morocco (F&S)
1957 Ghana (B)
1958 Guinea (F)

Phase II: French Africa, Belgian Africa, Spanish Africa, non-settler British Africa, and Indian Ocean Territories, 1960–1977

1960 Benin (F), Burkina Faso (F), Central African Republic (F), Cameroun (F&B), Chad (F), Congo-Kinshasa (Bl), Congo-Brazzaville (F), Cote d'Ivorie (F), Gabon (F), Madagascar (F), Mali (F), Mauritania (F), Niger (F), Nigeria (B), Senegal (F), Somalia (B&I), Togo (F)
1961 Sierra Leone (B)
1962 Burundi (Bl), Rwanda (Bl), Uganda (B), Tanganyika (B), Zanzibar (B)
1964 Malawi (B), Zambia (B)
1965 Gambia (B)
1966 Botswana (B), Lesotho (B)
1968 Equatorial Guinea (S), Swaziland (B), Mauritius (B)
1975 Western Sahara (S) [conquered by Morocco in 1976; territory remains disputed], Comoros (F)
1976 Seychelles (B)
1977 Djibouti (F)

Phase III: Lusophone Africa and Settler Colonies, 1962–1975

1962 Kenya (B)
1962 Algeria (F)
1975 Angola (P), Cabo Verde (P), São Tomé and Principe (P), Mozambique (P), Guinea Bissau (P)

Phase IV: Settler Colonies and Eritrea, 1980–1994

1980 Zimbabwe (cessation of white minority rule)
1990 Namibia (South Africa)
1993 Eritrea (I&Ethiopia)
1994 South Africa (cessation of white minority rule)

Notes

1. Jean Marie Allman, *The Quills of the Porcupine: Asante Nationalism in an Emergent Ghana* (Madison: University of Wisconsin Press, 1993), 18.

2. A. Bervin and Benito Sylvain, *Apôtre de relèvement social des noirs* (Port-au-Prince: La Phalange, 1969); and R. Pankhurst, "W. H. Ellis-Guillaume Enrique Ellesio: The First Black American Ethiopicist?" *Ethiopia Observer* 15:2 (1972): 89–121, as cited in M. B. Akpan, based on contributions from A. B. Jones and R. Pankhurst, "Liberia and Ethiopia, 1880–1914: The Survival of Two African States," in *General History of Africa*, vol. 7: *Africa under Colonial Domination, 1880–1935*, ed. A. Adu Boahen (Paris: UNESCO; London: Heinemann; Berkeley: University of California Press, 1985), 273.

3. Robert B. Edgerton, *Mau Mau: An African Crucible* (London: I. B. Tauris, 1990), 86–87, 176–77.

4. Compiled by the author.

IV

Globalization and Its Discontents

Part 4 offers an examination of the modern Atlantic World. The four chapters in this section illustrate that while changes were underway in the twentieth-century Atlantic World, those efforts were based largely on the institutions that had emerged in the previous four centuries across the Atlantic basin.

By exploring the roots of nationalism among European colonies in the Caribbean and Africa, E. G. Iweriebor and Amanda Warnock provide an excellent link between the Atlantic World that most scholars conceptualize and this more modern version. In that sense, Iweriebor and Warnock demonstrate the consequences of empire building—much of which, of course, was constructed on the backs of African slaves—that was covered earlier in the volume. Their depiction of the modern Black Atlantic reinforces the notion that in spite of geographical space and national differences, Atlantic people who shared racial and ethnic backgrounds found those Atlantic aspects of their lives to transcend space. Iweriebor and Warnock write, "Africans in Africa and Africans in the Caribbean, whether they interacted formally or not, they became part of global historical developments of a common segment of the world." Thus echoing the refrain of earlier chapters covering earlier periods, Iweriebor and Warnock advance our understanding of the contours of the modern Atlantic temporally and topically.

Likewise, Carol Anderson returns the twentieth-century Atlantic World to its roots in many respects. Though the ties that the NATO allies discussed were diplomatic, military, and political, Carol Anderson shows how the Cold War in Africa provoked African Americans to pressure the U.S. government on some of its decisions. Discussing primarily the role of the NAACP in the selection of a particular diplomat, Anderson's chapter illustrates the continuing linkages among Africans and peoples of African descent throughout the Atlantic World. In this case, the joint efforts between "African freedom fighters," the NAACP, and the Council on African Affairs further reinforces one of the central themes of this book: the pervasiveness of an Atlantic consciousness, whether in the early or modern history of the Atlantic World.

Venturing away from the political and diplomatic world and into the social arena, Amanda Warnock shows how modern gender and identity in the Atlantic World was just as important as Cold War events. In her chapter, Warnock advances the desire of the editors in bridging the temporal divide between the nineteenth century, when many Atlantic historians seem to think the Atlantic World ceased operating as a system, and its twentieth-century version.

Remaining doubters of that idea will certainly be convinced of the Atlantic World's continuing existence by Maxim Matusevich's chapter on globalization, reform, and reparations in the modern Atlantic. Necessarily examining the *longue durée* of the Atlantic World to fashion a solid context for understanding what is today called globalism, Matusevich covers the various efforts at ameliorating problems associated with globalization. The World Bank, the International Monetary Fund, reparations, anti-globalism, and neoliberalism can all be seen as natural consequences of the themes discussed earlier in the book.

CHAPTER TWELVE

The Diasporic Dimensions of Caribbean Nationalism, 1900–1959

E. G. Iweriebor and Amanda Warnock

In 1921 Marcus Garvey traveled to Cuba in an effort to garner support for the cause of Black Nationalism. During the trip he met with members of the twenty-five branches of the Universal Negro Improvement Association (UNIA) located on the island, as well as prominent figures of Havana's population of color. Although afforded the treatment of an important foreign dignitary by leaders of the Afro-Cuban community, within the black press editorials expressed doubts about Garvey's project, reflecting the rather tepid reception of his ideas among the majority of Afro-Cubans.

This episode highlights the contradictory nature of expressions of race and nationalism within the early twentieth-century Caribbean. As a country with a significant black population, Cuba seemed ideal ground for the expansion of the movement for the establishment of the Free State of Africa. Yet Garvey found that his primary base of support lay in the burgeoning population of Jamaican-born sugar cane cutters, while most Cuban-born blacks rejected his calls for Pan-African unity.[1] This episode was not without precedent. Although the race-based Partido Independiente de Color had met with some success before its suppression at the hands of the government in 1912, black Cubans since the mid-nineteenth century had fought alongside liberal whites in advancing the cause of national liberation. Both African descendants and white Cuban patriots espoused a doctrine of racial fraternity that subsumed distinctions of skin color and heritage to the goal of unity based on a shared national vision. To their sons and daughters support of an explicitly black political agenda signified potential treason to the ideals of Cuban independence.

Rather than interpreting Afro-Cubans as possessing a limited racial consciousness or debating the relative successes and limitations of Garvey's approach, this chapter seeks to understand the variety of tactics used by African-descendant women and men to contest colonial and neo-colonial rule in the early twentieth-century Caribbean. While the population of color in Cuba overwhelmingly allied themselves with the Liberal Party, other forms of political expression, such as labor organizing, religiosity, and the arts, drew on a cultural heritage that remained largely African. Although the patterns of mobilization differed considerably from the colonies of the British West Indies to the nominally independent nations of Cuba and Haiti, the movements that arose to challenge the legacies of slavery retained a decidedly African dimension.

The early twentieth-century Caribbean, with its intersection of empires and nation-states, provides fertile ground for an analysis of race and nationalist movements. During this period, Afro-Caribbean intellectuals and politicians generated a voluminous body of scholarship that addressed issues of race and racism and allied themselves with some of the most important struggles for social justice of our time. Their contributions to the creation of Pan-Africanism cannot be underestimated.

The goal of this chapter is to address Pan-Africanism as one aspect of the broader resistance of African descendants in the Caribbean to continued racism and colonial (and neo-colonial) domination. As peasants, urban workers, housewives, and political leaders, African-descendant women and men from coastal Colombia to the British West Indies constructed communities and mobilized a political vision that was largely based in their African heritage. Thus, although this essay recognizes the significance of the Pan-African movement, it considers, broadly, forms of cultural resistance and spaces of counter-hegemony that contested state power structures, whether explicitly or implicitly.

This chapter examines the period from the beginning of the century until the 1960s. It follows major developments in the expression of nationalism, as conceived of in the following ways: the political struggle against colonial rule, labor militancy against disadvantageous economic conditions, and cultural expression, such as religiosity and the arts that contested the European socio-cultural hegemony that denigrated African-based aesthetic forms.

Centering the African Caribbean

While it is common in academic literature to refer to the British Caribbean or the French Caribbean, this essay examines the African Caribbean, unencumbered by linguistic orientations, national boundaries, or imperial powers. Although many of the territories under scrutiny as island nations possess inherently limited borders, the people who live within them do not. For example, during the early twentieth century, West Indian men migrated to the Caribbean coasts of Central America and Florida to work in construction and agriculture, often returning to families left behind in Jamaica and Haiti and re-embarking when finances again became tight. In addition to regular human traffic, newspapers and radio, songs and stories, art and literature transmitted intellectual currents, political happenings, cultural developments and popular protest throughout the circum-Caribbean basin.

Within this essay we advocate broadening the lens through which we view nationalist movements to include a wider range of responses to colonial and neocolonial domination. Elements of social protest can be found in the music and literature of the period as well as in the organized resistance movements that developed in Haiti and the Dominican Republic in response to U.S. occupation. Additionally, we must consider how the variety of cultural movements and political struggles informed each other as in the case of Harlem Renaissance writers visiting with their Cuban counterparts, or Langston Hughes and Nicolas Guillén lending support to the Republican forces in the Spanish Civil War.

The last several decades have witnessed the veritable explosion of studies that treat the African Diaspora as a conceptual unit. Although the regular, human linkages of the trans-Atlantic trade end in the early to mid-nineteenth century, recent contributions to the literature on the Diaspora have addressed the sweeping social, political, economic, and cultural realignments of the post-abolition era. Moreover they have illuminated the crucial roles played by Africans and their descendants in the nation-building process.

Tiffany Ruby Patterson and Robin D. G. Kelly's "Unfinished Migrations: The Role of Africans in the Making of the Modern World," provides a theoretical elaboration of the African Diaspora in modern history. They advocate treating the African Diaspora as one unit of analysis in a larger global historical paradigm and suggest that commonalities in "diasporic" culture and experience should be interpreted as contingent and flexible rather than inevitable.[2] Their approach, therefore, centers any and all associations in which African-descendant women and men participated, such as labor and communist movements, rather than exclusively those in which race-based identification served as the primary organizational locus.[3]

Several outstanding works address the context of post-abolition societies and locate the roles of African descendants in nation-state formation. Laurent Dubois's *A Colony of Citizens: Revolution and Slave Emancipation in the French Caribbean, 1787–1804* at once provides a detailed account of the process of independence in the French Caribbean and demonstrates the ways in which the *gens du coleur* of Saint Domingue universalized the discourse of the "equality of men" coming out of the French Revolution. Kim Butler's *Freedoms Given, Freedoms Won: Post-Abolition São Paulo and Salvador* elaborates the post-abolition state policy and Afro-Brazilian responses in the cities of São Paulo and Salvador. In a comparative vein, the collection of essays by Frederick Cooper, Thomas Holt, and Rebecca Scott describes four different regions—French West Africa, Jamaica, Louisiana, and Cuba-state policy toward Africans and their descendants in the post-abolition era and the responses of the colonized populations to the new mechanisms of discrimination. For Cuba, works by Aline Helg, Ada Ferrer, Alejandro de la Fuente, and, most recently, Lillian

Guerra highlight the manifold challenges of independence and the efforts of Afro-Cubans to secure benefits from the new nation.[4]

Works by Ivor Miller and Stephan Palmié, like Kim Butler's work on Afro-Brazilians in Salvador, highlight the cultural dimensions of Afro-Cuban resistance to Spanish and later U.S. racism. Palmié's *Wizards and Scientists: Explorations in Afro-Cuban Modernity and Tradition* demonstrates how African-based religious culture developed as part of the same processes that formed the basis of modern Western institutions and advocates expanding the concept of rationality to encompass Afro-Cuban discourses on healing and spirituality.[5] Ivor Miller's work explores the specifics of African discourses on history and culture. Miller argues that West African–based Abakuá tradition, lore, and organization have played important roles in anti-colonial struggle since the establishment of the first group in Havana in 1836.[6]

A second variety of literature on Afro–Latin Americans in the nation-building process emphasizes, to borrow a phrase from Claudio Lomnitz, the "lateral bonds of fraternity" that developed between African-descendant women and men through the disparate regions of the African Diaspora.[7] The anthology *Between Race and Empire: African-Americans and Cubans before the Revolution*, edited by Lisa Brock and Digna Castañeda Fuertes, illuminates the many social, cultural, and political connections between African-Americans and Afro-Cubans in the post-abolition era. Frank Guridy's work on linkages between Afro-Cubans and African-Americans following World War II, like that of Brock and Castañeda Fuertes, demonstrates how anti-discrimination struggles in Cuba and the United States "cross-pollinated," to borrow Guridy's phrase, with each informing and contributing to the development of the other.[8] Additionally, biographies of individuals central to the development of Pan-Africanism, such as W. E. B. Du Bois and Marcus Garvey, provide an important perspective on the transnational relationships of solidarity between African-descended peoples throughout the United States, the Caribbean, and Africa.[9]

The Roots of Caribbean Nationalism

Although the majority of the West Indian islands did not achieve independence until the post–World War II era, the roots of Caribbean nationalism extend back more than 150 years to the Haitian Revolution. From the rebellions of the late eighteenth century, national self-determination was inextricably linked to the struggle to abolish slavery. Haitian independence, achieved in 1804, inspired the independence movement of Cuba in the 1860s. In Haiti, the black slave population united with the mostly mixed-race free population to overthrow colonial rule and abolish slavery. In Cuba, from the mid-nineteenth century onward, liberal whites allied themselves with blacks, many of whom were former slaves, to demand self-rule and the abolition of slavery. Although defeated by the Spanish, the multi-racial composition of the movement, combined with the black nationalist character of the Haitian leadership, provided two models of independence struggles, examples that were followed in subsequent nationalist movements in the Spanish, French, and British West Indies.

Yet, despite the discursive relationship between personal and political independence, throughout the British and French Caribbean independence did not accompany abolition. In discussing the African dimensions of nationalist movements, it is necessary to step back to the era of abolition and examine the evolving relationship between Afro-Caribbean peoples and the state. *De jure* freedom did not mean an end to racism and discrimination but rather the development of new forms of socio-economic, cultural, and legal oppression. Upon abolition in most regions of the Americas, the state enshrined racial inequality in government policy. Instead of compensating African descendants for the theft of their labor, governments from the United States to Brazil compensated the former slave owners for their loss of "property." Many administrations enacted vagrancy or apprenticeship laws as a new strategy to curtail freedoms, while scientists promoted theories of Social Darwinism or scientific racism to justify the supposed inferiority of people of color, thus providing the intellectual buttress for ongoing segregation.[10]

Within the Caribbean specifically, many African descendants faced the dual challenges of struggling against the race-based discrimination of the states' administrative structures while also struggling for independence and nationhood as a colonized people. Amid the barrage of attacks on African-based cultures, women and men of color throughout the Caribbean basin responded by promoting racial equality and an inclusive vision of nationhood.

Seeds of Nationalism, 1900–1929

With the explosion of the battleship *Maine* in Havana harbor in the spring of 1898 and the subsequent entrance of the U.S. military into the Cuban War for Independence, an era of expansionism and neo-colonialism began that would shape the politics and economies of the Caribbean throughout the twentieth century. The extension of U.S. imperialism occurred simultaneously with the social and political reconfigurations that surrounded the post-abolition era and helped shape nationalist struggles throughout the Caribbean region. Responses to U.S. political, economic, and, at times, military intervention varied considerably. In some cases Caribbean peoples viewed the United States as a benevolent, democratic alternative to the old colonial powers of Great Britain and Spain, while in others anger at the U.S. presence generated a substantial, and at times violent, backlash.

Throughout the Caribbean region, the first decades of the twentieth century saw the colonial and neo-colonial powers wield an unprecedented degree of control over politics, economy, society, and culture. Yet, Caribbean peoples reacted to these efforts to exercise and extend control by protesting with all the resources at their disposal. Wage cuts and high unemployment were met with riots and strikes while Afro-Caribbean women and men responded to ongoing racism and cultural imperialism with a flowering of the arts and literature detailing the struggle of an oppressed people.

In the mainland Caribbean countries of Honduras and Nicaragua, as well as in Haiti and the Dominican Republic, weak state structures allowed for the penetration of U.S. capital and subsequent political influence from the late nineteenth century on. The desire to maintain a political environment conducive to the steady flow of export commodities often translated into support for dictatorial, repressive governments. When these regimes failed to produce the desired results, direct military intervention and occupation often followed. From 1898 until 1917 the U.S. military intervened in Cuba, Puerto Rico (in both countries playing an active role in the armed struggle that secured independence from Spain), Haiti, the Dominican Republic, Nicaragua, Honduras, and Colombia (resulting in the "creation" of Panama).

The African-descendant population varied in its responses to the arrival of U.S. forces. In the case of Puerto Rico, many Afro-Puerto Ricans supported the U.S. intervention. As José Luis Gonzalez has argued, due to the race and class structure of the island in the nineteenth century, black Puerto Ricans viewed their struggle as against the white elite, the group which, following 1898, most identified with an anti-imperialist position. In contrast, in Haiti U.S. involvement met with a less welcome reception. As the second independent republic and the first black nation in the Americas, Haiti enjoyed a long history of freedom from slavery and a tradition of self-government. In reaction to the U.S. intervention and occupation from 1915 to 1934 and the establishment of the *corvée* (forced labor), a guerrilla resistance movement grew that targeted U.S. Marines. Militia groups fought heavily with the occupation forces, particularly from 1918 to 1920.

Nationalist struggles in Cuba proceeded down two major tracks: political and cultural resistance. With the victory over Spanish forces in 1898, the Cuban population of color, many of whom had fought in the war for independence, stood poised to create a republic based on José Martí's vision of a racially egalitarian society. A veteran of the conflict, Esteban Montejo described how Afro-Cuban soldiers in Cienfuegos attacked occupying American soldiers who disrespected Cuban women, thus asserting their place as guardians of the young nation.[11] Despite their sacrifices, during the occupation by U.S. forces from 1898 until 1902, Afro-Cubans found themselves disenfranchised and unable to reap the benefits of independence. Inspired by ideologies of Social Darwinism and scientific racism, under Governor General Leonard Wood, the military administration advocated measures to promote the whitening of the nation. These colonization plans brought hundreds of thousands of mostly single, male Spanish workers to toil in Cuba's sugar industry, though less than one quarter of the total are believed to have settled permanently there.[12] Despite the efforts of U.S.-backed politicians to mold Cuba into a "white" nation, the early twentieth century also witnessed the migration of thousands of West Indian migrants to work in the sugar industry. Cane cutters from Haiti and Jamaica, seeking better economic options outside of their homelands, came at the behest of mostly American capital interests seeking low-cost labor for their *centrales* (industrialized sugar mills).[13] Between 1915 and 1929, some 500,000 workers out of a population of 2 million left Haiti to work on plantations in Cuba and the Dominican Republic.[14]

In response to their political disenfranchisement a group of several hundred Afro-Cubans established the race-based Partido Independiente de Color (PIC) to lobby for their rights as African descendants, although the majority of the population of color continued to support the Liberal Party during the first decades of the century. Yet calls for racial justice were dismissed on the grounds that Marti's message of unity of all races preempted the creation of "racist" political parties. Near Santiago de Cuba in 1912, the rural guard attacked members of the PIC, their supporters, and many innocent Afro-Cubans, resulting in the massacre of at least 3,000.

Due to the late slave traffic, the influence of African culture remained strong in early twentieth-century Cuba. As a means of discouraging unity of the African population, in the larger cities of Havana, Matanzas, and Santiago de Cuba, African slaves throughout the nineteenth century had been encouraged to establish brotherhoods on the basis of ethnic origin. Among other responsibilities, these *sociedades de color* served the important functions of purchasing freedom for their members, celebrating religious festivals, and organizing work. The example of the Abakuá secret society provides an important window on Africanisms in Caribbean nationalism. Having first been organized in Havana in 1836, the secret brotherhoods of the Abakuá had played an important role in anticolonial struggle since the War of 1868. In contrast to Rastafarianism, which viewed Ethiopia as the symbolic homeland, the Abakuá societies considered themselves sovereign nations within the Cuban territory, maintaining their own language and complex rituals from the era of the slave trade. Although most societies forbade the divulgence of ritual chant, Ivor Miller has demonstrated that popular music from the 1920s and 1930s, much of it performed by Abakuá initiates, was infused with coded messages that spoke of the anti-colonial struggles of the Abakuá from the mid-nineteenth century through the Depression.[15]

This type of cultural resistance was common in disparate regions of the Caribbean basin. Kim Butler has demonstrated that the Afro-Brazilian population in Salvador responded to the racism of government and police by embracing their African heritage. Despite the criminalization of African-based cultural expressions, the practices of *candomblé* (a Yoruba-Brazilian religious tradition) and *capoeira* (an Afro-Brazilian martial art) flourished in the late nineteenth and early twentieth centuries. In Haiti as well the practice of *vodun* persisted, particularly among the lower classes, in spite of condemnation and criminalization incurred from the mostly mulatto elite.[16]

As opposed to Cuba, the Dominican Republic, and Puerto Rico, where a substantial white and mixed-race peasantry existed, in the French and British West Indies tensions between blacks and mulattos constituted the primary social cleavage, with mulattos comprising the numerically smaller elite. In the British Caribbean, early nationalist expression occurred at both elite and popular levels. From the beginning of the twentieth century black intellectuals in Europe, Africa, and the Americas created a movement for Pan-African unity. The first Pan-African Congress, convened by Trinidadian-born lawyer Henry Sylvester Williams, brought together representatives from Africa, the Americas, and Europe to develop and promote political reforms and challenge the discriminatory policies of the colonial and neo-colonial powers.

On a popular level Afro-Caribbean people used labor actions to protest against their social and political disenfranchisement. Since trade unions were outlawed in the British Caribbean until 1918, black workers relied on riots and general strikes to press their demands for wage increases and better working conditions. The Ruimveldt Riots in Demerara, British Guiana, provide a poignant example of transnational communication shaping anti-colonial struggle. In 1905 stevedores and plantation workers joined in a strike over stagnation of wages and their payment at a lower rate as the result of their categorization as "boys." The striking workers had been influenced by reports of major strikes in Great Britain, including a wave of strikes among dockworkers that took place during the 1890s.

Strikers in British Guiana provide but one example of transnational ties. Throughout the region, communication among Afro-Caribbean people played a vital role in shaping the resistance to discrimination and colonization. Much as the news of the Haitian Revolution inspired uprisings of the enslaved throughout the hemisphere, Haitians, Dominicans, and Cubans under U.S. domination were well aware of the lynchings of African Americans in the U.S. South. In addition to the personal linkages of workers and families that migrated throughout the Caribbean and the substantial communities of expatriates in the metropolitan centers of Paris, London, and New York, the black press disseminated news about current events in the Americas and Africa.

Sacrifice and Struggle, 1929–1939

With the onset of the worldwide economic depression in 1929, calls for reform were, in many regions, overpowered by cries of revolution. The Italian invasion of Ethiopia in 1935 generated increased support for Pan-African unity to repel the invaders while intellectuals voiced their support for the Republican faction in the Spanish Civil War. Throughout the Caribbean, peasants, students, and urban workers demanded relief from grinding poverty and unemployment. The movements that grew out of the Depression of the 1930s projected a powerful call for the redress for racial equality and, increasingly, for national self-determination.

As the heady decade of the 1920s gave way to the Depression of the 1930s, Caribbean economies suffered tremendous losses. Because the majority of the Caribbean islands provided the industrialized North with staple commodities (sugar, coffee, tobacco), the well-being of their populations depended in large part on the maintenance of stable, relatively high prices for exports on the world market. The steep decline in prices following the market crash launched the majority of Caribbean territories into severe economic depression. From 1928 to 1933 the prices for West Indian exports fell by 50 percent.[17]

The economic crisis of the 1930s touched off a profound social revolution that would attack domestic issues of race, color, and class and question the competence and legitimacy of colonial rule. From the mid-1930s onward a series of labor actions rocked the British and French West Indies. The deteriorating economic conditions of the Depression functioned as a catalyst for mobilizing heretofore unorganized groups of unemployed or underemployed workers, many of whom had recently returned from Cuba, Central America, or the United States. Central to the demands of workers and rioters was the idea that the imperial powers were mismanaging colonial affairs. Their links to the newly formed political parties and prominent position of Afro-Caribbean intellectuals proved a watershed in the development of nationalist movements.

In Jamaica, the economic hardships of the Depression had, by the late 1930s, led to increased organizational activity on the part of labor. Wages paid to laborers in the sugar sector constituted a mere one half to one quarter of wages paid on Cuban sugar *centrales*.[18] The Bustamante Industrial Trade Union (BITU), founded by Alexander Bustamante, had by 1938 gained the strength to pose a formidable challenge to the colonial administration. That year the BITU led dockworkers and sugar workers in a series of strikes that disrupted production and trade and resulted in rioting and the deaths of several workers. The influence of socialism and the militancy of workers led to the formation of the first political party in Jamaican history. The People's National Party, established by Norman Manley in 1938 and supported by Bustamante, would go on the shape Jamaica's future, winning important political victories during World War II.

In the French Antilles, economic deprivation led to the formation of unions by the workers and their legal recognition by the colonial administrations in the mid-1930s. In 1936 the Confédération Générale du Travail formed in Martinique, and in 1937 the Union Départmentale de la Confédération Française des travailleurs Chrétiens was established in Guadeloupe.[19] In addition to protesting against wage cuts and unemployment, in Haiti political agitation during the 1930s had an immediate goal: expulsion of the U.S. armed forces. From the late 1920s until 1934, scattered resistance to the U.S. occupation of Caribbean nations developed into a broader, organized movement of students, peasants, and workers. Although U.S. Marines withdrew from Haiti in 1934, they left a shattered economy in their wake.

In contrast to Haiti, where the 1930s saw the organization of a popular movement to extricate the country from U.S. influence, in the Dominican Republic the U.S.-supported president Rafael Trujillo continued his corrupt, dictatorial rule over the island. The Dominican Republic and Haiti had shared a long, interconnected history. Since the colonial period the Dominican-Haitian border had been relatively porous, resulting in communities of Haitian nationals residing on either side. In 1937, on the border between Haiti and the Dominican Republic, currents of race, nationalism, and dictatorship converged with disastrous results. Trujillo, in an appeal to knee-jerk nationalism, ordered the slaughter of all Haitians residing in the country. In a matter of days, the Dominican armed forces dispatched to the border had killed one-quarter to one-half of the 50,000 Haitians residing in the Dominican Republic.[20]

Elsewhere, populist leaders came to power with the stated goal of advancing racial plurality. The rise to power of populist leader Getulio Vargas in Brazil reflected the efforts of a multi-racial constituency to support an administration that would alleviate the social and economic problems plaguing the country. Amidst a worsening depression, the populist appeal of Vargas constituted a manifestation of nationalism, despite having been elevated to power in a military coup in 1930. Vargas embarked on a program of import substitution industrialization in an attempt to reduce dependency on the markets of the global north. His appeal among Afro-Brazilians rested on his acknowledgment of their specific disadvantages (higher rates of poverty and unemployment) and his willingness to extend the benefits of political patronage to them.

While Afro-Brazilians in the state of Bahia continued to embrace the religion and culture of their African ancestors, the creation of the Frente Negra Brasileira (FNB), active between 1931 and 1937, reflected the efforts Afro-Brazilians in the state of São Paulo to organize to fight racial discrimination and demand political reforms. Despite early successes in eliminating racial barriers to military service and fighting discrimination in public places, the middle-class leadership became increasingly alienated from its base: working-class Afro-Brazilian women and men. During the 1930s the FNB began its turn toward xenophobia, denouncing the European immigrants that entered Brazil looking for work, and by 1937 had fractured with one faction of leadership supporting the intellectual currents of European fascism popular at the time and others forming splinter organizations, including the Club of Social Culture and the Black Socialist Front.[21]

Cuba, too, experienced revolutionary upheaval during the 1930s. Dissatisfaction with the corruption of the Machado dictatorship gave rise to a broad-based movement for democratization. Afro-Cubans played a significant role in these anti-government actions, both as working women and men participating in trade union activity and as the middle-class members of Havana's black recreational societies, such as Club Atenas. While Garveyism had not made particularly strong inroads among Cuba's population of color, after the Revolution of 1933, which ousted dictator Gerardo Machado from power, many middle-class Afro-Cubans began to embrace communism and, along with their progressive white allies, waged a struggle against racial discrimination. This struggle did not occur in isolation. The movement's leaders were aided in their efforts through the active role played by the international black press and the relationships of solidarity that developed between Afro-Cubans and their North American counterparts. Throughout the 1930s the leadership of the Cuban and African American anti-discrimination movements kept in regular contact and helped shape each other's struggles. In 1937 the visit of African American U.S. congressman Arthur Mitchell to Havana led to protests by Afro-Cuban leaders when the staff of the Hotel Saratoga denied his delegation a table in the restaurant. Club Atenas also hosted other prominent African American intellectuals, artists, and political leaders such as Arturo (Arthur) Schomburg, Langston Hughes, Mary McCloud Bethune, and William Pickens.[22]

In addition to the gains of trade unions and political movements during the 1930s, popular responses to the deprivation of the Depression challenged the racism of the colonial system. In Jamaica, Marcus Garvey's return from the United States in 1927 reinvigorated the struggle of the poor black majority against the white colonial administration. Like Cubans and Brazilians, Jamaicans organized against racism and discrimination and advocated national self-determination through political and cultural channels. While the most militant protest movement of the 1930s in Jamaica, as in other regions of the British West Indies, was the labor movement, the growth of Rastafarianism from 1930 on represented a significant challenge to British rule. The roots of Rastafarianism lay in a statement made by Garvey that predicted the coming of an African king who would be a source of redemption for African peoples worldwide. Upon the coronation of Emperor Haile Selassie (born Prince Ras Tafari Makonnen) in 1930, many Jamaicans believed Garvey's prophecy had been fulfilled. Although early Rastafarian groups varied considerably in their beliefs, all supported a non-violent struggle against colonialism and sought to repatriate their fellow Jamaicans to Africa. Their efforts were buttressed by the 1935 Italian invasion of Ethiopia, which helped to unite disparate factions in the anti-colonial and Pan-African movements. From 1935 through World War II, outpourings of support for the Ethiopian government came from African descendants living in all parts of the world.

Inspired by the Harlem Renaissance of the 1920s, by the early 1930s Francophone intellectuals in Africa and the Caribbean were engaged in a literary and artistic movement that would come to be known as *la négritude. La négritude* advocated the embrace of African traditions and black skin color and promoted racial pride and a dismantling of colonialism. Aimé Césaire of Martinique, Léopold Sédar Senghor of Senegal, and Léon Gontran-Damas of French Guyana were considered the founders of the movement that drew both praise and criticism from intellectuals in the Americas, Europe, and Africa.

With the onset of World War II the Caribbean experienced a dramatic reversal of fortunes. The wartime economies of Europe and later the United States were once again capable of purchasing Caribbean-produced commodities. Yet the struggles of the 1930s and the organizations to which they had given rise would not accept being shunted aside by the colonial and neo-colonial powers. In the years during and following World War II Caribbean leaders would push for, and in many cases achieve, relative autonomy.

Toward Caribbean Independence, 1939–1960s

The post–World War II era saw decolonization of a vast area of the globe, ranging from Southeast Asia to West Africa to the Caribbean. From 1940 on, Caribbean leaders used the expediencies of war production and the advantageous socio-economic conditions of the post-war era to push nationalist agendas.

In the British Caribbean, the 1940s through the 1980s saw decades of anticolonial agitation result in the formation of independent nations. Propelled by the gains of the late 1930s, the Jamaican People's National Party and the Jamaica Labour Party secured universal suffrage and a measure of self-government in 1944. A revived economy, including diversification from the agricultural export model, provided the basis for substantial economic growth in the post-war era. In 1962, after almost two decades of relative autonomy, Great Britain granted Jamaican independence.

Barbados as well followed the model of trade unionism resulting in the formation of political parties which went on to push for independence. The Barbados Labour Party (BLP) was established in the aftermath of the labor agitation of 1937 and dominated Barbadian politics through the 1950s when the Democratic Labour Party (DLP) broke away and began to amass widespread public support. The leader of the BLP, Grantley Adams, shepherded Barbados into the West Indian Federation in 1958. Upon its failure in 1962, Barbados proceeded toward independence under Errol Barrow of the DLP, finally achieving it in 1966.

The World War II and post-war era also witnessed the emergence of reinvigorated anti-discrimination struggles in Cuba and the United States. Ongoing communication among intellectuals and artists and increased communication through the medium of Claude Barnett's Associated Negro Press so troubled the U.S. government that in 1943 the State Department began a propaganda campaign in an effort to mitigate the influence of communism among the latter. These actions by the State Department reflected a profound sense of unease with the increased mobilization of African descendants on both sides of the Florida Strait.[23] In the United States the Double V Campaign, begun in Pittsburgh in 1942, called for victory against the Axis powers and victory at home against discrimination and is generally credited with serving as the opening salvo in the twentieth-century movement for black civil rights. As many U.S. workers had used the passage of the National Labor Relations Act in 1935 to better their working conditions, predominantly African American unions seized upon the expediencies of war production to lobby for desegregation in the defense industries. In Cuba, the role of the Unión Revolucionaria Comunista, or Communist Party, in lobbying for racial equality had secured support for its agenda among a broad swath of the Afro-Cuban population. In anticipation of the coming Cold War, the State Department's efforts were largely successful, resulting in the purge of communists by a competing faction of Afro-Cuban leaders during the 1940s.[24]

Nationalist sentiment in Cuba, from the early 1950s on, took the form of a clandestine struggle against the dictatorship of Fulgencio Batista, who came to power in 1952 with the support of U.S. business and political leadership. By 1953 Batista's dictatorial leadership had alienated substantial segments of the Cuban population, particularly students, industrial workers, and much of the middle class.[25] On July 26th of that year a group of rebels, including a young Fidel Castro, led a failed assault on a military installation in the eastern end of the island. This episode was the beginning of what would develop into a nationalist revolution in Cuba. By 1956 Castro's band of guerrilla fighters had united with an underground urban insurgency in a protracted campaign to overthrow Batista. Leaders argued that Batista had permitted foreign (particularly U.S.) capital to dominate not only Cuba's economy but also its political life.

With the triumph of the Cuban Revolution on January 1, 1959, the island embarked on a massive program of expropriation and nationalization of resources. Within the next few years the new administration would implement a national literacy campaign, stabilize rents and redistribute housing, introduce fixed prices for staple goods, expand public education, and extend health care to all Cubans. While these measures alienated the U.S. government and business sector, the new administration's program of revolutionary change won support from the formerly most disenfranchised sectors of the population. Chief among the supporters of Fidel Castro's government were Afro-Cubans who benefited from the Revolution's efforts to eradicate racial segregation and socio-economic disparity.

Although today income from tourism has overtaken sugar and bananas as the crucial provider of state revenue, the Jamaican economy remains firmly tied to the vagaries of the international marketplace. Haiti, once the richest colony in the Americas, continues to have the highest infant mortality rate in the Western Hemisphere. Despite the significant economic changes and political reconfigurations that occurred from the 1940s through the 1960s, few, save the Cuban Revolution, addressed the structural inequalities that shape the lives of Caribbean women and men.

Conclusion

In the preceding pages we have attempted to sketch a picture of nationalist struggles in the early twentieth-century Caribbean. While nationalism can be, and often is, conceptualized as the struggle for political independence, we have endeavored to present a more inclusive definition of nationalism. For nationalism in the early twentieth-century Caribbean took on at least three major forms.

The first expression of Caribbean nationalism was the previously referred-to desire for political independence. The majority of the movements that developed along this track arose in opposition to British colonial and U.S. neocolonial influence in the Caribbean region. In Haiti, circa World War I, guerrilla forces engaged the U.S. military. More common, however, was the development of trade unionism and the subsequent growth of political parties to challenge colonial rule. In Jamaica, Barbados, and Trinidad and Tobago the inability of the British to alleviate the grinding poverty of the Depression led to labor riots and increased trade union activity by the late 1930s. From the early 1940s these industrial unions and the political parties to which they gave rise had begun to make substantial advancements, achieving universal adult suffrage and a measure of self-rule.

A second facet of nationalism in the Caribbean lay in the cultural expressions of Afro-Caribbean peoples. While workers organized strikes, boycotts, and underground networks of resistance, others looked to popular religion, art, literature, and music as a means of contesting their subordinate status. The continued practice of *candomblé* in Brazil, *vodun* in Haiti, and *santería* in Cuba, particularly in light of the nineteenth- and early twentieth-century criminalization of many African religions, speaks to the powerful presence of African heritage in resisting the apparatus of discrimination. The development of Rastafarianism in Jamaica in the 1930s and the flowering of the arts from the United States to Haiti during the 1920s and 1930s highlights the strength of African cultural resistance.

The third and final aspect of Caribbean nationalism concerns the development of transnational linkages throughout the Americas, Europe, and Africa. By emphasizing the relationships that developed across borders and the communication that was facilitated by individuals, agencies, and new technologies, this essay has sought to emphasize the inherently *international* nature of nationalist struggles in the Caribbean. Whenever and wherever writers and politicians exchanged letters and visited, organized, and debated, they were laying the groundwork of an international community of struggle. Often such events as the Pan-African conferences held from the beginning of the twentieth century onward and the friendships that were formed between writers of the Harlem Renaissance and those of the *négritude* movement occurred on the basis of a shared racial heritage. In other instances, such as Langston Hughes and Nicolas Guillen's support for the Republican faction in the Spanish Civil War, relationships developed on the basis of a shared support for communism, trade unionism, and many other social movements.

Although nationalist movements achieved significant gains by the mid-twentieth century, few went on to generate radical, structural changes in Caribbean societies. While independence produced some limited progress regarding political participation, education, and employment, in most Caribbean countries the gains of independence were, and are as yet, incomplete.

Notes

1. Lisa Brock and Digna Castañeda Fuertes, eds., *Between Race and Empire: African-Americans and Cubans before the Revolution* (Philadelphia: Temple University Press, 1998), 121–122.

2. Tiffany Ruby Patterson and Robin D. G. Kelly. "Unfinished Migrations: Reflections on the African Diaspora and the Making of the Modern World," *African Studies Review* 43:1, special issue on the Diaspora (April 2000), 11–45.

3. Frank Guridy, "Diaspora in Action: Afro-Cubans and African-Americans in the U.S.-Caribbean World" (forthcoming).

4. See Aline Helg, *Our Rightful Share: The Afro-Cuban Struggle for Equality, 1886–1912* (Chapel Hill: University of North Carolina Press, 1995); Ada Ferrer, *Insurgent Cuba: Race, Nation, and Revolution, 1868–1898* (Chapel Hill: University of North Carolina Press, 1999); Alejandro de la Fuente, *A Nation for All: Race, Inequality and Politics in Twentieth-Century Cuba* (Chapel Hill: University of North Carolina Press, 2001); and Lillian Guerra, "From Revolution to Involution in the Early Cuban Republic: Conflicts over Race, Class, and Nation, 1902–1906," in *Race and Nation in Modern Latin America*, ed. Nancy P. Applebaum, Anne S. Macpherson, and Karin Alejandra Rosemblatt (Chapel Hill: University of North Carolina Press, 2003).

5. Stephan Palmié, *Wizards and Scientists: Explorations in Afro-Cuban Modernity and Tradition* (Durham, N.C: Duke University Press, 2002).

6. Ivor Miller, "A Secret Society Goes Public: The Relationship between Abakuá and Cuban Popular Culture," *African Studies Review* 43:1 (April 2000): 161–188.

7. See Claudio Lomnitz's response to Benedict Anderson's *Imagined Communities*, "Nationalism as a Practical System: Benedict Anderson's Theory of Nationalism from the Vantage Point of Spanish America," in *The Other Mirror: Grand Theory through the Lens of Latin America*, ed. Miguel Angel Centeno and Fernando López-Alves (Princeton, N.J.: Princeton University Press, 2001).

8. Frank A. Guridy, "From Solidarity to Cross Fertilization: Afro-Cuban and African American Interaction during the 1930s and 1940s," *Radical History Review* no. 87 (Fall 2003): 19–48.

9. Recent biographies of Du Bois include David Levering Lewis's Pulitzer Prize–winning *W. E. B Du Bois: The Fight for Equality and the American Century, 1919–1963* (New York: Owl Books, 2001), and Manning Marable's updated *W. E. B. Du Bois: Black Radical Democrat* (Boulder, CO: Paradigm, 2005). Biographical pieces on Garvey include Tomás Fernandez Robaina, "Marcus Garvey in Cuba: Urrutia, Cubans, and Black Nationalism," in Brock and Castañeda, *Between Race and Empire*; and Tony Martin, "Marcus Garvey, the Caribbean, and the Struggle for Black Jamaican Nationhood," in *Caribbean Freedom: Economy and Society from Emancipation to the Present*, ed. Hilary Beckles and Verene Shepard (Princeton, N.J.: Markus Wiener, 1996).

10. The literature on the post-abolition era in the Americas and the Caribbean is very rich. For Brazil see Thomas E. Skidmore, *Black into White: Race and Nationality in Brazilian Thought* (New York: Oxford University Press, 1974), and George Reid Andrews, "Black and White Workers: São Paulo, Brazil, 1888–1928," *Hispanic American*

Historical Review 68:3 (August 1988): 491–524 (517). Rebecca Scott has published a number of important pieces on Cuba, including a comparative piece delineating similarities and differences in the post-abolition societies of Louisiana, Brazil, and Cuba. See Rebecca J. Scott, "Defining the Boundaries of Freedom in the World of Cane: Cuba, Brazil," and "Louisiana after Emancipation," *American Historical Review* 99:1 (February, 1994): 70–102 (78); Scott, *Slave Emancipation in Cuba: The Transition to Free Labor, 1860–1899* (Pittsburgh: University of Pittsburgh Press, 2000). Regarding emancipation in Jamaica see Thomas Holt, "The Essence of the Contract: The Articulation of Race, Gender, and Political Economy in British Emancipation Policy, 1838–1866," in *Beyond Slavery: Explorations of Race, Labor, and Citizenship in Postemancipation Societies*, ed. Frederick Cooper, Thomas C. Holt, and Rebecca J. Scott (Chapel Hill: University of North Carolina Press, 2000). For Puerto Rico, José Luis Gonzalez provides a description of changes in racial categories and understandings from the colonial period through U.S. colonization in his classic study, *Puerto Rico: The Four-Storeyed Country*, trans. Gerald Guiness (1980; trans., Princeton, N.J.: Markus Wiener, 1993).

11. Alejandro de la Fuente, *A Nation for All: Race, Inequality, and Politics in Twentieth-Century Cuba* (Chapel Hill: University of North Carolina Press, 2001), 36.

12. Alejandro de la Fuente, "Race, National Discourse, and Politics in Cuba: An Overview," in "Race and National Identity in the Americas," special issue, *Latin American Perspectives* 25:3 (May 1998): 43–69 (48).

13. On the subject of race, migration, and nation, see Aviva Chomsky, "'Barbados or Canada?' Race, Immigration, and Nation in Early-Twentieth-Century Cuba," *Hispanic American Historical Review* 80:3 (August 2000): 415–462.

14. Charles Arthur and Michael Dash, eds., *Libéte: A Haiti Anthology* (London: Latin America Bureau, 1999), 176–183.

15. Miller, "Secret Society Goes Public." Note that, although founded by West Africans and composed of a primarily Afro-Cuban membership, white Cubans could and did fully participate in the Abakuá brotherhood.

16. Arthur and Dash, *Libéte*, 255–258.

17. W. Arthur Lewis, "The 1930s Social Revolution," in Beckles and Shepard, *Caribbean Freedom*, 376.

18. Knight and Palmer, *Modern Caribbean*, 11.

19. Ibid., 13.

20. Arthur and Dash, *Libéte*, 42. The traditional interpretation of Dominican-Haitian relations suggests that the roots of the hatred that led to this massacre extended back to the Haitian occupation of the Dominican Republic from 1822 until 1844 and relate to questions of skin color and class. More recently, Lauren Derby has provided a compelling reinterpretation of issues of race, identity, and nationalism in the Dominican Republic. See Derby, "National Identity and the Idea of Value in the Dominican Republic," in *Blacks, Coloureds, and National Identity in Nineteenth-Century Latin America*, ed. Nancy Priscilla Naro (London: Institute of Latin American Studies, 2003).

21. George Reid Andrews, *Blacks and Whites in São Paulo Brazil, 1888–1988* (Madison: University of Wisconsin Press, 1991), 135–155. See also Kim Butler, *Freedoms Given, Freedoms Won: Post-Abolition São Paulo and Salvador* (New Brunswick, N.J.: Rutgers University Press, 1998), and Michael Hanchard, *Orpheus and Power: The Movimento Negro of Rio de Janeiro and São Paulo, Brazil, 1945–1988* (Princeton, N.J.: Princeton University Press, 1994), for discussions of Afro-Brazilian political action from abolition through the 1980s.

22. Guridy, "From Solidarity to Cross Fertilization," 19–48.
23. Ibid., 38–43.
24. Ibid., 41.
25. Batista had been close to the presidency since his tenure as the army chief of staff under Ramon Grau in 1933. He had also held the office of president prior to his 1952 coup, from 1940 through 1944.

CHAPTER THIRTEEN

The Cold War in the Atlantic World

Carol Anderson

World War II changed everything. Although the Allies denounced Aryan supremacy and defeated the Nazis, all in the cause of the principles of self-determination, they also undermined the very philosophical, moral, and legal pillars of European colonialism. Because of the war, white supremacy and brute control of other peoples and nations suddenly lost the aura of respectability that had permeated the nineteenth century's "Scramble for Africa."[1] Since the end of the World War II, historian Kenneth Twitchett noted, "colonialism, or more correctly the brand practised by the Western European powers, has come to be characterized as a fundamental evil" that had to be destroyed. In its place arose a new international regime that "enshrined the thesis that self-government is intrinsically superior to good government by an alien metropole."[2] Of course, Twitchett was only partially right because the "good government" was really not so good—especially *for* the Africans. While the Europeans tended to rhapsodize about their benevolence toward "the natives," the reality of that benevolence stretched from King Leopold's villainy in the Congo to the Germans' genocidal policies against the Hereros of South West Africa to the Italians' mass slaughter of Eritreans, Somalis, Ethiopians, and Libyans.[3] By the end of the World War II, therefore, the undeniable stirring of the African freedom struggle was clearly discernible. Kwame Nkrumah, the future prime minister of Ghana, summarized it best when he said that in "1942 . . . I was so revolted by the ruthless colonial exploitation and political oppression of the people of Africa that I knew no peace." World War II, therefore, had to be followed by a war of liberation. How that war would be fought depended in large measure on what kind of resistance the colonial powers would put up. Nevertheless, the war would be waged. Nkrumah was unequivocal. "[W]e are fighting against a system—a system which defiles the dignity of a man because of his race and the colour of his skin and, wherever we find that system in operation, it must be liquidated."[4]

That liquidation quickly became entangled in the U.S. rise to global dominance and obsession with communism, which provided both the opportunities for and obstacles to liberation. U.S. policymakers knew that colonialism was no longer viable and that to maintain it in its current form was to invite disaster. Nevertheless, despite the storm warnings, the United States wavered. According to Steven Metz, "The usual U.S. policy consisted of vague rhetoric about the right of self-determination coupled with insistence on the benefits of colonialism." Not surprisingly, this contradictory policy led the United States to "very nearly wait . . . until the winds of change had blown the roof from the house."[5]

Walter White, executive secretary of the National Association for the Advancement of Colored People (NAACP), who had traveled throughout Africa and Asia during the war, sensed a seismic change in the international atmosphere as well. He did not waver as he asserted that "A wind is rising—a wind of determination by the have-nots of the world to share the benefits of freedom and prosperity which the haves of the earth have tried to keep exclusively for themselves."[6] This refusal to accept white supremacy as the political and economic philosophy that would govern their lives led African freedom fighters to join with willing allies in the United States, such as the NAACP and the left-wing Council on African Affairs (CAA) in this struggle against "the civilizing mission," the "white man's burden," apartheid, and Jim Crow. Africans were also vigorously supported by the newly independent states in Asia, such as India, which used the United Nations to further delegitimize the rule of Europeans over people of color.[7] This would, however, be "no easy walk." Over the span of five decades, Africans tried every strategy at their command, from the International Court of Justice all the way through violent, protracted revolution, to end colonialism.[8] In too many cases, they had to fight and maneuver not only against the European metropole but against the United States as well.

For the American government, the only legitimate issue in the international system was the Cold War, officially launched in 1947 after a series of feints, missteps, and political calculations had irreparably severed the already strained bonds between World War II's victorious Allies. The United States and the Soviet Union grimly settled in for a war like no other. They amassed their resources, arrayed their allies, and set out on a global showdown to prove which economic and political system was superior. This winner-take-all ideological duel meant that liberation was no longer simply liberation but either a stunning triumph or humiliating defeat for either communism or capitalism. "Communist imperialists," the U.S. State Department concluded, were "busily engaged in a campaign to expand their power and domain by seizing anything that isn't nailed down. . . . Each acquisition increases their power and, by the same token, diminishes the free world's capacity for resistance." Convinced that "Africa would be a highly valuable prize for the Communist rulers," the United States was determined, despite the inevitable collapse of colonialism, to keep the continent safely locked down within the West's sphere of influence. Liberation, therefore, was only supposed to happen on America's terms, on America's timetable, led by those whom America trusted.[9] Of course, that philosophy so contravened the concept of self-determination that it put U.S. policy and the global freedom movement on a collision course.

U.S. Foreign Policy toward the European Colonial Powers

The refusal to honor its own wartime commitment to self-determination, particularly as espoused in the Atlantic Charter, was based first and foremost on the fact that imperial Europe was the centerpiece of America's Cold War strategy to contain communism and Soviet influence.[10] But, after World War II, Europe was in no position to be anyone's centerpiece as it quivered in bloodletting shock, barely holding together throughout the immediate post-war years of 1945, 1946, and 1947. With Europe's industrial infrastructure in ruins and firm grip on the resource and wealth-producing colonies severely weakened, its ability to play the role the United States wanted, that is, to deny the Soviets additional territory and influence, was seriously in question. Eastern Europe already hung behind the Iron Curtain of Soviet domination, and Western Europe looked particularly vulnerable. In 1947 State Department officials and President Harry Truman therefore crafted a series of policies to address what they viewed as the Soviets' serious threat to the democratic "Free World." Intent on stabilizing Western Europe, and hence America's global defense strategy, the United States allocated nearly 17 percent of its federal budget to rebuild Europe under the Marshall Plan. It enacted the Truman Doctrine that initially pledged an additional $400 million to stave off a possible communist takeover in Greece and Turkey; it constructed the North Atlantic Treaty Organization (NATO) to keep the Soviets hemmed up behind Eastern Europe; and it put enormous diplomatic, military, and financial power behind a policy of "containment" to keep the communist contagion from infecting any other area of the globe.

Implications of U.S. Cold War Foreign Policy on African Liberation

As a consequence, stability and the status quo became sacrosanct, while political change became synonymous with chaos, turmoil, and communism. American policymakers' fixation on the Cold War skewed their perceptions of African demands for independence and separated those demands from issues of African nationalism, self-determination, and the exploitive dimensions of colonialism. Moreover, the Cold War seriously curtailed American affinity for colonial revolutions. Although 1776 still resonated deeply in American iconography, "a tradition of ambivalence marked US attitudes about revolutions. American policymakers always had been wary about social and political upheavals, especially those arising from the left." At this point in particular, the United States could only countenance a "'good' revolution [which] needed to be conducted with a minimum of disorder, led by respectable citizens, harnessed to moderate political goals, and culminate in a balanced constitution safeguarding human and property rights."[11] As a result, the ferment for African independence, which included demands for not only political freedom but also for indigenous control of natural resources and "freedom from poverty and economic exploitation," was too often deemed little more than a Soviet-inspired plot to undermine America's European allies and trap millions of Africans behind another Iron Curtain.[12]

The second factor compelling the United States to support—either tacitly or explicitly—European ambitions in Africa was just plain old white supremacy, which, as one U.S. official fully admitted, was "[a]t the heart of the colonial system."[13] Africans were supposedly less evolved, less civilized, and too politically and emotionally immature to be entrusted with vouchsafing Africa for the West. "Africans," an article in *Look* asserted, are "among the most backward people." As a consequence, they are "prime targets for the siren song of abundance constantly drummed through the continent by busy agents of Moscow."[14] Decolonization, therefore, "was to proceed only when the allegiance of the new states to the Western alliance could be ensured. Often in Africa this criterion," at least as far as the United States was concerned, "could not be met."[15]

President Harry Truman, for example, asserted that while the people of Africa "are determined to establish their own free political and economic institutions," that determination held "great dangers" for the United States because "Communists or reactionaries can exploit the hopes and aspirations of these peoples for their own evil ends." "We must," the president insisted, "do all we can to keep this from happening."[16] This Red-phobic framework, of course, led to pervasive State Department "[w]arnings of the dangers of premature independence." A succession of assistant secretaries of state for African affairs, regardless of which political administration they served under, ruminated that "premature independence for primitive, uneducated peoples can do them more harm than good" because these "backward peoples" simply did not have the wherewithal to "handle the 'strenuous conditions of the modern world.'"[17]

This oft-repeated assumption exasperated the African leadership. Future Tanzanian premier Julius Nyerere directly questioned the right of the West to even ask about African fitness for independence. As he explained to former First Lady Eleanor Roosevelt, "If you come into my house and steal my jacket, don't then ask me if I'm ready for my jacket. The jacket was mine and you had no right to take it at all." In fact, Nyerere reiterated, "you have no right at all to ask me whether I was ready for my jacket . . . [because] the jacket is mine."[18] Similarly, Nkrumah insisted that the West, which had done everything in its power to keep Africans uneducated and impoverished, did not have the credibility or the authority to make any decisions concerning the timetable for African independence. The "right of a people to decide their own destiny, to make their way in freedom," Nkrumah made clear, "is not to be measured by the yardstick of colour or degree of social development. . . . [Instead,] a people's readiness and willingness to assume the responsibilities of self-rule is the single criterion of the preparedness to undertake those responsibilities."[19]

Self-determination and self-rule for people of color, however, was an extremely difficult notion for the virtually all-white, elitist State Department and foreign service to comprehend.[20] The more Africans insisted on their right to independence, the more U.S. policymakers saw "communist dupes" and "agitators," not national heroes.[21] In West Africa, completely ignoring African nationalism, disgust with disfranchisement, British expropriation of African-held land, and outrage over racialized labor and wage differentials, the American vice consul in Lagos, Robert C. Johnson Jr., identified communism and U.S.-educated Dr. Nnamdi "Zik" Azikiwe as the two major sources of political and labor unrest in Nigeria. Johnson informed his superiors "that communist literature has been coming into the country," and although "there is no evidence of communist funds or of entry into Nigeria of communist agents . . . Nigerian politicians are . . . aping the communists." This assessment was relatively easy for the United States to make because the "Zik Movement," based on African unity, organized labor, and strategic use of the UN, appeared rooted in the primary elements that the U.S. National Security Council had identified as indicators of communist activity. "Communism," the NSC stated authoritatively, "enters Africa overtly by means of . . . Africans, usually students returning from Europe or the United States with pro-Communist sympathies they acquired there, and . . . through contact with . . . labor leaders who are Communists or through contact with members of the UN Committees."[22]

Those intimations about Azikiwe "aping" the communists became outright assertions concerning the soon-to-be-assassinated Patrice Lumumba, who drew particular scorn because of his refusal to allow the mineral-rich Katanaga Province to be yanked away from the Congo and turned into an enclave for Belgian and American economic interests. "Lumumba," U.S. ambassador W. Averell Harriman observed, "will continue to cause difficulties in the Congo whether he is in control of the government, in jail or released. He is a rabble-rousing speaker, [and] a shrewd maneuverer with clever left wing advisers aided and encouraged by Soviet and Czech Ambassadors."[23] Similarly, the American Consul in Accra reported home that Nkrumah "is a dangerous man. . . . He is recognised as a communist . . . with a string of American degrees."[24] The fact that Nkrumah, Lumumba, and Azikiwe were first and foremost confirmed nationalists was ignored and, frankly, for the State Department, irrelevant. In American eyes, African nationalism was virtually synonymous with communism.

Tired of the American obsession with the issue, Nyerere shot back: "Look, . . . I don't like this attitude of the West hammering on communism and communist infiltration in Africa and all this business. What has communism to do with us?"[25] The real issues for him and other African leaders were political independence and economic development. Nyerere framed the goals of the struggle succinctly for African American labor leader A. Philip Randolph: "Very often people have a rather narrow view of our struggle for freedom. It is viewed as a negative desire to get rid of our rulers. It is not, it is a struggle for human dignity. Colonialism is incompetible [*sic*] with our dignity as human beings. But that is not all. Colonialism exploits us economically and keeps us down educationally."[26] The determination to have economic as well as political independence led Kenyan labor leader Tom Mboya to spend considerable time explaining to American audiences that African socialism, rooted in centuries of communal culture, was fundamentally different than the dreaded socialism that Americans equated with Marxism.[27] Less diplomatic and patient in his explanation was Guinea's Sekou Touré. In a frank conversation that led the State Department to define the African leader as someone who would be "difficult" to "deal . . . with," Touré "underline[d] his determination to develop in Guinea, without interference from East or West a social, economic and political system attuned to past and present African conditions."[28] Meanwhile, those fighting to rid themselves of South African control of then–South West Africa were equally unimpressed with the incessant questions about their ideological bent. "We want to tell you this," leaders of the South West African People's Organization (SWAPO) wrote, "we are not to be found for either Communism or the so-called Christian Western democracy under which we are now suffering, and the people of Angola, the Congo, Algeria and Asia are brutally being murdered. What we want is ONLY OUR FREEDOM and to bring a sane government in our country."[29]

All of these disparate but thematically unified African protestations were to no avail. The United States "demanded unconditional, uncritical obedience from non-White leaders."[30] The architect of the containment policy, George F. Kennan, "interpreted any unwillingness to ally wholeheartedly with the West against the Soviet bloc as evidence that nonwhite peoples were childlike and perhaps even canine, needing to be seized (by the scruff of the neck) and forced to defend their independence from the supposedly ubiquitous Soviet threat."[31]

Indeed, the Afro-Asian Conference of 1955, held in Bandung, Indonesia, truly exemplified the angst, the concern, and the inability of U.S. decision makers to view liberation through anything but a red-colored communist lens. Bandung, called by five newly independent states in Asia—Burma, Ceylon, India, Indonesia, and Pakistan—and with a guest list that deliberately excluded all the predominantly white nations, including the United States, Britain, France, and the Soviet Union, was a conference to articulate the economic and political development issues of the still colonized and newly emerging nations and to do so in a way independent of the dominant discourse of East or West.

That neutralism outraged the Eisenhower administration, which believed that there was only one global issue (communism), only one way to independence (through the West), and that many of the organizers of Bandung were, undoubtedly, "on the 'soft-side' of the cold war." Moreover, for the Eisenhower administration, the exclusion of the Soviet Union was essentially meaningless, particularly as long as the People's Republic of China would be in attendance. The Chinese posed a particular problem. Whereas "the Russians as white men couldn't take the masses over, the Chinese could claim that they are not white, [that] they are as anti-white as the Africans, and [say] 'play along with us and we will get rid of all white men.'"[32] Secretary of State John Foster Dulles, therefore, angrily viewed the conference's "sponsors as 'dupes' of the communist powers."[33] It was just incomprehensible to the administration that the newly independent nations did "not attach the same importance we do to Communist propaganda . . . and the direful threat of the new Soviet imperialism." Instead, much to the consternation of the United States, for the Afro-Asian nations, "anti-colonialism is accorded first place" as the most important issue facing the world.[34]

The administration, therefore, bandied about idea after idea on how to sabotage Bandung, limit participation of African Americans who wanted to attend the proceedings, pressure nations dependent on foreign aid to stay away, and have supposedly ultra-pro-Western allies such as the Philippines essentially hijack the meeting. President Eisenhower even "remarked facetiously that perhaps the best way for the United States to handle this matter was to give a few thousand dollars to each of the delegates. Indeed (again facetiously), the President added he would approve of any methods up to but not including assassination of the hostile delegates. The Vice President expressed the opinion that the best strategy for the United States would be to attempt to ensure the failure" of the conference, "rather than to attempt to get such an ill-assorted group of nations to take a position favorable to the Western democracies."[35] Organizing U.S. foreign policy to really do what it would take to make the Afro-Asian nations look favorably about the Western democracies, however, was not going to happen.

The Eurocentric nature of U.S. foreign policy, the racially degrading perceptions of Africans, and the vagaries of internal domestic politics stymied the development of a truly responsive and effective policy for dealing with the inevitable independence of African nations. When pushed by the U.S. representative on the Trusteeship Council, Mason Sears, to distance America from Europe's colonial policies and court the emerging African nations, the State Department bristled at the suggestion. The "United States positions on many colonial and trusteeship questions," one State Department official countered, were "the result of compromises reach[ed] by [the Departments of] Interior, Defense and State, and . . . among our Allies." Without understanding the full implications of how his words reflected the inadequacy of U.S. foreign policy in Africa, he proudly asserted that these compromises "reflect what is practical, what is safe, and what is right and diplomatically expedient."[36] For U.S. officials, then, communism was the issue, and trying to find a way to manage the inevitable transition from colonialism to national independence, and having to do so with Africans who carried all of the "the peculiarities of the native mind," such as being "half-educated" and "puerile," only increased the difficulty of a smooth, transformation of these "backward places."[37]

Africans' unrelenting demands for independence, as Kennan intimated, thus posed a substantial geo-strategic threat to U.S. national security and marked the third factor causing the United States to weigh in on the side of the colonial powers. A Central Intelligence Agency (CIA) report explicitly laid out the problem. "This shift of the dependent areas from the orbit of the colonial powers not only weakens the probable European allies of the United States but . . . [n]o longer can the Western Powers rely on large areas of Asia and Africa as assured sources of raw materials, markets, and military bases." The CIA, therefore, warned: "Should the recently liberated and currently emergent states become oriented toward the USSR, U.S. military and economic security would be seriously weakened."[38]

Yet, despite all of its misgivings about Africans and their independence, the United States also recognized that it was short-sighted and counter-productive to take a completely hard line against these aspirations for freedom. Old-style colonialism was dead. State Department official Benjamin Gerig summarized the political shift when he wrote: "the American people sense something which is repugnant in the rule of a people by an outside or alien people. They believe that this relationship is bad both for the ruler and the ruled. It denies the ruled 'certain inalienable rights' and it tends to cause the rulers to become arrogant, haughty and imbued with a false sense of superiority."[39] And, frankly, being on the side of the "arrogant" and "haughty" is not where the nation which had George Washington, Paul Revere, and Thomas Jefferson in its pantheon of heroes wanted to stand. Yet, on the other hand, "[s]ince the colonial or ex-colonial powers are our European allies," a State Department report acknowledged, "the traditional U.S. stance of anti-colonialism is compromised."[40]

Further complicating American decolonization policy was Jim Crow. Racial discrimination, as the National Security Council observed, had soured U.S.-educated Africans on American democracy and on America as the land of equal opportunity. Moreover, Africans, who had faced serious racial discrimination at the hands of colonial powers, were "very critical of racial segregation in the United States." In addition, "the absense [*sic*] of an energetic and unequivocal federal government (President) stand against discrimination causes Africans to doubt our sincerity about desiring to eliminate inequities."[41]

That is to say, 1776 was a long time ago, and African leaders demanded much more recent proof of America's anti-colonialism and commitment to the principle that "all men are created equal." Unfortunately for the United States, however, "Algeria, the Congo, and South Africa remain[ed] political concerns for all African leaders" and were the test cases that could either prove America's anti-colonial mettle or open the United States up to charges of "'fair weather' friendship and hypocrisy." Yet, each of these test cases carried major geo-strategic implications that the United States was unwilling to risk. Algeria was in a fierce war of liberation against NATO-ally France. The Congo was embroiled in secessionist turmoil that, because of the uranium-rich Katanga Province and the pro-Soviet tilt of Prime Minister Patrice Lumumba, carried high-stakes Cold War ramifications. Then there was South Africa, which reveled in white supremacy and the brutal suppression of the majority African population, yet it was also a staunch anti-communist, uranium-rich ally on the continent. Howard University historian Rayford Logan summarized the American Cold War dilemma in Africa. The "United States must walk a tight rope in Africa," Logan said. "On one hand, the United States must seek to avoid alienating our NATO Allies, especially those which have large stakes in Africa. . . . On the other hand, the United States must seek to avoid alienating the emergent and emerging so-called black nations of Africa. Without the natural and human resources of Africa, without strategic bases there, the West would be at a serious disadvantage in the event of war with the Soviet bloc and/or Communist China."[42] Staff members in the National Security Council had reached the same conclusion, envisioning the United States as precariously straddling an ever-widening canyon with Europe on one side, Africa on the other, and the abyss far, far below.[43]

Trying to "make friends with the Africans . . . without alienating our Allies" would, "of course, [be] difficult and require the greatest tact and diplomacy."[44] In many ways, it required a skill set that the United States just did not have. Too often the United States had "shown an increasing tendency to join the colonial powers in their opposition to the demands of the colonial peoples and their champions for self-government and human rights."[45] To offset this overt commitment to its European allies, the White House created a series of aid programs, such as Point IV, which would have allowed the United States to portray itself as doing everything possible to secure the economic and technical infrastructure necessary to prepare Africans for self-government and eventually independence.[46] This ostensible support for decolonization and development provided, in the words of historian George White Jr., a convenient "racial sanctuary" for white privilege that obliterated the harsh realities of colonialism and allowed the West to think of itself as helpful stewards of nation-building. "This discourse," White writes,

> erased the history and legacy of Europe as the scourge of the globe. Gone was the visage of the far-flung Western economic engine gorging itself on the fuel of the Atlantic slave trade. Gone was the image of dismembered Congolese hands, cut off by the Belgians for failure to meet rubber quotas. Gone were the stories of mass slaughters, like the one perpetrated by the Germans against the Maji Maji a generation before the Jewish Holocaust. In the place of these skeletons stood the new, tidy, innocent countenance of the Free World.[47]

The Role of African Americans in U.S. Foreign Policy in Africa

Of course, for so many, the Free World was not so free. During the height of the Cold War, arguing the cause for the African continent's liberation carried sizeable risk for African Americans. The Council on African Affairs (CAA), for example, which was founded in 1936 as an information conduit and advocate for Africa, came under increasing attack from the anti-communist wolves that the Cold War unleashed on American society.[48] The council, led by renowned entertainer and political activist Paul Robeson and by the former YMCA representative in South Africa, Max Yergan, had several major initiatives—its outstanding newsletter *New Africa*, famine relief efforts in Africa, and consultations with the State Department's Near East and Africa division—that signaled its commitment to African liberation. Early on, and throughout its history, however, some of the top leadership in the council had strongly suspected ties to the U.S. Communist Party (CP). Although that level of radical chic had some measure of acceptability in the politically fluid era of the Great Depression and hallowed wartime alliance with the Soviet Union, by the onset of the Cold War it had become a major liability.

In early 1948, afraid that the federal government would place the Council on African Affairs on the dreaded attorney general's list of subversive organizations, Yergan, who at one time flaunted his strong ties with the Communist Party, now insisted that the CAA publicly state that it was a democratic organization with no affiliation whatsoever to the Left. Robeson countered that the CAA's political orientation was irrelevant to the issues at hand, specifically colonialism and the subjugation of black people. And, he continued, to make Yergan's proposed public announcement in this politically charged era only served to kowtow to the red-baiting reactionaries who, in the name of democracy, were propping up the white supremacists and imperialists in Africa. Robeson, therefore, stood firm, and because he was the star power behind the council, his stance carried enormous weight. Yergan, however, would not concede. He boldly confided to a colleague that he was ready to have a major showdown with Robeson to get the CAA as far away from the communists as possible.

That showdown was as nasty, backbiting, and destructive as anyone could have imagined. Lies, charges, and countercharges filled the air. Philosophical issues about the direction of the organization quickly devolved into personal attacks on the character and integrity of Yergan and Robeson as their allies hurled accusation after accusation at the other. Desperate to shift the focus away from his own administrative and ethical shortcomings, Yergan called in the media and began to red-bait the council's leadership. Moreover, his supporters threatened to resign and take their influence with them unless Robeson relented and stated that the CAA was not tied in any shape or form to the communists or the Soviet Union. When Robeson refused, Yergan's supporters followed through on their threat. The ploy backfired and only served to shift the balance of power in the organization. The former YMCA representative was now, at least on the surface, outnumbered, out-maneuvered, and out in the cold.

By the fall of 1948, Yergan, ousted and enraged, eagerly crossed the line into the Cold War. He went to the FBI and began to systematically implicate his former colleagues in a communist conspiracy to undermine the foreign policy of the United States. Yergan claimed that Robeson and Robeson's chief ally, W. Alphaeus Hunton, "met repeatedly with the CP leadership and members of the Soviet Consulate in New York to determine how best to funnel money into the anti-apartheid movement in South Africa. He further offered that, under direct Soviet guidance and supervision, Hunton prepared reports 'regarding the treatment of the Negro both in the US and Africa,' which were then used by 'the Russian delegation at the United Nations . . . to attack British and American imperialism and discrimination against Negroes.'" Yergan insisted that one of the main conduits of this activity was the on-going relationship that Hunton had established with Soviet vice-consul Pavel I. Fedosimov and a cadre of communists and Africans in the UN, who had telephoned Hunton at the CAA's office on a regular basis.[49]

Yergan, however, was not yet done in trying to bolster his anti-communist credentials and his value to the Cold War–obsessed American government. He clearly understood, as the FBI shielded him from prosecution for extortion in exchange for his willingness to bring down the Council on African Affairs, that he could enjoy substantial legal protection and economic comfort by undermining the struggle for African liberation.[50] In a cover story in the May 1953 issue of *US News & World Report*, Yergan strongly supported the South African government's policy of apartheid, which created a migratory, disfranchised African labor pool used to extract uranium, diamonds, and gold from South Africa's mines. Without this cheap source of expendable labor, Yergan proffered, South Africa's considerable resources would remain unmined and unavailable for the economic and military defense of the West.[51]

Then, echoing a theme that played throughout U.S. foreign policy, which could not evaluate liberation movements as anything but Soviet-inspired, "America's Foremost Authority on Africa" claimed that the anti-apartheid movement, led by the African National Congress (ANC) and the Indian National Congress, was actually controlled by communists. And, as he made clear to the FBI, a considerable portion of the funding came from the Soviets and was laundered through the Council on African Affairs.

Yergan's support of apartheid and his eagerness to depict every attempt at black equality as communist-directed, did not end with South Africa. For example, he supported the unilateral declaration of independence by the white minority government of Rhodesia, even though this break from England was an act of defiance against British insistence on some level of racial equality as a condition for liberation. Yergan simply saw white anti-communist rule as vastly superior to African freedom.[52] The Congo also attracted his close attention. Through a well-financed ultra-conservative organization, he backed Moise Tshombe's separatist movement in the Katanga Province of the Congo, which would have severed that uranium-rich area from the rest of the country and the leadership of Soviet-educated Patrice Lumumba.[53]

The African American leadership, therefore, rightfully suspected that Yergan wanted to be tapped as "the 'expert' on Africa"—the State Department's own personal black gunslinger, who would publicly shoot down all liberation movements as communistic. Yergan, in fact, explained to his FBI handlers that although he was willing to serve as an informant, he did not want to testify in open court because it "would betray the confidence placed in him by certain African leaders. . . . adversely affect his work and goal as being recognized as an authority on African affairs," and "adversely affect the freedom which he has enjoyed up until the present in conducting interviews with young Africans concerning matters of communist infiltration in that area."[54]

Walter White, executive secretary of the NAACP, was visibly furious at Yergan. The association leader told Indian Prime Minister Jawaharlal Nehru that using a black, red-baiting front man for white supremacy was a time-honored strategy to divert attention away from the real cause of "unrest in . . . Africa. . . . hunger, frustration, colonialism, and racism."[55] White, therefore, set out to discredit the apologist for apartheid with a fiery letter to the *New York Times,* in which the executive secretary of the NAACP questioned virtually every shred of Yergan's career, motives, and commitment to anything and anyone but Max Yergan. Yergan's stinging response was quick and vicious. He publicly accused the NAACP and Walter White of attacking him, a patriot and true American, because the Association was cavorting with and shielding Fifth Amendment communists. That charge, which Yergan repeated to powerful Southern Democrats and members of the House Un-American Activities Committee, may help explain why it has been so difficult to understand the role of the nonleftist, progressive organizations in the African liberation struggles of the early Cold War. While left-wing organizations such as the Council on African Affairs were stool-pigeoned and prosecuted out of existence, and while former communists and African liberation supporters such as Max Yergan were baptized in the waters of the Cold War and became right-wing, born-again Americans, the activities of organizations such as the NAACP were much more subtle and therefore difficult to assess. Many historians, for example, contend that the onset of the Cold War compelled the Association not only to distance itself from the liberation movements in Africa but also, in a deal with the so-called American devil, to sell its soul (and sell out the struggle) to the U.S. government. The purported deal was simple. In exchange for silence on U.S. Cold War policies, including the support of the European colonial empires, the NAACP was to receive a dribble of civil rights concessions to buy off its discontented African American constituency.[56]

That, however, is not the case. Once the Cold War began, the Association astutely refined its tactics, chose its battles, and fought hard for the freedom of Africans, even when the State Department labeled the leaders of those liberation movements as "Communists." Because of the rabid anti-communism that dominated the American political landscape at the time, the NAACP's decision to align with these liberation struggles put the Association's reputation, access to the foreign policy inner circle, and domestic civil rights agenda at risk. But the NAACP forged ahead, nonetheless. Walter White insisted that "[w]hat is going on in the Union of South Africa, Nigeria, the former Italian colonies, Liberia and East Africa have in it the seeds of either disaster or freedom as has no other place in the world today."[57]

To avoid disaster and ensure freedom, the NAACP, decidedly anti-communist but fully aware of the degradation that raw capitalism brought to people of color, posited a "third way" of post-colonial nation building. Just like Mboya and Nyerere, the NAACP argued that human rights had to serve as the foundation for the political and economic transformation of colonies into nations. Without human rights, the Association contended, Africans would be unable to find any sense of justice and hope in their societies, political extremism would take root, and the result would be an endless cycle of violence, repression, deprivation, and war. Convinced that State Department officials such as George Kennan were wrong to disparage human rights as no more than Wilsonian idealism and irrelevant to national security, the NAACP responded that without human rights there could be no national security because, in the end, there would be no international security.[58]

Determined to elevate Africans' human rights to a national security issue, the Association capitalized on the government's eagerness to place "some outstanding Negro leaders" in high-profile positions on the American delegation to the United Nations, a move designed by the State Department to counter the negative publicity reverberating throughout the multi-racial colonial world about America's Jim Crow democracy. In many ways, the NAACP played its role as an "American organization" to perfection.[59] In return, the State Department rewarded the Association with prized spots on the delegation overseeing decolonization. With its hard-won entree into the corridors of power secured, the NAACP leadership used its position on the UN's Fourth Committee (Trusteeship) and influence with other progressive non-communist organizations to aid the liberation struggles in Namibia, Eritrea, Somalia, Libya, Kenya, Indonesia, and Tunisia.[60]

The significance of the NAACP's involvement is not just that the largest, most powerful civil rights organization was actively involved in trying to create a world free from colonial oppression. It is also important to assess why the Association was able to become so actively and effectively involved given the U.S. government's Cold War obsession and the McCarthyist witch hunts that had destroyed so many other anti-colonial advocates in the United States.

First and foremost was the nature of the NAACP itself. From a national perspective (as distinct from a southern viewpoint) the NAACP's devotion to the United States was simply unimpeachable, regardless of how hard Yergan and other supporters of white supremacy had tried to suggest otherwise. The Association's "Americanness" provided a level of protection from the McCarthy witch hunts that was unavailable to members of the black Left. That "Americanness," however, drew the line at racial inequality. Therefore, when both South Africa and former Nazi-ally Italy, pariah nations with horrific histories of human rights violations against people of color, demanded African territory in exchange for aligning with the anti-Soviet bloc, the NAACP fought to discredit these alliances and stop the transfer of African people and territory into the hands of white supremacists. The NAACP's refusal to tolerate racial inequality, even in the name of national security, gave it the moral compass that the black champion of apartheid, Max Yergan, never had.

The second factor that enabled the NAACP to move with a degree of political freedom was American ambivalence about colonialism. Despite its holdings in the Caribbean and the Far East, the United States simply did not consider itself a colonial power. Instead, the Americans maintained that they were merely caretaking, not colonizing, and pointed to the independence the United States granted the Philippines in 1946 to distinguish American administration of "dependent areas" from the less visionary actions of the Europeans. The British, therefore, worried aloud that the United States could neither be totally relied upon to "keep Negro Africa in its place" nor to admit that "colonialism is not necessarily a bad thing."[61] The NAACP leadership also sensed the American reluctance to be a full-fledged colonial power, understood that communism—not colonialism—was the prime motivator behind American actions in Africa, and exploited the contradictions and ambivalence in U.S. policy to assist the colonial liberation struggles.

The founding of the United Nations and its evolution into a powerful anticolonialist advocate was the third factor aiding the NAACP's surprising nimbleness. Although in the UN's initial incarnation the West believed that it had crafted an international organization with little or no authority in the colonial realm, the emergence of India as a power player within the UN, the coalescence of an Afro-Asian bloc of votes in the general assembly, and the creation of a number of anti-colonial committees that could not be easily controlled by the Western powers changed all of that. The Ad Hoc Committee on South West Africa, the Committee on Information from Non-Self-Governing Territories, and a host of others "turned the spotlight of international opinion on the colonial problem as it never had been turned before."[62]

Ironically, the Soviets were also essential in fostering the Association's internationalism. Not surprisingly, they hindered it as well. While the Kremlin eagerly backed the dissolution of the colonial empires, Moscow could not tolerate the sine qua non of national viability: human rights. On this issue, oddly enough, the United States and the USSR stood together. Because of America's

Jim Crow democracy on one hand, and Soviet pogroms, purges, and gulag system on the other, the superpowers jointly created, inserted, and then used the "domestic jurisdiction" clause in the UN Charter to prevent that organization from seriously investigating allegations of human rights violations. On the issue of colonialism, however, while the United States remained ambivalent and, thus, neutralized, the Soviets forged an alliance with the Afro-Asian delegates in the UN and chipped away at the imperial powers' claims of domestic jurisdiction in colonial affairs. This determined effort culminated in the UN's 1960 Declaration on the Granting of Independence to Colonial Countries and Peoples. It was, however, only a partial victory.

Despite the NAACP's attempt to fuse the struggle for human rights and the political liberation of colonial peoples into one movement, the stark disjuncture between the two goes to the core of the North-South issues that dominated questions about the place of newly emerged nations in the international system. The major industrialized powers' resistance to internationally enforceable human rights created a malformed hybrid that could countenance some level of political independence for colonial peoples but could provide no real support for the economic and cultural protections embodied in human rights. Thus, with no powerful nation serving as a champion for international human rights, with vulnerable populations in Asia and Africa being pulled into the labor vortex of modernization and a global economy, and with the exigencies of the Cold War leading the superpowers to "lend credibility to some of the worst leaders the world has ever known," repressive dictatorships, omnipresent violence, and grinding poverty were the results in all too many of the emerging nations.[63]

In short, America's Cold War fixation meant that the United States was not ideologically, politically, or culturally ready for the emergence of independent African nations. The U.S. representative on the UN Trusteeship Council, Mason Sears, perhaps feeling as insightful and as helpless as the mythical Cassandra, thus predicted that "there is going to be real trouble in Africa." The United States was on the wrong side. Instead of shutting off trade to the racially repressive regime in South Africa and bringing "the Nationalist Government to its knees," instead of valuing the goodwill and political benefits that would accrue from the Afro-Asian bloc for supporting America's oft-quoted commitment to self-determination, equality, and democracy, the United States had chosen instead to place a premium on gold, uranium, and anti-communism. Sears expressed his frustration that the United States would risk it all in the name of the Cold War by aligning its foreign policy with white supremacy. "In a continent of 200 million people it is ridiculous and out of all proportion," he asserted, "that a handful of perhaps less than 20,000 white die-hards in Colonial territories and say 2,000,000 split between the [colonies] of North Africa and the Afrikan [Boers] of South Africa can provide the flame to spark an international colonial-race issue which has become damaging in the extreme to the leading powers of the free world, including the United States."[64] But there the United States stood, in the middle of the flames of nationalism, looking for communists.

Notes

1. For the "Scramble," see David Levering Lewis, *Race to Fashoda: Colonialism and African Resistance* (reprint, New York: Henry Holt, 2001).

2. Kenneth J. Twitchett, "The Colonial Powers and the United Nations," *Journal of Contemporary History* 4:1 (January 1969): 167.

3. Adam Hochschild, *King Leopold's Ghost: A Story of Greed, Terror, and Heroism in Colonial Africa* (New York: Houghton Mifflin, 1999); Jeremy Silvester and Jan-Bart Gewald, *Words Cannot Be Found: German Colonial Rule in Namibia, An Annotated Reprint of the 1918 Blue Book* (Boston: Brill, 2003); Haile M. Larebo, *The Building of an Empire: Italian Land Policy and Practice in Ethiopia, 1935–1941* (Oxford: Clarendon Press, 1994), 18–27; I. M. Lewis, *A Modern History of Somalia: Nation and State in the Horn of Africa*, 2nd ed., (Boulder, Colo.: Westview Press, 1988), 92–95, 97, 111; "Memorandum to the United Nations from the Somali Delegation on the Future of Ex-Italian Somaliland," September 19, 1949, found in Reel 64, Papers of W. E. B. Du Bois (Sanford, N.C.: Microfilming, 1979), microfilm; "Report on Tripolitania: February 26–March 8, 1946," April 8, 1946, Box 6968, 865C.00/4–846, RG 59: Records of the Department of State, National Archives II, College Park, Md. (hereafter RG 59); Stephen R. Shalom, "The United States and Libya, Part 1: Before Qaddafi," Z (May 1990): 2.

4. Kwame Nkrumah, *Towards Colonial Freedom: Africa in the Struggle against World Imperialism* (London: Heinemann, 1962), ix; Kwame Nkrumah to Walter White, June 9, 1953, Box A4, File "Africa: General, 1952–53," Papers of the NAACP, Library of Congress, Washington, D.C.

5. Steven Metz, "US Attitudes toward Decolonization in Africa," *Political Science Quarterly* 99:3 (Fall 1984): 519.

6. Quoted in Brenda Gayle Plummer, *Rising Wind: Black Americans and US Foreign Affairs, 1935–1960* (Chapel Hill: University of North Carolina Press, 1996), frontispiece.

7. Richard M. Fontera, "Anti-Colonialism as a Basic Indian Foreign Policy," *Western Political Quarterly* 13:2 (June 1960): 423–424; Harold Karan Jacobson, "The United Nations and Colonialism: A Tentative Appraisal," *International Organization* 16:1 (Winter 1962): 37–56; "Measures to Counteract Adverse Effect of United Nations Voting against the UK over Colonies," CO 537/6568, Public Records Office/National Archives, Kew, United Kingdom.

8. South-West Africa Cases (Second Phase), Judgment of July 18, 1966, International Court of Justice, http://www.icj-cij.org/docket/index.php?p1=3&p2=3&k=f2&case=47&code=:S&p3=4 (accessed June 15, 2007); Matthew Connelly, *A Diplomatic Revolution: Algeria's Fight for Independence and the Origins of the Post–Cold War Era* (New York: Oxford University Press, 2002); Homer Jack, "Angola: Repression and Revolt in Portuguese Africa" (New York: American Committee on Africa, 1962).

9. "The Role of the United Nations in African Development," Box 1, File "26: Speeches and Writings: 'The Role of the United Nations in African Development, ca. 1960,'" Papers of Benjamin Gerig, Library of Congress, Washington, D.C.

10. Melvyn P. Leffler, *A Preponderance of Power: National Security, the Truman Administration, and the Cold War* (Palo Alto, Calif.: Stanford University Press, 1993).

11. On the symbolic power of the American Revolution see Michael Hunt, *Ideology and U.S. Foreign Policy* (New Haven, Conn.: Yale University Press, 1988); "Remarks

by the Honorable Francis B. Sayre," Press Release No. 244, October 2, 1947, in which he quotes Truman: "We are living in a time of profound and swiftly moving change. We see colonial peoples moving toward their independence. It is a process that we, as Americans, can understand and sympathize with, since it parallels our own struggle for independence." Quote found in Box 13, File "United Nations: Statements-Press Release," Papers of Francis B. Sayre, Library of Congress, Washington, D.C.; Francis B. Sayre to Harry S Truman, February 18, 1947, Box 12, File "United Nations: Correspondence, 1946–52," Papers of Francis B. Sayre; James Meriwether, *Proudly We Can Be Africans: Black Americans and Africa, 1935–1961* (Chapel Hill: University of North Carolina Press, 2002), 69–70.

12. Nkrumah, *Towards Colonial Freedom*, 43.

13. Mason Sears, *Years of High Purpose: From Trusteeship to Nationhood*, with a preface by Henry Cabot Lodge and an introduction by Julius Nyerere (Washington, D.C.: University Press of America, 1980), 22.

14. Bob Deindorfer, "Africa: Hot Spot for Red Propaganda," *Look*, 1951, found in Box A4, File "Africa: General, 1950–51," Papers of the NAACP.

15. Metz, "American Attitudes Toward Decolonization in Africa," 521.

16. "Address of the President at the National Conference on International Economic and Social Development," April 8, 1952, Box 61, File "Foreign Relations—Point IV (Conference)," Papers of George M. Elsey, Harry S. Truman Presidential Library.

17. Metz, "American Attitudes Toward Decolonization in Africa," 521–522; Francis B. Sayre, "The Problem of Underdeveloped Areas in Asia and Africa," Proceedings of the American Academy of Arts and Sciences 81:6 (April 9, 1952): 292, found in Box 13, File "United Nations: Printed Matter," Papers of Francis B. Sayre; Carol Anderson, *Eyes off the Prize: The United Nations and the African American Struggle for Human Rights, 1944–1955* (New York: Cambridge University Press, 2003), 50.

18. National Educational Television Presents Mrs. Eleanor Roosevelt: Prospects of Mankind, Program #6 B, *Africa: Revolution in Haste*, Box 1, File "Africa: Revolution in Haste, Script/Schedule/Background Info," *Papers of Henry Morgenthau III*, Franklin D. Roosevelt Presidential Library, Hyde Park, N.Y.

19. "Gold Coast's Claim to Immediate Independence," 1955, Box 14, File, "1: Writings by Kwame Nkrumah—Speeches and Statements: 1955, Gold Coast's Claim to Immediate Independence, Speech made in the National Assembly," Papers of Kwame Nkrumah, Moorland-Spingarn Research Center, Howard University, Washington, D.C.

20. Mary Renda, *Taking Haiti: Military Occupation and the Culture of U.S. Imperialism, 1951–1940* (Chapel Hill: University of North Carolina Press, 2001); Brenda Gayle Plummer, *Haiti and the United States: The Psychological Moment* (Athens: University of Georgia Press, 1992); Hugh Smythe to Rayford W. Logan, April 16, 1950, Box 20, File "15: Correspondence, Smythe, Hugh," Papers of Rayford W. Logan, Moorland-Spingarn Research Center, Howard University, Washington, D.C.; Michael L. Krenn, *Black Diplomacy: African Americans and the State Department, 1945–1969* (Armonk, N.Y.: M. E. Sharpe, 1999).

21. Roy Wilkins of the NAACP saw this same dichotomy on the domestic scene. "When Hungarians resist [Soviet] oppression," he remarked, "they are called heroes; when American Negroes legally and peacefully resist oppression they are called agitators. Our government sends observers to Hungary, organizes airlifts, sets up refugee camps, and opens immigration doors; but it does not say a mumbling word to the Deep South states about persecution, nor does it offer to aid a single black refugee." Address of Roy

Wilkins, New York City, executive secretary of the National Association for the Advancement of Colored People, at closing mass meeting of 48th Annual NAACP Convention, June 30, 1957, Box 94–13, File "333: Wilkins, Roy," Papers of Arthur B. Spingarn, Moorland Spingarn Research Center, Howard University, Washington, D.C.

22. Robert C. Johnson, Jr., to The Honorable Secretary of State [James F. Byrnes], October 10, 1946, 848L.5045/10–1046, Reel 4, US Confidential State Department Central Files: British Africa, 1945–1949 (Bethesda, Md.: University Publications of America); James M. Gilchrist, Jr., to The Honorable Secretary of State [Edward Stettinius], June 9, 1945, 848L.5045/6–945, ibid.

23. Fifth Message from Harriman, September 14, 1960, Box 430, File "Africa Visit, 1960," Papers of W. Averell Harriman, Library of Congress, Washington, D.C.

24. E. Talbot Smith to The Honorable Secretary of State [George C. Marshall], January 19, 1948, 848N.00/1–1948, Reel 5, British Africa, 1945–49.

25. National Educational Television Presents Mrs. Eleanor Roosevelt, Papers of Henry Morgenthau III.

26. Julius Nyerere to A. Philip Randolph, Box 4, File "Africa, 1949–68 + undated," Papers of Asa Philip Randolph, Library of Congress, Washington, D.C.

27. "Mboya Explains African Goals on U.S Tour," *Africa: Special Report* 4:4 (April 1959): 2, found in, Box 4, File "15: State Department: Africa, 1956–59," Papers of Benjamin Gerig; Tom Mboya, *Freedom and After* (London: Andre Deutsch, 1963), 163–203.

28. Harriman conversations with Sekou Touré, n.d., ca. August 1960, Box 430, File "Africa Visit, 1960," Papers of W. Averell Harriman.

29. Z. A. Shipanga, S. D. Haitengy, D. Muya, and John Cembo to K. C. Zonguizi, n.d., ca. 1961, File "2/17/3," Ruth First Papers, Institute of Commonwealth Studies, University of London, London, England (emphasis in original).

30. George W. White Jr., *Holding the Line: Race, Racism, and American Foreign Policy, 1953–1961* (New York: Rowman and Littlefield, 2005), 74.

31. Thomas Borstelmann, "Apartheid, Colonialism, and the Cold War: The United States and Southern Africa, 1945–52," Ph.D. diss., Duke University, 1990, 97–98.

32. Transcript of Background Press and Radio News Briefing, November 30, 1960, Box 6, File "Africa Trip, 1960," Papers of Loy Henderson, Library of Congress, Washington, D.C.

33. Wallace Irwin, Jr., to Richard L. Sneider, memo, August 27, 1953, Box 24, File "PSB 334 UN (8)," White House Office, National Security Council Staff: Papers, 1953–61, PSB Central Files Series, Dwight D. Eisenhower Presidential Library, Abilene, Kansas; Cary Fraser, "An America Dilemma: Race and Realpolitik in the American Response to the Bandung Conference, 1955," in *Window on Freedom: Race, Civil Rights, and Foreign Affairs, 1945–1988*, ed. Brenda Gayle Plummer (Chapel Hill: University of North Carolina Press, 2003), 116; Roy P. McNair to the Executive Officer, Operations Coordinating Board, memo, January 21, 1955, Box 85, File "OCB 092.3 [International Affairs Conferences and Boards] (File #1) (9) [January 1954–April 1955], White House Office, National Security Council Staff: Papers, 1948–61, OCB Central File Series, DDE; "A Transcript of Background Press and Radio News Briefing," November 30, 1960, Box 6, File "Africa Trip, 1960," Papers of Loy Henderson; Discussion at the Meeting of the National Security Council, memo, April 8, 1955, Box 6, File "244th Meeting of NSC April 7, 1955," Dwight D. Eisenhower: Papers as President, 1953–61 (Ann Whitman File), NSC Series, DDE.

34. Study Outline: United States Policy and the Colonial Question, January 23,

1956, Box 1, File "26: Speeches and Writings: United States Policy and the Colonial Question," Papers of Benjamin Gerig.

35. Fraser, "An America Dilemma," 117–118; Discussion at the Meeting of the National Security Council, memo, April 8, 1955, Box 6, File "244th Meeting of NSC April 7, 1955," Eisenhower: Ann Whitman File, NSC Series, DDE.

36. Gerig to Key, April 19, 1955, Box 4, File "16: State Department Colonial Policy: Memoranda and Correspondence including Alger Hiss Letter of 1945 on Yalta Conference," Papers of Benjamin Gerig; Key to Murphy, memo, April 20, 1955, ibid.; William J. Sebald to Murphy, April 27, 1955, ibid.

37. James M. Gilchrist, Jr. to The Honorable Secretary of State [Edward Stettinius], June 23, 1945, 848L.5045/6–2345, Reel 4, British Africa, 1945–1949; James M. Gilchrist, Jr. to The Honorable Secretary of State, July 6, 1945, 848L.5045/7–645, ibid.; Robert C. Johnson, Jr., to The Honorable Secretary of State [James F. Byrnes], October 10, 1946, 848L.5045/10–1046, ibid.

38. Central Intelligence Agency, "The Break-Up of the Colonial Empires and Its Implications for US Security," September 3, 1948, Box 214, File "Central Intelligence Reports: O.R.E.: 1948: 21–29 [April 2–November 9]," Papers of Harry S Truman: Personal Secretary File: Intelligence File, Harry S Truman Presidential Library, Independence, Mo.

39. "United States Attitude on the Colonial Question," n.d., Box 1, File "25: Speeches and Writings: United States Attitude on the Colonial Question," Papers of Benjamin Gerig.

40. Notes for Report, n.d., ca. September 1960, Box 430, File "Africa Visit, 1960," Papers of W. Averell Harriman.

41. Ibid. For Eisenhower's sluggish response to civil rights see Anderson, *Eyes off the Prize,* 211–215, 267–269; Kenneth O'Reilly, "Racial Integration: The Battle General Eisenhower Chose Not to Fight," *Journal of Blacks in Higher Education,* no. 18 (Winter, 1997–1998): 110; Michael L. Krenn, "Unfinished Business: Segregation and US Diplomacy at the 1958 World's Fair," *Diplomatic History* 20:4 (Fall 1996): 591–612.

42. Rayford W. Logan, "United States Policy toward African 'Neutralism' and 'Cold-War' Competition," Conference of American Committee on Africa, March 10, 1951, Box 26, File "71: Speeches, 1951, March 10, 'Neutralism' and 'Cold War' Competition," Papers of Rayford Logan.

43. Byron K. Enyart to Charles H. Taquey, memo, May 14, 1953, Box 18, File, "PSB 093," White House Office, National Security Council Staff: Papers, 1953–61, PSB Central Files Series; Charles H. Taquey to Acting Director of the Psychological Strategy Board, memo, August 24, 1953, ibid.

44. Key to Murphy, memo, April 20, 1955, Box 4, File "16: State Department Colonial Policy: Memoranda and Correspondence including Alger Hiss Letter of 1945 on Yalta Conference," Papers of Benjamin Gerig.

45. Donald Harrington and Judge J. Waties Waring to Friend, April 9, 1955, Box 3, File "Africa: American Committee," Papers of Asa Philip Randolph.

46. "Background Statement: Effect of the Reported Point IV Appropriations Cut," attached to Capus M. Waynick to W. Averell Harriman, July 7, 1950, Box 309, File "Point IV Program," Papers of W. Averell Harriman.

47. White, *Holding the Line,* 22.

48. Penny M. Von Eschen, *Race against Empire: Black Americans and Anticolonialism, 1937–1957* (Ithaca, N.Y.: Cornell University Press, 1997).

49. Anderson, *Eyes off the Prize*, 261–62.

50. David H. Anthony III, "Max Yergan and South Africa: A Transatlantic Interaction," in *Imagining Home: Class, Culture, and Nationalism in the African Diaspora*, ed. Sidney Lemelle and Robin D. G. Kelley (New York: Verso, 1994).

51. "Africa: Next Goal of Communists—an Interview with Dr. Max Yergan, America's Foremost Authority on Africa," *US News & World Report*, May 1, 1953.

52. Certificate of Appreciation, Box 1, File "30: Rhodesian Certificate, 1966," Papers of Max Yergan, Moorland-Spingarn Research Center, Howard University, Washington, D.C.

53. See Box 9, File "9: American Committee for Aid to Katanga Freedom Fighters, Correspondence," ibid.; "Goldwater Joins [James O.] Eastland, and Yergan in Outcries Against Unity in Congo," January 26, 1963, Box 1, File "Personal Papers—Newspapers articles about Yergan, 1952–1958," ibid.

54. Boardman to Bureau, teletype, November 16, 1953, FBI File on Max Yergan, Federal Bureau of Investigation, Washington, D.C. [FOIA]; SAC, New York, to Director, FBI, memo, June 12, 1957, ibid.; SAC, New York, memo, March 14, 1955, ibid.

55. Walter White to Jawaharlal Nehru, May 4, 1953, Box 675, File "Max Yergan, 1941–53," Papers of the NAACP.

56. Gerald Horne, *Black and Red: W .E .B. Du Bois and the Afro-American Response to the Cold War, 1944–1963* (Albany: State University of New York Press, 1986), 56; W. E. B. Du Bois to George Padmore, April 7, 1949, Papers of W. E. B. Du Bois, Reel 64; James Roark, "American Black Leaders: The Response to Colonialism and the Cold War, 1945–1953," *African Historical Studies* 4 (1971): 253–270; Robert L. Harris Jr., "Ralph Bunche and Afro-American Participation in Decolonization," in *The African American Voice in U.S. Foreign Policy since World War II*, ed. Michael L. Krenn (New York: Garland, 1999), 177; Von Eschen, *Race against Empire*, 107–118; Plummer, *Rising Wind*, 174–175, 178, 184, 188; Meriwether, *Proudly We Can Be Africans*, 2, 3–4, 83, 89; Kenneth Janken, *White: The Biography of Walter White, Mr. NAACP* (New York: New Press, 2003); idem, "From Colonial Liberation to Cold War Liberalism: Walter White, the NAACP, and Foreign Affairs, 1941–1955," *Ethnic and Racial Studies* 21:6 (November 1998): 1074–1075.

57. Walter White to Horace Mann Bond, October 25, 1950, Box A4, File "Africa: General, 1950–51," Papers of the NAACP.

58. Walter White to Chester Williams, October 25, 1948, Box 8, Folder "3," Papers of Rayford Logan; Walter White to Arthur [Spingarn], n.d., ca. February 1950, Box 6, File "Spingarn, Arthur B.," Walter Francis White and Poppy Cannon White Correspondence, Beinecke Rare Book and Manuscript Library, Yale University, New Haven, Conn.

59. Mary Dudziak, *Cold War Civil Rights: Race and the Image of American Democracy* (Princeton, N.J.: Princeton University Press, 2000); Thomas Borstelmann, *The Cold War and the Color Line: American Race Relations in the Global Arena* (Cambridge, Mass.: Harvard University Press, 2001); Walter White to Paul Hoffman, November 29, 1951, Box 636, File "Genocide," Papers of the NAACP; Anderson, *Eyes off the Prize*, 175–176, 186–188, 192–193.

60. Thomas Borstelmann, *Apartheid's Reluctant Uncle* (New York: Oxford University Press, 1993), 162; Tobias to White, November 12, 1952, Part 14, Reel 4, Papers of the NAACP in the International Arena; Summary Record of the 138th Meeting, November 27, 1949, A.C.4/SR/138, Box 81, File "Committee IV," Charles Fahy Papers, Franklin D. Roosevelt Presidential Library, Hyde Park, N.Y.; Provisional Verbatim

Record, September 28, 1953, A/PV.448, File "CO 936/97," PRO; Jones to Hickerson, Nov. 30, 1951, Box 2, File "6th General Assembly," RG 59; UK Delegation to the Foreign Office, November 23, 1951, File "CO 537/7137," PRO; UK Delegation to the Foreign Office, November 24, 1951, ibid.; Michael Scott, "South West African Referendum," n.d., Box 13, File "'S' (Folder 2)," Truman: Nash Papers, Harry S. Truman Library, Independence, Mo.; Walter White to Bureau of Immigration and Naturalization Service, July 23, 1954, Box A5, File "Africa: Kenya, 1952–55," Papers of the NAACP; "Land Hunger Seen as Crux of Kenya Issue," April 29, 1954, ibid.

61. Winston Churchill to Anthony Eden, August 8, 1952, File "PREM 11/300," PRO; Memorandum of Conversation, September 23, 1948, Box 55, File "US(P)/A/1–70," Record Group 84: Records of the US Mission to Foreign Posts, National Archives II, College Park, Md.

62. National Educational Television Presents Mrs. Eleanor Roosevelt: Prospects of Mankind, Program #6: Africa: Revolution in Haste, Box 1, File "Africa: Revolution in Haste, Script/Schedule/Background Info," Papers of Henry Morgenthau III.

63. Mark Huband, *The Skull beneath the Skin: Africa after the Cold War* (Boulder, Colo.: Westview Press, 2001), xi; Douglas Little, *American Orientalism: The United States and the Middle East since 1945* (Chapel Hill: University of North Carolina Press, 2002); Michael Wrong, *In the Footsteps of Mr. Kurtz: Living on the Brink of Disaster in Mobutu's Congo* (New York: Perennial, 2002); David F. Schmitz, *Thank God They're on Our Side: The United States and Right-Wing Dictatorships, 1921–1965* (Chapel Hill: University of North Carolina Press, 1999).

64. Mason Sears to Henry Cabot Lodge, Jr., memo, February 13, 1956, Box 2, File "PMS Africa 1955 (Notes/Misc.)," Papers of Mason Sears, Massachusetts Historical Society, Boston, Massachusetts.

CHAPTER FOURTEEN

Gender and Identity in the Twentieth-Century Atlantic World

Amanda Warnock

If, by the mid-nineteenth century, with the decline and ultimate suppression of the African slave trade, the theoretical construction of the "Atlantic World" shifts from regular, human linkages to infrequent contact and cultural vestiges, by the beginning of the twentieth century we find it even more ephemeral. The advent of modernity, as characterized by the extension of European colonialism, an increase in capitalist modes of production, and the ideology of liberalism, penetrated virtually every corner of the globe and shaped relations at all levels of society. While peoples throughout Africa and the Americas experienced some of the same effects of the integration of their nations into the orbits of the colonial and neo-colonial powers, these consequences were not confined to the Atlantic World, as it is traditionally understood by scholars of the fifteenth through nineteenth centuries. In recent contributions to the theoretical parameters of the African Diaspora, scholars have elaborated the many, diverse migrations taking place shortly prior to and for decades following abolition, and of the intertwined cultural destinies of people of African descent with migrants from other world regions arriving in the Americas as the result of the same processes.[1] Although a history of the twentieth century could include a discussion of, for example, the interactions between African descendants and South and East Asian migrants in the Caribbean, in the interest of maintaining geographic continuity, this chapter treats the Atlantic World as commonly conceptualized for the earlier period.

This piece discusses the admittedly broad subject of gender and racial identity in the twentieth-century Atlantic World. Although "gender" implies a conceptual framework that takes into account both women and men as historical actors as well as culturally constructed notions of female-ness and male-ness, the primary focus of the analysis is on how the profound social, economic, cultural, and political changes of the century have helped to shape the experiences of African and African-descendant women and their families.[2]

Following the abolition of slavery in the Americas and West Central Africa, Africans and African-descendant peoples remained committed to forming and maintaining their family units and lineage structures. In the wake of emancipation in the United States, one of the first actions of freed people was to leave plantations and search for family members who had fled or been sold away. Many freed people opted to remove women from the labor force with the idea of protecting the family unit.[3] In the case of Brazil, freed men and women aggressively sought to protect women and children from labor exploitation, in many cases removing them from wage labor altogether.[4] Much of the scholarship on West Central Africa as well supports the contention that, despite the effects of European colonialism, family and kinship groupings remained the main social channels through which women have constructed their own identities.

Yet, the twentieth century saw inconsistent gains for African and African-descendant women. Historically, African women have rarely organized themselves on the basis of sex. Rather, they have more frequently sought avenues for political participation within their family or lineage group or promoted an elite vision of social change and, in doing so, neglected to traverse boundaries of socioeconomic class to develop a broad, female-centered coalition. However, in the last decades of the century, women, facing vastly deteriorated circumstances as a result of World Bank– and International Monetary Fund–imposed stabilization and structural adjustment programs, combined with a pattern of mismanagement and corruption of national governments, have increasingly reached out to project a powerful call for change. While women throughout the Atlantic World began and ended the century obstructed by barriers of racism, sexism, and an economic position well below that of Europeans and European descendants, they have developed strategies for survival and political action that have begun to generate positive, albeit thus far limited, reforms for women and their families.

I divide the following discussion into two sections, which comprise the majority of Atlantic regions that provided and received enslaved Africans during the epoch of the transatlantic trade. The first covers the experiences of women in the United States, Latin America, and the Caribbean (particularly the United States, Brazil, and the Spanish Caribbean), and the second, West Central Africa, with a focus on the region that comprises present-day Nigeria. Due to the divergent political trajectories of the regions under scrutiny, the sub-themes and periodization differ considerably. However, the reader will note similarities, particularly regarding the processes of urbanization, family formation, and labor force participation. Addressing the wider-reaching impact of these trends remains beyond the scope of this work, but I refer the interested reader to several outstanding works in the bibliography.

Research on Gender and the Diaspora

While the title of this chapter implicitly assumes that this category "Atlantic World" remains conceptually legitimate in the twentieth century, a short review of the academic literature will be helpful in assessing the ways in which scholars have framed debates on the boundaries of Atlantic World history during this period and how gender, as a historical variable, has been addressed within this scholarship.

The pioneering work of W. E. B. Du Bois on the theoretical boundaries of the African Diaspora provided a model for subsequent scholarship that treats African descendants as part of a broad, international community rooted, metaphorically and geographically, in Africa. Contemporaries of Du Bois such as Melville Herskovits, Trinidad's C. L. R. James, Brazil's Raimundo Nina Rodrigues, and Cuba's Fernando Ortiz, to name but a few, expanded Du Bois's emphasis on the diasporic heritage of Africans in the Americas.[5] Although these scholars and others superficially addressed the unique circumstances of African and African-descendant women in the Americas, their analyses emphasized the shared experience of African-ness while downplaying sexual difference and ignoring the unique experiences of women of color.

Since the 1970s scholars have turned attention to the distinct experiences of women within the Diaspora. Scholars such as Filomina Chioma Steady have emphasized African feminist models and their applicability for African American women. Re-published in 1996, the work of Rosalyn Terborg-Penn and Andrea Benton Rushing, editors of the anthology *Women in Africa and the African Diaspora: A Reader*, emphasizes the ongoing intellectual and cultural linkages between African women and their counterparts throughout the Americas.

Another recent trend in global studies explores the contemporary category of "third world," "developing world," or "global south." Studies of this nature view Africa, Latin America, and often Asia as a periphery, subject to exploitation at the hands of the powerful in the "first world" or post-industrial economies of the north. An emerging sub-set of this field specifically treats women as powerful local and global actors and gender as integral to understanding economics and underdevelopment. Recent collections in this vein include Lourdes Beneria's *Gender, Development, and Globalization: Economics as If People Mattered*, Janet Henshall Momsen and Vivian Kinnaird's *Different Places, Different Voices: Gender and Development in Africa, Asia and Latin America*, and Haleh Afshar and Stephanie Barrientos's *Women, Globalization and the Developing World*.

In addition to scholarly contributions to Atlantic World studies, cultural production such as literary anthologies, symposia, and gatherings associated with diasporic cultural heritage have taken place with increasing frequency over the last several decades. These cultural workers have produced a body of material that addresses the unique experience of women and how the sexuality, intellect, family, and labor of African-descendant women has been rendered in art, literature, and music, as well as scholarship.

While the last twenty years have seen a surge in academic investigation into issues of race, gender, and identity, significant questions remain to be answered. As the process of globalization generates economic linkages between people and communities around the world, academics have begun to examine how women envision themselves as members of communities, be they local, national, or international. Thus, a gendered analysis of twentieth-century Atlantic World cultures reveals the possibilities and potential for future academic inquiry.

Women in the Americas: Family, Work, and State Policy

During the twentieth century, nations throughout the Americas experienced social upheaval associated with changing gender roles. As post-emancipation societies transitioned to capitalist labor relations, women confronted new possibilities and limitations as waged workers. Although expanded educational opportunities and increasing urbanization led to the growth of a professional class, women and men of color remained disproportionately represented in the lowest-paying, least stable sectors of the economy, often performing manual and domestic labor shunned by white women and men. As one consequence of this process, women, particularly women of color, who remained marginalized under the evolving social and economic order, faced increased challenges in forming, maintaining, and providing for their families. Throughout much of Latin America, economic fluctuations associated with reliance on often-unstable international markets for export commodities ensured a consistent pattern of boom and bust cycles. Although the beneficiaries of the former were inevitably foreign investors and national elites, women bore a disproportionate share of the burden in times of market contraction. Soaring rents and prices for basic foodstuffs, shortages, inadequate social services such as health care and child care, and the frequent migrations of men to industrial and urban centers in search of work have been but several of the effects of twentieth-century capitalism and globalization of production and markets on women and families in Latin America.

In addition to the expansion of capitalist modes of production, a second, no less important, set of forces that have shaped gender and identity in the twentieth-century Atlantic World have been the ideological and cultural movements that have influenced and been influenced by changing ideas about race, gender, and sexuality. With nineteenth-century emancipation came the imperative of the dominant, white classes to justify the ongoing subjugation of people of color. From the mid- to late nineteenth century through the early twentieth century, white intellectuals cultivated the theories of Social Darwinism or scientific racism to explain and justify the continued hierarchy of lighter-skinned over darker-skinned peoples throughout the Atlantic World. Social Darwinism exercised a profound influence from the United States to Brazil to Cuba, promoting racial "whitening" in an effort to "outbreed" the African elements of their respective populations. Thus, the sexual and reproductive capacities of women of color occupied an important space in debates over race and national identity.

The convergence of this ideological environment with the post-emancipation labor shortage led governments, teamed with private business interests, to encourage white (ideally northern and western, but more often southern and eastern) European immigration to the Americas. This process resulted in the disembarkation of millions of individuals in Atlantic ports during the late nineteenth to the early twentieth centuries, altering the demographics of these nations' populations and reinforcing discrimination against African descendants.

The social, economic, cultural, and intellectual changes of the late nineteenth to early twentieth centuries contributed to a radical restructuring of all levels of social interaction, from family relations to workplace relations to relations between women and the state. As women of both African and European descent moved from primarily performing reproductive and household labor into remunerated positions in the formal labor market, their presence, rather than providing the means to uplift them and improve their circumstances, more often than not, reinforced the second-class position of women in a male-dominated marketplace. As women enter into trades in substantial numbers, their presence has historically driven down wages throughout the industry. The entrance of people of color into an industry has tended to depress wages in a similar manner. Within this context and with a few, rare exceptions, women of color have occupied, and continue to occupy, the lowest rung in the socioeconomic ladder in countries as diverse as Argentina, Brazil, Cuba, Venezuela, Colombia, and the United States.

Export-Led Growth, 1900–1929: A Gendered Approach

Latin American historians have characterized the first several decades of the twentieth century as a period of export-led growth for the region. Economies throughout the Americas which had formerly depended on slave and indentured labor to produce agricultural products for export looked for new sources of labor and new methods of production to meet the increasing demands of the industrializing economies of the United States and Europe. The expansion of agrarian capitalism had several profound effects on women and families.

Shifting arrangements of land tenure affected the participation of women in agriculture and prompted a series of rural to urban migrations in the late nineteenth and early twentieth centuries. In an effort to raise agricultural productivity and secure larger profits, landowners throughout Latin America and the Caribbean sought to increase the size of their holdings. Buttressed by national political elites and often bankrolled by foreign investors, plantations expanded by buying out smaller operations. In Brazil, small *fazenderos*, affected by the instability of rural land tenure, lost their ability to remain competitive with larger-scale producers of coffee and sugar. The displacement of small farmers led many to migrate to the industrializing regions of Rio de Janeiro and São Paulo. In Cuba as well, the expansion of North American capitalists into the sugar sector led to the drastic growth of sugar-producing operations. Foreign firms such as Cuba Cane, the Cuban American Sugar Mills Company, and the United Fruit Company increased their holdings and consequent political leverage while Cuban farmers made the decision to either go to work for a large operation or move to the city.[6]

A second consequence of the process of land consolidation and transition to wage work was the desire to seek out new, readily exploitable workers for agricultural and industrial employment. This search for cheap labor, combined with an ideology rooted in Social Darwinism that stressed "whitening" of populations, inspired collaborations between government and the private sector to recruit European men, women, and families. In the United States, workers came from Eastern and Southern Europe to work in the established industrial economies of the Northeast and upstart industrial centers such as Chicago. In Brazil, European immigrants, the majority being of Portuguese and Italian extraction, traveled to rural areas as well as to the industrial cities of São Paulo and, to a lesser extent, Rio de Janeiro. In Cuba, the U.S. military occupation enacted a policy to encourage the migration of tens of thousands of mostly single, Spanish men to work in the sugar industry.

A third effect of the boom-bust cycle of agrarian capitalism was the increasing desire of financiers to diversify holdings, leading at times to greater opportunities, and, frequently, greater exploitation for women of color. Following the "dance of the millions" of 1920–1921, the subsequent contraction of the sugar industry in the face of lessened demand following World War I, and competition from European beet sugar producers, the decade of the 1920s saw Cuban policymakers and their foreign (mostly U.S.) collaborators seek out new opportunities for extracting profits from their investments in the island. In the face of declining revenues from sugar and the recent passage of prohibition legislation in the United States, investors began developing the infrastructure for a tourist industry in Cuba. Central to the lure of Cuba as a tourist destination was the exoticized sexuality of Cuba's black and mixed-race (referred to as *mulata*) women. Advertising posters from this era depict the Cuban *mulata* as a commodified sexual object available for North American consumption.

Finally, the experience of migration, often at the behest of state governments and private enterprise, shaped family life for African-descendant women and men. Although more substantial migrations occurred in the post–World War II era, the early twentieth century witnessed extensive out-migration from the West Indies, particularly Jamaica, Haiti, and the Lesser Antilles. In the majority of cases, these single, male workers traveled alone, leaving families behind and/or starting families upon arrival at their destination. West Indian workers traveled throughout the Caribbean and to the United States to work, most often in agriculture and construction. The United Fruit Company hired West

Indian workers to staff its banana plantations in Costa Rica, while the Panama Canal Company employed West Indian migrants to work in the Canal Zone. Conditions they encountered replicated the institutionalized racism of slavery, with a two-tiered system of living and working conditions that privileged whites over non-whites.[7] The Jamaican and Haitian cane-cutters, contracted to work for large sugar concerns in eastern Cuba faced frequent physical abuse in addition to a political environment that treated them as unwelcome interlopers.

In most cases, these social and economic transformations had disadvantageous consequences for women and men of color. In rural Brazil, the abolition of slavery in 1888 presented challenging circumstances for people with little capital, few tools, and limited education. Those families that opted to remain on rural estates faced competition from the European *colonos* recruited as agricultural labor. Employers often preferred hiring Europeans, who labored as a family and willingly subjected themselves to conditions resembling slavery, to Afro-Brazilians, who insisted on a work environment in which they retained autonomy to negotiate their employment and refused to provide the landowners with the free labor of women and children.[8]

Although many people of color sought better economic opportunities in urban centers, they had to compete with both African-descendant and newly arrived European workers for limited employment. Despite the presence of a substantial labor force of women and men of color in Brazil, employers opted to employ white workers, often favoring European over native-born workers. Within the textile industry—one of the nation's most developed early-twentieth-century industrial ventures—employers preferred women, who were assumed to be more docile and less likely to organize collectively, over men. Yet, employer preferences for female employees did not often translate into increased opportunities for women of color to enter the industrial marketplace. In the U.S. South as well, industrialists favored white employees for work in textile factories while women and men of color remained bound to sharecropping arrangements in the tobacco fields of the Carolinas.

The superficial prosperity of Cuba in the 1920s provided little in the way of substantial gains for the population of color. While mostly white, North American tourists indulged in the newly constructed yacht clubs and race tracks, they relied on Afro-Cuban men and women to transport them to their destinations, carry their baggage, prepare and serve their food and drink, and provide sexual companionship.[9] With the rise in North American tourism came the increasing commodification of Afro-Cuban forms of expression. White Cuban bandleaders co-opted and sanitized African music, art, and, at times, religion in order to appeal to the tastes of foreign tourists who desired an "exotic," though non-threatening experience.[10]

Within this context, African-descendant women continued to labor in the limited positions available to them, particularly domestic service, laundry, cottage industries, and prostitution. As a general rule, African-descendant men tended to confront more difficulties in securing steady employment. They faced significant barriers to industrial work, largely stemming from the racist ideologies that associated industry and technology with progress and viewed African descendants as "backward" and inferior to whites. Several scholars have suggested that the population of color in Brazil, as in other countries of the Americas, provided industrialists with an ample reserve labor force on which to rely in the case of labor agitation or work stoppages by white industrial workers.

Crisis and Transformation: 1929–1959

The stock market crash of 1929 and the ensuing economic depression profoundly affected the economies of the Americas, which had been heavily dependent on the markets of Europe and the United States. Prices for commodities such as Cuban sugar and Brazilian coffee fell sharply, perpetuating widespread unemployment. Cuba's burgeoning tourist industry, cultivated during the heady decade of the 1920s, declined precipitously and by the early 1930s lay in ruins. Throughout the continent, groups of industrial workers, communists, farmers, and, in the case of Cuba, university students responded to the economic crisis by rising against the leaders they perceived to have failed them. These multi-racial coalitions brought to power populist leaders who implemented social welfare programs and policies of import-substitution industrialization in an effort to minimize socio-economic inequality and decrease dependency on the markets of the north.

African-descendant and European women, most of whom already occupied a tenuous position in the labor force, felt the immediate effects of the economic crisis. Particularly in the United States and Cuba, those who participated in the limited professional options open to them, such as nursing or teaching, left or were forced out of the workforce altogether during the worst years of the Depression. Women of color, who had historically been represented in the workforce in considerably higher numbers than white women, suffered disproportionately. In New York City the participation of African American women in the labor market in 1920 was five times that of white women, with 90 percent employed in domestic service.[11] Due to high levels of African American male unemployment, women of color, almost half of whom were married and whose families relied heavily on their incomes, struggled to make ends meet amid wage cuts and job loss.[12] In Cuba as well, Afro-Cuban women's participation in the workforce was three to five times that of white women prior to the Depression. Between 1919 and 1931 their numbers declined by 10 percent, resulting in a rate of participation close to that of white women by 1931.[13]

As Europe and the United States moved toward war in the late 1930s, Latin American and Caribbean nations reassumed their traditional roles as the providers of raw materials for wartime industry. The increased productivity of the war economy, in general, led to greater employment and somewhat improved circumstances for women. In the United States during World War II the federal government and private enterprise encouraged women, both white and of color, and ethnic minorities who remained on the home front to aid in military production. Having been long excluded from industrial employment, many women joined in the wartime effort while unions relaxed their frequent "whites only" policies to allow men of color to join. The shared experience of war united African American soldiers from disparate geographical regions. The vastly different circumstances they encountered in Europe and the shared experience of discrimination in the United States led them to return home and organize the Double V campaign. Standing for victory against the Axis powers and victory against discrimination at home, the Double V campaign is now commonly acknowledged to have been the forerunner to the U.S. civil rights movement of the 1950s and 1960s.

Following the war, increased U.S. involvement in the Brazilian economy led the Brazilian elite, historically imitators of the intellectual currents of Europe, to adopt more features of the emergent U.S. middle-class consumer culture. With the growth of professional work and the consequent expansion of the middle class, white and African-descendant women played complementary, though unequal, roles in the evolving socio-economic order. Mid-century Brazilian society viewed women's work outside of the home as appropriate only inasmuch as the type of labor performed reflected their perceived skills as caregivers. White women who did opt to enter the professional labor force retained the responsibility of fulfilling the exalted role of *donas da casa* (housewives), managing their households and caring for their families. Of course, considering the impossibility of cooking, cleaning, and caring for children while nurturing a career, they continued to rely, as they had since the colonial period, on the labor of women of color to maintain their lifestyles and livelihoods. Afro-Brazilian women whose socio-economic status showed temporary gains during the wartime and post-war economy, remained constrained by the few professional options available to them and persisted in circumstances that required them to care for the households of white families, often, many argued, to the detriment of their own.

In Cuba, the post-war years saw the revival of the tourist industry, which brought thousands of mostly white, middle-class visitors to the country. The economic prosperity which led to more U.S. families having disposable income, combined with unions' successes in securing vacation time for employees, inspired a travel boom during the late 1940s and 1950s. Private investors and government functionaries alike worked to cultivate Cuba's image as an attractive destination. As they did in the 1920s, many visitors who came did so as much for Cuba's reputation as a den of iniquity, where one could have access to drugs, gambling, and as many women as money could buy, as they did for the beautiful beaches and rumba music.

Exploitation of Afro-Cubans and Afro-Cuban women in particular was central to generating these seemingly contradictory ideals of Cuba. Tourists in Havana could attend the glamorous Tropicana nightclub performances, displaying an idealized, sexualized, mixed-race Cuban woman in elaborate costume, while decidedly less glamorous women cleaned their hotel rooms and prepared their food. Prostitution, common and visible in Cuba since colonial times, flourished with the influx of single men traveling for business or pleasure.[14] Even revolutionary groups discursively couched their struggle in a metaphor of sexual domination, equating the *mulata* woman with Cuba and the white male tourist with the United States.

The Feminization of Poverty: 1960s–1990s

The 1960s to 1980s saw profound changes for women throughout the Atlantic World. The triumph of the Cuban Revolution in 1959 ushered in a new era of social and economic change that resonated throughout the hemisphere. Women and men of color built upon the gains of the civil rights movement in the United States to militate more vocally for change during the 1960s and 1970s. However, among these silver linings loomed the clouds of dictatorship and repression. In Brazil, a military-orchestrated coup brought dictatorship to power in 1964. The U.S. government met calls for racial justice with increased violence, actively pursuing and persecuting members of the Black Power movement. The social and political turbulence of the 1960s gave way to economic stagnation and hardship of the 1970s. The effects of the oil crisis of 1973 reverberated throughout the Americas, resulting in mushrooming national deficits and stabilization programs dictated by international lending agencies. Amid a climate of unemployment and higher prices for basic needs, women of color, normally among the first to suffer the effects of economic recession, devised strategies to provide for their families despite deteriorating circumstances.

Throughout the Americas, perhaps the most drastic consequences for women have occurred as the result of the restructuring of national economies by international lending agencies. From the 1960s through the 1990s, many American nations faced economic crises of severe proportions. In an effort to curb balance of payments deficits and lower soaring interest rates, administrations accrued debt from U.S.-dominated international lending agencies such as the World Bank and the International Monetary Fund (IMF). Conditions imposed in order to secure the loans often included privatization of state industries and a freeze or reduction in spending, particularly on social programs such as health care and education. The introduction of managed care programs in Argentina and Brazil, for example, has had the practical effect of diminishing the number of women who can access health-care services.[15] In this respect, national governments, at the behest of international lending agencies, have compromised the security of family units in an effort to maintain their own economic viability.

A second arm of foreign intervention that has hurt women and families has been the U.S.-supported militarization of many Latin American and Caribbean countries. Within the context of Cold War geopolitics, the United States increased its involvement considerably in the affairs of other nations, providing military aid in the form of arms and weapons, training, and logistical support to some of the most corrupt dictatorships in the hemisphere. Haiti and Brazil provide two examples of U.S.-backed dictatorships that have mismanaged the economy while repressing dissent and committing gross violations of human rights. Recent U.S. military involvement in Colombia under the guise of the "War on Drugs" has resulted in forced displacement for many Afro-Colombian communities.[16] In October 2004, Amnesty International denounced the belligerents—in particular, the paramilitaries—in Colombia's forty-year civil war for committing acts of violence against women, including rape, mutilation, disappearance, and murder.[17]

In many Caribbean countries, limited economic and educational opportunities and frequent political instability have led to a dramatic increase in migration, both to urban areas to work in the burgeoning export-processing industries and to the United States. Following the demise of the Trujillo dictatorship in the Dominican Republic in 1961 and the subsequent U.S. military occupation in 1965, hundreds of thousands of migrants have arrived in the United States, most of whom settled in New York City. Although the majority of Dominican migrants intended to return home after accumulating enough capital to purchase property, many cultivated "transnational" ties, spending time and maintaining contact with friends and family in both countries. Dominicans joined Puerto Ricans in New York and Haitians in Florida as a growing community of African descendants occupying the service sector in urban areas. Arrangements of this type altered family and kinship networks and shaped a new "migrant" identity among the Dominican community.

The case of Dominican migrants demonstrates how structural changes in the U.S. economy have shaped family relations. Due to the de-industrialization of the last several decades, the number of manufacturing jobs available has declined considerably, while service sector employment tends to favor women over men, particularly in the areas of housekeeping, laundry, and food preparation. These economic circumstances have strained family relations in many cases where men have been unable to find work for an extended time. At times female employability has led to improved economic circumstances within the household.[18] However, often the loss of patriarchal control with family migration to the United States has fostered resentment and backlash against women and children, resulting in domestic violence and divorce. By 1980, female-headed households accounted for 42 percent of Dominican families living in New York City.[19]

While the 1960s to the 1980s spelled economic stagnation and political repression throughout the Americas, in Cuba the 1960s saw radical transformations occur at all levels of society. Although the reforms of the early 1960s were aimed at reducing economic inequalities associated with social class, the disproportionate percentage of African descendants among the Cuban poor meant that social advances in Cuba, such as the campaign against illiteracy, land and housing redistribution, expansion of the public educational system, and extension of health benefits to all Cubans, generated strong support among the population of color. Women, who had long labored in a variety of marginal activities in order to eke out a living amid political turmoil and economic uncertainty, encountered a welcome change in the revolutionary government. Early success in organizing women under the banner of the Federación de Mujeres Cubanas (FMC) meant that, at least in theory, a forum existed in which to address concerns of sexual inequality. Early actions of the FMC included the implementation of programs to encourage women to enter the labor force and the establishment of free child-care centers. In 1975 the FMC, in cooperation with the revolutionary directorate, attempted to codify the new, liberated status of women into Cuban law with the Family Code. The code stated that women and men should shoulder equal responsibility for caring for household and family.[20] With the new "socialist morality" built into the law governing family responsibility and behavior, Cuban state policy attempted to change the most fundamental social relations: those that take place within the family.

Recently women have taken political leaders to task for the corruption and fiscal mismanagement that have led to poverty, violence, and instability. Women played crucial roles in Brazil's transition to democracy in the 1980s and in the coalition that brought Jean-Bertrand Aristide to power in Haiti in the early 1990s. Women's organizations such as MADRE have also addressed inequality and underdevelopment on an international level, arguing against neo-liberal policies, such as the proposed Free Trade Area of the Americas, on the grounds that they would reduce the often minimal protections offered by the state. While African-descendant women in the Americas frequently face the dual marginalization of racism and sexism, their minority status has frequently compelled them to unite with a variety of interest groups, such as labor, the Catholic Church, indigenous communities, landless workers, environmentalists, and students, in order to generate change. In recent years, such coalition building has been responsible for bringing to power leftist leaders such as Hugo Chavez in Venezuela, Luiz Ignacio Lula da Silva in Brazil, and Evo Morales in Bolivia and for putting issues of sustainable development, maternal health, domestic violence, education, and human rights high on national agendas.

In contrast to much of Latin America and the Caribbean, where weak state structures and dependence on international financial institutions have adversely affected women, Cuba has pursued an alternative path to development with mixed results. Although largely outside of the orbit of U.S. imperialism, women confronted economic hardships associated with the fall of the Soviet bloc in 1991. With an end to Soviet subsidies for Cuban sugar, the administration looked for alternative means of securing hard currency. The most obvious answer was to promote the long-dormant tourist trade in an effort to lure visitors (primarily European and Canadian) with money to spend. Tourism did indeed take hold and has produced a contradictory set of effects for Cuban women.

Revenues generated by the tourist trade have allowed Cuba to maintain social programs such as free health care, education, and food rationing. On the other hand, the influx of tourists to Cuba has reinforced both sexual and racial inequalities that the revolution has taken great pains to eliminate. As in the 1920s and the 1950s, tourists visit the island to exploit the ample supply of young women willing to sell sexual services in order to gain access to U.S. currency. While the pervasive structural racism that characterized the pre-1959 era virtually disappeared with the economic and social reforms of the 1960s, many Cubans still harbor racist attitudes. Reflecting this bias, employers regularly hire white or light-skinned Cubans over Afro-Cubans for jobs in the lucrative tourist economy. This lack of opportunity for participation in the formal sector has led an increasing number of women and men of color to join the informal sector, shunning higher education to work as unofficial tourist guides, street vendors, hustlers, and prostitutes.

Today women of color confront a cultural landscape radically altered by the changes of the preceding decades, while at the same time strikingly similar to the atmosphere that greeted them at the beginning of the century. Across the Americas, from Brazil to Jamaica, Venezuela to the United States, the story of both women and African descendants remains, in many ways, unchanged. On average, women continue to earn less than men, and darker-skinned women continue to earn less than lighter. In 1980, Afro-Brazilians lived, on average, 6.7 years less than white Brazilians, while African Americans lived 6.3 years less than white Americans. Cuba, the only country in the Americas to have undertaken a protracted campaign to address socio-economic inequality, was also the only country in the Americas where European-descendant and African-descendant Cubans enjoyed parity in the measure of life span.[21]

Few would argue that the nineteenth-century promises of freedom and equality for African-descendant women and men have been met. From the racism of early twentieth-century industrial employers to the late twentieth-century stabilization and structural-adjustment programs that have stripped away some of the most crucial protections from women and their children, the expansion of the electorate and the growth of wage labor has done little to resolve the structural inequities facing the Afro-descendant communities of the Americas.

Women in West Central Africa: Family, Work, and State Policy

The experiences of women in the twentieth century have been as diverse as one might expect in a geographic region as expansive as West Central Africa. While some women have retained their tribal affiliations and continue to practice local customs and observe tribal law, others have migrated to the more cosmopolitan cities of the coast where they receive a Western-style education, enter previously male-dominated professions, and choose their own marriage partners. However, despite the variations in life experiences of African women, virtually all have been shaped to some extent by European colonial rule, nationalist struggles and the formation of independent states, and the economic crises of the 1970s through the 1990s. It would be a mistake to say that women have either entirely accepted or rejected the transition to capitalism and the consequent effects on family and kinship organization. Although women have been the victims of much of the "progress" brought about as a result of colonialism, decolonization, and post-colonial national rule, they have continually fought to secure the economic advantages and new opportunities engendered by these changes.

1900s–1940s: Gender and Colonialism

The colonial consolidation of the 1880s to the 1920s significantly altered relations among and between traditional kinship groups. In their attempt to suppress the slave trade, British authorities encouraged enslaved women, often taken forcibly from the interior, to stay with their "husbands" rather than return to their tribal group. Although aimed at ensuring political stability and maintaining a productive coastal workforce, this act contributed to the accumulation of power in the hands of individual men and the erosion of the power of the traditional kinship organization. In the context of extending European hegemony, colonial authorities usurped communally held lands for the cultivation of cash crops. Women, who in pre-colonial times had frequently been the primary agricultural producers, could no longer exercise discretion over what crops to plant and when. Export agriculture increased the reliance on women's productive labor for the newly established coastal plantations while at the same time required that they retain the traditional responsibility of food preparation for the male workers.

In order to understand how abolition affected women and men, it is important to note the gendered nature of manumission in pre-colonial West Africa. In Igboland, as in other areas, a woman's status as slave or free was intimately bound up with that of her husband. A woman who married a free-born male received her freedom whereas a woman married to a slave normally remained a slave. In contrast, a male did not become free upon marriage to a free woman but, rather, could gain freedom through demonstrations of valor or land acquisition. The practices of nineteenth-century slavery dictated that a male effectively became manumitted when he purchased a parcel of land or eliminated an enemy of the community.[22] Although he might continue to work for a master one or two days a week, his higher status as a landholder set him apart from other male slaves. This path to landholding and the freedom it represented was not open to women. Thus, women's avenues to freedom were related to their status as wives, whereas men were tied to their status as a potential leader and landowner.

While many women in pre-colonial West Central Africa did own and cultivate parcels of land, the experiences of women in rural Ghana demonstrate how colonialism diminished women's access. The late nineteenth-century and early twentieth-century increase in cocoa prices had significant consequences for female small landholders. As in other regions of West Central Africa, when prices for export commodities rose, the stability of women's land tenure eroded. In matrilineal regions of Ghana that had enjoyed a history of cocoa production, patrilineal groups began to cultivate cocoa around the turn of the century. They would, in turn, divide cultivable land, formerly held by the kinship group, into individual parcels, most of which they gave to male children. Thus, while women often retained the rights to cultivate land, the right to designate an inheritor was increasingly reserved for men who, in turn, selected sons or nephews.[23]

The early colonial period also witnessed increased urbanization in West Central Africa. Unlike pre-colonial East Africa, large cities existed on the West coast at the time of colonization. In the early twentieth century the majority of migrants to urban areas, most often situated near the coast, were men. This rural out-migration affected women in both rural and urban areas. With the exception of the few opportunities in the informal economic market such as prostitute and petty trader, women in the city remained entirely excluded from the burgeoning political bureaucracy and limited professional sector. Rural women also found themselves squeezed by the process of urbanization. Colonial administrations relied on agricultural produce to support urban regions, maintain balance of payments and fund infrastructure. In doing so, women, increasingly important as agricultural producers with the departure of men for the cities, lost the ability to plant a variety of crops. Whereas prior to colonial rule women cultivated a mix of food crops and crops that could be sold in regional markets, under colonialism they shifted production toward the export economy, thus undermining the subsistence of their families and their control over production.[24]

Missionary activities carried out by Europeans buttressed colonial policy with the establishment of schools and churches. These institutions promoted the Western concepts of individual rights and freedoms and stressed a strict gender hierarchy and popular notions of Victorian womanhood. Although missionaries found many converts among former slaves, their teachings contrasted markedly with the experience of most women, many of whom remained enslaved well into the twentieth century. In urban areas market women purchased female slaves to run their errands, and in rural regions, with the shift to export-oriented production, men relied increasingly on arrangements of polygamy to secure plantation labor. In Nigeria, following the "Emancipation Declaration" of 1916, Igbo women continued to be victimized by "wife purchase" agreements, disguised under the tradition of bridewealth payments or dowries.[25]

The colonial attack on corporate conceptions of the family and traditional dual-sex organization expanded during the high colonial period, from roughly the 1920s through the 1960s. Although a virtual consensus exists on the decline of conditions for women under colonial rule, administrators made few direct efforts at changing the status of women for the better or worse. Rather, colonial institutions fostered values that promoted patriarchy and stressed proper—that is, European—gender roles. The co-optation of tribal chiefs both facilitated colonization and reinforced male supremacy. As European political power gained hegemony throughout West Africa, colonial administrations established laws that committed women to a status of legal dependency under men, further robbing them of their traditional inheritance rights and legal protections in marriage.

Although anti-colonial struggles began to generate significant changes following World War II, resistance movements existed throughout the entire colonial period, and women, directly and indirectly, contributed to their early victories. Perhaps the most cited example of direct, gender-based action is the 1929 protest against British taxation known as the Aba Women's War. In response to efforts by British colonial administrators to conduct a census of women for taxation purposes, thousands of Igbo women in southeastern Nigeria converged on the district centers, in many cases "sitting on" the warrant heads in non-violent protest and in other cases engaging in rioting and destruction of property.

The early to mid-twentieth century witnessed a decrease in options for women in rural areas. In addition to women's declining social status under colonialism, the commodification of their traditional productive tasks combined with a disruption in pre-existing systems of land tenure prompted an increasing number of women to migrate to urban centers, particularly after World War II. Decreased vigilance from the rural, often patriarchal, family meant increased freedom and increased uncertainty for women in cities. Undoubtedly this proved a tempting lure for women who previously lacked options for leaving an oppressive situation. For others, city life meant the loss of protection of the traditional family or kinship unit through which women had historically survived.

1940s–1960s: Gender and African State Formation

The past two decades have seen substantial advances in the scholarly literature on gender and nationalist movements. Although levels of participation varied by region, a virtual consensus exists that women significantly advanced nationalist goals. Recent work has also elaborated the gendered dimensions of the processes of decolonization and state formation. From supporting their striking husbands, brothers, and sons during Senegal's railway strike to organizing rallies in support of Ghanian independence, women worked alongside men and in some cases militated on their own in efforts to undermine European colonialism. Underlying their critique of colonial policy was the belief that the condition of women and children under colonialism had deteriorated significantly. Yet, rather than advance explicitly feminist goals aimed exclusively at raising the status of women, as in the case of many Western feminist movements, women supported the cause of nationalism with the understanding that indigenous African governments could and would more effectively respond to their needs.

During and following the Second World War, several major labor actions shook the colonial order in both French and British West Africa and laid the foundations for the creation of independent states. In the 1945 Nigerian general strike, workers demanded increased wages and family allowances based on claims to patriarchal respectability.[26] Although the female participants did not advance a woman-centered agenda per se, their militancy aimed to secure their own economic prosperity and challenged the colonial policies that failed to recognize the rights of African men and women to provide for their families. Women played significant roles in the coalition that developed in support of the strike. In addition to the support offered sons and husbands in the form of basic household maintenance (shopping, cooking, cleaning, child care, and the like), market women extended credit to striking workers and offered them lower prices for goods while other groups of women took to the streets to protest against shortages and high prices.[27]

Women in rural regions also protested their marginalization, albeit through different channels than women in urban areas. Following the mass migration of men to cities during the Depression, in the 1940s women increasingly sought compensation for their labor on farms in divorce proceedings.[28] Yet, the case of cocoa farmers in Ghana demonstrates how rural women were largely left out of the development of the post-war years. In fact, the increased agricultural productivity of the 1940s perpetuated a decline in prosperity for women. During good years, planters cultivated more cocoa, which Europeans stockpiled, leading to a drop in prices. In the 1950s larger farms could head off the crisis through diversification, while small farmers could not. By the 1960s male farmers could no longer afford to hire laborers from the north and turned to wives and children to compensate for the loss of waged workers.

In the political realm, nationalist leaders afforded women some minor concessions as a result of participating in the independence struggles. In some cases, the newly installed governments of African republics enacted legislation that benefited women. In Ghana, Kwame Nkrumah recognized women as an important base of support, as they were instrumental in establishing trade boycotts and financing nationalist groups. His administration responded by incorporating the National Council of Ghana Women into the Convention Peoples' Party, whose constitution dictated that ten parliamentary seats be reserved for women.[29] In Guinea, women who had actively participated in all levels of the nationalist struggle found ample rewards under President Sékou Touré. Legislation enacted for the benefit of women included an extensive marriage reform and laws governing women's participation in political and economic life.[30] Throughout West Central Africa, the expansion of the educational system allowed for more girls to attend primary and secondary schools and for a larger—though still small in relative terms when compared to men—number of women to receive education at the university level and enter the professional sector.

Unfortunately though, for most African women, the gains of nationalism proved fleeting and, ultimately, incomplete. Nationalism failed to provide the strong social supports and greater opportunities that many women had hoped for with the demise of colonial rule. In many cases corruption, weak popular support, and a general disinterest in generating change for women hindered administrations from putting forth any substantial policy aimed at furthering the condition of women. When viewed in a broad sense, nationalism failed to address the concerns of women in the wake of African state formation. Whether national governments might have come around under pressure to respond to women's concerns cannot be known as the financial crises of the 1970s and 1980s undermined the power of the nascent state structures, preventing them from addressing virtually all social issues. Women's rights and protections, which had never been the top priority of African states, were one casualty of the crisis.

1970s–1990s: The Feminization of Poverty

As in many Latin American and Caribbean nations, the revenues deposited with U.S. and European-dominated international banks and lending agencies during the 1970s had similar, negative consequences for women and families in West Africa. Constrained by international marketing agreements, many African republics attempted to stave off economic recession by mobilizing the resources at their disposal. Initial efforts at stabilization and resolving balance of payments deficits targeted the fragile social safety net. In this manner many states gutted programs designed to support the most vulnerable members of society. By neglecting the needs of women and children, these nations were able to project the picture of economic viability that international lending agencies demanded to see.

In addition to external pressures, internal obstacles to development have plagued West African nations. In many cases, mismanagement and corruption at all levels of government have exacerbated the effects of the economic crises facing African nations. In others, administrations have found themselves constrained by the imperative to maintain peace within states containing a number of ethnic groups. This has been the case in Nigeria, where policymakers have been obliged to reward constituencies rather than pursue a comprehensive development plan.[31] Recent research has demonstrated that structural adjustment programs in West Africa have rewarded the least productive sector of society—speculators—while harming the most productive sectors, particularly women.[32]

One major consequence of the privatization of state resources under pressure from international lending agencies has been a significant decline in the health and well-being of women in rural and urban areas. Though never the top priority of African states, public health has worsened significantly as the result of privatization schemes. Due to their responsibilities of managing the household, feeding the family, and caring for the sick, the curtailment of public health and sanitation programs has disproportionately affected women. Lapses in education, sanitation, and preventative health care have contributed to the recent resurgence of diseases such as malaria and cholera, while the privatization of vital services, such as water, has diminished access for the poorest women and their families.

In Nigeria, foreign capital combined with indebtedness to the West has shaped the national energy policy, which, in turn, has undermined the ability of women to fulfill their familial obligations. During the 1970s and 1980s, the Nigerian government began to rely heavily on oil exports. In the 1980s, facing a domestic economic crisis and burdened with considerable debt, the government developed an energy policy directed at the export of raw materials to the detriment of domestic consumption. Therefore, although endowed with ample reserves of petroleum, shortages have forced women to go to extra lengths to acquire cooking fuel, hauling firewood over long distances and waiting in lines to buy kerosene. Women have argued that the consequent difficulties in food preparation have been responsible for tension within families, which has led to higher rates of divorce.[33]

Even the best efforts of foreign capital and international development bodies have often proven negative for women. Development projects, in many cases, have undermined existing systems of land tenure through inconsistencies in the processes of land titling and resettlement. The Senegal River Basin Area is but one case of a development project funded by foreign capital and administered by a Senegalese state agency that has produced widely variable results in securing women's titles to their plots. Similarly, many female rice farmers in Gambia lost title to their land as the result of irrigation projects. While women had traditionally held the right to farm any land they cleared and to designate an heir to their property, with the advent of irrigation programs, married women's land often became folded into "household property," which shifted control to the husband. In other cases women have maintained control over their plots of land but have lost the right to transfer the property to their daughters.[34]

Lacking support of the state, women have shouldered the burden of providing for themselves and their families. Although West African women have a long tradition of non-cooperation, protest, and struggle, until recently such activity rarely included an explicitly feminist component. Yet, facing curtailment of their traditional protections and lacking the resources to adequately provide for their families, the last several decades offer many examples of strategies women have devised to secure their rights *as women*. In rural regions, women's resistance has taken the form of manipulating customary institutions or "reinventing" tradition to their benefit. Among the Nnobi of Nigeria, women have mobilized tradition in the form of female-to-female marriages in order to transfer land to female heirs.[35] In urban areas, women have formed political bodies to pressure the government on such issues as health care, education, and human rights. The 31st December Women's Movement of Ghana, for example, has championed concerns of women to the government while undertaking its own projects to promote political participation, literacy, clean drinking water, family planning, and the establishment of daycare centers.[36]

Most recently, women in Nigeria have responded to their ongoing marginalization at the hands of multi-national oil firms with tactics that combine both traditional and modern expressions of protest. In 2002 and 2003 women throughout the mineral-rich Delta region of Nigeria staged takeovers of oil-drilling facilities. Although not coordinated at the outset, word of their actions traveled fast, inspiring numerous occupations throughout the region. The demands of the women ranged from providing jobs for their sons and husbands to accepting responsibility for repairing the environmental damage to which they have subjected Delta communities in the course of their operations. Christiana Mene, of the Escravos Women's Coalition, summarized the group's position in the following:

> We want Chevron to employ our children. If Chevron does that we the mothers will survive, we will see food to eat. Our farms are all gone, due to Chevron's pollution of our water. We used to farm cassava, okra, pepper and others. Now all the places we've farmed are sinking, we cannot farm. We cannot kill fishes and crayfish. That is why we told Chevron that Escravos women and Chevron are at war.[37]

Addressing the social consequences of the presence of oil companies, a spokeswoman for women occupying Chevron-Texaco's Abiteye flow station explained that young women from outside the region come to areas of oil production to engage in prostitution, thus spreading disease within communities.[38]

In one of the more dramatic expressions of protest, women disrobed so as to pressure male executives at Shell and Chevron-Texaco into meeting their demands. This traditional shaming gesture, considered the most severe form of censure that a woman can bestow upon a man, epitomized the desperation of women whose families and household economies had been harmed, perhaps irreparably, by the oil companies.

In light of the incapacity of national governments to respond effectively to the concerns of women, calls for the redress of sexual inequalities both in the family and at the state level have become more urgent in recent years. As the twentieth century drew to a close, African women increasingly began mobilizing across the lines of class and ethnicity that had previously divided them. Organizations composed of mostly middle-class, Western-educated women such as the political action concern Women in Nigeria have joined with the more working-class Market Women Association in levying calls for democratization of the Nigerian state.[39]

Conclusion

In the preceding pages I have attempted to present a general sketch of some of the main issues in the history of gender and identity in the twentieth-century Atlantic World. While women have participated in sex-based political movements, the most profound changes influencing family, community, and patterns of subsistence have been negotiated in dialectic relationships existing at all levels of social interaction, be they with religious organizations, employers, local or national leadership, or international development bodies. Alliances between the state and private enterprise, for example, have spurred migrations, both domestic and international, that contributed to a destabilization of established power relations within the family unit. Changes in marriage patterns in Ibadan and Lagos, Nigeria, and Cotonou and Porto-Novo, Benin, and high rates of marriage dissolution among Dominicans in New York City reflect the experience of migration due to structural changes in Atlantic economies. In other cases, actions taken by and on behalf of women and their families—such as the decision to remove members of the group from waged labor in the United States and Brazil following emancipation—have inspired intervention by state and private interests, as in the development of programs to lure European workers in an effort to curb the labor shortage.

Although in many ways the political and economic trajectories of Latin America and the Caribbean have differed drastically from the nations of West Central Africa, state policies and the expansion of capitalist modes of production have unintentionally conspired to squeeze women economically, whether they opt to work within the family unit or outside of the home for wages. For African and African-descendant women, economic prosperity has often proven illusory. As we have seen in Brazil and the United States, success in securing waged work came with the drawback of depressing wages throughout an industry. Likewise, in Ghana a rise in prices for women's crops had the deleterious effect of inspiring men to take over their cultivation.[40]

Today, multi-national corporations and international financial institutions wield unprecedented power and influence over Latin America, the Caribbean, and Africa. Within the context of a global economy, non-governmental organizations (NGOs) and grassroots movements have increasingly utilized new technologies to organize across borders. Among their demands are transparency and accountability from the firms operating in their communities. From Colombia to the Ivory Coast, years of deprivation and marginalization have engendered a profound political consciousness in women.

Although women have made progress in lobbying for and securing their rights in marriage, work, and politics, vast socio-economic disparities based on gender and, particularly in the Americas, racial heritage have hampered their achievements. Even 150 years following the end of the slave trade, the legacies of oppression and exploitation continue to inform the daily lives of African and African-descendant women and men throughout the Atlantic World.

Notes

1. In particular see Tiffany Ruby Patterson and Robin D. G. Kelly, "Unfinished Migrations: Reflections on the African Diaspora and the Making of the Modern World," special issue on the Diaspora, *African Studies Review* 43:1 (April 2000): 11–45 (24–29).

2. For a substantive discussion on the implications of "gender" see Joan Scott's seminal article, "Gender: A Useful Category of Historical Analysis," *American Historical Review* 91:5 (December 1986).

3. Rebecca J. Scott, "Defining the Boundaries of Freedom in the World of Cane: Cuba, Brazil, and Louisiana after Emancipation," *American Historical Review* 99:1 (February, 1994): 70–102 (78).

4. George Reid Andrews, "Black and White Workers: São Paulo, Brazil, 1888–1928," *Hispanic American Historical Review* 68:3 (August, 1988): 491–524 (517).

5. For a more substantial historiography of scholarship on the African Diaspora see Patterson and Kelly, "Unfinished Migrations," 14–19.

6. While many cane cutters had lived in urban areas during the *tiempo muerto* (dead time) and migrated to the countryside for the *zafra* (harvest), the consolidation of large, sugar-milling operations increased corporate control over workers' lives, leading many to migrate to the cities on a permanent basis.

7. Aviva Chomsky, *West Indian Workers and the United Fruit Company in Costa Rica, 1870–1940* (Baton Rouge: Louisiana State University Press, 1996).

8. Andrews, "Black and White Workers," 517.

9. Rosalie Schwartz, "The Invasion of the Tourists," in *The Cuba Reader: History, Culture, Politics*, ed. Aviva Chomsky, Barry Carr, and Pamela Maria Smorkaloff, 244–252 (Durham, N.C.: Duke University Press, 2003).

10. Robin Moore, "The Commercial Rumba: Afrocuban Arts as International Popular Culture," *Latin American Music Review/Revista de Musica Latinoamericana* 16:2 (Autumn–Winter, 1995): 166–167.

11. Jaqueline Jones cited in Anne Stavney, "'Mothers of Tomorrow': The New Negro Renaissance and the Politics of Maternal Representation," *African American Review* 32:4 (Winter 1998), 533–561 (550, 559).

12. Ibid., 550.

13. Alejandro de la Fuente, "Race and Inequality in Cuba," *Journal of Contemporary History* 30:1 (January 1995), 131–168 (159).

14. The exploitation of women in the sex trades in 1950s Cuba has been well documented in testimonies collected following the Revolution. See Tomás Fernandez Robaina, *Recuerdos Secretos de Dos Mujeres Públicas* (La Habana: Editorial Letras Cubanas, 1984), and Oscar Lewis, Ruth M. Lewis, and Susan Migdon, *Four Women Living the Revolution: An Oral History of Contemporary Cuba* (Champaign: University of Illinois Press, 1977).

15. Celia Iriat, Howard Waitzkin, and Emerson Mehry, "HMO's Abroad: Managed Care in Latin America," in *Sickness and Wealth: The Corporate Assault on Global Health*, ed. Meredith Fort, Mary Anne Mercer, and Oscar Gish, 69–78 (Cambridge, Mass.: South End Press, 2004).

16. Aviva Chomsky, *Linked Labor Histories: New England and Colombia in the Long Twentieth Century*, Durham, N.C.: Duke University Press (forthcoming).

17. Amnesty International, "Colombia: Women's Bodies Used as a Battleground," October 13, 2004, http://web.amnesty.org/actforwomen/col-131004–action-eng.

18. Sherri Grasmuck and Patricia R. Pessar, *Between Two Islands: Dominican International Migration* (Berkeley: University of California Press, 1991), 148–149.

19. Ibid., 163.

20. Lois M. Smith and Alfred Padula, *Sex and Revolution: Women in Socialist Cuba* (New York: Oxford University Press, 1996).

21. De la Fuente, "Race and Inequality in Cuba," 143.

22. G. Ugo Nwokeji, "The Slave Emancipation Problematic: Igbo Society and the Colonial Equation," *Comparative Studies in Society and History* 40:2 (April, 1998), 318–355 (324).

23. Gwendolyn Mikell, "Ghanian Females, Rural Economy and National Stability," *African Studies Review* 29:3 (September, 1986): 67–88 (68–69). Leslie Gray and Michael Kevane, "Diminished Access, Diverted Exclusion: Women and Land Tenure in Sub-Saharan Africa," *African Studies Review* 42:2 (September, 1999), 15–39 (21–24).

24. Mikell, "Ghanian Females," 67–88.

25. Nwokeji, "Slave Emancipation Problematic," 337–338.

26. Lisa A. Lindsay, "Domesticity and Difference: Male Breadwinners, Working Women, and Colonial Citizenship in the 1945 Nigerian General Strike," *American Historical Review* 104:3 (June 1999), 783–812 (802).

27. Ibid., 794–799.

28. Mikell, "Ghanian Females," 70.

29. Kenneth Little, *African Women in Towns: An Aspect of Africa's Social Revolution* (London: Cambridge University Press, 1973), 70.

30. Ibid., 66.

31. Mikell, 1986, 68.

32. Kole Ahmed Shettima, "Engendering Nigeria's Third Republic," *African Studies Review* 38:3 (Dec., 1995), 61–98 (82).

33. D. J. Shehu, "Technology and the Fuel Crisis: Adjustment among Women in Northern Nigeria," in *African Feminism: The Politics of Survival in Sub-Saharan Africa, ed.* Gwendolyn Mikell (Philadelphia: University of Pennsylvania Press, 1997), 276.

34. Gray and Kevane, "Diminished Access," 25–26.

35. Ibid., 31.

36. 31st December Women's Movement of Ghana, http://www.dec31.org.gh/index.html.

37. As quoted in Terisa E. Turner and Leigh S. Brownhill, "'Why Women Are at War with Chevron': Nigerian Subsistence Struggles against the International Oil Industry" (New York: International Oil Working Group, 2003); reprinted in *Journal of Asian and African Studies* 39:1–2 (January 2004): 63–93.

38. Ibid.

39. Shettima, "Engendering Nigeria's Third Republic," 82–86.

40. Gray and Kevane, "Diminished Access," 20.

CHAPTER FIFTEEN

Reparation and Repair: Reform Movements in the Atlantic World

Maxim Matusevich

In the year 1441 a young Portuguese captain presented Prince Henry the Navigator with a gift of some dozen black slaves captured in the course of a raiding expedition down the shores of West Africa. More raids followed, and in 1455 a papal bull authorized Portugal to reduce to servitude all heathen people. A series of advancements in navigational science and Iberian Christian zeal were combined with an urgent proto-capitalist pursuit of profit to send Southern European explorers on the distant voyages of discovery. Christopher Columbus's arrival in 1492 in what turned out not to be India signified the emergence of an enormous intercommunicative zone of the Atlantic World. For centuries to come the circulation of human beings and goods across the Atlantic would be one of the most essential socio-economic components in the evolution of the system of world capitalism. The intense transatlantic exchanges defined the character of political orders on both sides of the ocean, forged cultural and national identities, and created a series of symbiotic economic relationships between the locales thousands of miles removed from each other.

We find in the Atlantic World the early manifestations of one of the most commonly discussed and debated of contemporary phenomena—that of globalization or the evolution of the interconnected world. Quite often such debates remain divorced from their relevant historical context. As recently observed by Frederick Cooper, the "globalization fad" has produced a global conversation that compensates in urgency and intensity for what it lacks in historical depth and analysis.[1] The Atlantic basin has long been the testing ground of modernity. It was also the stage for the grand show of Western capitalist expansion and growth. The Atlantic economy, based on a peculiar system of exchange which moved millions of humans across the water to work on the slave plantations of the Caribbean and the Americas for largely European consumption, fueled the accumulation of capital in Europe during the heyday of mercantilism and rise of the Enlightenment. New World plantation slavery, in association with Old World labor, spawned the global circular system of commercial exchange and human migration. Africans, forcibly integrated into this scheme as labor, capital, and currency, shaped the parameters of the integration process.[2] The Atlantic slave trade, that proverbial "ghost of globalization past," became a major contributing factor in the European industrial expansion, the economic fact of life readily recognized as such by its contemporaries.[3]

Scholars have long looked at the Atlantic zone as one of the main sources of European modernization. As early as 1944, Eric Williams, in his seminal *Capitalism and Slavery,* considered the impact of the direct profits from slavery and the slave trade on Britain's economy and society. More significantly, Williams saw the primary impact of slaving in the dynamism it imparted upon world trade between the fifteenth and the nineteenth centuries, as well as in the creation of the radically new structures of capital, labor, production, and services. By the mid-eighteenth century the Atlantic peripheries were responsible for the bulk of European trade statistics, and in the case of Britain they represented the country's fastest growing markets. Importantly, these New World markets guaranteed employment to virtually millions of European workers.[4] It is equally significant that prior to the rise of factory-based production in England and on the continent, the Caribbean sugar plantations operated as the largest in scale and the most labor and capital intensive enterprises in modern history. Not unlike modern corporations, plantations often had management, which was divorced from ownership and finance. British, French, and Dutch governments protected large-scale business by controlling, owning, or chartering their respective overseas companies, while the distribution of produce was organized through increasingly sophisticated marketing and advertising strategies. Gangs of free, semi-free, and slave workers toiled in a structured and task-oriented environment under strict discipline, thus becoming the forerunners of the European working classes. Indeed, the Old World was tugged into the modern by the New.

Just as European humanitarian and religious leaders were beginning to challenge the moral legitimacy of slave trade, the American and French revolutions marked the transition from the cosmopolitan values of the age of Enlightenment to new kinds of national territoriality within the world economy. The idea of a nation state became in effect a new global commodity. Revolutionary nationalist ideas reached far afield, creating a ripple effect all across Europe, precipitating the liberation of Latin America after 1808, and even inspiring the first Hindu reform movement, the predecessor of modern-day Indian nationalism. The former global connections were increasingly becoming international in nature and could be upheld or disrupted as a result of a dialogue (or the lack thereof) between nation-states. The states with an enhanced sense of loyalty to their physical space and to their populations sought to consolidate control over resources within their boundaries. This transformation from the age of kings and multi-ethnic empires to the age of peoples and nations went hand in hand with the rise of national entrepreneurial classes. Adam Smith, one of the fathers of economic liberalism, among others, took a universal view of national issues. His "invisible hand" of free competition operated in the environment shaped by economic contests between national capitalist elites. The shift from eighteenth-century mercantilism to nineteenth-century free trade also meant that nation-states were willing to render political and military support to the expanding national enterprises around the world. *Economic imperialism* as represented by "gunboat diplomacy," so fashionable toward the middle part of the nineteenth century, became a standard feature of transnational economic transactions. The United States expanded over land and into Latin America, as the British along with the French and the Dutch expanded into Asia and then Africa. By the mid-nineteenth century a world regime of national expansion had become virtually institutionalized, with the British Navy fighting the victorious Opium Wars to protect the rights of British merchants to conduct the opium trade in China, or with the indefatigable US *Admiral Perry* forcing the Japanese to open up to American trade.

In the nationalist discourse the "nation" is often juxtaposed with the "empire." Yet it is also true that the rise of European nationalism would eventually contribute to European imperial expansion. In fact, a number of scholars have argued that overseas expansion, imperialism, and empire were directly linked to the growth of European nation-states. A. G. Hopkins has suggested that the nineteenth century nation-state needs to be placed in the center of the history of globalization, which was consistent with the existence of such a state and also reinforced it.[5] "There has never been a great power without great colonies," wrote one French publicist in 1877. "Every virile people has established colonial power," echoed the famous German historian Heinrich von Treitschke. The 1884 Berlin Conference on Africa projected the rivalries between European nations onto another continent whereby international protocols were utilized for the conduct of national competition on a world scale.

Following the "Scramble for Africa" the consolidation of colonial states led to the creation of regions of the world with their own distinct economic specializations, integrated into one world system of production. The advent of free international trade implied that spaces were being created for the movement of commodities between the empires and around the world. The main actors (for example, Britain) became keenly interested in the creation of multinational structures to uphold the emerging multilateral business links. By the end of the century we see British shipping providing freight for other nations or British financial institutions getting involved in the distribution of manufactured goods produced by other nations. Intercontinental trade was facilitated enormously by the Suez and Panama canals. In 1913 the value of world trade was roughly $38 billion, or about twenty-five times what it had been in 1800. The operation of such a system required the creation of a single world of rules and regulations based on new international organizations. Thus the inauguration of the International Telegraph Union in 1865 can be seen as a precursor of the international non-governmental organizations (INGOs) that have become such prominent features of modern-day globalization. Statesmen and champions of European empires around the fin de siècle embraced positivist visions of integrated system of international trade based on the achievements of a concomitant revolution in communications. Global advertising and grandiose international exhibitions, such as the Chicago World's Fair in 1893 or a similar event in Paris in 1900, helped to extend universal imagery to the general national and imperial audiences. As the English historian James Bryce noted in 1901, it seemed as if "a new sort of unity is being created among mankind," and the world, it seemed, was becoming a much smaller place.

Globalization both originates and results in motion, in the movement of commodities, technologies, and ideas, and also—invariably—in the transfer of populations. The advent of colonial rule re-energized old and created new patterns of migrations. Colonial communications greatly extended historical linkages between the older centers of globalization and new frontier economies. By the late nineteenth century new networks of labor migrations drew on the earlier labor systems of the Atlantic World while giving prominence to the migrations of unskilled labor. Other movements sought to reverse the earlier crossings—such as the African ex-slaves who resettled in Sierra Leone, Liberia, Gambia, and Kenya. In fact, colonialism made some of its subjects migrants several times over. Empires provided migratory umbrellas, while also supplying new opportunities to move populations. So we observe movements of Africans to new locations (the case of "Bombay Africans," for example) or an influx of Asian labor to new settler colonies in Africa and the Caribbean. At least 3 million Chinese, Japanese, Indians, and Filipinos—to name only the four most important groups—moved abroad before 1920. Whether directed by colonial states or spontaneous and opportunistic in nature, these migrations created the world of diasporic connections and sensibilities that endure to this day.

During the imperial age, as before, the New World became the destination point for the most significant numbers of international migrants. The main difference, of course, lay in a simple fact that the late-nineteenth-century migrations overwhelmingly originated in Europe and were voluntary in nature. About 60 million Europeans undertook the voyage from the resource-scarce and labor-abundant Europe to the resource-abundant and labor-scarce New World in the century following 1820. Three-fifths of European migrants went to the United States. By the 1880s the cumulative European migration had exceeded that of African slaves during the previous centuries. The overwhelming majority of new European immigrants arrived in the Americas. Even though the United States remained the most important destination, there were significant outflows to South America (mostly to Argentina and Brazil) and to Canada after the beginning of the twentieth century. A much smaller but persistent migratory stream linked the United Kingdom to Australia, New Zealand, and

South Africa. In the era of Western imperial expansion there were bound to emerge tensions between European and non-European migratory groups. Whether in East Africa or Australasia, European settlers favored strict controls on Asian migration and proceeded to build *great white walls*—discriminatory laws designed to keep to minimum the influence of non-European migrants in the spaces open to new settlement. These practices contributed to the increasingly lopsided nature of the globalizing world on the eve of the World War I. The gap between the industrializing regions (mainly Europe and North America, but also such areas of European settlement as South Africa and Australia) and the non-industrialized ones (mainly Africa, Asia, and Latin America) became an essential and persistent feature of the world economy. In fact, through the processes of industrialization and imperial and migratory expansion, the West institutionalized the patterns of uneven global development and the resulting global inequality.

The liberal hopes and dreams of a Europe-centered global community were dashed in the summer of 1914 when European nations plunged the world into the turmoil of the first total war. Ironically, the reality of an increasingly interconnected world was largely responsible for the carnage almost immediately taking on truly global dimensions.

The war and its aftermath (particularly the rise of totalitarian ideologies) inflicted a staggering blow on nineteenth-century European liberalism and some of its core beliefs. A number of scholars went so far as to suggest that the World War I and the following interwar period witnessed a reversal of the processes of globalization, a closing of the nineteenth-century open economy. Others have argued that, measured both in the amount of mass family migration and in the volume of international trade and capital flows relative to GDP, the pre-1914 international economy was in many respects more integrated than the present one.[6] Yet another argument contends that no clean break with the past had occurred during the war, but rather the national economies reflected the profound disillusionment with the positivist thinking of the nineteenth-century liberals. For the post–World War I generation globalization manifested itself primarily in the all-engulfing and technologically advanced killing and, after the New York Stock Exchange crash of October 29, 1929, in the global character of the Great Depression. Rather than completely disappearing, globalization stagnated or hibernated. Traumatized by the war, social upheavals, and economic slumps, the states did their best to protect national economies from outside threats. In 1931–1932, with economic liberalism temporarily all but forgotten, Britain, Canada, the United States, and the Scandinavian countries abandoned the gold standard, traditionally considered the foundation of international exchanges. In 1936 these states were followed by Belgium, the Netherlands, and France. Symbolically, in 1931 Great Britain abandoned Free Trade, which had been so central to the British economic identity. Even the international flow of capital seemed to virtually disappear with international lending between 1927 and 1933 dropping by more than 90 percent. Western nations, especially the United States, began increasingly to look inward, giving preference to internal economic and social concerns. The redemption was to be found inside the nation while the outside world became the source of potential danger and disruptive influences.

The total defeat of Nazi Germany and its allies in World War II created the conditions for a remarkable recovery by the war-ravaged Western nations. It seemed for a while that after more than thirty years of turmoil and anxiety, the "war to end all wars" had been finally won. The period of prolonged economic prosperity, with the United States as its undisputed center of gravity, began in the West. The aftermath of the war witnessed a drive toward the establishment of an equitable international arrangement providing for collective security. The newly founded United Nations set out on an ambitious path of creating the "family of nations." This family was growing by leaps and bounds. After the war, the formerly mighty European empires found themselves weakened and incapable of sustaining the far-flung colonial domains. One after another the former colonial possessions in what now was referred to as the Third World attained their independence. The process of decolonization born out of the worldwide crisis of colonialism spread with a remarkable speed around the globe. Starting in Asia, it eventually reached Africa, where Ghana proclaimed its independence in 1957. Almost all of the remaining British, French, and Belgian colonies in Africa became independent in 1960–1962, with most of the rest following shortly. By the end of the decade whose beginning was marked by the "Year of Africa" (1960), the last vestiges of formal colonialism would be found only in Portuguese possessions and in the areas controlled by the independent settler states. But even there the trend toward eventual liberation was unmistakable.

The newly liberated nations of the Third World asserted their sovereignty within the framework of a peculiar international setup. Within months (if not weeks) after the end of the war, it became clear that the world had once again failed to become one. On the contrary, the world was effectively split in two between the new superpowers—the United States and the Soviet Union. The Cold War often required the newly independent nations to situate themselves internationally vis-à-vis the two ideological camps. Interchangeably wooed and exploited by the big players, the developing nations had to navigate the murky waters of Cold War politics dominated by the East-West confrontation. In this situation, a significant number of them recognized the opportunities offered by the acquisition of a non-aligned status. To this end, twenty-nine African and Asian nations met at Bandung, Indonesia, in 1955. The conference participants sought to establish a common economic and cultural ground between nations of the newly liberated Third World. Only united and non-aligned, argued Indonesian President Sukarno, Indian Prime Minister Neru, and other speakers at the conference, can the young developing nations survive in the post-colonial world. The Non-Aligned Movement, launched in 1961, was intended to upgrade the bi-polar world by introducing a third independent force on the scene.

Yet the concept of the Third World, largely defined by the logic of the Cold War, didn't survive the test of time. The dream of anti-colonial solidarity remained largely a dream or yet a rhetorical tool of convenience as the ruling elites in the Third World lined up behind their respective superpower sponsors. Another problem lay in the very diversity of the newly independent nations, not all of them properly "poor." While the gap in per capita GNP between the "developed" and the "developing" world continued to widen (the first group averaged 14.5 times the GNP per capita of the second in 1970 and over twenty-four times the "less fortunate" countries' GNP per capita in 1990[7]), some parts of the Third World were either rapidly enriching themselves through oil (Arab Gulf states) or else rapidly industrializing (the "Pacific Tigers"). By mid-1970 it was difficult to see such nations as Saudi Arabia and Nigeria as belonging to the same geo-economic clan. The modern-day globalization thus arrived in the world, where the split between the rich "North" and the poor "South" was as real as it was nuanced. It took the end of the Cold War to reveal the poignancy and intricacy of this issue.

Globalization after the Cold War

At the height of Mikhail Gorbachev's *perestroika* in the Soviet Union, Francis Fukuyama penned a much-talked-about article in which he heralded the final triumph of liberal democracies. According to the author, Western liberalism, having prevailed over both fascism and communism, has finally reached the "end of history."[8] Fukuyama predicted the demise of ideological rivalries that shaped much of the twentieth-century history, and the rise, in their stead, of "Common Marketization" of international relations geared toward "the endless solving of technical problems, environmental concerns, and the satisfaction of sophisticated consumer demands." Life in such a "post-historical" world would be anything but exciting—no large-scale wars between states, no major economic or environmental calamities to distract us from the boredom of everyday prosperity. Fukuyama's argument goes to the core of the modern-day discourse on globalization—whether or not the world we inhabit in the beginning of the twenty-first century, with its shrinking distances and instantaneous communications, with its "McDonaldization" of national economies and the dominance of multinational corporations, is the inevitable final destination of our civilization.

By definition, globalization is a multi-faceted phenomenon. Its economic dimension becomes evident to anyone who checked the national origins of products purchased at shopping malls and supermarkets on several continents. In the new global economy neither distance nor national boundaries can slow down the flow of commerce. The radical reduction in transportation costs, the breaking down of communication barriers, and the emergence of a uniform informational space are bound to result in a closer integration of the countries and the people of the world. In this respect, globalization should be perceived as something more than just trade and financial transactions. As noted by Ulrich Beck, globalization calls into question one of the first premises of modernity, according to which the contours of society largely coincide with those of the national state. This is not to say that the nation-state is on the verge of dissolution, yet we observe the transformation of social spaces where identities, situations, and processes become increasingly transnational in nature.[9] Transnational space provides for a natural flow of ideas and values across invisible borders with a seemingly obvious end result: the creation of a universal civil society based on shared cultural principles, be it internationalized pop culture or human rights ideals. However, one doesn't have to be a Marxist to see that in its present form the emerging society of the global is firmly attached to the bandwagon of Western (especially American) capitalism. Champions and foes of globalization alike tend to recognize the primacy of international capitalist economics in shaping the outlines of what they hope or fear to be our global future. Both camps direct their intense attention to the main institutions governing globalization.

Institutions of Globalization

The International Monetary Fund (IMF), the World Bank, and the World Trade Organization (WTO) are the three key institutions at the center of economic transformations in the last two decades. The IMF and the World Bank both owe their origins to the post–World War II reconstruction effort expressed through the decisions of the UN Monetary and Financial Conference at Bretton Woods, New Hampshire, in July 1944. With much of the world still remaining in the colonial preserve, the reconstruction of war-ravaged Europe remained for a while the primary concern of the newly established bodies.

The decisions made at the Bretton Woods conference were profoundly influenced by the ideas of one of its participants—John Maynard Keynes, the British economist who had devoted much of his efforts to analyzing and explaining the origins of the Great Depression. Keynes's analysis produced a simple set of prescriptions for preventing global economic downturns. Governments, Keynes argued, could stimulate aggregate demand (and thus avoid economic depressions) by either increasing expenditures or cutting taxes. This kind of thinking was behind the creation of the IMF, the organization saddled with an all-important task of preventing another global economic meltdown. Just as the creators of the United Nations relied on joint international efforts in maintaining world peace, the founders of the IMF believed that economic stability could only be achieved through collective actions at a global level. The IMF functions as a public institution supported by taxpayers around the world, but it reports to the countries' central banks and ministries of finance. Because the bulk of taxpayers' money flows to the IMF from the major developed countries, and because the voting arrangement within the IMF is somewhat archaic (it is based on the economic prowess of the nations at the end of World War II), the institution continues to be dominated by the "usual suspects"—the industrial nations of the North, with only one country, the United States, exercising the right of veto.

By a strange historic irony, the IMF has undergone a profound metamorphosis in the six decades since its inception. From an institution inherently suspicious of markets, it has turned into a champion of free market forces. This change in institutional values and priorities began to materialize in the 1970s and greatly accelerated with the rise of neoliberalism (see more below) and the coming to power of two of its erstwhile proponents on the opposing shores of the Atlantic—Ronald Reagan in the United States and Margaret Thatcher in the United Kingdom. From the early 1980s onward, the IMF and the World Bank have sought to impose the free market paradigm on the Third World. Instead of simply lending for specific projects in developing countries, the World Bank was now providing comprehensive support to countries that met specific conditions imposed by the IMF. Through implementation of such structural adjustment programs the IMF reinvented itself as an integral part of the developing world.

This trend toward treating the world as a business venture was reflected in the creation of a number of organizations which placed economics at the center of global management. A club of European corporate leaders first gathered in the Swiss village of Davos in 1971. The so-called Davos club effectively reaffirmed Adam Smith's much earlier conclusions by articulating a very particular view of the world where the public good had to come out of trade, competition, and self-interest. Davos foreshadowed the arrival in 1975 of the G6 (now G8), the grouping of the world's largest economies, which together examined the world from the standpoint of commercial self-interest. The nations' economic power was dramatically shifting into the global market place, where it translated itself into a potent integrationist drive. So the economies of Canada and the United States were brought closer together under the 1988 Free Trade Agreement, with Mexico following suit after the signing of the North American Free Trade Agreement (NAFTA).

Sixty years ago the Bretton Woods agreement envisioned the creation of an economic organization to oversee and regulate international trade relations and to encourage the free flow of goods and services. The General Agreement on Tariffs and Trade (GATT) aimed at lowering tariffs by which countries upheld their economies at the expense of their neighbors. While succeeding in significantly reducing tariffs, the GATT never realized a genuinely global trade model. It took a fifty-year gestation period and the dissolution of the bi-polar international order to bring to life what can probably be considered globalization's most symbolic institution—the World Trade Organization (WTO). Launched in 1995, the WTO became a powerful centralized body to oversee commercial trade issues as well as a forum for trade negotiations. The WTO, a true pinnacle of globalization, treated global space as essentially commercial and thus subject to universally applied canons of trade. Needless to say, such categorical casting of the world in commercial terms required a comprehensive ideological substantiation.

Neoliberalism

If Adam Smith could be resurrected and introduced to some of the features of neoliberalism, he would probably find them extreme. Yet neoliberalism as an ideology of market capitalism in the age of globalism derives directly from the *Wealth of Nations*. Such classic market liberals as Adam Smith or David Ricardo firmly believed in the moral necessity of market forces in the economy. Early liberals saw the entrepreneur as an inherently positive social agent, someone giving civilization a sense of direction and ethical content. Economic liberals of the past advocated *laissez-faire* or the abolition of government intervention in the matters of the economy; they argued for the removal of restrictions on manufacturing, for the elimination of commercial barriers and tariffs. Individual enterprise stimulated by the conditions of "free trade" was essential for propelling nations toward economic prosperity. Modern day neoliberals build their arguments on a two-hundred-year-old theoretical foundation:

> The natural effort of every individual to better his own condition, when suffered to exert itself with freedom and security, is so powerful a principle, that it is alone, and without any assistant, not only capable of carrying on the society to wealth and prosperity, but of surmounting a hundred impertinent obstructions with which the folly of human laws too often encumbers its operations.[10]

Advocates of neoliberalism (also known as neoconservatism) adhere passionately to the old liberal belief in the magic powers of the market. Born out of the economic difficulties of the 1970s (especially exacerbated by the 1973 oil embargo) and the profound disillusionment with the efficacy of Western governments and "collectivist structures," neoliberalism aspires to a global free market society. Neoliberalism is far more than an economic theory; rather, it is a worldview focusing on repeated and increasingly frequent transactions between business units and members of the society alike. As befits an all-inclusive philosophy, neoliberalism supplies answers to stereotypical philosophical questions. The meaning of life in neoliberal interpretation is organically connected to participation in the market, where every human being becomes an entrepreneur managing his own life. The free market turns into a mechanism to determine "collective choice" on an individual basis. In other words, the market principle is being extended to non-economic areas of life.

In political terms, neoliberals advocate a "minimal state" unburdened by excessive intervention in the economy and social life. Governments, in their opinion, become coercive when they interfere with people's own capacity to determine their interests. And so do trade unions when they attempt to interfere with the free-flowing and market-oriented labor process. It is natural for a neoliberal to argue for the reduction of public expenditure for social services as well as for the reorientation of perceptions of public and communal good towards individualism and individual responsibility. Based on the above we can summarize some of the guiding principles behind the ideology of neoliberalism:

- Sustained economic growth is the way to human progress.
- Free markets without government "interference" would be the most efficient and socially optimal allocation of resources.
- Wealth, accumulated at the top, will "trickle down" to benefit the society at large.
- Economic globalization would be beneficial to everyone.
- Privatization removes inefficiencies of the public sector.
- Governments should function mainly to provide the infrastructure to advance the rule of law with respect to property rights and transactions.

At the international level this would additionally translate to:

- Freedom of trade in goods and services.
- Unimpeded circulation of capital.
- Freedom to invest.

The champions of neoliberalism herald the arrival of a new global world order defined by the withering away of traditional nation-states. In accordance with this line of thinking, nationalism presents an impediment to progress—yet not a moral or ethical impediment. Rather, nation-states are viewed as "unnatural and even impossible business units" in the world of borderless and denationalized economies where national governments are transforming into transmission belts for global market forces. In other words, "where states were once the masters of markets, now it is the market which, on many critical issues, is the master over the government of states . . . the declining authority of states is reflected in a growing diffusion of authority to other institutions and associations."[11] Globalization has evoked in its supporters, elites, and ideologues the sense of new transnational identity reinforced by their attachment to neoliberal economic orthodoxy. The global spread of Western liberal democracy will, in the neoliberal view, inadvertently result in the retreat of cultural particularism and in the rise of new civilization characterized by universal standards of political and economic order. This breathtaking vision of a "Brave New World" based on and directed by the market has an enormous appeal, particularly for those who have already benefited from the globalized economic arrangement. Yet not everybody has benefited from it. Moreover, there is a growing realization among the critics of globalization that not everybody will.

Globalization vs. Anti-globalization

As the second millennium was drawing to its close amid widespread fears of major global network disruptions, an estimated 50,000 protesters rallied in Seattle to shut down the opening conference of the World Trade Organization. The events in Seattle of November–December 1999 and their sporadically violent follow-ups in Washington, D.C., Genoa, and Prague moved the globalization debate to the front pages of newspapers across several continents. A motley assemblage of left-wing radicals, trade unionists, environmentalists, anarchists, young idealists, and Third World activists challenged the neoliberal dogma and its institutional manifestations. Behind the smashed windows of McDonald's restaurants and the torched skeletons of German-designed and Mexican-manufactured cars the observers of the protests could discern a powerful and passionate ideological opposition to some of the sacred postulates of global capitalism. For the growing number of skeptics and critics of globalization the phenomenon represents the latest stage in the history of capitalist accumulation with multinational capital taking over political power of nation-states. The agendas of the two opposing camps increasingly appear irreconcilable. "After the Cold War, the fourth world war has started," declared the icon of the antiglobalization movement, a mysterious Zapatista Sub-Commandante Marcos. And this battle cry has resonated around the world.

The idea of globalization, its opponents argue, serves to justify and legitimize the neoliberal global project, which in fact is the creation of a global free market for Western (particularly American) capitalism within the world's major economic regions. For this purpose the ideology of globalization operates as a myth and as a propaganda tool to discipline and convert the citizenship to the demands of the global marketplace. Orthodox Marxists go even further in their critical analysis of globalization, which they interpret as a key element in traditional capitalist expansionism. Continuous expansion of its geographical reach is in the nature of national capitalism. The history of the modern world is often reduced by Marxists to the history of Western capitalist powers dividing up and redividing the world into exclusive economic zones. The formal empires of the past, they assert, have been replaced by a new global arrangement based on mechanisms of multilateral control and supervision such the G8 group, the World Bank, and so forth. Marxists are reluctant to utilize the language of globalization and instead consider the current period as a new form of Western imperialism born out of the needs of finance capital within the world's major capitalist states. Yet another brand of criticism focuses on geopolitics by assigning the overwhelming globalizing agency to the major economic and military powers. The internationalization of economic and political relations is seen as contingent on the policies and preferences of the super powers of the day since only they have sufficient economic resources and military muscle to enforce their will. In the unipolar world of today, the United States is the only power capable of effectively exercising its hegemony, and, therefore, globalization should be understood as an American-facilitated project. Globalization, for these critics, equals Americanization.

So what about the more specific criticisms of globalization put forward by its adversaries? The most common of those looks at the polarizing effect globalization has allegedly had on the "family of nations." Contrary to the promise of the "world as one," globalization, its detractors allege, accentuated the fault lines between the developed industrialized North and the developing South, where 1.3 billion people currently live on less than $1 a day. The benefits of globalization remain disproportionately confined to the developed regions of the world while the developing nations continue to be bedeviled by economic disparities and poverty. Similar polarization is taking place within the developing countries themselves between the minority of economic and political elites and the vast majority of the population. In other words, globalization has conditioned a new polarization and stratification of the world population into globalized rich and localized poor. As Zigmunt Bauman put it, "some have the planet as their residence, while others are chained to the spot." Globalization seems to be unable to reverse the global spread of inequality—first, between the North and the South; second, within the industrialized developed nations where the underclass has been growing as a result of outsourcing; and third, within the developing countries of the Third World. The following table reveals the decreasing share of global income going to the poorest 20 percent of the global population over the period 1960–1990 and the increasing share going to the richest 20 percent over the same period.

Another important criticism of globalization draws attention to the impact of the spreading global capitalist project on national cultures. Cultural nationalists insist that Western-style consumer culture has effectively subverted local traditional aesthetics. Local cultural productions are being filtered by Western demand for voguish multiculturalism, which, by the way, has also become a marketable commodity in the West. Revelers in a trendy Afro-beat club in Manhattan may have difficulty imagining that back in Nigeria the overwhelming majority of the population is too busy surviving or living up to a Western consumer dream to appreciate the privileged New Yorkers' infatuation with Fela Kuti. For those people "in the street" the developed world comes across less like a benevolent and culturally sensitive giant and more like an exclusive club for the supranational elites as inaccessible as those tennis courts behind the guarded walled compounds of Western oil corporations. Since globalization has arrived in the Third World in the form of an elitist operation, many individual citizens in the developing countries these days feel left out, powerless, and alienated from their natural social and cultural environment.

The supporters of globalization have long promised the withering away of nationalist conflicts and rivalries in the world where the borders between nation-states were becoming less rigid and more open to the flow of goods, ideas, and information. Yet the skeptics disagree. They emphasize the enduring qualities and the continuous emotional appeal of national identities, especially when compared with the "rootless" and ersatz nature of the transnational commercial culture. Furthermore, the doubters point out the special role played by new communication systems in the consolidation of various nationalist projects. While technological achievements of the fiber-optic age have created access

Table 15.1. Global Income Distribution, 1960–1990

Year	Share of global income going to richest 20% (%)	Share of global income going to poorest 20% (%)	Ratio of richest to poorest
1960	70.2	2.3	30:1
1970	73.9	2.3	32:1
1980	76.3	1.7	45:1
1990	82.8	1.3	64:1

Source: Caroline Thomas and Peter Wilkin, eds., *Globalization and the South* (New York: St. Martin's, 1997), 3.

to distant others, they can also generate an acute awareness of differences and stimulate unprecedented interest and involvement in local affairs. In some respects, the critics argue, globalization has rendered local cultures even more robust and insulated.

The nation-state remains very much alive, and the reports of its demise, it seems, have been greatly exaggerated. In fact, a number of observers have suggested that by the end of the twentieth century nationalism and the nation-states were stronger than they had been when globalization began. The bloody ethnic wars in the Balkans during the 1990s were happening just as international elites were declaring the irrelevance of nation-states. And so globalization's triumph with the creation of the WTO in 1995 coincided with the Dayton Accords, which paved the way for the creation of new nation-states in the Balkans. The "world without borders" was also apparently incapable or unwilling to stop the Rwandan genocide of 1994 when some 800,000 people were slaughtered over a period of several weeks. As the massacres proceeded in Central Africa, the old-fashioned assemblage of nation-states at the United Nations soundly failed to rally an international intervention to prevent the killing. Since the Rwandan tragedy the mass-scale ethnic and racial murders proceeded almost unabated in the Congo, in the Sudan, and elsewhere. Obviously the widely celebrated accomplishments of global economic governance have been spectacularly irrelevant in the crisis areas of the world. The era of globalization has also proved to be the time of an accelerated political meltdown and the increased levels of nationalist violence.

To Repair or to Repay?

As the reality of global inequality and the dire economic predicament of much of the developing world have become painfully clear, even the moderates have begun to raise their voices for a coordinated set of measures to curtail the excesses of globalization and to soften its impact on the developing world. In his recent memoir-reflection on globalization, the Nobel Prize winner Joseph Stiglitz recognized the necessity for reform and general overhaul of the established institutions and strategies of globalization. Stiglitz refuses to reject globalization, while acknowledging its apparent deficiencies. One of the most influential voices in the current debate, Stiglitz suggests several possible venues of reform. As with any major undertaking the reform of globalization requires a change in the mindset of those in charge of it. The developed nations need to acquire a greater sensitivity to—and understanding of—local conditions. The captains of globalizing efforts need to differentiate between local, national, and global operational levels. The latter should entail collective action through systems of global governance. When the issues associated with global peace, global health, and global environment are at stake, the world community has a special responsibility for global collective action—such as in cases of genocide, AIDS, and global warming. To this end—that is, to make globalization work for everybody—changes in governance are a must. The supporters of reform argue that a sure way to make the international economic institutions more responsive to the needs of the poor, to the environment, and to broader social and political concerns is to increase their openness and transparency, to eradicate the "culture of secrecy" permeating the structures of the IMF, the WTO, or the World Bank. These institutions need to respect the citizens' *right to know*, as recognized through laws such as America's Freedom of Information Act.

On a more practical level the reformists call for a restructuring of the global financial architecture whereby the IMF would limit itself to managing crises without micromanaging the economies of transition. Responses to various financial crises should be placed within an appropriate social and political context. The conditions that the IMF imposes on countries in crisis need to be more narrowly defined and more situation-specific. In a similar vein, the proponents of reform argue against the imposition of a myriad of conditions, often political in nature, as a precondition for assistance to the developing countries where such *conditionality* has routinely undermined democratic processes. The recipients of aid should be allowed to choose for themselves their own development strategies. In addition, the lending institutions are encouraged to reconsider and even forgive some of the developing nations' debts. It has been noted that when the IMF and the World Bank had lent money to notoriously corrupt regimes (such as Zaire under Mobutu), they should have known that they were not contributing to the economic prosperity of those unhappy nations. In so many words, the developing world stands to benefit from globalization with a human face which, freed from the heavy-handedness of its governing institutions, provides for openness and fairness vis-à-vis the poor nations.

In the last few years the moderate calls for reforms have sometimes been overshadowed by more radical appeals to the West to repair past and present injustices inflicted on the Third World. Such demands have been articulated by the growing global anti-capitalist movement representing a vast and diverse array of social movements and non-governmental organizations (NGOs), from anarchists to social democrats to left-wing Third World activists. The movement has attracted world attention through its globally coordinated campaigns of protest against the subordination of human and ecological security to the interests of global market. Besides mass street actions at all major globalization summits, the movement launched several highly publicized single-issue campaigns such as Jubilee 2000 seeking debt cancellation for poor countries, mobilization against the Multilateral Agreement on Investment proposing a global charter of rights for multinational companies (MNCs), or the most recent campaign for a Tobin tax on global financial speculation.

Even more radical appear to be the demands for a more substantive change in the system of global governance with the introduction of alternative systems which would privilege people over profits and the local over global. These committed critics of globalization seek to de-legitimize its purposes and institutions and to contest the existing distribution of wealth and resources in the world. One of the ways to undermine the status quo is to question the legitimacy of the present world order by revealing its exploitative nature and origins. The currently raging debates over the issue of reparations to the descendants of African slaves or to the poor nations that have borne the brunt of Western industrialization should be viewed in this context. The 2001 World Conference Against Racism, Racial Discrimination, Xenophobia and Related Intolerance (WCAR) in Durban, South Africa, acknowledged the trans-Atlantic slave trade as a crime against humanity yet stopped short of demanding reparations from the developed world. This did not satisfy the reparations camp. In considering the trans-Atlantic slave trade and colonialism as the historical sources of present-day globalization, the pro-reparation argument invariably places the processes and outcomes of globalization within the general framework of Atlantic history:

> The damage done to Africa by slavery, the trans-Atlantic Slave Trade and colonialism is irreparable yet the provision of reparations is a measure of protection for the future generations and a deterrent to insure that such barbaric crimes will never be committed against the continent again. . . . The current international economic regime was built on a biased and discriminatory order that favors the expropriation and exploitation of resources of the poor underdeveloped countries to the benefit of rich nations thus consolidating and entrenching racism and racial discrimination.[12]

Even though the outcome of the current debate on reparations is far from certain, it undoubtedly succeeded in bringing the dark past of globalization into the limelight of public scrutiny. From its beginnings as a fringe phenomenon, the reparations movement has evolved into one of the most hotly contested (and most divisive) issues in the current discourse on globalization. At the very least it adds another powerful dimension to the moral argument for a just and equitable management of the world shaped by the processes of global integration.

From Global Resistance to Regional and Local Initiatives

Even the most vociferous opponents of "Washington Consensus," or the neoliberal model of our world's global future, recognize and appropriate the reality of globalization. And here global ideas and local actions merge. A good example of this could be found in the proliferation of NGOs that often operate outside of national and corporate discourses. According to David Henderson, the rise of NGOs in the last decades of the twentieth century represented the fulcrum of the "global anti-globalist movement."[13] Even though NGOs are overwhelmingly supranational, and thus intrinsically tied to the processes of globalization, they more often than not articulate anti-liberal and anti-capitalist positions. NGOs routinely advocate self-reliance and local initiatives while remaining critical of such manifestations of global capitalism as multinational enterprises and an unrestricted cross-border flow of trade and capital investment. As a counterbalance to global capitalism, NGOs launch and support initiatives at grassroots levels fomenting alternative economic enterprises and financing local social programs directed toward the marginalized subjects.[14] On a practical level, by stimulating local initiatives, the NGOs in fact attempt to bring about a reversal of the aspects of globalization viewed as damaging and unfair to the developing world. Some anti-globalist activists have conceived of this process in terms of de-globalization, or the movement toward a plural arrangement, a world where, in words of Sub-Comandante Marcos, many worlds fit.

The Zapatista uprising in Chiapas led by the enigmatic Marcos encapsulated the very essence of this drive to rearrange the modern "global village." The Zapatistas declared war on neoliberal globalization on January 1, 1994, the very day when the North American Free Trade Agreement (NAFTA) went into effect. From the very beginning the Zapatista rebellion became the focal point of a broadly based international civil society movement against neoliberalism and for social justice. In a manifest departure from the usual dichotomy of global capitalism versus the traditional left, the Zapatistas articulated a new brand of "local-global" politics. They did draw the world's attention to the dire consequences of globalization in the South, yet in doing so they took full advantage of the global communication networks and infused their message with postmodern global symbolism. In 1996, the Zapatista National Liberation Army (EZLN) organized and hosted two major events designed to stimulate a "local-global" dialogue. Both the Continental Gathering and the Intercontinental Encounter for Humanity and Against Neoliberalism embraced the rhetoric of a democratic transformation directed by civil society on a scale that was nothing short of planetary (the latter gathering also dabbed itself the Intergalactic Encounter).

In many respects the global resistance networks (many of them inspired by the Zapatistas) are the mirror image of their arch foe, the neoliberal world of global capitalism and its institutions. Global activism combines the concern for localism and autonomy among the participants with cosmopolitan appeals for cross-cultural solidarity. "Global" activists, for example, welcomed the opportunity to attend such "official" global meetings as the UN-sponsored summits in Rio and Beijing. The Zapatistas' example fueled the growth of many groups who challenge neoliberal globalization through horizontally structured yet global solidarity movements. The People's Global Action (PGA) became one such organization that can trace its genesis back to the jungle of Chiapas. Founded in Geneva in 1998 by hundreds of delegates from seventeen different countries, the PGA is a diverse and egalitarian coalition of autonomous actors (from Sri Lanka fishermen to Brazilian peasants to Dutch squatters) whose intention is to provide logistic support and global coordination for massive transnational protests against neoliberalism.[15] The huge protest rallies against the World Bank and the IMF paralyzed parts of Washington, D.C., in April 2000. Even though demonstrators failed to disrupt the ongoing meetings of the WTO, they nevertheless could claim to their credit a remarkable degree of coordination, much of it through such global activist networks as transnational gender alliances and environmental justice movements. Just as the protesters marched through Washington, the Group of 77, an organization claiming to represent the governments of 80 percent of the world's population, convened its meeting in Havana, Cuba. In his address to the gathering South African president Thabo Mbeki voiced sentiments similar to those championed by the Zapatistas: "We believe consciousness is rising, including in the north, about the inequality and insecurity globalization has brought."[16] In other words, the global neoliberal agenda not only stirred up the local actors but also created a truly global backlash of activism and resistance.

The same tendency to fuse local sensibilities and concerns with global outreach is evident in a number of alternative social and economic initiatives, many of them originating in and focused on the South. The recent United Nations' *Report on the Implementation of South-South Cooperation* indicates that the developing countries are placing renewed emphasis on South-South cooperation in efforts to reduce growing gaps between rich and poor countries. There is a growing consensus among the developing nations of the South (many of them disaffected with the structural adjustment programs, or SAPs, of the previous two decades) that South-South relations would enable countries adversely impacted by globalization to learn winning development strategies through mutual exchange of ideas, resources, skills, and country-specific know-how.[17] It is no coincidence that the first World Social Forum (WSF I), held in Porto Alegre, Brazil, in January 2001, organized some 10,000 participants around the rallying cry "Another World Is Possible." This new world, the argument has it, would leave behind the age-old patterns of inequality and the legacy of exploitation of the poor developing South by the rich industrialized North.

The trend toward South-South cooperation manifests itself in the creation or in some cases reinvention of regional institutions. In 1999–2002, the African

Union (AU) succeeded the ailing Organization of African Unity (OAU) as the premier organization promoting the processes of socio-economic integration on the continent. The founders of the AU justified the creation of the new continent-wide body by citing Africa's numerous social, economic, and political problems compounded by "certain negative aspects of globalization."[18] The recently increased visibility of the Economic Community of West African States (ECOWAS) and the expanding economic reach of the South American Common Market (MERCOSUR) provide representative examples of the growing commitment in the developing world to foster sub-regional cooperation as a forerunner to full regional integration.

The champions of South-South cooperation are hopeful that local alternative economies will successfully challenge the dominant neoliberal paradigm. Partly a response to the rigidity and cultural insensitivity of SAPs and partly a corollary to sheer economic desperation of local populations, the new "post-modern" economies are often driven by grassroots movements, which improvise and create new alternatives from the bottom up. The interests of small-scale producers are clearly behind Brazil's Landless movement (Sem-Terra), which takes over idle or ill-used land and then sets up cooperatives and provides infrastructure necessary for the social and economic viability of the rural poor. Autonomous communities with integrated economic and social programs, such Gaviotas in Colombia or the Zapatistas' projects in Chiapas, Mexico, stress self-reliance and symbolize the rise of the marginalized economic actors in the Third World. Roger Burbach has identified a linkage between these essentially rural movements and the new urban activism. The struggles of the cocoa farmers in Bolivia and the Indian uprisings in Ecuador were often led by those who had spent time in the cities and participated in the activities of the municipal and community-owned enterprises. Even more remarkable is the fact that many of these struggles, while originating in local circumstances, seek to situate themselves in a transnational and transcontinental context. The Landless movement in Brazil, for example, routinely secures international funding and solicits NGOs' support for its alternative economic projects, while socially responsible investment companies have financed several community-oriented and alternative economic enterprises in South Africa.[19]

It is probably not a mere coincidence that by the end of the twentieth century significant challenges to the "Washington Consensus," or the neoliberal vision of globalization, emerged in the areas geographically or historically linked to the Atlantic basin. For centuries the Atlantic World served as an immense laboratory of globalization. The cross-Atlantic travels, conquests, trade, cultural exchanges, and migrations have defined much of modern civilization. Since, after decades of unequal exchanges, profound economic and structural inequality between the developed North and the largely impoverished South continues to be the essential feature of this civilization, there exists, especially at the grassroots levels, a growing realization of the defectiveness of current global arrangement. Disillusioned with the industrial nations' unwillingness or simply inability to adequately address the concerns of the poor nations and their populations, local actors begin to take matters into their own hands. Ironically, the very strategies of their resistance often reaffirm the global nature of the modern world and the new subjects' intrinsic connection to and their awareness of the Atlantic history.

Notes

1. Frederick Cooper, "What Is the Concept of Globalization Good For? An African Historian's Perspective," *African Affairs* 100:399 (2001): 189–213.
2. Richard Drayton, "The Collaboration of Labour: Slaves, Empires, and Globalizations in the Atlantic World, *c.* 1600–1850," in *Globalization in World History*, ed. A. G. Hopkins (London: Pimlico, 2002), 98–114.
3. Milton Meltzer, *Slavery: A World History* (New York: Da Capo Press, 1993) 2:44.
4. David Richardson, "The Slave Trade, Sugar, and British Economic Growth, 1748–1776," *Journal of Interdisciplinary History*, 17 (1987): 757–763.
5. See A .G. Hopkins, "The History of Globalization—and the Globalization of History?" in Hopkins, *Globalization in World History*, 11–46.
6. Jeffrey G. Williamson, "Globalization, Convergence and History," *Journal of Economic History*, 56:2 (June 1996): 277–306; also see Paul Hirst and Grahame Thompson, *Globalization in Question: The International Economy and the Possibilities of Governance* (Cambridge: Cambridge University Press, 1996), 18–31.
7. *World Tables 1991* (Washington, D.C.: World Bank, 1991).
8. Francis Fukuyama, "The End of History?" *National Interest*, no. 16 (Summer 1989): 3–18.
9. Ulrich Beck, *What Is Globalization?* (Maiden, Mass.: Blackwell, 2000).
10. Adam Smith, *An Inquiry into the Nature and Causes of the Wealth of Nations*, quoted in Brink Lindsey, *Against the Dead Hand: The Uncertain Struggle for Global Capitalism* (New York: John Wiley, 2002), 256.
11. Susan Strange, *The Retreat of the State: The Diffusion of Power in the World Economy* (Cambridge: Cambridge University Press, 1996).
12. "Statement on Item 6: Racism, Racial Discrimination, Xenophobia, and All Forms of Discrimination. Joint Written Statement by Fédération Mondiale Démocratique, Centre Europe-Tiers Monde, Nord-Sud XXI," *Human Rights Commission*, 2002 (E/CN.4/2002/NGO/21).
13. David Henderson, "Anti-Liberalism 2000: The Rise of New Millennium Collectivism," in *Thirtieth Wincott Lecture 12 October 2000* (London: Institute of Economic Affairs, 2000), 19–20.
14. For a thoughtful discussion of the rise and functions of NGOs see Roger Burbach, *Globalization and Postmodern Politics: From Zapatistas to High-Tech Robber Barons* (London: Pluto Press, 2001), 97–98.
15. Lesley J. Wood, "Bridging the Chasms: The Case of Peoples' Global Action," in *Coalitions across Borders: Transnational Protest and the Neoliberal Order*, ed. Joe Bandy and Jackie Smith (New York: Rowman and Littlefield, 2005), 95–120.

16. See "Poor Nations Leaders Back Washington Protestors," *Washington Post*, April 16, 2000, A31.

17. *Report on the Implementation of South-South Cooperation*, Executive Board of the United Nations Development Programme and of the United Nations Populations Fund (June 7, 2004).

18. See "African Union in a Nutshell," African Union, http://www.africa-union.org/root/AU/AboutAu/au_in_a_nutshell_en.htm, accessed June 8, 2007.

19. Burbach, *Globalization and Postmodern Politics*, 112.

Bibliography

Abimbola, Wande. *Ifa Divination Poetry.* New York: Nok, 1977.

Adams, John. *Remarks on the Country Extending from Cape Palmas to the River Congo.* London: G. and W. B. Whittaker, 1823.

Adams, Richard E. W., and Murdo J. MacLeod, eds. *The Cambridge History of the Native Peoples of the Americas.* Vol. 2, *Mesoamerica.* Cambridge: Cambridge University Press, 2000. 2 vols.

Afshar, Haleh, and Stephanie Barrientos. *Women, Globalization and Fragmentation in the Developing World.* New York: St. Martin's, 1999.

Agorsah, Kofi E. "Ethnoarchaeological Consideration of Social Relationship and Settlement Patterning among Africans in the Caribbean Diaspora." In *African Sites Archaeology in the Caribbean,* ed. Jay B. Haviser, 38–64. Princeton: Markus Wiener, 1999.

Ali, Hakim, and Marika Sherwood. *Pan-African History: Political Figures from Africa and the Diaspora since 1787.* London: Routledge, 2003.

Alpers, Edward A. "The Impact of the Slave Trade on East Central Africa in the Nineteenth Century." In *Forced Migration,* ed. J. E. Inikori, 242–273. New York: Africana, 1982.

Altman, Ida, and James Horn, eds. *"To Make America": European Emigration in the Early Modern Period.* Berkeley: University of California Press, 1991.

Amadiume, Ifi. *Male Daughters, Female Husbands: Gender and Sex in African Society.* London: Zed Books, 1987.

——. *Reinventing Africa: Matriarchy, Religion and Culture.* London: Zed Books, 1997.

Andrews, George Reid. "Black and White Workers: São Paulo, Brazil, 1888–1928." *Hispanic American Historical Review* 68:3 (1988): 491–524.

Andrien, Kenneth. *Transatlantic Encounters: Europeans and Andeans in the Sixteenth Century.* Berkeley: University of California Press, 1991.

Anstey, Roger. *The Atlantic Slave Trade and British Abolition.* Atlantic Highlands, N.J.: Humanities Press, 1975.

Aptheker, Herbert. *Afro American History: The Modern Era.* Seacaucus, N.J.: Citadel Press, 1971.

———. *American Negro Slave Revolts.* New York: Columbia University Press, 1943.

Armitage, David, and Michael J. Braddick, eds. *The British Atlantic World, 1500–1800.* New York: Palgrave Macmillan, 2002.

Arthur, Charles, and Michael Dash, eds. *Libéte: A Haiti Anthology.* London: Latin America Bureau, 1999.

Astley, Thomas. *A New General Collection of Voyages and Travels: Consisting of the most Esteemed Relations which have hitherto been published in any Language.* London: Frank Cass, 1st ed., 1745–1747.

Bailyn, Bernard. "The Idea of Atlantic History." *Itinerario* 20:1 (1996): 38–44.

———. *The Peopling of British North America.* New York: Alfred A. Knopf, 1986.

Bandy, Joe, and Jackie Smith, eds. *Coalition across Borders: Transnational Protest and the Neoliberal Order.* New York: Rowman and Littlefield, 2005.

Barry, Boubacar. *Senegambia and the Atlantic Slave Trade.* New York: Cambridge University Press, 1998.

Bartlett, Robert. *The Making of Europe: Conquest, Colonization, and Cultural Change, 950–1350.* London: Penguin, 1993.

Bascom, William. *Shango in the New World.* Austin: African and Afro-American Research Institute, 1972.

———. "Two Forms of Afro-Cuban Divination." In *Acculturation in the Americas,* ed. Sol Tax, 169–179. Chicago: University of Chicago Press, 1952.

Bauman, Zygmunt. *Globalization.* Cambridge: Cambridge University Press, 1998.

Beck, Ulrich. *What Is Globalization?* Maiden, Mass.: Blackwell, 2000.

Beckles, Hilary. *Natural Rebels: A Social History of Black Women in Barbados.* New Brunswick, N.J.: Rutgers University Press, 1989.

Beckles, Hilary, and Verene Shepard, eds. *Caribbean Freedom: Economy and Society from Emancipation to the Present.* Princeton, N.J.: Markus Wiener, 1996.

Beier, Ulli. "Festival of the Images." *Nigeria* 45 (1954): 14–20.

Beneria, Lourdes. *Gender, Development, and Globalization: Economics as If People Mattered.* New York: Routledge, 2003.

Benezet, Anthony. A *Cautions and A Warning to Great Britain and Her Colonies in a Short Representation of the Calamitous State of the Enslaved Negroes in the British Dominions.* Philadelphia: 1766; London: 1767; New York: 1969.

———. *A Short Account of that part of Africa, Inhabited by the Negroes.* Philadelphia, 1762; Paris, 1767; London and Dublin, 1768.

———. *Some Historical Account of Guinea, Its Situation, Produce and General Disposition of Its Inhabitants. With an Inquiry into the Rise and Progress of the Slave Trade Its nature and Lamentable Effects.* Philadelphia: 1771; London: 1772.

Berger, Iris, and E. Frances White. *Women in Sub-Saharan Africa: Restoring Women to History.* Bloomington: Indiana University Press, 1999.

Berlin, Ira. "From Creole to African: Atlantic Creoles and the Origins of African American Society in Mainland North America." *William and Mary Quarterly,* 3rd ser., 53 (1996): 251–288.

———. *Many Thousands Gone: The First Two Centuries of Slavery in North America.* Cambridge, Mass.: Belknap, 1998.

———. *Slaves without Masters: The Free Negro in the Antebellum South.* New York: Pantheon Books, 1974.

Bethell, Leslie. *The Abolition of the Brazilian Slave Trade: Britain, Brazil, and the Slave Trade Question, 1807–1869.* Cambridge: Cambridge University Press, 1970.

Bisnauth, Dale. *A History of Religions in the Caribbean.* Jamaica: Kingston Publishers, 1989.

Blackburn, Robin. *The Making of New World Slavery: From the Baroque to the Modern, 1492–1800.* London: Verso, 1997.

———. *The Overthrow of Colonial Slavery.* London: Verso, 1988.

Boxer, C. R. *The Portuguese Seaborne Empire, 1415–1825.* New York: Alfred A. Knopf, 1969.

Brewer, John. *The Sinews of Power: War, Money, and the English State, 1688–1783.* New York: Alfred A. Knopf, 1989.

Brock, Lisa, and Digna Castañeda Fuertes, eds. *Between Race and Empire: African-Americans and Cubans before the Revolution.* Philadelphia: Temple University Press, 1998.

Brooks, George E. *Landlords and Strangers: Ecology, Society, and Trade in Western Africa, 1000–1630.* San Francisco: Westview, 1993.

Brown, Kathleen M. *Good Wives, Nasty Wenches and Anxious Patriarchs.* Chapel Hill: University of North Carolina Press, 1996.

Bruns, Roger, ed. *Am I Not a Man and a Brother: The Antislavery Crusade of Revolutionary America: 1688–1788.* New York: Chelsea House, 1977.

Buckley, Gail. *American Patriots: The Story of Blacks in the Military from the Revolutionary War to Desert Storm.* New York: Random House, 2001.

Burke, Edmund. *Collected Works.* Vol. 5. London, 1852.

Burkholder, Mark A., and Lyman L. Johnson, *Colonial Latin America.* Oxford: Oxford University Press, 1998.

Bush, Barbara. *Slave Women in Caribbean Society, 1650–1838.* Bloomington: Indiana University Press, 1990.

Butler, Kim. *Freedoms Given, Freedoms Won: Afro-Brazilians in Post-Abolition São Paulo and Salvador.* New Brunswick, N.J.: Rutgers University Press, 1998.

———. "From Black History to Diaspora History: Brazilian Abolition in Afro-Atlantic Context." *African Studies Review* 43:1 (2000): 125–139.

Calloway, Colin. *New Worlds for All: Indians, Europeans, and the Remaking of Early America.* Baltimore: Johns Hopkins University Press, 1997.

Campbell, Mavis C. *The Maroons of Jamaica, 1655–1796.* Trenton, N.J.: African World Press, 1990.

Canny, Nicholas, ed. *Europeans on the Move: Studies on European Migration, 1500–1800.* Oxford: Clarendon Press, 1994.

Carroll, Joseph C. *Slave Insurrections in the United States, 1800–1865.* Boston: Chapman and Grimes, 1938.

Caulfield, Sueann. *In Defense of Honor: Sexual Morality, Modernity, and Nation in Early-Twentieth-Century Brazil.* Durham, N.C.: Duke University Press, 2000.

Chafer, Tony. *The End of Empire in French West Africa: France's Successful Decolonization?* Oxford: Berg, 2002.

Chomsky, Aviva, Barry Carr, and Pamela Maria Smorkaloff, eds. *The Cuba Reader: History, Culture, Politics.* Durham, N.C.: Duke University Press, 2003.

Cipolla, Carlo M. *Guns, Sails, and Empires.* Manhattan, Kans.: Sunflower University Press, 1965.

Clarkson, Thomas. *The History of the Rise, Progress and Accomplishment of the Abolition of the Slave Trade by the British Parliament.* 2 vols. London, 1808.

Clendinnen, Inga. *Ambivalent Conquests: Maya and Spaniard in the Yucatan, 1517–1570.* Cambridge: Cambridge University Press, 1987.

Cobley, Alan G., and Thompson, Alvin, eds. *The African-Caribbean Connection: Historical and Cultural Perspectives.* Barbados: University of West Indies, 1990.

Coe, Michael D., and Rex Koontz. *Mexico: From the Olmecs to the Aztecs.* 5th ed. London: Thames and Hudson, 1994.

Collins, Robert O., ed. *Documents from the African Past.* Princeton, N.J.: Marcus Wiener, 2001.

"The Colonial and Post Colonial Experience: Five Centuries of Spanish and Portuguese America." Quincentenary supplement to *Journal of Latin American Studies* 24 (1992).

Connelly, Matthew James. *A Diplomatic Revolution: Algeria's Fight for Independence and the Origins of the Post–Cold War Era.* Oxford: Oxford University Press, 2002.

Conniff, Michael, and Thomas J. Davis. *Africans in the Americas: A History of the Black Diaspora.* New York: St. Martin's, 1994.

Cook, Noble David. *Born to Die: Disease and New World Conquest, 1492–1650.* Cambridge: Cambridge University Press, 1998.

Cooper, Frederick. "What Is the Concept of Globalization Good For? An African Historian's Perspective." *African Affairs* 100 (2001): 189–213.

Costa, Emilla Viotti da Costa. *The Brazilian Empire: Myths and Histories.* Chicago: University of Chicago Press, 1985.

Craton, Michael. *Testing the Chains: Resistance to Slavery in the West Indies.* Ithaca, N.Y.: Cornell University Press, 1982.

Crawford, Vicki L., Jacqueline Anne Rouse, and Barbara Woods, eds. *Women in the Civil Rights Movement: Trailblazers and Torchbearers, 1941–1965.* Bloomington: Indiana University Press, 1993.

Crosby, A. W. *The Columbian Exchange: Biological and Cultural Consequences of 1492.* Westport, Conn.: Greenwood, 1972.

Cugoano, Ottabah. *Thoughts and Sentiments on the Evil and Wicked Traffic of Slavery and Commerce of the Human Species.* 1787; reprint, New York: Penguin, 1999.

Curtin, Philip D. *The Rise and Fall of the Plantation Complex: Essays in Atlantic History.* Cambridge: Cambridge University Press, 1990.

David, T. J. *A Rumor of Revolt: "The Great Negro Plot" in Colonial New York.* New York: Free Press, 1985.

Davis, David Brion. *The Problem of Slavery in the Age of the American Revolution.* Ithaca, N.Y.: Cornell University Press, 1975.

———. *The Problem of Western Culture.* Ithaca, N.Y.: Cornell University Press, 1966.

Deagan, Kathleen A. *Columbus's Outpost among the Tainos: Spain and America at La Isabela, 1493–1498.* New Haven, Conn.: Yale University Press, 2002.

DeCorse, Christopher. "Historical Archaeological Research in Ghana, 1986–1987." *Nyame Akuma* 29 (1987): 27–31.

De la Fuente, Alejandro. "Myths of Racial Democracy: Cuba, 1900–1912." *Latin American Research Review* 34:3 (1999): 39–73.

———. "Race and Inequality in Cuba." *Journal of Contemporary History* 30:1 (1995): 131–168.

———. "Race, National Discourse, and Politics in Cuba: An Overview." *Latin American Perspectives* 25:3 (1998): 43–69.

Denzer, LaRay. "Yoruba Women: A Historiographical Study." *International Journal of African Historical Studies* 27:1 (1994): 1–39.

Dickerson, Dennis C. *Out of the Crucible: Black Steelworkers in Western Pennsylvania, 1875–1980.* Albany: State University of New York Press, 1986.

Dorigny, Marcel, and Bernard Gainot. *La Société des Amis des Noirs, 1789–1799.* Paris: UNESCO, 1998.

Douglass, Frederick. *The Life and Writings of Frederick Douglass.* Ed. Philip S. Foner. Vol. 4. New York: International Publishers, 1975.

Drewal, John H. "Art or Accident: Yoruba Body Artists and Their Deity Ogun." In *Africa's Ogun: Old World and New,* ed. Sandra T. Barnes, 235–260. Bloomington: Indiana University Press, 1997.

Drewal, Margaret T. "Dancing for Ogun in Yorubaland and in Brazil." *In Africa's Ogun: Old World and New,* ed. Sandra T. Barnes, 199–234. Bloomington: Indiana University Press, 1997.

Du Bois, W. E. B. *The Suppression of the African Slave Trade to the United States of America, 1638–1870.* New York: Russell and Russell, 1898.

Edwards, Paul, and James Walvin. *Black Personalities in the Era of the Slave Trade.* Baton Rouge: Louisiana State University Press, 1983.

Eltis, David. "Free and Coerced Transatlantic Migrations: Some Comparisons." *American Historical Review* 88 (1983): 251–280.

———. *The Rise of African Slavery in the Americas.* Cambridge: Cambridge University Press, 2000.

Eltis, David, Stephen D. Behrendt, David Richardson, and Herbert S. Klein. *The Trans-Atlantic Slave Trade: A Database on CD-ROM.* Cambridge: Cambridge University Press, 1999.

Eltis, David, and David Richardson. *Routes to Slavery: Direction, Ethnicity and Mortality in the Transatlantic Slave Trade.* London: Frank Cass, 1997.

Equiano, Olaudah. *The Life of Olaudah Equiano or Gustavas Vasa, The African Written by Himself.* 1789; reprint, New York: Penguin Books, 1995.

Eze, Emmanuel. *Race and the Enlightenment: A Reader.* Cambridge, Mass.: Blackwell, 1997.

Fagan, Brian M. *Kingdoms of Gold, Kingdoms of Jade: The Americas before Columbus.* London: Thames and Hudson, 1991.

Falola, Toyin, ed. *Africa.* Vol. 4: *The End of Colonial Rule, Nationalism and Decolonization.* Durham, N.C.: Carolina Academic Press, 2002.

Ferguson, Leland. *Uncommon Ground: Archaeology and Early African America, 1650–1800.* Washington, D.C.: Smithsonian Institution Press, 1992.

Fernández Armesto, Felipe. *Before Columbus: Exploration and Colonization from the Mediterranean to the Atlantic, 1229–1492.* Philadelphia: University of Pennsylvania Press, 1987.

Fick, Carolyn. *The Making of Haiti: The Saint Domingue Revolution from Below.* Knoxville: University of Tennessee Press, 1990.

Findlay, Eileen J. Suarez. *Imposing Decency: The Politics of Sexuality and Race in Puerto Rico, 1870–1920.* Durham, N.C.: Duke University Press, 1999.

Foner, Laura. "The Free People of Color in Louisiana and St. Domingue: A Comparative Portrait of Two Three-Caste Societies." *Journal of Social History* 3 (1970): 406–430.

Foner, Philip. *History of Black Americans.* Westport, Conn.: Greenwood, 1975.

Foster, James, D.D. *Discourses on ALL The Principle Branches of the Natural Religion, And Social Virtue.* Vol. 1. London, 1749.

Fox, George. *Gospel, Family-Order, Being a Short Discourse Concerning, the Ordering of Families, Both of Whites, Blacks and Indians.* London, 1676.

Franklin, John Hope, and Alfred A. Moss. *From Slavery to Freedom: A History of African Americans.* New York: McGraw Hill, 2000.

Frederickson, George M. *Black Liberation: A Comparative History of Black Ideologies in the United States and South African.* New York: Oxford University Press, 1995.

———. *White Supremacy: A Comparative Study in American and South African History.* Oxford: Oxford University Press, 1981.

Freyre, Gilberto. *The Masters and the Slaves: A Study in the Development of Brazilian Civilization,* trans. from the Portuguese by Samuel Putnam. New York: Alfred A. Knopf, 1964.

Frost, J. William, ed. *The Quaker Origins of Antislavery.* Norwood, Penn.: Norwood Editions, 1980.

Fukuyama, Francis. "The End of History?" *National Interest* 16 (1989): 3–18.

Games, Alison. "Migration." In *The British Atlantic World, 1500–1800, ed.* David Armitage and Michael Braddick. New York: Palgrave Macmillan, 2002.

———. *Migration and the Origins of the English Atlantic World.* Cambridge, Mass.: Harvard University Press, 1999.

Gaspar, David Barry. *Bondmen and Rebels: A Study of Master-Slave Relations in Antigua.* Durham, N.C.: Duke University Press, 1985.

Genovese, Eugene. *From Resistance to Revolution: Afro-American Slave Revolts in the Making of the New World.* Baton Rouge: Louisiana University Press, 1979.

———. *Roll, Jordan, Roll: The World the Slaves Made.* New York: Vintage, 1972.

Gibson, Arrell Morgan. *The American Indian: Prehistory to the Present.* D. C. Heath, 1980.

Gilpin, Robert. *Global Political Economy.* Princeton, N.J.: Princeton University Press, 2001.

———. *Globalization: Challenge and Opportunity.* New York: Council on Foreign Relations, 2002.

Gilroy, Paul. *The Black Atlantic: Modernity and Double Consciousness.* 1993; reprint, Cambridge, Mass.: Harvard University Press, 2003.

Godechet, Jacques. *France and the Atlantic Revolution of the Eighteenth Century, 1770–1799.* New York: Free Press, 1965.

Godwyn, Morgan. *The Negro's and Indian's Advocate.* London, 1680.

Goucher, Candice. "African-Caribbean Metal Technology: Forging Cultural Survivals in the Atlantic World." In *African Sites: Archaeology in the Caribbean,* ed. Jay B. Haviser, 143–156. Princeton, N.J.: Markus Wiener, 1999.

Graham, Gerald S. *Great Britain in the Indian Ocean, 1810–50.* Oxford: Clarendon, 1967.

Grasmuck, Sherri, and Patricia R. Pessar. *Between Two Islands: Dominican International Migration.* Berkeley: University of California Press, 1991.

Gray, Leslie, and Michael Kevane. "Diminished Access, Diverted Exclusion: Women and Land Tenure in Sub-Saharan Africa." *African Studies Review* 42:2 (1999): 15–39.

Hall, Jaquelyn Dowd, James Leloudis, Robert Korstad, Mary Murphy, Lu Ann Jones, and Christopher B. Daly. *Like a Family: The Making of a Southern Cotton Mill World.* New York: W. W. Norton, 1989.

Handler, Jerome S. "An African-Type Healer/Diviner and His Grave Goods: A Burial from a Plantation Slave Cemetery in Barbados, West Indies." *International Journal of Historical Archaeology* 1:2 (1997): 91–130.

Harding, Vincent. *There Is a River: The Black Struggle for Freedom in America.* New York: Harcourt Brace Jovanovich, 1981.

Hassig, Ross. *Mexico and the Spanish Conquest.* New York: Longman, 1994.

Hatton, T. J., and Joel G. Williamson. *The Age of Mass Migration: An Economic Analysis.* New York: Oxford University Press, 1998.

Haviser, Jay B. "Identifying a Post-Emancipation (1863–1940) African-Curacaoan Material Culture Assemblage." In *African Sites: Archaeology in the Caribbean,* ed. Jay B. Haviser, 221–263. Princeton, N.J.: Markus Wiener, 1999.

Hay, Margaret Jean. "Queens, Prostitutes and Peasants: Historical Perspectives on African Women, 1971–1986." *Canadian Journal of African Studies* 22:3 (1988): 431–447.

Hayward, Jack. *Out of Slavery: Abolition and After.* London: Frank Cass, 1985.

Held, David, and Anthony McGrew. *Globalization/Anti-Globalization.* Malden, Mass.: Blackwell, 2002.

Herbert, Eugenia W. Iron, *Gender and Power: Rituals of Transformation in African Societies.* Bloomington: Indiana University Press, 1993.

Herskovits, Melville J. *The Myth of the Negro Past.* Boston: Beacon, 1941.

Hirst, Paul, and Grahame Thompson. *Globalization in Question: The International Economy and the Possibilities of Governance.* Cambridge: Cambridge University Press, 1996.

Hobsbawm, Eric. *The Age of Extremes.* New York: Vintage Books, 1994.

——. *The Age of Revolution, 1789–1848.* New York: World, 1962.

Holland, R. F. *European Decolonization, 1918–1981: An Introductory Survey.* New York: St. Martin's, 1985.

Hopkins, A. G. "The Compatibility of the Slave and Palm Oil Trades in the Bight of Biafra." *Journal of African History* 17:3 (1976): 353–364.

——. "Economic Imperialism in West Africa, Lagos, 1880–92." *Economic History Review* 21:3 (1967): 580–606.

——, ed. *Globalization in World History.* London: Pimlico, 2002.

Horowitz, Michael M. *Peoples and Cultures of the Caribbean: An Anthropological Reader.* Garden City, N.Y.: Natural History Press, 1971.

Horsmanden, Daniel. *The New York Conspiracy.* 1744; reprint, New York: Beacon, 1971.

Hudson, Blaine J. "The African Diaspora and the 'Black Atlantic': An African American Perspective—Cover Story." *Negro History Bulletin,* Oct–Dec, 1997.

Huntington, Samuel. *The Clash of Civilizations and the Remaking of World Order.* New York: Simon and Schuster, 1996.

Isichei, Elizabeth. *The Ibo People and the Europeans: The Genesis of a Relationship to 1906.* New York: St. Martin's, 1973.

——. *Igbo Worlds: An Anthology of Oral Histories and Historical Descriptions.* Philadelphia: Institute for the Study of Human Issues, 1978.

James, C. L. R. *The Black Jacobins: Toussaint L'Ouverture and the San Domingo Revolution.* New York: Vintage, 1963.

——. *A History of Pan African Slave Revolts,* Washington, D.C.: Drum and Spear, 1969.

Johnson, Cheryl. "Grass Roots Organizing: Women in Anti-Colonial Activity in Southwestern Nigeria." *African Studies Review* 25:2/3 (1982): 137–157.

Johnson, Michael P., ed. *Lincoln, Slavery and the Civil War: Selected Writings and Speeches.* Boston: Bedford, 2001.

Jordan, Winthrop D. *White over Black: American Attitudes towards the Negro, 1550–1812.* New York: W.W. Norton, 1968.

Klein, Herbert S. *African Slavery in Latin America and the Caribbean.* New York: Oxford, 1986.

Klooster, Wim. "The Rise and Transformation of the Atlantic World." In *The Atlantic World: Essays on Slavery, Migration, and Imagination,* ed. Wim Klooster and Alfred Padula. Upper Saddle River, N.J.: Pearson/Prentice Hall, 2004.

Kottak, Conrad Phillip. *Assault on Paradise: Social Change in a Brazilian Village.* 2nd ed. New York: McGraw-Hill, 1992.

Kriger, Colleen. "Textile Production and Gender in the Sokoto Caliphate." *Journal of African History* 34:3 (1993): 361–401.

Laguerre, Michel S. *Diasporic Citizenship: Haitian Americans in Transnational America.* New York: St. Martin's, 1998.

Larner, John. *Marco Polo and the Discovery of the World.* New Haven: Yale University Press, 1999.

Law, Robin, and Kristin Mann. "West Africa in the Atlantic Community: The Case of the Slave Coast." *William and Mary Quarterly,* 3rd ser., 56:2 (1999): 307–334.

Lawal, Babatunde. "Yoruba Sango Sculpture in Historical Retrospect." Ph.D. diss., Indiana University, 1970.

Lindsey, Brink. *Against the Dead Hand: The Uncertain Struggle for Global Capitalism.* New York: John Wiley, 2002.

Linebaugh, Peter, and Marcus Rediker. *The Many Headed Hydra: Sailors, Slaves, Commoners and the Hidden History of the Revolutionary Atlantic.* Boston: Beacon, 2000.

Little, Kenneth. *African Women in Towns: An Aspect of Africa's Social Revolution.* London: Cambridge University Press, 1973.

Locke, John. *Two Treatises of Government: A Critical Edition with an Introduction and Apparatus Criticus,* ed. Peter Lasslett. Cambridge: Cambridge University Press, 1960.

Lovejoy, Paul E., ed. *Identity in the Shadow of Slavery.* London: Continuum, 2000.

———. *Transformations in Slavery: A History of Slavery in Africa.* 2nd ed. Cambridge: Cambridge University Press, 2000.

MacGaffey, Wyatt. *Art and Healing of the BaKongo: Commented by Themselves.* Stockholm: Folkens Museum; Bloomington: Indiana University Press, 1991.

Macqueen, Norrie. *The Decolonization of Portuguese Africa: Metropolitan Revolution and the Dissolution of Empire.* London: Longman, 1997.

Mandela, Nelson. *Long Walk to Freedom: The Autobiography of Nelson Mandela.* Boston: Little, Brown, 1994.

Manning, Patrick. *Slavery and African Life.* Cambridge: Cambridge University Press, 1990.

———. *Slavery, Colonialism, and Economic Growth in Dahomey, 1640–1960.* New York: Cambridge University Press, 1982.

Martinez-Echazabel, Lourdes. "Mestizaje and the Discourse of National/Cultural Identity in Latin America, 1845–1959." *Latin American Perspectives* 25:3 (1998): 21–42.

Mazrui, Ali A., ed. *General History of Africa.* Vol. 8, *Africa since 1935.* London: Heinemann, 1993.

McFarlane, Anthony. "Rebellions in Late Colonial Spanish America: A Comparative Perspective." *Bulletin of Latin American Research* 14:3 (1995): 313–338.

Meinig, D. W. *The Shaping of America: A Geographical Perspective on 500 Years of History.* Vol. 1, *Atlantic America, 1492–1800.* New Haven, Conn.: Yale University Press, 1986.

Mikell, Gwendolyn, ed. *African Feminism: The Politics of Survival in Sub-Saharan Africa.* Philadelphia: University of Pennsylvania Press, 1997.

——. "Ghanian Females, Rural Economy and National Stability." *African Studies Review* 29:3 (1986): 67–88.

Miller, Joseph C. "Central Africa during the Era of the Slave Trade, c. 1490s–1850s." In *Central Africans and Cultural Transformations in the America Diaspora*, ed. Linda M. Heywood, 21–69. Cambridge: Cambridge University Press, 2002.

——. "The Slave Trade of Congo and Angola." In *The African Diaspora: Interpretive Essays,* ed. Martin Kilson and Robert Rotberg, 75–113. Cambridge, Mass.: Harvard University Press, 1976.

——. *Way of Death: Merchant Capitalism and the Angolan Slave Trade, 1730–1830.* Madison: University of Wisconsin Press, 1988.

Mintz, Sidney, and D. Hall. *The Origins of the Jamaican Internal Marketing System.* Yale University Publications in Anthropology no. 57. New Haven, Conn., Department of Anthropology, Yale University, 1991.

Mintz, Sidney M., and Richard Price. *The Birth of African-American Culture: An Anthropological Perspective.* Boston: Beacon, 1992.

Momsen, Jane Henshall, and Vivian Kinnaird. *Different Places, Different Voices: Gender and Development in Africa, Asia and Latin America.* London: Routledge, 1995.

Montesquieu, Baron de. *The Spirit of the Laws.* Cambridge: Cambridge University Press, 1989.

Morgan, Edmund C. *American Slavery, American Freedom: The Ordeal of Colonial Virginia.* New York: W. W. Norton, 1975.

Morrisey, Marietta. *Slave Women in the New World: Gender Stratification in the Caribbean.* Lawrence: University Press of Kansas, 1989.

Morton-Williams, Peter. "The Oyo Yoruba and the Atlantic Trade, 1670 to 1830." In *Forced Migration,* ed. J. E. Inikori, 167–186. New York: Africana, 1982.

Murphy, Craig C. *International Organizations and Industrial Change: Global Governance since 1850.* Cambridge: Cambridge University Press, 1994.

Nadel, G. H., and P. Curtis, eds. *Imperialism and Colonialism.* New York: Macmillan, 1964.

Nadel, Siegfried F. A *Black Byzantium: The Kingdom of Nupe in Nigeria.* London: Oxford University Press, 1942.

Newitt, M. D. D. A *History of Portuguese Overseas Expansion, 1400–1668.* London: Routledge, 2005.

Northrup, David. *Africa's Discovery of Europe, 1450–1850.* Oxford: Oxford University Press, 2002.

——. "The Compatibility of the Slave and Palm Oil Trades in the Bight of Biafra." *Journal of African History* 17:3 (1976): 353–364.

——. *Trade without Rulers: Precolonial Economic Development in South-Eastern Nigeria.* Oxford: Clarendon, 1978.

O'Brien, Thomas F. *The Revolutionary Mission: American Enterprise in Latin America, 1900–1945.* Cambridge: Cambridge University Press, 1996.

Olwell, Robert. *Masters, Slaves and Subjects: The Culture of Power in the South Carolina Low Country, 1740–1790.* Ithaca, N.Y.: Cornell University Press, 1998.

O'Meara, Patrick, Howard Mehlinger, and Matthew Krain, eds. *Globalization and the Challenges of a New Century: A Reader.* Bloomington: Indiana University Press, 2000.

Onimode, Bade. *Africa in the World of the 21st Century*. Ibadan, Nigeria: Ibadan University Press, 2000.

O'Rourke, Kevin, and Jeffrey Williamson. *Globalization and History: The Evolution of a Nineteenth-Century Atlantic Economy*. Cambridge, Mass.: MIT Press, 1999.

Owensby, Brian P. *Intimate Ironies: Modernity and the Making of Middle-Class Lives in Brazil*. Stanford, Calif.: Stanford University Press, 1999.

Palmer, R.R. *The Age of the Democratic Revolution*. Vol. 1, *The Challenge, 1760–1800*. Princeton, N.J.: Princeton University Press, 1959. Vol. 2, *The Struggle*. Princeton, N.J.: Princeton University Press, 1964.

Parry, J. H. *The Spanish Seaborne Empire*. 1966; reprint, Berkeley: University of California Press, 1990.

Patai, Daphne. *Brazilian Women Speak: Contemporary Life Stories*. New Brunswick, N.J.: Rutgers University Press, 1993.

Patterson, Tiffany Ruby, and Robin D. G. Kelly. "Unfinished Migrations: Reflections on the African Diaspora and the Making of the Modern World." *African Studies Review* 43:1 (2000): 11–45.

Patton, Sharon F. *African-American Art*. Oxford: Oxford University Press, 1998.

Petras, J., and H. Veltmeyer. *Globalization Unmasked: Imperialism in the 21st Century*. London: Zed Books, 2001.

Pole, L. M. "Decline or Survival? Iron Production in West Africa from the Seventeenth to the Twentieth Centuries." *Journal of African History* 23:4 (1982): 503–513.

Posnansky, Merrick, and L. B. Crossland. "Pottery, People, and Trade at Begho, Ghana." In *The Spatial Organisation of Culture*, ed. Ian Hodder. Pittsburgh: University of Pittsburgh Press, 1978.

Price, Richard, ed. *Maroon Societies: Rebel Slave Communities in the Americas*. New York: Anchor, 1973.

Raboteau, Albert J. *Slave Religion: The "Invisible Institution" in the Ante-bellum South*. New York: Oxford University Press, 1978.

Reis, Joào Jose. *Slave Rebellion in Brazil: The Muslim Uprising of 1835 in Bahai*. Baltimore: Johns Hopkins University Press, 1993.

Richardson, David. "The Atlantic Slave Trade Scale, Structure and Supply Slave Exports from West and West—Central Africa, 1700–1810: New Estimates of Volume and Distribution." *Journal of African History* 30:1 (1989): 1–22.

——. "The Slave Trade, Sugar, and British Economic Growth, 1748–1776." *Journal of Interdisciplinary History* 17 (1987): 757–763.

Ringrose, David R. *Expansion and Global Interaction, 1200–1700*. New York: Longman, 2001.

Robbins, Richard. *Global Problems and the Culture of Capitalism*. Boston: Allyn and Bacon, 1999.

Roberts, Kevin D. *African American Issues*. Westport, Conn.: Greenwood, 2005.

——. "The Influential Yoruba Past in Haiti." In *The Yoruba Diaspora in the Atlantic World*, ed. Toyin Falola and Matt Childs, 177–184. Bloomington: Indiana University Press, 2004.

Robertson, Claire, and Martin Klein, eds. *Women and Slavery in Africa*. Madison: University of Wisconsin Press, 1983.

Rodney, Walter. *A History of the Upper Guinea Coast: 1545–1800*. New York: Monthly Review Press, 1970.

Rotberg, Robert I. *Ending Autocracy, Enabling Democracy: The Tribulations of South-*

ern Africa, 1960–2000. Cambridge, Mass.: World Peace Foundation; Washington, D.C.: Brookings Institution Press, 2002.

Rout, Leslie B. *The African Experience in Spanish America: 1502 to the Present Day.* Cambridge: Cambridge University Press, 1976.

Salomon, Frank, and Stuart B. Schwartz, eds. *The Cambridge History of the Native Peoples of the Americas.* Vol. 3, *South America.* Cambridge: Cambridge University Press, 1999. 2 vols.

Sanneh, Lamin. *Abolitionists Abroad: American Blacks and the Making of Modern West Africa.* Cambridge, Mass.: Harvard University Press, 1999.

Sarduy, Pedro, and Jean Stubbs, *Afro Cuba: An Anthology of Cuban Writing on Race Politics and Culture.* Melbourne: Ocean Press, 1993.

Sassen, Saskia. *Globalization and Its Discontents.* New York: New Press, 1998.

Schuler, Monica. *Alas, Alas, Kongo: A Social History of Indentured African Immigrants into Jamaica, 1841–1845.* Baltimore: Johns Hopkins University Press, 1980.

Schwartz, Stuart B. *Sugar Plantations in the Formation of Brazilian Society: Bahia, 1550–1835.* Cambridge: Cambridge University Press, 1985.

Scott, Joan Wallach. *Gender and the Politics of History.* New York: Columbia University Press, 1988.

Scott, Rebecca J. “Defining the Boundaries of Freedom in the World of Cane: Cuba, Brazil, and Louisiana after Emancipation.” *American Historical Review* 99:1 (1994): 70–102.

——. *Slave Emancipation in Cuba: The Transition to Free Labor.* Princeton, N.J.: Princeton University Press, 1985.

Sharp, Granville. *A Representation of the Injustice and Dangerous Tendency of Tolerating Slavery in England.* London: 1769.

Shepherd, Verene, Bridget Brereton, and Barbara Bailey, eds. *Engendering History: Caribbean Women in Historical Perspective.* New York: St. Martin’s, 1995.

——. *Women in Caribbean History.* Kingston, Jamaica: Ian Randle, 1999.

Sherlock, Phillip, and Hazel Bennett. *The Story of the Jamaican People.* Kingston, Jamaica: Ian Randle, 1998.

Shettima, Kole Ahmed. “Engendering Nigeria’s Third Republic.” *African Studies Review* 38:3 (1995): 61–98.

Sieber, Roy. “Kwahu Terracottas, Oral Traditions and Ghanaian History.” In *African Art and Leadership,* ed. Douglas Fraser and Herbert Cole, 173–183. Madison: University of Wisconsin Press, 1972.

Smith, Carol A. “Race-Class-Gender Ideology in Guatemala: Modern and Anti-Modern Forms.” *Comparative Studies in Society and History* 37:4 (1995): 723–749.

Smith, Robert. “Yoruba Armament.” *Journal of African History* 8:1 (1967): 87–106.

Spear, Jennifer. “Colonial Intimacies: Legislating Sex in French Louisiana.” *William and Mary Quarterly,* 3rd ser., 60 (January 2003): 75–98.

Stavney, Anne. ““Mothers of Tomorrow”: The New Negro Renaissance and the Politics of Maternal Representation.” *African American Review* 32:4 (1998): 533–561.

Stiglitz, Joseph E. *Globalization and Its Discontents.* New York: W.W. Norton, 2002.

Strange, S. *The Retreat of the State.* Cambridge: Cambridge University Press, 1996.

Stuckey, Sterling. *Going through the Storm: The Influence of African American Art in History.* New York: Oxford University Press, 1994.

Terborg-Penn, Rosalyn, and Andrea Benton Rushing, eds. *Women in Africa and the African Diaspora: A Reader.* 2nd ed. Washington, D.C.: Howard University Press, 1996.

Thomas, Caroline, and Peter Wilkin, eds. *Globalization and the South.* New York: St. Martin's, 1997.

Thomas, Hugh. *The Slave Trade.* New York: Simon and Schuster, 1997.

Thompson, Robert F. *Flash of the Spirit.* New York: Vintage Books, 1983.

Thornton, John. *Africa and Africans in the Making of the Atlantic World, 1400–1800.* Cambridge: Cambridge University Press, 1992.

Tise, Lawrence. *Proslavery: A History of the Defense of Slavery in America, 1701–1840.* Athens: University of Georgia Press, 1987.

Vansina, Jan. *Kingdoms of the Savanna.* Madison: University of Wisconsin Press, 1966.

———. *Paths in the Rainforests: Toward a History of Political Tradition in Equatorial Africa.* Madison: University of Wisconsin Press, 1990.

Verger, Pierre. "Nigeria, Brazil, and Cuba." *Nigeria Magazine* (Oct. 1960): 113–123.

———. *Trade Relations between the Bight of Benin and Brazil, 17th–19th Century.* Trans. Evelyn Crawford. Ibadan, Nigeria: Ibadan University Press, 1976.

Vlach, John M. *The Afro-American Tradition in Decorative Arts.* Cleveland: Cleveland Museum of Art, 1978.

Voss, Stuart F. *Latin America in the Middle Period, 1750–1929.* Wilmington, Del.: Scholarly Resources, 2002.

Wallace, George. *A System of the Principles of the Laws of Scotland.* Edinburgh: W. Millar, 1760.

Wallace, Michele. *Black Macho and the Myth of the Superwoman.* New York: Dial Press, 1979.

Weinstein, Barbara. "Unskilled Worker, Skilled Housewife: Constructing the Working Class Woman in São Paulo, Brazil." In *The Gendered Worlds of Latin American Women Workers: From Household and Factory to the Union Hall and* Ballot Box, ed. John French and Daniel James, 73–99. Durham, N.C.: Duke University Press, 1997.

White, Deborah Gray. *Ar'n't I a Woman? Female Slaves in the Plantation South.* New York, W. W. Norton, 1985.

Williams, Eric. *Capitalism and Slavery.* Chapel Hill: University of North Carolina Press, 1944.

Williamson, Jeffrey G. "Globalization, Convergence and History." *Journal of Economic History* 56 (1996): 277–306.

Wilkie, Laurie A. "Evidence of African Continuities in the Material Culture of Clifton Plantation, Bahamas." In *African Sites Archaeology in the Caribbean,* ed. Jay B. Haviser, 264–275. Princeton, N.J.: Markus Wiener, 1999.

Wilson, Samuel M., ed. *The Indigenous People of the Caribbean.* Gainesville: University Press of Florida, 1997.

Winbush, Raymond A., ed. *Should America Pay? Slavery and the Raging Debate on Reparations.* New York: HarperCollins, 2003.

Winch, Julie. *A Gentleman of Color: The Life and Times of James Forten.* New York: Oxford University Press, 2002.

Wolfe, Joel. *Working Women, Working Men: São Paulo and the Rise of Brazil's Industrial Working Class, 1900–1955.* Durham, N.C.: Duke University Press, 1993.

Wright, Donald R. *The World and a Very Small Place in Africa: A History of Globalization in Niumi, the Gambia.* New York: M. E. Sharpe, 2004.

Zeleza, Paul Tyambe. *Rethinking Africa's Globalization.* Trenton, N.J.: Africa World Press, 2003.

Websites

African American Religion: A Documentary History Project. "Part One: African-American Religion in the Atlantic World, 1441–1808." http://www.amherst.edu/~aardoc/Atlantic_World.html.

The Atlantic World: An Electronic Exploration. http://muweb.millersville.edu/~winthrop/atlantic.html.

The Atlantic World Workshop at NYU. http://www.nyu.edu/pages/atlantic/.

Carolina Lowcountry and Atlantic World Program, College of Charleston. http://www.cofc.edu/atlanticworld/.

International Seminar on the History of the Atlantic World, 1500–1825, Harvard University. http://www.fas.harvard.edu/~atlantic/.

Transatlantic History Doctoral Program, Department of History, University of Texas at Arlington. http://www.uta.edu/history/transatlantic/index.htm#programs.

Virtual Jamestown. http://www.virtualjamestown.org/.

Contributors

Carol Anderson is an associate professor of history at the University of Missouri–Columbia. Her research focuses on U.S. international relations and public policy, especially concerning human rights and African Americans. She is author of *Eyes off the Prize: The United Nations and the African American Struggle for Human Rights, 1944–1955*, which was the recipient of the Gustavus Myers and Myrna Bernath book awards.

Ken Aslakson completed his Ph.D. in history at the University of Texas in 2007 under the direction of James Sidbury. His dissertation, "Making Race: The Role of Free Blacks in the Development of New Orleans' Three-Caste Society, 1791–1812," excavates the ways that free people of African descent in New Orleans built an autonomous identity as a third "race" in what would become a unique racial caste system in the United States. He is an assistant professor of history at Union College, specializing in African American and early American history. Prior to graduate school, he received his law degree from the University of Texas and practiced law in Dallas. His work centers on the intersection of law and culture, especially race, in early America and the Atlantic World.

Timothy R. Buckner is an assistant professor of history at Troy University. He earned his Ph.D. in history from the University of Texas at Austin. His dissertation deals with slavery and identity formation in the Old South town of Natchez, Mississippi. He earned his M.A. from Florida State University and his B.A. from Georgia State University.

David Cahill is a professor of modern history at the University of New South Wales. He has taught at the University of Liverpool, the University of Bielefeld, and the École des Hautes Études en Sciences Sociales, Paris. Among his recent publications are *From Rebellion to Emancipation in the Andes: Soundings from Southern Peru, 1750–1830* (2002); *Habsburg Peru: Images, Imagination and Memory* (2000), authored with Peter

Bradley; and *New World, First Nations: Native Peoples of Mesoamerica and the Andes under Colonial Rule* (2006), edited with Blanca Tovías. In 2003 he was awarded the Conference on Latin American History Prize. He is currently completing a book on the Great Andean Rebellion of 1780.

Douglas B. Chambers, Ph.D., teaches at the University of Southern Mississippi. A specialist in Atlantic Africa in the era of transatlantic slave trade, he is author of *Murder at Montpelier: Igbo Africans in Virginia* (2005). He is editor of the journal *Southern Quarterly* and is currently working on the slave trade from the Bight of Biafra, ca. 1650–1850.

Toyin Falola, editor of a five-volume series on Africa, is the Frances Higginbotham Nalle Centennial Professor in History at the University of Texas at Austin. He is the author of numerous books, including *Key Events in African History: A Reference Guide* and *Nationalism and African Intellectuals*, and many edited books, including *Tradition and Change in Africa* and *African Writers and the Readers*. He is co-editor of the *Journal of African Economic History*, series editor of Rochester Studies in African History and the Diaspora, and series editor of the Culture and Customs of Africa. He has received various awards and honors, including the Jean Holloway Award for Teaching Excellence, the Texas Exes Teaching Award, and the Ibn Khaldun Distinguished Award for Research Excellence. For his contribution to the study of Africa, his students and colleagues have presented him with a festschrift edited by Adebayo Oyebade, *The Transformation of Nigeria: Essays in Honor of Toyin Falola*.

Alison Games teaches Atlantic history at Georgetown University, where she is the Dorothy M. Brown Distinguished Professor of History. She is author of *Migration and the Origins of the English Atlantic World* (1999), winner of the Theodore Saloutos Prize in Immigration and Ethnic History. She is author (with Douglas R. Egerton, Kris Lane, and Donald R. Wright) of *The Atlantic World: A History, 1440–1888* (2007) and editor (with Adam Rothman) of "Major Problems in Atlantic History" (forthcoming). She has written extensively on different aspects of Atlantic history, and her articles have appeared in such journals as *Slavery and Abolition, Itinerario, American Historical Review,* and *William and Mary Quarterly*.

Timothy P. Grady is an assistant professor of history at the University of South Carolina–Upstate. He earned his Ph.D. in history from the College of William and Mary. His dissertation is a regional study of Anglo-Spanish interaction across the borderland region between South Carolina and Spanish Florida in the seventeenth and early eighteenth centuries. The study seeks to illustrate cultural, economic, and political changes between the two colonies during this period as well as the accommodations and responses of the Indian populations that both imperial powers sought to influence. His broader interests include Atlantic World studies concentrating on early Spanish and English colonialism. He received his M.A. from Virginia Tech and his B.A. from Tennessee Tech.

Michael Guasco is an associate professor of history at Davidson College. He received his Ph.D. in history from the College of William and Mary in 2000. His research interests include early colonial settlement, cross-cultural encounters, and the development of Anglo-American slavery. He is currently completing a book-length manuscript entitled "Slaves and Englishmen: Human Bondage and the Making of an Anglo-Atlantic World."

E. G. Iweriebor is a graduate of the University of Ibadan, Nigeria. He obtained his Ph.D. from Columbia University, New York. He specializes in colonial and contemporary Nigerian and African intellectual history and the history of contemporary African political and economic development. He has published several articles and is a commentator on current affairs in Nigerian newspapers. His current research is in contemporary economic history, with special reference to endogenous innovative responses to economic crisis, technological developments, and the growth of autocentric perspectives and actions among Nigerian entrepreneurs. His books include *Radical Politics in Nigeria, 1945–1950: The Significance of the Zikist Movement* (1996); *The Age of Neo-colonialism in Africa* (1997); and, with Dr. Martin Uhmoibhi, *UN Security Council: The Case for Nigeria's Membership* (1999). He taught in the Department of History, University of Ilorin, Nigeria, and was pioneer chair of the Department of African Studies at Manhattanville College, Purchase, New York. He is currently an associate professor in the Department of Black and Puerto Rican Studies, Hunter College, City University of New York.

Maurice Jackson is an assistant professor of Atlantic and African American history at Georgetown University in Washington, D.C. He specializes in social protest movements, culture, and ideology in the African Diaspora. He is at work on a social biography of Anthony Benezet (1731–1784), the French-born Huguenot who became a Quaker educator and founded the African Free School. Based in Philadelphia, Benezet reenergized the Atlantic antislavery zeal of the era, through his many pamphlets and through correspondence with antislavery leaders throughout the Atlantic World.

Maxim Matusevich is Assistant Professor of World History at Seton Hall University and Visiting Research Fellow at the W. E. B. Du Bois Institute for African and African American Research at Harvard University. A native of St. Petersburg, Russia, he received his B.A. from the University of Oklahoma and then obtained his M.A. and Ph.D. in African studies and African history from the University of Illinois at Urbana–Champaign. In 1999 he served as Visiting Research Fellow at the Nigerian Institute of International Affairs in Lagos, Nigeria. His first book, *No Easy Row for a Russian Hoe: Ideology and Pragmatism in Nigerian–Soviet Relations, 1960–1991* (2003), reflected an enduring interest in the history of political and cultural encounters between Africa and the Soviet Union. Most recently he edited and contributed to an interdisciplinary volume, *Africa in Russia, Russia in Africa: Three Centuries of Encounters* (2006).

Patricia Pearson is a doctoral student at the University of Texas at Austin.

Kevin D. Roberts is the founder and headmaster of Pope John Paul II Academy in Lafayette, Louisiana. He earned his Ph.D. in history from the University of Texas at Austin. A specialist in slavery and the history of the American South, he has published *African American Issues* (2005) and several articles on African ethnicities in the New World.

Joel E. Tishken is an associate professor of history at Columbus State University in Columbus, Georgia. He is the author of numerous articles and chapters on Africa, religion, world history, and pedagogy. His forthcoming projects include being co-editor of a volume on the Yoruba deity Sango and author of a monograph examining prophecy and leadership within Afro-Christian churches. His professional specialties include central and southern Africa, Christianity, prophecy, and the Caribbean.

Aribidesi A. Usman is Associate Professor of Anthropology and African & African American Studies at Arizona State University. His research and publication focus on African history and archaeology, especially precolonial and contact period, African urbanism, regional political and economic interaction, social transformation, frontier dynamics, Africans and the trans-Atlantic contact, and Cultural Resource Management. His current research is a book on the Yoruba Frontier: regional history of community formation, experience, and changes in West Africa (ca. 1200–1900 AD).

Amanda Warnock is a Ph.D. candidate in the history department at the University of Texas at Austin. Her dissertation explores how merchants in New England and Cuba worked to integrate Havana into global trade networks during the late eighteenth and early nineteenth centuries. Her research interests include gender and state building, international communication networks, and the economic and cultural history of New England, Latin America, and the African Diaspora. She is editor, along with Toyin Falola, of the *Encyclopedia of the Middle Passage* (2007).

Index